2016/17

THE GUIDE TO

EDUCATIONAL GRANTS

FOURTEENTH EDITION

Gabriele Zagnojute and Jodie Huyton

Additional research by:
Jennifer Reynolds, Rachel Cain, Ian Pembridge
and Denise Lillya

dsc
directory of social change

Published by the Directory of Social Change (Registered Charity no. 800517 in England and Wales)

Head office: 24 Stephenson Way, London NW1 2DP

Northern office: Suite 103, 1 Old Hall Street, Liverpool L3 9HG
Tel: 08450 77 77 07

Visit www.dsc.org.uk to find out more about our books, subscription funding websites and training events. You can also sign up for e-newsletters so that you're always the first to hear about what's new.

The publisher welcomes suggestions and comments that will help to inform and improve future versions of this and all of our titles. Please give us your feedback by emailing publications@dsc.org.uk.

It should be understood that this publication is intended for guidance only and is not a substitute for professional or legal advice. No responsibility for loss occasioned as a result of any person acting or refraining from acting can be accepted by the authors or publisher.

First published 1988
Second edition 1992
Third edition 1994
Fourth edition 1996
Fifth edition 1998
Sixth edition 2000
Seventh edition 2002
Eighth edition 2004
Ninth edition 2006
Tenth edition 2009
Eleventh edition 2011
Twelfth edition 2013
Thirteenth edition 2014
Fourteenth edition 2016

ISBN 978 1 78482 006 0

British Library Cataloguing in Publication Data
A catalogue record for this book is available from the British Library

Cover and text design by Kate Griffith
Typeset by Marlinzo Services, Frome
Printed and bound by Page Bros, Norwich

Contents

Foreword   iv

Preface   iv

Introduction   v

Grant-making charities – their processes and
   effectiveness   xiv

About this guide   xiv

How to use this guide   xvi

How to identify sources of help – a quick
   reference flowchart   xvii

How to make an application   xviii

Using the application form template for
   financial assistance   xix

Application form template   xx

About the Directory of Social Change   xxii

National and general sources of help   1

Livery companies, orders and membership
   organisations   125

Local charities   129

Statutory grants and student support   313

Types of schools in the UK and their funding   315

Alternative routes to employment:
   apprenticeships   319

Company sponsorships   321

Funding for gap years and overseas
   voluntary work   323

Contacts and sources of further information   325

Index   329

Foreword

Access to education has never been more important: as national president of the National Union of Students, I see and hear evidence of this fact every day. Both from our research and from talking to students' unions it is obvious that access to education is still restricted by family background or household income. In fact, it may even be getting worse in some areas with part-time student numbers falling consistently.

For too many this means some courses are entirely out of reach, with education often out of reach altogether. But getting into education itself is not the only barrier that students are facing. We have to change the idea that access is only about getting through the door. If students cannot afford books or equipment, cover the cost of the bus or get access to mental health services they are unable to participate, either as well as they should or even at all. Students from lower-income families are also having to struggle holding down a part-time job just to pay the rent and are often locked out from extra-curricular activities that their richer peers take advantage of.

The government's own Social Mobility Commission has warned that there remains a mountain to climb if the poorest are to have the same opportunities as the wealthiest, but it is also the government's own policies which are making the chance that the poorest can have these opportunities even more remote. George Osborne's decision to scrap maintenance grants and nursing bursaries will hit the poorest students hardest. The continuing failure to provide adequate learner support in further education and rates of poverty pay under the inadequate apprenticeship minimum wage are also damaging to students' life chances.

Targeted support for the poorest students through maintenance grants are a lifeline, and we have been fighting to save them. But we've also been working to increase student income and reduce the costs of study and living that students face. *The Guide to Educational Grants* is an essential resource in this endeavour. There are so many charities and trusts that can help students to access education. This accessible and comprehensive guide can help those in need and their advisers identify the funds that can assist them. Whether the sums awarded are small or large, they very often make the difference between access and exclusion for those who receive them.

The generosity, commitment and hard work of charities in supporting students in need is often overlooked. This guide is so important at showing the incredible range of organisations supporting students and underlines the extent of their contribution and the need for public support. This is particularly important at the time when charities and third sector organisations face increased scrutiny of their fundraising.

NUS proudly supports and champions students' unions and their role in supporting students, and we are just as proud to support the Directory of Social Change in their efforts to support grant-making charities in theirs.

Megan Dunn
NUS National President

Preface

During what has been a troubling and challenging year for the charity sector, it has been rewarding to take part in the research for this guide and to read of the dedicated and tireless work undertaken by trustees and charity workers, both those who are paid and those volunteers who work for no monetary reward. It is a great shame that the press when they point the finger at a particular charity for 'mismanagement' or 'fraud' can have an almost unchallenged field day and spread rumours which have little foundation in fact.

The good news that the press should be communicating to the general public is the care and dedication given by those running charities to people who are struggling and who are forced to access charity funds because the state has failed to identify and/or meet their most basic needs. The press should be applauding the professionalism and excellence within the charity sector, the compassion of its volunteers and staff and the dedication of its trustees who work without pay, developing strategy, meeting ever increasing and often new demands, setting higher standards and working within strict regulatory lines (dealing with miles of red tape). This is to benefit those who are not in good health, are on low, or no income, those who struggle with making their benefits go around, and those who care for others – the list could go on. We could say those who are, for one reason or another, having to apply to charities for help and often through no fault of their own because there is little available from the state.

The Research Team at DSC applauds those who work to help others in disadvantaged situations financially or otherwise, and appreciates being a part of a long-established sector which has maintained its high standards and developed to accommodate an ever-changing society and its needs.

Denise Lillya
Research Team Manager,
Directory of Social Change

Introduction

Welcome to the fourteenth edition of *The Guide to Educational Grants 2016/17*. The main objective of this guide is to provide information on grant-making charities which offer financial support for individuals who are in education or training. This edition contains over 1,000 grant-making charities with a total of £55.6 million available in grants to individuals for educational purposes. Many of the organisations included in this guide also give grants to individuals in need for welfare purposes. These are detailed in the guide's sister publication *The Guide to Grants for Individuals in Need 2016/17*, also published by the Directory of Social Change (DSC).

Challenges for charities

During the course of research for *The Guide to Educational Grants 2016/17*, the Research Team at DSC has systematically analysed information from annual reports, accounts and websites of over 1,000 charitable grant-makers in the field of education to explore their experiences, and to discover the impact of the changing social and economic environment that grant-makers and beneficiaries face. What we have identified is a continuance, and in some cases magnification, of prevailing trends, as well as the occurrence of new challenges for charities. Throughout our research, we have seen how grant-makers have adapted their policies and practices in order to meet the increasing complexity of issues their beneficiaries face following the changes in statutory educational and welfare provision.

We discussed in the previous edition of this guide the initial impact of government cuts on charities and their beneficiaries under the 2010–15 coalition government but it seems that repercussions of these political decisions are still affecting charitable organisations and people they serve today.

Among those that continue to be affected is The Royal Masonic Trust for Girls and Boys – a charity funded by freemasons which aims to relieve poverty and advance education for children and young people. The trustees describe the ongoing effect of policy changes on the trust's beneficiaries:

> *Externally, changes to government policy and educational funding and provision continue to affect the families we support. The petitions committee continues to review the impact of those changes and made appropriate adjustments to the types and levels of grants paid for beneficiaries.*
>
> RMTGB 2015

The current climate

The changes brought in by the Welfare Reform Act 2012 and major shifts in the role of local government have reshaped the landscape of social security dramatically. The introduction of Universal Credit aims to consolidate working-age benefits in a simplified, single payment and to encourage transition into employment, with new responsibilities for those seeking work. Disability Living Allowance is being replaced with Personal Independence Payment, while Employment Support Allowance is offered to those suffering from 'illness or incapacity', conditional upon reviewed Work Capability Assessments to judge these criteria. The so-called 'bedroom tax' introduced additional penalties on under-occupancy – a housing policy with significant welfare implications.

Throughout our research period, we have identified how changes to social welfare provision have had a knock-on effect in the field of education in relation to a wide range of issues, such as parents' ability to afford school uniforms and other educational essentials. Furthermore, the drastic cuts in statutory funding to early years services (such as Sure Start children's centres), schools, further education, and higher education are also having a devastating impact.

Statistical analysis produced by the Department for Education shows that pupils from disadvantaged backgrounds achieve lower results in GSCEs or equivalent evaluations and make poorer progress in mathematics and English – the attainment gap between disadvantaged pupils and all other pupils is more than 27% across all four key indicators measured (Easby 2015). As Laura McInerney in *The Guardian* points out, tighter budgets also mean that parents are less able to pay for educational 'extras', such as revision guides and internet access, that could help pupils improve their results. Unfortunately, libraries and youth services that would normally help fill this gap are also facing closures or severe budget cuts (McInerney 2013).

Since the beginning of 2011, when 'departmental spending cuts have begun to bite', the public sector workforce experienced a fall of around 300,000 (Cribb *et al.* 2014). People working in the private sector have also been affected – there has been a decline in the number of retail stores as well as employees across the country and the forecasts suggest that, in the worst-case outcome, by 2025 there may be 'as many as 900,000 fewer jobs in retail' (BRC 2016). While redundancy alone is a significant factor affecting individuals' lives, people with disabilities and their families are additionally burdened with having to deal with changes to Disability Living Allowance and struggle with the impact of the punitive bedroom tax.

Evidence we found over the course of our research suggested that government education and welfare policies continue to have a negative impact on access to education. The following sections will outline the landscape within which the grant-makers in this guide operate, focusing on government reforms and funding cuts at different stages of education.

Children's centres

Children's centres are the frontline service in the communities they support and there is as big a demand as ever for the services they provide. Children's charity 4Children has published the findings of its annual Children's Centre Census, which provides an overview of the major trends and developments taking place in children's centres across the country. 4Children's findings show that 'demand for services is at record levels, with over one million families supported and receiving services delivered through Children's Centres on a regular basis'. The census identified that children's centres make an important difference to the lives of parents and children, with 79.4% of parents reporting that being unable to use their local children's centre would make life harder for them and their families. Children's centres have developed strong relationships with a wide range of statutory and non-statutory organisations in their local areas and have embedded themselves in communities. They provide a wide range of services and have a key role in providing mental health and employment support (4Children 2015).

Emily Dugan in *The Independent* highlights the importance of children's centres and illustrates, using the following personal case study, the vital support they provide to individuals' lives:

> *I didn't know anything about children's centres or what they did until I was pregnant, but it's been invaluable. I went there for my first midwife appointment and my partner had just left me. I was on my own and there was lots of emotional stuff going on. I told the midwife about it and the next day the manager of the centre called to ask if I'd like to come in. The staff helped me find everything I needed. I had a job, as a rehab support worker for people with brain injuries, but they took me to the job centre to help me set up child benefit and tax credits. They also subsidised counselling for me so I only had to pay £10 a week to see someone. That was a big help as my partner of four years had left me soon after I found out I was pregnant. They even offered an informal mediation service and now Logan's dad comes every week. It's a bold statement but if the centre hadn't been there at that time I don't think I'd be the strong woman and mother I am now. At the moment Weybridge isn't under threat of closure but there's always the risk; it's quite frightening, the idea that it could close, because having that service for free has been invaluable.*
>
> Dugan 2015

Despite the clear need for children's centres, two-thirds of centre managers have had their annual budget cut, reflecting a long-term trend of budget decreases (4Children 2015). It is evident that 'cuts have led to the closure of many Sure Start children's centres which provide a lifeline for many families in these difficult economic times' (Unison 2016). Budget cuts are having a tangible impact – 57.5% of managers who have experienced a budget reduction say they will have to cut back services, and 32% say they will be unable to reach as many families as before (4Children 2015). There is considerable uncertainty about the future, and the threat of closure remains very real for many. 4Children recommends that the government should prioritise children and families, maximise the existing infrastructure of children's centres, and recognise their value and potential to deliver a range of services at a time when resources are stretched.

Schools

Chris Belfield and Luke Sibieta from the Institute for Fiscal Studies argue that 'under the coalition government, school spending in England was relatively protected at a time when other areas of government saw large cuts'. The new Conservative government has equally provided considerable security to school spending by 'committing to protecting day-to-day spending per pupil in cash terms over the current parliament' (Belfield and Sibieta 2015).

According to Unison (2016), regardless of government pledges to protect schools from cuts, 'some school support staff are facing redundancy as headteachers struggle to balance their books'. Belfield and Sibieta go on to explain that increasing costs and higher numbers of pupils mean that resources per child are likely to fall significantly. Their forecasts at the Institute for Fiscal Studies show that 'school spending per pupil is likely to fall by around 8% in real terms (based on a school-specific measure of inflation) between 2014–15 and 2019–20'. They note that this is likely to come as a new experience for those working in the school sector, as the last real-terms cuts were experienced in the mid-1990s. Furthermore, 'a significant challenge on the teacher workforce over the next five years will be recruiting the required number of teachers, and of sufficient quality and motivation, at a time of continued public pay restraint and rising pupil numbers'. However, it should be remembered that schools are still relatively protected compared with many other areas of education spending – 'further education and sixth form spending fell by 14% in real terms under the last parliament' (Belfield and Sibieta 2015).

Further education

Unison notes that college staff serve to help people gain new skills and retrain in order to get back into work; unfortunately, 'a wave of job losses has swept through further education as colleges are pressured into ever fiercer competition for funding and students' (Unison 2016). Funding cuts in adult further education of about 24% in 2015–16 were announced by the Skills Funding Agency early in 2015 (Lauener 2015). According to University and College Union this, while protecting the apprenticeships budget, will result in 'a further blow to colleges which have already sustained significant funding reductions since 2009' (UCU 2015). As noted in the previous edition of this guide, this age group has already been hit by the abolition of the Educational Maintenance Allowance (EMA). Unison describes EMA as 'a key tool for improving access to further education' and suggests that by abolishing it the government is 'recreating elitist tertiary education where only those who can afford it get it' (Unison 2016).

On a positive note, our research suggests that grant-makers are fully aware of the cuts within the further education sector and realise the significance of the support they provide. An example of this is reflected in the following extract:

> *Trustees consider grants to support young people who now have to stay on at school or undertake a programme of training until the age of 18 as particularly important since, in effect, the abolition of Educational Maintenance Allowance, (EMA). This has doubtlessly placed a greater financial strain on families.*
>
> Norwich Town Close Estate Charity 2015

Higher education

The Higher Education Funding Council states that 'higher education is one of the nation's most valuable assets; it enriches, inspires and transforms people's lives as well as bringing huge economic, social and cultural benefits'. There have been some significant changes in higher education in the UK in recent years which may threaten this asset, however. This includes the introduction of variable tuition fees (at various times for different parts of the country) and a shift in 2012 towards students funding their education with loans rather than grants and university fees increasing to up to £9,000 per year (HEFCE 2013). Indeed, data from a House of Commons briefing paper demonstrated that 'the total number of applicants to UK universities in 2012 was down by 6.6% or 46,500, compared to 2011, and there were larger percentage falls in groups directly affected by the fee increase' (Bolton 2015).

Chris Tansley, Unison president, reflects on the potential impact of the 2012 reforms on his own family to illustrate how other individuals will also likely be affected:

'My daughter was lucky enough to get to university before the government's huge increase of tuition fees. My son isn't going to be so lucky. He's looking at having to find fees of £8–9,000 a year. It's going to make him and thousands more of our brightest youngsters – who don't come from wealthy families – think hard about whether it's worth going into higher education at all.'

Unison 2016

Part-time and mature students

According to the Higher Education Funding Council for England, following the 2012 reforms, there was considerable concern over a decrease in part-time course attendants, with 'a significant decline in part-time entrants at both undergraduate and postgraduate levels'. Furthermore, 'the general state of the economy and fluctuations of the labour market are likely to affect the take-up of part-time study'. Part-time provision is 'an important factor in enabling the adaptability of individuals in the labour market, and improving flexibility in the wider economy'; nevertheless, because of economic challenges, the risk of lower investment in learning increases (HEFCE 2013).

Similarly, there has been some concern over the levels of mature students entering higher education courses, and specifically among applicants aged over 30. Indeed, the greatest decline in mature students following the 2012 reforms was among applicants aged 40 or over (HEFCE 2013). Later Higher Education Funding Council research shows that mature students are also more likely to drop out from higher education and some recent evaluation of yearly data suggests that there are 'early signs of emerging trends, particularly among mature students' with some potential relation to the increase in tuition fees (HEFCE 2016).

There is a correlation between part-time study and mature students. The Higher Education Funding Council also showed that in 2010 a total of 79% of students enrolling on part-time undergraduate courses were over 25, compared with 13% enrolling on full-time courses. The report states that 'part-time students are more likely to be non-traditional learners and are more likely to be mature' (HEFCE 2013). More recent findings reveal that the number of part-time undergraduate students entering higher education has fallen 55% from 2010–11 to 2014–15 (HEFCE 2015).

Students from disadvantaged backgrounds

Despite the much-feared deterrent effect on students from disadvantaged backgrounds, there are suggestions that poorer students are entering higher education more than before. The UCAS figures from the January 2013 applications deadline suggested an increase in application rates (from 18.4% to 19.5%, which was the highest level recorded) from the most disadvantaged neighbourhoods (HEFCE 2013). Furthermore, the latest UCAS *End of Cycle Report 2015* states that the entry rates for disadvantaged 18-year-olds 'have increased every cycle since 2006, making disadvantaged young people in England 30 per cent more likely to enter university in 2015 than five years ago, and 65 per cent more likely to enter higher education than in 2006' (UCAS 2015). This unexpected state of affairs may have occurred because grants for these students also increased at the same time as this rise (Britton *et al.* 2015).

Nevertheless, despite this considerable progress, the gap in participation rates between the most and least disadvantaged since the 2012 reforms has been and remains wide. The Higher Education Funding Council, reporting on the impact of the 2012 reforms, stated that 'students from different backgrounds tend to go to different types of universities and colleges'. Furthermore, it is apparent that 'those 18-year-olds living in advantaged areas are typically between six and nine times more likely to go to institutions that have higher entry requirements than those in disadvantaged areas' (HEFCE 2013). This is reiterated by the UCAS (2015) end-of-cycle report which notes that the gap in participation rates between the most and least disadvantaged remains wide: 'young people in the more advantaged areas [are] substantially more likely to enter higher education and hold A levels than those living in more disadvantaged areas'.

The role of grant-making charities

While undertaking our research for this publication we were able to witness how trustees of grant-making charities are accommodating the needs of higher education students, recognising the challenges students face and the importance their support can make to a struggling student. An example of such a charity is the Helena Kennedy Foundation, which 'exists to overcome social injustice by providing financial bursaries, mentoring and support to disadvantaged students from the further and adult education sectors' in order to enable students 'to complete their studies in higher education and move on successfully into employment or further studies' (HKF 2016). The trustees' annual report for 2013/14 gives the following account:

With the costs associated with studying in higher education continuing to rise and a challenging employment market impacting on opportunities for students to gain access to part time work to support their studies, this support remains more relevant and important to students' needs than ever.... Our bursary awards provide financial support that makes a real difference to our students' ability to meet the rising costs associated with studying. It remains the primary reason for students' application to the Foundation.... The wider economic climate also presents additional challenges for small charities like ours.... We continue our efforts to secure greater numbers of sponsors for bursary awards that we know are of enormous value to our students.

HKF 2015

INTRODUCTION

The experiences and reports of charitable sector, and the wider statistical analysis, suggest that government reforms and cuts to statutory funding have contributed to the pressures of the education system. With this changing educational and social climate in mind, what effect has this had on the grant-makers in this guide?

Levels of demand

Some grant-making charities reported an overall rise in demand for their services in their latest annual report. Others recorded a continuation of long-term increases and noted record numbers of applications received. For instance, the trustees of the Consolidated Charity of Burton upon Trent (2015) stated in their annual report that 'this year [2014] there were 70 applicants, compared to 49 applications in 2013; this was a substantial increase on last year'. Similarly, the Norwich Town Close Estate Charity (2015) described in its annual report that 'the number of grants made to individuals increased significantly, from 116 in 2013/14 to 142 in 2014/15, a 22% rise'.

We identified that some charities were able to keep up with the rise in demand by increasing their grants budget, either generally or to meet a specific need. However, we also found that not all charities were able to meet the increased demand, and had to become more selective in the application process. For example, the trustees of Peter Alan Dickson Foundation note that they receive more applications than they can support and, therefore, have to be selective – as part of the selection process the foundation looks to support those most in need (PAD Foundation 2016).

There are various factors which can contribute to the level of demand a charity experiences each year. Some charities attributed higher numbers of applications to a change in their publicity approach, such as advertising their services more prominently or developing their online presence. Bishop Laney's Charity notes in its 2014/15 annual report that 'the trustees established a web page last year and are entering into other incentives to increase the number of applicants' (Bishop Laney's 2015).

Other charities have used various ways to attract applicants. For example, the trustees of Chippenham Borough Lands Charity, as noted in their 2014/15 annual report, 'aim to encourage applications from the local community and have employed methods such as drop-in sessions targeting specific groups; monthly press releases on grants awarded; networking at local community events; and placing flyers in local shops, cafes, community notice boards, as well as the local library' (CBLC 2015).

A number of charities, however, experienced a decrease in demand for their services. The trustees of Dr Edwards and Bishop King's Fulham Charity stated in their 2013/14 annual report 'that the overall take up of grants in this year has been surprisingly low, given the economic climate, as a result of which the charity has decided to be more robust in its self-promotion' (DEBK 2015). In some cases, the reduction in applications has been explained by exceptionally high demand in the previous year. For instance, the trustees of the Gardeners' Royal Benevolent Society note that: 'The 5% decrease in clients in 2014 is partly due to an unusually high 15% increase in clients in 2013, when a combination of very bad weather, the new benefits system and high fuel bills led to over twice the rate of increase experienced in each of the previous three years' (Perennial 2015).

Partnerships and collaborations

In the course of our research we have found that a number of charities are partnering with other organisations in order to continue to meet their aims and objectives. The trustees of the IAPS Charitable Trust state that 'the trust will seek to identify other partners with whom it can work to efficiently deliver its objectives and may consider further mergers with other charities if they will fit within the objectives' (IAPS 2015). Similarly, the trustees of The Book Trade Charity noted in the 2014 annual report: 'During the year, BTBS worked closely with the Matthew Hodder Charitable Trust (MHCT) to provide programmes of support towards education and training objectives. With MHCT, BTBS launched a new programme to give additional resources and financial assistance to talented young people who would otherwise be unable to enter, grow and develop in the book trade' (BTBS 2015).

For charities that are increasingly being approached by beneficiaries with multiple complex needs, partnerships can provide a cost-effective way of supporting them. We have also found that many grant-makers are relying on other organisations and agencies, such as Citizens Advice, or occupational bodies, to refer individuals to their services. The Richmond Parish Lands Charity trustees state in their 2013/14 annual report: 'Multiple local agencies refer applications to the RPLC for support for those who have encountered hard times and require crisis funding.... Trustees are grateful to the dedicated teams from the referring agencies including the Citizens Advice Bureau, the Resettlement Team, Achieving for Children and the local Community Mental Health Teams' (RPLC 2014).

Rising to the challenge

The DSC Research Team has been inspired during the research process by the remarkable work that charities do and the difference they make to individuals' lives. It was interesting to note how charities are adapting to meet the needs of their beneficiaries despite the challenges they face. The Sacro Trust provides a range of services and grants to help individuals in Scottish communities in the process of rehabilitation. This trust is an example of the resilience of charities in the face of a challenge, as demonstrated in the following extract from the trust's 2013/14 annual report:

Years of budget cuts and a widespread programme of austerity – which still shows no sign of receding any time soon – had resulted in our organisation examining how we go about our business to achieve the best possible outcomes for our service users. It meant rethinking how we deliver services, develop our people, influence policy and manage ourselves. This was not always an easy or straightforward process but we are reaping the benefits of those changes now. Major investment in IT infrastructure has improved how we communicate and how we manage and measure our performance.... We have developed existing services, initiated new ones and formed partnerships to make collaborative working among the voluntary and statutory sectors a reality. We have revisited the effectiveness of the board and its committees and greatly increased the visibility and involvement of board members in these strategic areas.

Sacro 2014

The Reedham Children's Trust has been around helping children for over 170 years and has adapted its services as times have changed: 'always seeking the most innovative ways to meet the needs of vulnerable children'. The trust started as one of the first orphanages, operated as a residential school from 1950 until the closing in 1980 and since then has offered 'a unique grants programme supporting vulnerable children with their care and education at boarding schools' (Reedham 2016). The trust describes ways in which it adapted to the economic climate:

The trust works in conjunction with other trusts and schools to achieve its aims and make up a 'package' of support'.... Volatile economic conditions continued to impact on the trust's income from donations and cash deposits.... The Board agreed to reduce the grants budget available for its main grants programme to £300,000 for 2013/14. Whilst this means a reduction in the number of new grants available, it will give the Trust an opportunity to begin working on some more locally focused projects. The Board agreed to ring-fence some funding for 2013/14 for a new initiative focusing on identifying and supporting children from the London borough of Croydon.... It is the intention to build and further develop relationships with business and the corporate sector in order to secure further financial support.... The Board is developing a fundraising strategy that aims to raise £250,000 to support its current grants programme as well as its new initiatives within the next two years. It has recognised that as well as investing in research, investment will be required in the production of new publicity materials, computer systems, social media, and staff training to ensure it is in the best position to attract funds.

Reedham 2013

The Miners' Welfare Educational Fund 'makes grants to assist mineworkers, former mineworkers and their dependants to take higher education courses' (Miners' Welfare National Educational Fund 2016). The fund is aware of increasing dependence on assistance from charities and encourages students to take full benefit of the support available, as described in its 2013/14 annual report:

Students have become much more reliant on such charitable support with the decline in support available from the government and through local authorities, and the move into student loans. With further cuts in funding to be made available to Universities, and therefore increases in tuition fees to be paid by students, this situation will be exacerbated. The Trustees and Selection Committee are all too aware of the benefits and wider opportunities that participation in higher education can bring and would wish to continue to encourage as many as possible from mining communities to participate. It is

hoped that by working with other charitable groups, and funds specific to mining communities and beneficiaries it can help many more to achieve their full potential.

Miners' Welfare National Educational Fund 2015

The Winston Churchill Memorial Trust provides funds 'to investigate inspiring practice in other countries, and return with innovative ideas for the benefit of people across the United Kingdom' (WCMT 2016). The trustees of the charity explain how the trust has had a life-changing impact on individuals' lives, as noted in the 2013/14 annual report:

The Winston Churchill Memorial Trust carries forward [Sir Winston Churchill's] legacy by funding British citizens of all ages and all backgrounds to travel overseas and bring back inspiration and examples of best practice, for the benefit of others in their communities and professions. The Winston Churchill Memorial Trust aims to award over 100 Fellowships each year and has supported over 4,952 to date. The impact on the lives of these Churchill Fellows has been transformational; many have emerged as role models and experts in their local communities and workplaces. The opportunity provided by the Winston Churchill Memorial Trust has consistently inspired Fellows and their networks and improved life for people in the UK.

WCMT 2015

These and other examples we identified illustrate how grant-makers strive to overcome the challenges they face in order to continually meet the needs of their beneficiaries against all odds. The impact that the help from the charities make to the lives of many individuals is truly remarkable.

Case studies

Case studies provide a direct insight into the experiences of grant-making charities and beneficiaries and demonstrate the problems they face and the real difference that charities make. We have collected a few to share from The Prince's Trust and Able Kidz.

The Prince's Trust

The Prince's Trust helps disadvantaged 13- to 30-year-olds who are unemployed, struggling at school or at risk of exclusion to get their lives back on track. These young people include individuals who are leaving care, face social issues such as homelessness or mental health problems, or have been in trouble with the law. Help delivered by the trust through its programmes 'gives vulnerable young people the practical and financial support needed to stabilise their lives, helping develop self-esteem and skills for work' (Prince's Trust 2016). The Prince's Trust quantifies in its 2013/14 annual report the achievements it has made throughout the year:

The Prince's Trust helped 58,804 young people – more than we have helped in any single year since we were founded by HRH The Prince of Wales in 1976.... Our positive outcomes have continued to rise and now stand at 77%; more than three in four of our young people are in education, employment, training or volunteering, three months after completing a programme. 44% of our clients either found a job or entered self-employment – a climb of four per cent since the year before. These achievements are a real credit to our staff, volunteers, partners and supporters. As the economy returned to a cautious growth, overall levels of youth unemployment started to fall. Yet, at the end of the financial year, around 900,000 young people were still out of work.... For those young people who've never had the chance of a steady job, the road to recovery is long and slow; it would be a tragedy if they were left behind. This motivates us to do more, to ensure every young person has the chance to succeed. Our programmes help young people across the UK and we provide concentrated support in the areas where young people are most vulnerable. During the year we expanded our network of Prince's Trust centres, opening new sites in Belfast, Stoke and Burnley and moving to an improved location in Bristol. In the year ahead a further centre will open in London and we will continue to expand the opportunities for young people at each of our sites.

Prince's Trust 2014

Case study: The Prince's Trust

The charity's website provides case studies of some of its beneficiaries, explaining the difference the charity made to their lives:

Tara, 22, from North London, had to deal with abandonment from her father and felt like an outcast throughout her time at school. Tara struggled to connect with people and suffered with severe depression, after the death of her good friend Tara decided to turn her life around. Her support worker put Tara in touch with jobs in mind – a mental health charity – who then showed Tara a Prince's Trust leaflet for a Get Started with Fashion programme. Tara had always loved fashion and realised this was a perfect opportunity for her. Tara explained the support she received from the staff at the Prince's Trust was amazing; they provided her with advice and support when she needed it. The course helped Tara develop skills that were valuable for the work place. At the end of the course Tara was able to secure a permanent job at Zara. Tara now has the privilege of being a young ambassador for the Prince's Trust and hopes to help and encourage other people to change their lives.

Prince's Trust 2016

Khiry, 23 from Haringey, had to deal with the death of his mum at the age of 10, which affected his behaviour at school and led to depression. School wasn't a great time for Khiry, he was diagnosed with learning difficulties, including dyslexia and was coping with the loss of his mum. He was depressed, had few qualifications and felt unsupported by the people around him. However after a visit to the Prince's Trust, Khiry spoke to a member of staff who signed him up for the Fairbridge programme, the programme gives young people the chance to try new activities and learn new skills. Khiry received regular one-to-one support from staff at the centre which helped his confidence grow and slowly he started to trust people again. Then an opportunity came up for Khiry to take part in a Get into Retail programme, in partnership with Tesco, which gives young people intensive training and experience in that sector. Khiry thrived on the course and impressed staff so much that he was offered a job. He now works at a local Tesco store and was recently awarded a permanent contract. He is also a young ambassador for the Prince's Trust and he hopes to inspire more young people, like him, to achieve their goals.

Prince's Trust 2016

Case study – Able Kidz

The Able Kidz Educational Trust 'provides support for children and young adults with disabilities, seeking to improve their education in order to attain a greater level of independence and self-reliance in the face of adversity' (Able Kidz Educational Trust 2016).

The charity's website provides case studies explaining the difference Able Kidz has made to the lives of its beneficiaries:

Danielle was twelve and failing academically, her mother suspected she was dyslexic, her school said she would need to be independently tested by the institute of dyslexia but that she would have to bear the cost herself. Danielle's mother applied to Able Kidz for the fee, which they granted. An assessment process by the educational psychologist officially diagnosed Danielle with dyslexia this meant her school where now duty bound to offer her all the help and support that the educational psychologist considered appropriate. In the last two years Danielle's educational progress has gone from strength to strength and last year she was awarded the school prize for most improved student. Danielle is now expected to gain at least the 5 GCSE passes and she has set her heart on becoming a nurse.

Able Kidz 2016

These are only two examples of activities undertaken by grant-makers that are contained in this guide but they illustrate the vital support these organisations provide to individuals. The complexity of cases that charities have to deal with has increased following the welfare reforms, but the grant-makers do their best to adapt their policies and practices in order to accommodate the needs of those beneficiaries affected and often confused by the changes in the benefits' system.

A focus on higher education funding

The following article was contributed by DSC Researcher Rachel Cain.

Many of the grant-makers in this guide provide support for students in higher education. This article aims to explore the implications on students of two of the most significant policy changes currently affecting the funding of higher education, and to highlight the value of charitable grants in this context.

Maintenance grants and loans

Perhaps the most notable recent policy change in funding for undergraduate students was the announcement in the Chancellor's 2015 Summer Budget that the means-tested maintenance grants previously provided by the government will, for students entering higher education from September 2016 onwards, be scrapped and replaced by expanded maintenance loans.

The amount on offer by way of maintenance loans is set to rise to £8,200 for students from the lowest-income groups, resulting in an increase in disposable income (Bolton

2016). This will be welcomed by many, as the cost of living is indeed a great cause of concern for many students. Research by the National Union of Students found that, on average, students face a funding shortfall of almost £7,700 each year for the cost of living (NUS 2013). This is a gap that many of the grant-making charities in this guide help to fill.

Unlike a grant, however, a loan must be repaid. According to the analysis by the Institute for Fiscal Studies, this arrangement will mean that the average student will have to contribute an additional £9,000 overall towards the cost of their degree, and the heaviest increase will fall upon graduates from low-income backgrounds who reach the top 30% graduate earnings bracket (Britton *et al.* 2015).

Even if many graduates do not ultimately repay the entire loan over their lifetime, an important question is whether the prospect of this debt will deter students from entering higher education, particularly those from the lowest-income households.

As we noted earlier in this introduction, there was evidence that the rise in fees in 2012 did not reduce participation rates of the poorest students in higher education; however, grants for these students also increased at the same time as this rise (Britton *et al.* 2015). It may be that the up-front living costs are a greater priority for many students, and the expansion of maintenance loans could offset these concerns. However, for students from low-income backgrounds, particularly those who are debt-averse, the long-term prospect of having such increased levels of already significant graduate debt could be a strong deterrent from entering university. The Sutton Trust (2015), for example, has pointed out that participation in higher education has risen significantly in lower-income groups since the introduction of grants, and there is a risk that this change could 'tip the balance' for students from low- and middle-income groups against going to university.

This could make the grants in this guide even more important for supporting these individuals, by lessening the long-term financial impact of studying at university. This policy change represents a shift from the state being primarily responsible for funding higher education, towards the individual facing the whole burden, and the charities in this guide are there to support those individuals who are less able to bear this cost.

Students with disabilities

Disabled Students Allowance (DSA), the government's grant provision for students with a disability, long-term health condition or specific learning difficulty, is also undergoing a reform, with universities becoming responsible for more of the provision than in the past, and students also contributing more in some cases.

DSA is provided to fund support such as specialist equipment, non-medical helpers, additional travel expenditure and other course-related costs that occur due to a disability. Under reforms enacted from September 2016 onwards, higher-education providers become responsible for directly funding support for those with lower-level difficulties, while DSA will be used to fund more specialised support (Hubble and Bolton 2016). For example, while DSA could previously be used to provide standard laptops to meet students' needs, it will now only cover specialist computers and students will be expected to contribute £200 towards the cost. The most specialist non-medical support will still be directly funded by DSA, while higher-education providers are expected to fund expenditure such as additional accommodation costs, apart from in exceptional cases.

In 2014/15, 7% of full-time students in the UK who are studying for their first degree were in receipt of DSA (HESA 2015). Research by the Equality Challenge Unit, however, found that only around 50% of students who declare having a disability receive DSA and, as such, there are many students with disabilities who do not receive DSA (ECU 2015). This number may increase under the reformed provision due to the restrictions on eligibility and the transfer of responsibility for evaluating eligibility to higher-education providers. While these changes will give higher-education providers more control over their provision for students with disabilities, these providers are not charged with clear, specific obligations, creating uncertainty and the risk that provision for students with disabilities could vary greatly between universities.

Many of the charities in this guide that assist those with disabilities provide additional support to those receiving DSA, but also meet the needs of those who do not receive DSA, but whose disability or condition still affects their studies.

The value of a grant for higher education

Higher education is clearly a worthwhile investment. Funding just one undergraduate degree is estimated to bring an average return of £94,000 to the government, as well as countless non-monetary benefits for the individual, for the state and for society (Tatlow and Conlon 2013).

In awarding a grant, a funder demonstrates that they believe an individual is worth investing in, and that they have the potential to achieve and to contribute to society. This is an empowering message to send to a student. A grant allows a student not only to meet their short-term needs but also to shape their future, and the repayment of this faith and investment on the part of the trustees is in the individual's contribution to society.

The grants in this guide continue to be ever more valuable in the current higher education funding environment, and they demonstrate that education is a worthwhile investment – for the individual, and for society as a whole.

Finally...

Both educational and charitable sectors are experiencing difficult and uncertain times. However, the attitudes of grant-making charities are as inspiring as ever, with most ready to go the extra mile to help those in need. We put together the following sections to help both the grant-making charities and those requiring assistance. Information includes:

▷ 'Grant-making charities – their processes and effectiveness': our recommendations for grant-makers

INTRODUCTION

▶ 'About this guide': a description of the types of charities that are included, how they are ordered in the guide and the type of help that they give

▶ 'How to use this guide': an explanation of a typical entry and a flowchart to show you how to identify sources of help

▶ 'How to make an application': some advice on making applications, including an application form template

Most importantly, ensure that you read all eligibility criteria accurately. Do not apply if you are not eligible because the charities will not be able to fund you and it simply wastes everyone's time, including your own. Follow application procedures precisely and make sure that you meet any deadlines. More and more, we are seeing organisations expanding their support beyond just financial grants, and many are offering advice services as well, so take full advantage of these.

We wish you the best of luck in your search for funding.

Acknowledgements

We would like to offer a special thank you to Megan Dunn of the NUS for her contribution to this introduction.

We are extremely grateful to the many charity trustees, staff and volunteers who have provided up-to-date details for inclusion in this guide, and others who have helped. To name them all individually would be impossible.

How to give feedback to us

The research for this guide was done as carefully and thoroughly as we were able, but there will still be relevant charities that we have missed and some of the information may be incomplete or will become out of date. If you come across omissions or mistakes in this guide please let us know by calling or emailing DSC's Research Team (0151 708 0136; email: research@dsc.org.uk) so that we can rectify them for the future.

We are always looking to improve our guides and would appreciate any comments, positive or negative, about this guide, or suggestions on what other information would be useful for inclusion when we research the next edition.

References

4children (2015), *Children's Centre Census 2015: A national overview of children's centres in 2015* [PDF report], available at www.4children.org.uk, accessed 10 February 2016

Able Kidz Educational Trust (2016), 'Home' and 'Success Stories' [web pages], www.ablekidz.com, accessed 26 January 2016

Belfield, Chris and Luke Sibieta (2015), 'English schools will feel the pinch over the next five years' [web article], Institute for Fiscal Studies, www.gov.uk, 21 October 2015, accessed 15 January 2016

Bishop Laney's (2015), annual report and accounts 2014/15, Cambridgeshire, Bishop Benjamin Laney's Charity

Bolton, Paul (2015), *Tuition Fee Statistics* [PDF briefing paper no. 917], House of Commons Library, available at researchbriefings.files.parliament.uk, accessed 15 March 2016

Bolton, Paul (2016), *HE in England from 2012: Funding and finance* [PDF briefing paper no. 6206], House of Commons Library, available at researchbriefings.files.parliament.uk

BRC (2016), *Retail 2020: Fewer but better jobs* [PDF report], British Retail Consortium, available at www.brc.org.uk, accessed 15 March 2016

Britton, Jack, Claire Crawford and Lorraine Dearden (2015), *Analysis of the Higher Education Funding Reforms Announced in Summer Budget 2015* [PDF report; briefing note BN174], London, Institute of Fiscal Studies, available at www.ifs.org.uk, accessed 13 March 2016

BTBS (2015), annual report and accounts 2014, London, The Book Trade Charity

CBLC (2015), annual report and accounts 2014/15, Wiltshire, Chippenham Borough Lands Charity

Consolidated Charity of Burton upon Trent (2015), annual report and accounts 2014, Staffordshire, Consolidated Charity of Burton upon Trent

Cribb, Jonathan, Richard Disney and Luke Sibieta (2014), *The Public Sector Workforce: Past, present and future* [PDF report; briefing note BN145], Institute for Fiscal Studies, available at www.ifs.org.uk, accessed 15 March 2016

DEBK (2015), annual report and accounts 2013/14, London, Dr Edwards and Bishop King's Fulham Charity

Dugan, Emily (2015), 'Family services at risk as thousands of children's centres face budget cuts', *The Independent*, 18 October 2015

Easby, Jenny (2015), *Statistical First Release: GCSE and equivalent attainment by pupil characteristics, 2013 to 2014 (Revised)*, Department for Education, available at www.gov.uk, accessed 15 March 2016

ECU (2015), *Equality in Higher Education: Statistical report 2015 part 2: students* [PDF report], London, Equality Challenge Unit

HEFCE (2013), *Higher Education in England: Impact of the 2012 reforms* [PDF report], available at www.hefce.ac.uk, accessed 10 February 2016

HEFCE (2015), *Higher Education in England: Key facts* [PDF report], Higher Education Funding Council for England, available at www.hefce.ac.uk, accessed 15 March 2016

HEFCE (2016), 'Have higher fees affected the number of students dropping out?' [blog article], Higher Education Funding Council for England, 13 January 2016, available at blog.hefce.ac.uk, accessed 15 March 2016

HESA (2015), 'UKPIs: Widening participation of students in receipt of DSA' [web page], Higher Education Statistics Agency, www.hesa.ac.uk, accessed 29 February 2016

HKF (2015), annual report and accounts 2013/14, Chessington, Helena Kennedy Foundation

HKF (2016), 'What we do' [web page], www.hkf.org.uk, accessed 26 January 2016

Hubble, Susan and Paul Bolton, P. (2016), *Reform of the Disabled Students' Allowance in England* [briefing paper no. 7444], House of Commons Library

IAPS (2015), annual report and accounts 2014/15, London, IAPS Charitable Trust

Lauener, Peter (2015), 'Allocations for the funding year 2015 to 2016' [letter to the providers], Skills Funding Agency, 26 February 2015, available at www.feweek.co.uk, accessed 15 March 2016

McInerney, Laura (2013), 'Why welfare and education are inextricably linked', *The Guardian*, 15 April 2013, available at www.theguardian.com/education, accessed 29 February 2016

Miners' Welfare National Educational Fund (2015), annual report and accounts 2013/14, Sheffield, Miners' Welfare National Educational Fund

Norwich Town Close Estate Charity (2015), annual report and accounts 2014/15, Norwich, Norwich Charitable Trusts

NUS (2013), 'NUS figures show new students face cost of living crisis' [press release], National Union of Students, available at www.nus.org.uk/en/news/press-releases, accessed 29 February 2016

PAD Foundation (2016), *Grant programme: Guidance for applicants and application form* [PDF guide], Peter Alan Dickson Foundation, available at www.tarncourt.com, accessed 26 January 2016

Perennial (2015), annual report and accounts 2014, Leatherhead, Gardeners' Royal Benevolent Society (Perennial)

Prince's Trust (2014), annual report and accounts 2013/14, London, The Prince's Trust

Prince's Trust (2016), 'About the trust' and 'Success stories' [web pages], www.princes-trust.org.uk, accessed 26 January 2016

Reedham (2013), annual report and accounts 2012/13, Surrey, Reedham Children's Trust

Reedham (2016), 'Home' [web page], www.reedhamchildrenstrust.org.uk, accessed 26 January 2016

RMTGB (2015), annual report and accounts 2013, London, The Royal Masonic Trust for Girls and Boys

RPLC (2014), annual report and accounts 2013/14, Guildford, Richmond Parish Lands Charity

Sacro (2014), annual report and accounts 2013/14, Edinburgh, Sacro Trust

Sutton Trust (2015), 'Sutton Trust response to maintenance grants cuts set out in today's Budget' [press release], 8 July 2015, available at www.suttontrust.com, accessed 29 February 2016

Tatlow, Pam and Gavan Conlon (2013), *What's the Value of a UK Degree?* [PDF report], London, million+ and London Economics, available at www.millionplus.ac.uk, accessed 29 February 2016

UCAS (2015), *End of Cycle Report 2015* [research paper], available at www.ucas.com, accessed 15 March 2016

UCU (2015), *UCU Briefing on 24% Cuts to Adult Further Education Budget in England* [briefing paper], University and College Union, available at www.ucu.org.uk, accessed 15 March 2016

Unison (2016), 'Cuts in education services' and 'Real stories' [web pages], www.unison.org.uk, accessed 10 February 2016

WCMT (2015), annual report and accounts 2013/14, London, Winston Churchill Memorial Trust

WCMT (2016), 'About fellowships' [web page], available at www.wcmt.org.uk, accessed 26 January 2016

Note: All annual reports and accounts are available on the Charity Commission for England and Wales website.

Grant-making charities – their processes and effectiveness

The Directory of Social change has a vision of an independent voluntary sector at the heart of social change. Based upon this vision and our experience of researching this publication for over 25 years, we would like to suggest some ways in which charities that give grants to individuals could seek to encourage greater fairness and more effective practices in grant-making. We suggest that they:

- Seek to collaborate with others that have similar objectives. By sharing knowledge and best practice, organisations can contribute towards improving the wider grant-making landscape.
- Do as much as possible to decrease the amount of ineligible applications they receive. This is a joint responsibility with applicants, who should make sure that they read criteria carefully and not apply to charities for funding for which they are not eligible. However, grant-makers should facilitate this by ensuring that eligibility criteria and applications guidelines are transparent and easily available. Our research suggests that a growing number of charities choose to move towards electronic application forms and also sometimes consider a two-stage application process. Many willingly offer help and guidance with filling in the application form.
- Ensure, where they are local, that they are very well known within their area of benefit by writing to local Citizens Advice Bureaux, local authorities, schools and other educational establishments and community centres. As evidenced by the comments of the charity trustees during our research, an effective measure of raising the organisation's profile remains word of mouth, particularly with smaller charities. Ideally charities should aim to ensure that needs can be met as rapidly as possible, for example by empowering the clerk or a small number of trustees to make small emergency grants. If trustees can only meet twice a year to consider applications these should cover the peak times, namely: May to June when people are running out of money at the end of the academic year or looking forward to funding courses beginning in September; and November to December when people who have started their courses have a much clearer picture of how much money they need.
- Form clear policies on who they can support and what they can provide, targeting those most in need. A small number of charities in this guide are restricted to making grants to inhabitants of relatively wealthy areas and appear to have great difficulty finding individuals in need of financial support. In these cases, it would be appropriate for the trustees of these charities to consider applying to the Charity Commission for amendments to their governing document. The majority, however, receive a high volume of applications and they cannot support all of them.

About this guide

What charities are included?

We have included in this guide grant-making charities that give or have the potential to give:

- At least £500 a year in educational grants (most give considerably more)
- Grants based upon need rather than academic performance
- Funding for levels of education from primary school to first degree level: there may be some that will support pre-school education or postgraduate degrees as well ('education' is defined in its loosest sense, and therefore includes all types of vocational education and training, extra-curricular activities and personal or professional development)
- Grants to students of more than one educational establishment

We have not included those that (except where they appear to be particularly relevant to people in need):

- Give grants that are solely for postgraduate study
- Provide awards or scholarships for academic excellence

About 30% of the charities in this guide also give grants to individuals in need for the relief of poverty and hardship. These, along with many others, are included in the guide's sister publication *The Guide to Grants for Individuals in Need 2016/17*. The charities in this guide often support educational charities, youth organisations, community groups and educational establishments as well; however, the information given relates only to that which is relevant for individuals. *The Directory of Grant Making Trusts*, also published by the DSC, contains funding sources for organisations.

How charities are ordered

The grant-making charities in this guide are listed in five sections. The majority of grant-makers featured in the first four sections operate nationally, with criteria defined by something other than the geographical area of the applicant, although there are a few exceptions.

The five sections are:

- Charities by need (for example, general educational needs, further and higher education, illness and disability, independent and boarding schools)
- Subjects
- Occupation or parent's occupation
- Livery companies, orders and membership organisations
- Local charities (grant-makers which support individuals living in specific geographical areas – see page 129 for details about how to use this section)

What are grants given for?

Generally the charities in this guide offer one-off grants for a specific purpose or recurrent support for the duration of the individual's course or project. In some instances support may be given for a specific number of years or, in some rare instances, throughout the individual's education. The majority of the support given is intended to be supplementary and applicants will often need to secure money from different sources; however, small costs of necessities or sometimes even bigger projects may be covered in full. A handful of the grant-makers listed may offer low-interest or interest-free loans as well.

Grant-makers in this guide can give supplementary help with small grants for:

▶ Uniforms and other school clothing, sport kits, specialist outfits for professionals and clothes for a job interview
▶ Books, training materials, equipment, tools and specialist instruments
▶ Small-scale fees associated with the course or training, such as exam, registration or workshop fees
▶ Living expenses and maintenance costs or accommodation
▶ Travel costs both in the UK and overseas, including for overseas study, educational trips, voluntary and gap year experience, field studies or research purposes
▶ Course, school or training fees, particularly those for professional, technical or vocational courses and qualifications
▶ Extra-curricular activities aimed at the physical and social development of the individual, including sports, outdoor activities, music (including musical instruments, or the loan of musical instruments), arts and so on

▶ Specialist equipment related to disability that cannot be funded from statutory sources
▶ Childcare costs, particularly for mature students
▶ Expenses associated with apprenticeships or entering a trade or profession (this can sometimes include business start-up costs)
▶ Vouchers, such as for the local school uniform shop

Supporting information and advice

This guide also contains supporting information and advice on:

▶ Statutory grants and student support (see page 313)
▶ Types of schools in the UK and their funding (see page 315)
▶ Alternative routes to employment: apprenticeships (see page 319)
▶ Company sponsorships (see page 321)
▶ Funding for gap years and overseas voluntary work (see page 323)
▶ Contacts and sources of further information (see page 325)

How to use this guide

Below is a typical charity entry, showing the format we have used to present the information on each of the charities.

On the following page is a flowchart. We recommend that you follow the order indicated in the flowchart to look at each section of the guide and find charities that are relevant to you. You can also use the information in the sections 'About this guide' and 'How to make an application' to help inform your applications.

The Fictitious Charity

£24,000 (120 grants)

Correspondent: Ms I M Helpful, Charity Administrator, 7 Pleasant Road, London SN0 0ZZ (020 7123 4567; email: admin@fictitious.org.uk; website: www.fictitious.org.uk).

CC Number: 112234

Eligibility
Children or young people up to 25 years of age who are in need. Preference is given to children of single-parent families and/or those who come from a disadvantaged family background.

Types of grants
Small one-off grants of up to £250 for a wide range of needs, including school uniforms, books, equipment and educational trips in the UK and abroad. Grants are also available for childcare costs.

Annual grant total
In 2014 the charity had an income of £25,000 and an expenditure of £27,000. Grants awarded to 120 individuals totalled £24,000.

Other information
The charity also gives relief-in-need grants to individuals.

Exclusions
No grants are given for private school or university fees.

Applications
Applications can be made using a form available from the correspondent. They can be submitted directly by the individual, or by the parent or guardian for those under 18. Applications are considered in January, April, July and October.

Award and no. of grants
This shows the total (or estimated) amount given in grants during the financial year in question. Where further information was available, we have also included the total number of grants made.

Correspondent
This shows the name and contact details of the charity's correspondent. In many cases, this correspondent is the same contact listed on the Charity Commission's online register; however, in cases where we could find a more appropriate correspondent on a charity's website, we've included their name here instead.

Charity Commission number
This is the number given to a charity upon registration with the Charity Commission. A small number of the grant-makers detailed in this guide are not registered charities and so do not have a Charity Commission number.

Eligibility
This states who is eligible to apply for a grant. Criteria can be based on, for example, place of residence, age, subject studied or occupation.

Types of grants
Specifies whether the charity gives one-off or recurrent grants, the size of grants given and for which items or costs grants are actually given. This section will also indicate if the charity runs various schemes.

Annual grant total
This section shows the total amount of money given in grants to individuals in the last financial year for which there were figures available. Other financial information may be given, where relevant.

Other information
This section contains other helpful or interesting information about the charity.

Exclusions
This field gives information, where available, on what the charity will not fund.

Applications
Information on how to apply, who should make the application (i.e. the individual or a third party) and when to submit your request.

How to identify sources of help - a quick reference flowchart

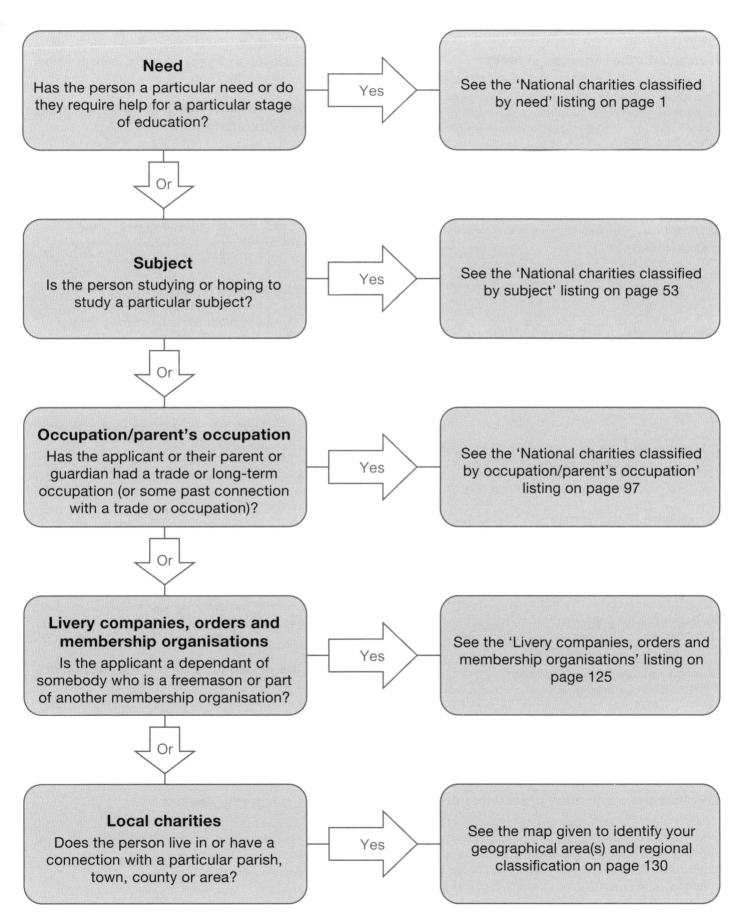

Need
Has the person a particular need or do they require help for a particular stage of education?

Yes → See the 'National charities classified by need' listing on page 1

Or

Subject
Is the person studying or hoping to study a particular subject?

Yes → See the 'National charities classified by subject' listing on page 53

Or

Occupation/parent's occupation
Has the applicant or their parent or guardian had a trade or long-term occupation (or some past connection with a trade or occupation)?

Yes → See the 'National charities classified by occupation/parent's occupation' listing on page 97

Or

Livery companies, orders and membership organisations
Is the applicant a dependant of somebody who is a freemason or part of another membership organisation?

Yes → See the 'Livery companies, orders and membership organisations' listing on page 125

Or

Local charities
Does the person live in or have a connection with a particular parish, town, county or area?

Yes → See the map given to identify your geographical area(s) and regional classification on page 130

How to make an application

This section gives you some information on how to make an application, with additional tips from funders' perspectives.

1. Exhaust other sources of funds

All sources of statutory funding should have been applied for and/or received before applying to a charity. Applications, therefore, should include details of these sources and any refusals. Where statutory funding has been received but is inadequate, an explanation that this is the case should be made. A supporting reference from a relevant agency may also be helpful.

If the applicant attends an educational establishment it should also have been approached to see if there are any funds that may give financial support or a reduction in fees is available.

> 'The best way to get help for individual funding is to start by helping yourself – try every avenue to raise as much of the money yourself before and while you approach others for a contribution to your cause. If they can see how determined you are and how hard you've worked already, they'll naturally feel motivated to help you find the remainder.'
>
> BBC Performing Arts Fund

Other possible sources of funding and advice are listed on page 325.

2. Use the flowchart on page xvii to identify potential sources of funding

Once you have found a grant-maker that may be relevant to you…

3. Check eligibility criteria

Submitting ineligible applications is the biggest mistake that applicants make. A charity cannot fund you if you are not eligible and you merely waste both your and the charity's time and resources by applying. If you are in any doubt, contact the grant-maker for clarification. Please remember that many charities are run by volunteers and their time is particularly valuable.

> 'Always read carefully a charity's criteria for eligibility. We, for example, are only allowed to help the children of actors, but three quarters of the applications I receive do not match this basic requirement. You are wasting your time and hopes by applying to a trust which clearly is not allowed to help you.'
>
> TACT

4. Follow the application procedures precisely

Wherever they are available, we have included application procedures in the entries; applicants should take great care to follow these. If there is an application form, use it! Please read any guidelines thoroughly and take note of deadlines. Some charities can consider applications throughout the year; others may meet monthly, quarterly or just once a year. Very urgent applications can sometimes be considered between the main meetings. Make sure that the appropriate person submits the application; this could be the individual, their parent or guardian or a professional such as a social worker.

Evidence from our research shows that the majority of organisations welcome initial contact before a full application is made, so if you are unsure about anything, get in touch with them.

5. Give details of any extenuating or unforeseen circumstances

Potential applicants should think carefully about any circumstances which put them at a disadvantage from other families or students, such as coming from a low-income background, being in receipt of state benefits, being a single parent, having a health problem or disability and so on. Where relevant, try and show how the circumstances you are now in could not have been foreseen (for example, illness, family difficulties, loss of job and so on). Charities are often more willing to help if financial difficulties are a result of unforeseen circumstances rather than a lack of forward planning. The funding in this guide is aimed at those facing the most barriers to education or training.

6. Give clear, honest details about your circumstances, including any savings, capital or compensation

Most trustees will consider the applicant's savings when they are awarding a grant, although sometimes this does not need to affect the trustees' calculations. In circumstances where you are certain that your savings are not relevant to grant calculations, you should explain this in the application.

> 'Be open and honest about your circumstances. We have to ensure that we have all the information we need to put your case forwards. If essential details emerge at a later date, this can affect your application. Be honest about how much you want to apply for and don't ask for the most expensive item. If you show that you've done your research, then that helps us too.'
>
> Fashion and Textile Children's Trust

7. Tailor the application to suit the particular charity

For example, if an application is being made to a trade charity on behalf of a child whose parent had lengthy service in that particular trade, then a detailed description (and, where possible, supporting documentation) of the parent's service would be highly relevant.

8. Ask for a suitable amount

Ask for an amount that the organisation is able to give. If a charity only makes small grants, try asking for help with books, travel, childcare expenses and similar costs, and apply for fees elsewhere.

9. Mention applications to other charities

Explain that other charities are being approached, when this is the case, and state that any surplus money raised will be returned.

10. Offer to supply references

For example, from a teacher, college tutor, support worker and/or another independent person. If the individual has disabilities or medical needs then a report from a GP would be necessary.

11. Be honest and realistic, not moralising and emotional

Some applicants try to morally bribe trustees into supporting the application, or launch into tirades against the current political regime. It is best to confine your application to clear and simple statements of fact.

12. Be clear, concise and provide sufficient detail

Give as much relevant information as possible, in the most precise way. For example, 'place of birth' is sometimes answered with 'Great Britain', but if the charity only gives grants in Liverpool, to answer 'Great Britain' is not detailed enough and the application will be delayed pending further information. Make sure that you write clearly and do not use jargon so that your application is easily understood.

13. Say thank you

Charitable organisations generally like to be kept informed of how their grants have made a difference. It is also important to keep in touch if you are in need of recurrent funding. Feedback also helps charities in their future grant giving.

'Don't consider the moment the grant appears in your bank account as the end of your relationship with the grantmaker – try to provide updates on the work the grant has helped you to undertake, including photos, videos and other resources.'

Royal Geographical Society

So remember to thank grant-makers for their support and let them know how their funding has helped you and others.

See below for notes on the application form template.

Using the application form template for financial assistance

Over the page is a general-purpose application form. It has been compiled with the help of the Gaddum Centre. It can be photocopied and used whenever convenient and should enable applicants (and agencies or persons applying on behalf of individuals) to state clearly the basic information required by most grant-makers.

Alternatively, applicants can use it as a checklist of points to include in the letter. Applicants using this form should note the following things in particular:

1 It is worth sending a short letter setting out the request in brief, even when using this application form.

2 Because this form is designed to be useful to a wide range of people in need, not all the information asked for in the form will be relevant to every application. For example, not all applicants are in receipt of state benefits, nor do all applicants have HP commitments.

In such cases, applicants should write N/A (not applicable) in the box or on the line in question.

3 If, similarly, you do not have answers for all the questions at the time of applying – for example, if you have applied to other charities and are still waiting for a reply – you should write 'Pending' under the question: 'Have you written to any other charities? What was the outcome of the application?'

4 The first page is relevant to all applications; the second page is only relevant to people applying for school or college fees. If you are applying for clothing or books for a schoolchild then it may be worth filling in only the first page of the form and submitting a covering letter outlining the reasons for the application.

5 Filling out the weekly income and expenditure parts of the form can be worrying or even distressing. Expenditure when itemised in this way is usually far higher than people expect. It is probably worth filling out this form with the help of a professional.

6 You should always keep a copy of the completed form in case the trust has a specific query.

7 This form should not be used where the trust has its own form, which must be completed.

Application form template

Purpose for which grant is sought	Amount sought from this application £
Applicant (name)	Occupation/School
Address Telephone no.	
Date of birth Age	Place of birth
Nationality	Religion (if any)

☐ Single   ☐ Married   ☐ Divorced   ☐ Partnered   ☐ Separated   ☐ Widow/er

Family details: Name	Age	Occupation/School
Parents/ Partner	. . . . . .	. . . .
Brothers/Sisters/ Children	. . . . . .	. . . .
. . . .	. . . . . .	. . . .
. . . .	. . . . . .	. . . .
Others (specify)	. . . . . .	. . . .

Income (weekly)	£	p	Expenditure (weekly – *excluding course fees*)	£	p
Father's/husband's wage	. . . . . .		Rent/mortgage	. . . . . .	
Mother's/wife's wage	. . . . . .		Council tax	. . . . . .	
Partner's wage	. . . . . .		Water rate	. . . . . .	
Income Support	. . . . . .		Electricity	. . . . . .	
Jobseeker's Allowance	. . . . . .		Gas	. . . . . .	
Employment and Support Allowance	. . . . . .		Other fuel	. . . . . .	
Pension Credit	. . . . . .		Insurance	. . . . . .	
Working Tax Credit	. . . . . .		Fares/travel	. . . . . .	
Child Tax Credit	. . . . . .		Household expenses (food, laundry etc.).	. . . . . .	
Child Benefit	. . . . . .		Clothing	. . . . . .	
Housing Benefit	. . . . . .		School dinners	. . . . . .	
Attendance Allowance	. . . . . .		Childcare fees	. . . . . .	
Disability Living Allowance	. . . . . .		HP commitments	. . . . . .	
Universal Credit	. . . . . .		Telephone	. . . . . .	
Personal Independence Payments	. . . . . .		TV rental	. . . . . .	
Maintenance payments	. . . . . .		TV licence	. . . . . .	
Pensions	. . . . . .		Other expenditure (specify)	. . . . . .	
Other income (specify)	. . . . . .				
. . . .	. . . . . .				
. . . .	. . . . . .				
. . . .	. . . . . .				

Total weekly income £ [   ]   **Total weekly expenditure** £ [   ]

Name of school/college/university:

Address

Course:

Is the course ☐ full-time? ☐ part-time?

Date of starting course:

Date of finishing course:

Name of local education authority:

Have you applied for a grant? ☐ YES ☐ NO

What was the outcome of the application?

Give details of any other grants or scholarships awarded:

Have you applied to your school/college/university for help? ☐ YES ☐ NO

What was the outcome of the application?

Have you applied to any other charities? ☐ YES ☐ NO

What was the outcome of the application?

Have you applied for any loans? ☐ YES ☐ NO

What was the outcome of the application?

How much are your school/college fees?

£

Have they been paid in full? ☐ YES ☐ NO

If NO, please give details:

Other costs (e.g. books, clothing, equipment, travel etc.):

How much money do you need to complete the course? £

Examinations passed and other qualifications

Previous employment (with dates)

Any other relevant information (please continue on separate sheet if necessary)

Signature:

Date:

About the Directory of Social Change

DSC has a vision of an independent voluntary sector at the heart of social change. The activities of independent charities, voluntary organisations and community groups are fundamental to achieve social change. We exist to help these organisations and the people who support them to achieve their goals.

We do this by:

▶ Providing practical tools that organisations and activists need, including online and printed publications, training courses, and conferences on a huge range of topics
▶ Acting as a 'concerned citizen' in public policy debates, often on behalf of smaller charities, voluntary organisations and community groups
▶ Leading campaigns and stimulating debate on key policy issues that affect those groups
▶ Carrying out research and providing information to influence policy makers

DSC is the leading provider of information and training for the voluntary sector and publishes an extensive range of guides and handbooks covering subjects such as fundraising, management, communication, finance and law. We have a range of subscription-based websites containing a wealth of information on funding from charities, companies and government sources. We run more than 300 training courses each year, including bespoke in-house training provided at the client's location. DSC conferences, many of which run on an annual basis, include the Charity Management Conference, the Charity Accountants' Conference and the Charity Law Conference. DSC's major annual event is Charityfair, which provides low-cost training on a wide variety of subjects.

For details of all our activities, and to order publications and book courses, go to www.dsc.org.uk, call 08450 777707 or email cs@dsc.org.uk

National and general sources of help

The entries in this first section are arranged in three groups: 1) classified by need, 2) classified by subject, and 3) classified by occupation of parent or applicant. Charities appear in full in the section that is most relevant (usually the section which occurs first) and are then cross-referenced.

This breakdown is designed to be the easiest way to identify charities which might be of relevance and as such we have attempted to make the terms as specific as possible. There is some crossover between sections; for instance, mature university students could identify charities in the 'Adult education and training' and 'Further and higher education' sections, with various other categories possibly being relevant dependent on personal circumstances.

There are a number of grant-makers which do not fall into any specific category; these appear in the 'General' section.

Charities are arranged alphabetically within each category. We always caution against using these lists alone as a guide to sources of money. Read each main entry carefully as there will usually be other criteria that must be met; for example, someone who is blind should not simply apply to all the charities in the 'sensory impairment' section. See the advice in the 'How to make an application' section on page xviii for more information on how to apply.

Classification by need

National charities classified by need 3

Adult education and training 9

Business start-up 9

Carers 9

Children and young people 10

Further and higher education 13

Gender 17

Illness and disability 19

    Sensory impairment 23

    Special educational needs 26

Independent and boarding schools 26

Miscellaneous 29

Overseas students 30

Personal development and extra-curricular activities 37

Religion 38

    Christianity 39

    Judaism 41

Specific circumstances 43

    People who have offended 43

    Refugees and asylum seekers 45

Study, work and voluntary work overseas 45

    Study/work 47

    Volunteering 48

Vocational training and apprenticeships 51

Classification by subject

Formal sciences 53

Humanities 53

    Arts 54

    History 66

    Languages 66

Natural sciences 67

    Earth sciences 67

    Physics 67

Professional and applied sciences 67

    Business and finance 68

    Construction 69

    Education 69

    Engineering 70

    Environment and agriculture 74

    Heritage and conservation 77

    Hospitality 78

    Law 79

    Media, journalism and communication 79

    Medicine 80

    Nautical subjects 83

    Public services 84

    Social work 85

    Sports 85

Religion 87

Skilled crafts 90

Social sciences 93

    Archaeology 93

    Cultural studies 94

    Geography 95

Classification by occupation of applicant or parent

Armed forces 97

    Army 99

    Royal Air Force 100

    Royal Navy and Marines 100

Arts and culture 102

    Acting 103

NATIONAL AND GENERAL SOURCES OF HELP

Dance 104

Music 104

Business, financial services and insurance
105

Education and training 107

Environment and animals 108

Hospitality and retail 109

Information and communication 109

Legal professions 111

Manufacturing 111

Mariners 112

Medicine and health 113

Mining and quarrying 116

Public and government sector 117

Emergency services 118

Religion 120

Sciences and technology 121

Secretarial and administration 122

Skilled crafts and trades 122

Sports 123

Transport and storage 124

National charities classified by need

General educational needs

Al-Mizan Charitable Trust

£11,300 (41 grants)

Correspondent: Zahra Shirzad, Grants Officer, 2 Burlington Gardens, London W3 6BA (email: admin@almizantrust. org.uk; website: www.almizantrust.org. uk)

CC number: 1135752

Eligibility
British citizens, those granted indefinite leave to remain in the UK and asylum seekers who are living in a condition of social or economic deprivation. Preference is given to the following groups:

▶ Orphans (a child who has lost either both parents or one parent who was the main bread-winner in the family)
▶ Children and young people under the age of 19 years (particularly those in care or who are carers)
▶ Individuals who have a disability, are incapacitated or terminally ill (particularly those who have a severe mental disability)
▶ Single parents (particularly divorcees and widows/widowers with children)
▶ Estranged or isolated senior citizens
▶ Individuals with severe medical conditions or their families
▶ Ex-offenders or reformed drug addicts or alcoholics
▶ Victims of domestic violence and/or physical or sexual abuse
▶ Victims of crime, anti-social behaviour and/or terrorism

Prisoner Training Fund: Serving prisoners, including foreign nationals, in custody of HMPS at any one of the following prisons in the North West: HMP Manchester; HMP Styal; HMP Forest Bank; HMP Wymott; HMP Kirkham; HMP Lancaster Farms; and HMP Hindley.

Applicants must have demonstrated good behaviour and/or have taken part in a regular programme of academic/ vocational learning, work or skills development workshops, and must have successfully acquired match-funding and/or made a personal contribution towards their training costs.

The trust prioritises the following groups:
▶ Individuals who are unable to read or write to an adequate standard
▶ Foreign nationals
▶ Individuals with a physical, mental or learning disability

Types of grants
Mainly one-off grants, which in 2013/14 ranged from £34 to a maximum of £500, with an average grant being £232. Interest-free loans can also be given. Grants are awarded with the aims of: providing access to education and/or vocational skills; increasing employability; and encouraging excellence in education, sport and/or the arts. They are also made to help relieve welfare needs and to break the cycle of poverty for individuals and families.

Prisoner Training Fund: The trust runs a specialist grants programme to help support the training and rehabilitation of prisoners in the UK. Grants of up to £200 are available for prisoners and detainees who are looking to access funding for vocational courses and/or books in prison that will assist their personal development and/or rehabilitation.

Annual grant total
In 2013/14 the trust had assets of £150,500 and an income of £127,500. Grants totalled £39,000, of which 41 grants for educational and employability purposes amounted to £11,300 (or around 29% of the grants' total).

Exclusions
The trust cannot help with: general appeals; applications from organisations or formal groups (except when assisting an individual or family); applicants who are not claiming all benefits for which they are eligible; applicants who have received funding from the trust in the last 12 months; applications for items or costs that have already been paid for; expenses relating to the practise or promotion of religion; debts, including rent and council tax arrears; fines or criminal penalties; university tuition fees; gap year projects; immigration costs; funeral expenses; gifts (including birthdays or festivals); holidays (however, the trust will consider funding trips for children and/or young people which 'enrich learning opportunities or very occasionally where a short vacation may serve a medical or social need'); international travel; applications for more than £500 (the trust will consider match-funding requests if the rest of the required amount is raised from other sources); products/services which contravene the ethos and values of the trust.

Prisoner Training Fund:
▶ Individuals who have served less than six months
▶ Individuals who have been awarded a grant from the trust within the last 12 months
▶ Individuals who are on remand or serving a sentence for offences related to terrorism
▶ Applications for training which will not have been completed by the end of the individual's sentence (applications for training beginning after the individual's release from prison should be made to the general fund)

- Applications which support a second undergraduate course or postgraduate study

Applications

All applications for grant funding must be submitted using the trust's online application system. They can be submitted directly by the individual or by a third party (with the individual's permission). Only one application can be considered per household at any time. The trust states the following information on its website:

We have developed a seven stage application process that includes an assessment of the need of the applicant based on individual social circumstances, telephone interviews and/or home-visits, analysis of the income and expenditure of applicants in relation to recognised models as well as reference and security checks.

Prisoner Training Fund: Applicants must ask a member of prison staff to download and print the application form from the trust's website. The trust will not post forms to individual prisoners. Although the form may be completed by a member of prison staff, the trust does expect the applicant to write a supporting letter or note. A referee (who must be a member of prison staff with an official prison email address) must sign the completed application before returning it to the trust by post or by email (as a single PDF file to grants@almizantrust.org.uk). The website states: 'Applications are considered in March and September each year. The deadline for receipt of applications is the 15th of the previous month. Applications received after the deadline will be allocated to the next round of grant-making.'

Note that, in order to reduce administrative costs, the trust does not accept enquiries by telephone.

Other information

In 2013/14 the trust launched – along with four partner organisations – a food bank to serve the boroughs of Brent, Harrow and Ealing. The partner organisations have pledged an annual investment of £35,000 to maintain the service, as well as a range of additional services in support of individuals who are experiencing poverty. In the food bank's first year, Al-Mizan Charitable Trust contributed £10,000.

The trust has an informative website and detailed annual report with case studies.

Lawrence Atwell's Charity (Skinners' Company)

£102,000 (124 grants)

Correspondent: S. Morris, Atwell Administrator, The Skinners' Company, Skinners' Hall, 8 Dowgate Hill, London EC4R 2SP (020 7213 0561; email: atwell@skinners.org.uk; website: www.skinnershall.co.uk/charities/lawrence-atwell-charity.htm)

CC number: 210773

Eligibility

The following information is taken from the 2013/14 annual report:

The Charity considers requests from young people between 16 and 26 who are focused on a particular vocational goal and who need help with the costs of vocational and pre-vocational training or to begin work. There is a particular interest in reaching those with additional barriers in life, employment and training (e.g. with no or few qualifications, caring responsibilities, family estrangement or separation through having to seek asylum, people affected by a disability, ex-offenders or those at risk of offending)

Applicants must be UK citizens, refugees with leave to remain in the UK or asylum seekers in the process of obtaining leave to remain.

Types of grants

Support towards:
- Vocational training below the level of a first undergraduate degree, for example, NVQ Level 3, BTEC National Diplomas, City and Guilds courses
- 'First step' qualifications to help people become qualified for work, such as NVQ Level 1/2, BTEC First Diplomas/Certificates and access and foundation courses
- Costs of finding a job, including the costs of attending an interview or buying tools to get someone started

Grants are given according to need, usually in the range of £100–£1,500, and can be one-off or recurrent (re-application each year is required). The majority of grants are given towards tuition, enrolment, registration and examination fees; however, help is also given towards general living expenses, travel costs, household bills, accommodation and specific items, tools, childcare costs or clothing.

Annual grant total

In 2013/14 the charity had assets of £15.3 million and an income of £416,000. The amount of grants given to individuals totalled £102,000.

Exclusions

Grants are not provided:
- To people under the age of 16 and over the age of 27
- To international or foreign students who have not lived in the UK for three years prior to the start of their course (including people from EU countries)
- For non-vocational courses such as GCSEs, A-levels, or GNVQs
- For higher education courses or courses for which government funding (such as a student loan) is available
- For courses at Level 4 or above
- For undergraduate/first degrees
- For postgraduate/second degrees
- Towards dance and drama courses which take place at private schools and colleges
- To individuals who are already qualified to work or who have had significant work experience
- To people whose current qualifications are Level 3 or above
- To cover any already existing fees or debts (including loans)
- In cases where it is unclear that the applicant will realistically be able to raise the balance of funds to complete the entire course
- Towards expeditions, travel or study abroad
- For business enterprises or start-up costs

If you are unsure about the level of your qualification see the Qualifications and Curriculum Authority website or visit the Quality Assurance Agency website.

Applications

Applicants are asked to first complete a short pre-application questionnaire available on the charity's website. Eligible applicants can then proceed with an online application. Guidelines for applicants and a useful FAQ section are also available to view on the website. The grants committee meets bi-monthly, in July, September, November, January, April or May, to consider new grant applications from individuals; however, emergency grants can also be made.

All applicants complete a standard online form and provide formal documentation of their identity and chosen training course; where appropriate, a statement of parental income is also submitted for assessment. Grant payments are usually made termly; they are only continued where the training or educational establishment certifies satisfactory attendance and progress.

The charity welcomes informal contact via phone (except on Wednesdays) or email to discuss applications. When making enquires make sure to leave your name, address, day-time phone number and/or your email address.

Other information

The charity also provides assistance to organisations and support to the Skinners' Company's voluntary-aided schools. In 2013/14 grants to schools and organisations totalled £131,000.

Black Family Charitable Trust

£10,000

Correspondent: Dr Thomas Black, Trustee, PO Box 232, Petersfield, Hampshire GU32 9DQ (email: enquires@bfct.org.uk; website: www.bfct.org.uk)

CC number: 1134661

Eligibility

Schoolchildren, further and higher education students who are in need. The trust's website states that the charity 'primarily aims to help young people to access high quality education, focusing its support particularly on those who would otherwise be denied appropriate education due to a lack of financial resources'.

Types of grants

Means-tested bursaries/scholarships and merit-based prizes/awards. Projects or research can also be supported.

Annual grant total

In 2013/14 the trust had an income of £19,500 and a total expenditure of £85,000. In previous years most of the support was given to universities and organisations. We estimate that around £10,000 was awarded to individuals for educational purposes.

Applications

Apply in writing to the correspondent.

Other information

Grants are also given to schools (also in developing countries) and other organisations.

The Alan Brentnall Charitable Trust

£10,000 (1 grant)

Correspondent: Roger Lander, Trustee, Spinney Corner, Green Lane, Aspley Guise, Milton Keynes, Bedfordshire MK17 8EN (01908582958)

CC number: 1153950

Eligibility

People in education who are in need.

Types of grants

Grants are made to help individuals with their education.

Annual grant total

In 2014 the trust had assets of £1.4 million and an income of £1.5 million. The trust made £17,500 in grants distributed as follows: £10,000 for educational support at Redroofs Theatre School for an individual; £5,000 to Derbyshire Children's Holiday Centre; £1,500 to Home-Start Erewash; and £1,000 to Derbyshire Asbestos Support.

Applications

Applications may be made in writing to the correspondent.

Other information

Awards are also made to registered charities in the areas of health, education and the relief of poverty.

M. R. Cannon 1998 Charitable Trust

See entry on page 51

The Chizel Educational Trust

£1,400

Correspondent: Geoffrey Bond, Trustee, Burgage Manor, Southwell, Nottingham NG25 0EP (016360816855)

CC number: 1091574

Eligibility

People under the age of 25 throughout the UK who are in need of financial assistance.

Types of grants

Bursaries, maintenance allowances and grants towards equipment, clothing, instruments, books and travel in the UK or abroad. Grants can be made to people entering a trade. The trust states that due to the present level of funds only small grants are available.

Annual grant total

In 2013/14 the trust had an income of £2,700 and an expenditure of £3,000. Financial support is also given to organisations; therefore, we estimate that the total amount of grants to individuals was around £1,400.

Applications

Applications should be made in writing to the correspondent. They must be submitted in May or November for consideration in June and December, respectively. An sae must be enclosed.

Other information

Financial assistance is also provided towards the maintenance of Ackworth

School Yorkshire and the Inverness Royal Academy Mollie Stephens Trust.

The Coffey Charitable Trust

£1,500

Correspondent: Christopher Coffey, Trustee, Oak Tree House, Over the Misbourne Road, Denham, Uxbridge, Middlesex UB9 5DR (01895 831381; email: coffeytrust@gmail.com)

CC number: 1043549

Eligibility

People in need in the UK.

Types of grants

Occasional one-off and recurrent grants are given according to need.

Annual grant total

In 2013/14 the trust had an income of £12,300 and a total expenditure of £6,500. We estimate grants to individuals for educational and social welfare purposes to be around £3,000.

Applications

Applications may be made in writing to the correspondent.

Other information

This trust mainly provides grants to Christian organisations and events.

Peter Alan Dickson Foundation

See entry on page 33

Family Action

£137,000

Correspondent: The Grants Service, 24 Angel Gate, City Road, London EC1V 2PT (020 7254 6251 (Wednesday and Thursday only between 2pm and 4pm); email: info@family-action.org.uk; website: www.family-action.org.uk)

CC number: 264713

Eligibility

Family Action helps people 'experiencing poverty, disadvantage and social isolation across England'. Educational support is given to individuals over the age of 14 who wish to enter further education, undertake training/retraining and otherwise pursue their career. Applicants must be studying at an organisation affiliated to Family Action's Educational Grants Service, attending a further education course (including pre-access and access), living on a low income (primarily in receipt of benefits) and must have a right of residency in the UK (EU students included).

Preference is given to people undertaking commercial subjects (for example IT, book keeping or accounting).

Types of grants

The charity states on its website:

> Many individuals face challenges during their time at school which may mean they are unable to complete their studies and pursue their future career goals. For others, their life situation may change meaning they need to re-train to gain employment that suits their family life. Family Action's Educational Grants Programme helps individuals to begin their studies as well as supporting existing students to continue and complete their studies.

Educational grants are normally in the region of £200–£300 and can be made towards costs associated with a course of study, for example clothing and/or equipment required for the course, travel, examination costs or computers/ laptops.

The charity's accounts state that they have also provided support towards school uniforms and travel costs to educational courses.

Annual grant total

In 2013/14 the charity had assets of almost £12.3 million and an income of £20.2 million. A total of 556 grants totalling £175,000 were made for the alleviation of need and a total of £137,000 was spent as other costs under the educational grants advice, which we take to refer to the grant expenditure.

Exclusions

Funding is not given for:

- Course fees
- Costs already incurred
- Items provided by the college for the course
- Childcare
- Study outside the UK
- Higher education courses
- Postgraduate study
- Asylum seekers and overseas students

Applications

Applications have to be submitted online by authorised members of staff (this will often be the student welfare advisors or an equivalent body) from the affiliated organisation.

Further details on support available can be obtained via phone or email (egas.enquiry@family-action.org.uk). The charity's website states: 'With regret we are unable to acknowledge or respond to postal enquiries.'

Other information

Family Action provides a range of advice and support services across the country – see the 'Find us' facility on the website to find your local office. Support is given to help in the areas of some of the most complex issues, including financial hardship, mental health problems, social isolation, learning disabilities, domestic abuse, or substance misuse and alcohol problems. It is aimed to improve the lives of children and families, help through the early years of child development and ensure adult mental health and well-being.

Fenton Trust

£24,000

Correspondent: Fiona MacGillivray, Correspondent, Family Action, 501–505 Kingsland Road, London E8 4AU (020 7241 7609; email: grants. enquiry@family-action.org.uk; website: www.family-action.org.uk)

CC number: 264713-33/247552

Eligibility

Any dependant of a member of professional class undergoing a course of education or training or 'poor and deserving members of the professional or middle classes and their dependants'.

Types of grants

Grants are normally of about £200–£300 and can be given to assist with general educational costs.

Annual grant total

In 2013/14 the trust had an income of £17,500 and an expenditure of £26,000. We estimate that about £24,000 was given in grants.

Exclusions

Grants are not available for private school fees, loan repayments, childcare costs, living expenses or to postgraduate students.

Applications

The trust is administered by the Family Action. Enquiries should be directed to the correspondent.

Other information

Our research suggests that the grant is paid to the governing body not the individual.

The Carol Hayes Foundation

£7,000

Correspondent: Carol Hayes Management, Carol Hayes Management, London LTD, 5–6 Underhill Street, London NW1 7HS (020 7482 1555; email: carol@carolhayesmanagement.co. uk)

CC number: 1153269

Eligibility

Young people from disadvantaged backgrounds.

Types of grants

Financial support and the provision of specialist equipment for those is need which will enable them to pursue a trade, career apprenticeship or similar vocational training and allow them to participate in society.

Annual grant total

In 2014 the foundation had both an income and an expenditure of around £7,200. We estimate that the amount of grants given to individuals totalled about £7,000.

Applications

Apply in writing to the correspondent.

George Heim Memorial Trust

£2,800

Correspondent: Paul Heim, Trustee, Wearne Wyche, Picts Hill, Langport TA10 9AA (01458252097; email: peheim@pictshill.com)

CC number: 1069659

Eligibility

People under the age of 30 who are in education or training. Our research suggests that further/higher education students are particularly supported.

Types of grants

Grants range up to £1,000 and are given to 'encourage [beneficiaries] in education'.

Annual grant total

In 2013/14 the trust had an income of £2,700 and an expenditure of £3,000. We have estimated that the annual total amount of grants awarded was around £2,800.

Applications

Applications may be made in writing to the correspondent.

Leverhulme Trade Charities Trust

£1.8 million (343 grants)

Correspondent: Paul Read, Administrator, 1 Pemberton Row, London EC4A 3BG (020 7042 9881; fax: 020 7042 9889; email: pread@ leverhulme.ac.uk; website: www. leverhulme-trade.org.uk)

CC number: 288404

Eligibility

Students at a recognised UK university who are in need and whose parent or spouse has worked as commercial traveller, grocer or chemist for at least five years.

Individuals are still eligible if their parent/spouse is unemployed (or deceased) but who fell within one of the three categories when the employment ceased (or at the time of death).

Types of grants

One-off or recurrent grants of up to £3,000 a year to full-time undergraduate students and of up to £5,000 a year to postgraduate students. Support is given towards general educational needs, including tuition and examination fees, living expenses, books, equipment, travel costs and accommodation. Awards are paid to the applicant's university.

Annual grant total

In 2013/14 the trust had assets of £62 million and an income of £2.2 million. Bursaries to 343 individuals totalled around £1.8 million, consisting of £1.4 million in 278 undergraduate bursaries and £360,000 in 65 postgraduate bursaries.

Applications

Application forms for undergraduate funding together with full guidelines can be accessed from the trust's website. They should be submitted by 1 March or 1 November for consideration in the following six weeks.

The closing date for postgraduate applications is 1 October.

Where application numbers exceed the amounts allocated for bursaries, awards are reduced or declined based on the financial need of the applicant.

Other information

In 2013/14 grants to institutions totalled £359,000.

P. and M. Lovell Charitable Trust

£6,000 (20 grants)

Correspondent: The Trustees, Administrator, KPMG, 100 Temple Street, Bristol BS1 6AG (0117 905 4000; fax: 0117 905 4065)

CC number: 274846

Eligibility

People in education who are in need.

Types of grants

One-off grants of up to £500 (generally of £300).

Annual grant total

In 2013/14 the trust had assets of £2.3 million, an income of £74,000 and made grants totalling £48,000. Awards to 20 individuals totalled £6,000. The trustees' annual report from 2013/14 states 'The income of the trust is to be distributed solely for charitable purposes to charitable institutions or individuals. The capital may be applied for charitable purposes or retained by the trustees at their discretion.'

Applications

Apply in writing to the correspondent.

Other information

Grants are mostly made to organisations (around £42,000 to 83 institutions in 2013/14).

The Osborne Charitable Trust

£2,200

Correspondent: John Eaton, Trustee, 57 Osborne Villas, Hove, East Sussex BN3 2RA (01273 732500; email: john@eaton207.fsnet.co.uk)

CC number: 326363

Eligibility

People in need undertaking education in the UK and overseas.

Types of grants

One-off and recurrent grants are given according to need and one-off grants in kind are given. According to our research, awards are made to schoolchildren for equipment/instruments and to people with special educational needs towards fees and equipment/instruments.

Annual grant total

In 2014/15 the trust had an income of £7,200 and a total expenditure of £10,100. We estimate that around £2,200 was given in grants to individuals for educational purposes.

Exclusions

Grants are not made for religious or political purposes.

Applications

Our research suggests that the trust does not respond to unsolicited applications.

Other information

The trust can also make grants to individuals for social welfare purposes and supports organisations (especially children's charities).

The Prince's Trust

£1.8 million (6,737 grants)

Correspondent: Sarah Haidry, Secretary, Prince's Trust House, 9 Eldon Street, London EC2M 7LS (020 7543 1234; fax: 020 7543 1200; email: info@princes-trust.org.uk; website: www.princes-trust.org.uk)

CC number: 1079675, SC041198

Eligibility

Young people between the ages of 13 and 30 who are not expecting to achieve five GCSEs (or equivalent) grades A-C, who struggle at school, are not in education or training, are in or leaving care, are long-term unemployed or have been in trouble with the law.

Types of grants

The Prince's Trust aims to change the lives of young people, helping them to develop confidence, learn new skills and get practical and financial support. The following support is offered:

▶ Development awards – cash grants of between £50 and £500 that are available to assist young people aged 14 to 25 to access education, training or employment. For example, previous awards have funded young people to buy essential equipment for college courses or pay for childcare enabling young mothers to access training

▶ Enterprise programme – assists young people aged between 18 and 30 to start their own business through the provision of financial and mentoring support. The programme helps young people who are interested in self-employment. The focus of the programme is on supporting young people to choose and achieve the outcome which is best for them. It also helps those who believe they are ready to start a business to plan and test their ideas thoroughly, improving the quality of their propositions and, therefore, increasing their chances of success

Annual grant total

In 2013/14 the trust had assets of £38.7 million and an income of £60.5 million. A total of £1.8 million was distributed in grants to individuals, consisting of:

| Enterprise programme | 1,475 | £1 million |
| Development awards | 5,262 | £818,000 |

Exclusions

The trust will not fund:
▶ Retrospective grants
▶ Gap year or overseas projects
▶ Medical treatment
▶ Course fees that are far above the £500 funding limit

- NVQ Level 4, HNC, HND, university degree or postgraduate courses (or courses of an equivalent level)

Applications

Initial enquiry forms should be completed online on the trust's website. Eligible applicants will then be advised on further procedure.

Potential applicants are also invited to make queries by phone at 0800 842842, or text 'Call Me' to 07983 385418 to discuss an application.

Other information

The Prince's Trust also runs many programmes which provide young people with personal development, training and opportunities to help them move into work. Details of these can be found on the trust's website.

Professionals Aid Council

£21,000 (62 grants)

Correspondent: Finola McNicholl, Chief Executive, 10 St Christopher's Place, London W1U 1HZ (020 7935 0641; email: admin@professionalsaid.org.uk; website: www.professionalsaid.org.uk)

CC number: 207292

Eligibility

The dependants of people who are graduates or have worked in a professional occupation requiring that level of education, or those who have a first degree themselves, studying in the UK.

With regard to assistance for college or university students, the charity states the following information on its website:

We may be able to assist you if you are studying in the UK and are:

- a UK citizen or have indefinite leave to remain
- an EU or overseas student undertaking studies in the UK
- a medical, dental or veterinary student in the final two years of your course

Types of grants

Grants are given for:
- Children's education – modest grants to assist with the costs of uniforms, (in some circumstances) school travel expenses, and other school-related costs (books, stationery, etc.)
- College and university students – grants, usually in the range of £300 to £500, are given for (in some circumstances) course-related travel expenses (e.g. work or research placements) and other related course expenses (stationery, books, thesis production, etc.)

Annual grant total

In 2014 the charity had assets of £2.2 million and an income of £101,000. In total, the charity assisted 228 beneficiaries during the year. Grants totalled £121,500, of which £101,000 was given in general assistance. Grants from the Educational Fund amounted to £21,000, and assistance was received by 26 families towards children's education and by 36 higher and further education students.

Exclusions

The charity does not assist with: extra-tutorial fees; study abroad; ordination or conversion courses; intercalated years or medical elective periods; or IELTS, ORE or PLAB tests for overseas doctors.

Applications

Initial enquiries can be made using the form on the website or, alternatively, by writing to the charity's Administration Department. Grants are means-tested.

Other information

The organisation also offers advice and assistance. Grants are also made for welfare purposes.

Scarr-Hall Memorial Trust

£9,500

Correspondent: Donna Thorley, Administrator, Baker Tilly, Festival Way, Festival Park, Stoke-on-Trent, Staffordshire ST1 5BB (email: donna.thorley@bakertilly.co.uk)

CC number: 328105

Eligibility

People in education and training throughout the UK.

Types of grants

One-off grants are usually in the range of £100–£500.

Annual grant total

In 2014 the trust had an income of £25,000 and an expenditure of £10,000. We estimate the annual total amount of grants awarded to individuals to be around £9,500.

Applications

Applications can be made in writing to the correspondent providing an sae and stating all the relevant individual circumstances, reasons why the grant is needed and how much is required.

The Talisman Charitable Trust

£26,000 (20 grants)

Correspondent: Philip Denman, Trustee, Basement Office, 354 Kennington Road, London SE11 4LD (020 7820 0254; email: talismancharity@gmail.com; website: www.talismancharity.org)

CC number: 207173

Eligibility

People in the UK who are living on a very low income.

Types of grants

One-off and recurrent grants are given according to need.

Annual grant total

In 2013/14 the trust had assets of £10.4 million and an income of £205,500. Grants totalled £205,000, of which £172,000 was awarded to individuals. 20 educational grants to individuals were made, amounting to £26,000.

An additional £146,000 was paid in 147 social welfare grants to individuals, and organisations received a further £33,000.

Applications

Applications should be made in writing to the correspondent through a social worker, Citizens Advice or similar third party. They should be on headed paper and include the individual's full name and address, a summary of their financial circumstances, what is needed and how much it will cost. A brief history of the case and a list of any other charities approached should also be included, as should the payment details of the third party organisation to which the grant will be paid. Supporting evidence such as medical documentation, a letter from the applicant's school or written quotations would also be helpful. The trust stresses that original documentation should not be submitted, as it cannot be returned. Applications are considered throughout the year. Only successful applications will receive a reply. See the website for full guidelines on how to apply.

Other information

This trust was previously called The Late Baron F. A. D'Erlanger's Charitable Trust.

The trust cannot accept applications made by recorded delivery or 'signed for' services.

Toby and Regina Wyles Charitable Trust

£7,000

Correspondent: Ross Badger, Trustee, 3rd Floor, North Dukes Court, 32 Duke Street, St James's, London SW1Y 6DF (020 7930 7797; email: ross.badger@hhllp.co.uk)

CC number: 1118376

People in need of assistance to enter or continue their education.

Types of grants
Grants are given towards general educational costs.

Annual grant total
In 2014/15 the trust had an income of £5,600, and a total charitable expenditure of £142,000. Most of the trust's funding is given to other charitable organisations. The amount of grants awarded to individuals was not specified; however, previously grants to individuals have totalled £7,000.

Applications
Apply in writing to the correspondent.

Other information
Grants are mainly made to organisations.

The Zobel Charitable Trust

£1,600

Correspondent: Stephen Scott, Trustee, Tenison House, Tweedy Road, Bromley, Kent BR1 3NF (020 8464 4242 (ext. 402))

CC number: 1094186

Eligibility
People in education in the UK, particularly in the Christian field.

Types of grants
Small, one-off grants according to need.

Annual grant total
In 2013/14 the trust had an income of £1,000 and an expenditure of £3,400. We estimate that about £1,600 was given in grants to individuals.

Exclusions
Grants are not made for school, university or postgraduate fees.

Applications
Our research indicates that this trust does its own research and does not always respond to unsolicited applications.

Other information
Grants are also made to organisations.

Adult education and training

Diamond Education Grant (DEG)
See entry on page 17

Monica Eyre Memorial Foundation

£1,400

Correspondent: Michael Bidwell, Trustee, 53 Oliver's Battery Road North, Winchester SO22 4JB (email: monica.eyre@gmail.com)

CC number: 1046645

Eligibility
Mature students in need, particularly those with disabilities/special needs in the UK.

Types of grants
Grants towards fees to enable mature students to start or continue courses.

Annual grant total
In 2014/15 the foundation had both an income and a total expenditure of £5,800. Grants are made to individuals and organisations for a wide range of charitable purposes. We estimate that educational grants to individuals totalled £1,400.

Applications
Apply in writing to the correspondent. The foundation vets course content and validates enrolment before awarding any funding.

Business start-up

The Oli Bennett Charitable Trust

£11,000

Correspondent: Joy Bennett, Administrator, Camelot, Penn Street, Amersham HP7 0PY (01494 717702; email: info@olibennett.org.uk; website: www.olibennett.org.uk)

CC number: 1090861

Eligibility
Young people between 18 and 30, who are self-employed and are UK residents.

Types of grants
Grants in the range of £1,000–£1,500 for people starting up their own businesses.

Annual grant total
In 2014 the trust had an income of £5,500 and an expenditure of £11,500. We estimate that grants made to individuals totalled around £11,000.

Applications
Application forms are available on the trust's website. Applications are considered every three months. A business plan is required to assess the viability of the idea.

Other information
The trust was set up in memory of Oli Bennett, who died in the September 11 2001 attacks in New York.

Carers

Carers Trust

£35,000

Correspondent: Grants Team, 32–36 Loman Street, London SE1 0EH (0844 800 4361; fax: 0844 800 4362; email: info@carers.org; website: www.carers.org)

CC number: 1145181

Eligibility
Unpaid carers in the UK, especially those who live near a Princess Royal Trust for Carers Centre.

Types of grants
One-off grants are awarded, usually of up to £300. Funding is given to provide support to carers towards equipment, essential items, personal and skills development or other educational activities.

Annual grant total
In 2013/14 the trust had assets of £8.4 million and an income of £11.4 million. The amount of grants given to individuals totalled £70,000. We estimate that educational grants to individuals totalled £35,000, with funding also given for social welfare purposes.

Applications
Applications should be made via your local Carers Service centre. Direct applications are not considered.

Other information
The trust was formed by the merger of The Princess Royal Trust for Carers and Crossroads Care in April 2012 and acts as a resource body, providing advice, information and support for carers. Carers who are in need of support can contact the online support team by

emailing support@carers.org. The support team is available over the Christmas and New Year period.

In 2013/14 grants were also paid to institutions, totalling £273,500, and to the trust's Network Partners, amounting to more than £1.4 million.

Children and young people

The Athlone Trust

£30,000

Correspondent: David King-Farlow, Trustee, 36 Nassau Road, London SW13 9QE (07496653542; fax: 020 7972 9722; email: athlonetrust@outlook.com; website: www.athlonetrust.com)

CC number: 277065

Eligibility

Adopted children under the age of 18 who are in need.

Types of grants

According to our research, the trust can give grants for school fees (including private education). The trust marks that support is increasingly given to families with children who have serious disabilities such as Asperger's Syndrome or Attention Deficit Hyperactivity Disorder (ADHD). In exceptional circumstances one-off grants can be provided to help with the cost of educational essentials for schoolchildren.

Annual grant total

In 2013 the trust had an income of £17,000 and an expenditure of £32,000, which is the highest in the past five years. We estimate that the annual total amount of grants awarded was around £30,000. At the time of writing (July 2015) the information provided was the latest available.

Exclusions

People at college or university are not supported.

Applications

Apply in writing to the correspondent. Applications should be submitted by the applicant's parent/guardian and are usually considered in May and November.

Other information

The trust may consider assisting people who are 19 years old providing they are still at school.

John Collings Educational Trust

£7,500

Correspondent: Anthony Herman, Trustee, 11 Church Road, Tunbridge Wells, Kent TN1 1JA (01892 526344)

CC number: 287474

Eligibility

Children, normally up to the age of 14, who are in need.

Types of grants

Support towards general educational needs, including books, fees, equipment/instruments and other essentials for schoolchildren.

Annual grant total

In 2013/14 the trust had an income of £27,000 and an expenditure of £14,800. We estimate that grants awarded to individuals totalled around £7,500.

Exclusions

Grants are not available to people at college or university.

Applications

Apply in writing to the correspondent. Previously the trust has noted that its income is accounted for and new applicants are unlikely to benefit.

Other information

Grants can also be made to organisations.

The EAC Educational Trust

£38,000 (28 grants)

Correspondent: Daniel Valentine, Trustee, Sherwood, The Street, Brook, Ashford, Kent TN25 5PG (01580 713055)

CC number: 292391

Eligibility

Children and young people, normally between the ages of 8 and 16, from single parent families, poor families and, particularly, sons and daughters of the Church of England clergymen.

Types of grants

According to our research, grants are almost exclusively given for school fees, including boarding expenses. The trust has a close link with one particular school which specialises in educating the families of clergy but other applications are also accepted, especially for the education of children in choir schools or other establishments with musical or dramatic emphasis. Individual grants almost never exceed one-third of the pupil's annual fees.

Annual grant total

In 2013/14 the trust had assets of £41,000 and an income of £44,000. A total of around £38,000 was awarded in grants to 28 individuals.

Applications

Apply in writing to the correspondent. Applications are normally considered in spring.

Other information

The main objectives of the charity are the relief of poverty and advancement of education for the benefit of the public and particularly amongst the families of clergy of the Church of England, single parent families or other poor families.

The French Huguenot Church of London Charitable Trust

£76,000 (51 grants)

Correspondent: Duncan McGowan, Clerk to the Trustees, haysmacintyre, 26 Red Lion Square, London WC1R 4AG (02079695500; email: dmcgowan@haysmacintyre.com)

CC number: 249017

Eligibility

People under the age of 25. Support is given in the following priority: people who/whose parents are members of the Church; people of French Protestant descent; other people as trustees think fit (see the 'Types of grants' section for preferences).

Types of grants

Annual allowances, bursaries and emergency or project grants to school pupils, further/higher education students, people in training or those entering a trade/starting work. Preference is given to French Protestant children attending French schools in London, choristers at schools of the Choir Schools Association, girls at schools of the Girls' Day School Trust and United Learning, and boys in selected independent day schools (list can be received upon request from the trust).

Support can be given for various educational needs, including outfits, necessities, equipment and instruments, books, study of music or other arts, also home/overseas projects. Special allowances for people of French protestant descent are given in modest one-off payments towards books.

Annual grant total

In 2014 the trust had assets of £11.5 million and an income of £352,500. Educational grants and bursaries to 51 pupils totalled £76,000, including grants to four young people totalling £700 for overseas projects.

Applications

Applications for grants and bursaries from members of the Church and French Protestant children attending schools in London should be made to the Secretary of the Consistory, 8–9 Soho Square, London W1V 5DD.

Requests for special allowances to people of French Protestant descent and for project grants should be addressed to the correspondent.

Applications from choristers and pupils at the selected schools should be addressed to the educational institution concerned, mentioning the applicant's connection (if any) with the French Protestant Church.

Other information

In addition to the educational fund there also are church and hardship funds mostly supporting organisations.

In 2014 awards totalling £78,500 were made to organisations working with people in hardship, and £41,500 to educational organisations, including an annual postgraduate scholarship of £2,500 for Huguenot research at the Institution of Historical Research at the University of London.

The William Gibbs Trust

£7,500

Correspondent: Antonia Johnson, Trustee, 40 Bathwick Hill, Bath BA2 6LD

CC number: 282957

Eligibility

Children and young people in education who are of British nationality.

Types of grants

One-off and recurrent grants are given according to need are given towards general educational needs.

Annual grant total

In 2013 the trust had an income of £9,400 and an expenditure of £15,300. We estimate the annual total amount of grants awarded to individuals to be around £7,500.

At the time of writing (October 2015) the information provided was the latest available.

Applications

The trust has previously stated that it does not respond to unsolicited applications as the funds are already allocated. Any enquiries should be made in writing.

Other information

Grants are also given to organisations for educational purposes.

The Lloyd Foundation

See entry on page 107

The McAlpine Educational Endowments Ltd

£103,500 (23 grants)

Correspondent: Brian Arter, Trustee, Eaton Court, Maylands Avenue, Hemel Hempstead, Hertfordshire HP2 7TR (01442 233444; email: b.arter@sir-robert-mcalpine.com)

CC number: 313156

Eligibility

Children and young people in need at a public or an independent school and at any technical college or University.

Types of grants

According to the trustees' annual report for 2014, support is given for 'an academic year by year basis, but can be renewed for subsequent years subject to a satisfactory school report for the academic year and the availability of funds'.

According to our research, grants normally reach up to £1,800 and are mainly given towards the cost of independent school fees for children attending ten schools selected by the trustees. Applicants normally are of academic ability, sound character and leadership potential but, for reasons of financial hardship, would otherwise have to leave the school.

Annual grant total

In 2014 the charity had assets of £135,500, an income of £99,500 and made grants to individuals totalling £103,500. During the year 23 bursaries were made.

Exclusions

Grants for people at specialist schools (such as ballet or music schools, or schools for children with learning difficulties) are not normally considered.

Applications

Apply in writing to the correspondent. The trustees' annual report form 2014 states that the charity 'carries out its objectives by receiving applications from individuals or parents in connection with mainstream education'. Applications should normally be made through the selected schools, the list of which is available from the correspondent. Applications are considered during the summer before the new academic year. Note, that because of the long-term nature of the charity's commitments, very few new grants can be considered each year.

The Northern Counties Children's Benevolent Society

£71,000 (29 grants)

Correspondent: Glynis Mackie, Secretary, 29A Princes Road, Gosforth, Newcastle upon Tyne NE3 5TT (0191 236 5308; email: info@gmmlegal.co.uk)

CC number: 219696

Eligibility

Children in need through sickness, disability or other causes who live in the counties of Cheshire, Cleveland, Cumbria, Durham, Greater Manchester, Humberside, Lancashire, Merseyside, Northumberland, North Yorkshire, South Yorkshire, Tyne and Wear and West Yorkshire. Preference is given to individuals who have lost one or both of their parents.

Types of grants

One-off and recurrent grants are available mainly towards school fees and clothing. The society has previously stated that support is also given for necessities, equipment, computers, or, in a limited number of cases, the provision of special equipment of an educational or physical nature for children with disabilities. In almost every case the need for assistance arises through the premature death of the major wage earner or the break-up of the family unit. Applications are treated in strict confidence and the financial circumstances of each applicant are fully and carefully considered by the trustees before an award is made.

Annual grant total

In 2014 the society had assets of £1.5 million and an income of £61,000. Grants totalling £71,000 were awarded to 29 individuals.

Applications

Application forms are available from the correspondent. Grants are normally considered in January, April, July or October. The trustees will usually undertake home visits and may ask a report from a third party, such as a medical professional or a teacher.

Victoria Shardlow's Children's Trust

£4,500

Correspondent: Liz Clifford, Charities Administrator, 9 Menin Way, Farnham GU9 8DY (email: Victoriashardlowtrust@googlemail.com)

Eligibility

Children or young people up to the age of 18 who are coping with 'difficult circumstances and are disadvantaged to participate and benefit from formal or non-formal education'.

Types of grants

Small, one-off grants are awarded towards equipment, fees (excluding for independent schools), transportation costs and educational trips in the UK or abroad. The maximum available grant is £3,000.

Annual grant total

In previous years, the trust has awarded grants totalling around £4,500.

Exclusions

Grants are not given for university fees, gap year activities, independent school fees or for personal computers.

Applications

Application forms can be obtained from the correspondent and should be submitted either directly by the individual or by the parent/guardian. Applications are considered in January, April, July and October.

Other information

Support can be given to small registered groups providing educational opportunities for disadvantaged children. The trust has also informed us that larger amounts are given to organisations.

This trust is very small and, therefore, is not registered with the Charity Commission. The correspondent has confirmed that the trust's beneficial area is not restricted and, in practice, applications can be made from anywhere in the world.

Dr Meena Sharma Memorial Foundation

See entry on page 19

The Stanley Stein Deceased Charitable Trust

£15,000

Correspondent: Michael Lawson, Trustee, Burwood House, 14–16 Caxton Street, London SW1H 0GY (020 7873 1000; email: michael.lawson@ williamsturges.co.uk)

CC number: 1048873

Eligibility

People under the age of 21 who are in need.

Types of grants

One-off and recurrent grants are given according to need towards general educational costs.

Annual grant total

In 2013/14 the trust had an income of £11,200 and a total expenditure of £32,500. Grants are made to individuals for both educational and social welfare purposes. We estimate that educational grants totalled around £15,000.

Applications

Applications can be made on a form which is available from the correspondent.

Thornton-Smith and Plevins Trust

£203,000 (96 grants)

Correspondent: Moore Stephens, Moore Stephens LLP, Russell Square House, 10–12 Russell Square House, London WC1B 5LF (020 7509 9000; fax: 01582 890995; email: thornton.smithypt@ ntlworld.com)

CC number: 1137196

Eligibility

Currently the trust mostly supports young people aged 16–19 who are in distressed circumstances.

Support may also be given to people under the age of 25 who are in need, including people undertaking work practice or apprenticeships in any trade or profession and young people in preparatory, secondary, higher or further education. Assistance is also given to individuals of the professional or business classes who have fallen into poverty and are unable to make adequate provision for their retirement or old age.

Types of grants

Support is given in grants and loans towards school fees and associated costs or in scholarships to travel overseas for educational purposes. Grants are means-tested and are paid per term, subject to reasonable progress. The average award is around £2,700. Preference is given to short-term applications primarily in relation to A-levels.

Annual grant total

In 2013/14 the trust had assets of £11.3 million and an income of £383,000. Grants were made to 96 individuals totalling £203,000 and consisted of £201,000 in individual grants and loans to assist with school fees and expenses and £2,000 given in scholarships for educational travel abroad (Kew Scholarship).

Exclusions

Our research suggests that grants are not normally given for first degree courses. Support will not be given in circumstances where parents were not in a position to fund the fees when entering the child for the school.

Applications

Apply in writing to the correspondent. Applications should include details of candidates' education and their parents' financial situation. If the applicant is considered eligible further enquiries are made. Applications are normally considered by 31 March and awards commence in September.

Other information

This trust was formerly the Thornton-Smith Young People's Trust which has been combined with the Wilfred Maurice Plevins Trust, Thornton-Smith Plevins Common Investment Fund and The Thornton-Smith Trust for efficiency.

To be assisted by The Wilfred Maurice Plevins fund, beneficiaries must also be aged ten or over and be the children of a professional. Beneficiaries older than 25 may only receive assistance from The Thornton-Smith fund.

The trust is directing most grants towards education although support was continued for existing elderly beneficiaries (£3,500 in 2013/14).

The T. A. K. Turton Charitable Trust

£11,500

Correspondent: Mrs R. Fullerton, Trustee, 47 Lynwood Road, London W5 1JQ (020 8998 1006; email: nopublicaddress@charity.com)

CC number: 268472

Eligibility

The trust usually supports three pupils in the UK and three in South Africa who are in need. Applicants should demonstrate good academic records (for example good GCSE results or equivalent). Support is given to cover a proportion of the school fees for a two-year period, normally leading to A-levels or equivalent university entrance qualifications. Applications are only accepted from schools which have awarded the candidate a bursary of at least 25% of the fees.

Types of grants

Grants are awarded to cover part of the school fees, normally to pupils in their final years of school education. Up to about £3,000 can be awarded per year.

Annual grant total

In 2013/14 the trust had an income of £15,500 and an expenditure of £12,000. We estimate the annual total amount of grants awarded to be around £11,500.

Applications

According to our research, applications should be made in writing to the correspondent through the school where the candidate proposes to study.

Other information

Our research suggests that, since grants are normally given for a two-year period, new applications from UK students can now only be considered every two years.

Further and higher education

The Emmott Foundation Ltd

£373,500 (101 grants)

Correspondent: Julie and Paul Spillane, Education Officers, 136 Browns Lane, Stanton-on-the-Wolds, Nottinghamshire NG12 5BN (0115 937 6526; email: emmottfoundation@btinternet.com; website: emmottfoundation.org)

CC number: 209033

Eligibility

Students aged 16–18 in fee-paying schools (including state boarding schools) who have high academic achievements (a majority of actual or predicted As or As at GCSE).

The following is taken from the 2013/14 trustees' annual report:

> Accordingly grants are primarily intended for children whose parents or guardians can no longer meet their considered financial commitments for education in either state or independent sixth forms as a result of a family crisis such as death, severe illness, accident, divorce, desertion or loss of employment. Consequently support is often given to children of families where the household income is very low. Consideration will also be given to cases where there is a major educational or pastoral problem, including the impact of parental drug and/or alcohol abuse, domestic violence and bullying.

Awards may be granted to students with lower grades in circumstances of exceptional need or where there is a major educational, social or pastoral problem, including domestic violence, bullying, parental drug/alcohol abuse.

Note: Grants are made only where the school is willing to make a significant contribution to the fees.

Types of grants

Grants are for sixth form only. Their purpose is to enable pupils to enter or remain in the sixth form in their present school. The grants help only with basic fees, not with incidental expenses (music lessons, travel, books, expeditions and so on). Grants are usually of between £500 and £1,500 per term, paid directly to the school at the start of each sixth form term.

Annual grant total

In 2013/14 the foundation had assets of £9.9 million and an income of £972,000. Direct individual fee assistance totalled £367,500. Annual scholarships of £2,000 each were awarded to three sixth form pupils by the Arkwright Scholarship Trust for Design Technology.

Exclusions

Students in other age groups than specified above are not considered.

Applications

Initial applications should be made in writing to the correspondent. Application forms will be sent to eligible applicants. The trustees meet in March, June and November to consider applications.

Enquiries and applications should be made to the correspondent.

The Follett Trust

£36,500

Correspondent: Jamie Westcott, Administrator, The Follett Office, Broadlands House, Primett Road, Stevenage, Hertfordshire SG1 3EE (01438 810400; email: folletttrust@ thefollettoffice.com)

CC number: 328638

Eligibility

Students in higher education. Some priority may be given to the arts and medical/health concerns.

Types of grants

One-off and recurrent scholarships and grants according to need.

Annual grant total

In 2013/14 the trust had assets of £61,000 and an income of £174,000. A total of £211,000 was spent in charitable expenditure, of which £36,500 was awarded in grants to individuals.

Applications

This is a private family trust and the trustees' annual report from 2013/14 states: 'The majority of successful applications, come from persons and organisations known to the Trustee or in which the Trustees have a particular interest.' Generally successful applications come this way and the trust is unable to accept unsolicited appeals.

Gilchrist Educational Trust

£27,500 (49 grants)

Correspondent: Val Considine Acis, Secretary, 20 Fern Road, Storrington, Pulborough, West Sussex RH20 4LW (01903 746723; email: gilchrist.et@ blueyonder.co.uk; website: www. gilchristgrants.org.uk)

CC number: 313877

Eligibility

Full-time students at a UK university who either 'have made proper provision to fund a degree or higher education course but find themselves facing unexpected financial difficulties', or 'those who, as part of a degree course, are required to spend a short period studying in another country'.

Types of grants

Both study and travel grants are usually of around £500. Four book prizes are also available to students achieving high grades at Birkbeck College, London University's Department of Extra-Mural Studies.

Annual grant total

In 2014/15 the trust had assets of £2 million, an income of £90,000 and a total charitable expenditure of £87,000. The amount of grants given to individuals totalled £27,500, consisting of 30 travel grants (£15,000) and 19 study grants (£12,500). Gilchrist Fieldwork Award totalled £15,000 and four book prizes were awarded totalling £200.

Exclusions

The trust's website states that support is not given to the following:

- part-time students
- people seeking funds to enable them to take up a place on a course
- students seeking help in meeting the cost of maintaining dependents
- students who have, as part of a course, to spend all or most of an academic year studying in another country
- those wishing to go abroad under the auspices of independent travel, exploratory or educational projects

Applications

Individuals should contact the Grants Officer via the above email or by post to the following address: 13 Brookfield Avenue, Larkfield, Aylesford ME20 6RU. Following an initial enquiry, eligible applicants will be sent further list of details required for application. Individuals can submit their applications at any time by post only.

Other information

The trust also gives grants to organisations (£24,500 in 2014/15) and

British university expeditions for scientific research (£8,000 in 2014/15).

Helena Kennedy Foundation

£130,000 (88 grants)

Correspondent: Foundation Administrator, Room 243A, University House, University of East London, Water Lane, Stratford E15 4LZ (020 8223 2027; email: enquires@hkf.org.uk; website: www.hkf.org.uk)

CC number: 1074025

Eligibility

Socially, economically or otherwise disadvantaged students attending a publicly funded further education institution in the UK who are progressing to university education. The main aim of the foundation is to 'tackle social injustice by supporting those who face multiple barriers to participation in education and work to fulfil their potential'. Applicants must be intending to undertake a higher diploma or undergraduate degree for the first time. Students taking a gap year will also be considered.

Types of grants

One of bursaries of £1,500 'are awarded to individuals who have successfully completed a programme of study at a further education sector college and are progressing on to a course in higher education'.

Annual grant total

In 2013/14 the foundation had assets of £591,000 and an income of £329,000. A total of £130,000 was awarded in bursaries to 88 individuals.

Exclusions

Funding is not available to:
- People who have already undertaken a higher education course
- Postgraduate students
- Students at private institutions
- Previous bursary recipients
- Students at international institutions

Applications

Applicants are encouraged to visit the foundation's website or contact the foundation to enquire about eligibility criteria. Application forms can be obtained from the foundation's website. Candidates will need to demonstrate severe financial hardship and barriers to accessing higher education. All applications must be supported by the applicant's educational institution.

Other information

The foundation also provides mentoring, information, one-to-one advice, specialist and practical support, skills training and work experience opportunities.

The trustees' annual report for 2013/14 states:

> In 2013/14 we developed our partnerships with universities and now work with 17 higher education institutions. The project boasts 15 graduates, 29 students who are entering into their second or final year of study and we anticipate a further 25 will commence an undergraduate degree programme this autumn.

The Leathersellers' Company Charitable Fund

£171,000 (77 grants)

Correspondent: David Santa-Olalla, Clerk, The Leathersellers' Company, 21 Garlick Hill, London EC4V 2AU (020 7330 1444; fax: 020 7330 1454; email: dmsantao@leathersellers.co.uk; website: www.leathersellers.co.uk)

CC number: 278072

Eligibility

Higher education students on a full-time degree course at any UK university. Applicants must have a an unconditional offer for, or be enrolled on, a full-time course. Preference given to people from Greater London and those studying engineering or subjects connected with the leather trade.

Twice a year applications are also welcomed from graduates and undergraduates intending to take holy orders.

Types of grants

Grants of up to £4,000 are given to support higher education.

Annual grant total

In 2013/14 the fund had assets of £50.8 million, an income of £1.5 million and a total charitable expenditure of £1.6 million. During the year 77 individual grants were made to students totalling £171,000.

Exclusions

Funding is not given for one-year professional conversion courses.

Applications

Applications can be made using an online application form available from the Leathersellers' company's website.

Other information

The company also gives grants to organisations for both educational and a wide range of welfare causes.

Both successful and unsuccessful applicants are informed in due course and the fund requests not to be contacted with queries regarding the outcome of the application, unless your contact address has changed.

The Joseph Nickerson Charitable Foundation

£13,700

Correspondent: Eric White, Foundation Administrator, Villa Office, Rothwell, Market Rasen, Lincolnshire LN7 6BJ (01472 371216; email: j.n.farms@farmingline.com)

CC number: 276429

Eligibility

Young people, normally aged 18 or over, in further or higher education. Preference may be given to people from Lincolnshire.

Types of grants

Grants to assist with general educational expenses.

Annual grant total

In 2013/14 the foundation had an income of £45,500 and a charitable expenditure of £28,000. A total of £13,700 was awarded in educational grants to young people.

Applications

Apply in writing to the correspondent. Our research suggests that applications for grants starting in September should be made by the end of June for consideration in July.

The James Pantyfedwen Foundation (Ymddiriedolaeth James Pantyfedwen)

£159,000 (39 grants)

Correspondent: Richard Morgan, Executive Secretary, Pantyfedwen, 9 Market Street, Aberystwyth, Ceredigion SY23 1DL (01970 612806; email: pantyfedwen@btinternet.com; website: www.jamespantyfedwenfoundation.org.uk)

CC number: 1069598

Eligibility

Postgraduate applicants who have been resident in Wales sometime during the three years immediately preceding the date of application (excluding the term-time address as a college/university student) and who (or whose parents) were born in Wales, or who have studied at any educational institution in Wales for at least seven years. Currently some priority is given to students undertaking postgraduate research.

Types of grants

One-off and recurrent grants for postgraduate studies. Most grants are for fees and, in very exceptional circumstances, living costs. The average grant is of around £3,900 but where the fees are higher grants may be awarded of up to £7,000. People training for Christian ministry can also be supported.

Annual grant total

In 2013/14 the foundation had assets of £14.9 million and an income of £539,000. Charitable expenditure totalled £415,500 and a total of £157,500 was awarded in grants to 37 postgraduate students (a maximum of £7,000 in each case). Undeb Cymru Fydd scholarships of £1,250 each were also paid to two postgraduate students.

Exclusions

According to the application guidelines, the foundation does not support the following:

- undergraduate courses
- courses at institutions which have not been approved by the department of education
- higher degrees where students already have a higher degree (this does not exclude progress from a master's degree to a PhD)
- accounting training courses
- private tuition
- PGCE courses
- postgraduate training courses in social work
- CPE Course in law (but legal practice courses are permitted)
- master's courses of more than one year's duration (where a student is pursuing a two year's master's course on a full-time basis the foundation is prepared to consider assistance for the second and final year of study)

Support is not given to supplement awards provided by the local authorities and research councils.

Applications

Application forms are available from the foundation's website.

Other information

During 2013/14 a total of £56,250 was awarded to religious buildings and £13,200 was given to special projects.

The Sidney Perry Foundation

£191,500 (202 grants)

Correspondent: Mrs L. Owens, Secretary, PO Box 2924, Faringdon SN7 7YJ (website: www.the-sidney-perry-foundation.co.uk)

CC number: 313758

Eligibility

The foundation's primary aim is to assist first degree students. Applicants must be under the age of 35 when the course starts. Eligible foreign students studying in Britain can also apply. Students undertaking medicine as their second degree and, therefore, not qualifying for any support are welcomed to apply (see particular exclusions relating to the medicine degree).

Types of grants

One-off and recurrent grants from £300 onwards with an average award of around £900. The maximum general award is of £1,000 and the maximum 'super grant' – of £1,500. In no cases will support exceed £3,000 per individual. Grants are usually towards books and equipment/instruments.

The foundation's website notes that 'grants are considered to be supplemental and to go part of the way to bridge a gap with the applicant finding the bulk of funding elsewhere'.

Annual grant total

In 2013 the foundation had assets of £4.3 million, an income of £193,000 and grants totalled £223,000. During the year a total of 202 grants (amounting to £191,500) were payable to individual applicants to assist them to undertake educational courses. In addition 21 grants were awarded through the Philharmonia Orchestra/Martin Musical Scholarship Fund, four grants through the Guildhall School of Music and five grants through the Open University. At the time of writing (July 2015) the latest financial information available was from 2013 accounts.

Exclusions

According to the accounts for 2013, the foundation is unable to assist:

- the first year of a (three or four year) first degree, save for veterinary, medicine and in exceptional circumstances
- medical students during their first year if medicine is their second degree
- medical students during elective periods and intercalated courses
- second degree courses where the grade in the first is lower than a 2:1, save in exceptional circumstances
- second degree courses or other postgraduate study unrelated to the first unless they are a necessary part of professional training (e.g. medicine or dentistry)
- expeditions or courses overseas, emergency funding or clearance of existing debts
- students over the age of 35 when their course of study commences, save in the most exceptional circumstances
- A Level and GCSE examinations
- students on access, ESOL, HNC, HND, BTEC, GNVQ and NVQ levels 1–4 and foundation courses

- those with LEA/SAAS funding, except in exceptional circumstances
- Open University courses (except engineering, which is supported)

Distance learning, correspondence, part-time and short-term courses may only be considered according to circumstances.

Applications

Application forms are available from the foundation's website or the correspondent. Together with a covering letter and other supporting documentation they can be submitted directly by the individual via post by November (the year before the academic year when assistance is necessary). In exceptional circumstances late applications may be considered, with a final cut-off date of 31 January. Incomplete forms will be disregarded. Enclosure of an sae would be appreciated. Applications have to be in writing and supported by signed original references (one of which must be academic). Students are expected to have a confirmed place at an educational establishment and most of the necessary funding already secured before approaching the foundation. Previous beneficiaries should include details of the previous award (amount granted, year received and grant number).

Other information

The foundation is generally unable to deal with student debt or financial problems needing a speedy resolution.

The following is taken from the 2013 annual report:

> The Governors continue to provide grants to assist in a professional or other career. During the year approximately 1060 application forms were sent out and of those 243 were considered by the Governors. 202 awards were given, 20 refused and 21 referred for further consideration or deferred. 17 'supergrants' of between £1,200–£1,500 were awarded. Twenty one awards totalling £18,000 were given to promising young musicians through auditions organised by the Philharmonia Orchestra/ Martin Musical Scholarship Fund. Vocal awards totalling £12,000 were awarded to students of the Guildhall School of Music. Five awards totalling £5,050 were given to Open University students to encourage promising engineers working towards professional status. In total grants paid amounted to £226,525.

Thornton-Smith and Plevins Trust

See entry on page 12

TIKO Foundation

£26,000 (2 grants)

Correspondent: Kirill Ozerov, 1 Douglas Path, London E14 3GR (07983632444; email: info@tikofoundation.org; website: www.tikofoundation.org)

CC number: 1145979

Eligibility

Students must be entering a first (undergraduate) degree and have already received an offer from a high-ranking university/universities. Candidates must be academically gifted, reside in the UK and come from a low-income background.

Eligibility will initially be checked through an application form and supporting documents.

Types of grants

The foundation's grant will finance an applicant's education expenses, including tuition and accommodation, for the duration of his or her academic course. Advice and support from the trustees is offered throughout the grant award period.

Annual grant total

In 2013/14 the foundation had assets of £19,800 and an income of £27,000. During the year two grants were awarded totalling £26,000.

Exclusions

According to its website, the foundation will not provide:

- funding for a postgraduate degree (for example, MA or BSC), employment training programmes, internships or a first degree already started
- any other expenses other than course fees and accommodation
- funding for fees already incurred throughout a degree
- funding towards anyone who does not meet **all** foundation's eligibility criteria

Applications

Application forms can be found on the foundation's website. Completed electronic copies should be emailed to the correspondent together with any supporting documentation and a completed Financial Eligibility Checker, which is also available from the website. The application round usually opens in October and runs until the end of May in the following year.

Other information

The award is not part of an employee training programme and the foundation will not offer any post-graduation work placements or internships.

The award is subject to the applicant achieving excellent grades, taking part in regular monitoring and evaluation of progress, and participating in marketing events.

Williamson Memorial Trust

£2,300

Correspondent: Colin Williamson, Trustee, 6 Windmill Close, Ashington, Pulborough, West Sussex RH20 3LG (01903 893649; email: cpjgwilliamson@ yahoo.co.uk)

CC number: 268782

Eligibility

Students on first degree courses.

Types of grants

Grants of not more than £200 a year are made to help with books, fees, living expenses and study or travel abroad. Grants are limited to £200 a year to overseas students too – the trust is not able to make a more significant contribution towards the higher fees and living expenses that overseas student incur.

Annual grant total

In 2014/15 the trust had an income of £9,100 and a total expenditure of £9,500. Grants are made to individuals and organisations for educational and social welfare purposes. We estimate that educational grants to individuals totalled £2,300.

Exclusions

Grants are not made to postgraduate students.

Applications

Due to a reduction of its funds and the instability of its income, the trust regrets that very few new applications will be considered to ensure it can meet its existing commitments. Support will generally only be given to cases known personally to the trustees and to those individuals the trust has existing commitments with.

S. C. Witting Trust

£900

Correspondent: Trust Administrator, Friends House, 173 Euston Road, London NW1 2BJ

CC number: 237698-10

Eligibility

Students following a course of study at a university, who are ordinarily resident in England.

Types of grants

Small, one-off grants (on average of about £75) are made for clothing, books and equipment/instruments.

Annual grant total

The correspondent has informed us that the budget for educational grants was £900 in 2015.

Exclusions

Grants are not made to help reduce debts or in the form of loans.

Applications

Applications must be made in writing with a letter of support from a tutor. They must give a short case history, reasons for the need and the amount needed. Requests are considered monthly and unsuccessful applications will not be acknowledged unless an sae is provided. The trust **does not** welcome any phone calls or emails.

Other information

Grants are also made to benefit individuals under the age of 15 or over the age of 60 for welfare purposes.

This trust is linked to Friends Trust Limited (Charity Commission no. 237698).

The WR Foundation

£6,000 (2 grants)

Correspondent: John Malthouse, Trustee, Malthouse and Co., 8B Rumford Place, Liverpool L3 9DD (0151 284 2000; email: mail@malthouse.com)

CC number: 1003546

Eligibility

People who need support to 'continue with their work and/or studies'. Our research suggests that grants are mainly awarded to higher education students.

Types of grants

One-off grants, normally between £500 and £2,500.

Annual grant total

In 2013/14 the foundation had assets of £4,800 and an income of £32,500. There were a total of 11 grants made totalling about £20,500, including two awards to individuals totalling £6,000.

Applications

Applications may be made in writing to the correspondent.

Other information

Most grants are made to organisations and the amount awarded to individuals varies each year. The charity's income is mainly generated through WR Ltd.

Gender

Altrusa Careers Trust

£9,000

Correspondent: Correspondent, PO Box 6160, Orkney KW16 3WY (email: admin@altrusacareerstrust.org.uk; website: www.altrusacareerstrust.org.uk)

OSCR number: SC009390

Eligibility
Women permanently resident in the UK or the Republic of Ireland who wish to further their career prospects or to retrain after bringing up a family but are prevented from doing so by lack of means.

Types of grants
Grants are of up to £500. Loan schemes are also available.

Annual grant total
In 2013/14 the trust had an income of £3,000 and an expenditure of £9,200. We estimate the annual total amount of grants awarded to individuals to be around £9,000.

Exclusions
Support is not provided to school leavers and PhD students.

Applications
Application forms are available from the correspondent. Applications will require a passport sized photo of the candidate and names and addresses of two referees. The deadline by which submissions should be made is posted on the website and applications are only considered once a year. Payments are normally made in July directly to the institution and not the applicant. Do not provide any additional information if it is not requested in the application form. If you have not been contacted by the end of May, you should presume your application to have been unsuccessful.

Other information
The charity's income is derived from donations, gifts and legacies.

Diamond Education Grant (DEG)

£6,000

Correspondent: Charity Administrator, 2nd Floor, Beckwith House, 1 Wellington Road North, Stockport, Cheshire SK4 1AF (0161 480 7686; email: hq@soroptimistgbi.prestel.co.uk; website: sigbi.org/our-charities/deg)

CC number: 1139668

Eligibility
Women permanently resident in one of the countries of the Federation of Soroptimist International Great Britain and Ireland who wish to refurbish their skills after an employment break or acquire new ones to re-enter the employment market and improve their opportunities of employment/ promotion.

Types of grants
Grants, on average of around £390, are available towards the course fees, books or equipment. Grants are normally paid for one year but may be extended in exceptional circumstances.

Annual grant total
In 2013/14 the charity had an income of £13,500 and a total expenditure of £6,500. We estimate that the amount of grants given to individuals totalled around £6,000.

Exclusions
Living expenses cannot be supported.

Applications
Applications can be made through the nearest local branch of Soroptimist International. The deadline for applications is 15 April each year.

Other information
Grants are only paid after the successful applicants have started their courses.

Edinburgh Association of University Women – President's Fund

£15,500

Correspondent: Alison MacLachlan, Trustee, 6/5 Craigleith Avenue South, Edinburgh EH4 3LQ

OSCR number: SC004501

Eligibility
Women in their final year of study for a degree (postgraduate or undergraduate) at UK universities who face unexpected financial hardship.

Types of grants
One-off modest grants, usually between £150 and £500. Awards are intended to help with costs of books, equipment and maintenance/living expenses. Applicants receive only one award which is intended to help them to complete the current study.

Annual grant total
In 2014 the fund had an income of £22,500 and an expenditure of £16,000. We estimate that the amount of grants given to individuals totalled around £15,500.

Exclusions
Grants are not given to begin a new course, towards diplomas, certificates, access courses, study or work outside the UK, childcare, one-year undergraduate and one-year postgraduate degrees.

Applications
Application forms can be requested by writing to the correspondent. Requests must be submitted directly by the applicant (not third parties). Academic references are required. The trustees usually meet in February, April/May, October and November to consider grants.

Other information
The fund has previously stated that 'applications which disregard the exclusions will not be acknowledged'.

The Girls of The Realm Guild (Women's Careers Foundation)

£14,500

Correspondent: Beth Hayward, Secretary, 2 Watch Oak, Blackham, Tunbridge Wells, Kent TN3 9TP (01892 740602)

CC number: 313159

Eligibility
Women over the age of 21 who are UK citizens and are seeking assistance to begin or continue studies for a career. Younger applicants (over the age of 16) may be supported for music or dance studies.

Types of grants
One-off grants and loans to help with any costs relating to education or training, preferably leading to a career. Awards can reach up to £1,000 but on average total around £250.

Annual grant total
At the time of writing (October 2015) the latest financial information available was from 2013. In 2013 the charity had an income of £11,500 and an expenditure of £15,000. We estimate that the annual total amount of grants awarded was around £14,500.

Exclusions
Grants are not generally given for PhD or postgraduate studies, particularly if the subject indicates a complete change of direction.

Applications
Application forms and further guidelines can be requested from the correspondent. Candidates are requested to provide an sae. Applications should be submitted between 1 September and 31 January for the following academic year. It is strongly advised to submit

applications well in advance. The correspondent has previously stated that timing is crucial: 'so many people write for immediate help which we cannot give'.

Other information

Note that this charity is small and has limited resources.

The Marillier Trust

£29,000

Correspondent: William Stisted, Trustee, 38 Southgate, Chichester, West Sussex PO19 1DP (01243 787899; email: ws@andersonrowntree.co.uk)

CC number: 1100693

Eligibility

Boys between the ages of 5 and 13.

Types of grants

Grants are given for education other than formal teaching in class. The trust will support educational and recreational opportunities, residential trips, after-school activities and so on. Loans are also made to individuals.

Annual grant total

In 2013/14 the trust had assets of £742,500 and an income of £33,500. Charitable expenditure totalled £297,000. A total of £29,000 was awarded in grants to individuals (£10,800 for residential trips and £18,200 for after-school activities).

Applications

Apply in writing to the correspondent.

Other information

A total of £267,000 was awarded to institutions (2013/14).

The Hilda Martindale Educational Trust

£23,000 (15–20 grants)

Correspondent: Secretary to the Hilda Martindale Trust, c/o The Registry, Royal Holloway, University of London, Egham TW20 0EX (01788 434455; fax: 01784 437520; email: hildamartindaletrust@rhul.ac.uk; website: www.royalholloway.ac.uk/aboutus/governancematters/thehildamartindaletrust.aspx)

Eligibility

Women over the age of 21 pursuing a profession or career requiring vocational training in the areas where women are underrepresented. Applicants must be British nationals.

Courses/training must be a full academic year in length and preferably start in September/October. Priority is given to undergraduates in their final year of study.

Types of grants

A small number of one-off grants in the range of £200–£3,000 are offered for training courses and are normally paid in three instalments, in October, January and April. Awards can be used for fees, books, equipment, living expenses or childcare and so on.

A limited number of awards can also be given towards the costs of any graduate training (MSc/MA and PhD) in an area which is underrepresented by women (for example science, technology, engineering, architecture, some branches of medicine (such as surgery), leadership roles in all fields) at a UK institution approved by the trustees.

Annual grant total

The trust generally awards 15–20 women each year totalling £20,000–£25,000.

Exclusions

Assistance is not given for:

- Short courses
- Access courses
- Courses attended abroad
- Elective studies
- Intercalated BSc years during a UK medical, dental, veterinary or nursing course
- Wholly academic courses
- Academic research
- Special projects in the UK or abroad
- First year undergraduates
- People holding grants from research councils, British Academy and other public sources
- Retrospective awards

Funding can only be given to women who cannot access any other funding. Medical, dental, or veterinary students will only be considered if they are pursuing an area within that field where women are underrepresented.

Applications

Application forms are available from the Council of Royal Holloway website. Applications, together with two references and a personal statement, should be submitted by February for the courses taking place in the following academic year. Submissions can be made by email or via post, providing an sae. The trustees normally meet in April to consider awards.

Other information

The trust only invites applications from candidates who exactly suit its eligibility criteria. The correspondent has requested us to direct potential applicants to the Council of Royal Holloway website where the application forms and detailed guidelines can be found and are regularly updated.

The Muirhead Trust

£7,500

Correspondent: Ann Prentice, Trust Administrator, c/o Franchi Law LLP, Queens House, 19 St Vincent Place, Glasgow G1 2DT (email: ann@franchilaw.co.uk; website: www.themuirheadtrust.org.uk)

OSCR number: SC016524

Eligibility

Female students of Scottish origin and almost exclusively those who are studying in Scotland. Support is available to students of medicine, veterinary science, pharmacy, nursing, dentistry, science and engineering.

Types of grants

Grants of around £2,000–£3,000 are available for two years, after which the student is eligible for a statutory grant for the further three years.

Annual grant total

In 2014/15 the trust had an income of £7,500 and a total charitable expenditure of £8,000. We estimate the annual total amount of grants awarded to be around £7,500.

Exclusions

Biomedical or forensic science students are outside the remit of the trust.

Applications

Application forms can be downloaded from the trust's website and should be submitted together with a CV or a resume and an academic transcript. The deadline for applications is 31 August annually.

The NFL Trust

£92,000 (22 grants)

Correspondent: Margot Chaundler, Secretary, 9 Muncaster Road, London SW11 6NY (020 7223 7133; email: nfltrust@mail.com; website: www.nfltrust.org.uk)

CC number: 1112422

Eligibility

Girls between the ages of 11 and 18 who are attending schools and colleges in the UK (primarily fee-charging institutions). Support is given in line with 'Christian principles'.

Types of grants

Recurrent bursaries (up to the end of course, usually by the age of 18) are awarded subject to means-testing and annual financial review. Individual needs of the child and parents' commitment are also taken into account when considering grants.

Annual grant total

In 2013/14 the trust had assets of £4.2 million and an income of £50,000. During the year bursaries were given to 22 pupils totalling £92,000. Eight new bursaries were awarded, all of them to girls with difficult family circumstances or medical conditions. 14 existing bursaries were reviewed and were renewed later in the year. The trustees made three grants from the Diana Matthews Trust Fund at a total of £1,000.

Applications

Application forms and further details can be requested from the correspondent.

Note: Families of applicants should apply in the academic year *before* the year in which a bursary is required.

Other information

The trustees of The NFL Trust also administer the designated funds of a small Diana Matthews Trust Fund. They are used to provide educational extras for girls in need, whether or not they benefit from the NFL bursary.

Dr Meena Sharma Memorial Foundation

£6,000

Correspondent: Vivek Sharma, Executive, 14 Magdalene Road, Walsall, West Midlands WS1 3TA (01922629842; fax: 01922632942; email: gwalior@onetel. com; website: www.msmf.chandri.com)

CC number: 1108375

Eligibility

Children and women in the UK and India, especially those who have disabilities or are disadvantaged or underprivileged. Teachers, other educational professionals and medical personnel or medical students may also be supported.

Types of grants

Small awards up to £500 (generally £100–£250) are available to help children and women. Awards may include scholarships, travel grants and other educational costs. Support can be given to teachers, other educational professionals and medical personnel or medical students to assist their training and professional development.

Annual grant total

In 2014/15 the foundation had an income of £22,500 and a total expenditure of £22,000. We estimate that about £6,000 was given in educational support to individuals.

Applications

Eligible candidates should apply in writing to the correspondent via post, providing an sae. Requests should give full contact details (including an email address) and reasons for seeking a grant. Applications can be made at any time. Only successful applicants are informed. The foundation's website notes: 'If you do not hear from us within six weeks of next round of meetings from your application, it has been unsuccessful. You may re-apply for next round if desired.'

Other information

Grants are also made to organisations, especially in India, and individuals may be supported for welfare needs.

Yorkshire Ladies' Council of Education (Incorporated)

£23,500

Correspondent: Phillida Richardson, Secretary, Flat 4, Forest Hill, 11 Park Crescent, Leeds LS8 1DH (01132691471; email: admin@ylce.org; website: www. ylce.org.uk)

CC number: 529714

Eligibility

British women over the age of 21 who are in need of financial assistance towards their education at a British educational institution and who do not qualify for local authority support.

A separate fund has been set up in association with the Sir James Knott Trust, to enable grants to be offered exclusively to applicants from the North East of England (defined as Tyne and Wear, Northumberland, County Durham inclusive of Hartlepool but exclusive of Darlington, Stockton-on-Tees, Middlesbrough, Redcar and Cleveland).

Types of grants

Grants in the range of £100 to £500 (the average grant of £200–£300) are given for the course fees only. The award is available for one year but can be renewed for up to three years.

Annual grant total

In 2013/14 the charity had assets of £569,500 and an income of £42,000. A total of £34,000 was spent in charitable activities, of which £23,500 was awarded in scholarships and educational grants.

Exclusions

Members, and the dependants of members, of Yorkshire Ladies' Council of Education are not eligible for support.

Applications

Application forms can be found on the charity's website together with detailed guidelines. A completed form and an sae should be submitted directly by the individual by 1 January, March, June or September for consideration later in the month. The awards committee meets four times a year.

Applicants for grants from the Sir James Knott Trust (who may be asked for proof of residency) should label their form 'SPECIAL FUND'.

Other information

The charity also provides grants to local community bodies and institutions.

Illness and disability

Able Kidz

£14,500

Correspondent: Cathryn Walton, Trustee, 43 Bedford Street, London WC2E 2HA (0845 123 3997; email: info@ablekidz.com; website: www. ablekidz.com)

CC number: 1114955

Eligibility

Children with disabilities and young adults under the age of 18 in the UK.

Types of grants

One-off and recurrent grants are given according to need. Grants are typically made for specialist educational equipment and extra tuition.

Annual grant total

In 2013/14 the charity had an income of £14,700 and a total expenditure of £15,200. We estimate that grants awarded tolled around £14,500.

Applications

Apply in writing to the correspondent. Applications are not means-tested. They should include the following:

- A summary of the child's circumstances
- What the child requires and how Able Kidz might be able to help
- An outline of the costs involved

The British Kidney Patient Association

£23,500

Correspondent: Fiona Armitage, Correspondent, 3 The Windmills, St Mary's Close, Turk Street, Alton GU34 1EF (01420 541424; fax: 01420 89438; email: info@britishkidney-pa.co.uk; website: www.britishkidney-pa.co.uk)

CC number: 270288

Eligibility

Dialysis patients and their families who are on low incomes. Also, other patients, including transplant patients and those receiving conservative care, if their health and quality of life is being seriously affected by their renal condition.

Types of grants

Grants to help with, where appropriate, the cost of university or college fees, or the cost of books, equipment, accommodation or other expenses involved with educational and job opportunities.

Annual grant total

In 2014 the association had assets of £33.1 million and an income of £1.4 million. Grants totalled more than £1.8 million, of which £900,500 was given to support hospital projects and post funding ('staff posts that hospital trusts cannot fund but which local medical teams feel are critical to ensure good quality of care'). Patient aid amounted to £931,500, with grants for social welfare purposes amounting to £907,500. Around £23,500 was given for patients' further education.

Exclusions

Grants are not made: to reimburse patients for bills already paid; for telephone bills, court fines, home improvements, the repayment of credit cards or loans, medical equipment, or council tax payments; or to help with the costs of getting ongoing dialysis.

Applications

Application forms, along with guidelines, are available to download from the association's website. The form must be submitted by a renal social worker or a member of the patient's renal team, who must sign the form and attach a detailed social report on the hospital's headed paper. The association gives the following helpful information on its website: 'if there's no member of staff able to help, the BKPA's Counsellor Jacquie Fraser can be contacted by calling the main BKPA telephone number'.

Other information

The charity makes grants to hospitals and, as part of its work, supports the Ronald McDonald Houses at children's hospitals in Liverpool (Alder Hey), Birmingham, Bristol, London (Evelina Children's Hospital), Manchester and Glasgow (Royal Hospital for Sick Children, Yorkhill), which provide support for the families of young renal patients attending the units at these hospitals.

It also funds non-laboratory research and provides support services, information and advice to kidney patients, amongst other projects.

CLIC Sargent (formerly Sargent Cancer Care for Children)

Correspondent: Grants Department, Horatio House, 77–85 Fulham Place, London W6 8JA (0300 330 0803; website: www.clicsargent.org.uk)

CC number: 1107328

Eligibility

Children and young people aged 24 or under who are living in the UK and are receiving treatment for cancer.

Types of grants

We had little information on the types of educational assistance the charity may have given previously. In general, financial assistance from the CLIC is aimed at supporting children and young people with the additional costs brought on by a cancer diagnosis.

Annual grant total

In 2013/14 the charity distributed more than £1 million in grants to young people and their families. Our research suggests that educational grants usually account for only a minimal portion of this expenditure, with the majority of grants given to young people and their families for welfare needs. In previous years, grants for educational purposes have totalled around £6,000.

Exclusions

Previous research indicates that no grants are given for school fees.

Applications

Applications should be made through a healthcare or social care professional, such as a CLIC Sargent Social Worker.

Other information

Details of other grants and services offered by CLIC Sargent are available from a CLIC Sargent Social Worker or the charity's informative website. Alternatively, call 0300 330 0803 for more information, advice and support.

CLIC Sargent was formed in 2005 following a merger between CLIC and Sargent Cancer Care for Children.

The National Association for Colitis and Crohn's Disease (Crohn's and Colitis UK)

£50,000

Correspondent: David Barker, Chief Executive, 45 Grosvenor Road, St Albans AL1 3AW (01727 830038; email: info@crohnsandcolitis.org.uk; website: www.crohnsandcolitis.org.uk)

CC number: 1117148, SC038632

Eligibility

People who are aged between 15 and 25 who have ulcerative colitis, Crohn's disease or related inflammatory bowel diseases (IBD). Candidates must have been resident in the UK for at least six months and be on a low income.

Types of grants

Grants of up to £500 are made towards any educational or training needs, including tuition fees, books, equipment, additional costs of university/college en-suite, and travel passes. Grants are also given for special educational needs, retraining purposes or other items and services arising as a consequence of having IBD.

Annual grant total

In 2014 the charity had assets of £2.9 million and an income of £3.7 million. 262 personal grants amounted to £100,500. We have taken these figures to include both Personal and Young Person's Grants. We estimate that Young Person's Grants, which are given for educational and vocational support, amounted to around £50,000.

Exclusions

Ongoing household bills or debts cannot be considered.

Applications

Application forms are available to download from the charity's website, along with guidance notes. The form has two extra sections, one of which should be completed by a doctor to confirm the individual's illness and one to be filled in by a social worker (or health visitor, district nurse, Citizens Advice advisor, or another professional). Completed applications should be sent to the Personal Grants Fund Secretary at: PO Box 334, St Albans, Herts AL1 2WA. Grant payments are normally made directly to the retailer/provider. See the website for details of application deadlines and subsequent Grants Panel

Meeting dates. Note that, apart from in exceptional circumstances, individuals may only apply for one grant every five years.

Further information on grants can be obtained from Julia Devereux (telephone: 0800 011 4701 or 01727 759654; email: julia.devereux@ crohnsandcolitis.org.uk).

Other information

Grants are also made for welfare purposes and to institutions for research. Occasionally local grants are made to hospitals. The main role of the association is to provide information and advice to people living with IBD.

The Hylton House Fund

£4,200

Correspondent: Grants Administrator, County Durham Community Foundation, Victoria House, St John's Road, Meadowfield Industrial Estate, Durham DH7 8XL (0191 378 6340; fax: 0191 378 2409; email: info@cdcf.org.uk; website: www.cdcf.org.uk)

CC number: 1047625–2

Eligibility

People in the North East (County Durham, Darlington, Gateshead, South Shields, Sunderland and Cleveland) with cerebral palsy and related disabilities, and their families and carers. Applicants (or their family members, if aged under 18) must be on income support or a low income or have a degree of disability in the family, which creates a heavy financial demand. People who live in Burnhope and require specialist equipment due to poor health or a disability may also be assisted.

Types of grants

Grants of up to £500 are made towards specialist equipment and up to £200 – towards domestic equipment. Our research suggests that support can be made for needs associated with education, training and therapy, such as sound and light therapy, specialist clothing or tools, communication and mobility aids, travel costs (for example, taxi and rail fares to attend a specific activity if no alternative transport is available). Respite support can also be given. This may include visiting a specialist centre where full-time extensive care is provided or assitance where the needs of the applicant require them to be accompanied by an employed carer.

Annual grant total

In 2013/14 grants from the fund were approved totalling £8,400.

Exclusions

According to our research awards are not generally made for:
- Legal costs
- Ongoing education
- Medical treatment
- Decorating and/or refurbishment costs (unless the work is due to the nature of the applicant's disability)
- Motor vehicle adaptations
- Motor insurance, deposits or running costs
- Televisions or DVD players
- Assessments

Only one grant can be held in each financial year starting in April and retrospective funding is not available.

Applications

Application forms are available to download from the County Durham Community Foundation website or can be requested from the correspondent. All appeals must include a reference from a social worker or health-care professional, with a telephone number and the individual's permission for them to be contacted about an application. A full breakdown of costs should also be included. A confirmation from an occupational therapist, doctor, physiotherapist or other professional advisor that the equipment requested is recommended/suitable is also required.

Requests are generally considered in January, April, July and October and should be received before the start of the month. Urgent appeals can be considered between these dates within a month of application, but the applicant will need to request this and provide a reason why an exception to the usual policy needs to be made.

Other information

The fund is managed by the County Durham Community Foundation (Charity Commission no. 1047625). See a separate entry for the details of the foundation on page 228.

The Joseph Levy Memorial Fund

£50,000

Correspondent: Roland Gyallay-Pap, Grants Administrator, 1st Floor, 1 Bell Street, London NW1 5BY (020 7616 1207; email: roland@jlef.org.uk; website: www.jlef.org.uk)

CC number: 1079049

Eligibility

Children and young adults up to the age of 25 who have cystic fibrosis.

Types of grants

Grants are available to help individuals develop their career through further/ higher education or professional qualifications. Support is given for tuition fees, examination fees, living costs and similar expenses to progress the applicant's career.

Annual grant total

In 2013/14 the fund had an income of £28,000. Grants totalled £50,000.

Applications

Applications can be made using a form available on the fund's website, or from the correspondent. The deadline for applications is 30 March and awards are decided mid-June.

Other information

The fund is administered by the Cystic Fibrosis Trust.

The Dan Maskell Tennis Trust

See entry on page 86

Meningitis Now (formerly known as Meningitis Trust)

£132,500

Correspondent: The Community Support Officer, Fern House, Bath Road, Stroud GL5 3TJ (01453 768000; fax: 01453 768001; email: info@ meningitisnow.org; website: www. meningitisnow.org)

CC number: 803016/SC037790

Eligibility

People in need who have meningitis or who have disabilities as a result of meningitis and reside in the UK.

Established researchers based in universities, hospitals and other research institutions in the UK can receive research grants.

Types of grants

Financial Support Grants
One-off and recurrent grants are given towards specialist equipment and computer software, retraining and special training or tuition, such as sign language lessons or driving lessons, also short-term education support where a child is waiting for an SEN assessment.

Research Grants
Awards are made for work towards the prevention of meningitis and associated disease in the UK, for example vaccine development, understanding risk factors associated with infection and carriage or understanding mechanisms of pathogenesis which could ultimately inform novel preventative strategies. Grants are given up to £250,000 over three years (must not exceed £100,000

per year). They can cover the costs of project staff, consumables, and other expenses.

Annual grant total

In 2013/14 the charity had assets totalling £1.3 million and an income of nearly £3.4 million. Grants for individuals totalled £265,000. This amount was not broken down; therefore, we estimate that educational awards were made totalling about £132,500.

Exclusions

Support may not be given for the following:

▶ Services or items which should normally be supplied by a statutory body (e.g. NHS or local authority)
▶ Home adaptations on rented property
▶ Holidays
▶ Payment of domestic bills
▶ Arrears (e.g. mortgage payments)
▶ Bedding, furniture or clothing
▶ Domestic appliances
▶ Swimming pools

Applications

Application forms are available from the correspondent or can be downloaded from the website, where criteria are also posted. An initial telephone call on 0808 801 0388 or an email to helpline@ meningitisnow.org to discuss the application process is welcomed. Applications should be submitted through a third party and are reviewed on a monthly basis. They will need to include the confirmation of the diagnosis and a supporting letter from a professional involved in the care or support of the person who had meningitis (this is **not** required for applications for funeral or headstone costs).

Preliminary application forms and full details for those interested in *research grants* are given on the charity's website or can be obtained via phone on 01453 768000 or by emailing research@ meningitisnow.org.

Other information

Meningitis Now was formed following the merger of Meningitis Trust and Meningitis UK.

The charity runs 'Believe and Achieve' weekends for young people aged 11–18 who have had meningitis or meningococcal disease. The two day events are free for families to attend and include refreshments, meals and Saturday night accommodation. You can find out more by calling 0345 120 4530 or emailing believe@meningitisnow.org.

The charity also offers a range of professional counselling, home visits, therapy and information services and runs campaigns. Funding for research totalled £532,500 in 2013. There is an informative website.

The MFPA Trust Fund for the Training Of Handicapped Children in the Arts

£10,500

Correspondent: Tom Yendell, Trustee, 88 London Road, Holybourne, Alton, Hampshire GU34 4EL (01420 88755)

CC number: 328151

Eligibility

Children with physical or mental disabilities between the ages of 5 and 18 living in the UK.

Types of grants

One-off and recurrent grants towards participation in arts, crafts, painting, music, drama and so on. Awards can be given towards, for example, books, educational outings, equipment and materials or school fees. The maximum grant available is £6,000.

Annual grant total

In 2013/14 the fund had an income of £150,000. Awards to children totalled £10,500. Grants to individuals are erratic and previously have fluctuated between few hundreds and about £20,000.

Applications

Apply in writing to the correspondent. Applications can be made directly by the individual or through a third party such as their school, college or educational welfare agency. They are considered throughout the year. Candidates should also enclose a letter explaining their needs and a doctor's letter confirming the disability.

Other information

The fund also gives grants to organisations (£40,000 in 2013/14).

The Adam Millichip Foundation

£16,000

Correspondent: Stuart Millichip, Trustee, 17 Boraston Drive, Burford, Tenbury Wells WR15 8AG (07866 424286; email: apply@adammillichip foundation.org; website: adammillichip foundation.org)

CC number: 1138721

Eligibility

People with disabilities in the UK who wish to participate in sports, with the aim of improving the quality of their lives.

Types of grants

Grants have previously been awarded for riding lessons, a specialist bike, ski

lessons and a ski slope pass and swimming lessons.

Annual grant total

In 2013/14 the foundation had an income of £11,500 and an expenditure of £16,000. We estimate that grants totalled around £16,000.

Exclusions

Our research suggests that grants cannot be awarded for competitive purposes.

Applications

There is a six stage application process which is begun on the website. Applications are processed on a first come, first served basis and can take up to two months once all the information has been gathered.

Other information

This foundation was established in memory of Adam Millichip.

Richard Overall Trust

£9,500

Correspondent: Nicholas Overall, Trustee, New Barn Cottage, Honey Lane, Selborne, Alton GU34 3BY (01420 511175)

CC number: 1088640

Eligibility

Young people with disabilities participating in physical education.

Types of grants

Examples of applications for which funding may be made include equipment, training, clothes, transport and support costs towards sporting events.

Annual grant total

In 2013/14 the trust had an income of £15,000 and an expenditure of £10,000. Grants made totalled approximately £9,500.

Applications

Application forms are available from the trust's website.

Snowdon Trust (Formerly known as The Snowdon Award Scheme)

£147,500 (93 grants)

Correspondent: Paul Alexander, Chief Executive Officer, Unit 18, Oakhurst Business Park, Wilberforce Way, Southwater, Horsham, West Sussex RH13 9RT (01403 732899; email: info@ snowdonawardscheme.org.uk; website: www.snowdontrust.org)

CC number: 282754

Eligibility

Students with physical or sensory disabilities who are in or about to enter further/higher education or training in the UK and, because of their disability, have financial needs which are not met elsewhere. Preference is given to people between the ages of 17 and 25.

Types of grants

Bursaries for up to two years are available to people in further/higher education and those training towards employment. Support is aimed to cover additional costs incurred due to the disability which cannot be met in full from statutory sources, including human support (for example sign language interpreters or people to take notes), translators for deaf students, computer equipment, specialist software, adapted or additional accommodation, travel costs, wheelchairs and other mobility equipment or similar expenses.

Grants are normally between £250 and £2,000 but in exceptional circumstances awards of up to £2,500 can be awarded.

Annual grant total

In 2013/14 the trust had assets of £1.2 million and an income of £223,000. Grants were made to 93 students totalling £147,500.

Exclusions

The trust does not normally cover expenses for tuition fees or standard living, accommodation and childcare costs, but can occasionally help with the tuition fees if the need is justifiably and directly related to the applicant's disability. Retrospective awards are not made.

Applications

Application forms can be completed online or downloaded (along with guidelines) from the trust's website. Applicants are required to provide academic and personal references and supporting documentation such as medical information of disability, if applicable.

Other information

This trust also provides mentoring support and advice to beneficiaries and occasionally undertakes research.

Student Disability Assistance Fund (SDAF)

£10,000

Correspondent: Patricia Esswood, Administrative Secretary, University of Nottingham Health Centre, Cripps Health Centre, University Park, Nottingham NG72 2QW (07982040005; website: www.studenthealthassociation. co.uk)

CC number: 253984

Eligibility

Students over the age of 18 on a higher education course in the UK who are affected by a disability or illness. Candidates are expected to apply for Disabled Students Allowance (DSA) before applying to the fund. Priority is given to individuals who are not eligible for funding from the local authorities and those who do not qualify for DSA.

Types of grants

One-off grants of up to £500 towards educational aids made necessary by the student's illness or disability. For example, support can be given for special computer equipment and software, additional books, photocopying, extra travel costs for those with mobility problems, cost of note-takers or signers and other special equipment.

Annual grant total

In 2014 the fund had an income of £11,900 and an expenditure of £10,200. We estimate the annual total amount of grants awarded to be around £10,000.

Exclusions

Funding is not given for general educational expenses incurred by all students (for example, fees, living costs or compulsory textbooks) and for medical treatment or equipment, unless it is specifically aimed at helping with studies.

Applications

Eligible applicants are asked to apply on an online form on the fund's website. Supporting evidence will have to be posted to the correspondent (full list of required documentation can be found on the website). The deadlines for applications are normally 1 March, 1 June and 1 November each year. Incomplete applications are not accepted.

Note that the fund 'cannot respond to any telephone enquiries or give information about prospective or pending applications'.

Other information

The fund was formerly known as BASHE (The British Association of Health Services in Higher Education). It can also offer guidance, advice and information.

Sensory impairment

The Christina Aitchison Trust

£500

Correspondent: Revd Roger Massingberd-Mundy, Trustee, The Old Post Office, The Street, West Raynham, Fakenham NR21 7AD

CC number: 1041578

Eligibility

Young people under the age of 25. Support can particularly be provided to people who are blind or suffering from any ophthalmic disease or disability. Some preference may be given to individuals in the north east or south west of England.

Types of grants

One-off or recurrent grants for up to £300 are made to support young people in educational activities, including arts and music. Awards are made in the form of books, equipment, fees, bursaries and fellowships.

Annual grant total

In 2013/14 the trust had an income of £1,900 and an expenditure of £2,200. We estimate that approximately £500 was given for educational purposes to individuals.

Applications

Application forms are available from the correspondent and should generally be submitted in March or September for consideration in April or November.

Other information

Relief-in-need grants are also given to assist people who have an ophthalmic disease or who are terminally ill and to organisations.

The Amber Trust

£92,000 (180 grants)

Correspondent: Julia Walport, Trustee, 64A Princes Way, London SW19 6JF (020 8788 9755; email: info@ambertrust. org; website: www.ambertrust.org)

CC number: 1050503

Eligibility

Children and young people up to and including the age of 18 who are blind or partially sighted and have a talent or love for music.

Types of grants

One-off and recurrent grants for up to one year are awarded to fund three terms of music lessons, music therapy sessions, one-off events, the purchase of musical instruments, specialist software (such as Sibelius), concert tickets or travel to musical activities. After one year applications can be made again but using a re-application form which allows the trust to monitor the impact of their funding. The average award is of £380.

Annual grant total

In 2013/14 the trust had assets of £160,000 and an income of £64,000, primarily from general donations. During the year 134 awards were made to 132 individuals. A total of £39,000 was approved and distributed in grants and further £53,000 had been approved but had not been paid out by the end of the year.

The website notes that most recently a total of 180 awards were given, including 59 new applicants.

Exclusions

The trust will not make retrospective grants. In some instances the charity will not be able to fund the full costs and the balance will have to be raised from other sources, but the applicants are welcomed to use the Amber pledge to encourage other funding.

Applications

Application forms can be found on the trust's website. Applications should be completed by the child's parents or carers, but can be assisted or prepared by a support worker or teacher. Applications for the purchase of instruments or software should include prices and supplier details. Applications for lessons or music therapy sessions must include full details of the teacher's or therapist's qualifications, experience and CRB clearance. The trustees meet three times a year, in March, July and November. Applications should be received by the end of February, June and October, respectively. All eligible applications will be acknowledged in writing.

When applying for the second and subsequent times, remember to use a re-application form which can also be found on the website.

Other information

If parents have not found a suitable music teacher or therapist for their child, they are encouraged to get in touch with RNIB's Music Advisory Service providing information and advice on music education at all levels. The service can be contacted on 020 7391 2273 or at mas@rnib.org.uk.

The trust's annual report and accounts for 2013/14 state:

> As the number of applications for Music Awards continues to grow, and to be able to help more children, the trust is increasing its fundraising budget to £80,000 for 2014 rising to £100,000 to 2015 whilst carefully monitoring the increase in demand, particularly for individual music therapy sessions.

Beacon Centre for the Blind

£500

Correspondent: Phil Thomas, Company Secretary, Wolverhampton Road East, Wolverhampton WV4 6AZ (01902 886781; email: enquiries@beaconvision. org; website: www.beaconvision.org)

CC number: 216092

Eligibility

People who are registered blind or partially sighted and live in the metropolitan boroughs of Dudley (except Halesowen and Stourbridge), Sandwell and Wolverhampton, and part of the South Staffordshire district council area.

Types of grants

One-off grants of up to a maximum of £250 for specific items or improvements to the home. The charity also aims to facilitate employment opportunities for visually impaired people.

Annual grant total

In 2014/15 the charity had assets of £9.5 million and an income of £2.5 million. Most of the charity's expenditure, which totalled £1.8 million, is spent in relation to service provision. There were seven grants made to individuals totalling almost £1,000 for both social welfare and educational purposes.

Applications

Applications may be made in writing to the correspondent. They should state the degree of vision and age of the applicant as well as their monthly income and expenditure. Applications can be submitted through a social worker or school, and are considered throughout the year.

Other information

The charity's main concern is the provision of support services and facilities to blind and partially sighted people. It provides domiciliary care for up to 71 older blind and partially sighted people. Its activities involve day centres, therapeutic activities, gym facilities, outreach and a talking newspaper. In 2015 it started running the Beacon Bus – a mobile low vision service.

The Blatchington Court Trust (BCT)

£51,000 (155 grants)

Correspondent: Anthony Schofield, Clerk to the Trustees, 6A Hove Park Villas, Hove, East Sussex BN3 6HW (01273 727222; fax: 01273 722244; email: info@blatchington-court.co.uk; website: www.blatchington-court.co.uk)

CC number: 306350

Eligibility

People under the age of 30 who live in the Sussex area and are visually impaired.

Types of grants

One-off and recurrent support to people at any school, university, college or other institution of further education and training, approved by the trustees. The trust provides equipment, mobility aids, books and other study necessities (including those for the study of music and other arts) which will assist in the pursuit of education, training and employment or business development. Assistance will also be given in connection with preparation to enter a school, profession, trade, occupation or service. Most grants awarded are under £3,000.

Annual grant total

In 2013/14 the trust had assets of £12.4 million, an income of £505,000 and a total charitable expenditure of £279,000. A total of £51,000 was awarded in grants to individuals, consisting of 76 computer grants totalling £22,500 and 79 personal grants totalling £28,500.

Exclusions

The trust does not give cash grants or bursaries and will not normally provide funding for wheelchairs, school fees, holidays or travel costs.

Applications

Apply in writing to the correspondent. Applications should normally be made by September.

The following is stated on the trust's website:

> Applications need to describe costed proposals or schemes which fit with the Trusts objective – to assist the development of vision impaired individuals aged from birth to 30. It must be clear that the proposals or schemes will make a real difference in the development of the young people who will benefit – and confirm that any other finance required is in place or promised.

Other information

The trust also runs the Annual Awards Scheme that, according to the latest accounts, can:

> Award grants for the provision of recreational and leisure facilities (or contributions towards such facilities), which enable vision impaired people to develop their physical, mental and moral capacities; and make grants to any voluntary or charitable organisation approved by the Trustees, the objects of which include the promotion of education, training and/or employment of vision

impaired young people and their general well-being in pursuance of all the foregoing.

Elizabeth Eagle-Bott Memorial Fund

£25,000

Correspondent: Fund Administrator, Music Advisory Service, RNIB, 105 Judd Street, London WC1H 9NE (email: mas@rnib.org.uk; website: www.rnib.org.uk)

Eligibility

Musicians, normally aged 18 and over, who are blind or partially sighted. Candidates must be registered as sight impaired or seriously sight impaired (partially sighted or blind) and be UK citizens.

Types of grants

Previously grants have been awarded for the purchase of instruments, vocal tuition, music course fees, transcriber and reader costs, purchase or development of accessible and assistive music technology, costs associated with staging concerts and so on.

There are three types of grants, explained on the website as follows:

A. Major awards for individuals, of up to £10,000 per bid, to blind or partially sighted, UK citizens, aged 18 and over, to support their music making. These are awarded annually.

B. Major awards, of up to £15,000 per bid, for those working on behalf of the music making of blind or partially sighted, UK musicians. These are awarded annually.

C. Minor awards for individuals, of up to £500 per bid, to blind or partially sighted, UK citizens, aged 18 and over, to support their music making. These are awarded quarterly.

Annual grant total

In 2013/14 the fund held assets of £39,000 and had an income of £28,000. A total of £50,000 was spent in charitable activities. We estimate that the amount of grants given to individuals totalled around £25,000.

Applications

Application forms are available from the correspondent. To request an application form or to discuss your application email mas@rnib.org.uk.

All requests will be considered by an expert Panel, with their decisions approved by RNIB. The closing time for applications for awards A and B is noon on 31 March each year.

The closing time for applications for award C:

▶ 31 March for awards valid between 1 June and 31 August

▶ 31 July for awards valid between 1 September and 30 November
▶ 31 October for awards valid between 1 December and end of February
▶ 31 January for awards valid between 1 March and 31 May

There are separate application forms for each type of award, A, B and C.

Other information

The fund is administered by The Royal National Institute of Blind People (Charity Commission no. 226227). We use financial figures relating to the fund only.

Grants may also be given to support organisations and individuals assisting blind or partially sighted musicians in their music making.

Gardner's Trust for the Blind

£19,200

Correspondent: Angela Stewart, Correspondent, 117 Charterhouse Street, London EC1M 6AA (020 7253 3757)

CC number: 207233

Eligibility

Registered blind or partially-sighted people who live in the UK.

Types of grants

Grants are mainly for computer equipment, music equipment and course fees.

Annual grant total

In 2013/14 the trust had assets of £3.5 million and an income of £85,000. Grants to individuals, for both educational and social welfare purposes, were distributed as follows:

Annual grants (paid quarterly)	£23,500
Education and trade grants	£19,100
General aid grants	£9,400
Music grants	£100

Exclusions

Loans are not given.

Applications

Apply in writing to the correspondent. Applications can be submitted either directly by the individual or by a third party; however, direct applications must also be supported by a third party who can confirm that the applicant has a disability and that the grant is needed. Requests are considered in March, June, September and December and should be submitted at least three weeks before the meeting.

The Society for the Education of the Deaf

£35,000

Correspondent: Nancy Ward, Administrator, c/o Alexander Sloan, Chartered Accountants, 38 Cadogan Street, Glasgow G2 7HF (0141 204 8989; fax: 0141 248 9931; email: nancy.ward@ alexandersloan.co.uk; website: www. gsedd.org.uk)

OSCR number: SC003804

Eligibility

Individuals who are deaf and/or speech impaired.

Types of grants

Grants are mainly awarded towards British sign language courses or similar activities and educational courses that will improve applicants' ability to communicate with others. Previously the society has also offered assistance towards specialist equipment such as radio aids, computers and so on.

Annual grant total

In 2013/14 the society had an income of £39,000 and an expenditure of around £37,500. We estimate that the amount of grants given to individuals totalled about £35,000.

Exclusions

Grants are not given for taster or introductory courses. Grant applications will only be considered from individuals and not course organisers or businesses.

Applications

Application forms can be completed online on the society's website or printed off and sent to the correspondent. Applications can be submitted directly by the individual or through a third party and are normally assessed within three to eight weeks.

Other information

In 2012 the Glasgow Society for the Education of Deaf and Dumb became a company limited by guarantee and changed its name to The Society for the Education of the Deaf.

Webster and Davidson Mortification for the Blind

£13,500

Correspondent: G. Fulton, Administrator and Secretary, Thorntons Law LLP, Whitehall House, 33 Yeaman Shore, Dundee DD1 4BJ (01382 229111; fax: 01382 202288; email: gfulton@ thorntons-law.co.uk; website: www.

thorntons-law.co.uk/practice-areas/wills,-trusts,-executries/charitable-trusts)

OSCR number: SC004920

Eligibility

Blind or partially sighted people who are undertaking musical education and are resident, or normally resident, in Britain. Preference will be given to people from Scotland.

Types of grants

Grants, normally of around £1,000, to support the learning and appreciation of music and for a specific musical purpose. Generally, but not exclusively, grants are given at secondary school level or to further/higher education students.

Annual grant total

In 2014 the charity had an income of £24,000 and an expenditure of £27,000. We estimate that music awards to individuals totalled around £13,500.

Exclusions

The bursary is not intended to take the place of or supplement Scottish students' allowances or other awards derived from public funds.

Applications

Application forms, guidance notes and referee report forms (also available in Braille) can be obtained from the correspondent or downloaded from the Thorntons Law LLP website. Applications should be submitted by 31 March.

Other information

Grants are also given to organisations working with visually impaired people to provide funding for educational visits to places of historical or other interest. Organisations from Dundee, Tayside or elsewhere in Scotland are preferred.

Special educational needs

The Joseph and Annie Cattle Trust

£10,500

Correspondent: Roger Waudby, Administrator, PO Box 23, Patrington, Hull HU12 0WF (01964 671742; fax: 01964 671742; website: www.jacattletrust.co.uk)

CC number: 262011

Eligibility

Schoolchildren who have dyslexia and live in Hull or the East Riding of Yorkshire area.

Types of grants

One-off grants, usually of £200 to £500.

Annual grant total

In 2013/14 the trust had assets of £8.6 million and an income of £367,000. The annual report and accounts state that £319,000 was distributed during the year but a breakdown of grants to individuals and awards to organisations was not provided. In previous years, grants to individuals for both social welfare and educational purposes have totalled around £21,000

Exclusions

The trust cannot accept applications from, or make grants to, individuals directly. It only deals with charitable organisations or statutory authorities.

Applications

Individuals may not apply directly, but a welfare body (charitable or statutory) may apply on their behalf. Application forms can be downloaded from the website and should be printed and completed by hand before being returned to the trust by post or fax. Supporting papers should accompany the form where necessary.

Note that Hull City Council agencies should not use the application form, but should instead contact Hull Advice (01482 300303).

Dyslexia Institute Ltd (Dyslexia Action)

£96,000

Correspondent: Anne Frater, Company Secretary, Dyslexia Action House, 10 High Street, Egham, Surrey TW20 9EA (01784 222300; email: GetInvolved@dyslexiaaction.org.uk; website: www.dyslexiaaction.org.uk)

CC number: 268502, SC039177

Eligibility

People in the UK who have dyslexia or literacy difficulties and are from low-income families.

Types of grants

A small number of grants are made from the Learning Fund for subsidised assessment and specific periods of tuition based on educational needs related to dyslexia and literacy difficulties. Grants for one term's tuition are for approximately £400, totalling £2,400 for six terms. A contribution from the individual or their family is required at a minimum of £5 per week. The fund is solely reliant on fundraising activities; therefore, the amount of grants given is restricted and varies each year.

The majority of bursary-funded pupils attend the nationwide centres of Dyslexia Action for 1.5 or 2 hours of multi-sensory tuition each week during the academic year.

Annual grant total

In 2013/14 the charity had assets of £2.5 million, an income of £8.8 million and a total charitable expenditure of £6.9 million. Individuals are awarded grants from the Learning Fund, which provided support totalling £96,000.

Exclusions

Applicants from families where joint annual income is in excess of £22,000 will not be considered without evidence of exceptional circumstances.

Applications

Applicants should contact the Dyslexia Action Centre at which they wish to have tuition. Applications are considered three times a year (one meeting each academic term). Applicants for tuition grants should indicate the family's income and severity of dyslexia – a full educational psychologist's assessment is normally required.

Note that while a grant is awarded to an individual, the payment of fees for tuition is made directly to the Dyslexia Action centre where the tuition will take place.

Other information

The charity also organises training events, conferences, fundraising events, provides guidance and advice and supports schools across England working with children with dyslexia and literacy difficulties who are on free school meals and live in deprived communities.

Independent and boarding schools

The BMTA Trust Ltd

£182,000 (153 grants)

Correspondent: Mrs L. Dolphin, Secretary, Wild Wood, Fairfield Road, Shawford, Winchester SO21 2DA (01962 715025; email: bmtatrust@yahoo.co.uk)

CC number: 273978

Eligibility

Children between the ages of 13 and 16 who are already attending an independent school with a preference for those whose families are connected with the motor industry. Children in exceptional circumstances of social need are occasionally supported to begin attending an independent or boarding school. The trustees 'aim to consider, primarily, cases brought about by unforeseen disaster rather than giving assistance to fund over-ambitious plans'.

The annual report and accounts state:

> The intention is that qualifying educational cases should be supported up to GCSE level with further education being funded only in exceptional cases where alternative state-funded arrangements are for some reason not practical.

Types of grants

Short-term educational grants are given to enable children to complete their current stage of schooling when families have suffered unforeseen financial difficulties.

Assistance may be given up to GCSE level and further education is only funded in exceptional circumstances.

Annual grant total

In 2013/14 the trust had assets of £4.8 million and an income of £223,000. Grants to 153 individuals totalled £182,000, with an average grant of £1,200.

Applications

Apply by contacting the correspondent via email, letter or phone.

Other information

A total of 153 grants were paid to individuals and none to organisations, 90% being for educational purposes and the balance – for welfare purposes.

Buttle UK – School Fees Programme

£892,000 (312 grants)

Correspondent: Hazel Sewell, Small Grants Officer, 15 Greycoat Place, London SW1P 1SB (02078287311; email: info@buttleuk.org; website: www. buttleuk.org)

CC number: 313007

Eligibility

Children and young people over the age of 11 with medical, emotional, social difficulties or those within precarious households. The following groups are eligible to apply: adopted children and young people; children and young people cared for by grandparents, other relatives or friends; children and young people from single parent families; children and young people with two carers, where one is severely incapacitated through illness or disability, or is terminally ill. Support is only available where the state education system has been unable to meet the applicant's needs.

Types of grants

The charity funds places within UK-based boarding or independent day schools.

Annual grant total

In 2013/14 the charity had assets of £48.8 million and an income and of £4.2 million. Charitable expenditure totalled £4.7 million, of which 312 grants were awarded to children totalling £892,000. Of the total amount awarded, 37% comprised new awards and the remainder were renewals. The split between day schools and boarding is now 40:60, which is a shift towards more boarding.

Exclusions

The charity cannot assist: children or young people who are looked after by the local authority or other statutory body; where a school has been chosen because of special facilities for a learning or developmental difficulty; where needs could be met within the state day system; children or young people who do not have 'settled' status in the UK or who are normally resident abroad; where the school has been chosen for a particular type of education, such as music, drama or sports.

Applications

To apply, email info@buttleuk.org detailing how you meet the criteria. An enquiry form is also available from the charity's website. The charity will then decide if it can send you an application form.

Alternatively you can write to the following address: Buttle UK, 15 Greycoat Place, London SW1P 1SB, including your full postal address and contact details and telling clearly if the grant required is for the current or new academic year.

Other information

The charity also runs the Small Grants Programme helping individuals in need.

Fishmongers' Company's Charitable Trust

£30,000

Correspondent: Peter Woodward, Trustee, Fishmongers' Hall, London Bridge, London EC4R 9EL (020 7626 3531; fax: 020 7929 1389; email: ct@ fishhall.org.uk; website: www.fishhall.org. uk/Education–Grants)

CC number: 263690

Eligibility

Children and young people under the age of 19 who are in need of a sum of money to complete schooling. Preference is given to children of single parent families and/or those with a learning difficulty or disability, or those who come from a disadvantaged or unstable family background. People studying fishery-related subjects are also favoured.

Types of grants

Small, one-off grants to assist in cases of short-term need. The company has previously been giving assistance with school fees, the maximum grant being of around £1,800.

The following information is taken from the latest trustees' annual report:

> The Trust accepts applications from both institutions and, for educational purposes only, from individuals. Applications are reviewed against specific criteria and all applications are considered by a Committee formed from a number of the Court members of the Worshipful Company of Fishmongers.

> The Trust's main objective is the provision of charitable grants for educational purposes, fishery-related bodies, the environment and heritage, and the relief of hardship and disability. The Trust also provides grants to projects that advance medical science and grants for the advancement of religious and social work in accordance with the Christian faith. The Trust makes grants to institutions whose criteria meet those objectives and to individuals for educational purposes and the relief of hardship.

Annual grant total

In 2014 the trust had assets of £25.5 million, an income of £751,000 and a total charitable expenditure of £555,000. Around £428,000 was awarded in educational grants, of which almost £30,000 was given in grants to individuals.

Applications

Application forms can be requested from the correspondent. They can be submitted directly by the individual or by a parent/guardian for those under the age of 18. The trustees usually meet in March, June/July and October/ November.

Other information

The company also gives to organisations for welfare, medical, environment and heritage causes. The largest recipient of the trust's funding is Gresham's School in Norfolk, but a number of other schools are also supported.

IAPS Charitable Trust

£27,000

Correspondent: Richard Flower, Secretary, 11 Waterloo Place, Leamington Spa, Warwickshire CV32 5LA (01926 887833; email: rwf@ iaps.uk; website: iaps.uk/about/our-charities)

CC number: 1143241

Eligibility

Children in early, primary or middle school years (i.e. up to the age of 13), both in the UK and overseas. Support is also given to 'children of members or deceased members of the teaching profession to continue their education in independent senior schools, where their families' financial circumstances would otherwise prevent them from doing so'.

Children between the ages of 8 and 14 are supported to attend residential music courses in the UK (principally supported courses are the National Schools Symphony Orchestras (NSSO and Young NSSO), the National Preparatory School Orchestras and the Junior Eton Choral Courses).

Teachers may be awarded grants for research.

Types of grants

Grants are available to support children's education, including training in music, and also to teachers for training and research.

The trust also provides bursaries of up to £2,500 per year per pupil. Priority is given where 'pupils have already started their education in independent schools and whose families' financial circumstances have changed. The support of the school, or intended school, is essential and all awards are subject to an annual needs assessment review.'

Annual grant total

In 2014/15 the trust had assets of £1.2 million and an income of £558,500. Grants totalled £54,500, of which £28,500 was given to individuals. A breakdown of grants distributed was not included in the annual report and accounts; however, they did provide the following information:

> The restricted funds were used to make bursary grants to support the on-going education of four children in senior schools, benevolent grants to support six individuals and Harrison fund grants to twenty eight children so that they could attend courses. Two further children were assisted by grants from unrestricted funds.

We estimate educational grants to individuals to have totalled around £27,000.

Exclusions

Support is not given where public funding is available. Gap year students are not assisted.

Applications

Apply in writing to the correspondent. Applications for general grants are considered at termly meetings, although urgent cases can be decided in between these.

Enquiries about bursary applications should be made to Charles Abram, Bursary Secretary (cncabram@gmail.com) and for music grants to John Brett, Harrison Memorial Fund Secretary (johnbrett62@yahoo.com). Enquiries about general grants should be made to Richard Flower, Secretary and Treasurer (rwf@iaps.uk).

Other information

In 2012 the IAPS Benevolent Fund and the IAPS Bursary Trust, and in 2013 the IAPS Orchestra Trust, merged with the trust allowing to extend its work.

The trust is also known as 'itrust'.

Reedham Children's Trust

£296,000 (116 grants)

Correspondent: Sarah Smart, Secretary, 23 Inwood Avenue, Coulsdon, Surrey CR5 1LP (020 8660 1461; fax: 020 8763 1293; email: info@reedham-trust.org.uk; website: www.reedham-trust.org.uk)

CC number: 312433

Eligibility

Children (normally between the ages of 11 and 16) who are in need of boarding care, due to the death, disability or absence of one or both of their parents (whether natural or through adoption), or their own disability, or other domestic or personal circumstances, such as domestic violence or parental drug/alcohol abuse.

The trust focuses on social need for boarding, not an educational need or academic ability; however, it closely monitors the progress (both academic and social) of the children assisted.

Types of grants

Boarding grants for children who are in need of care.

Annual grant total

In 2013/14 the trust had assets of £8.2 million and an income of £1 million. Expenditure totalled £312,000 and grants were awarded totalling £296,000 (excluding restricted grants of £16,000) in support of 116 children at 46 schools in the UK.

Exclusions

The trust will not give support in cases where the local authority should bear the responsibility (for example where a care order is in place).

Children below the age of 11 are supported only in exceptional circumstances and funding after GCSEs can only be continued following a review of the home situation.

Applications

Applications can be downloaded from the trust's website. Eligible applicants should contact the trust via email or phone for further guidance on the application process. The trust will need confirmation from a professional that boarding is in the interest of the applicant.

The following is stated on the trust's website:

> Due to high demand and for the foreseeable future, we are only able to consider cases where children live within a 60 mile radius of our office here in Purley, Surrey. If you live outside the area please telephone the office on 020 8660 1461 to discuss your case prior to completing any of our forms.

Other information

The trust has a restricted North East Fund to support children in that specific area.

Royal National Children's Foundation

£1.1 million (349 grants)

Correspondent: John Marshall, Correspondent, Sandy Lane, Cobham, Surrey KT3 4AW (01932 868622; fax: 01932 866420; email: admin@rncf.org.uk; website: www.rncf.org.uk)

CC number: 310916

Eligibility

Children between the ages of 7 and 18 who have suffered a trauma, tragedy, neglect or are at risk in some other way, and whose family cannot meet the costs of boarding education unaided.

Types of grants

The foundation provides support towards state and independent boarding school fees. Some pupils in independent day schools are also assisted (normally younger children aged 7–13). Emphasis is on boarding need rather than on educational need.

Annual grant total

In 2013/14 the foundation had assets of £23.6 million and an income of £1.2 million. A total of £1.1 million was spent in support to 349 children.

Exclusions

Support cannot be given on the sole basis of financial difficulties, educational preferences or special needs.

Applications

Eligible applicants should make initial contact with the foundation via phone or email. Application forms will then be provided and should be completed by a parent/guardian or other third party (such as a legal or medical professional, school or welfare agency, if applicable). Consideration can take around 8–12 weeks. Informal enquiries prior to the application are also welcomed.

Other information

The Royal Wanstead Children's Foundation and Joint Educational Trust have merged to form Royal National Children's Foundation, retaining the registered charity number of the former.

Miscellan-eous

Conservative and Unionist Agents' Benevolent Association

£10,000

Correspondent: Sally Smith, Hon. Secretary CABA, Conservative Campaign Headquarters, 30 Millbank, London SW1P 4DP (020 7984 8172 (Tuesdays 11am–5pm); email: sally.smith@conservatives.com; website: www.conservativeagentscharity.org.uk)

CC number: 216438

Eligibility

Children of deceased Conservative or Unionist Agents or Women Organisers.

Types of grants

One-off and recurrent grants towards books, equipment, instruments and fees for schoolchildren.

Annual grant total

In 2013/14 the charity had assets of £2.8 million and an income of £92,500. Grants totalled £57,000, of which, we estimate, around £10,000 was given for educational purposes.

Exclusions

Loans are not given. The charity is not able to provide support to serving or retired Conservative Party staff who are not qualified agents.

Applications

Initial enquiries can be made by post, email or telephone to the correspondent, who will then discuss the possibilities available for the applicant. A member of the Management Committee or a local serving agent will then visit the applicant to discuss their application and their need for support, which is based on an assessment of the applicant's household income and other circumstances. Every beneficiary is reassessed annually, either in winter or summer.

Other information

The majority of the association's grants are made for relief-in-need purposes.

Rouben Foundation

Correspondent: Patrick O'Driscoll, Trustee, 4th Floor, Millbank Tower, 21–24 Millbank, London SW1P 4QP (020 7802 5014; fax: 020 7802 5002; email: contact@reubenfoundation.com; website: www.reubenfoundation.com)

CC number: 1094130

Eligibility

Children and young people from disadvantaged backgrounds who attend University of Oxford, University of Cambridge or any of the Ark Schools and show academic potential.

Types of grants

Reuben Scholarships are given to undergraduates at partnership schools. There are 30 students supported at University of Oxford each year, four at Ark schools and 30 at University of Cambridge.

In connection with UK Friends of the Association for the Wellbeing of Israel's Soldiers (UK AWIS), the foundation also gives Impact Scholarships to discharged soldiers from disadvantaged backgrounds to enable them to 'realise their potential by pursuing higher education goals'.

Annual grant total

In 2014 the foundation had assets of £79.3 million and an income of £4.2 million. The vast majority of support is given to organisations (almost £3.8 million during the year) but we believe that around £2 million of this was given as part of the foundation's scholarship programmes, as shown below:

Oxford University	£877,500
ARK	£480,000
Cambridge University	£472,500
University College London	£150,000
Impact Scholarships	£20,500

Applications

The foundation has partnerships with University of Oxford, University of Cambridge and ARK schools to identify applicants. Interested pupils enrolled at any of these schools should make enquiries at the school and not to the foundation.

Other information

The foundation was established in 2002 as an outlet for the philanthropic giving of billionaire property investors David and Simon Reuben. The foundation was endowed by the brothers with a donation of $100 million (£54.1 million), with the income generated to be given to a range of charitable causes, particularly in the fields of healthcare and education.

The Vegetarian Charity

£6,500

Correspondent: Susan Lenihan, Grants Secretary, PO Box 496, Manchester M45 0FL (01249 443521; email: grantssecretary@vegetariancharity.org.uk; website: www.vegetariancharity.org.uk)

CC number: 294767

Eligibility

Vegetarians and vegans up to the age of 26 who are in need. Although UK-based, the charity will consider applications from most countries.

Types of grants

One-off and recurrent grants of up to £500 can be made for educational courses and other needs. Priority will be given to first degrees. According to the website, the charity is 'keen to receive more applications from young people and parents experiencing financial hardship'. Applications for help towards school clothing, school trips, shoes, coats and other essential items for children will receive careful consideration from the trustees.

The charity also offers a fully-funded Vegan Cookery course for young people (aged 16–25).

Annual grant total

In 2013/14 the charity had assets of £1.15 million and an income of £56,500. There were 51 grants paid during the year to individuals and organisations totalling £26,000. A further breakdown was not available; therefore, we estimate that the amount of grants given to individuals for educational purposes totalled around £6,500.

Exclusions

The charity's website states: 'In the current economic climate postgraduate applications are only considered in exceptionally difficult personal circumstances.'

Applications

Application forms are available on the website or from the correspondent. They can be submitted by individuals directly or by a parent/guardian on a child's behalf, preferably by email. You will be asked to provide details of any other grants received, your income and expenditure (bank statements), a CV, a letter of recommendation from a tutor or confirmation of acceptance on the course, school reports and a covering letter. Two professional references are also required to verify the applicant's commitment to vegetarian or vegan diet.

It takes about three months to complete the consideration of an application. Requests are considered throughout the year. The trustees take into account efforts made by applicants to improve their financial situation and any evidence of employment or efforts made to find work (or conversely, reasons why they have been unable to do so, such as medical certificates) should be included.

Applications for the cooking course open in January – see the website for further details.

The charity asks all communication to be via email or post.

Other information

Grants are also made to organisations which promote vegetarianism/veganism among young people (excluding business projects) and for relief in need.

The Vegetarian Charity is an amalgamation of The Vegetarian Children's Charity and The Vegetarian Home for Children and was formed in 1986.

Overseas students

The Alvechurch Grammar School Endowment

See entry on page 188

The Anglo-Czech Educational Fund

£41,000

Correspondent: Paul Sheils, Trustee, Moon Beever Solicitors, Bedford House, 21A John Street, London WC1N 2BF (02074007770; email: info@moonbeever.com)

CC number: 1110348

Eligibility

Students from the Czech Republic who wish to study primarily in the UK, USA and European countries.

Types of grants

Grant and loans.

Annual grant total

In 2013/14 the fund had assets of 1.4 million and an income of £147,500. During the year, a grant of £41,000 was awarded to Karlova Univerzita to distribute as grants.

Applications

Apply in writing to the correspondent.

Anglo-Swedish Literary Foundation

£9,500

Correspondent: Ann Nilsen, Cultural Affairs Officer, Embassy of Sweden, 11 Montagu Place, London W1H 2AL (02079176465; website: www.swedenabroad.com/en-GB/Embassies/London/Contact/Anglo-Swedish-Literary-Foundation)

CC number: 230622

Eligibility

Individuals connected to studies of Swedish language and literature, translation work and research. The foundation aims develop the 'cultural intercourse between Sweden and the British Islands through the promotion and diffusion of knowledge and appreciation of Swedish culture in the British Islands'.

Types of grants

Grants are given for translation and publishing subsidies, travel to Sweden for educational/research purposes and similar causes.

Annual grant total

In 2013/14 the foundation had an income of £8,000 and an expenditure of £10,000. We estimate the annual total amount of grants awarded to be around £9,500.

Applications

Apply in writing to the correspondent. Applicants should outline their project or activity, state funding required and give details of any other funding applied to/secured. Applications must be received by 1 May or 1 November.

Other information

The foundation established the Bernard Shaw Translation Prize which awards £2,000 every three years for the best translation into English of a Swedish work, published for the first time by a UK publisher. This prize is administered by the Society of Authors.

Armenian General Benevolent Union London Trust

£55,000

Correspondent: Camilio Azzouz, Trustee, 29 Garway Road, London W2 4PH (07455165223; website: www.agbu.org.uk)

CC number: 282070

Eligibility

University students of Armenian descent studying full-time at accredited UK educational institutions. Both undergraduate and postgraduate programmes are eligible. Preference can be given for courses in Armenian studies or subjects which may benefit the Armenian community.

There is a specific AGBU Religious Education Assistance Program available to Armenian clergy and lay leaders for professional development.

Types of grants

Scholarships generally range from £1,000 to £3,000 and are awarded annually for up to three years. Support is both need and merit based and is normally intended to cover educational fees or to contribute to essentials, books or maintenance. The trust offers both grants and interest-free loans.

Students studying performing arts or religious studies should apply for AGBU Performing Arts Fellowship (study in the UK) or AGBU Religious Studies Fellowship, as they will not be eligible for the general scholarship.

Our research suggests that student grants are occasionally given to Armenians with significant financial hardship or for refugees in the UK. Grants have also been given towards teaching, arts and research papers connected with Armenian culture.

Annual grant total

In 2014 the trust had an income of £148,000 and a total expenditure of £71,000. We estimate that student grants and loans totalled around £55,000. At the time of writing (October 2015) the annual report and accounts for the year were not available to view.

Exclusions

Citizens of Armenia studying in Armenia are not eligible for the scholarship. The trust does not offer travel grants, support for conferences, semesters of study abroad, non-degree courses, research studies and similar short-term educational or professional experience.

Applications

Applications can be made online on the AGBU Scholarship program website. There is a convenient eligibility checking programme. Applications for scholarships must be made by 31 August and for fellowships by 31 July. Note that application deadlines are very strict and submissions past the designated dates will be disregarded.

Applications for the AGBU Religious Education Assistance Program can be made on a form downloadable from the website.

Other information

Support is also given to Armenian schools, nurseries and cultural groups in the UK and overseas, usually towards running costs for Armenian language, history, religion and culture classes. Occasionally welfare grants can be given to people in need.

The AGBU scholarship website also suggests a number of other sources of help. The trust itself is connected with the Armenian Education Trust (Charity Commission no. 313930).

The Benlian Trust

£52,000 (18 grants)

Correspondent: Maral Ovanessoff, Administrator, 15 Elm Crescent, Ealing, London W5 3JW (02085671210; email: benliantrust@gmail.com)

CC number: 277253

Eligibility

Children of Armenian fathers. Applicants must be members of the Armenian Church studying at universities and colleges in the UK.

Types of grants

Scholarships to Armenian people in higher education. Grants are given towards the cost of fees and/or living expenses. Priority is given to undergraduates. Scholarships are awarded in the range of £1,000 to £4,500.

Annual grant total

In 2013/14 the trust had assets of £2.7 million, an income of £108,000 and a total charitable expenditure of £97,000. Scholarships were made totalling £52,000 to 18 students studying at various colleges and universities in the UK. A further £31,500 was awarded towards the costs of eight Armenian cultural and educational activities in London.

Applications

Apply in writing to the correspondent via post or email. Completed applications should be returned before 30 April. Three references are required (two academic and one social).

Other information

The trustees' annual report for 2013/14 states:

> The trust specifies that 3/5ths of its income is to be distributed in scholarships, 1/4th towards activities connected with the cultural life of the London Community of Armenians, including the maintenance and support of Armenian House, 1/10th in advancement of medical research, 1/10th to the Armenian Hospital in Istanbul and L'Ecole Mixte Armeniennes (France) in equal shares, and 1/20th in provision of amenities for nurses at the Middlesex Hospital.

The Bestway Foundation

£80,000 (34 grants)

Correspondent: Mohammed Sheikh, Trustee, Abbey Road, Park Royal, London NW10 7BW (020 8453 1234; fax: 020 8453 8219; email: zulfikaur. wajid-hasan@bestway.co.uk; website: www.bestwaygroup.co.uk/page/Bestway-Foundation.html)

CC number: 297178

Eligibility

Higher education students who are of Indian, Pakistani, Bangladeshi or Sri Lankan origin.

Types of grants

One-off and recurrent scholarships, grants and loans towards tuition fees. Payments are normally made directly to academic institutions.

Annual grant total

In 2013/14 the foundation had assets of £7 million, an income of £648,000 and a charitable expenditure of £400,000. During the year 34 individuals were supported. A total of £156,000 was awarded to individuals and foreign charities. Amount given to students was not specified in the accounts; however, previously grants to individuals have totalled around £80,000.

Applications

Applications can be made in writing to the correspondent by post (enclosing an sae) or by email. Applications are normally considered in January.

Other information

Grants are also made to organisations in the UK and overseas (17 grants were made during the year).

British Council

Correspondent: Alison Coutts, Secretary, 10 Spring Gardens, London SW1A 2BN (email: trustees@ britishcouncil.org; website: www. britishcouncil.org)

CC number: 209131

Eligibility

People who are looking to work, study or volunteer abroad. See the website for more information.

Types of grants

For information on the type of grants available see the 'Study, Work, Create' section of the British Council website.

Annual grant total

The British Council provides scholarships for people looking to work, study or volunteer abroad.

Applications

Applications should be made online via the British Council website.

The British Institute for the Study of Iraq (Gertrude Bell Memorial)

£27,500 (20 grants)

Correspondent: Lauren Mulvee, Administrator, 10 Carlton House Terrace, London SW1Y 5AH (020 7969 5274; fax: 020 7969 5401; email: bisi@ britac.ac.uk; website: www.bisi.ac.uk)

CC number: 1135395

Eligibility

People undertaking research, projects, conferences or development events on Iraq, and Iraqi scholars visiting the UK for a study. The charity can support scholars in areas relating to Iraq and neighbouring countries in anthropology, archaeology, geography, history, language and related disciplines within the arts, humanities and social sciences.

Types of grants

Grants are available for research projects, to cultural heritage professionals of Iraq for retraining and re-equipment, also for educational events that develop the understanding of Iraq's society, history and culture.

Research and conference grants are awarded to people in the field of humanities and social sciences. Assistance is available for direct educational expenses (such as equipment, travel costs, consultancy fees) and can be of up to £4,000. Applicants must be employed by, or have an official connection with, a UK higher education institution.

Pilot project grants are given to support up to one year of preliminary research on Iraq, the arts, humanities or social sciences that has a potential to turn into a long-term project. The award can reach up to £8,000. Application criteria are the same as for regular research grants.

Outreach grants, usually of up to £500, can be awarded for various public engagement events and projects (such as lectures or study days) relating to Iraq. Applicants should normally be UK residents.

Visiting Iraqi Scholarships are offered each year to two Iraqi scholars and cultural heritage professionals for research, training and collaborative projects in the UK, particularly those who already work in partnership with UK institutions/academies. These awards are available for institutional fees (excluding tuition fees), living and travel expenses and emergency travel insurance.

Annual grant total

In 2013/14 the charity had assets of £2.7 million, an income of £106,000 and a total charitable expenditure of £180,000. During the year 20 individuals were awarded grants totalling £27,500. The grants can be broken down as follows:

Research and conference grants	£12,000
Pilot project grants	£8,000
Outreach grants	£4,500
Publications support grant	£3,000

Exclusions

Visiting Iraqi Scholarships would not cover salary expenses, tuition fees or routine medical expenses. Research grants cannot be offered for institutional overheads, salary costs, PhD studentships or living costs.

Applications

Application forms for different schemes can be found on the charity's website or requested from the correspondent. The deadlines are: 1 October for Outreach grants (applications must be emailed providing two references) and 1 February for Research grants (applications must be made both by email and post) and Visiting Iraqi Scholarships.

Other information

The charity also organises public events, lectures, study days, conferences, also publishes books and a journal.

The British Institute of Archaeology at Ankara (British Institute at Ankara)
See entry on page 93

The Canadian Centennial Scholarship Fund UK (CCSF)

£48,500 (16 grants)

Correspondent: Leith McKay, Trustee, Canadian Centennial Scholarship Fund, c/o Canadian Women's Club, Canada House, Trafalgar Square, London SW1Y 5BJ (020 7228 0698; email: info@canadianscholarshipfund.co.uk; website: www.canadianscholarshipfund.co.uk)

CC number: 313966

Eligibility

Canadian citizens who are in need of financial assistance for a postgraduate study or training in the United Kingdom. Applicants also must:

- Demonstrate high academic standards
- Be currently enrolled on a postgraduate (or equivalent) course
- Be attending a full-time UK university (or similar institution) at the time of application
- Have completed at least one term of study with at least one term remaining

Types of grants

The fund offers scholarships ranging from £1,000 to £5,000 which can be used towards fees, travel expenses, books, maintenance and living expenses.

Annual grant total

In 2013/14 the fund had assets of £58,500 and an income of £33,000. The amount of grants given to individuals totalled £48,500. Each year 16 individuals are selected for the award.

Exclusions

Applicants undertaking a one-year programme are not accepted.

Applications

Apply in writing to the correspondent.

Other information

Among the 16 annual grants the fund gives two special awards: The Belle Shenkman Award for the Study of Arts and the Mary Le Messurier Award for the Study of History.

Unsuccessful applicants are not notified.

Sir Ernest Cassel Educational Trust (The Cassel Trust)

£37,000

Correspondent: Kathryn Hodges, Secretary, 5 Grimston Park Mews, Grimston Park, Grimston, Tadcaster LS24 9DB (01937 834730; email: casseltrust@btinternet.com; website: www.casseltrust.co.uk)

CC number: 313820

Eligibility

Overseas students from the Commonwealth countries studying in the UK who are in the final year of their studies and are experiencing unforeseen financial difficulties.

Postdoctoral students of humanities and other fields in the UK universities undertaking research overseas.

Types of grants

The trust offers grants to individuals in the following two categories:

- Mountbatten Memorial Grants – for overseas students from the Commonwealth countries who are facing financial difficulties in their final year at a UK university to help them finish the course by

contributing towards the living expenses only
- Postdoctoral Travel Grants – awards of up to £1,000 to assist with the travel costs to postdoctoral students who are at a university in the UK undertaking research overseas in the humanities and other fields.

Annual grant total

In 2014/15 the trust had assets of £1.5 million, an income of £64,000 and a total expenditure of £64,500. Grants to individuals were made in the following categories:

Mountbatten Memorial Grants	£18,000
Mountbatten Memorial Grants provision for exceptional grants	£11,000
Overseas research grants	£8,000

Exclusions

Grants are not intended to cover or contribute to the course fees. The trust will not provide retrospective grants, repayment of debts or support to overseas students who are UK-registered for fees purposes. Student on a one-year course are unlikely to be supported.

Applications

The Mountbatten Memorial Grants are administered by either Churches International Student Network Hardship Fund or through a Block Grant Scheme currently active in the following universities: Birmingham, Cardiff, Glasgow, Leeds, Leicester, Manchester, Nottingham, Reading, Imperial College London and University College London. Candidates from these institutions should apply directly to their student welfare office responsible for overseas students. Students at any other university should apply to: The Grants Secretary, CISN Hardship Fund, 2/27 Pentland Drive, Edinburgh EH10 6PU (tel: 0131 445 4015, email: dphilpot@cofscotland.org.uk).

Applications should include the following:
- A CV and details of the intended career
- Details of the course or research degree and the completion date
- Current financial position and the nature of the unforeseen circumstances causing the difficulty
- Any other grants and outstanding applications for financial assistance
- A letter of support/statement of attendance from an academic supervisor

The trustees meet once a year to consider applications, usually in July.

Applications for the Postdoctoral Travel Grants are administered by the British Academy and should be made on the small research grant form available from the academy at: The Research Grants Department, The British Academy,

10 Carlton House Terrace, London SW1Y 5AH (tel: 020 7969 5200). Applications are considered in spring each year.

Church Burgesses Educational Foundation
See entry on page 308

Churchill University Scholarships Trust for Scotland

£26,500

Correspondent: The Trustees, c/o MacRae and Kaur LLP, 6th Floor, Atlantic House, 45 Hope Street, Glasgow G2 6AE (0141 611 6000)

OSCR number: SC013492

Eligibility
Students in Scotland.

Types of grants
Grants are given for one-off educational projects of benefit to the community, for example, medical electives or voluntary work overseas in a student's gap year or holiday.

Annual grant total
In 2013/14 the trust had an income of £19,500 and an expenditure of £27,000. Grants totalled approximately £26,500.

Exclusions
Grants are not made for any other educational needs, such as course fees, books or living expenses.

Applications
Apply in writing to the correspondent.

The Frank Denning Memorial Charity
See entry on page 216

Peter Alan Dickson Foundation

£2,300

Correspondent: Conchita Garcia, Correspondent, Robins Roost, Thruxton, Andover SP11 8NL (email: conchita@ thefsi.org or info@padfoundation.org; website: www.tarncourt.com/wp-content/uploads/2013/04/pad-guidance-for-applicants-and-application-form.pdf)

CC number: 1129310

Eligibility
The foundation's education fund provides financial support to individuals who cannot pursue education or develop their skills and abilities because of

poverty or other circumstances. The focus specifically, but not exclusively, is placed on people in financially developing countries.

Preference may be given to applications in the areas of marine biology or the food and beverage industry but all applications will be given full consideration.

Types of grants
Individual bursaries to help with tuition fees and related educational expenses. Grants can range from £250 to £1,000.

Annual grant total
In 2013/14 the foundation had an income of £12,000 and an expenditure of £7,300. We estimate that the annual total amount of grants awarded to individuals for educational purposes was around £2,300.

Exclusions
The foundation will not:
▷ Give support where central/local/ national government should be responsible for the provision of assistance
▷ Provide for people in independent education sector
▷ Offer retrospective funding

Applications
Application forms are available on the foundation's website together with full guidelines.

Other information
The foundation also assists charitable organisations, families and communities in relation to educational causes, youth support and development, and disaster or poverty relief.

English Speaking Union of the Commonwealth (English Speaking Union)

£1.3 million

Correspondent: Charity Administrator, Dartmouth House, 37 Charles Street, London W1J 5ED (020 7529 1550; email: esu@esu.org; website: www.esu.org)

CC number: 273136

Eligibility
People involved in teaching the English language overseas and other education-related or cross-cultural projects. There are scholarships relating to the clergy, library professionals, literary translators, scientists, young musicians, teachers and students of various subjects.

Types of grants
The union administers a number of grant and scholarship awards for students and professionals, often in the

form of travel scholarships. For details of individual funds, applicants are advised to refer to the union's website.

Annual grant total
In 2013/14 the charity had assets of £39 million and an income of £3.6 million. A total of £1.3 million was spent in scholarships and other educational programmes.

Applications
Applications vary for the different scholarships; therefore, applicants should refer to the website.

Some schemes require applicants to attend an interview/audition.

Other information
The organisation offers training, initiates youth and academic exchanges, organises educational programmes, conferences and meetings as well as cultural activities.

Erasmus Mobility Grants

Correspondent: The Erasmus Team, British Council, 10 Spring Gardens, London SW1A 2BN (029 2092 4311; email: erasmus@britishcouncil.org; website: www.erasmusplus.org.uk)

CC number: 209131, SC037733

Eligibility
Students from the EU who wish to study (for a period between 3 and 12 months) or work as a trainee (for a period between 2 and 12 months) abroad. Applicants must be following any higher education studies leading to a recognised degree or other recognised tertiary level qualification up to and including the level of doctorate or be enrolled on a vocational education course, including foundation degree courses, or undertaking apprenticeships.

Academics, trainers, adult education staff, school teachers are eligible for staff mobility programmes (both teaching and training) for a period between two days and two months.

Opportunities are also available to youth workers and young people.

Types of grants
Grants for students carrying out study or work placements. Support is given based on the duration of the period abroad and can cover travel costs, foreign language preparation, living costs or other extra costs arising from studying abroad. Amounts awarded will depend on the country where the applicant is travelling and roughly range from 150 to 500 euros per month.

Individuals with special needs, students in traineeship and students from disadvantaged backgrounds are entitled to additional support.

Students from outermost programme countries and regions (Cyprus, Iceland, Malta, overseas countries and territories) will receive higher support to reflect the travel costs.

Annual grant total

The Erasmus+ programme has been allocated an overall budget of £14.7 billion for the seven-year period from 2014 to 2020. The sum is divided between education and training (78%), youth (10%), sport (2%) and other (10%) categories.

Exclusions

University students cannot apply during their first year.

The Erasmus+ programme is new; therefore, previous participants of Erasmus Life Learning Programme can apply again but the organisations may be more likely to select individuals with no previous experience in Erasmus opportunities.

Applications

Applications have to be made through organisations. Students should contact the Erasmus co-ordinator at their home university to enquire about the programme.

Other information

The Erasmus+ programme started operating from January 2014. It integrates the previously run Erasmus programmes.

The British Council website notes that 'most UK universities and many other UK institutions of higher/further education have some involvement with the Erasmus student mobility programmes. The involvement varies from institution to institution but overall every subject area is covered.' New applications are welcomed from institutions, groups, organisations, charities and so on.

Ruth Hayman Trust

£21,000

Correspondent: The Trustees, PO Box 17685, London N6 6WD (email: info@ ruthhaymantrust.org.uk; website: www. ruthhaymantrust.org.uk)

CC number: 287268

Eligibility

Adults (aged over 16) in state-funded education or training who have come to settle in the UK and who speak English as their second or other language. Applicants must be resident in the UK as citizens of the UK/EU, spouses of citizens or as asylum seekers/refugees.

Types of grants

One-off and recurrent grants of up to £500 (on average £150) are available to help with the cost of fees (registration, course or exam), joining the professional bodies (if it is essential for the course) or disclosure and barring service fees. Depending on the finances available, the trust can also assist with the cost of equipment and instruments. Grants towards travel costs are also made to people with disabilities who can provide a statement from the doctor. The trust also suggests that for a limited period the £500 maximum can be increased for those on courses at Level 3 and above or for membership of professional associations where fees are very high. Cheques are usually paid to the educational institution directly.

There is an additional annual Rose Grant Special Award of £500 available to 'applicants who can show exceptional academic achievement, an outstanding commitment to the community or human rights as well as financial need'.

Annual grant total

In 2013/14 the trust had an income of £19,000 and a total expenditure of £21,500. We estimate that £21,000 was awarded in grants.

Exclusions

Grants cannot be given towards travel costs (except for people with disability), childcare, living expenses, postgraduate education (unless it leads directly to employment) or private education courses (unless the course is only available in specialist private training).

People studying as overseas students are not supported and individuals on distance learning courses can only be supported if they are unable to travel to the place of education.

Applications

Application forms can be found on the trust's website or requested from the correspondent. Grants are awarded about five times a year and applications should be submitted in February, late April, late June, early September or late November. Candidates are required to provide an academic reference.

Applications for the Rose Grant Special Award should be made on the same form providing evidence that the candidate satisfies the additional requirements.

The trust reminds that it is crucial to fill in the application form in full (do not forget to demonstrate financial need, state your first language, include a reference and specify what the support is needed for). Further application guidelines can be found on the website, read them carefully to avoid your application being rejected on technical grounds.

Other information

The full name of the trust is 'The Ruth Hayman Trust for the Advancement of the Education of Adults Resident in the United Kingdom Whose First Language is not English'.

The Nora Henry Trust

£26,000

Correspondent: Fiona MacGillivray, Head of Deputy Service, Family Action, 501–505 Kingsland Road, London E8 4AU (020 7254 6251; email: grants. enquiry@family-action.org.uk; website: www.family-action.org.uk)

CC number: 264713-56/313949

Eligibility

Students from any country with a preference for students from financially developing countries who are studying subjects which will be of use when the student returns to that country.

Students can study sociology, economics, ecology, philosophy or training of a professional, technological, technical, scientific or artistic nature.

Types of grants

One-off grants usually ranging from £100 to £200 can be given towards books, fees, living expenses, travel and childcare.

Annual grant total

In 2013/14 the trust had assets of £1.6 million, an income of £49,000 and a total expenditure of £27,500. We estimate that grants totalled £26,000.

Exclusions

No grants are given for study or travel overseas for British students, or for student exchanges.

Applications

Application forms are available from the correspondent. Applications should be submitted directly by the individual and supported by an academic referee. They are considered all year round. The trust is administered by Family Action.

The Hertfordshire Educational Foundation
See entry on page 264

The British and Foreign School Society – International Link Scholarship Scheme
See entry on page 46

The Jeremi Kroliczewski Educational Trust

£7,500

Correspondent: Simeon Arnold, Trustee, Montage Lambert and Co., 41–41A Haven Green, London W5 2NX (020 8997 2288; email: sarnold@ montaguelambert.com)

CC number: 1051524

Eligibility

Polish students under the age of 25 who are in further/higher education in England or Wales. The trust's funds are fully committed years in advance.

Types of grants

Grants are given according to need for general educational purposes, including fees, maintenance and living expenses, books, equipment and other necessities.

Annual grant total

In 2013/14 the trust had an income of £7,000 and a total expenditure of £8,000. We estimate the annual total amount of grants awarded to be around £7,500.

Applications

The trustees have confirmed that the trust's funds are fully committed at least five years in advance; therefore, new applications are not currently invited.

Mihran Essefian Charitable Trust (The Mihran and Azniv Essefian Charitable Trust)

£38,500 (412 grants)

Correspondent: Maral Ovanessoff, Administrator, 15 Elm Crescent, Ealing, London W5 3JW (02085671210; email: benliantrust@gmail.com)

CC number: 275074

Eligibility

University students of Armenian origin studying in Armenia or Armenian students in the UK.

Types of grants

The trust offers scholarships to university students. Grants range from around £30 to £200 per student.

Annual grant total

In 2013/14 the trust had assets of £1.7 million, an income of £55,000 and a total charitable expenditure of £47,000. Grants to 412 individuals totalled £38,500.

Applications

Apply in writing to the correspondent. The deadline for applications is usually the end of April each year.

Other information

Grants are also given to organisations and institutions promoting educational, cultural and charitable activities of the Armenian community (£8,500 in 2013/14).

Viquaran Nisa Noon and Firoz Khan Noon Educational Foundation (Noon Educational Foundation)

£77,500

Correspondent: Dr Paul Flather, Chair, c/o Mansfield College, University of Oxford, Mansfield Road, Oxford OX1 3TF (01865 284482; fax: 01865 284481; email: info@noon-foundation. org)

CC number: 1017002

Eligibility

People who are from Pakistan, have spent at least 12 years studying in Pakistani schools/colleges/universities and wish to undertake a higher education course in the natural sciences, social sciences or arts and humanities at either Oxford or Cambridge University. Applicants must be able to demonstrate academic merit, excellent command of the English language, financial need and evidence that they have not previously had the opportunity to study abroad at a western university. They must also show that they intend to return to Pakistan and potentially contribute to the local community upon completion of their course.

Types of grants

Full and partial scholarships are generally given for postgraduate study but suitable undergraduates will also be supported.

Annual grant total

In 2013/14 the foundation had an income of £41,000 and a total of £77,500 was awarded in grants, but had not been paid by the year end, to Cambridge and Oxford providing partial support for students.

Applications

There is no specific application form. Candidates should make applications directly to the universities. The foundation's website provides links to the relevant sections. Applicants should indicate that they wish to apply for the Noon Foundation grant on the general scholarships application form that accompanies their application to study at either the University of Oxford or Cambridge. Scholarships are decided by July each year, in preparation for the coming academic year.

Other information

The foundation reminds that 'it receives many more applications for funding than it can offer'.

The Puri Foundation

£1,800 (2 grants)

Correspondent: Nathu Ram Puri, Trustee, Environment House, 6 Union Road, Nottingham NG3 1FH (0115 901 3000; website: www.purico.co.uk/ charitable_functions)

CC number: 327854

Eligibility

Individuals in need living in Nottinghamshire who are from India (particularly the towns of Mullanpur near Chandigarh and Ambala). Employees/past employees of Melton Medes Group Ltd, Blugilt Holdings or Melham Inc. (and their dependants) who are in need are also eligible. The foundation wants to support people who have exhausted state support and other avenues, in other words to be the 'last resort'. Eligible people can receive help at any stage of their education, including postgraduate and mature students.

Types of grants

One-off and recurrent grants are given according to need. The maximum donation is usually between £150 and £200.

Annual grant total

In 2013/14 the foundation had assets of nearly £3.2 million and an income of £345,000. Grants were made totalling £284,500, with a major grant of £227,000 being given to Puri Foundation for Education in India. Grants to three individuals were listed in the accounts totalling £3,400, one of them being for general support and two for education and cultural purposes.

Applications

Applications may be made in writing to the correspondent, either directly by the individual or through a social worker.

Other information

Note that the vast majority of charitable giving is in grants to organisations. Individual support is given occasionally. General welfare grants can also be made.

Schilizzi Foundation in Memory of Eleutherios and Helena Veniselos (The Schilizzi Foundation)

£90,000

Correspondent: Stephen Schilizzi, Trustee, Chacombe Priory, Chacombe, Banbury OX17 2AW (01295 710356; email: admin@schilizzifoundation.org.uk; website: www.schilizzifoundation.org.uk)

CC number: 314128

Eligibility

Greek nationals pursuing an undergraduate degree course (normally for three years) or vocational training in Great Britain who can demonstrate need and financial hardship. Priority is given to students in their final year of study but postgraduates and other students will be considered too.

Children of Greek nationals resident in Great Britain can also be eligible for support to further their education in the language, history, literature and institutions of Greece.

Types of grants

The foundation's website notes that its present policy is to 'provide financial assistance in two main areas: hardship grants for students currently at British universities and further education scholarships awarded in conjunction with Kings College London'.

Hardship grants are awarded for the tuition fees, cost of books or living expenses. Support can also be given for expenditure outside Great Britain provided it has been incurred in pursuance of education.

Education scholarships for further education in the UK can be one-off or recurrent and are awarded to selected students; therefore, direct applications will not be considered.

Annual grant total

In 2013/14 the foundation had assets of £2.3 million and an income of £84,000. Grants totalled £90,000 and were distributed as follows: special awards (£59,000); scholarship grants (£25,500); and other grants (£5,500).

Applications

Application forms for hardship grants can be requested from the secretary at the following address: The Secretary, The Schilizzi Foundation, Rowan, Turweston, Brackley, Northamptonshire NN13 5JX. Applications should be then submitted through the student counsellor/adviser at the candidate's college.

The Sloane Robinson Foundation

£133,000

Correspondent: Michael Wilcox, Trustee, Old Coach House, Sunnyside, Bergh Apton, Norwich NR15 1DD (01508 480100; email: info@wilcoxlewis.co.uk)

CC number: 1068286

Eligibility

Overseas students wishing to study at British universities and British students wishing to study overseas.

At an undergraduate level emphasis is placed on liberal arts, orthodox sciences (but not religion), social sciences and languages. At postgraduate level no restrictions apply. With regards to overseas studies emphasis should be placed on the subjects in which the country offers better courses.

The foundation is also interested in funding research into controversial issues (for example prison policy, decriminalisation of cannabis, population issues) and supporting young people to work in financially developing countries on projects which transfer knowledge and skills to the local people.

Types of grants

Grants and scholarships according to need.

Annual grant total

In 2013/14 the foundation had assets of £13.2 million, an income of £192,000 and a total charitable expenditure of £471,000. Grants made to individuals totalled £133,000 (all to pupils of Latymer School).

Applications

The foundation is 'continuing to develop long-term relationships with a number of academic institutions, with the ultimate goal of establishing scholarships and bursary schemes'. Our research suggests that applications should be made directly through educational establishments. The trustees meet at least twice a year.

Note that 'only successful applicants are notified, in order to avoid increased administrative costs for the foundation'.

Other information

The foundation mainly provides funding to educational institutions (£338,300 in 2013/14).

The Charles Wallace India Trust

£148,000

Correspondent: Richard Alford, Secretary, 36 Lancaster Avenue, London SE27 9DZ (02086702825; email: cwit@btinternet.com; website: www.wallace-trusts.org.uk/cwt_india.html)

CC number: 283338

Eligibility

Students, scholars and professionals of Indian nationality and citizenship (generally between the ages of 25 and 38) studying in the UK in the field of arts, heritage, conservation or humanities. Applicants should normally be resident in India and intend to return there at the end of their study. Certain short-term awards are available for people aged between 25 and 45.

Types of grants

Grants and scholarships towards educational courses, research or professional development in the fields of arts, heritage, conservation and humanities. Most awards are given at a postgraduate level to supplement other sources of funding or constitute completion of study awards for those whose scholarships have run out.

A limited number of postdoctoral or post-professional research grants are awarded. Support includes fully-funded awards, visiting fellowships in agreed subjects at specific institutions, grants for research and professional visits, grants for doctoral study and grants to attend the Scottish Universities' Summer School or specialist training.

Annual grant total

In 2013/14 the trust had assets of £6.7 million and an income of £293,500. There was a total expenditure of £195,500 and £148,000 was awarded in grants and scholarships.

Exclusions

Studies relating to economic development or leading to professional legal, business or administrative qualifications are not normally considered.

Applications

Apply in writing to the correspondent. Applications can be found on the British Council website together with respective deadlines. Applicants are required to identify what benefit an award will bring not only to them personally but also to the people of India.

Other information

There are separate, smaller Charles Wallace Trusts for Bangladesh, Burma and Pakistan. All of the trusts are registered charities in the UK with separate and independent boards of trustees.

Note: The British Council facilitates and advises on the visas but the cost must be borne by the applicant. Further enquiries can also be addressed to the British Council in New Delhi at: cwit@in.britishcouncil.org.

World Friendship

£11,500

Correspondent: The Applications Secretary, 15 Dudlow Lane, Liverpool L18 0HH (0151 722 9700; email: worldfriendship@hotmail.co.uk; website: www.worldfriendship.merseyside.org)

CC number: 513643

Eligibility

International students studying at universities in the Diocese of Liverpool. Preference is given to people in the final year of their course and individuals from Anglican dioceses and Christian communities overseas. Applicants must intend to return to their home country.

Types of grants

One-off grants of about £500 towards relieving unexpected hardships which have arisen since the beginning of the course and which would prevent individuals from completing their studies.

Annual grant total

In 2014 the charity had an income of £14,500 and an expenditure of £12,000. We estimate that the amount of grants given to individuals totalled around £11,500.

Exclusions

Grants are not given to those whose place of study is outside the Diocese of Liverpool. Students from an EU country, those who are intending to stay in the UK at the end of their course, or applicants from overseas who are not yet studying in Liverpool are not usually supported.

Applications

Application forms should be sought from student support offices at relevant institutions or can be requested from the correspondent. For details of the relevant contact see the charity's website.

Personal development and extra-curricular activities

The Arrol Trust

£13,000

Correspondent: Callum Kennedy, Trust Administrator, Lindsays, Caledonian Exchange, 19A Canning Street, Edinburgh EH3 8HE (0131 229 1212)

OSCR number: SC020983

Eligibility

Young people between the ages of 16 and 25 who are disadvantaged because of their social/economic circumstances or physical/mental disabilities.

Types of grants

Grants are given for activities which will 'broaden individuals' horizons'. Support can be given towards travel in the UK and overseas, educational trips and gap year or volunteering opportunities.

Annual grant total

In 2014/15 the trust had an income of £13,500 and an expenditure of £16,000. We estimate the annual total amount of grants awarded to individuals to be around £13,000.

Exclusions

Grants are not made for direct educational expenses, such as course fees.

Applications

Application forms can be requested from the correspondent and must be supported by a reference from the applicant's teacher or employer. Potential candidates may be invited for an interview with the trustees and asked to report back on the completion of their activity.

Jim Bishop Memorial Fund

£2,000

Correspondent: Roger Miller, Trustee, c/o Young Explorers Trust, 6 Manor Road, Burnham on Sea, Somerset TA8 2AS (01278 784658; email: ted@theyet.org.uk; website: www.theyet.org)

Eligibility

People under 19 who wish to participate in any adventure activity.

Types of grants

Grants of between £50 and £150. Recent grants have been given to enable participation in expeditions abroad, at sea and in the UK.

Annual grant total

Grants from the Jim Bishop Memorial Fund generally total around £2,000 and are awarded to individuals for educational purposes.

Exclusions

University expeditions will not be supported.

Applications

Application forms are available from the correspondent or to download from the Young Explorers' Trust website. Applications should include an sae and be submitted by the end of March.

Other information

Jim Bishop was an outstanding young engineer, scientist and explorer who was tragically killed whilst on an international expedition to the Karakorum. He was originally inspired by mountains and adventure as a teenager and he always regarded this initial experience as an important factor in his subsequent life. He always endeavoured to encourage this taste for adventure in the young and the Jim Bishop Awards were established by his family and friends to help further these ideals.

The fund is administered by the Young Explorers' Trust.

The Alec Dickson Trust

£1,000

Correspondent: Emily Evans, Trustee, 18–24 Lower Clapton Road, Hackney, London E5 0PD (02076431360; email: alecdickson@gmail.com; website: www.alecdicksontrust.org.uk)

CC number: 1076900

Eligibility

Young people under 30 years of age who are involved in volunteering or community service in the UK.

Types of grants

The trust's mission is to support young people who are able to demonstrate that through volunteering or community service they can enhance the lives of others, particularly those marginalised by society. The trust particularly welcomes applications from innovative projects in the spirit of Alec Dickson. Grants of up to £500 are available.

Annual grant total

In 2013/14 the trust had no income and an expenditure of £1,500. We estimate that grants totalled around £1,000.

Applications to the trust are managed and administered by Volunteering Matters.

Exclusions

No grants are given for gap years, projects based outside the UK, equipment, uniforms, expenditure for a fundraising event or for personal benefit (e.g. university course fees or a laptop for personal use).

Applications

Application forms are available from the correspondent or to download on the website. Applications can be submitted at any time.

Other information

In the spirit of the trust, all the trustees are aged under 30 and have a connection to voluntary or community service.

The Duveen Trust

£7,000

Correspondent: Alan Kaye, Trustee, 1 Beauchamp Court, Victors Way, Barnet, Hertfordshire EN5 5TZ (020 8216 2520; email: administrator@ theduveentrust.org.uk; website: www. theduveentrust.org.uk)

CC number: 326823

Eligibility

Individuals aged up to 25 who wish to get involved with projects which require initiative and which give something back to the community, and who are in need of financial support. Educational assistance to enable individuals to work in a community project specialising in the social education of young people.

Types of grants

One-off grants of £100 to £500.

Annual grant total

In 2013/14 the trust had an income of £17,000 and a total expenditure of £7,500 we estimate that grants totalled around £7,000. The website states that the trust has a grant potential of up to £15,000 per annum.

Exclusions

Grants are unlikely to be made to support formal education, except for courses leading to qualifications in youth and community work.

Applications

Application forms and guidelines are available from the correspondent or from the website and should be accompanied by a report from the organising agency, and a copy of the programme of the scheme that the applicant wishes to participate in.

The Pain Trust (The Pain Adventure Trust)

£26,500

Correspondent: The Secretary, 15 Rolle Street, Exmouth, Devon EX8 1HA (01395 275443; email: admin@pain-trust. org.uk; website: www.pain-trust.org.uk)

CC number: 276670

Eligibility

Boys and young men aged between 11 and 21 (on the day of the expedition or activity, not on the date of application) who live in the East Devon area or within eight miles of Exmouth Town Hall, excluding the area to the west of the estuary of the river Exe. In considering awards the trust takes into account whether the applicants: are away from home for the first time; are having their first trip abroad; show self-sufficiency and integration within a group; are pursuing a new activity never attempted before. Preference may be given to activities undertaken as a part of the group rather than individually.

Types of grants

One-off grants towards travel and adventure to further physical development, character building, leadership training or fostering a team spirit. Examples of projects include bungee jumping in New Zealand, skiing in Europe and the USA, train rides to China via Russia, camping on Dartmoor, canoeing in Norway, surfing in Australia, assisting charity projects in Brazil, community work in Zambia and so on.

Annual grant total

In 2013/14 the trust had assets of £72,000 and an income of £52,000. A total of £26,500 was awarded in grants to 18 individuals and 11 groups.

Exclusions

The following are not supported:
- Competitive sport or the pursuit of excellence in sport
- Purchase of equipment
- Activities considered to be within the responsibilities of the government/ local authorities
- Activities which could be considered to be a part of the national curriculum
- Retrospective applications
- Activities during term time for those in full-time education

Applications

Application forms are available on the trust's website. The trust invites potential applicants to contact the correspondent to discuss their application or for further guidance. Applications must be submitted at least 16 days before a meeting, the dates of

which can be found on the website. Last year there were eight meetings held. Applications must be accompanied by a detailed itinerary with costs and demonstrate adequate evidence of background research into the proposed expedition. Repeat applications can be considered as long as they fulfil the objectives for funding.

The Bassil Shippam and Alsford Trust
See entry on page 279

The Torch Trophy Trust
See entry on page 87

Religion

Charities of Susanna Cole and Others

£1,600

Correspondent: Tony Pegler, Trustee, Central England Quakers Office, Friends Meeting House, 40 Bull Street, Birmingham B4 6AF (0121 682 7575)

CC number: 204531

Eligibility

Quakers in need, with preference to those who live within the 1910 Worcestershire boundaries or belong to Central England Area Quaker Meeting. Some favour is also given to younger children (for education).

Types of grants

One-off and recurrent grants for education or retraining, also starting work or a business.

Annual grant total

In 2014 the charity had an income of £12,300 and a total expenditure of £4,600. We estimate grants to individuals for educational purposes to be around £1,600.

Applications

It has previously been noted in the charity's annual report: 'For a new application the trustees require a letter or email from the applicant's overseer outlining the situation. To make this easier the trustees have a named trustee for each local meeting who can be consulted about the matter.'

Our research suggests that requests should be received by early March and October for consideration later in the same months.

Other information

Grants are made for both welfare and educational purposes.

The charity also administers the income from the Bursary Fund belonging to Central England Area Quaker Meeting, which is kept in a separate and restricted fund and is used solely to help with care home fees for elderly members or attenders of Central England Area Quaker Meeting.

Christianity

Catenian Association Bursary Fund Ltd

£110,000 (944 grants)

Correspondent: Mark Allanson, Company Secretary, 2nd Floor, 1 Copthall House, Station Square, Coventry CV1 2FY (024 7622 4533; email: bursary@thecatenians.com; website: www.thecatenians.com/pages/bursary_fund/bursary_fund1/default.aspx)

CC number: 1081143

Eligibility

Young Catholics (between the ages of 16 and 25) who want to work on projects around the world to assist local communities. Grants are also made to young people working as helpers on diocesan and HCPT pilgrimages.

Types of grants

Bursaries to help with the expenses related to undertaking overseas projects which 'have a clear benefit for others as well as widening the individual's life experience'. Awards may cover travel costs, medical expenses, essential clothing, personal subsistence and other needs. Any activity must have clear Christian ethos.

Most recently funding for any diocesan or ordinary workers on pilgrimages to Lourdes were worth £45 and for HCPT workers – £75.

Annual grant total

In 2013/14 the fund had assets of £408,500 and an income of £121,000. Grants were made totalling £110,000 to 944 individuals.

Exclusions

The guidance notes state:

> Awards are not made for medical electives, projects that are part of an educational course or for gap years. However an award may be made for a specific project undertaken during the year between School and University, or during the time between University and employment.

Funding is not given retrospectively.

Applications

Application forms for both overseas projects and pilgrimages, as well as guidance notes, are available online on the association's website. Two references are required. Application should be submitted to the correspondent via email (do **not** send the form as a PDF file) at least three weeks before the trustees' meeting – for the dates of upcoming meetings see the application form – and no less than two months before the project\expedition is due to start. All receipts are acknowledged by email.

Note: Individuals applying as young workers who are joining official pilgrimages to Lourdes are not required to submit the form online as signatures are required from their parish priest/chaplain and group leader/Diocesan Pilgrimage Director.

Other information

The fund's objectives note:

> The projects will involve the implementation of Christian, particularly Catholic, principles and may be undertaken solely or jointly with other people or under the aegis of organisations operating under the same principles. Grants are awarded according to the merits of each individual application.

There is also Catenian Association Benevolent and Children's Fund (Charity Commission no. 214244) which supports members of the association and their dependants who are in need.

The fund's website notes:

> The Catenian Association is an international body of proudly Catholic laymen who meet at least once a month in local units called Circles, to enjoy each other's company and thereby strengthen their family life and faith through friendship. It is open to practising Catholic laymen from the age of 18 years.

Daily Prayer Union Charitable Trust Ltd

£31,000

Correspondent: Mrs C. Palmer, Administrator, 12 Weymouth Street, London W1W 5BY (email: dputrust@hotmail.co.uk)

CC number: 284857

Eligibility

Christians undertaking religious training or education.

Types of grants

Grants to support Christian training and education.

Annual grant total

In 2013/14 the trust had assets of £35,000 and an income of £46,000. Charitable expenditure totalled £39,000 and grants to individuals totalled £31,000.

Applications

Apply in writing to the correspondent.

The Duchess of Leeds Foundation for Boys and Girls

£44,000 (25 grants)

Correspondent: John Sinfield, Clerk to the Trustees, 19 Kenton Road, Harrow, Middlesex HA1 2BW (020 8422 1950)

CC number: 313103

Eligibility

Roman Catholic children attending Catholic schools who are resident in England, Wales or the Channel Islands and who are either orphaned/fatherless or whose fathers do not support them sufficiently. Our research suggests that help is concentrated on secondary education and children in primary school are helped only in exceptional circumstances.

Types of grants

One-off awards and recurrent grants in the range of around £300–£400 per term. According to our research, support is normally given towards the cost of school fees. Grants may continue until the end of an A-level course.

Annual grant total

In 2014 the foundation had an income of £45,000 and an expenditure of £48,500. Grants totalled 44,000 which supported 25 individuals.

Applications

Apply in writing to the correspondent. Applications can be submitted directly by the individual or their parents/guardians. The deadline for applications is normally by the end of January.

Milton Mount Foundation

£101,500 (12 grants)

Correspondent: Revd Erna Stevenson, Secretary, 11 Copse Close, Slough, Berkshire SL1 5DT (01753 748713; email: erna.stevenson@blueyonder.co.uk)

CC number: 306981

Eligibility

The children of ministers of the United Reformed Church, the Congregational Federation, the Evangelical Fellowship of Congregational Churches and the Unaffiliated Congregational Churches. The children of members of these churches can also be supported.

Types of grants

Bursaries and grants are available to children aged 11–18 towards school fees and other educational needs, including school uniforms and necessities.

The following is stated in the latest annual report:

> The Governors give educational grants to children of ministers and members of The United Reformed Church and Congregational Churches. Priority is given to the children of ministers in respect of school fees. Grants are targeted to those with limited means and are subject to a graded means test in relation to income of the parents of the children being assisted.

Annual grant total

In 2013/14 the foundation had assets of £3.2 million and an income of £128,000. Annual bursaries to individuals totalled £101,500 and can be broken down as follows:

Bursaries in other schools (girls)	£56,000
Bursaries to Bournemouth Collegiate School (girls)	£34,000
Bursaries in other schools (boys)	£7,500
Outfitting and other allowances	£4,000

Applications

Apply in writing to the correspondent providing information about the family income. Applications are normally considered in May and June.

The Mylne Trust

£24,000

Correspondent: Robin Twining, Secretary, PO Box 530, Farnham GU9 1BP (email: admin@mylnetrust.org. uk; website: www.mylnetrust.org.uk)

CC number: 208074

Eligibility

Members of the Protestant faith who have been engaged in evangelistic work, including missionaries and retired missionaries, and Christian workers whose finances are inadequate. Married ordinands with children are also supported when all other sources of funding have failed to cover their needs.

Types of grants

Grants are given towards educational training at theological colleges, for the cost of books and living expenses to undergraduates and overseas students.

Annual grant total

In 2014/15 the trust had assets of £2.1 million and an income of £59,500. Grants totalled £48,500. We estimate that grants for educational purposes amounted to £24,000

Exclusions

The trust cannot support individuals who are not of a Protestant denomination.

Applications

The trust notes the following helpful information on its website:

The trust has reviewed and, in 2013, changed its policy and procedure for making grants. Most grants are now being handled with partners already in Christian mission work. (Applications based on earlier procedures, using the old application forms, will no longer be considered by the trust.)

Worldwide except Africa
In principle, the only grant applications that will be considered by direct application to the trust are those from candidates for mission work who are studying or planning to study within the UK. Such applicants are invited to contact the Clerk to the Mylne Trust at admin@mylnetrust.org.uk requesting a current application form.

Africa
There are special arrangements for applicants who are based in Africa.

We would advise potential applicants to visit the website for more information before applying.

North of Scotland Quaker Trust

£5,000

Correspondent: The Trustees, Quaker Meeting House, 98 Crown Street, Aberdeen AB11 6HJ

OSCR number: SC000784

Eligibility

People who are associated with the Religious Society of Friends in the North of Scotland Monthly Meeting area and their dependants.

Types of grants

Grants are given to schoolchildren and to people studying in further or higher education for books, equipment, instruments and educational outings. Grants for travel and conferences are also available.

Annual grant total

In 2014 the trust had an income of £14,700 and a total expenditure of £30,000. Grants are made to individuals and organisations. We estimate that the amount of grants given to individuals for educational purposes totalled around £5,000.

Exclusions

No grants are given to people studying above first degree level.

Applications

Apply in writing to the correspondent.

Other information

Grants are also given for welfare purposes.

The Norwich French Church Charity

£8,000

Correspondent: Samantha Loombe, Correspondent, Hansells Solicitors, 13–14 The Close, Norwich NR1 4DS (01603 275814; email: samantha.loombe@ hansells.co.uk)

CC number: 212897

Eligibility

Children and young people, primarily of French Protestant descent, who are under the age of 25 and live in Norwich. Applicants from Norfolk can also be considered.

Types of grants

Grants, ranging from £250 to £500, for schoolchildren and college students for uniforms/other school clothing, books, equipment/instruments, maintenance/living expenses, childcare, educational outings in the UK, study or travel abroad, etc. A preference is given to applicants of Huguenot descent.

Annual grant total

In 2013 the charity had an income of £13,000 and an expenditure of £9,000. We estimate that around £8,000 was distributed in grants to individuals for education.

The 2013 accounts were the latest available at the time of writing (October 2015).

Applications

Application forms are available from the correspondent which can be submitted directly by the individual or through the individual's college or educational welfare agency, or another third party, at any time.

The Podde Trust

£4,000

Correspondent: Peter Godfrey, Trustee, 68 Green Lane, Hucclecote, Gloucester GL3 3QX (01452 613563; email: thepodde@gmail.com)

CC number: 1016322

Eligibility

Individuals involved in Christian work in the UK and overseas.

Types of grants

One-off and recurrent grants.

Annual grant total

In 2013/14 the trust had assets of £3,000 and an income of £46,000. There were 33 grants to individuals totalling £8,500. The purposes for which awards were given were not specified. We estimate grants for educational purposes to have totalled around £4,000.

Applications

Applications may be made in writing to the correspondent. Note, the trust has previously stated that it has very limited resources, and those it does have are mostly already committed. Requests from new applicants, therefore, have very little chance of success.

Other information

Organisations involved in Christian work in the UK and abroad are also supported (£36,000 was given to 40 organisations in 2013/14). The trust awards grants for charitable purposes, including the advancement of religion, of education and the relief of poverty.

The annual report and accounts for 2013/14 note the following: 'Contributions made in the past financial year include Pacific Partnership Trust working with students in New Zealand, Operation Mobilisation and TEAR Fund to name but a few.'

Saint George's Trust (FSJ (UK) TA SSJE)

£14,500

Correspondent: Linden Sheffield, Administration Officer, 11 Mayhew Crescent, High Wycombe HP13 6BX (01494 446636; email: lindensheffield@ fsje.org.uk; website: www.fsje.org.uk/ sgeorges.php)

CC number: 253524

Eligibility

Members of the Church of England – Anglican clergy, seminarians and students.

Types of grants

Small, one-off grants of up to £350 are made towards specific projects in the UK or abroad. Support can be given to:
- Clergy undertaking a recognised study during their sabbaticals towards travel and accommodation costs
- Seminarians in Anglican theological colleges or on ministerial courses for the costs of pastoral placements that are part of the formation (three members of a college/course may apply each year)
- Students between the ages 18 and 25 towards the work on a Christian mission and service (usually as a gap year activity)

Annual grant total

In 2014 the trust had an income of £13,000 and an expenditure of £15,000. We estimate the annual total amount of grants awarded to be around £14,500.

Exclusions

The trust will not provide any long-term financial support and cannot contribute towards restoration projects or education fees.

Applications

Apply in writing to the correspondent. Applicants should give full details of the project, include estimated costs, note any other funds available and provide a brief letter of reference (from an educational or clerical authority). An sae needs to be provided for a reply from the trust. The trustees encourage applications early in the year.

Other information

In 2006 the administration of the trust was transferred to The Fellowship of Saint John (UK) Trust Association.

The Stewardship Trust Ripon

£8,500

Correspondent: Anne Metcalfe, Trustee, Hutton Hill, Hutton Bank, Ripon HG4 5DT (01765602887; email: stewardship.ripon@gmail.com)

CC number: 224447

Eligibility

People connected with Christian causes and studies.

Types of grants

One-off and recurrent grants for people training in Christian ministry, engaged in studies of Christianity or working for Christian causes.

Annual grant total

In 2013/14 the trust had an income of £3,700 and a total expenditure of £47,000. Most of the trust's support goes to organisations. In previous years the total amount of grants awarded to individuals has reached up to £8,000–£9,000.

Applications

Apply in writing to the correspondent. Our research suggests that the trust's funds are usually fully committed and new applications are only considered if there is extreme need.

Other information

The trust also supports various churches, societies and the Christian Institute.

The Stokes Croft Educational Foundation

£18,000

Correspondent: Frances Webster, Trustee, 7 Remenham Park, Bristol BS9 4HE

CC number: 311672

Eligibility

People aged 11 to 50 with family connections with the Unitarian Church in Bristol, the Stokes Croft (Endowed) School or the Western Union of Unitarian and Free Christian Churches.

Types of grants

Grants are given for maintenance allowances, overseas travel, books, clothing and equipment/instruments for beneficiaries looking to enter a particular profession, trade or calling. Grants range from £50 to £500.

Annual grant total

In 2014 the foundation had an income of £20,500 and an expenditure of almost £19,000. We estimate that educational grants totalled £18,000.

Applications

Apply in writing to the correspondent.

Judaism

The Anglo Jewish Association

£142,000 (103 grants)

Correspondent: Jonathan Walker, Trustee, 75 Maygrove Road, West Hampstead, London NW6 2EG (email: info@anglojewish.org.uk; website: www.anglojewish.org.uk)

CC number: 256946

Eligibility

Undergraduate and postgraduate Jewish students in need who are studying a full-time course at a UK university or further education college, regardless of their nation of origin. Preference is given to courses on high-rated institutions.

Types of grants

Scholarships range between £500 and £3,000 a year.

Annual grant total

In 2013 the association had assets of £1.9 million and an income of £98,500. The amount of grants given to individuals totalled £142,000 and was awarded to 103 students.

At the time of writing (November 2015), these were the most recent accounts available for the charity.

Applications

Application forms are available from the association's website or can be requested from the correspondent. Applications should be submitted by 30 April. They must also include two academic references, a CV, a covering letter, a copy of a letter of acceptance from the educational institution and details of the applicant's personal history.

Scholarships are for one academic year and individuals may apply for the part or the whole of an additional academic year by submitting another complete application, prior to the closing date for the relevant year. The award of a second, third or fourth scholarship is not automatic.

Application forms for the Finnart House School Trust and the Stuart Young Foundation are also available from the website.

The trust welcomes applicants to contact them via email to discuss an application.

Other information

The association also administers a number of other funds offering help to students studying in the fields of medicine, science or more general areas of study. It has historical links with a number of humanitarian and grant-making organisations, which it may also support.

Applicants can be given direct financial support, general advice and guidance on education in the UK or be signposted to other bodies that may help.

Finnart House School Trust

£167,000

Correspondent: Sophie Reindorp, Correspondent, The Charities Advisory, Radius Works, Back Lane, London NW3 1HL (07804 854905; email: info@finnart.org; website: www.finnart.org)

CC number: 220917

Eligibility

Finnart Scholarships applicants must be:
- Jewish and able to provide proof of this (applicants must have Jewish parents, a Jewish mother or evidence of conversion by a Rabbinic authority)
- Attending a college/university course at a recognised UK institution which ends in a recognised qualification (a degree or diploma)
- Under the age of 21 at the time of starting the course
- Going directly from 6th Form to university without taking a gap year
- Eligible for UK home fees
- In financial need (scholarships are means-tested – an applicant's family income will usually be below the national average and there may be several dependants). Applicants are required to provide information on their family's income and savings

Types of grants

Finnart Scholarships range between £1,000 and £3,000 per year for courses between three and seven years in length.

Bursaries are distributed through a number of secondary schools.

Annual grant total

In 2013/14 the trust had assets of £5.1 million and an income of £178,000. From 31 applications, 30 Finnart Scholarships were awarded during the year, amounting to £160,000. Two grants, which, we believe, were redistributed as bursaries, were given to schools, totalling £7,000.

Exclusions

Only members of the Jewish faith can be supported. Funding is not given for study abroad or to international students.

Applications

Bursaries are awarded via schools. Scholarship applications are made by the individual using an application pack, which is available to download from the website. Applications should usually be completed and returned to the trust by the end of April.

Gur Trust

£18,500

Correspondent: Trust Administrator, 1st Floor Offices, 1 Bridge Lane, London NW11 0EA (020 8801 6038)

CC number: 283423

Eligibility

People connected to the Jewish Orthodox faith in the UK.

Types of grants

One-off and recurrent grants for education and personal development. The trust aims to support education in and the religion of Orthodox Jewish faith.

Annual grant total

In 2013/14 the trust had assets of over £1.3 million and an income of £43,000. Charitable activities totalled about £53,500; however, further breakdown was not given. It would appear that support is mainly given for educational needs, even though the information on the trust on the Charity Commission's records notes that welfare needs are also supported. We estimate that educational grants to individuals totalled around £18,500.

Applications

Applications may be made in writing to the correspondent. Our research notes that the trust has previously stated that 'all calls for help are carefully considered and help is given according to circumstances and funds then available'.

Other information

The trust also makes grants to organisations, Talmudical colleges and

may provide some relief in need for individuals.

The Jewish Widows and Students Aid Trust

£56,000 (27 grants)

Correspondent: Alan Philipp, Trustee, 5 Raeburn Close, London NW11 6UG (email: alan@gapbooks.com)

CC number: 210022

Eligibility

Jewish students from the UK, Ireland, Israel, France and the British Commonwealth who are aged 16 to 30 years old.

Types of grants

The trust also offers interest-free loans ranging from £1,000 to £1,500 mainly for course fees, although living expenses, books, travel or similar necessities can also be supported. Awards are made on the basis of academic excellence and need. On occasions grants can also be given to schoolchildren over the age of 10.

Annual grant total

In 2013/14 the trust had assets of £769,000 and an income of £64,000. Charitable expenditure totalled £60,000 and 27 individual grants were awarded totalling £56,000.

Applications

Apply in writing to the correspondent including a CV and confirmation of acceptance at an educational establishment.

Other information

Grants are also given to widows with young children.

Allan and Gerta Rank Educational Trust Fund

£3,000

Correspondent: Nikki Spencer, Trustee, 16 Eyre's Gardens, Ilkeston DE7 8JE (0115 849 9216; email: nikki.spencer@geldards.com)

CC number: 1091456

Eligibility

Students who are of the Jewish faith and are either living or studying within a 50-mile radius of Nottingham city centre.

Types of grants

One-off and recurrent grants to students in college or university.

Annual grant total

In 2014/15 the charity had no income and a total expenditure of £3,200. We estimate that educational grants to individuals totalled around £3,000.

Applications

Applications may be made in writing to the correspondent.

Specific circum- stances

Prisoners of Conscience Appeal Fund

£38,000

Correspondent: Kirsty Bennett, Grants Officer, PO Box 61044, London SE1 1UP (020 7407 6644; fax: 020 7407 6655; email: grantsofficer@ prisonersofconscience.org; website: www. prisonersofconscience.org)

CC number: 213766

Eligibility

Prisoners of conscience and/or their families, who have suffered persecution for their conscientiously-held beliefs. The fact that the person is seeking asylum or has been a victim of civil war is not sufficient grounds in itself. The fund's website states: 'A degree of personal persecution has to be established.'

Applicants for bursaries must also have previously completed an undergraduate degree (not necessarily in the UK) and must be able to provide evidence of the postgraduate or conversion course at the time of application.

Types of grants

Mainly one-off grants of about £350 each for travel, resources, equipment, some vocational conversion courses (such as PLAB and IELTS) and re- qualification costs.

Bursary grants are also made for tuition fees for postgraduate study and professional conversion courses. The website states: 'funding will be provided towards tuition fees for one academic year. A commitment for funding subsequent years cannot be given but applicants can re-apply to be considered again the following year.'

Annual grant total

In 2014 the fund had assets of £157,000 and an income of £270,000. The fund's annual report for 2014 states that 104 grants were made to individuals and families during the year, totalling £105,500. During the year, 11 new bursaries totalled £38,000. We were unable to determine the amount given in one-off grants for educational purposes.

Exclusions

No support is given to people who have used or advocated violence or supported a violent organisation. Funding cannot be given retrospectively.

Applications

Applications are not considered directly from individuals but rather from approved referral organisations that apply on behalf of individuals. The fund advises the following on its website:

> You can ask your solicitor to make an application or you can contact the many local Citizens Advice Bureaux who may apply to us on your behalf. If you are in touch with any other refugee organisations or official bodies, you could also ask them to make an application. If you do not know of any organisation who might be able to assist you, please contact us grantsofficer@prisonersof conscience.org and we will try to help.

Referral agencies must register with the fund's online system in order to apply for a grant. See the website or contact the correspondent for more information.

Other information

The fund was initially established in 1962 as the relief arm of Amnesty International, but is now a charity in its own right. It is the only agency in the UK making grants specifically to prisoners of conscience – individuals who have been persecuted for their conscientiously-held beliefs, provided that they have not used or advocated violence. Grant recipients include political prisoners, human rights defenders, lawyers, environmental activists, teachers and academics who come from many different countries such as Burma, Zimbabwe, Sri Lanka, Tibet, Iran, Cameroon and Eritrea.

The charity's aim is to raise and distribute money to help them and/or their families rehabilitate themselves during and after their ordeal. Financial grants cover general hardship relief, furniture, medicines, travel costs, family reunion costs, education, requalification and resettlement costs and medical treatment and counselling after torture.

People who have offended

The Frank Longford Charitable Trust (Longford Trust)

£32,000

Correspondent: Peter Stanford, Director, Frank Longford charitable Trust, 42 Callcott Road, London NW6 7EA (020 7625 1097; email: info@ longfordtrust.org; website: www. longfordtrust.org)

CC number: 1092825

Eligibility

Ex-offenders or those awaiting release in the near future whose sentence was or is still being served in a UK prison and who cannot afford education. Applicants must have identified a specific course they want to study at degree level offered by an institute of higher education (including Open University) and have obtained a provisional offer of a place (eligibility remains open for up to five years after release). The chosen course should improve the applicant's career chances and advance the rehabilitation process.

Types of grants

Scholarships are given to enable individuals to continue their rehabilitation through education at a UK university or equivalent institute.

A small number of awards are made under the Patrick Pakenham Awards' Scheme to those who want to study law or criminology.

Both awards are worth up to £5,000 per annum. The Longford Scholarship is extendable for up to three years on receipt of suitable reports of academic progress. Grants are intended to cover both the cost of tuition fees on higher education courses and offer a contribution to living expenses, books, other course material and basic sustenance.

Annual grant total

In 2013/14 the trust had an income of £210,500 and total charitable expenditure of £152,500. Grants made directly to individuals totalled £32,000.

Exclusions

Grants are not made for postgraduate study. Applicants should be ineligible for student loans or other financial support.

Applications

Application forms can be made online on the trust's website or can be downloaded, printed off and posted to the correspondent. Applications for courses beginning in September must be made by 1 June in that year.

Other information

The Longford Trust was established in 2002 by friends, family and admirers of Lord Longford (1905–2001) to celebrate his achievements and to further the goals he pursued in the fields of social and prison reform.

The following is taken from the 2013/14 annual report:

The trust has three programmes of work: its annual Longford Lecture on a subject of social or penal reform; its annual Longford Prize, given to an individual or organisation doing exceptional work in the field of prison reform; and the Longford scholarship programme, which gives financial and mentoring support to young serving- and ex-prisoners who wish to continue their rehabilitation by studying for degrees at UK higher education institutions.

NIACRO

Correspondent: Gareth Eannetta, Service Manager, Amelia House, 4 Amelia Street, Belfast BT2 7GS (028 9032 0157; email: gareth@niacro.co.uk; website: www.niacro.co.uk)

CC number: NIC101599

Eligibility

Prisoners, people who have offended and their immediate relatives in Northern Ireland in need of support. People in detention seeking access to education, training and/or employment who cannot obtain help from other sources may be supported financially.

A number of projects are available to children and young people at risk of (re)offending.

Types of grants

Support is given to help individuals access academic qualifications and vocational training which will advance their integration back into society and the job market. One-off and recurrent grants are given according to need can be given towards degrees, vocational qualifications, NVQs, HGV driving licenses or other training and associated needs.

Annual grant total

In 2014/15 the charity had assets of £1.7 million, an income of £4.3 million and a total programme expenditure of £4.1 million (on 'Children and Young People', 'Adults in the Community' and 'People in Prison and their Families'). The vast majority of support is available through specific advice services, although some grants can be provided to individuals referred to the organisation. We have been unable to determine the amount given in grants to individuals for educational purposes for this financial year. Note that the overall expenditure is not representative of the charity's grant-giving.

Exclusions

Grants are not normally given for computer hardware, capital equipment or set-up costs of small business initiatives.

Applications

Individuals in need of support should contact the correspondent to find out more about the support available and the application procedure.

Other information

The organisation's main activities are providing support, advice and guidance to prisoners, people who have offended and their relatives. A number of projects are undertaken in partnership with other bodies.

There are also regional offices.

Prisoners' Education Trust

£453,500

Correspondent: Rod Clark, Company Secretary, Prisoners' Education Trust, The Foundry, 17 Oval Way, London SE11 5RR (020 3752 5680; fax: 020 8648 7762; email: info@prisonerseducation.org.uk; website: www.prisonerseducation.org.uk)

CC number: 1084718

Eligibility

Individuals over the age of 18 who are serving a custodial sentence in the UK and still have at least six months of their sentence to serve. People leaving prison may also be eligible for resettlement support up to six months after their release.

Types of grants

Grants from the Access to Learning programme to pay fees for distance learning and resettlement courses, including Open University courses (funded by a contract from The Department for Business, Innovation and Skills), A-levels, GCSE and vocational qualifications, including both accredited and non-accredited courses. Grants are also available for arts and crafts, hobby materials, course-related necessities.

Annual grant total

In 2014 the trust had assets of £764,000 and an income of £1.4 million. A grant total of £453,500 was awarded in grants in the following categories:

General education courses and arts/ hobby material	£359,000
Open University courses	£95,000

Applications

Apply in writing to the correspondent by sending a completed application form (which can be downloaded from the trust's website) and a letter stating what kind of support is needed and why it would be useful. An endorsement by a prison education manager is essential. Applications are considered every month and the outcome is communicated to all applicants.

Other information

The organisation also provides advice about distance learning courses and how they relate to employment paths and possibilities. It supports learners in prisons, trains people to act as peer learning mentors and commissions research, projects, reports and conferences to help in evaluating and advancing prison education.

Note that applications are welcomed from any prison in the UK (including HMP La Moye, in Jersey).

The Royal London Society

£60,000 (313 grants)

Correspondent: Peter Cox, Grant Administrator, Royal London Society, Commercial House, High Street, Hadlow, Kent TN11 0EE (01622 230737; email: office@royallondonsociety.org.uk; website: www.royallondonsociety.org.uk)

CC number: 214695

Eligibility

People who are serving a prison sentence or ex-offenders recently released from prison who are resident in South East or Greater London. Candidates who demonstrate efforts to obtain funds elsewhere and make a personal contribution (if possible) are favoured.

Types of grants

One-off grants, generally around £300. Support is given towards equipment, tools and work clothing, resettlement education, vocational training and associated needs that will lead to employment, generally in the immediate future or within the next six months.

Annual grant total

In 2014 the society had assets of £937,000 and an income of £338,500. Grants to 313 individuals totalled £60,000.

Exclusions

Grants are not given for:
- Accommodation costs, rent, leases, licences or deposits
- Household items, furniture or appliances
- Debts or loans
- Driving lessons for domestic purposes
- Computer and associated equipment not related to employment
- Open University or distance learning courses not related to employment
- Personal clothing not related to employment

The charity does not normally consider grants for hobbies and recreation, unless the applicant still has at least 12 months to serve.

Applications

Application forms are available from the society's website. They should be posted to the correspondent together with all the supporting documentation – written references from a prison officer, probation officer, trade instructor, education department or other agency, such as social services or a housing association. Applications are considered at quarterly meetings but urgent applications may be dealt with more quickly.

Other information

Grants are also made to organisations (£2,000 in 2014).

Sacro Trust

£2,400

Correspondent: The Trust Fund Administrator, 29 Albany Street, Edinburgh EH1 3QN (0131 624 7270; fax: 0131 624 7269; email: info@national. sacro.org.uk; website: www.sacro.org.uk)

OSCR number: SC023031

Eligibility

People living in Scotland who are subject to a license/court order or who have been released from prison in the last two years, and their families.

Types of grants

Grants are usually to a maximum of £300, including those for fees, driving lessons, books and equipment, or other needs assisting the individual in the process of rehabilitation.

Annual grant total

In 2013/14 the trust had an income of £83,500 and a total expenditure of £44,500. It 'awarded 41 grants totalling £4,900 to help individuals in Scotland with the process of rehabilitation'. We estimate that about £2,400 was given for educational needs.

Exclusions

Grants are not made where financial help from other sources is available.

Applications

Applications can only be accepted if they are made through a local authority, voluntary sector worker, health visitor or so on. The forms may be obtained from the correspondent and are considered every two months. Payments are made to the organisation making the application rather than directly to the individual. Other sources of funding should be sought before applying to the trust.

Other information

The trust also gives grants for social welfare purposes. The Sacro Annual

Review for 2013/14 states: 'The Sacro Trust is constitutionally separate and aims to provide small grants to individuals in the process of rehabilitation.'

Sacro (OSCR no. SC016293) provides advice and information, mediation services, criminal and youth justice services, and also conducts research and policy work. Full details of service provision are given on the website. In 2013/14 it spent over £7 million in the areas of criminal justice, youth justice and community mediation. The trust's website notes: 'Founded over 40 years ago, Sacro works independently and collaboratively within Scotland's communities to provide support, prevent conflict and challenge offending behaviour wherever the need arises.'

The Sheriffs' and Recorders' Fund

£42,000 (85+ grants)

Correspondent: The Secretary, c/o Central Criminal Court, Old Bailey, Warwick Square, London EC4M 7BS (020 7248 3277 (Tue and Wed 11am – 4.45pm); email: secretary@srfund.net; website: www.srfund.org.uk)

CC number: 221927

Eligibility

People on probation and families of serving prisoners in the Greater Metropolitan Area of London. The charity is also concerned with the rehabilitation of drug and alcohol abusers.

Types of grants

One-off grants for education and training at any level following release. Support may be given for training, including vocational courses, tools and equipment, clothing and household items, such as white goods and furniture. Grants to families primarily seek to enable children to enjoy holidays and other recreational activities. Awards are made according to need and have ranged from £250 to £10,000.

Annual grant total

In 2013/14 the charity had assets of over £1.3 million and an income of £218,000. Grants were made to 1,284 individuals totalling £164,000. There were 85 grants totalling £16,000 made for education and training purposes and a further £26,000 was awarded in the provision of tools (including donations to the charity Bounce Back).

Applications

Application forms are available from the correspondent and must be submitted through probation officers or social workers. They are considered throughout

the year. The fund's website states: 'The Probation Service and other Social Welfare agencies recommend people for grants, mainly in the first weeks after release when ex-prisoners are at most risk of re-offending.'

Other information

Grants are also made for welfare purposes and to organisations for special projects (three awards totalling £11,000 in 2013/14).

The charity's website has a list of useful organisations where support may also be available.

Refugees and asylum seekers

Ruth Hayman Trust

See entry on page 34

See entry on page 34

Study, work and voluntary work overseas

The Winston Churchill Memorial Trust

£882,000 (137 grants)

Correspondent: Alexandra Sibun, Trust Secretary, 29 Great Smith Street (South Door), London SW1P 3BL (020 7999 1660; fax: 020 7799 1667; email: office@ wcmt.org.uk; website: www.wcmt.org.uk)

CC number: 313952

Eligibility

British citizens resident in the UK who are over 18. Preference is given to individuals who are unlikely to obtain funding from other sources.

Types of grants

Grants are made to people with a specific project which involves travelling overseas (normally for four to eight weeks) in order to bring back knowledge and best practice for the benefit of others in their professions, communities and the UK as a whole. Support can cover return travel, daily living, insurance, travel within the countries being visited and occasionally assistance with home expenses. Categories are drawn from the following fields: crafts and makers; designers; education; the arts and older people; early years prevention and intervention; environment and sustainable living; medicine, health and patient care; prison and penal reform; science technology and innovation; young people; and other worthwhile projects not falling within the above categories.

Annual grant total

In 2013/14 the trust had assets of £35.7 million and an income of £2 million. Grants totalled £882,000 which was awarded in 137 fellowships.

Exclusions

Awards are not made for attendance of courses, academic studies, student grants, gap year projects, electives, degree placements, internships and postgraduate studies (unless real and wider benefits to others in the UK can be clearly demonstrated). Projects involving less than four weeks of travel are not eligible. Existing fellows may not re-apply.

Applications

Applications can be made online on the trust's website. Applications open in May of each year and should be submitted by the end of September. Shortlisted candidates will be asked to attend an interview in January or early February.

Other information

The following is taken from the 2013/14 trustees' annual report:

> The WCMT aims to fulfil its objects by the granting of over 100 Travelling Fellowships a year. It also provides up to ten Bursaries annually to undergraduates at Churchill College, Cambridge and one Archive By-Fellowship each year. Occasionally further grants are awarded to individuals and or organisations for purposes that fit with the WCMT's objects.

The Cross Trust

See entry on page 137

Go Make it Happen: A Project In Memory of Sam Harding

See entry on page 52

Hazel's Footprints Trust

£10,600 (13 grants)

Correspondent: Joan Aiton, Company Secretary, Legerwood, Earlston, Berwickshire TD4 6AS (01896 849677; fax: 01896 849677; email: info@ hazelsfootprints.org; website: www. hazelsfootprints.org)

OSCR number: SC036069

Eligibility

People of any age from the UK and Europe who want to take part in voluntary projects abroad. Proposed projects must be of an educational nature (teaching, community development work and so on) and should last no less than six months (the preferred project duration is one year).

Types of grants

'Footprinter' grants to people who want to take part in voluntary work abroad but are struggling to cover the whole costs themselves.

Annual grant total

In 2013/14 the trust had assets of £608,000 an income of £37,000 and a total expenditure of £101,500. During the year a total of £10,600 was awarded to 13 'footprinters'.

Applications

Application forms can be downloaded from the trust's website. They should be typed and emailed to the correspondent. If you have any photographs of the project or the community that you are applying on behalf of do send them. All applicants are notified of the outcome of their application. Candidates may be invited for an interview.

Other information

A total of £72,500 was awarded to nine overseas educational projects including a final payment of £17,000 to Nubri school in Nepal (2013/14).

The British and Foreign School Society – International Link Scholarship Scheme

Correspondent: Belinda Lawrance, Scheme Administrator, Maybrook House, 97 Godstone Road, Caterham, Surrey CR3 6RE (01883 331177; email: enquiries@bfss.org.uk; website: www. bfss.org.uk)

CC number: 314286

Eligibility

Individuals from the UK who wish to engage in educational activities in developing countries. Awards can also be made to students coming to the UK from developing countries to acquire skills and knowledge which will be useful to their home country. Applicants must be in financial need and be supported by one of the link organisations with which the society works. The society states that 'link organisations have been encouraged to put forward young people from a more diverse social, cultural and

educational background than previously'.

Types of grants

Grants of up to £12,000 depending on the length of the overseas placement. Grants are made to enable volunteers going overseas to teach or undertake other educational activities to support the local community.

Annual grant total

Refer to 'Other information'.

Applications

Applications must be submitted through one of the link organisations with which the society works using the form available on the society's website, where details of application deadlines can also be found.

Other information

The British and Foreign School Society (BFSS) is a grant-giving organisation and offers funding for educational projects in the UK and around the world. The society also offers a small number of grants for organisations and individuals through its subsidiary charities and this award scheme. Eligibility criteria for these subsidiary/linked charities depend on area of residence and/or particular field of educational activity. In March 2014 we were informed by Steven Ross, a trustee of the society, that money was available from these funds.

Note:

The society itself no longer makes grants directly to individuals although it does administer the following linked funds which do:

Alfred Bourne Trust: helps those undertaking education up to the age of 30. The trust generally has an income of about £1,000 per year. Following a review of administrative arrangements, these funds are now distributed by London South Bank University where applications can be made through Student Services.

Berridge Trust: supports the training of teachers of cookery or nutrition. It generally has an income of about £1,000 per year. Use the BFSS application form for individuals.

The BFSS Trust: provides annual grants to the student welfare fund at London South Bank University. Grants are made by the university and students should apply to the university directly.

The British School Charity: provides grants in support of education in the Saffron Walden area for students up to the age of 25. The charity's annual income is around £7,000 and most support goes to schools and educational institutions but some grants are made to individuals living in the area. There is a separate application form for individuals.

Old British School, Bratton: supports the education of people under the age of 25 who are in need of financial assistance and who live within a radius of 20 miles from Bratton, Wiltshire. Grants may be made to individuals or organisations. Note that 'grants are no longer made direct to individuals other than through the Wiltshire Community Fund'.

The Rowlett Educational Foundation: supports training and education of students under 25 in Corby. The foundation generally has an income of around £1,000 per year. Potential applicants should contact Belinda Lawrence by emailing enquiries@bfss.org.uk in the first instance.

South Church Educational Fund: supports educational initiatives in the area of the District of Wear Valley. The fund generally has an income of around £1,000. Grants may be made to individuals or organisations. There is a separate application form for individuals.

Sarah Walker and Spafford Fund: provides an annual grant to Durham University for student travel. Students should apply to the university directly.

Visit the BFSS website for information on the set criteria.

The Sloane Robinson Foundation

See entry on page 36

Study/work

Sir Ernest Cassel Educational Trust (The Cassel Trust)

See entry on page 32

The Worshipful Company of Cutlers General Charitable Fund – Captain F. G. Boot Scholarships

£7,000 (7 grants)

Correspondent: Rupert Meacher, Clerk, The Worshipful Company of Cutlers, Cutlers' Hall, 4 Warwick Lane, London EC4M 7BR (020 7248 1866; fax: 020 7248 8426; email: clerk@cutlerslondon. co.uk; website: www.cutlerslondon.co. uk)

CC number: 283096

Eligibility

Students between the ages of 17 and 25 travelling abroad for at least six months to develop a second language and learn about other cultures. Applicants should either be awaiting entry to further education or be studying abroad as a part of their university degree.

Types of grants

At least five scholarships are awarded each year. Grants can range between £500 and £1,000 depending on the individual's circumstances.

Annual grant total

In 2013/14 the fund had assets of £2.1 million, an income of £188,000 and a total expenditure of £85,500. A total of £7,000 was awarded in seven Captain F.G. Boot Scholarships.

Exclusions

Grants are not available to Project Trust applicants.

Applications

Application forms can be downloaded from the charity's website. Application forms, completed in handwriting, should be accompanied by two references and posted to the fund before 12 June. Shortlisted applicants will be invited for an interview.

Other information

The fund also: provides a number of specific awards to students at nominated universities/schools/colleges; gives recurrent grants to charitable organisations; offers an annual Surgical Prize to scientist developing the design or application of surgical instruments or surgical techniques.

Gilchrist Educational Trust

See entry on page 13

The Peter Kirk Memorial Fund

£18,000 (9 grants)

Correspondent: Kirsten Sampson, Secretary, 1A Meadow Close, Liphook, Hampshire GU30 7BJ (01428727789; email: mail@kirkfund.org.uk; website: www.kirkfund.org.uk)

CC number: 1049139

Eligibility

Citizens of any European country aged between 18 and 26 (under some circumstances an older candidate up to the age of 29 might be considered). Applicants must have been in full-time education at some time during the 12 months preceding the application.

Types of grants

Scholarships are awarded to undertake research in a European country.

Annual grant total

In 2013/14 the charity had assets of £494,000 and an income of £25,500. During the year nine scholarships were awarded totalling £18,000.

Exclusions

Peter Kirk Scholarships are awarded for independent study projects. Scholarships cannot be used to pay for course work which is required as part of an academic qualification but applicants sometimes find it possible to undertake an independent project alongside studies abroad. Contact mail@kirkfund.org.uk if uncertain of your position.

Applications

Application forms can be downloaded from the website. Applications must be submitted by 2 November, with selection/interviews normally being completed by the end of December (check the website for the most up-to-date deadlines). Interviews take place in London at the applicant's expense. To submit an application download the application form, complete it, and send to mail@kirkfund.org.uk.

Other information

The charity has a very helpful and informative website.

The Link Foundation

£62,500

Correspondent: Administrative Secretary, New Zealand House, 80 Haymarket SW1Y 4PD (email: nz-uk. link@hotmail.co.uk; website: www. nzuklinkfoundation.org)

CC number: 802457

Eligibility

People wishing to participate in a vocational exchange between the UK and New Zealand, through specific joint educational schemes in a range of economic, social, cultural and scientific disciplines. The schemes are advertised through the governing bodies and specialist press belonging to these areas. Applicants must be either nationals or permanent residents of New Zealand or the UK.

Types of grants

Scholarships, grants, allowances and prizes towards educational and cultural exchange linked to a vocation, including for research.

Annual grant total

In 2013/14 the foundation had an income of £30,500 and a total expenditure of £104,000. During the year, the foundation granted fellowships totalling £62,500.

Exclusions

Grants are not made to individuals seeking funds for one-off trips such as medical residencies or to applicants wishing to visit countries other than Britain or New Zealand.

Applications

Application forms or relevant links for schemes can be found on the website.

Other information

A list of scholarships and fellowships offered by the foundation and details of its fellowship partners are available on its informative website.

The North Yorkshire Fund Educational Travel Award

£1,800 (2 grants)

Correspondent: Philip Ingham, Trustee, Suite 1.34, The Innovation Centre, York Science Park, York YO10 5DG (01904 435277; email: office@trcf.org.uk; website: www.trcf.org.uk)

CC number: 1084043

Eligibility

In previous years the fund has been open to full-time students who are studying at a British university and living in North Yorkshire or within the former West Riding boundary. However, the award is currently closed as the award criteria are being updated. Consult the website for the new criteria when the fund re-opens.

Types of grants

Two grants ranging from £250 to £1,000 are given each year. Financial assistance is available to students to give them the opportunity to study abroad as part of their full-time degree course.

Annual grant total

In 2013/14 two grants were made totalling £1,800.

Applications

Apply online through the Two Ridings Community Foundation website.

Other information

Two Ridings Community Foundation supports a number of community groups, projects and organisations. This particular award is only a small part of the charity's activities.

The Nottingham Roosevelt Memorial Travelling Scholarship Fund

£26,500

Correspondent: Ellen Burns, Trustee, 8 Mornington Crescent, Nuthall, Nottingham NG16 1QE (0115 975 5669; website: www.rooseveltscholarship.org)

CC number: 512941

Eligibility

People between the ages of 21 and 30 (cut-off date is 1 August of the current year) who work and/or live in the city or county of Nottingham and are primarily engaged in trade, commerce or 'the professions'.

Types of grants

A scholarship to enable an individual to visit the USA for a period between one and three months. Scholars are expected to travel widely throughout the USA and learn about the American way of life – an ambassadorial role. It is expected that some aspects linked to the work of the applicant will be investigated during the trip. The value of each scholarship can be up to about £3,200, plus a return flight to New York.

Annual grant total

In 2014 the fund had an income of £22,500 and an expenditure of £27,000. We estimate the annual total amount of grants awarded to be around £26,500.

Applications

Detailed guidelines, application forms and submission deadlines can be found on the trust's website. Applications are usually invited in spring. The fund prefers to receive them via email. Shortlisted candidates are required to attend interviews.

Other information

Applicants do not need to be in full-time education/employment or have any formal qualifications.

Further queries can be submitted online on the fund's website.

The Trans-Antarctic Association

£12,500

Correspondent: Dr James Smith, Grants Secretary, Trans-Antarctic Association, c/o British Antarctic Survey, High Cross, Madingley Road, Cambridge CB3 0ET (01223 728222; email: taagrants@bas.ac.uk)

CC number: 205773

Eligibility

Citizens of the UK, Australia and New Zealand seeking to further knowledge or exploration of the Antarctic region.

Types of grants

Grants are given to support expeditions to the Antarctica, including travel and equipment costs, as well as research and publication expenses. Awards normally are up to £1,500.

The total funds available for distribution in any one year typically ranges between £10,000 and £15,000. One third of available funds are awarded to New Zealand nationals, with the remainder being awarded to nationals from Australia, South Africa and the United Kingdom.

Annual grant total

In 2014 the organisation had an income of £12,500 and an expenditure of £13,000. We estimate that individual grants totalled around £12,500.

Exclusions

People who are not nationals of the countries named above are not normally supported.

Applications

Application forms and full guidelines are available on the association's website. The submission deadline is 31 January each year.

Volunteering

The Barnabas Trust

See entry on page 87

Reg Gilbert International Youth Friendship Trust (GIFT)

£12,000

Correspondent: Pamela Brewster, 23 Linnet Way, Frome BA11 2UY (01373 465225; email: yorkie77pam@aol.com; website: giftfriendshiptrust.org.uk)

CC number: 327307

Eligibility

UK citizens aged between 14 and 25 who are visiting a developing country on a project lasting at least six weeks. Applicants must live and volunteer within an indigenous community in the host country, preferably in a homestay environment. Candidates need to demonstrate their own fundraising initiatives, research and preparation for the visit. Normally they would have to be vetted and accepted by an approved overseas project agency but independent travellers may be considered provided a comprehensive and verifiable breakdown of their travel arrangements is submitted.

Types of grants

Grants of up to £500 are given to travellers who can demonstrate need and have already started preparation for the project.

Annual grant total

In 2014/15 the trust had an income of £6,000 and an expenditure of £12,500. We estimate the annual total amount of grants awarded to be around £12,000.

Exclusions

Grants are not available for proposals leading to academic or vocational qualifications.

Applications

Application forms can be downloaded from the trust's website after the eligibility criteria has been read and understood. An independent academic or professional reference is required together with the application.

Other information

The charity is an autonomous trust under the supervision of the Rotary Club of Frome.

Roger and Miriam Pilkington Charitable Trust

£5,800 (11 grants)

Correspondent: Jane Fagan, Trust Administrator, c/o Brabners, Chaffe Street, Horton House, Exchange Flags, Liverpool L2 3YL (0151 600 3000; email: jane.fagan@brabners.com)

CC number: 261804

Eligibility

The trustees' report from 2014/15 states that grants are given to:

> Enterprising young people, particularly those who are undertaking imaginative projects abroad which could be said to broaden horizons, giving them experiences which they may not otherwise have; increase awareness of other cultures and ways of living; or help them understand something of social problems outside their immediate environment.

Grants are awarded to those between the ages of 16 and 25.

Types of grants

One-off grants only, usually around £500. Due to a great demand grants are spread across a wide selection of projects.

Annual grant total

In 2014/15 the trust had assets of £927,000 and an income of £32,000. A total of almost £46,000 was spent in

charitable activities. Annual grants to 11 individuals totalled £5,800.

Exclusions

The trustees do not offer support where it should be provided by the education authorities. Long term funding is not available.

Applications

Applications should be submitted in writing to the correspondent. Applications can be made directly by individuals at any time for consideration in March and August. All grants are contingent on the applicant raising a significant proportion of the funds through their own efforts.

Other information

The trust is currently running a grant scheme in seven schools or colleges in the UK and Jersey with applicants being selected by the staff and approved by the trustees. In 2013/14 the grant scheme was allocated £30,000.

The Sir Philip Reckitt Educational Trust Fund

£32,000 (409 grants)

Correspondent: John Lane, Trustee, Rollits LLP, Rowntree Wharf, Navigation Road, York YO1 9WE (01904 625790; email: andy.cook@rollits.com; website: www.spret.org)

CC number: 529777

Eligibility

People in full-time education who live in Kingston upon Hull, East Riding of Yorkshire, or the county of Norfolk.

Types of grants

Grants are given towards educational travel such as Raleigh International, working in the developing world, Outward Bound-type courses and so on. Travel must be connected with the extra-curricular projects of the course. Grants can also be used to help with residence and attendance at conferences, lectures and short educational courses.

Annual grant total

In 2014 the fund had assets of £982,500 and an income of £36,500. Educational grants to individuals totalled £32,000.

Exclusions

Awards will not normally be made to people under the age of 14 on the date of travel. Repeat applications for identical activities are not normally considered.

Applications

An application form can be completed and submitted online or can be downloaded and posted to the appropriate address after completion. A

reference from the head of the institution of study, an employer or other suitable referee is required.

Note: Applications should be received by the charity more than six weeks before the intended departure date. Those submitted later are not normally considered. Successful applicants must complete a report to be returned to the trustees within three months of the end of the project or period of study.

Other information

Contacts

Kingston upon Hull and East Riding of Yorkshire – The Trustees, Sir Philip Reckitt Educational Trust, Rollits, Wilberforce Court, High Street, Hull HU1 1YJ (email: christine.atherton@rollits.com

Norfolk – The Trustees, Sir Philip Reckitt Educational Trust, c/o Mrs J. Pickering, 99 Yarmouth Road, Ellingham, Bungay NR35 2PH (email: spretrust@googlemail.com).

The Rotary Foundation Scholarships

£1 million

Correspondent: Foundation Administrator, Rotary International in Great Britain and Ireland, Kinwarton Road, Alcester, Warwickshire B49 6PB (01789 765411; fax: 01789 764916; email: info@ribi.org; website: www.ribi.org)

Eligibility

Scholarships to further international understanding for secondary school students, graduates, undergraduates, teachers and professional journalists.

Types of grants

Global Grant Scholarships overseas are available to graduates and are given towards achieving sustainable high-impact outcomes in the areas of peace and conflict prevention/resolution, disease prevention and treatment, water and sanitation, maternal and child health, basic education and literacy, economic and community development.

District Grant Scholarships are available for smaller scale projects locally or abroad. Clubs and districts create their own scholarships funded through district grants.

The purpose of the scholarships is to further international understanding and friendly relations among people of different countries, rather than to enable beneficiaries to achieve any particular qualification.

Annual grant total

Previously about £1 million has been spent in charitable support.

Applications

Applications can only be made through a rotary club in the district where the applicant lives, studies or works. Applications are normally considered throughout the year but the foundation encourages making enquiries well in advance of the planned activity.

The Shelroy Trust

£500

Correspondent: Jenny Bevan, Grants Manager, Norfolk Community Foundation, St James Mill, Whitefriars, Norwich NR3 1TN (01603 623958; fax: 01603 230036; email: jennybevan@ norfolkfoundation.com)

CC number: 327776

Eligibility

Young people living in East Norfolk and Norwich who are taking part in voluntary service overseas. Projects must have a Christian and/or humanitarian objective.

Types of grants

One-off grants, usually ranging from £200 to £300.

Annual grant total

In 2013/14 the trust had assets of £908,500 and an unusually high income of £1.75 million, the vast majority of which was received thanks to a bequest. This was a factor in the trust's unusually high grants total for the year, which amounted to £1.6 million.

The trust principally makes grants to organisations, although in the year it also assisted 19 individuals who have disabilities or who were facing disadvantage and distributed an additional 108 Christmas parcels to individuals in need.

Two young people who were carrying out humanitarian projects were also supported and, although we were unable to determine an exact amount, we estimate that this support totalled around £500.

Applications

Applications can be made in writing to the correspondent at any time. Individuals applying for grants must provide full information and two referees are required. Applications can be made directly by the individual or through a social worker, Citizens Advice or other third party. They are considered at the trustees' quarterly meetings in March, June, September and December. The trust is not able to reply to unsuccessful applicants unless an sae is provided.

W. W. Spooner Charitable Trust

£16,000

Correspondent: Michael Broughton, Trustees, 2 Elliot Road, Watford, Hertfordshire WD17 4DF (email: jo@ eisenerz.co.uk)

CC number: 313653

Eligibility

Our research suggests that young people who are taking part in voluntary overseas projects and expeditions can be supported. Preference is given for those living in Yorkshire (especially West Yorkshire) and former employees of the Spooner Industries Ltd or their dependants. Scholarships can also be awarded 'for the encouragement of young employees'.

Types of grants

One-off and recurrent grants are available.

Annual grant total

In 2013/14 the trust had assets of £1.7 million and an income of £71,500. A total of £114,000 was spent in charitable activities, of which donations and grants totalled £33,000. According to our research, previously around £16,000 has been awarded in grants to individuals.

Applications

Applications can be made in writing to the correspondent, normally by the end of March, July or October.

Other information

The trust mainly supports charitable and community organisations, clubs/groups.

The Erik Sutherland Gap Year Trust

£6,500

Correspondent: Viki Sutherland, Correspondent, Erik's Gap Year Trust, Torren, Glencoe, Argyll, Scotland PH49 4HX (01855 811207; fax: 01855 811338; email: info@eriks-gap year-trust. com; website: www.eriks-gap year-trust. com)

OSCR number: SC028293

Eligibility

School leavers living in the UK.

Types of grants

Grants are given to young people who wish to take a gap year or take part in voluntary work overseas before entering university or college. The trust primarily gives partial funding in instances where the young person has a shortfall in funds, although in exceptional cases the

trust may 'possibly bear the whole cost of a year out'. The trust aims to help one or more school leavers each year.

Annual grant total

In 2013/14 the trust had an income of £900 and an unusually high total expenditure of £6,700. We estimate that the amount of grants given to individuals totalled around £6,500.

Applications

An application form is available to download from the website.

Virgin Atlantic Be The Change Volunteer Trip Scholarship

£15,700 (30 grants)

Correspondent: Alice Likely, Charity Administrator, 7–11 St John's Hill, London SW11 1TR (020 7978 5225; email: ukyouth@freethechildren.com; website: www.freethechildren.co.uk/ virgin-atlantic-volunteer-trip)

CC number: 1138645

Eligibility

Volunteering travel scholarships are available to UK students between the ages of 12 and 18 (at the application deadline) 'who have demonstrated a commitment to global issues or community volunteerism'.

The charity's website states:

Applicants will be selected based on personal interest, merit, and demonstrated commitment to raising awareness in their local community. The ideal candidates are young people who are already working to improve their local or global community, and who will use this experience to motivate and inspire others to take action.

Types of grants

Each summer 30 scholarships are given to travel to one of Free The Children 'Adopt a Village' communities in India.

Annual grant total

In 2013/14 the charity's Scholarship Fund had an income of £22,000 and an expenditure of £24,000 (of this sum £8,100 was spent on salaries and related costs). The annual report and accounts for 2013/14 state that a total of £15,700 was spent in grants and other project costs relating to Scholarship-Volunteer trips. We use the latter figure as the grant total.

Exclusions

Note that a scholarship will not cover 'certain incidentals, including passport, visa, vaccinations, insurance, travelling costs to a London airport and spending money'. The website notes: 'We will work with students to help them fundraise for these costs, should this become a barrier to travel.'

Applications

Application forms can be accessed online and should be submitted by 23 March (references – 27 March) for August 2015 trips. Successful applicants will be notified by phone or email. Students can apply directly or may be recommended by a third party.

Other information

Scholarships are provided by the Virgin Atlantic Foundation in partnership with Free The Children UK (Charity Commission no. 1138645) and run by *Me to We*, Free The Children's charity partner.

Vocational training and apprentice- ships

The William Barry Trust

£151,500

Correspondent: Keiko Iwaki, Trustee, Flat 56, Avenue Close, Avenue Road, London NW8 6DA (020 7722 3974; email: williambarrytrust@gmail.com)

CC number: 272551

Eligibility

People in vocational studies and training, such as hospitality, hotel management, technical crafts or artistic occupations (singing, dancing, acting and so on).

Types of grants

One-off cash grants in range of £750 and £1,000. Support is available for general educational expenses, fees and maintenance/living costs.

Annual grant total

In 2013/14 the trust had an income of £234,000 and an expenditure of £177,000. A total of £151,500 was awarded in grants.

Exclusions

Grants are not available for career development or postgraduate degrees.

Applications

Apply in writing to the correspondent. Applications can be submitted directly by the individual or a family member.

Other information

The trust also supports organisations and has limitations on grants to individuals.

M. R. Cannon 1998 Charitable Trust

£32,000

Correspondent: Chris Mitchell, Trustee, 53 Stoke Lane, Westbury-on-Trym, Bristol BS9 3DW (0117 377 6540)

CC number: 1072769

Eligibility

Young people who wish to undertake vocational training or studies. Preference is given to individuals from Bristol, County Durham, Dorset, North Devon and North Yorkshire.

Types of grants

One-off and recurrent grants are given according to need.

Annual grant total

In 2013/14 the trust had assets of £3.3 million, an income of £34,000 and a total charitable expenditure of £52,000. The amount of grants given to individuals totalled £32,000.

Applications

Apply in writing to the correspondent.

Other information

Support can also be given to medical/health charities, conservation and countryside-related initiatives or small local projects. Grants made to ten institutions totalled £19,500 in 2013/14.

City and Guilds Bursaries

£78,500

Correspondent: David Miller, Administrator, City and Guilds of London Institute, 1 Giltspur Street, London EC1A 9DD (fax: 020 7294 2400; email: david.miller@cityandguilds.com; website: www.cityandguilds.com/ qualifications-and-apprenticeships/ support/bursaries)

CC number: 312832

Eligibility

Applicants must be completing a City and Guilds/ILM qualification and must be able to demonstrate in their application that they are in genuine financial need that would otherwise prevent them from completing their qualification. Applicants must currently be resident and wish to study in the UK for a City and Guilds/ILM qualification.

Types of grants

Educational grants are available for course and exam fees, living costs, books/equipment, travel costs, childcare and other needs. Around 40–60 awards are made each year. Awards are agreed on a case by case basis and determined by the individual course costs.

Annual grant total

In 2013/14 the charity had income of £129.8 million, a total expenditure of £122.4 million and awarded bursaries totalling £78,500.

Exclusions

Retrospective payments, grants for career development or deferred loans taken out with a college or bank are not covered.

Applications

Applications can be made online via the charity's website. For specific deadlines and the bursary timetable see the website. Candidates are invited to an interview in London.

Other information

City and Guilds primarily exist to provide qualifications, awards, assessments and support across a range of occupations in industry, commerce and the public services.

The charity warns that the awards are very competitive.

Henry Dixon's Foundation for Apprenticing – administered by Drapers' Charitable Fund

Correspondent: Andrew Mellows, Charities Administrator, The Drapers' Company, Drapers' Hall, Throgmorton Avenue, London EC2N 2DQ (020 7588 5001; fax: 020 7628 1988; email: charities@thedrapers.co.uk; website: www.thedrapers.co.uk)

CC number: 251403

Eligibility

Apprentices, students, schoolchildren, school leavers and people in vocational training under the age of 25. Particular regard may be given to those studying in the fields of technical textiles and art or design, with preference for inner city London.

Types of grants

One-off grants are made towards vocational training initiatives and apprenticeships, as well as activities in sports, arts and music, including support towards books, clothing, equipment/ instruments, fees, travel costs and other educational needs.

Annual grant total

In 2013/14 the foundation had assets of £2.1 million and an income of £45,000. No grants were made in 2013/14, but grants have previously totalled around £45,000.

Applications

Grants are normally made through educational institutions; therefore, applications should be made to the university or college rather than the foundation.

Other information

The foundation's funds have been transferred to the Drapers' Charitable Fund and are administrated as a restricted fund. Previously the charity was registered under the number 314292.

Go Make it Happen: A Project In Memory of Sam Harding

£8,600

Correspondent: Keith Harding, Administrator, 72 New Caledonian Wharf, 6 Odessa Street, London SE16 7TW (020 3592 7921, 07790 622381 (mob); email: keithhard@ hotmail.co.uk; website: www. gomakeithappen.co.uk)

CC number: 1145369

Eligibility

People between the ages of 18 and 30 who want to build a career in the tourism and travel industry. The charity has a particular, but not exclusive, focus on young people who have not necessarily followed a conventional academic route and wants to help them 'achieve things in their lives that they would not otherwise be able to achieve'.

Types of grants

Funding is available for training courses, travel expenses and other educational opportunities in the UK and overseas. Some examples include: support for volunteering and internships, language learning, skills-based qualifications and so on.

Annual grant total

In 2014/15 the charity had an income of £7,400 and an expenditure of £9,000. We estimate that grants totalled around £8,600.

Applications

Applications can be made online on the charity's website. The charity will normally make contact within two weeks and may arrange for an interview.

Other information

The charity also provides information and advice on opportunities for working overseas and in travel or tourism generally (both in the UK and abroad).

It also campaigns for cycling safety and driver awareness in memory of Sam's tragic death.

The Thomas Wall Trust

£42,000 (32 grants)

Correspondent: Deborah French, Chief Accountant, Skinners' Hall, 8 Dowgate Hill, London EC4R 2SP (020 7213 0567; email: information@thomaswalltrust.org. uk; website: www.thomaswalltrust.org. uk)

CC number: 206121

Eligibility

People who are over the age of 16 and have been resident in the UK for at least three years prior to the beginning of the course to be attended and who are facing financial difficulties preventing them from entering education or employment. Applicants should not have any qualifications for work and should be unable to fund their courses through any other means (for example, statutory grants or loans). The courses should be below degree level and lead to employment.

Types of grants

Small, one-off grants (generally of up to £1,000) to overcome financial barriers to work or education. Awards are given towards fees, equipment and other expenses related to vocational, skill-based or technical study and professional training. Interest-free loans can also be made. Both full-time and part-time courses are considered for support.

Annual grant total

In 2013/14 the trust had assets of £3.3 million and an income of £136,500. Charitable expenditure totalled £65,500 and grants to 32 individuals totalled £42,000.

Exclusions

Grants are not given:
- For undergraduate and postgraduate degree courses or PhD students
- Towards higher education courses that qualify for Student Loan Company funding
- To people earning above £26,000 per year
- To individuals with a family income above the average salary (£26,000 per year)
- To people who are considered 'employable' or 'qualified to work'
- For travel, study or work overseas
- For elective periods or intercalated courses
- Towards business start-up costs
- For GCSEs or A-levels
- To schoolchildren

Applications

Apply in writing to the correspondent.

Other information

Grants are also given to charitable organisations in the fields of education and social welfare, especially those that are small or of a pioneering nature.

The trustees' annual report for 2013/14 states:

> As in previous years, grants were made to assist individuals wanting to break through the barriers in their lives and life chances by pursuing technical or skill-based training, which will improve their prospects of finding paid work. Grants to charities were aimed at funding small organisations that are active in serving the social and/or education needs of their communities, especially where a grant can make a real impact in improving the lives of local people.

National charities classified by subject

Formal sciences

The Ogden Trust

£699,500 (87 grants)

Correspondent: Tim Simmons, Chief Executive, Hughes Hall, Wollaston Road, Cambridge CB1 2EW (01223 518164; fax: 01223 761837; email: office@ ogdentrust.com; website: ogdentrust.com)

CC number: 1037570

Eligibility

Academically gifted young people in the areas of science, physics and maths who have previously been educated in the state sector and who wish to attend a selection of independent secondary schools at sixth form level to study science subjects at A-level with the intention of studying physics at university. Undergraduate students who are already associated with the trust are also supported (for a list of groups members of which are considered to be associated with the trust, see the website). Applicants must be of British nationality and have a combined parental income of less than £50,000.

Types of grants

The trustees aim to continue to encourage and promote the teaching and learning of science through the sponsorship of:

- Talented students studying maths and physics at sixth form and undergraduate level
- Undergraduate and postgraduate students who wish to become science (specifically physics) teachers
- Programmes and projects supporting maths and science teaching in primary and secondary schools

Annual grant total

In 2013/14 the trust had assets of £48.9 million and an income of £610,000. Bursaries and scholarships totalled £699,500 which consisted of £399,500 in 37 bursaries and £300,000 in 50 undergraduate scholarships.

Exclusions

Postgraduate degrees are not supported (except PGCE physics students).

Applications

The sixth form scholarships operate through schools associated with the trust and a list be found on the website. Applicants should apply to the school directly using the enquiry form which can be downloaded from the trust's website. Undergraduate science scholarship applications can be found on the trust's website. Applications should be accompanied by an academic reference and supporting documentation.

The Worshipful Company of Scientific Instrument Makers

£29,500

Correspondent: The Clerk, Glaziers Hall, 9 Montague Close, London SE1 9DD (020 7407 4832; email: theclerk@wcsim.co.uk; website: www. wcsim.co.uk)

CC number: 221332

Eligibility

Schoolchildren, sixth formers, undergraduates and postgraduates with outstanding ability in science and mathematics and a creative and practical interest in branches of engineering connected with instrumentation and measurement.

Students must attend one of the following universities: Brunel, Cambridge, City, Glasgow Caledonian, Imperial, Oxford, Teesside, UCL, UMIST, Warwick.

Types of grants

The Young Engineers Program supports people to attend national and international events, competitions, prizes and travel support plus apprenticeships. There are also scholarships of £300 for sixth formers.

Postgraduate awards of £2,000 for 'exciting research and design and a postdoctoral award of £5,000 for up to 3 years'.

Annual grant total

In 2013/14 the charity held assets of £2.3 million and had an income of £74,500. Charitable expenditure totalled £58,500 and £29,500 was awarded in grants for scholarships.

Applications

See the charity's website for details of how to apply to each separate scheme. Students must apply through the university and not directly to the charity.

Humanities

Council for British Research in the Levant

£108,000 (28 grants)

Correspondent: Charity Administrator, 10 Carlton House Terrace, London SW1Y 5AH (020 7969 5296; fax: 020 7969 5401; email: cbrl@britac.ac.uk; website: www.cbrl.org.uk)

CC number: 1073015

Eligibility

British citizens or those ordinarily resident in the UK, Isle of Man or the Channel Islands carrying out research in arts, humanities, social and related sciences in connection with the countries of the Levant (Cyprus, Israel, Jordan, Lebanon, Palestine, Syria and adjacent territories).

Types of grants

The charity administers a range of support for scholars, currently:

▶ Arabic Language Training – grants to cover the cost of full tuition, air travel and accommodation to members of academic staff at a UK university, or academic staff (faculty) with a UK PhD and CBRL membership participating in the CBRL Academic Arabic Programme;

▶ Visiting Research Fellowships and Scholarships – for scholars in university posts, early career postdoctoral candidates and students conducting PhD/DPhil research to spend a period of time at CBRL's overseas institutes to conduct primary research, develop contacts, give lectures and write up project results/ publications derived from a thesis/ research;

▶ Pilot Study Awards – up to £7,500 to enable postdoctoral scholars to undertake initial exploratory work or a feasibility study as a preliminary to making major funding applications to a research council, the British Academy or another body;

▶ Travel Grants – up to £800 to cover costs of travel and subsistence of students, academics and researchers undertaking reconnaissance tours or smaller research projects in the countries of the Levant;

▶ Conference and Outreach Funding – lectures, seminars, workshops and conferences in London, Amman, and Jerusalem, as well as occasional meetings elsewhere, mostly initiated by the CBRL (formal applications for support towards conferences, exhibitions, or other forms of outreach are also encouraged)

Awards range from £700 to around £12,000.

Annual grant total

In 2013/14 the charity had assets of £336,500 and an income of £918,500. During the year 28 individuals were awarded grants totalling £108,000 under the following categories: research awards, pump-priming awards, visiting research fellowships, travel grants, scholarships and direct support.

Exclusions

Grants are not normally made towards maintenance, fees, group tours, books or equipment.

Applications

Separate application forms for each of the awards together with extensive guidance notes and conditions are available on the charity's website. Applicants should also refer to the website for application deadlines as these vary.

Other information

This charity has an extremely comprehensive website which should be referred to by any interested applicants.

A report is required to be submitted after the completion of the research which is then made publicly available.

The Hanna and Zdzislaw Broncel Charitable Trust (The Broncel Trust)

£7,500

Correspondent: Trust Administrator, 371 Uxbridge Road, London W3 9RH (020 8992 9997; email: info@akpp.co.uk)

CC number: 1103737

Eligibility

People involved with Polish history, literature, art or social sciences. The trustees are prepared to consider a varied range of requests.

Types of grants

The trust awards scholarships, financial assistance for research and grants for publishing Polish works of literature.

Annual grant total

In 2013/14 the trust had an income of £4,000 and an expenditure of £15,000. We estimate the annual total amount of grants awarded to individuals to be around £7,500.

Applications

Apply in writing to the correspondent.

Other information

Grants are made to both organisations and individuals. Occasional financial support can be provided for libraries, museums and exhibitions.

Society of Antiquaries of London

£56,000 (21 grants)

Correspondent: John Lewis, General Secretary, Burlington House, Piccadilly, London W1J 0BE (020 7479 7080; fax: 020 7287 6967; email: admin@sal.org.uk; website: www.sal.org.uk)

CC number: 207237

Eligibility

People in higher education (including postgraduates), early career researchers and scholars studying archaeological, antiquarian, architectural subjects, art history, documentary and undertaking research projects focusing on material cultural heritage.

Types of grants

The society offers a number of research and travel grants in the range of £500–£5,000. Awards are given on an annual basis with a potential renewal up to two years.

A number of specific awards named after various benefactors are offered in addition to the general grants. See the website for the details of these individual funds.

Annual grant total

In 2013/14 the society had assets of £14.6 million and an income of £1.5 million. Charitable expenditure totalled £1.4 million and a total of £56,000 was awarded for research grants to 21 individuals.

Exclusions

Research and travel grants are not made for work contributing to an undergraduate or postgraduate degree.

Some of the awards are not available to students.

Applications

Applications can be made online or downloaded from the society's website. Applications should not exceed four A4 pages and, together with a reference, should be submitted by 15 January for consideration in March. Applicants will be notified of a decision by 31 March.

Other information

The society also awards William and Jane Morris Fund (Church Conservation Grant Awards) grants to churches, chapels and other places of worship in the United Kingdom.

Arts

The Amber Trust

See entry on page 23

The Artistic Endeavours Trust

£4,000

Correspondent: Richard Midgley, Trustee, Macintyre Hudson LLP, 30–34 New Bridge Street, London EC4V 6BJ (020 7429 4100)

CC number: 1044926

Eligibility

Students undertaking education in the arts or entering artistic professions.

Types of grants

Grants to graduates and undergraduate students for fees, clothing, equipment, books, travel, general subsistence, also living expenses to those who are unable to secure employment for a period not exceeding two years.

Annual grant total

At the time of writing (October 2015) the latest financial information available was from 2013. In 2013 the trust had an income of £23,000 and a total expenditure of £7,800. We estimate that around £4,000 was awarded to individuals.

Applications

Apply in writing to the correspondent.

Other information

The trust also gives grants to organisations for various creative projects.

It is possible for donors to indicate a particular individual or individuals who they wish to support and channel the money through the trust.

The Lionel Bart Foundation

£31,500

Correspondent: John Cohen, Trustee, Clintons, 55 Drury Lane, London WC2B 5SQ (02073796080; email: jc@clintons.co.uk)

CC number: 1086343

Eligibility

Undergraduate and postgraduate students who are aiming to become actors, composers, lyricists, book writers, playwrights, designers, choreographers, directors and anyone who wishes to make the theatre their career.

Types of grants

Grants towards tuition fees are given in the range of £200–£3,000.

Annual grant total

In 2013/14 the foundation had an income of £97,500 and a total expenditure of £53,000. The amount of grants given to individuals totalled around £31,500.

Applications

Apply in writing to the correspondent. Applications should be made between January and May each year.

Other information

The foundation also invites applicants through various theatre schools.

Benney Arts Foundation

£5,800

Correspondent: Paul Benney, Trustee, Somerset House, Strand, London WC2R 1LA (07973 373 220; email: info@benneyartsfoundation.org)

CC number: 1154043

Eligibility

Young artists over the age of 18 who have financial difficulties and would not have sufficient funds to continue their education with an established artist.

Types of grants

The foundation's website states: 'The BAF offers bursaries up to £15,000 dependent on means and period of apprenticeship'

'Our funding provides a bursary for the apprentice as well as a stipend for the established artist, creating a professional environment where all parties will be motivated to focus and make the most of the apprenticeship.'

Annual grant total

In 2014 the foundation had an income of £15,200 and an expenditure of £6,000. We estimate that the amount of grants given to individuals totalled around £5,800.

Applications

Applications are available from the correspondent. Completed forms should be returned to: West Hall B at Hackney Downs Studios, Amhurst Terrace, London E8 2BT.

Other information

The following information is from the foundation's website:

> The Benney Arts Foundation's goal as a charity is to provide art apprenticeships and sustained funding for young artists with financial difficulties who otherwise would not have sufficient funds to continue their education as an apprentice to an established artist. Our aim is to place young artists in a working studio environment where they will have the opportunity to get first hand experience of the various aspects of making a living in the arts; from practical techniques to how to gain exposure in the wider art world. We hope this will provide candidates with the experience and support needed to develop their own independent art practice.

The Richard Carne Trust

£35,000

Correspondent: Karen Wall, Administrator, Kleinwort Benson Trustees Ltd, 14 St George Street, London W1S 1FE (0203207 7356; email: Karen.Wall@kleinwortbenson.com; website: richardcarnetrust.org)

CC number: 1115903

Eligibility

Young people in the performing arts who are in need. Preference is given to those studying music and theatre.

Types of grants

Grants are given according to need.

Annual grant total

In 2014 the trust had an income of £495,500 and a total expenditure of £228,000. We estimate that around £35,000 was awarded in grants to individuals. At the time of writing (July 2015) full accounts were not available to view on the Charity Commission's website.

Applications

The trust's website states: 'Please note that the Richard Carne Trust does not respond to individual applications for financial help. Assistance is provided via the various academic and cultural institutions which the trust supports.'

Other information

The following is taken from the trust's website: 'Working mainly with the major music academies and drama schools, the trust provides bursaries and scholarships to students selected by those institutions, both on the basis of talent and financial need.'

The Costume Society

£1,500

Correspondent: Jill Salen, Hon. Secretary, Rose Cottage, Crofft Y Genau, St Fagans, Cardiff CF5 6DU (029 2056 8622; email: awards@costumesociety.org.uk or info@costumesociety.org.uk; website: www.costumesociety.org.uk)

CC number: 262401

Eligibility

Students in the history and theory of design (fashion and textiles), dress, costume, theatre wardrobe and related fields. Support is given to students engaged in further and higher education, including postgraduate courses and also to researchers and trainee museum curators.

Types of grants

The society offers the following awards:

- **Museum Placement Award** – of up to £1,000 to student volunteers to undertake a placement (full- or part-time for a minimum of two months) in a public museum in the UK
- **Conference Student Bursary** – covers costs of full attendance at the Costume Society's annual three-day conference (excluding transport to and from the event). It is open to UK full-time and part-time students at a graduate and postgraduate level engaged in research directed towards

the presentation of a dissertation or thesis

▶ **The Patterns of Fashion Award** – award of £500 open to students in costume and fashion-related education courses who 'produced a reconstructed garment from a pattern in one of the Janet Arnold *Patterns of Fashion* books that reflect the high standards presented in the books'

▶ **The Yarwood Award** – of up to £500 plus one-year membership available to master's students 'engaged in high quality research into the history of dress and/or textiles with expenditure relating to the completion of their dissertation'. The award is intended to cover specific expenses, such as 'travel to a library, archive or collection, subsistence while away and archive reproduction fees' not the overall cost of the degree

▶ **Jubilee Award** – in 2015, as part of the celebration of The Costume Society's 50th anniversary, there was additional opportunity to increase rewards for winning the existing competitions. Support of up to £2,000 could be given for The Yarwood, Museum Placement and Patterns of Fashion awards and Conference Student Bursary Award could be increased by up to £500 to include costs associated with transportation to the conference

Annual grant total

In 2014 the society had assets of £338,000 and an income of £62,000. Awards from restricted funds totalled £1,500 and consisted of: Patterns of Fashion Awards (£700); Yarwood Award (£500); Student Fashion Design Award (£300).

Applications

Application procedures and deadlines are different for each of the awards. Detailed eligibility and application guidelines are available on the society's website and are also published in *Costume*, the annual journal of the society. Applicants are encouraged to approach the society with initial enquiries.

Other information

The **Student Design Award** of £250 is not open to the public and forms part of the society's symposium. Fashion courses at art schools close to the symposium venue are invited to participate.

The society's aims are the promotion of the study and preservation of historic and contemporary dress.

Craft Pottery Charitable Trust

£2,000

Correspondent: John Higgins, Trust Secretary, Taplands Farm Cottage, Webbs Green, Soberton, Southampton SO32 3PY (023 9263 2686; email: JohnHigginsceramics@gmail.com; website: www.cpaceramics.co.uk/craft-potters-charitable-trust)

CC number: 1004767

Eligibility

People involved in the field of ceramics (regardless of the membership of the Craft Potters Association). Applicants must be British citizens or have permanent resident status, as defined by UK Visas and Immigration, and meet the definition of a professional artist.

Types of grants

The trust offers awards through the Annual Grant Scheme. According to the application guidelines, awards of up to £1,000 can be used:

> For a period of independent research and creation of a body of work, the development of prototypes, participation in artists' residencies and specialised professional development activities (such as workshops or specialised training), as well as production of work for confirmed public exhibitions in the UK and/or abroad.

In the past bursaries of £500 were also made to new graduate makers to undertake individual postgraduate projects.

Support may be used towards training, travel, conference attendance, preparation of books or films and other projects relevant to the education of the public in craft pottery.

Annual grant total

In 2014 the trust had an income of £18,000 and a total expenditure of £4,600. We estimate that about £2,000 was given in grants to individuals.

Applications

Application forms and further guidelines can be obtained from the correspondent via email or by post including an sae. Further information is also given on the trust's website. The closing date for applications for the annual award is 15 December. These grants are then considered within the following two months.

Other information

Grants may also be made to organisations.

The Thomas Devlin Fund

See entry on page 133

The Ann Driver Trust

£18,500

Correspondent: Penny Neary, Administrator, 10 Stratford Place, London W1C 1BA (07939 556574; email: secretary@anndrivertrust.org)

CC number: 801898

Eligibility

Young people wishing to pursue an education in the arts, particularly music.

Types of grants

Scholarships and bursaries for the advancement of education in the arts, principally music.

Annual grant total

In 2013/14 the trust had an income of £27,500 and assets of £814,500. Grants were made totalling £18,500 for scholarships and bursaries.

Applications

Application forms should be requested by the principle or head of department at place of study.

The Fenton Arts Trust

£17,220

Correspondent: Shelley Baxter, Trust Manager and Administrator, PO Box 68825, London SE23 9DG (website: www.fentonartstrust.org.uk)

CC number: 294629

Eligibility

People who are making, or who aspire to make, a worthwhile contribution to the artistic and cultural life of the UK. Grants are made towards the creative arts, principally painting and drama. Students should have British nationality and be aged under 35.

Types of grants

Scholarships and bursaries to charitable bodies and to individuals or organisations to support work or performance by those early in their careers.

Annual grant total

In 2013/14 the trust had an income of £148,000 and assets totalling almost £4.2 million. Grants made during the year to individuals and organisations totalled £98,000. In the previous year grants to individuals totalled £17,220.

Applications

Applications for scholarships and bursaries can come from any institution which provides study opportunities and wishes to offer scholarships and bursaries to its students.

Applications for other grants can be made in writing directly by the individual to the administrator. Requests should include a fully budgeted proposal with the amount requested and information regarding other sponsors to the project.

Applications should preferably be sent nine months to a year in advance.

The trustees meet to discuss applications three times a year.

Other information

The trust also provides grants to organisations.

The Haworth Charitable Trust

£14,500

Correspondent: Sarah Cordwell, Trustee, 3 The Mews, London N1 7AZ (07515 941621)

CC number: 803029

Eligibility

Young musicians and painters in their final year of full-time study or the first year of their professional career. Preference is given to applicants from the north west of England, Herefordshire, Shropshire, The Wrekin and London.

Types of grants

Grants of £1,000 to £2,000 for one year only, paid in instalments over the year. Grants are for any purposes to further the establishment of a career in music, painting and the fine arts. Grants are not made for general welfare purposes.

Annual grant total

In 2013/14 the trust had an income of £15,000 and an expenditure of £15,000. We estimate that grants totalled around £14,500.

Exclusions

Loans are not made and mature students cannot be funded.

Applications

Applications should be made by letter, with a CV, to the correspondent, and must be supported by a recommendation of a tutor of a full-time course.

IdeasTap Ltd

£576,000

Correspondent: Simon Johnson, Trustee, Wool Yard, 54 Bermondsey Street, London SE1 3UD (020 7232 5465; email: sjohnson@ideastap.com; website: www.ideastap.com)

CC number: 1132623

Eligibility

Artists, particularly (but not exclusively) young people under the age of 25.

Support is provided in the areas of music, acting, performing arts, photography, gaming, creative writing, film production, design and other arts.

Types of grants

The organisation operates similarly to a community foundation and administers a number of schemes in partnership with various arts organisations and 'creative corporations'. The support available ranges from grants and scholarships to networking opportunities and career development events, to paid experience or opportunities to showcase an artwork.

Annual grant total

During 2013/14 the charity had assets of £1.4 million an income of £2.9 million. Grants were made totalling £576,000.

Applications

Apply in writing to the correspondent.

Other information

One of the bigger schemes administered by IdeasTap is Sky Academy Scholarships (currently in its fourth year) distributing bursaries to the value of £150,000 each year together with one-to-one mentoring and career development opportunities.

IdeasTap also provides funding to organisations to deliver projects, although support to individuals is currently the charity's main activity.

The charitable company is a wholly owned subsidiary undertaking of The Peter De Haan Charitable Trust.

The Philip Bates Trust

£3,300

Correspondent: Karen Moulton, Trustee, 5 Fern Close, Rugby CV23 0UQ (01788 561148; email: info@philipbatestrust.org.uk; website: www.philipbatestrust.org.uk)

CC number: 1094937

Eligibility

People under 25 pursuing creative and artistic achievement. Preference is given to musicians and applicants in the West Midlands.

Types of grants

One off, and in exceptional circumstances recurrent, grants of £100 to £300 and musical instrument loans. There are also four prizes for composition awarded each year.

Annual grant total

In 2014 the trust had both an income and an expenditure of £6,600. We estimate that grants awarded to individuals for educational purposes totalled around £3,300.

Exclusions

Grants to individuals will not be made to more than one sibling per family.

Applications

Applications should normally be submitted in December or June for consideration in January and July. Where possible, trustees prefer to receive a personal request from the applicant rather than from a parent, guardian or other person on their behalf.

Other information

The trust also supports projects or workshops which aim to develop creative and artistic interests and skills in young people.

Peggy Ramsay Foundation

£115,500

Correspondent: Neil Adleman, Trustee, Hanover House, 14 Hanover Square, London W15 1HP (020 7667 5000; fax: 020 7667 5100; email: prf@harbottle.com; website: www.peggyramsayfoundation.org)

CC number: 1015427

Eligibility

Playwrights who are resident in the British Isles (UK, Republic of Ireland, the Channel Isles and the Isle of Man) who have had at least one full length play in English professionally produced for a run for an audience of adults or young people (also see 'Exclusions'). The website specifies: 'By full length the Trustees usually mean a play of more than one hour and that a run implies performance for more than one week.'

Types of grants

One-off grants. Individual grants ordinarily do not exceed a standard commissioning fee. Grants are sometimes made for equipment, such as laptops, and for expenditure which makes writing possible.

Annual grant total

In 2014 the foundation had assets of £5.95 million and an income of £227,000. During the year, 94 grants were made to individuals totalling £231,000. We estimate that social welfare grants to individuals amounted to £115,500

Exclusions

The foundation's website states the following information:

The Trustees will not accept as qualification books for musicals, pantomime scripts, puppet plays, foreign language plays, translations or school plays. Adaptations and plays intended primarily for younger audiences are accepted only in special circumstances which imply wider originality.

Plays in other media and scripts for film or television are not a qualification but are relevant in a CV.

The Foundation does not support production costs or any project which does not have a direct benefit to individual playwrights or writing for the stage. Commissioning costs are usually considered as part of production costs. Fees for training or courses of any kind are not supported. Scripts, publicity material and reviews should not be sent. References are not needed.

Applications

Apply by writing a short letter to the correspondent. The letter should explain the need, the amount requested and the way in which the grant would be spent. A full CV 'not limited to writing' should also be sent.

Applicants are also asked to provide answers to the following questions:
- When and where the first professional performance of a play of theirs took place?
- Who produced the play which qualifies them for a grant?
- When and where was their qualifying play produced, how long was it, what was its approximate playing time and has it been revived?
- For that production were the director and actors all professionals engaged with Equity contracts?
- Did the audience pay to attend?

Scripts and publicity material must not be included, and references are not needed. The trustees meet quarterly and, although applications are dealt with between meetings, it may take six to eight weeks before a definitive answer is received.

Rhona Reid Charitable Trust
See entry on page 82

The Society for Theatre Research

£5,000

Correspondent: Secretary, c/o The Royal Nat Theatre Archive, 83–101 The Cut, London SE1 8LL (email: contact@str.org.uk; website: www.str.org.uk)

CC number: 266186

Eligibility

People involved with research into the history, historiography, art and practice of the British theatre, including music-hall, opera, dance, and other associated performing arts. Applicants should be aged 18 or over. There are no restrictions on status, nationality, or the location of the research.

Applications are not restricted to those engaged in formal academic work and academic staff, postgraduate students, theatre professionals and private researchers are all equally eligible.

Types of grants

Annual theatre research awards ranging between £200 and £1,000.

Annual grant total

In 2013/14 the charity had an income of £45,500 and an expenditure of £44,500. We estimate that research awards totalled around £5,000. At the time of writing (September 2015) full accounts were not available to view on the Charity Commission's website.

Exclusions

Exclusively literary topics are not eligible.

Applications

Application forms can be downloaded from the society's website.

The South Square Trust

£36,500 (36 grants)

Correspondent: Nicola Chrimes, Clerk to the Trustees, PO Box 169, Lewes, East Sussex BN7 9FB (01825 872264; website: www.southsquaretrust.org.uk)

CC number: 278960

Eligibility

Students over the age of 18 years who are studying full-time practical degree courses in the fine and applied arts, especially those related to gold, silver and metalwork, also music, drama and dance.

Preference is given to students who have been mainly educated in the UK, those in their third year of an undergraduate degree or postgraduate students.

Types of grants

The trust assists students directly and also provides scholarships and bursaries to a number of schools/colleges. Individual awards can be given towards fees or for living expenses.

Annual grant total

In 2013/14 the trust had assets of £4.2 million and an income of £208,500. Grants to 36 individuals totalled £36,500.

Exclusions

Grants are not given for:
- People under 18
- Part-time or short courses
- Expeditions or travel outside the UK
- Courses outside the UK
- Film, architecture and interior design courses
- Foundation courses and research degrees
- Purchase of equipment
- Private lessons

Applications

Application forms can be completed online on the trust's website. Individual applications are invited from 1 January to 30 April each year. Two references (preferably from the applicant's current tutors) and a photograph are required (along with photographs of work if on an arts-related course).

Initial enquiries by telephone are also welcomed.

Other information

In 2013/14 bursaries and scholarships to nine schools and colleges totalled £57,000. The trustees have set up scholarship awards with a number of Colleges and institutions. A full list of these can be obtained from the correspondent.

Split Infinitive Trust

£21,000

Correspondent: Heather Stoney, Trustee, PO BOX 409, Scarborough YO11 9AJ (email: splitinfin@ haydonning.co.uk; website: www. splitinfinitivetrust.co.uk)

CC number: 1110380

Eligibility

People in arts education and artists requiring funding for a specific project. Performance arts courses (such as music, drama or dance) are favoured, although other arts areas may be considered. The trust asks applicants to check with the correspondent if their course might be eligible prior to applying.

Types of grants

Grants are given for arts education associated needs and specific arts projects. Awards are generally under £1,000.

Annual grant total

In 2013/14 the trust had assets of £66,000 and an income of £31,000. There were 108 grants totalling over £46,000, of which over £21,000 was given to individuals. During the year four students were given grants of £1,000 each; the remainder consisted of grants under £1,000.

Education	£17,200
Training	£3,300
Productions	£1,000

Exclusions

Note that 'repeat grants are rare and although previous recipients are welcome to re-apply, the fact of a previous grant is no guarantee of a future one'.

Applications

Application forms are available on the trust's website and should be completed electronically, although hand-written and posted copies will also be accepted. Supporting evidence – a covering letter, an acceptance from the course of study (for students) or evidence of the project/commission and/or a CV (for non-students) – must be attached.

The trustees meet every three months, normally in March, June, September and December, but this can vary.

Other information

The trust supports both individuals and organisations. According to the website, currently the trustees' efforts are focused on supporting students.

The trust's website reminds:

> The Trust aims to award grants to support individuals, or projects by companies or organisations with charitable status that support the arts in general and in education. The Trust will also look to support projects that alleviate sickness, poverty, hardship and distress, primarily within the Yorkshire area.

> Grants made are solely at the trustees' discretion and correspondence regarding their decisions will not be entered into.

The Talbot House Trust

£10,500

Correspondent: Jayne Day, Pothecary Witham Weld Solicitors, 70 St George's Square, London SW1V 3RD (020 7821 8211; email: charities@pwwsolicitors.co.uk; website: www.pwwsolicitors.co.uk/funding-applications/11-the-talbot-house-trust)

CC number: 1010214

Eligibility

UK-resident students aged 16 to 25 who come from a low-income household and are undertaking courses in the UK in performing arts, such as drama, dance and music.

Types of grants

One-off grants to students in further/higher education to help with the cost with the costs of fees. In exceptional circumstances a contribution towards equipment and instruments or maintenance and living costs will be considered. The grants are intended to be supplementary only and applicants will be expected to raise funds through their own efforts.

Annual grant total

In 2014/15 the trust had an income of £10,000 and a total charitable expenditure of £11,000. We estimate the annual total amount of grants awarded to be around £10,500.

Exclusions

Postgraduate students are not supported.

Applications

Applications should be made on a form available upon request from the correspondent. Applications must be received by March for consideration in May. Applicants should include details of any financial hardship and any other reason why special consideration should be given to their application.

The John Thaw Foundation

£50,000

Correspondent: Foundation Administrator, PO Box 477, Amyand Park Road, Twickenham TW1 9LF (email: clare.eden@talk21.com)

CC number: 1090668

Eligibility

People wishing to pursue a career in the theatre and performing arts. Preference is given to individuals who are underprivileged and disadvantaged.

Types of grants

The foundation provides scholarships and bursaries of around £3,000 towards fees through specifically chosen training programmes at established schools or youth groups.

Annual grant total

In 2013/14 the foundation had assets of £168,000 and an income of £158,000. A total of £123,500 was spent in grants to individuals and organisations. We estimate the annual total amount of grants awarded to individuals to be around £50,000.

Applications

Apply in writing to the correspondent. Note that awards are mainly made through specific bursary programmes and, therefore, applications should be made through appropriate institution.

Other information

The foundation works with a number of partner bodies and also supports educational organisations.

The Wall Trust

£31,500 (13 grants)

Correspondent: Charles Wall, Trustee, Flat 19, Waterside Point, 2 Anhalt Road, London SW11 4PD (020 7978 5838)

CC number: 291535

Eligibility

Exceptionally talented students of performing arts who are nominated by an organisation with which the trust has a scholarship scheme (see 'Applications' section). Scholarships are given on the basis of outstanding talent and genuine financial need. Individuals aged 16 or over may be undertaking further, higher or postgraduate education or vocational training in music, drama or dance.

Types of grants

The trust provides scholarships (which normally range between £1,000 and £3,000) towards the cost of tuition and training. Payments are made directly to the educational establishment. Recurrent grants may be made for the duration of the course (normally three years), provided the candidates continue to progress.

Annual grant total

In 2013/14 the trust had assets of £212,500 and an income of £27,000. A total of £35,000 was spent in charitable activities, of which £31,500 was awarded in 13 scholarships (five involved with dance, seven drama and one in music).

Exclusions

Unsolicited applications are not normally accepted. Funding is supplementary and cannot be given for maintenance/living expenses.

Applications

Applications should only be made by an organisation with which the trust has a scholarship scheme. Applicants will be auditioned and interviewed by the trustees.

Sydney Dean Whitehead's Charitable Trust

£33,000 (17 grants)

Correspondent: Moore Stephens, Moore Stephens, Chartered Accountants, 30 Gay Street, Bath BA1 2PA (01225 486100; fax: 01225 448198; email: mark.burnett@moorestephens.com)

CC number: 207714

Eligibility

Children under the age of 18 who have special artistic talents, especially in music, dance or ballet, and whose 'parents are unable to provide them with an education suitable to their position or abilities'. Preference will be given to applicants who demonstrate efforts of raising funds themselves.

Types of grants

Grants are given mainly towards school fees but support may also be given to help fund one-off purchases (for example musical instruments). The awards range from £500 to £2,500.

Annual grant total

In 2013/14 the trust had assets of £1.2 million, an income of £52,000 and made 17 grants to individuals totalling £33,000.

Applications

Application forms can be obtained from the correspondent providing an sae. They can be submitted directly by the individual. The trustees meet once a year, in June.

Other information

Grants are also made to small local charities (£2,500 in 2013/14).

The Marie Duffy Foundation

£3,700

Correspondent: Michael Pask, Trustee, 4A Flaghead Road, Poole, Dorset BH13 7JL (01202 701173; email: enquiries@marie-duffy-foundation.com; website: www.marie-duffy-foundation.com)

CC number: 1145892

Eligibility

People over the age of 12 who are passionate about excellence in dance, music, composition or choreography of Irish Dance.

Types of grants

The foundation provides 'financial assistance to aspiring dancers, musicians and choreographers so they may fulfil their dreams in the world of Irish Dance'.

Awards may include support towards fees, seminars, bursaries, projects, competitions and so on. The website notes that 'applications can be made for funding Irish Dance related projects which exhibit creativity, flair and entrepreneurship in the promotion of Irish Dance skills, performance, scholarship or business acumen'.

Annual grant total

In 2013/14 the foundation had an income of £8,000 and a total expenditure of £7,800. We estimate that about £3,700 was given in grants to individuals.

Applications

Application forms are available on the foundation's website. They should be submitted by 31 of December.

Other information

Grants are also made for Irish Dance projects by groups or organisations.

Lisa Ullmann Travelling Scholarship Fund

£13,500

Correspondent: The Secretary, Breach, Kilmington, Axminster, Devon EX13 7ST (01297 35159; email: emma.r.mcfarland@gmail.com; website: www.lutsf.org.uk)

CC number: 297684

Eligibility

UK residents (for at least five years) over the age of 18 working in the field of movement and dance (choreographers, performers, lecturers/teachers, writers, therapists, administrators and so on) who wish to travel in the UK or abroad to attend a conference, undertake research or a short course of study to develop their skills and knowledge. Travel must originate and end in the UK

Types of grants

Grants are available for travel expenses, generally in the range of £600, but occasionally larger.

Annual grant total

In 2013/14 the fund had an income of £9,000 and a total expenditure of £14,500. We estimate that the amount of grants given to individuals totalled £13,500.

Exclusions

The fund will not support:

- Course or conference fees
- Applications relating to undergraduate or master's degree courses
- Full-time courses or courses extending over one, two or three years, including most diploma, certificate, and postgraduate degree courses (doctoral studies will be considered)
- Gap year travel, degree placements or fieldwork
- Joint or group projects (individuals who are part of a larger project team may be considered)
- Travel insurance, visas, additional baggage costs, travel to/from the airport
- Projects which directly support the work of companies, institutions or organisations
- Set-up costs of projects or festivals
- Previous recipients of a scholarship may be considered for a second award after at least five years have passed and/or in exceptional circumstances

Applications

Application forms and guidelines are available on the foundation's website by November of each year or can be requested from the correspondent providing an sae. Four copies of a completed application form should be submitted by post no later than 15 January. Forms sent by email or fax are not acceptable. Individuals will be informed about the outcome of their application by the end of March. Applications should demonstrate passion and commitment and projects should have clear and achievable outcomes, be carefully thought through and show evidence of preliminary research.

The Tom Acton Memorial Trust

£3,000

Correspondent: Alan Gage, Trustee, Hamilton House, Cobblers Green, Felsted, Dunmow CM6 3LX (01371 820382; website: tomactonorg.wordpress.com/home)

CC number: 1088069

Eligibility

People in musical education who are under the age of 25, were born or are resident in Essex and have been largely educated in Essex.

Types of grants

Financial assistance is available towards the costs of musical education fees, purchase or loan of an instrument, travel expenses in respect of musical education or performance, music-related physical and psychological health needs. Grants can reach up to a maximum of £800 and are awarded according to need.

Annual grant total

In 2014/15 the trust had an income of £3,000 and an expenditure of £3,200. We estimate the annual total amount of grants awarded to be around £3,000.

Applications

Application forms can be requested from the correspondent or downloaded from the website. Candidates are asked to include a teacher's reference to support the application which should be submitted by the end of May. Applicants who are successful in their initial application are invited for an audition, usually in July.

The Australian Music Foundation in London

£30,000

Correspondent: Sally-Ann Shepherdson, Administrator, 51 Musgrove Road, London SE14 5PP (07778 313 479; email: sas@australianmusicfoundation.org; website: australianmusicfoundation.org)

CC number: 270784

Eligibility

Australian musicians, conductors and composers under 30 years of age for study in Europe, the United Kingdom and the United States of America.

Types of grants

Grants are usually made towards the costs of musical equipment, study and development. This may include: fees for a course of study at an 'outstanding' overseas music institution; contributions towards the maintenance costs of a student attending a full-time course at an overseas institution; or payment for private tuition, language courses, purchase of musical instruments, travel costs or other strategic items necessary for the applicant's musical development. In the case of tuition fees, funds are normally paid directly to the appropriate institution. The foundation's website states: 'Typically awards are in the range of AUD 1,000 to 30,000, or the equivalent amounts in an international currency.'

Annual grant total

In 2013 the foundation had an income of £12,200 and a total expenditure of £30,700. We estimate that grants totalled £30,000.

The 2013 accounts were the latest available at the time of writing (November 2015).

Applications

The application process consists of two stages:

- Stage 1 – An online application form can be found on the foundation's website and should be submitted with accompanying video audition files. There is a £10 administration fee
- Stage 2 – Applicants who have been successful at Stage 1 will be notified and invited to attend a live audition, usually in September. Awards are then granted to the successful auditionees

Opening and closing dates for applications are available on the foundation's website, as is a sample application form and a helpful list of FAQs.

Note: Composers should apply using the standard online form, but should instead include scanned copies of scores (or PDF files), as well as audio files of their music recordings.

Other information

There is a separate award jointly funded by the Australian Music Foundation and Sir Charles Mackerras, which is specifically for young Australian conductors of merit. Potential applicants should request further information from the Australian Musical Foundation.

Awards for Young Musicians

£80,500 (125 grants)

Correspondent: Hester Cockcroft, PO Box 2754, Bristol BS4 9DA (0117 904 9906; email: enquiries@a-y-m.org.uk; website: www.a-y-m.org.uk)

CC number: 1070994

Eligibility

Musicians aged 5 to 17 who are in financial need and have exceptional musical potential. Applicants must ideally have achieved a distinction in their last music exam or be able to show evidence of this level of ability.

Types of grants

£200 to £2,000 for instruments, music lessons, weekend music schools, music courses, orchestra fees and travel. Awards are not paid directly to students or their families.

Annual grant total

In 2014 the charity had assets of £297,000 and an income of £227,500. Awards to 125 individuals totalled £80,500.

Exclusions

No support is given for singers or students about to enter their first undergraduate year. No retrospective funding.

Applications

Application forms are available on the website to be submitted by mid-March each year. Dates of deadlines are given on the website. Applications must include three references – one each from the applicant's music teacher, headteacher and recommending organisation – as well as evidence of family income. All applications are means-tested.

The applications panel recommends two strands of award beneficiaries: Strand 1, for those awarded funding up to £500, and Strand 2, for those awarded funding of over £500. Applicants in Strand 2 will be invited to audition.

Other information

Awards for Young Musicians also provides advice, support and mentoring to young musicians.

BBC Performing Arts Fund

£190,000 (19 grants)

Correspondent: Miriam O'Keeffe, Director, 4th Floor Bridge House, MediaCityUK, Salford Quays M50 2BH (0161 836 0303; email: performingartsfund@bbc.co.uk; website: www.bbc.co.uk/performingartsfund)

CC number: 1101276

Eligibility

Individuals involved in performing arts, including drama, singing, musical composition, script writing for television, theatre, media presentation, mime and dance. The fund seeks to support people who lack means to achieve their full potential.

Eligibility differs for each scheme so it is recommended that applicants refer to the terms and conditions and other information on open schemes on the fund's website.

Types of grants

The following is taken from the 2013/14 annual report:

Our Fellowship Scheme, starting with Dance in 2012, Music in 2013, and Theatre in 2014, offers developmental residencies within professional arts organisations across the country plus networking opportunities and mentoring and advice co-ordinated by the BBC PAF team. Our 19 Fellows this year, and their host organisations, have demonstrated some remarkable achievements; both personal growth for young: professionals at the beginning of ambitious and promising careers as well as the considerable benefits which have accrued to the organisations which have hosted the Fellows.

Our Community Scheme this year awarded 58 grants to organisations across the whole of the UK. Grants awarded through this scheme allow groups to carry out training, attract new audiences, encourage new members and raise their profile in their communities. The Fund also hopes to encourage groups to take on more challenging projects through commissions and encouraging collaboration with professional theatre makers and other local organisations.

Annual grant total

In 2013/14 the fund had assets of £596,500 and an income of £401,500. Charitable expenditure totalled £419,000. Grants totalled £190,000 and were awarded in 19 fellowships.

Applications

Eligibility criteria, deadlines and online application forms are available for open schemes on the fund's website. The trustees meet a minimum of four times a year to approve grants.

Other information

The fund supports individuals, organisations and community groups, such as choirs, community orchestras, samba bands or drumming circles. The Theatre Fellowship scheme aims to support individuals through the early stages of their theatre careers, helping them to establish themselves in the professional world through bespoke placements within existing theatre organisations.

The following is taken from the 2013/2014 trustees' annual report: 'Rather than awarding grants directly to individuals themselves, we encouraged applications from theatre companies, organisations, venues and festivals from across the UK.'

The charity is mainly funded through the incidental revenue from the voting lines of BBC entertainment programmes such as Strictly Come Dancing, The Voice and Sports Personality of the year. All income is unrestricted.

The Rainer and Doreen Burchett Charitable Foundation (The Burchett Foundation)

£15,000 (10+ grants)

Correspondent: Rainer Burchett, Trustee, Watermillock House, Watermillock, Penrith CA11 0JH (01768 486191; email: burchett.foundation@ gmail.com)

CC number: 1076739

Eligibility

People in education and those involved in music and athletics.

Types of grants

Grants given according to need.

Annual grant total

In 2013/14 the foundation had an income of £24,000 and an expenditure of £29,000. In previous years the total amount awarded in grants to individuals was around £15,000 and the foundation was capable of accommodating over ten students at any given year. Specific information on the grants in 2013/14 was not available on the Charity Commission's record.

Exclusions

Unsolicited applications will not be accepted or acknowledged.

Applications

The foundation has decided to no longer accept unsolicited applications. The charity will be reaching its beneficiaries through a small number of relevant bodies, such as educational organisations.

Other information

The trustees have decided to concentrate the awards on the following three areas: education, music and athletics.

The Choir Schools' Association Bursary Trust Ltd

£261,000 (120 grants)

Correspondent: Susan Rees, CSA Administrator, 39 Grange Close, Winchester, Hampshire SO23 9RS (01962 853508; email: admin@ choirschools.org.uk; website: www. choirschools.org.uk)

CC number: 1120639

Eligibility

Pupils or proposed pupils between the ages of 7 and 13 at a member school of the Choir Schools' Association.

Ex-choristers over the age of 13 may also be supported from the money donated by the School Fees Insurance Agency.

Types of grants

Grants of up to £1,500 are available to pay the fees of choristers attending member schools of the Choir Schools' Association. Applications are means-tested.

Annual grant total

In 2013/14 the trust had assets of £1.3 million and an income of £961,000. Grants were awarded totalling £261,000 to 120 individuals.

Applications

Applicants should contact the head of the choir school concerned. Applications should normally be submitted by 15 March, 31 August and 15 December for consideration in May, October and February respectively.

The Else and Leonard Cross Charitable Trust

£20,000

Correspondent: Helen Gillingwater, Trustee, The Wall House, 2 Lichfield Road, Richmond, Surrey TW9 3JR (020 8948 4950; email: helengillingwater@ hotmail.com)

CC number: 1008038

Eligibility

Young musicians, particularly pianists, between the ages of 11 and 27 who are in need.

Types of grants

Scholarships are normally made through specialist musical institutes to help with fees, living and maintenance expenses, purchase of instruments or performance-related costs.

Annual grant total

In 2013/14 the trust had an income of £4,500 and an expenditure of £22,000. We estimate the annual total amount of grants awarded to individuals to be around £20,000.

Applications

Applications should be made through the individual's educational institution.

Other information

Occasional grants can be given to music-related festivals and events.

Miss E. B. Wrightson's Charitable Settlement

£23,500 (43 grants)

Correspondent: N. Hickman, Administrator, Swangles Farm, Cold Christmas Lane, Thundridge, Ware SG12 7SP (email: info@wrightsontrust. co.uk; website: wrightsontrust.co.uk)

CC number: 1002147

Eligibility

Young musicians, usually between the ages of 8 and 18, who are in financial hardship.

Types of grants

One-off and recurrent grants ranging from £100 to £800 are given for instruments, lessons, choir/orchestra fees, Saturday conservatoires, travel costs and similar expenses. Recurrent grants would not normally be renewed more than three times per person. The charity prefers to make payments directly to the teachers/instrument dealers/ conservatoires and so on.

Annual grant total

In 2013/14 the charity had assets of £1.1 million and an income of £27,000. A total of £23,500 was awarded in grants to 43 individuals.

Exclusions

People over the age of 21, undergraduates and postgraduates are not normally supported. Assistance cannot be given for tuition fees.

Applications

Application forms can be found on the trust's website and should be submitted in three copies. Applications should be accompanied with two letters of support from the applicant's tutor/teacher to prove the candidate's musical abilities and potential, a CV (for those over 12), reasons for applying, any other sources of funding applied to and any other relevant information about the individual's circumstances and financial situation. The trustees meet regularly to consider applications.

Other information

The charity also supports organisations, makes grants to assist young children in their personal development and runs a boat, Lady Elsa.

Elizabeth Eagle-Bott Memorial Fund

See entry on page 25

EMI Music Sound Foundation

£154,500

Correspondent: Janie Orr, Chief Executive, Beaumont House, Avonmore Road, London W14 8TS (020 7550 7898; email: enquires@emimusicsound foundation.com; website: www. emimusicsoundfoundation.com)

CC number: 1104027

Eligibility

Young people in the UK who are undertaking music education. Applicants must have been resident in the UK for a minimum of three years and: be a British citizen; a national of a member state of the European Economic Area; have been granted leave to enter or remain in the UK for an indefinite period; or hold a certificate of right of abode in the UK. Due to increased demand the foundation focuses on those in most need.

Note: Individuals resident in the UK for the purpose of education or attending a course of study are not eligible.

Types of grants

Grants, usually of up to £2,000, towards the purchase of instruments and music equipment in primary, secondary and tertiary education. Funding may also be given to music teachers to further their training and undertake courses.

The foundation also operates a bursary scheme of £5,000 for students at selected musical colleges and institutes. These are: Birmingham Conservatoire, Brighton and Bristol Institute of Modern Music, Centre for Young Musicians, English National Opera, International World Music Centre, Limerick, National Children's Orchestra, Royal Academy of Music, London, Royal Conservatoire of Scotland, Royal Welsh College of Music and Drama, Tech Music Schools (London).

Annual grant total

In 2013/14 the foundation had assets of £7.9 million and an income of £439,000. The amount of grants given to individuals totalled £154,500.

Exclusions

Grants are not provided to:

- Applicants based outside the UK and Ireland
- Community groups based outside the school
- Applications for tuition fees and living expenses (other than through the bursary scheme)
- Applications for more than £2,000

- Independent music teachers
- Cover the teaching of the national curriculum or peripatetic teaching
- Help with music therapy costs

Applications

Application forms for instrument/equipment grants can be downloaded from the foundation's website or requested from the correspondent. They should be submitted by individuals or their school via post, together with all the relevant documentation and references a month before the trustees' meeting. The meetings are held twice a year, normally in October and March (for exact dates consult the website, as they may change). Candidates are invited to approach the foundation with queries prior to application.

Applications for bursaries should be made through the individual's educational establishment.

Other information

The foundation also gives grants to a number of secondary schools to fund music education. In 2013/14 a total of £90,500 was also awarded to institutions. During the year 574 individual and school applications were approved.

The Gerald Finzi Trust

£12,300 (12 grants)

Correspondent: The Administrator of The Finzi Trust, PO Box 137, Stour Row, Shaftesbury, Dorset SP7 0WX (email: admin@geraldfinzi.org; website: www. geraldfinzi.org)

CC number: 313047

Eligibility

Musicians and music students between the ages of 18 and 80. Formal training, qualifications or previous professional experience are not prerequisite.

Types of grants

The trust offers grants for the purchase of musical instruments and scholarships for projects in the UK and overseas which 'might show a creative initiative or could involve engaging in some practical experience, education or research, perhaps giving a personal change of direction'. The projects would ideally last between three and eight weeks. If a project involves travel then the trust can meet these expenses along with the cost of accommodation, subsistence and equipment for the period involved. Scholarships awarded in recent years have covered studies in Estonia, Finland, France, Germany, India, Ireland, Italy, South America, Sweden, the UK and the USA.

Annual grant total

In 2013/14 the trust had assets of £182,000 and an income of £65,500. A

total of £36,500 was spent in charitable activities. Grants to three individuals totalled £9,000 and scholarships to nine students totalled £11,400.

Exclusions

Grants are not given for attendance of courses, to support academic degree qualifications and for fees or living expenses. Group applications are not considered and awards are not likely to be made to previous recipients of either a Finzi Scholarship or a Winston Churchill Memorial Trust Fellowship.

Applications

Application forms can be found on the trust's website or requested from the correspondent providing an sae. Applications should include an outline of the proposal and an estimate of the costs involved. The deadline for applications is the beginning of November. Candidates who are successful with their initial application are invited for an interview which is normally held in January, in London.

Other information

Grants are also made to organisations (£11,700 in 2013/14).

The Jean Ginsburg Memorial Foundation

£3,500

Correspondent: Ian Henry, Trustee, The Garden Flat, Flat 1, 3 Heath Drive, London NW3 7SY (07774435130; email: info@jeanginsburg.com)

CC number: 1104077

Eligibility

Undergraduate and postgraduate students who are training to pursue a career in medicine or people under the age of 30 training as classical musicians, especially pianists.

Types of grants

Scholarships, bursaries and grants towards general educational needs.

Annual grant total

In 2013/14 the foundation had an income of £100 and an expenditure of £7,000. We estimate that about £3,500 was distributed in grants to individuals.

Applications

Applications may be made writing to the correspondent, preferably via email.

Other information

The foundation also provides scholarships at The Royal Free Medical School, The Royal Academy of Music in London and Somerville College, Oxford University. Previously students in Cardiff, Newcastle and Sheffield universities have been supported.

The Kathleen Trust

£65,000 (33 grants)

Correspondent: Edward Perks, Administrator, Currey and Co., 21 Buckingham Gate, London SW1E 6LS (020 7828 4091)

CC number: 1064516

Eligibility

Young musicians of outstanding ability who are in need.

Types of grants

Loans in the form of musical instruments and sometimes bursaries to attend music courses, ranging between £500 and £3,000.

Annual grant total

In 2013/14 the trust had assets of £1.2 million and an income of £28,000. Grants were made to 33 individuals and totalled £65,000.

Applications

Apply in writing to the correspondent.

The Macfarlane Walker Trust

£5,500 (4 grants)

Correspondent: Sophie Walker, Administrator, 4 Shooters Hill Road, London SE3 7BD (020 8858 4701; email: sophiewalker@mac.com)

CC number: 227890

Eligibility

Music students over 18 who are in need, with a preference for those who live in Cheltenham and Gloucestershire.

Types of grants

One-off grants ranging from £500 to £2,500, for the purchase of musical instruments for music students.

Annual grant total

In 2013/14 the trust had an income of £34,500 and an expenditure of £28,500. Four individuals were awarded grants totalling £5,500

Exclusions

The trust does not provide financial assistance towards tuition fees or gap year trips. Large charities, animal charities, foreign charities or major building projects are not supported.

Applications

Apply in writing to the correspondent. Applications should be made directly by the individual, giving the reason for applying and an outline of the project with a financial forecast. According to our research, an sae and references from an academic referee must accompany the initial application.

Other information

The charity also supports various projects in the field of music, drama and fine arts. The trust assists in provision of educational facilities particularly for scientific research.

The Music Libraries Trust

£2,500

Correspondent: Edith Speller, Secretary to the Trustees, c/o Jerwood Library of the Performing Arts, Trinity Laban Conservatoire of Music and Dance, King Charles Court, Old Royal Naval College, Greenwich, London SE10 9JF (020 8305 4422; email: secretary@ musiclibrariestrust.org; website: www. musiclibrariestrust.org)

CC number: 284334

Eligibility

Music librarians in the UK and Ireland involved in education or training and people carrying out research into music librarianship, music bibliography, musicology and related disciplines.

Types of grants

The trust's website states:

> The trust has a regular programme of allocating grants in support of projects, research and course attendance with a preference for supporting those who have been unable to receive financial support from elsewhere.

> Awards of between £100 and £5,000 have been given for initial funding, with second grants being considered in exceptional cases. Funding is normally only awarded to projects, research and course attendance directly related to music libraries, music librarianship and/or music bibliography.

Examples of previous awards and suggested potential projects can be found on the trust's website.

Annual grant total

In 2013/14 the trust had an income of £5,500 and an expenditure of £5,300. We estimate that the amount of grants given to individuals totalled around £2,500.

Exclusions

The trust will not provide funding for general undergraduate and postgraduate studies.

Applications

To apply for research support you should write to the correspondent at any time to be considered in the following trustees' meeting. The meetings take place three times a year. Applications should provide full details of the project, state other sources of funding considered and give a full analysis of anticipated expenses. References may also be required. The trust welcomes informal discussions by email.

Further details about bursaries may be requested from Megan Dyson, Bursaries Administrator (tel: 0113 222 3400 ext. 3458; email: bursaries@ musiclibrariestrust.org).

Other information

Support is also given to organisations. In addition to regular funding, the trust also offers bursaries and a memorial prize.

Bursaries

Bursaries of £200–£300 are available to 'students and library staff to attend study weekends and courses organised by International Association of Music Libraries (UK & Ireland)' with priority being given to those 'who would otherwise be unable to attend and who have no other sources of funding'. Applicants must be paid-up personal or institutional members of the association.

E.T. Bryant Memorial Prize

The award (£250 in 2014) is made in conjunction with International Association of Music Libraries (UK and Ireland) 'to a student of Library and Information Science or to a librarian in the first five years of the profession for a significant contribution to the literature of music librarianship'.

The Ouseley Trust

£58,000 (16 grants)

Correspondent: Martin Williams, Clerk to the Trustees, PO Box 281, Stamford, Lincolnshire PE9 9BU (01780 752266; email: ouseleytrust@btinternet.com; website: www.ouseleytrust.org.uk)

CC number: 527519

Eligibility

Children, generally between the ages of 9 and 16, who are (or are about to become) choristers in recognised choral foundations in the Church of England, Church of Ireland or Church in Wales.

Types of grants

Grants are given towards the choir school fees for up to two years. They usually range from £1,000 to £5,000. In special circumstances awards may also be given for organ tuition.

Annual grant total

In 2013 the trust had assets of £4.4 million, an income of £259,000 and made grants totalling £88,000. Awards for fees totalled £58,000 given to 16 students.

A further £31,000 was given from specific endowments to be distributed in scholarships and bursaries.

At the time of writing (July 2015) the 2013 accounts were the latest available.

Exclusions

Help is not available for choristers at Brecon, Ely, Norwich, Rochester and St Alban's cathedrals where the trust has donated funds to be used for scholarships. Awards are not made for music lessons or for a period exceeding two years.

Applications via fax or email are not accepted.

Applications

Application forms and guidelines can be requested from the correspondent by the school, church, choir or choral foundation concerned, not by choristers or their parents. A statement of financial resources by the child's parents or guardian will be required as well as references. Applications are considered at the biannual meetings in March and October and should be submitted by 28 February or 30 June, respectively.

The trust stresses that applicants are strongly advised to obtain and study the guidelines for applications.

Other information

The trust's annual report for 2013 states:

> At present, the trustees' policy is to concentrate their resources on making grants for: courses of instruction; endowment grants; choir school fees; and the purchase of music. In addition, careful consideration is given to other applications that involve unique or imaginative ways of fulfilling the trust's object.

The Royal College of Organists

£12,000

Correspondent: Philip Meaden, 4 Sherbourne Drive, Leeds LS6 4QX (01132743313; email: admin@rco.org.uk; website: www.rco.org.uk)

CC number: 312847

Eligibility

People studying organ playing or choral directing and similar or those engaged in research in these areas. Most awards are given to members or student members of the Royal College of Organists.

Types of grants

The charity offers various scholarships and awards. One-off and recurrent grants range from £100 to £1,500 and can be awarded for travel costs, purchase of instruments/equipment, music books, additional lessons or courses, tuition fees and other purposes. For specific details of each scholarship, see the 'awards fact sheet', which can be found on the charity's website.

Annual grant total

In 2013/14 the charity had assets of £2.3 million, an income of £747,000 and a total charitable expenditure of £482,000. Scholarships and prizes totalled £12,000.

Applications

Application forms can be downloaded from the charity's website and should be submitted by April (or by February for two specific courses) together with any required documentation, such as a letter of support or an outline of the travel plans.

The Rushworth Trust

£5,000

Correspondent: The Grants Team, Liverpool Charity and Voluntary Services, 151 Dale Street, Liverpool L2 2AH (0151 227 5177; email: grants@lcvs.org.uk)

CC number: 1076702

Eligibility

Music students living within a 60-mile radius of Liverpool Town Hall. Grants can be awarded to a wide range of musicians, including composers, young conductors, young performers, student singers and instrumentalists, choirs and choir singers and so forth.

Types of grants

One-off grants of around £300 to help with the cost of the study of music and to develop taste and appreciation of music. Financial assistance is available for music publishing, promotion, training, equipment/instruments, music tours and concerts. Our research suggests that grants can only be made if the individual is not eligible for grants from any other source and awards are not usually repeated.

Annual grant total

In 2013/14 the trust had an income of £4,000 and an expenditure of £5,500. We estimate the annual total amount of grants awarded to be around £5,000.

Exclusions

Grants are not available for course fees and maintenance.

Applications

Application forms can be requested from the correspondent and should be submitted in advance of the trustee meetings which are normally held in March, June, September and December.

Other information

The trust has been formed by the merging of The William Rushworth Trust, The Thew Bequest and The A K Holland Memorial Award.

The Stringwise Trust

£900

Correspondent: Michael Max, Trustee, Lion House, Red Lion Street, London WC1R 4GB (020 8455 9308)

CC number: 1048917

Eligibility

People who play stringed instruments, particularly children and aspiring teachers.

Types of grants

Bursaries and scholarships to enable attendance at any training courses or experiential events.

Annual grant total

In 2014 the trust had an income of £5,000, which is the highest in the past five years and a total expenditure of over £900, which is the lowest in the past five years. We estimate that grants totalled around £900.

Applications

Applications may be made in writing to the correspondent.

The Wessex Young Musicians Trust

£7,500

Correspondent: Sandrey Date, Trustee, 7 Southbourne Coast Road, Bournemouth BH6 4BE (01202 423429; email: sandreydate@yahoo.co.uk)

CC number: 1100905

Eligibility

Young musicians who live in Dorset and Hampshire, particularly, but not exclusively, the participants and supporters of the Centre for Wessex Young Musicians.

Types of grants

Grants towards equipment and facilities, also loans, scholarships, bursaries and prizes, not usually provided by the statutory authorities.

Annual grant total

In 2013/14 the trust had an income of £8,000 and a total expenditure of £8,000. We estimate that around £7,500 was awarded in grants to individuals.

Applications

Apply in writing to the correspondent.

History

The Catherine Mackichan Trust

£2,600

Correspondent: David Mackichan, Treasurer, 2 Hutton Avenue, Houston PA6 7JS (email: david.mackichan@sky.com; website: www.mackichantrust.co.uk)

OSCR number: SC020459

Eligibility

Grants are available to students of history, particularly (but not exclusively) Celtic and/or West Highland history or medieval history. People who are researching various aspects of Scottish history, including archaeology, genealogy and language studies are equally eligible.

The trust's website also states: 'Applicants will receive particular consideration if they demonstrate that they are unable to obtain funding via normal channels, or if their work is an extension of a topic previously funded through one of these channels.'

Types of grants

Grants range from £200 to £500 but in exceptional circumstances greater amounts can be awarded. Support can be given for specific costs of research. For example, this might include the costs of travel for site visits, excavations, access to specialist services such as radiocarbon dating, and documentation or publication.

Assistance is available to postgraduate students, individuals without formal attachment to any institute of education, local history societies, amateur historians or school groups.

Annual grant total

In 2013/14 the trust had an income of £2,100 and an expenditure of £2,800. We have estimated that around £2,600 was distributed in grants to individuals.

Exclusions

Grants are given to people whose education or research should be funded by statutory sources. Support is not provided for university undergraduate or postgraduate fees or living expenses whilst studying for a degree.

Applications

Application forms can be obtained by contacting the correspondent via email. They should be submitted between 1 January and 16 April and are usually considered before the end of June. The trust's website mentions that 'it is desirable, but not essential, that the names and addresses of two referees accompany each application'.

Other information

Grants are also given to schools, groups and local history societies for local history and archaeological purposes.

The Stuart Rossiter Trust Fund

£8,100

Correspondent: Rex Dixon, Trustee, 39 Braybank, Bray, Maidenhead, Berkshire SL6 2BH (01628 628628; email: rexdixon@btinternet.com; website: www.rossitertrust.com)

CC number: 292076

Eligibility

Anyone of any nationality undertaking original research into postal history with a view to publication. Applicants can be students seeking a higher degree at university, amateurs or professionals, as long as the research is original, approved, likely to lead to publication for the benefit of a wider public, and adds to the stock of publicly available material. English language is preferred in published or electronic form to promote accessibility.

Types of grants

Grants towards translations, cost of hire of researchers, publication costs and costs of research. Part or the entire grant may be recovered from sales of the publication.

Annual grant total

In 2014 the charity had assets of £513,500 and an income of £25,500. Grants for research and publications totalled £8,100.

Exclusions

The charity only gives grants for research into postal history with a view to publication.

Applications

Application forms are available from the correspondent.

Other information

Grants are also made to organisations.

Languages

John Speak Foundation Foreign Languages Scholarships Trust Fund (John Speak Trust)

£11,500

Correspondent: Sandy Needham, Bradford Chamber, Devere House, Vicar Lane, Bradford BD1 5AH (01274 230090; email: john.speak@wnychamber.co.uk; website: www.johnspeaktrust.co.uk)

CC number: 529115

Eligibility

British-born citizens over the age of 18 who are studying at a recognised college or university, wish to advance their abilities in foreign language while residing overseas and who, preferably, intend to follow a career in the UK export trade.

A good basic knowledge (at least GCSE or equivalent) of the foreign language is essential. While abroad, candidates will be required to live within the local community rather than with English speakers, volunteer for a business firm in the country or, alternatively, attend a school/university/training course and provide short monthly reports in both English and the foreign language to the charity.

Types of grants

Grant recipients will receive monthly payments for the period of their stay (normally between six and ten months). Usually, the support is given to cover living expenses and sometimes towards travel costs. Awards are aimed at people who are intending to follow a career connected with the export trade of the UK, so applicants should usually be (or should stand a reasonable chance of becoming) a representative who will travel abroad to secure business for the UK. Grants can range from £1,500 to £2,500.

Annual grant total

In 2013/14 the charity had an income of £13,000 and an expenditure of £12,000. We estimate that £11,500 was awarded in grants.

Applications

Applications can be made online on a form available on the charity's website. Potential applicants are invited for an interview with the trustees and will be expected to read, translate and converse in their chosen language. References from a current/prospective employer or the principal/head of languages of the applicant's school may be required.

The Norwich Jubilee Esperanto Foundation (NOJEF)

£6,700

Correspondent: Clare Hunter, Correspondent, c/o Esperanto-Asocio de Britio, Esperanto House, Station Road, Barlaston, Stoke-on-Trent ST12 9DE (email: clare.hunter@esperanto.org.uk; website: www.nojef.org)

CC number: 313190

Eligibility

People under the age of 25 who either are British or live in the UK and can demonstrate efficiency in the study of Esperanto. Our research shows that preference among non-Britons is normally given to those whose native language is not English, since contact with such is more useful to British students of Esperanto.

Research funding is available for applicants who are British or at British institution and is only given upon condition that a copy of research will be available (in English or Esperanto) for the Butler Library. Larger grants will be given for research which is in the public domain, for proposals at a higher academic level and depending on the extent of focus on Esperanto in the proposal.

Types of grants

The foundation can provide the following financial assistance:

- One-off grants to cover travel, accommodation, entrance fee and related costs for British students attending approved Esperanto events
- Support towards research with a maximum grant of £1,000 for a PhD thesis. Non-Esperantists are welcome to request funding

Annual grant total

In 2014/15 the foundation had an income of £16,300 and an expenditure of £7,000. We estimate that the annual total amount of grants awarded was about £6,700.

Exclusions

Financial support cannot be made retrospectively.

Applications

Applications for travel grants should be made by sending a letter in Esperanto to the Secretary, Tim Owen (email: secretary@nojef.org), giving some details of the travel plans and likely costs. New applicants are also asked to introduce themselves and give details of a referee who could confirm the applicants' efforts in learning Esperanto and provide a character reference.

Applications for research funding should be made by emailing the secretary at tim.owen@nojef.org with the research proposal including any anticipated costs.

Other information

All grants are given on the condition that a written report in Esperanto will be provided following the event. Further grants for different events will only be considered if the reports are delivered within reasonable time and at respectable length.

Natural sciences

Earth sciences

The Institute of Materials, Minerals and Mining (IOM3)

£30,000

Correspondent: Julija Bugajeva, Head of Finance, The Institute of Minerals and Mining, 297 Euston Road, London NW1 3AQ (020 7451 7300; fax: 020 7839 1702; email: directorate@iom3.org; website: www.iom3.org)

CC number: 269275

Eligibility

People studying minerals, mining and metallurgy disciplines. Preference is given to current and former members of the institution and their dependants. Membership is a requirement for some grants and some awards are restricted to people under the age of 35. Refer to the charity's website for details on specific awards.

Types of grants

The institute offers support through one-off and recurrent grants, bursaries, scholarships and other awards. Travel grants are available to members (usually up to the age of 35) to travel long distances to conferences (usually abroad), preferably to present papers. Scholarships and bursaries are awarded in the range of £500 to £14,400.

Annual grant total

In 2014 the institute had assets of £21.7 million, an income of £19 million and spent over £6 million in charitable activities. Grants, scholarships, awards and prizes from the restricted funds totalled £30,000.

Applications

Applications can be made online on the institute's website. Separate forms can also be downloaded or requested from the correspondent.

Note: Different grants and awards may have different deadlines, eligibility requirements and correspondents. Candidates are advised to see the website for specific details.

Other information

The institute's website has detailed information on all grants available as well as the assistance from other bodies. There are a variety of prizes and awards offered.

The institute also runs the School Affiliate Scheme to provide help, advice and teaching materials to schools and to engage children in the science subjects.

Physics

The Ogden Trust

See entry on page 53

Professional and applied sciences

Air Pilots Trust

£63,000

Correspondent: Paul Tacon, Trustee, Cobham House, 9 Warwick Court, Gray's Inn, London WC1R 5DJ (020 7404 4032; email: office@airpilots.org; website: www.airpilots.org/about-the-company/trusts/apt)

CC number: 313606

Eligibility

British or Irish citizens who are or intend to be engaged professionally as air pilots or navigators in commercial aviation.

Types of grants

Grants and scholarships to assist education and training in aviation.

Annual grant total

In 2013/14 the trust had assets of £586,000 and an income of £93,000. Awards were made totalling £63,000, distributed as follows:

Scholarships	£34,500
Flying bursaries	£10,200
Academic bursaries	£9,000
Donations	£6,900
P B Saul Prize (restricted)	£2,000
Trophies and awards	£300
J. Landymore award (restricted)	£150

Applications

According to the website, requests should be made to the correspondent. Application forms for bursaries and scholarships awarded by The Honourable Company of Air Pilots are accessible online.

Other information

Awards are made to both organisations and individuals. The trust also promotes the study and research of aviation and flight, runs lectures and disseminates information relating to aviation.

The trust is administered by The Honourable Company of Air Pilots which also manages Air Safety Trust and

The Benevolent Fund of Air Pilots (see a separate entry on page 124).

Business and finance

Company of Actuaries Charitable Trust Fund

£38,500 (44 grants)

Correspondent: Patrick O'Keeffe, Administrator, Broomyhurst, Shobley, Ringwood, Hampshire BH24 3HT (01425 472810; email: almoner.cact@ btinternet.com)

CC number: 280702

Eligibility

Further and higher education students progressing towards actuarial qualifications.

Types of grants

One-off grants to help students with course/exam fees so that they can complete their training for the profession.

Annual grant total

In 2013/14 the fund had assets of £363,500, an income of £216,000 and made grants totalling £38,500. The fund made 44 bursaries of £750 each totalling £33,000, prizes for university students totalled £3,000 and prizes for the Institute and Faculty of Actuaries students totalled £3,000.

Applications

Application forms are available from the correspondent.

Other information

The fund also gives grants to organisations.

Gustav Adolph and Ernest Koettgen Memorial Fund

£12,400

Correspondent: Fiona MacGillivray, Administrator, Family Action, 501–505 Kingsland Road, London E8 4AU (020 7254 6251; email: grants. enquiry@family-action.org.uk; website: www.family-action.org.uk)

CC number: 313291

Eligibility

Undergraduate students (including mature students) of British nationality whose means are insufficient to afford higher education or tuition for a higher commercial career. Preference is given to employees of John Batt and Company (London) Ltd or members of their families.

Types of grants

One-off grants from £200 to £500 are available towards the cost of books, fees, living expenses and childcare. According to our research, applicants are only considered if they are in their final year of a course and if they have managed to raise almost the whole amount needed or if they encounter unexpected difficulty, as these grants are only intended to be supplementary.

Annual grant total

In 2013/14 the fund had an income of £8,600 and a total expenditure of £12,600. We have estimated that the annual total amount of grants awarded was around £12,400.

Exclusions

Our research suggests that postgraduate studies are not supported.

Applications

Application forms can be obtained from the correspondent. Applications can be submitted directly by the individual but will need to be supported by an academic reference.

Other information

The fund's trustees are Family Action.

The AIA Education and Benevolent Trust

£3,500

Correspondent: Mr T. Pinkney, Staithes 3, The Watermark, Metro Riverside, Tyne and Wear NE11 9SN (0191 493 0272; fax: 0191 493 0278; email: trust. fund@aiaworldwide.com; website: www. aiaworldwide.com)

CC number: 1118333

Eligibility

Those wishing to undergo training and education in accountancy.

Types of grants

Grants for training and education in accountancy.

Annual grant total

In 2014 the trust had an income of £3,500 and a total expenditure of £7,000. We estimate that educational grants totalled around £3,500. Funding is also awarded to fellows and associates of the institute, and their close dependants, for social welfare purposes.

Applications

Apply in writing to the correspondent using the form available from the trust's website. Applications are received on an ongoing basis.

Anderson Barrowcliff Bursary

£4,500

Correspondent: Hugh McGouran, Administrator, Wallace House, Falcon Court, Preston Farm Industrial Estate, Stockton-on-Tees TS18 3TX (01642 260860; email: info@ teesvalleyfoundation.org; website: www. teesvalleyfoundation.org)

CC number: 1111222

Eligibility

Students from Tees Valley on a full-time undergraduate degree in accountancy, maths or business studies at a UK university. Decisions are made based on A-level results, UCAS personal statement and financial circumstances.

Types of grants

A bursary of £4,500 over three years.

Annual grant total

Payments of around £500 per term over three years.

Applications

Application forms are available on the Tees Valley Community Foundation website, when the application round opens.

Other information

This fund is administrated by the Tees Valley Community Foundation.

The successful applicant will have to take part in a six- to eight-week placement with Anderson Barrowcliff during the summer vacation.

The Institute of Actuaries Research and Education Fund

£1,600

Correspondent: David Burch, Correspondent, Institute of Actuaries, Staple Inn Hall, 1–3 Staple Inn, London WC1V 7QJ (020 7632 2194; email: david. burch@actuaries.org.uk; website: www. actuaries.org.uk)

CC number: 274717

Eligibility

Actuarial students at any educational establishment approved by the actuarial profession.

Types of grants

Awards, scholarships and grants for professional training and research in actuarial science.

Annual grant total

In 2014/15 the fund had an income of £5,400 and a total expenditure of £1,800.

We estimate that grants totalled around £1,600.

Applications

Applications may be made in writing to the correspondent.

Construction

Alan Baxter Foundation (ABF)

£5,700

Correspondent: Julia Gavin, Correspondent, c/o Alan Baxter and Associates LLP, Cowcross Court, 70–77 Cowcross Street, London EC1M 6EL (020 7250 1555; email: aba@alanbaxter.co.uk)

CC number: 1107996

Eligibility

People involved in the study or research of the built and natural environment.

Types of grants

Grants are available according to need for general educational costs, research and projects.

Annual grant total

In 2013/14 the foundation had an income of £9,800 and a total expenditure of £22,000. Previously about 26% of the overall expenditure has been given in grants to students. We use this figure to estimate that about £5,700 was given in grants to individuals.

Applications

Applications may be made in writing to the correspondent.

Other information

Grants are also made to various organisations supporting education and research relating to the built and natural environment. The foundation also organises educational activities to publicise research and other information on the topic.

Scottish Building Federation Edinburgh and District Charitable Trust

£9,000

Correspondent: Fiona Watson, Charity Accounting Services, Scott-Moncrieff (Secretaries and Treasurers), Exchange Place 3, Semple Street, Edinburgh EH3 8BL (0131 473 3500; email: fiona.watson@scott-moncrieff.com; website: www.scott-moncrieff.com/services/charities/charitable-trusts)

OSCR number: SCO29604

Eligibility

Students studying skills relating to the building industry at the following universities and colleges: Heriot-Watt University; Napier University; West Lothian College; Edinburgh College.

Types of grants

Scholarships for study, research and travel associated with the building industry and grants for course expenses such as books, equipment and travel.

Annual grant total

In 2014 the trust had an income of £51,500 and a total expenditure of £57,000. Grants are made to individuals for both social welfare and educational purposes but we were unable to determine a precise figure for awards made during the year. The trust is administered by Scott-Moncrieff, whose website provides the following information: 'Up to £9,000 per annum is available for scholarships to deserving students.'

Applications

Applications can be made by completing the form, which is available to download from the Scott-Moncrieff website, and forwarding it to the appropriate university or college department. Representatives of the trust liaise with universities and colleges to arrange applications and interviews and to decide which applications should be funded.

Education

The Higher Education Academy

Correspondent: Sean Mackney, Senior Deputy Chief Executive, Innovation Way, York Science Park, York YO10 5BR (01904 717500; fax: 01904 717505; email: enquiries@heacademy.ac.uk; website: www.heacademy.ac.uk)

Eligibility

Anyone who is responsible for the student learning experience working in higher education institutions in the UK that subscribe to the Higher Education Academy, and students of those institutions.

Types of grants

Previously support has been provided: towards teaching development projects that aim to encourage innovation in learning and teaching; in travel awards to staff and students to enable them to engage in events and meetings; and to further good practice in learning, teaching and assessment within higher education.

Annual grant total

Currently, grants are not provided.

Applications

Guidelines, terms and conditions and FAQs for the support will be available on the website, should the funding resume.

Other information

The academy's website states that:

> We work with institutions across the world to improve the student learning experience, particularly within our key themes: employability, retention and attainment, and assessment and feedback. When research funding opportunities are available we will post the details here.

We are maintaining the entry, as the organisation has noted that new plans are being developed and should funding become available grant-making can resume and will be based in the lines of: curriculum design and innovative pedagogies; and transitions for both students and higher education staff.

The organisation is an independent organisation funded by the four UK higher education funding bodies, by subscriptions and grants.

The Hockerill Educational Foundation

£69,000 (126 grants)

Correspondent: Derek Humphrey, Secretary, 3 The Swallows, Harlow, Essex CM17 0AR (01279 420855; fax: 05603 140931; email: info@hockerillfoundation.org.uk; website: www.hockerillfoundation.org.uk)

CC number: 311018

Eligibility

The foundation awards grants widely for causes related to religious education, which are usually given under the following categories:

- Students and teaching assistants taking teaching qualifications, or first degrees leading to teaching
- Teachers, teaching assistants and others in an educational capacity seeking professional development through full-time or part-time courses
- Those undertaking research related to the practice of Religious Education in schools or further education
- Students taking other first degree courses, or courses in further education
- Others involved in teaching and leading in voluntary, non-statutory education, including those concerned with adult and Christian education

Grants are also made for gap year projects with an educational focus to those whose home or place of study is in the Dioceses of Chelmsford and St Albans.

Types of grants

Grants of £500 to £1,000 are available to students for help with fees, books, living expenses and travel. Priority is given to those training to be teachers, with a preference to those teaching religious education, but if funds are available other students with financial difficulties will be funded.

Annual grant total

In 2013/14 the foundation had assets of £6.6 million and an income of £214,000. Grants totalling £69,000 were made to 126 individuals consisting of:

- 37 training for primary education
- 64 for secondary education
- 24 for higher or degrees or diplomas in education
- 1 gap year student

Exclusions

No grants are given: to schoolchildren; to those studying for Christian ministry or mission (unless continuing in teaching, and for visits, study or conferences abroad); for gap year activities; for courses in counselling, therapy or social work; or for courses leading specifically to non-teaching careers such as medicine, law or accountancy. Grants are no longer made to overseas students.

Applications

Application forms are available from the foundation's website and should be returned by 31 March.

The foundation's website states: 'If you have not finalised your course until later in the summer you can still apply in April and May, and these applications will be considered in June.'

Other information

The charity states that the majority of annual funding is committed to long-term projects or activities in education, but funding is also given to other projects, namely:

- Training and support for the Church of England's educational work, particularly in the dioceses of Chelmsford and St Albans
- Research, development and support grants to organisations in the field of Religious Education

The charity also supports conferences for new RE teachers and a 'Prize for Innovation in the Teaching of RE'.

Engineering
The Douglas Bomford Trust

£20,500 (18+ grants)

Correspondent: Paul Miller, Secretary, 46 Howard Close, Haynes, Bedford MK45 3QH (01234 381342; fax: 01234 751319; email: enquiries@dbt.org.uk; website: www.dbt.org.uk)

CC number: 1121785

Eligibility

People involved in education, research and practice of agricultural engineering and mechanisation who are aiming to become professional engineers or scientists and intend to work applying their expertise to agricultural and land-related problems. Priority is given to individuals who work in the areas of particular national or technical importance and those who can receive part of the costs from other sources. Some connection with the UK is required, either through nationality, residency, or place of learning/registration.

Types of grants

The trust can offer: travel scholarships for educational tours overseas, conferences and for presenting papers at international conferences; scholarships to undergraduate students; support towards postgraduate study and research; discretionary awards in cases of hardship; and various prizes to students showing high academic achievements or to the authors of papers published in allied journals.

Annual grant total

In 2013/14 the trust had assets of £4 million, an income of £130,000 and a total charitable expenditure of £117,000. The amount of grants given to individuals totalled £20,500. The amount given can be broken down as follows:

Studentships	8	£7,000
Discretionary awards	Not specified	£6,500
Travel grants	10	£6,000
Other awards	Not specified	£1,000

Applications

There are different grant schemes for travel awards, undergraduate students, postgraduate research and other awards. Application details for each of them can be found on the trust's website.

Other information

The trust also awards grants to organisations (in 2013/14 a total of £96,500 which included £38,000 to Cranfield University and £1,500 to Riseholme College).

The Coachmakers and Coach Harness Makers Charitable Trust 1977

£7,500 (7 grants)

Correspondent: Commander Mark Leuning, Administrator, Royal Navy, The Old Barn, Church Lane, Glentham, Market Rasen, Lincolnshire LN8 2EL (07505 089841; email: clerk@coachmakers.co.uk; website: www.coachmakers.co.uk)

CC number: 286521

Eligibility

People studying/working in the aerospace, automotive and coach making or associated industries.

Types of grants

Grants are available to individuals in technical education and training, including apprenticeships. Awards are usually given towards general educational needs, research, study/travel overseas and maintenance expenses.

Bursaries are given for individuals studying motor vehicle design at The Royal College of Art and aerospace sciences at Cranfield University.

There is also a 'flying scholarship for an individual who, in competition, has shown aptitude and determination to become a pilot' and an annual 'Award to Industry' made 'to promote excellence in design, technical development and commercial significance'.

Annual grant total

In 2013/14 the trust had assets of £1.4 million and an income of £132,500. A total of £7,500 was awarded in grants to seven individuals in the motor, aircraft and coach making industries.

Exclusions

The trust's website states that 'awards are as substantial as possible, but bursaries are allocated on an annual basis and, because funds cannot always be guaranteed, the Livery cannot accept commitments to individuals for long-term educational courses'.

Applications

Apply in writing to the correspondent. Applications should normally be submitted in December and October for consideration in January and November respectively.

The Worshipful Company of Engineers Charitable Trust Fund

£25,000

Correspondent: Anthony Willenbruch, Clerk, Wax Chandlers' Hall, 6 Gresham Street, London EC2V 7AD (020 7726 4830; fax: 020 7726 4820; email: clerk@engineerscompany.org.uk; website: www.engineerstrust.org.uk)

CC number: 289819

Eligibility

Qualified engineers and those training to be chartered engineers, incorporated engineers and engineering technicians. Eligibility criteria differs depending on the award being applied for. See the website for more information.

Types of grants

The charity supports a number of award schemes to encourage excellence in engineering. Grants are also made to support engineers who are facing hardship, particularly whilst they are in education.

Annual grant total

In 2014 the charity had assets of £1.5 million and an income of £116,000. The annual report for the year stated: 'Monetary prizes to the value of £21,900 (2013 £16,000) were made to 7 (2013) individuals and grants to a total value of £632,700 (2013 £11,735) were made to individuals and organisations.' Unlike those for 2013, these accounts did not include a breakdown of grants awarded and so we were unable to determine an exact figure for educational grants to individuals. In previous years, these grants have accounted for the majority of grants made to individuals. We estimate that educational grants during the year totalled around £21,000.

Applications

Specific application details for different awards can be found on the charity's website. Some schemes require candidates to be nominated by their educational institution.

Other information

The charity supports welfare needs, engineering research and can award grants to organisations in the City of London that further the interest of the history, traditions and customs of the city.

The Benevolent Fund of the Institution of Civil Engineers

£9,000 (9 grants)

Correspondent: Lindsay Howell, Caseworker, 5 Mill Hill Close, Haywards Heath, West Sussex RH16 1NY (01444 417979 or 0800 587 3428 (free 24 hour helpline); email: info@icebenfund.com; website: www.icebenfund.com)

CC number: 1126595

Eligibility

Student members of Institution of Civil Engineers (ICE), who have disabilities or are otherwise disadvantaged and undertaking an ICE accredited course at a UK university or further education establishment. You must have been a member for at least a year to be eligible.

According to the guidelines for applicants, the following are more likely to be favoured:

- students with dependants, especially lone parents
- students aged 25 and over with extra financial commitments
- students who were previously in Local Authority Care
- students estranged from their parents
- students repeating a year due to reasons beyond their control
- second, third, and final year students who have lost their initial source of funding

Types of grants

Educational grants of up to £1,000 per term are made towards living costs, travel, equipment or course materials but not normally the course or examination fees.

Annual grant total

In 2014 the charity had assets of £15.3 million and an income of £1.2 million. Grants were made to a total of 168 individuals (148 in the UK and 20 overseas) totalling £516,000, including support for nine students. There was no breakdown of support in the accounts but the majority of awards are made for social welfare purposes. We have estimated that the amount awarded to individuals for educational purposes was around £9,000.

Exclusions

Grants are not made for students who:

- Have not started their university course or have yet to be offered a university place
- Have mismanaged their finances and simply run out of money
- Are studying for a Civil Engineering degree not accredited by ICE
- Are undertaking a postgraduate course

- Are in their first year of study (unless there are exceptional circumstances)

Funding may not be used to clear old debts, indulge in social activities, to purchase non-essential equipment and materials or cover tuition fees.

Applications

Application forms are available from the website or the correspondent. They can be submitted at any time during the academic year and *must* be accompanied supporting documents, including a reference or letter of support from the Head of Department, or their nominee.

Other information

The fund owns properties in West Sussex and has nomination rights to the Hanover Housing Association which it uses to help current and former members and their families who are facing difficult circumstances and need somewhere to live.

It also runs a 24-hour helpline (0800 587 3428) which offers support and advice on a wide range of issues, including counselling, stress management, relationship problems, financial troubles, parenting, illness and well-being and work life. Face-to-face support can also be arranged. There is the 'Back to Work' scheme operating providing advice and coaching for people who have been out of work for at least three months.

The Institution of Engineering and Technology (IET)

£403,000

Correspondent: Andrew Wilson, Correspondent, The Institution of Engineering and Technology, 2 Savoy Place, London WC2R 0BL (020 7344 5415; email: governance@theiet.org; website: www.theiet.org)

CC number: 211014, SC038698

Eligibility

The following list of regulations applies as a general rule to all scholarships and prizes (however, candidates should refer to the website to ensure they fit the specific criteria of different awards):

- Students must be studying or about to study (in the next academic session) on an IET-accredited degree course at a UK university (for a list of accredited programmes see the website)
- Each candidate should be supported by the head of the educational or training establishment, the course tutor, the university head of department or by a chartered member of the IET (for some awards it is necessary to become a member)

- A candidate who is shortlisted for an award may be required to attend an interview at the IET
- The scholarship will be paid in instalments, as determined by the IET (it will be withdrawn and any unpaid instalments withheld if the holder leaves the course)
- Successful candidates must not hold any other IET scholarship or grant at the same time
- Applicants should demonstrate passion to engineering and/or high academic achievements

Types of grants

The IET offers a range of scholarships, prizes and travel awards ranging up to £10,000. These include undergraduate and postgraduate scholarships, travel grants to members of the IET (for study tour, work in the industry, to attend a conference), apprenticeship and technician awards and various prizes for achievement and innovation. International scholarships for study in India and America and various scholarships at participating universities are also available.

The Diamond Jubilee Scholarship Fund also offers £1,000 for each year of the degree to students applying for IET accredited courses in Computing, Electrical, Electronic and Manufacturing Engineering. During 2014, 70 students received the award.

Further information about the type of grants available can be found on the website.

Annual grant total

In 2014 the charity had assets of almost £146 million and an income of £51.5 million. The amount of grants given to individuals totalled around £403,000.

Exclusions

There may be certain conditions attached to separate awards, for example, undergraduate grants are not intended to cover placement years and IET postgraduate scholarships are not currently given for MSc degrees (but awards from specific funds offer support). Applicants are advised to read the guidelines for specific awards carefully.

Applications

Further details and application forms are available from the institution's website. Generally applications should be made on an online system. The deadlines vary for different awards.

Other information

The institution also administers a number of restricted funds to assist training and education in engineering and electrical engineering.

The institution's website contains extensive information on all awards available.

The Benevolent Fund of the Institution of Mechanical Engineers (IMechE) – known as Support Network

£55,500

Correspondent: Maureen Hayes, Casework and Support Officer, 1–3 Birdcage Walk, Westminster, London SW1H 9JJ (020 7304 6816; fax: 020 7973 1262; email: info@support network.org.uk; website: www.support network.org.uk)

CC number: 209465

Eligibility

Financially disadvantaged students or students who have disabilities or long-term health conditions, who are IMechE members and are studying mechanical engineering on an IMechE accredited undergraduate course at a UK university.

Preference is given to the following: students on IMechE accredited courses; students who have disabilities; final year students; students with dependants, especially those with care responsibilities; students with children under the age of 18, especially single parents; students aged 25 and over with extra financial commitments; local authority care-leavers; students who are estranged from their parents; students who have significant debts before starting their university course; students who are repeating a year of study due to circumstances outside their control; students who have no access to other sources of funding.

Types of grants

One-off grants of up to around £1,000 (up to £1,500 for final year students) for financially disadvantaged students for living costs, travel and accommodation, equipment costs and course materials, such as software and books.

Annual grant total

In 2014 the charity had assets of £21.7 million and an income of £1.2 million. All grants to individuals were listed as relief of poverty and totalled £278,500. Although educational/ training grants are not separately listed, this may be because most of the criteria for educational/training grants appear to include a financial qualification as well. We estimate that grants for educational purposes totalled around £55,500.

Exclusions

No grants are made for people who are studying outside the UK; those who have not been offered a university place or started their studies; those who have mismanaged their finances and run out of money.

Applications

The charity's website notes: 'Please check with your university's student services department to make sure you are receiving all the statutory assistance available and/or any help from university funds. After this, contact us to confirm eligibility and we will send you an application form.'

Other information

The charity's website states that students studying at levels other than undergraduate and/or students who are the dependants of IMechE members can apply for assistance from its general funds via info@supportnetwork.org.uk.

Support Network offers a range of support and advice services which also includes grants for social welfare purposes, sheltered housing and residential care, and help with job seeking.

Free expert advice is available through a telephone helpline run by the charity's partner organisation, Advice Express. For advice on 'all sorts of everyday problems and queries' call 01275 376029 (Monday–Friday 8am–8pm and 9am–noon on weekends), mentioning that you are calling from the IMechE. There are also financial and legal advice helplines, more details of which are available from the website.

The ISTRUCTE (Institution of Structural Engineers) Educational Trust

£3,600 (7 grants)

Correspondent: Darren Byrne, Trustee, 47–58 Bastwick Street, London EC1V 3PS (020 7201 9138; email: edtrust@istructe.org; website: www. istructe.org/about-us/funds-and-donations/educational-trust)

CC number: 1001625

Eligibility

Structural engineers, students and pupils considering career in the field.

Types of grants

The trust awards bursaries, scholarships, travel grants, prizes and so on in order to encourage young people to enter structural engineering career. The following are available:

Competitions and Travel Grants

Engineering Architecture Prize – biennial essay competition awarding £500 (each) to an A-level student and two students/graduate members of the institution.

The Pai Lin Li Travel Award – research grants between £1,000 and £3,000 to institution members to spend four to six weeks abroad studying.

The Young Structural Engineers' International Design Competition – three-annual competition awarding prizes of £1,000 to £5,000 in four categories.

Academic Bursaries and Scholarships

Arkwright Scholarship Trust – two scholarships are supported by the institution for study of A-levels, International Baccalaureate, National Diploma or Scottish Highers/Advanced Highers (15- to 16-year-olds).

Interdisciplinary Design for the Built Environment (IDBE) Bursary – an annual bursary is sponsored by the institution ('the IDBE course is a part-time master's degree at the University of Cambridge offered jointly by the departments of architecture and engineering').

Research Grants

Undergraduate Research Grants – up to ten grants of a maximum of £800 each (£200 to student and up to £600 to university) are available for the best innovative project ideas.

MSc Research Grants – grants of £500 (£200 to student and £300 to university) for projects carried out as part of a full or part-time MSc degree programme; an additional £500 is given to the best report and poster.

EEFIT Research Grant Scheme – two awards of £1,500 are given for 'short-term projects that will benefit earthquake (and related hazards) disaster mitigation and post-disaster reconnaissance efforts'.

In 2013 the Young Structural Engineer of the Year Award, made by the institution and supported by the trust, was also offered to engineers under the age of 28.

Annual grant total

In 2013 the trust had an income of £59,000 and an expenditure of £17,600. Seven awards were made to individuals totalling £3,600. At the time of writing (August 2015) the information provided was the latest available.

Applications

The application procedure is specific for different awards – see the website for details and deadlines or contact the correspondent for more information on each.

Other information

Both individuals and organisations are supported. The trust can provide schools with teaching materials and also participates in various educational projects and partnerships with institutions. Examples include: sponsoring Maths Inspiration events; The Scottish Romanian universities exchange (SRUE) programme; Engineers Without Borders; and others.

The Educational Trust is a charity connected to and receiving donations from the Institution of Structural Engineers.

Mining Institute of Scotland Trust

£12,500

Correspondent: Keith Donaldson, Hon. Secretary/Treasurer, 14/9 Burnbrae Drive, Edinburgh EH12 8AS (0131 629 7861; website: www.mining-scotland.org/trust.htm)

OSCR number: SC024974

Eligibility

Individuals who are taking a university course with a mining element to it (see the 'Types of grants' information for details of specific awards).

Our research indicates that the trust has a preference for supporting people from Fife in the first instance, and, secondly, those who are of Scottish origin, although other people can be considered. Applicants who are not already members of the institute will be invited to join. Members and former members of the Mining Institute of Scotland, and their dependants, can also receive hardship grants.

Types of grants

The trust's webpage describes the three components of its educational fund:

- Norman Henderson Prize – each year the trustees can purchase a medal for presentation to the author of any paper considered by them to be of outstanding merit
- Sam Mavor Travelling Scholarship – bursaries or prizes can be awarded to an MIS student or students to allow them to visit places, works or mines in any such place of special interest to them as may be determined by the trustees
- Cunningham Scholarship – scholarships for education in the science of mining, insight into contemporary mining methods, or visiting/studying mines anywhere in the world may be provided

Annual grant total

In 2014 the trust had an income of £33,000 and a total expenditure of £43,000. Our research suggests that the trust has about £25,000 available to give in grants each year for both education and social welfare.

Applications

Applications for assistance can be made in writing to the correspondent.

Other information

Organisations are also supported.

The Mott MacDonald Charitable Trust

£57,000 (15 grants)

Correspondent: Steve Wise, Administrator, Mott MacDonald House, 8–10 Sydenham Road, Croydon CR0 2EE (020 8774 2090; email: carole.teacher@mottmac.com; website: mottmac.com/article/5901/mott-macdonald-charitable-trust)

CC number: 275040

Eligibility

People undertaking higher education in the fields of civil, structural, mechanical, electrical or allied engineering (disciplines directly related to the work of Mott MacDonald company).

Types of grants

Undergraduate bursaries (generally on an annual basis) and recurring scholarships mainly to master's students (or occasionally PhD). The amount of money available to any person is a maximum of £12,000. Awards are given to cover the course fees.

Annual grant total

In 2014 the trust had assets of £136,000 and an income of £179,500. A total of 15 scholarships totalling £57,000 were made during the year.

Exclusions

Funding is not given retrospectively.

Applications

Apply in writing to the correspondent. Applications should be submitted by 30 March for the courses starting later in that year. The trustees meet in May. Candidates should have obtained a conditional offer of acceptance and provide details of fees. Each application is acknowledged and if the consideration is taken further the trust will ask for some more clarification.

Applicants employed by Mott MacDonald need to supply two employer references and those that do not work in the company need to supply two academic or one academic and one employer references.

Other information

The trust also awarded £11,000 for research and development during the year.

South Wales Institute of Engineers Educational Trust

£8,000

Correspondent: Administrative Officer, Suite 2, Bay Chambers, West Bute Street, Cardiff CF10 5BB (01792 879409; website: www.swieet2007.org.uk)

CC number: 1013538

Eligibility

People entering or practising engineering in Wales – school pupils deciding on their career, undergraduate students on engineering courses, graduates starting work in engineering industry, apprentices and equivalent.

Types of grants

One-off and recurrent grants are given according to need, generally from £100 to £1,000. The trust has funded engineering education from pre-GCSE level through to postgraduate/professional qualifications.

Annual grant total

In 2013/14 the trust had assets of £940,000 and an income of £29,500. A total of £33,000 was spent in charitable grants, of which 8,000 was awarded to individuals.

Applications

The trust's office should be contacted directly to find out the details of the current year's awards/prizes and to discuss an application.

Other information

Grants to organisations to support engineering education totalled £25,000 in 2013/14.

The Institution of Works and Highway Management (Bernard Butler) Trust

£37,500

Correspondent: Geoff Porter, Trustee, 27 Ashley Park, Ringwood BH24 2HA (01425 837790; email: info@bernardbutlertrust.org; website: www.bernardbutlertrust.org)

CC number: 1063735

Eligibility

People studying or working in the fields of engineering who are in need.

Types of grants

Grants, of at least £1,000, can be one-off or recurrent. Assistance can be given to college/university students (including mature and postgraduate), people in vocational training or individuals who wish to undertake courses to improve their skills and professional qualifications. Support is available towards various course-related costs (including fees, necessities, books), travel and accommodation costs to attend seminars/conferences/meetings, also childcare or costs of dependants, and any other project or expenses which will enable individuals to advance their education. The trust is interested in supporting work on 'improving the standards of safety, education and quality of engineering processes and methods of construction'.

Annual grant total

In 2014/15 the trust had an income of £8,000. A total expenditure of £38,000 we estimate that £37,500 was awarded in grants to individuals.

Applications

Application forms are available from the trust's website or can be requested from the correspondent. They can be submitted at any time. The remit of support available is very wide and the trust welcomes informal enquires to discuss applications.

Other information

Grants can also be made to organisations.

Environment and agriculture

Alan Baxter Foundation (ABF)

See entry on page 69

The Alice McCosh Trust

£800

Correspondent: Grace Carswell, Administrator, 49 Cluny Street, Lewes, Sussex BN7 1LN (email: info@thealicemccoshtrust.org.uk; website: www.thealicemccoshtrust.org.uk)

OSCR number: SC035938

Eligibility

People of any age undertaking work or study related to natural history and/or the environment. Preference will be given to individuals from (or work relating to) Scotland, England and Turkey.

Types of grants

One-off grants in the range of £600 to £1,000 can be given, for example, to cover the cost of a school field trip or project, an expedition as part of a research project or the development of new teaching materials for schools or institutes of higher education.

Annual grant total

In 2013/14 the trust had an income of £17,000 and a total expenditure of £900. We estimate that around £800 was distributed in grants to individuals for education.

Exclusions

Projects involving joining an existing commercial organisation on a pre-paid tour or expedition will not be considered.

Applications

Application forms are available from the website along with guidelines. Applications should be emailed to the correspondent between 1 October and 30 November each year (applications received at other times, or sent by post, will not be considered). Applications should be concise (no more than four typed pages) and include two referee statements.

The Merlin Trust

£30,000

Correspondent: Chloe Wells, 30 Moor Lane, Chessington KT9 1BW (email: info@merlin-trust.org.uk; website: www.merlin-trust.org.uk)

CC number: 803441

Eligibility

Horticulturists of British or Irish nationality resident in Britain or Ireland only. Foreign nationals may apply but they must be studying in a British or Irish horticultural training establishment and be 18–35 years of age (or if over 35 years then within the first five years of a career in horticulture).

Types of grants

Grants towards visiting gardens in different parts of the country or abroad, or travelling to see wild plants in their native habitats. Any suitable project, large or small, will be carefully considered.

Previous support has been awarded for an expedition to southern Chile to observe the range of beautiful plants, a trip to New York's community gardens and a visit to Peru in search of orchids.

Applicants will be considered for two annual prizes awarded by the trustees, the Christopher Brickell Prize for the best written report and the Valerie

Finnis VMH Prize for the report demonstrating photographic excellence.

Annual grant total

In 2013/14 the trust had an income of £22,000 and a total expenditure of £31,500. We estimate that grants totalled around £30,000. At the time of writing (November 2015) accounts were not available to view on the Charity Commission's website.

Exclusions

Grants are not given towards postgraduate study or to fund highly technical laboratory-based research.

Applications

Application forms are available to download from the website. The form should be completed and emailed to the secretary along with a one page description of your project and a CV. A signed copy of the form should also be posted to the secretary. The trust welcomes telephone enquiries. A written report must be presented within three months of the project being completed.

The Monmouthshire Farm School Endowment

£39,000

Correspondent: The Trustees, Education Finance Department, County Hall, Croesyceiliog, Cwmbran, Gwent NP44 2XH (01633 644495)

CC number: 525649

Eligibility

Awards to students in need of assistance who attend Usk Agricultural College, or any other educational institution that pursues courses of study in agricultural subjects. Preference is given to people aged under 25.

Types of grants

Grants of between £500 and £1,000 to help with the costs of study at the Usk College of Agriculture or any other farm institute, school, university or department of agricultural education approved by the governors. Grants can be for books, equipment/instruments, fees, living expenses and educational outings in the UK.

Annual grant total

In 2013/14 the charity had assets of £679,000 and an income of £61,500. Grants totalled £39,000.

Applications

Application forms are available from the correspondent which can be submitted at any time directly by the individual including an estimate of costs.

Applications are considered in October and January.

Other information

The following is taken from the 2013/14 trustees' annual report:

> The primary object of the Charity, as stated in its governing document, is to make awards to students in need of assistance to attend Usk Agricultural College, or at the discretion of the governing body, any other college, institution or university to pursue courses of study in agricultural subjects. The governing body can use its discretion to apply any unawarded income to provide funding towards the cost of their facilities or amenities at Usk College which would benefit these students.

The NFU Mutual Charitable Trust Centenary Award

£23,500 (3 grants)

Correspondent: James Creechan, Administrator, Tiddington Road, Stratford-upon-Avon, Warwickshire, Cv37 7BJ (email: centenary_award@nfumutual.co.uk; website: www.nfumutual.co.uk/company-information/charitable-trust/centenary-award)

CC number: 1073064

Eligibility

Postgraduate students in agriculture. Students should have gained/be expecting a 2:1 or above in agriculture or a closely related degree and have been accepted/provisionally accepted on a master's or PhD course in agriculture in the UK. Successful applicants will show excellent academic achievements and commitment to the future of agriculture.

The following three topic areas have been specifically identified in the latest accounts:

- sustainable agriculture and climate change
- international agriculture development
- the application of science and innovative technology to the agricultural industry

Types of grants

Annual bursaries to pay up to 75% of the course fees for selected postgraduate students in agriculture (master's or PhD).

Annual grant total

In 2014 awards were made to three individuals totalling £23,500. The awards came from the restricted fund which represents the funding available under The NFU Mutual Charitable Trust Centenary Award Scheme.

Applications

Application forms together with further details can be requested by emailing the correspondent. Full details of application deadlines can be found on the charity's website.

Other information

According to the website, 'the Centenary Award is a long-term scheme, run by NFU Mutual Charitable Trust, and was launched in 2010 to celebrate the 100th birthday of NFU Mutual'.

Note that we use the figures for the restricted fund. Charitable activities of The NFU Mutual Charitable Trust are of greater extent and are aimed at organisations. The trust receives most of its income from NFU Mutual.

Nuffield Farming Scholarship Trust

£115,500 (21 grants)

Correspondent: Mike Vacher, Director, Southill Farmhouse, Staple Fitzpaine, Taunton, Somerset TA3 5SH (01460 234012; email: director@nuffieldscholar.org; website: www.nuffieldscholar.org)

CC number: 1098519

Eligibility

UK residents between the ages of 22 and 45 who have been working for at least two years in farming, horticulture, forestry, rural land-based industries, countryside management, food industries or agricultural associated industries and intended to remain within the sector. Applicants must be three years post-tertiary education. The trust is looking for 'candidates who they believe will contribute and innovate in their respective industries on return from their scholarship, whilst also benefiting as an individual from a unique, often life changing experience'.

Types of grants

Awards are of £6,000 and can be given towards travel and subsistence expenses. Support is intended to encourage the study of practices and techniques employed anywhere in the world within farming, food, horticulture, rural and associated industries.

Annual grant total

In 2013/14 the trust had assets of £905,500 and an income of £390,000. Grants totalled £115,500 and were awarded in scholarships to 21 individuals. Approximately 20 scholarships are awarded each year.

Exclusions

Funding cannot be given for academic courses, gap year or research projects and to people in full-time education.

Applications

Application forms can be obtained from the trust's website. The closing date for applications is 31 July, scholarships are then awarded in October and must be used within 18 months. Shortlisted applicants are invited for an interview.

Other information

Note that no academic qualifications are required to apply for the scholarship.

A number of other specific awards are offered, such as The Young Nuffield (Bob Matson) Award for young entrepreneurs, Frank Arden Memorial Award to UK residents working in the fields of food, farming or forestry and various special interest awards. Further details can be found on the trust's website.

The John Oldacre Foundation

£225,000 (11 grants)

Correspondent: Stephen Charnock, Trustee, 35 Broadwater Close, Hersham, Walton-on-Thames KT12 5DD

CC number: 284960

Eligibility

Undergraduate or postgraduate students who are carrying out research in the agricultural sciences which is meaningful to the UK agricultural industry. The research must be published.

Types of grants

One-off and recurrent grants are given according to need towards structured research in the UK and overseas. Previously funded research included projects on pig welfare, drought effect on rape, UK food security, potato diseases, soil fertility, wheat vulnerability to environmental stress, sustainable crops and so on.

Annual grant total

In 2013/14 the foundation had assets of £8.8 million and an income of £144,000. During the year 11 awards were made totalling £225,000.

Applications

Apply in writing to the correspondent. Applications are usually considered twice a year.

Other information

Grants are made through organisations and educational establishments, not to individuals directly.

The Royal Bath and West of England Society

£25,000

Correspondent: Paul Hooper, Company Secretary, The Showground, Shepton Mallet, Somerset BA4 6QN (01749 822200; email: paul.hooper@ bathandwest.co.uk; website: www. bathandwest.com)

CC number: 1039397

Eligibility

People studying any aspect of agriculture, horticulture, forestry, veterinary, conservation or any form of food production or marketing. Other projects that have been supported previously include livestock photography, overseas study tour and rural leadership.

Artists between the ages of 21 and 30 working on artwork on the theme of rural life in the UK.

Types of grants

Scholarships and grants for personal development and projects in furtherance of agriculture and rural economy. In the past money has been used to assist funding in many different areas from assisting youngsters through agricultural college and veterinary schools.

An art scholarship is awarded bi-annually and in addition to prize money, the artist has the unique opportunity to exhibit a selection of their work at the show.

Annual grant total

In 2014 the society had assets of £2 million and an income of £3.8 million. In previous years the society has awarded grants totalling around £25,000.

Applications

Application forms can be requested from Marry Holmes (mary.holmes@ bathandwest.co.uk). They are normally considered twice a year, in spring and autumn.

To apply for the Art Scholarship contact the Chair of the Art Committee, Mrs Fran Wood.

Other information

The society aims to promote agriculture, rural economy, manufacture, commerce, arts and crafts through conferences, seminars, study tours, open days, exhibitions and other initiatives to individuals and rural businesses.

The Royal Horticultural Society (RHS)

£116,000 (100 grants)

Correspondent: Shalimar Turner, Administrator, 80 Vincent Square, London SW1P 2PE (020 7821 3034; email: info@rhs.org.uk; website: www. rhs.org.uk/Learning/Education/bursaries. htm)

CC number: 22879, SC038262

Eligibility

Professional and student gardeners/ horticulturalists, plant and soil scientists, botanists, agriculturalists, landscapers, botanical artists and related professionals. While priority is given to professional horticulturists and students, applications are also considered from serious amateur gardeners. Eligible proposals must be closely identified with horticulture.

Types of grants

Grants can be awarded for horticultural project, expeditions, study tours, voluntary work placements, conferences, educational and training courses, taxonomy, research and so on.

Two separate bursaries are offered: Susan Pearson Bursary for a one-year paid traineeship at a UK garden open to public; and Dawn Jolliffe Botanical Art Bursary for painting or drawing plants in their natural habitat or exhibiting work at an RHS show.

Annual grant total

In 2013/14 the society had assets of £94.7 million and an income of £73.1 million. A total of £116,000 was awarded in bursaries. The annual report states that a total of 143 applications were received 70% of which received a bursary.

Exclusions

Grants are not normally made for salary costs, tuition fees, exam fees or living costs for educational courses.

Applications

Application forms can be obtained from the society's website or the correspondent. Completed forms should be submitted via email by 31 March, 30 June, 30 September or 15 December. Applications for the traineeship and for botanical artwork must be submitted by 31 March.

Other information

Organisations, charities and gardens open to the public may be supported.

The Royal Horticultural Society administers a number of bursary funds, established and maintained through generous bequests and donations, to support professional and student gardeners/horticulturalists.

Studley College Trust

£96,500 (95 grants)

Correspondent: Christine Copeman, Secretary, Old Post Office, Hill Road, Lower Boddington, Daventry NN11 6YB (01327 260165; email: studleyct@ btinternet.com; website: www. studleytrust.co.uk)

CC number: 528787

Eligibility

British or Irish nationals aged 18 to 30 (except cases of genuine career change) enrolled on a college/university course connected with UK land-based activities (agriculture, horticulture, forestry, fish farming, agri-food technology, agricultural or horticultural marketing, arboriculture, game keeping and estate skills and agricultural engineering) whose progress is obstructed by lack of funds. Practical experience and/or strong rural background are required.

The trust is looking to support students in their early qualifications and master's degrees or PhD studies are not likely to be supported.

Types of grants

One-off and recurrent (up to three years) grants towards examination and external test fees, books, study material, transport, travel, clothing, equipment, accommodation, living expenses and food. Grants can be of up to £2,000, according to circumstances.

The Trust provides scholarships through the Professional Gardeners' Guild, Nuffield Farming Scholarships Trust and Tresco Abbey Gardens.

Annual grant total

In 2013/14 the trust had assets of £2.6 million and an income of £116,500. A total of around £96,500 was paid in grants and bursaries to 95 students.

Exclusions

No grants are available for hire purchase payments, overdraft and loan repayments, support for dependants or long-term housing costs. Students on industrial experience for over six weeks are not supported.

Applications

The trust has made partnerships with six land-based colleges and students at these should apply through their institution's student support office (a list of partner colleges is available on the trust's website). Applications for sponsored scholarships should be made through the appropriate organisations, details of which can be found on the website.

Applications from other university/ college students and for travelling scholarships or traineeships can be submitted directly to the trust. Application forms can be requested on the website or from the correspondent. The trustees consider applications in July and October, the deadlines are 1 June and 1 October, respectively.

The trust's website states:

> If you are intending to study at a college or university that is not listed on the College Bursaries page, or if you have any other enquiry that needs clarification, you can email the Studley College Office and seek clarification, or request the forms to make direct application to the Trust.

Other information

The trustees' annual report from 2013/14 states:

> In order to reduce administration costs the Trust has increasingly made grants through partnership arrangements with selected land-based colleges and other institutions. Direct applications will still be considered subject to eligibility and availability of funds. The Trust's website has been updated to inform applicants as to procedural requirements for applications.

The Water Conservation Trust

£73,000

Correspondent: Trust Administrator, HQS Wellington, Temple Stairs, Victoria Embankment, London WC2R 2PN (0118 983 3689; email: waterloo@aol.com)

CC number: 1007648

Eligibility

People who are working or studying in the fields of water or environment conservation and industry, and their dependants.

Types of grants

The trust offers one-off grants to individuals and runs a bursary programme for postgraduate studies and research in environment/water at nine UK universities.

Annual grant total

In 2013/14 the trust had assets of £466,500 and an income of £44,000. Charitable expenditure totalled £79,500 and a total of £73,000 was spent in grants for educational purposes, broken down as follows:

Bursary and/or dissertation support at various universities	£72,000
Grants to individuals	£500
Pupil prizes	£300

Exclusions

Unsolicited applications are not invited.

Applications

When funds are available applicants for scholarships are invited through the water and environmental press. Applications should then be made via specific universities.

Other information

The trust also awards grants to environmental organisations, promotes environmental education in schools and the community and supports activities with environmental focus for people with a disability.

Heritage and conservation

The Zibby Garnett Travelling Fellowship

£15,500

Correspondent: Martin Williams, Trustee, 20 Rutland Terrance, Stamford, Lincolnshire PE9 2QD (01636 636288; email: info@zibbygarnett.org; website: www.zibbygarnett.org)

CC number: 1081403

Eligibility

Students, craft apprentices or young professionals working in the fields of historic and decorative crafts, architectural conservation, historic landscape and gardens, traditional building skills, sculpture, artefacts and similar or associated areas, who wish to travel abroad for educational purposes or research.

Types of grants

Grants and bursaries in the range of £300–£3,000 are given to allow individuals to travel overseas for practical study and conservation work. The trustees are looking for 'imaginative and unusual ideas likely to broaden the applicant's understanding of their subject and widen their horizons'. Preference will be given to projects which are not part of the academic curricular but rather the applicant's own initiative. The awards are not restricted to British nationals but overseas students should plan projects outside their country of origin.

Annual grant total

In 2013/14 the charity had an income of £8,000 and an expenditure of £16,000. We estimate that the annual total amount of grants awarded was around £15,500.

Exclusions

Grants are not given retrospectively, for placements in the UK, for conferences/ formal courses or holidays. Support is intended for practical work in conservation, not new work.

Applications

Application forms can be found on the charity's website. Applications are considered once a year and the submission deadline is 12 noon of the last working day in February annually. Applicants who are successful with their initial application are invited for an interview (usually in March) which is held in London and in Lincoln/Newark.

Anna Plowden Trust

£35,500 (35 grants)

Correspondent: Francis Plowden, Trustee, 4 Highbury Road, London SW19 7PR (020 8879 9841; email: info@ annaplowdentrust.org.uk; website: www. annaplowdentrust.org.uk)

CC number: 1072236

Eligibility

People who want to train for a qualification in conservation of movable heritage and professionals who are looking to develop their skills in conservation.

Types of grants

The trust offers conservation bursaries to individuals (usually graduates) seeking to obtain qualifications to enter conservation profession and awards continuing professional development grants covering up to 50% of the costs for short, mid-career skills development opportunities. In 2015 applications were invited for the Award for Research and Innovation in Research – a prize awarded as part of the Conservation Awards organised by Icon (The Institute of Conservation) (see the website for more specific details).

Annual grant total

In 2013/14 the trust had assets of £558,500 and an income of £64,000. A total of £35,500 was awarded in grants. During the year the trust awarded 17 bursaries and 18 conservators received the CPD grants.

Exclusions

Courses on the conservation of non-moveable heritage are not eligible (for example, building or natural environment conservation).

Applications

Application forms and further guidelines are available from the trust's website. Bursary applications are considered once a year, usually in May. For specific deadlines see the website. Applications for funding are also invited through advertisements in the national conservation journals.

Other information

The following is taken from the trustees' annual report for 2013/14:

> The Trust is delighted once more to be offering the Anna Plowden Trust Award for Research and Innovation in Conservation as part of Icon's Conservation Awards. The Trustees were delighted that Icon secured support from BEKO for the Conservation Awards 2015 and that others, such as the Pilgrim Trust, are once again offering awards. The Award is publicised on the Trust's and Icon's websites.

Hospitality

ABTA LifeLine (The ABTA Benevolent Fund) Bursary

£2,000 (1 grant)

Correspondent: Isabel O'Riordan, Business and Marketing Assistant, 30 Park Street, London SE1 9EQ (020 3693 0171; email: lifeline@abtalifeline. org.uk or apatel@abta.co.uk; website: www.abtalifeline.org.uk)

CC number: 295819

Eligibility

Anyone who is currently working for an ABTA (Association of British Travel Agents) Member and is unable to consider further or higher education without support.

The charity's website states: 'ABTA LifeLine are especially interested in people who work in small or medium sized companies (fewer than 250 employees) front line travel agents or individuals who feel that in order to reach their full potential they currently lack an appropriate qualification.'

Types of grants

The bursary is offered to 'an individual in [the] travel community who does not have the means to further their education and develop their career potential within the industry'. The maximum grant available is £2,000 a year for a maximum of three years and is aimed to help with the course fees for a relevant vocational or professional qualification. The candidate must demonstrate their commitment and progression in order to receive funding for years two and three.

Successful applicants will also be allocated a senior mentor from the travel industry to offer support and enable the bursary recipients to attend key industry events and 'may be invited to spend a day with an ABTA Member company, Midcounties Cooperative or Kuoni, to gain experience of a different organisation'.

Annual grant total

In 2014 the charity had assets of £530,500 and an income of £119,500. One bursary of £2,000 was awarded.

Applications

Application forms are available from the correspondent or can be downloaded from the website.

Other information

The bursary was established in 2014 in partnership with Travel Weekly in memory of Colin Heal.

The charity mainly provides social welfare support. In 2014 grants to 27 individuals totalled £43,500.

The Geoffrey Harrison Foundation

£4,500

Correspondent: Richard Harrison, Secretary, Oxford House, Oxford Road, Thame, Oxon OX9 2AH (email: enquiries@geoffreyharrisonfoundation. org.uk; website: www. geoffreyharrisonfoundation.org.uk)

CC number: 1142242

Eligibility

People in education or training in the hotel, restaurant and hospitality industries. Currently support is mainly aimed at Year 10 and 11 students attending the Junior Chefs Academy courses at selected institutions, and individual students in the 16–18 age groups at Westminster Kingsway College and the University of West London, who show exceptional talent and would benefit from specific support.

Types of grants

Grants to support education and training connected with the catering and hospitality industries.

Annual grant total

In 2013/14 the foundation had assets of £147,500 and an income of £92,000. Student support totalled £4,500.

Applications

Apply in writing to the correspondent.

Other information

The main activity of the foundation is to contribute to the Saturday Morning Junior Chefs Academy courses held at University of West London, Ealing and the Westminster Kingsway College, Victoria. In 2013/14 amount spent for the courses totalled £60,000.

Law

The Airey Neave Trust

See entry on page 93

Media, journalism and communication

Royal Television Society

£75,000 (25 grants)

Correspondent: Anne Dawson, Bursary Consultant, Kildare House, 3 Dorset Rise, London EC4Y 8EN (020 7822 2810; email: bursaries@rts.org.uk; website: www.rts.org.uk/education-training/rts-bursaries)

CC number: 313728

Eligibility

UK students studying full-time accredited undergraduate degree courses in television production, broadcast journalism or technology (computer and engineering). A full list of eligible universities and courses can be found on the society's website. The trust will **only** consider applicants who:

▶ Are from households with an annual income below £25,000 for a Production and Broadcast Journalism Bursary/£35,000 for a Technology Bursary
▶ Are new to higher education
▶ Are home and full-time students
▶ Have accepted an offer as their firm choice to study full-time on one of the Creative Skillset or Broadcast Journalism Training Council accredited undergraduate programmes (for TV Production and Broadcast Journalism bursaries) or one of the undergraduate programmes listed by the society (for Technology Undergraduate bursaries)
▶ Meet the application deadline

Types of grants

The society offers two bursary schemes for undergraduates – Television Production and Broadcast Journalism Bursary and Technology Bursary. Grants of £3,000 are awarded towards living costs, paid in yearly instalments of £1,000, for undergraduates on specified relevant courses. Successful applicants will also receive a free student membership of the Royal Television Society while studying and one year's free full membership after graduation, affiliate membership of the Hospital Club while studying and the trust will aim to set up a mentoring or placement with one of its industry members in the final year of the applicant's course. Full

guidance notes and an FAQ section are available on the society's website.

Annual grant total

Bursaries are generally made to 25 students each year, totalling £75,000.

Exclusions

The society's website provides an exhaustive list of eligible institutions and courses. Students enrolling on any other course that is not listed on the website would **not be eligible to apply**.

Applications

Application forms can be found on the society's website. All applications have to be sent electronically and must be accompanied by a copy of the applicant's UCAS personal statement. Applicants **must** also include a link to an example of their work or attach a file. Further guidelines on completing the application form and the shortlisting criteria are on the website. Note that the application criteria and deadlines are subject to change and it is best to consult the society's website for any updates before applying.

Note the following request by the society: 'Please do not leave [the application] until the last minute, as IT systems are likely to be busy, and it may take some time to upload your application.'

The society may contact the applicant to arrange a short telephone interview.

Other information

The society receives approximately 200 applications annually.

The Stationers' Foundation

£94,000

Correspondent: Pamela Butler, Administrator, Worshipful Company of Stationers and Newspaper Makers, Stationers Hall, Stationers Hall Court, Ave Maria Lane EC4M 7DD (020 7246 0990; email: foundation@stationers.org; website: www.stationers.org)

CC number: 1120963

Eligibility

UK residents under the age of 25 who are in need and studying stationer's trade, printing, papermaking, publishing and distribution, journalism, librarianship, typography, book and graphic design, photography, conservation of books and manuscripts, packaging, advertising, website creation and all relevant electronic communication and publishing. Preference is given to people who are former pupils of Stationers' Company School, also to sons and daughters of liverymen and freemen of the company.

Types of grants

The foundation offers support through the following schemes:

▶ Scholarships and Awards – a number of various awards to people studying a trade of the guild, or the children of liverymen and freemen towards general educational costs, such as fees, travel in the UK and abroad, projects, living expenses and so on
▶ Postgraduate Bursary – up to 12 annual awards of £6,000 each to postgraduates studying trades of the guild

Annual grant total

In 2014 the foundation had assets of £4 million and an income of £336,000. A total of around £94,000 was awarded in educational grants, including £60,500 in postgraduate bursaries and £33,500 in general awards.

Exclusions

People over the age of 25 are only supported in exceptional circumstances.

Applications

Application forms are available from the foundation's website along with detailed guidance notes, specific to each award. Applicants are advised to phone the correspondent in the first instance, to discuss an application. The trustees meet at least quarterly but generally candidates are invited to submit their applications between September and December.

Other information

The foundation also supports a number of specific schools, organises and sponsors Shine School Media Awards, funds three Saturday supplementary schools for disadvantaged children in London, holds a welfare fund to support people within the industry and administers a library for the use of people involved in historical studies related to printing, publishing, bookselling, bookbinding, newspaper making and similar trades.

George Viner Memorial Fund

£30,500 (5 grants)

Correspondent: Gayle Baldwin, Administrator, National Union of Journalists, Headland House, 308–312 Gray's Inn Road, London WC1X 8DP (020 7843 3728; email: georgeviner@nuj.org.uk; website: www.nuj.org.uk/rights/george-viner-memorial-fund)

CC number: 328142

Eligibility

Students from black and Asian backgrounds who have received a formal offer of a place on a National Union of Journalists-recognised media course in the fields of print, broadcasting, online or photo journalism but have not yet commenced their studies. Applicants must be UK or Irish citizens who intend to continue their education or start a career within the UK/Ireland media industry.

Types of grants

Grants are given for tuition fees, travel expenses, accommodation, books, equipment and other necessities. Mentoring and career guidance are also provided. Payments are made directly to institutions.

Annual grant total

In 2013/14 the fund had an income of £25,500 and a total expenditure of £31,000. The annual total amount of grants awarded to individuals amounted to £30,500 and was given to five scholars.

Exclusions

Individuals who have already received a student loan/sponsorship and previous recipients of an award from the fund are not supported.

Applications

Application forms can be obtained from the fund's website once the funding round opens, which happens at the end of May. The deadline for applications is mid-August. It is crucial to include the estimated costs for the course, including fees, travel, accommodation, books and other equipment. Note that handwritten applications or late submission are not accepted.

Other information

The following is taken from the 2013/14 annual report:

> This year our charity was able to award bursaries to five scholars: two scholars are studying for NCTJ Diplomas one is on the foundation course and the other is undertaking the Multimedia course. The three remaining scholars are all studying for their Masters in Broadcast Journalism.

> For the second year running we were able to offer our current scholars two to three week unpaid work placements at the BBC to gain experience in their chosen field of journalism. The charity paid them a daily allowance to cover food and met their travel costs.

Yr Ymddiriedolaeth Ddarlledu Gymreig (The Welsh Broadcasting Trust)

£6,500

Correspondent: Mali Parry-Jones, Secretary, Islwyn, Lôn Terfyn, Morfa Nefyn, Pwllheli, Gwynedd, North Wales LL53 6AP (01758 720132; email: gwybod@ydg.org.uk; website: www.ydg. org.uk)

CC number: 700780

Eligibility

People who wish to expand and improve their knowledge and skills in television, film, radio and new media. Applicants must either have been fully resident in Wales for at least two years prior to applying, or be born in Wales or be Welsh speakers.

Types of grants

The trust supports participation in appropriate training or career development courses and attendance at educational courses at higher degree level.

Annual grant total

In 2013 the trust had an income of £15,000 and an expenditure of £26,000. We estimate that around £6,500 was awarded in grants to individuals. The 2013 financial information was the latest available at the time of writing (November 2015).

Exclusions

The trust does not fund undergraduate entry to courses.

Applications

Application forms are available from trust's website or can be requested from the correspondent.

Other information

Grants are also made to training bodies or companies which offer specific training/educational programmes.

Medicine

Ted Adams Trust Ltd

£39,000 (32 grants)

Correspondent: Rosie Stables, Administrator, 208 High Street, Guildford, Surrey GU1 3JB (email: tedadamstrust@live.co.uk; website: www. tedadamstrust.org.uk)

CC number: 1104538

Eligibility

Students of nursing/midwifery, whether pre- or post-registration, working or attending courses in the Guildford area. Individuals or nursing service managers are also eligible to apply for funding towards the course fees or associated costs to further their professional education and development. The trust is 'particularly keen to fund individuals where the outcomes of their course/ study will enhance patient care in the local area.'

Types of grants

Grants are awarded towards the course fees, training, travel costs, research and similar expenses and activities undertaken in pursuance of educational and professional development.

The trust also offers special prizes for clinical excellence to the final year undergraduate students (including the diploma in higher education in nursing studies and midwifery studies at the University of Surrey in Guildford). Potential prize winners are nominated by their mentors. The awards are: £500 to the overall winner in all branches and £250 for each winner in children's nursing, mental health nursing and adult nursing (two awards).

Annual grant total

In 2013/14 the trust had assets of £161,000 and an income of £114,500. Charitable expenditure totalled £119,000 and grants to 32 individuals totalled £39,000.

Exclusions

The trust does not offer support towards living expenses, childcare or debts.

Applications

The following is taken from the trust's website :

> The applicant completes the on-line application form and returns it to the Ted Adams Trust. The application will be considered by at least two of the Trustees who will either agree the application in principle, or refuse it. This decision will be notified to the applicant. If funding is confirmed the applicant will be informed when this will become available and the address for forwarding the invoice for the agreed amount. Confirmation of attendance may also be requested.

The Worshipful Society of Apothecaries General Charity Ltd

£36,000 (36 grants)

Correspondent: Secretary, Apothecaries Hall, Black Friars Lane, London EC4V 6EJ (020 7236 1189; email: clerk@ apothecaries.org; website: www. apothecaries.org)

CC number: 284450

Eligibility

Penultimate and final year medical and pharmaceutical students who are in need. Undergraduates taking courses in history of medicine and the ethics and philosophy of healthcare can also be supported.

The charity also supports a student at the Guildhall School of Music and Drama and provides awards at the London medical schools, Christ's

Hospital School and the City of London Academy (Southwark).

Types of grants
One-off and recurrent grants of about £1,000 a year.

Annual grant total
In 2013/14 the charity had assets of £1.4 million and an income of £97,500. During the year 36 undergraduate medical students were given a total of £36,000 in grants.

Applications
Every year the trustees write to the deans of all 28 medical schools, schools of pharmacy and to the Royal Pharmaceutical Society of Great Britain's Benevolent Fund requesting nominations of eligible students, to be submitted by 30 June. Recommendations are considered in July and the grants are disbursed in August. Additional meetings can also be held as required.

Other information
Donations to City of London charities, and other institutions totalled £6,500 in 2013/14.

BMA Charities Trust Fund

£125,000 (55 grants)

Correspondent: Marian Flint, Principal Officer, BMA House, Tavistock Square, London WC1H 9JP (020 7383 6142; email: info.bmacharities@bma.org.uk; website: bma.org.uk/about-the-bma/what-we-do/bma-charities)

CC number: 219102

Eligibility
Medical students who are taking medicine as a second degree at a UK medical school.

The annual report for 2014 states: 'Access to the [Medical Education] Fund is limited to students who can demonstrate that they are over £25,000 in debt, thus ensuring that only the neediest students receive help.'

Types of grants
Grants of up to £2,500 are given towards fees and living costs.

Annual grant total
In 2014 the fund had assets of over £4.6 million and an income of £283,500. During the year, £125,000 was awarded to 55 beneficiaries from the Medical Education Fund.

Welfare grants to individuals from the Hastings Fund, which were authorised to a total of £31,500 but amounted to £21,500 in the accounts, were made to 30 beneficiaries (including 22 refugee doctors, two other doctors and six

medical students in financial need). A further £30,000 was awarded to two external charities.

Exclusions
No grants are made to students who benefit from the NHS bursary scheme or from student loans.

Applications
Application forms are available from the correspondent. Grants are made once a year and application packs are only available between November and mid-January each year.

Other information
The BMA Charities Trust Fund incorporates the Hastings Benevolent Fund and the BMA Educational Fund.

British Society for Antimicrobial Chemotherapy

£5,600

Correspondent: Tracey Guise, Executive Officer, Griffin House, 53 Regent Place, Birmingham B1 3NJ (0121 236 1988; email: grants@bsac.org.uk; website: www.bsac.org.uk)

CC number: 1093118

Eligibility
Postgraduate and undergraduate students and members of the society involved in research and training in antimicrobial chemotherapy.

Types of grants
The society currently offers the following grants:
- Project Grants – up to £15,000 for projects of up to one year duration
- Research Grants – up to £50,000 for projects of up to one year duration
- Overseas Scholarships – up to £1,250 per calendar month, to enable workers from other countries the opportunity to work in the UK departments for up to six months
- Vacation Scholarship – £180 per week for up to ten weeks, designed to give undergraduate experience in research for candidates on a full-time first degree course in the sciences, medicine, veterinary medicine or dentistry
- Travel Grants – up to £1,500, restricted to BSAC members, to enable individuals to attend the annual meetings of ECCMID and ICAAC
- PhD Studentships – up to £25,000 for up to four years to first-class students in the field of antimicrobial chemotherapy (award made biannually)

- Education grants – up to £50,000 for research projects and initiatives of benefit to the field

Annual grant total
In 2013/14 the society had assets of £6.5 million and an income of £1.7 million. During the year a total of £5,600 was awarded in travel grants to individuals and £160,500 was distributed through institutions in other types of awards, including vacation grants (£8,700).

Applications
Each programme has specific application forms, guidance notes and deadlines. See the society's website for full details for each programme and note that changes are likely to have been made.

The society also warns that the awards are very competitive, subject to a stringent peer review process and require two to three independent referees.

Other information
The society makes large grants to institutions to fund research and liaises with organisations across the globe in promoting medical research.

British Veterinary Nursing Association

£3,000

Correspondent: The Bursary Administrator, 79 Greenway Business Centre, Harlow Business Park, Harlow, Essex CM19 5QE (01279 408644; fax: 01279 408645; email: bvna@bvna.co.uk; website: www.bvna.org.uk/members/bursaries)

Eligibility
People undertaking education and training in veterinary nursing and veterinary nurses seeking to develop their professional skills. Applicants must be members of the association.

Types of grants
The association administers a number of bursary schemes, further details of which can be found on the website (details of 2016 bursaries will be released in January). Current schemes include:
- **BVNA Educational Bursary** – up to £500 to help veterinary nurses or students in training or furthering their veterinary nursing education
- **The Kennel Club Charitable Trust Bursary** – 'a fund of £2,500 is available to help defray the costs of veterinary nurse training', including course fees or other educational expenses, such as travel and accommodation
- **The Kennel Club Charitable Trust Degree Bursary** – £3,000 (distributed equally over a period of three years) is

available for one degree student 'to help defray the costs associated with training', including course fees or other educational costs, such as travel and accommodation

Annual grant total

About £3,000 is available each year through the three current bursary schemes.

Applications

Full details of schemes open to applications are published on the association's website.

Other information

Other schemes may be added and current one may close – for the most up-to-date information see the association's website. Other funding opportunities are also advertised on the website.

The Chartered Society of Physiotherapy Charitable Trust

£63,500 (65 grants)

Correspondent: Stuart De Boos, Administrator, 14 Bedford Row, London WC1R 4ED (020 7306 6646; email: debooss@csp.org.uk; website: www.csp.org.uk/charitabletrust)

CC number: 279882

Eligibility

Qualified, associate and student members of the society.

Types of grants

Grants can be given for fees of academically accredited research courses, UK and overseas presentations, overseas development projects, research visits, master's research dissemination and student elective placements. Educational awards are generally in the range of £150 to £3,000.

Annual grant total

At the time of writing (October 2015) the latest financial information available was from 2013. In 2013 the society had assets of £4.3 million, an income of £2.7 million and made grants totalling £858,500. A total of £63,500 was given in 65 educational grants.

Applications

Application for educational awards should be submitted using the CSP ePortfolio which can be accessed on the society's website. The deadlines for applications for different awards vary – for the most up-to-date information see the website.

Other information

Awards can also be made for experienced researchers and those only starting their research career. Research funding

comprises Physiotherapy Research Foundation awards, paediatric research funding and a special care of older people research award. For specific details and latest available awards in this category, see the website.

The Jean Ginsburg Memorial Foundation
See entry on page 63

The Nightingale Fund

£33,500

Correspondent: Rebecca Stanford, Honorary Secretary, Half Thatch, Deers Green, Clavering, Safron Walden, Essex CB11 4PX (01799550668; email: rlstanford@thenightingalefund.org.uk; website: www.thenightingalefund.org.uk)

CC number: 205911

Eligibility

Nurses, midwives and community public health nurses who are registered with the Nursing and Midwifery Council and healthcare assistants in the UK.

Types of grants

Grants in the range of £500 to £2,000 are given for the course fees only. Support is given towards further education and training to allow individuals to improve and develop their nursing practice.

Annual grant total

In 2013/14 the fund had an income of £24,500 and a total expenditure of £34,000. We estimate that £33,500 was awarded in grants.

Applications

Application forms can be downloaded from the fund's website and should be emailed to the correspondent together with a current CV. Grants are considered three times a year, in March, July and November. The deadline for applications is stated on the website. Applicants are required to attend an interview either in person or by telephone.

The Queen's Nursing Institute

£5,900 (14 grants)

Correspondent: Joanne Moorby, Welfare and Grants Officer, 1A Henrietta Place, London W1G 0LZ (020 7594 1400; fax: 020 7490 1269; email: mail@qni.org.uk; website: www.qni.org.uk)

CC number: 213128

Eligibility

Working and retired nurses, midwives and health visitors undertaking post-

qualification and community nursing courses.

Eligible training includes: specialist community practitioner qualification; specialist community public health nursing (school, health, district, general practice nursing, children's, mental health, learning disabilities nursing, or return to nursing/health visiting); advanced nurse practitioner qualifications; or other community nursing courses.

Types of grants

Grants of up to £500 towards education and training to improve nursing skills. The institute's website notes that only 'accredited education courses and modules promoting excellence in community nursing' can be considered for funding.

Annual grant total

In 2014 the institute had assets of more than £10 million and an income of nearly £2.4 million. Educational grants totalled £5,900 awarded to 14 individuals.

Applications

Application forms are accessible on the institute's website. You will need a copy of your latest bank statement and a utility bill too. Initial contact may also be made to Joanne Moorby (020 7549 1405; joanne.moorby@qni.org.uk) to discuss the application. Requests can be made at any time.

Other information

Welfare support is also given to nurses. The institute undertakes campaigning, lobbying and various projects. Organisations are also assisted (nine grants totalling £38,500 in 2014).

The RCN Foundation
See entry on page 114

Rhona Reid Charitable Trust

£22,000

Correspondent: K. Clayton, Rathbone Taxation Services, Port of Liverpool Buildings, Pier Head, Liverpool L3 1NW (0151 236 6666; email: karen.owen-jones@rathbones.com)

CC number: 1047380

Eligibility

People involved in the study and advancement of medicine (especially ophthalmology), music and the arts.

Types of grants

One-off and recurrent grants are given according to need for necessities and activities which would be 'supporting excellence in the chosen field'.

Annual grant total

In 2014/15 the trust had an income of £14,500 and an expenditure of £44,000. We estimate the annual total amount of grants awarded to individuals to be around £22,000.

Applications

Apply in writing to the correspondent. Applications are considered in March and September.

Other information

Grants are also made to organisations and people who are blind, visually impaired or have another disability.

Sandra Charitable Trust

£100,000 (147 grants)

Correspondent: Martin Pollock, Secretary to the Trustees, Moore Stephens LLP, 150 Aldersgate Street, London EC1A 4AB (020 7334 9191)

CC number: 327492

Eligibility

Nurses and nursing students who are in financial need. Postgraduate, overseas and part-time students can all be supported.

Types of grants

One-off and recurrent grants are given according to need, for courses, equipment and other necessities.

Annual grant total

In 2013/14 the trust had assets of £19.4 million, an income of £503,000 and a total charitable expenditure of around £505,000. Grants to 147 individuals totalled £100,000.

Applications

Application forms can be requested from the correspondent. Previously the trust has stated that its funds are largely committed. The trustees meet on a frequent basis to consider applications.

Other information

Grants are also made to organisations (in 2013/14 a total of £408,000).

The following is taken from the trustees' annual report for 2013/14:

The aims of the Charity are to support a wide variety of beneficiaries including nurses and charities involved in animal welfare and research, environmental protection, relief of poverty and youth development and to maintain resources at a reasonable level in order to continue to provide general charitable assistance in the foreseeable future.

The Swann-Morton Foundation

£10,200

Correspondent: Michael Hirst, Administrator, Swann-Morton Ltd, Owlerton Green, Sheffield S6 2BJ (0114 234 4231)

CC number: 271925

Eligibility

People studying or working in the fields of surgery and medicine, particularly concerned with physical and mental disabilities.

Types of grants

One-off and recurrent grants are given according to need are available to students of medicine and surgery for general educational expenses and research projects.

Annual grant total

In 2013/14 the foundation had assets of £112,000 and an income of £55,000. A total of £44,000 was spent to cover donations and legacies, of which about £10,200 was awarded in student grants and electives.

Applications

Apply in writing to the correspondent. The annual report and accounts for 2013/14 state that 'applicants are invited to submit a summary of their proposals in a specific format'.

Other information

The foundation welcomes applications from individual students, charities and hospitals. Support can also be given to current or former employees of W R Swann and Co. Limited.

Nautical subjects

The Corporation of Trinity House, London

£5,000

Correspondent: Graham Hockley, Secretary, Trinity House, Tower Hill, London EC3N 4DH (020 7481 6914; email: graham.hockley@thls.org; website: www.trinityhouse.co.uk)

CC number: 211869

Eligibility

Candidates must be between 16 and 18½ years old with five GCSE at grade C or above and must also have passed the Department of Transport medical examination. Applicants must also be British and permanently resident in the British Isles. Applicants must be applying to become an officer in the Merchant Navy.

Types of grants

The Trinity House Merchant Navy Scholarship Scheme provides financial support for young people seeking careers as officers in the Merchant Navy. The website states: Cadets undertake a three or four year programme split between nautical college and time at sea in a variety of British-managed vessels. Cadets can train as either Deck or Engineer Officers or pursue a Marine Cadetship encompassing both disciplines.

Annual grant total

The charity's significant assets are no reflection of the money available for grant-making which is a very small part of its activities.

In 2013/14 the corporation had assets of £201.4 million and an income of more than £8 million. Grants were made to 28 retired seafarers in financial need at a rate of £676 per year. This totalled £24,500. A further £11,500 was awarded in grants to individuals, some of which was distributed for educational purposes. We estimate this to be around £5,700.

The vast majority of the charity's grants were distributed to organisations, with more than £1.5 million awarded during the year.

Applications

Details of the scholarship scheme are available upon application in writing to the correspondent.

Other information

The following information is taken from the corporation's website: 'The safety of shipping, and the well being of seafarers, have been our prime concerns ever since Trinity House was granted a Royal Charter by Henry VIII in 1514.'

Today there are three distinct functions:

▶ The General Lighthouse Authority (GLA) for England, Wales, the Channel Islands and Gibraltar. The remit is to provide Aids to Navigation to assist the safe passage of a huge variety of vessels through some of the busiest sea-lanes in the world

▶ A charitable organisation dedicated to the safety, welfare and training of mariners

▶ A Deep Sea Pilotage Authority providing expert navigators for ships trading in Northern European waters

The Honourable Company of Master Mariners and Howard Leopold Davis Charity

£71,500

Correspondent: The Clerk, HQS Wellington, Temple Stairs, Victoria Embankment, London WC2R 2PN (020 7836 8179; fax: 020 7240 3082; email: info@hcmm.org.uk; website: www. hcmm.org.uk/activities/charitable-giving)

CC number: 1127213

Eligibility

People who are serving in the Merchant navy, those intending to serve, and also individuals who have an interest in seamanship or sail training.

Types of grants

Grants are made to encourage the education, instruction and training of individuals.

Annual grant total

In 2014 the charity had an income of £104,500 and a total expenditure of £153,000. At the time of writing (November 2015) the charity's annual report and accounts were not yet available to view online at the Charity Commission. Based on previous years, we estimate that the amount of grants given to individuals for both social welfare and educational purposes totalled around £143,000.

Applications

In the first instance, applications should be made to The Merchant Navy Welfare Board or SSAFA. Members of the company who are seeking assistance should instead apply directly to the correspondent.

Other information

This charity is an amalgamation of four separate funds: the Education Fund, the Benevolent Fund, the London Maritime Institution and the Howard Leopold Davis Fund.

The Marine Society and Sea Cadets

See entry on page 112

Reardon Smith Nautical Trust

£108,500

Correspondent: Sarah Fox, Administrator, Fox SE Consultancy, 4 Bessemer Road, Cardiff CF11 8BA (02920890383; email: sarah@ foxseconsultancy.co.uk)

CC number: 1153623

Eligibility

Residents of Wales up to the age of 25 studying recognised nautical or maritime courses in the UK or abroad. These should relate to shipping, maritime law and commerce, navigation, sailing, oceanography or marine-related environmental issues, in particular those which give the individual first hand practical experience of being at sea. Preference is given to residents of city and county of Cardiff.

Types of grants

Grants, scholarships, exhibitions and bursaries towards general educational expenses.

Annual grant total

In 2014/15 the trust had assets of £3.1 million and an income of £110,000. Grants awarded to institutions totalled £108,500. Grants to individuals are made through institutions.

The following is taken from the 2014/15 annual report: 'Grants are made to those individuals who apply to the trustees for financial support. Grants are paid through sail training providers, these include Island Trust, Tall Ships Youth Trust and Challenge Wales'

Applications

Applications should be made through a relevant educational establishment or sail training provider.

Sailors' Society

£12,000

Correspondent: Welfare Fund Manager, 350 Shirley Road, Southampton SO15 3HY (023 8051 5950; email: bkidd@sailors-society.org; website: www. sailors-society.org)

CC number: 237778

Eligibility

Students or nautical cadets preparing for a career at sea in the merchant navy (of any country) and enrolled at a recognised college or academy of nautical education. Seafarers who have already entered the profession and have been accepted on a course of study by an accredited institution to further their qualifications.

Applicants must be able to demonstrate that they have no other source of funds to pursue their nautical education.

Types of grants

One-off and recurrent grants are given towards course study fees, related books and necessary course materials.

Annual grant total

In 2014 the society had assets of £17 million and an income of £3.7 million. Educational grants to individuals totalled £12,000.

Applications

In the first instance, contact the correspondent via email.

Other information

The society maintains a network of chaplains at the various key ports around the world, who carry out ship visiting routines and minister to seafarers. It also provides centres and clubs for seafarers and associated maritime workers at strategic seaports.

The society administers the Leith Aged Mariners' Fund and the Dundee Seaman's Friend Society.

Public services

Institution of Fire Engineers

£10,000

Correspondent: Charity Administrator, IFE House, 64–66 Cygnet Court, Timothy's Bridge Road, Stratford-upon-Avon CV37 9NW (01789 261463; fax: 01789 296426; email: frstt@ife.org.uk; website: www.ife.org.uk/Charitable-Educational-Foundation-CEF)

OSCR number: SC012694

Eligibility

All fire professionals, members of fire research organisations and the fire engineering profession or students of these areas in the UK.

Types of grants

More information on support currently available can be requested from the correspondent via email. Our research suggests that educational grants can be given for assistance with fees, books or research associated with a project/degree/general course work. Scholarships for major pieces of work and research grants are also available.

Annual grant total

The income for the institution is donated by another charity (The Fire Service Research and Training Trust), and varies greatly. In 2014 the institution had an income and a total expenditure of £1 million. Grants usually total around £10,000 each year.

Applications

Further guidelines and information on applications are available from the correspondent.

Other information

The institution makes grants on behalf of the Fire Service Research and Training Trust.

Social work

The Social Workers' Educational Trust

£21,000

Correspondent: The Hon. Secretary, 16 Kent Street, Birmingham B5 6RD (012 622 3911; email: swet@basw.co.uk; website: www.basw.co.uk/financial-support/social-workers-educational-trust)

CC number: 313789

Eligibility

Qualified social workers, with at least two years of post-qualifying experience, who work or are looking for work in the UK, and are undertaking post-qualifying training to improve their knowledge and skills for social work practice. British Association of Social Workers membership will be taken into account.

Types of grants

One-off and recurrent grants of up to £500 for fees, travel costs, childcare and books. Grants for courses of more than one year are made on an annual basis and are dependent on the recipient's successful completion of the year's training and the trust's level of funds. Part-funding of fees or expenses may also be considered should the additional funding be available from another source.

The trust's webpage states that it is usually able to make around 50 grants each year.

Annual grant total

In 2013/14 the trust had an income of £18,000 and a total expenditure of £21,500. We estimate that grants totalled £21,000.

The following is stated on the trust's website: 'The Trust's income usually allows it to make about 50 grants of up to £500 each year.'

Exclusions

The trust cannot assist those undertaking initial social work training or qualifications. Successful applicants may not re-apply within three years of the completion of a supported training course or project.

Applications

Application forms are available from the correspondent or to download from the website along with guidelines. Applications can be submitted at any time and are normally considered in February, June, September and November.

Other information

The trust also manages funds bequeathed or subscribed in memory of colleagues.

'These funds provide more substantial scholarships which are awarded annually through competition.' Enquiries for these larger annual scholarships should be made to the correspondent.

Sports

Athletics for the Young

£10,000

Correspondent: Alan Barlow, Trustee, 12 Redcar Close, Hazel Grove, Stockport SK7 4SQ (0161 483 9330; email: runalan55@hotmail.com; website: www.englandathletics.org)

CC number: 1004448

Eligibility

Young people under the age of 23 who are in full-time education, active in athletics and eligible to compete for England.

Types of grants

One-off educational grants towards athletic pursuits, including equipment and travel expenses.

Annual grant total

In 2013/14 the charity had an income of £20 and a total charitable expenditure of £19,500. We estimate the annual total amount of grants awarded to individuals to be around £10,000.

Exclusions

People already receiving funding from other sources are not normally supported.

Applications

Application forms can be downloaded from the England Athletics website or requested from the correspondent. The deadline for applications is mid-February. Note that applications should be completed in handwriting and provide a reference.

Other information

Grants can also be made to organisations and projects benefitting young athletes.

The Dickie Bird Foundation

£4,500

Correspondent: Edward Cowley, Trustee, Flat 3, The Tower, The Tower Drive, Pool in Wharfedale, Otley, West Yorkshire LS21 1NQ (email: info@thedickiebirdfoundation.co.uk; website: www.thedickiebirdfoundation.org)

CC number: 1104646

Eligibility

Disadvantaged young people under the age of 17 who are participating in sport.

Types of grants

One-off grants usually ranging from £100 to £1,000, according to need. Grants are usually given for items of sports clothing such as shirts, shorts and footwear, and for equipment and travel within the UK.

Annual grant total

In 2014/15 the foundation had an income of £3,600 and an expenditure of £5,300. We estimate that grants totalled around £4,500.

Exclusions

Grants cannot be given for:
- Professional fees of any kind, including club membership, or club fees
- Travel outside the UK
- Scholarships, summer/winter/training camps
- Equipment that is available for use elsewhere
- Overnight accommodation

Applications

Guidelines, which are available on the foundation's website, should be read before submitting an application. Applications also need to be supported by two independent referees.

Other information

The foundation's website notes:

The vision of the Foundation is to assist young people under 16 years of age to participate, to the best of their ability, in the sport of their choice irrespective of their social circumstances, culture or ethnicity and to ensure that, in doing so, they improve their chances both inside and outside sport.

The Rainer and Doreen Burchett Charitable Foundation (The Burchett Foundation)

See entry on page 62

Francis Drake Fellowship Trust Fund

£1,000

Correspondent: Joan Jupp, Correspondent, 24 Haldane Close, London N10 2PB (020 8883 8725)

CC number: 248302

Eligibility

Dependants of deceased members of the fellowship who are in full-time education.

Types of grants

Our research suggests that allowances of £52 per month per child is given to children in full-time education, up to the end of their A-levels.

Annual grant total

In 2014 the charity had an income of £100 and a total expenditure of £2,300. We estimate that the total awarded to individuals for educational purposes was around £1,000.

Applications

Application forms may be requested from the correspondent. They should be submitted through the bowling clubs Francis Drake Fellowship delegate. Applications are accepted two years after the date of the member's death.

Other information

Grants are also given to widows, orphans and other dependants of deceased members of the fellowship.

The Monica Elwes Shipway Sporting Foundation

£3,600

Correspondent: Simon Goldring, Trustee, c/o Trowers and Hamlins LLP, 3 Bunhill Row, London EC1Y 8YZ (020 7423 8000; email: sgoldring@trowers. com)

CC number: 1054362

Eligibility

Children and young people in full-time education engaged in sporting activities who have limited resources.

Types of grants

Onc-off grants of up to £300 towards clothing, equipment and fees in relation to sport activities.

Annual grant total

In 2013/14 the foundation had an income of £1,800 and an expenditure of £3,900. We have estimated that the annual total amount of grants awarded was around £3,600.

Exclusions

General university fees are not supported. Help is not available to individuals with sufficient resources.

Applications

Applications may be made in writing to the correspondent. They are considered throughout the year.

Other information

Some support may also be given to or through organisations.

The Brian Johnston Memorial Trust (The Johnners Trust)

£14,500 (24 grants)

Correspondent: Tim Berg, Administrator, c/o The Lord's Taverners, Brian Johnston Memorial Trust, 10 Buckingham Place, London SW1E 6HX (020 7821 2828; email: tim. berg@lordstaverners.org; website: www. lordstaverners.org)

CC number: 1045946

Eligibility

Young promising cricketers between the ages of 11 and 19 who are in need of financial assistance to further their personal and cricketing development.

Types of grants

Scholarships of around £500 towards travel, equipment and coaching.

Annual grant total

In 2014 the trust had assets of £28,000 and an income of £64,500. A total of £43,000 was spent in charitable activities. Brian Johnston Scholarships totalled £14,500 and were given to 24 individuals.

Applications

Apply in writing to the correspondent. Scholarships are awarded on the recommendation of the ECB Performance Department. The awards committee meets at least once a year.

Other information

Grants are also paid to cricket associations to assist participation of visually impaired and blind cricketers.

The Dan Maskell Tennis Trust

£12,000

Correspondent: Trust Administrator, c/o Sport Wins, PO Box 238, Tadworth KT20 5WT (01737 831707; email: danmaskell@sportwins.co.uk; website: www.danmaskelltennistrust.org.uk)

CC number: 1133589

Eligibility

UK citizens resident in the UK who have disabilities (including mobility, hearing, visual impairments or learning disabilities) and are playing tennis or wish to engage in this sport.

Types of grants

Individuals may apply for their own tennis wheelchair. The delivery costs will have to be covered by the applicant.

Individuals may also apply for specific needs, for example, tennis rackets,

coaching lessons with the Lawn Tennis Association (LTA) licensed coach or course fees for official LTA development or coaching courses.

The maximum grant for individuals is £500.

Annual grant total

In 2014 the trust had assets of £569,000 and an income of £77,000. Grants to 37 individuals and groups totalled about £46,000. The proportion granted to individuals was not specified in the accounts; therefore, we estimate that about £12,000 was given in support for individuals for educational purposes.

During the year the trust approved 37 grant applications, which included 14 individual tennis wheelchairs, six tennis wheelchairs for separate groups, nine tennis equipment bags, and 37 grants to individuals/groups.

Applications

Application forms are available on the trust's website. The trustees meet at least three times a year, usually in May, September and December so applications should be submitted by the middle of April, August and the beginning of November. The exact dates are likely to change so applicants are advised to see the website. Completed application forms can be returned by post or scanned and emailed to the correspondent.

Applicants are requested to provide as much information as possible, including details of their tennis activities, and provide details of estimated costs for each item or service.

Other information

Groups, clubs and specific projects can also receive support for one or more wheelchairs designed for general use at grass root level, also help with equipment, facilities or coaching fees. A deposit of £250 is required. Tennis equipment bags, containing rackets, balls, mini net and coaching aids (such as cones and throw down marker lines) are also available and will be delivered directly by the trust. The maximum grant for groups or projects is £1,500.

The trustees' annual report states: 'the trust works closely with The Tennis Foundation in liaising on grant applications and supporting the Foundation's disability programmes where appropriate. It also liaises with The Lord's Taverners in providing tennis wheelchairs for suitable (junior) applicants.'

The Torch Trophy Trust

£23,500

Correspondent: Liaison Officer, 4th Floor, Burwood House, 14–16 Caxton Street, London SW1H 0QT (020 7976 3900; fax: 020 7976 3901; email: Sbarker@sportandrecreation.org.uk; website: www.torchtrophytrust.org)

CC number: 306115

Eligibility

Volunteers working for any organisation involved in sports or outdoor activities within local communities who want to improve their skills and whose governing body is keen to help out but is unable to provide the necessary funding.

Types of grants

Bursaries from £100 to £1,000 to take courses to qualify as club coaches or officials/administrators. The award will not cover more than 50% of the total costs involved, although exceptional circumstances may be considered.

Annual grant total

In 2014 the trust had an income of £16,700 and an expenditure of £24,000. We estimate that awards to individuals totalled around £23,500.

Applications

Application forms can be requested from the correspondent or found on the trust's website (when the application cycle begins). A supporting letter from the relevant governing body must be included. For submission deadlines and further details see the trust's website.

Other information

Grants can also be made to organisations, although main support is given to individuals.

The trust also presents annual Trophy Torch Awards to the most outstanding nominated volunteers in the UK.

Religion

The Andrew Anderson Trust

£34,500

Correspondent: Andrew Anderson, Trustee, 1 Cote House Lane, Bristol BS9 3UW (0117 962 1588)

CC number: 212170

Eligibility

People studying theology.

Types of grants

One-off and recurrent grants are given according to need.

Annual grant total

In 2013/14 the trust had assets of £11.7 million and an income of £367,500. Charitable expenditure totalled £308,000 and grants to individuals for education purposes totalled £34,500.

Applications

The trust states that it rarely gives to people who are not known to the trustees or who have not been personally recommended by people known to the trustees. Unsolicited applications are, therefore, unlikely to be successful.

Other information

In 2013/14 a total of £239,000 was awarded to institutions.

The Barnabas Trust

£25,000

Correspondent: Richard Padfield, Trustee, Lawn Farm, Pillows Green Road, Corse, Gloucester GL19 3NX (01452 840371; email: richard@padfield.me.uk)

CC number: 900487

Eligibility

The trust defines its objectives as 'being an efficient channel of funds to the individuals and organisations supported by the trust'. People involved in Christian work and missionaries, particularly overseas, are eligible. Support may also be given to individuals on religious education courses.

Types of grants

Grants are given according to need. The trust works 'for individuals and organisations by administering their voluntary income and donations, including banking and recording income, applying for Gift Aid and forwarding funds on to their banks at home or overseas'.

Annual grant total

In 2014/15 the trust had assets of £5,400 and an income of £28,500. A total of £29,500 was spent in charitable activities. Grants made to individuals totalled around £25,000.

Applications

Apply in writing to the correspondent. Our research suggests that normally applications should be submitted by the end of February. The trustees meet quarterly.

The Duncan Trust

£120,000

Correspondent: Trust Administrator, c/o Thorntons Law LLP, Brothockbank House, Arbroath, Angus DD11 1NE (01241 872683; fax: 01241 871541)

OSCR number: SC015311

Eligibility

Students who are training or intend to train for the Ministry of the Church of Scotland on either regular or modified course. Preference is given to individuals within the Presbytery of Angus and Mearns.

Types of grants

Bursaries and scholarships.

Annual grant total

In 2013/14 the trust had an income of £117,500 and a total charitable expenditure of £123,500. We estimate that the annual total amount of grants awarded was around £120,000.

Applications

Apply in writing to the correspondent.

The Elland Society

£7,000

Correspondent: Revd Colin Judd, Trustee, 57 Grosvenor Road, Shipley BD18 4RB (01274 584775; email: elland@saltsvillage.co.uk; website: www.ellandsocietygrants.co.uk)

CC number: 243053

Eligibility

Men and women training for the ordained ministry of the Church of England who are evangelical in conviction and outlook (further guidance on the latter requirement is available on the website). The society will give priority to the ordinands sponsored by dioceses in the province of York or who will serve their title there.

Types of grants

One-off grants and general cash contributions according to need are given to those who have already started training at residential or non-residential theological college. Previously grants have been awarded for clothing/footwear, household items, living expenses, travel expenses, study overseas, books and educational equipment. Our research suggests that grants rarely exceed £500 per person.

Annual grant total

In 2014/15 the society had an income of £7,500 and an expenditure of £7,500. We estimate the annual total amount of grants awarded to be around £7,000.

Exclusions

Grants are not provided for the items already included in the main church grant.

Applications

Application forms can be downloaded from the society's website or requested from the correspondent.

Other information

The society prefers communication by email.

Lady Hewley's Charity

£54,500

Correspondent: Neil Blake, Correspondent, Military House, 24 Castle Street, Chester CH1 2DS

CC number: 230043

Eligibility

Young men or women preparing for United Reformed and Baptist Church ministries. Preference will be given to students who were born in the north of England.

Annual grant total

In 2013/14 the charity had assets of £16.4 million and an income of £381,500. The amount of grants given to individuals totalled £153,000, of which £54,500 was given in student grants.

Exclusions

No grants will be given when local authority funds are available.

Applications

Applications for grants are invited through contact with respective churches at both local church, regional and province levels. Individual applications are considered twice a year and grants are made according to an individual's personal and financial circumstances.

The Hockerill Educational Foundation
See entry on page 69

The Leaders of Worship and Preachers Trust

£3,800

Correspondent: Adrian Needham, Executive Officer, PO Box 2352, Watford WD18 1PY (01923 231811; fax: 01923 296899; email: lwptoffice@lwpt.org.uk; website: www.lwpt.org.uk)

CC number: 1107967

Eligibility

Individuals who wish to pursue their vocation in ministry, including individuals who are 'in the early stages of exploring their calling to preach'. Applicants should be committed Christians and active members of a church.

Types of grants

Grants can be made to assist with fees or materials for any recognised course or conference that enables the applicant to explore or develop their preaching skills. This can include gap year or similar courses and those to continue professional development. Grants can vary in size but are generally in the region of £500.

Annual grant total

In 2013/14 the trust had assets of £582,500 and an income of £848,000. Grants totalled £11,200, of which £3,800 was given to individuals in vocational grants.

Exclusions

Grants are not made to assist with accommodation or subsistence. Applicants are normally awarded only one grant within a twelve month period.

Applications

An application form is available to download from the website along with guidance notes. Information about the applicant's financial circumstances will be requested by the trust in order to determine the need for support. Applicants must have the support of a member of their church staff, who will be asked for a reference confirming the individual's interest and potential ability in preaching, their Christian faith and their character.

Applications must be submitted by 30 June for a grant in September or by 30 October for a grant in January. In exceptional circumstances, requests for support outside these time frames may be accepted.

Other information

The trust notes on its website: 'It is important to note before making an application, that your church may be able to offer you financial support.'

The Leathersellers' Company Charitable Fund
See entry on page 14

The James Pantyfedwen Foundation (Ymddiriedolaeth James Pantyfedwen)
See entry on page 14

Powis Exhibition Fund

£5,500

Correspondent: John Richfield, 39 Cathedral Road, Cardiff CF11 9XF (029 2034 8200; fax: 029 2038 7835)

CC number: 525770

Eligibility

People who are training as ordinands of the Church in Wales. Applicants must be born or be resident in Wales and speak Welsh.

Types of grants

Grants are available only for the period of study and can range up to £700 per year.

Annual grant total

In 2014 the fund had an income of £12,500 and an expenditure of £6,000. We estimate that the annual total amount of grants awarded was around £5,500.

Applications

Application forms are available from the correspondent or from individual dioceses.

The Sheffield West Riding Charitable Society Trust

£4,900

Correspondent: Malcolm Fair, Diocesan Secretary, Diocesan Church House, 95–99 Effingham Street, Rotherham, South Yorkshire S65 1BL (01709 309100; email: malcolm.fair@sheffield.anglican.org; website: www.sheffield.anglican.org)

CC number: 1002026

Eligibility

Clergy children at school and in further education in the Diocese of Sheffield.

Types of grants

Only a small proportion of grants are educational. They are given to help with the cost of books, clothing and other essentials.

Annual grant total

In 2014 the trust had an income of £13,900 and a total expenditure of £10,100. We estimate that grants for purposes related to education totalled £4,900.

Applications

An application form is available from the correspondent.

Other information

Welfare grants are also made to the clergy, housekeepers and disadvantaged families in the diocese.

Sola Trust

£330,000 (117 grants)

Correspondent: Simon Pilcher, Trustee, Green End Barn, Wood End Green, Henham, Bishop's Stortford CM22 6AY (01279 850819; email: admin@solatrust.org.uk)

CC number: 1062739

Eligibility
Individuals training at a theological college or at a church (in a form of an apprenticeship) for full-time Christian work, as well as to those already involved in full-time ministry.

Types of grants
Grants are usually one-off or up to one year and intended to be supplementary only. Support is available towards books, other necessities, conferences, training courses, retreats and other expenses. Additionally the charity aims to relieve the financial hardship of those involved in Christian ministry.

Annual grant total
In 2013/14 the trust had assets of £151,000 and an income of £334,000. Charitable expenditure totalled £559,000. Grants totalled £330,000 and were distributed to 117 individuals consisting of:

Theological and ministry training grants	£288,800
Other ministry grants	£26,000
PhD studies	£14,000
Relief of poverty	£1,000

The trust further notes that 'the majority of the people and institutions supported were in the UK (with no particular geographical focus within the UK)' with a significant minority being in a variety of European and Australasian countries, South Africa and the USA.

Applications
Apply in writing to the correspondent. Where appropriate, grants may be routed through a church or equivalent body that is providing training to individuals. The trustees meet several times a year to consider applications. Applicants are required to provide a budget detailing anticipated income and expenditure. References are also required.

The following is taken from the trust's website:

Your application should include:
- What you are applying for funding for
- Christian background
- Age, education, Christian ministry and other work (eg, non-Church paid employment)
- Hopes, ambitions and plans
- An annual budget – accounting for any spouse, children or other dependents

See the trust's website for more details.

Other information
The trustees' annual report for 2013/14 states that:

The charity also seeks to facilitate the strategic placement of trained gospel workers – working in new geographical areas (areas of the country where there is little or no biblical ministry at present) and in new types of ministry (for example youth or women's ministry).

48 grants were also made to institutions consisting of theology and ministry grants, church plant grants other church ministry grants totalling £229,000.

The Spalding Trust

£69,500

Correspondent: Tessa Rodgers, Secretary, PO Box 85, Stowmarket IP14 3NY (website: www.spaldingtrust.org.uk)

CC number: 209066

Eligibility
People undertaking research projects into the great religions of the world, particularly comparative studies, who are in need of financial support. Projects must primarily have a religious concern, rather than sociological or anthropological.

Types of grants
Awards of up to £2,000 for the comparative study of the major religions. Support is available for research projects, publications, occasionally travel costs, conferences and related expenses. Applications may not necessarily be academically orientated, provided they have sufficient practical and beneficial aspect. Recurrent grants extending over one year are only considered in exceptional circumstances.

Annual grant total
In 2014 the trust had an income of £82,500 a total expenditure of £90,500 and grants totalled £69,500.

Exclusions
Grants are not given retrospectively and will rarely be provided towards expenses related to a first degree.

Applications
Apply in writing to the correspondent providing:
- An outline of the proposal/course
- A copy of the applicant's CV, specifying their own religious commitment, if any
- Details of the budget and of other possible sources of funding that have been applied for (this should be done using a copy of the financial statement available on the trust's website)
- Preferably two academic references

- Daytime and evening phone numbers and an email address

Applications should be submitted by post. Further application guidelines are available on the trust's website. The trustees meet once a year to decide on major proposals but smaller grants are considered on a monthly basis (it may take up to three months to reach a decision).

Other information
The trust also makes grants to institutions, such as libraries, colleges, other educational establishments.

A subsidiary of the trust, the Ellen Rebe Spalding Memorial Fund, makes grants to disadvantaged women and children.

The Foundation of St Matthias

£41,500 (63 grants)

Correspondent: Karine Prescott, Clerk to the Trustees, Hillside House, First Floor, 1500 Parkway North, Newbrick Road, Stoke Gifford, Bristol BS34 8YU (0117 906 0100; email: stmatthiastrust@bristoldiocese.org; website: www.stmatthiastrust.org.uk)

CC number: 311696

Eligibility
Further and higher education students, including mature students and occasionally postgraduates, who are studying in accordance with the doctrine of the Church of England. This includes:
- People who are, or intend to become, engaged in social welfare work as social workers, community workers, youth workers, teachers or supervisors of pre-school groups, etc.
- People who are intending to become ministers of the Church of England or of a church in communion with the Church of England

Preference is given to applicants from the dioceses of Bath and Wells, Bristol and Gloucester, although applicants from elsewhere are considered.

Types of grants
One-off grants usually ranging from £200 to £1,000. Grants can be given for books, fees, maintenance/living expenses, childcare and for some study or travel abroad. Overseas courses may be supported only if the visit is integral to the course or research.

Annual grant total
In 2014 the foundation had assets of £6.4 million and an income of £271,000. The amount of grants given to individuals totalled £41,500, of which 47 grants were of less than £1,000 and 16 were of £1,000 or more.

Exclusions

No retrospective grants are made.

Applications

Applicants should telephone in the first instance to discuss the nature of study and so on. Applications must be made on a form available from the foundation's website. They should be submitted by 31 May for consideration in July or 30 September for consideration in November.

Other information

The foundation advises applicants to apply to as many sources of funding as possible as funding is not guaranteed and often, the foundation cannot offer the full amount requested. There is a link to other religious education charities on its website.

The foundation is not able to cover the costs of fees, maintenance or travel, etc. of students from overseas, but small contributions may be offered should evidence be supplied that substantial funding is available from other sources.

The Thornton Fund

£2,800

Correspondent: Dr Jane Williams, Trustee, 93 Fitzjohn Avenue, Barnet EN5 2HR (020 8440 2211; email: djanewilliams@dsl.pipex.com)

CC number: 226803

Eligibility

Students at Unitarian colleges or training for Unitarian ministry.

Types of grants

Grants, usually of between £250 and £1,500, to help with books, equipment, instruments, living expenses, study exchange and study or travel abroad.

Annual grant total

In 2014 the fund had an income of £20,500 and a total expenditure of £11,300. Grants are made to individuals for both welfare and educational purposes, and occasionally to Unitarian and Free Christian churches for special projects. We estimate that training grants to individuals totalled £2,800.

Applications

Applications can be made by writing to the correspondent through a third party such as a minister. Applications should include the total and annual estimated costs of study. They are considered on an ongoing basis.

Torchbearer Trust Fund

£30,000

Correspondent: Phil Burt, Secretary, Capernwray Hall, Carnforth, Lancashire LA6 1AG (01524 733908; fax: 01524 736681; email: info@capernwray.org.uk; website: www.capernwray.org.uk)

CC number: 253607

Eligibility

People engaged in full-time Christian instruction or training. Preference is given to students and former students of Torchbearer Bible schools.

Types of grants

One-off grants and bursaries according to need.

Annual grant total

In 2013/14 the charity had assets of £132,000 and an income of £70,500. Grants totalled £60,000, a breakdown of which was not available in the accounts. We estimate that grants for educational purposes totalled around £30,000.

Applications

At the time of writing (August 2015) the charity stated the following on its Charity Commission record: 'All funds are fully allocated at present and so applications for funding will not receive a response.'

Women's Continuing Ministerial Education Trust

£50,000

Correspondent: The Adminstrator, Archbishops' Council, Church House, Great Smith Street, London SW1P 3AZ (020 7898 1000; email: webmaster@ churchofengland.org; website: www.cofe. anglican.org)

CC number: 1093320

Eligibility

Women (ordained or not) who are licensed into a nationally recognised ministry in the Church of England or the Scottish Episcopal Church (with the exception of Readers). Religious Sisters and retired clergy who are involved in active ministry can also apply.

Types of grants

Grants are given for continuing ministerial education. Support is given towards general educational needs, conferences, educational fees (where possible, any costs of fees will be awarded). Grants are intended to supplement funds available from the applicant's diocese.

Accommodation, travel costs or childcare is not normally covered, but anticipated costs of those needs should be included in the budget in order to allow better assessment of the application.

Due to limited funds the trust focuses on applications for courses/projects that clearly relate to assisting the minister in their work and professional development.

Annual grant total

In 2014 the trust had an income of £250 and a total expenditure of £55,500. Generally about £50,000 is given a year.

Exclusions

The trust does not normally fund courses in IME 4–7 and retreats/ sabbaticals.

Applications

Application forms can be accessed from the Church of England website. Applications must be endorsed by the Diocesan CME Officer or Dean of the Women's Ministry. Grants are normally considered quarterly, in February, May, July and October and the deadline for applications is in the preceding month. Candidates are informed about the outcome of their application in the following month.

Skilled crafts

The Worshipful Company of Butchers' Educational Charity

£1,800

Correspondent: The Clerk, Butchers' Hall, 87–88 Bartholomew Close, London EC1A 7EB (020 7600 4106; fax: 020 7606 4108; email: clerk@butchershall.com; website: www.butchershall.com)

CC number: 297603

Eligibility

People involved in the meat trade who are studying courses related to the trade.

Applicants for the Nuffield Farming Scholarship must be UK residents aged between 25 and 45 who have been in the industry for at least two years and intend to remain involved in the sector.

Types of grants

One-off grants towards further and higher education fees.

The company also provides one Nuffield Farming Scholarship each year to enable someone who is active in the meat and livestock industries to study a topic of their choice carrying out a tour anywhere in the world to further their knowledge and understanding.

Annual grant total

In 2013/14 the charity had assets of £827,500 and an income of £32,500. The amount of grants given to individuals totalled £1,800. A further £40,000 was given to organisations.

Applications

Apply in writing to the correspondent. Applications should be submitted directly by the individual for consideration monthly.

To apply for the Nuffield Farming Scholarship contact Bob Bansback on bob@bansback.co.uk.

The Carpenters Company Charitable Trust

£3,000 (1 grant)

Correspondent: Brigadier Tim Gregson, Clerk, Carpenters' Hall, 1 Throgmorton Avenue, London EC2N 2JJ (020 7588 7001; email: info@carpentersco.com; website: www.carpentersco.com/pages/charities/carpenters_company_charitable_trust1)

CC number: 276996

Eligibility

The trust was established to support the craft i.e. people wishing to set up in or to study carpentry.

Types of grants

Educational grants are awarded up to £2,400 to help with fees, maintenance, equipment and other necessities.

Annual grant total

In 2014/15 the trust had assets of £24.6 million (comprising mainly endowment, restricted and designated funds) and an income of £1.1 million. One grant of £3,000 was awarded to an individual during the year. A further £967,000 was awarded in grants to 18 organisations.

Applications

Application forms are available from the correspondent or from the website. Applications are considered in March, July and November.

Coats Foundation Trust

£17,500

Correspondent: Andrea McCutcheon, Coats Pensions Office, Cornerstone, 107 West Regent Street, Glasgow G2 2BA (0141 207 6800; email: cft@coats.com; website: www.coatspensions.co.uk/about-us/coats-foundation-trust)

CC number: 268735

Eligibility

University students living in the UK who are studying textile and thread-related subjects. Those with a long-term future in the UK and without a previous degree are prioritised by the trust.

Types of grants

One-off grants according to need. Grants are made to college students, undergraduates and mature students for fees, books and equipment/instruments. Schoolchildren may also receive grants for books and equipment/instruments.

Annual grant total

In 2013/14 the trust had an income of £1,200 and a total expenditure of £77,000. Grants are made to both individuals and organisations for social welfare and educational purposes. We estimate that the amount of grants given to individuals for educational purposes totalled around £17,500.

Applications

Applications can be made using the application form, which is available to download from the website along with a financial statement, which must also be completed. Details should be provided on other sources of funding that have been applied to or from which the applicant may expect help. Any other relevant information that may help the trustees when considering the applicant's case should be included. Payments are not made to other charities as the trust's intention is to assist individuals directly.

The Goldsmiths Arts Trust Fund

£30,000 (26 grants)

Correspondent: The Clerk, The Goldsmiths' Company, Goldsmiths' Hall, Foster Lane, London EC2V 6BN (020 7606 7010; fax: 020 7606 1511; email: charity@thegoldsmiths.co.uk; website: www.thegoldsmiths.co.uk)

CC number: 313329

Eligibility

University and college students, postgraduates, recent graduates and apprentices studying silversmithing and precious metal jewellery. Specific programmes are also available to support school teachers.

Types of grants

The fund offers bursaries and grants reaching up to over £1,000 to students at universities and colleges of art or apprentices. Support can be given towards exhibitions, specific projects, provision of materials and tools, skills development programmes, masterclasses

and courses that advance the arts, design and craftsmanship.

The fund's website also notes that the funding is currently focused on four major projects: supporting seven selected primary schools; providing science teachers with free residential courses; allowing primary and secondary school teachers to undertake professional and personal development; and assisting postgraduate medical students who have turned to medicine as their second degree (support administered through British Medical Association only).

Annual grant total

In 2013/14 the fund had assets of £112,500 and an income of £772,500. A total of £30,000 was awarded in bursaries and grants to 26 individuals.

Exclusions

According to our research, grants are not normally made for fees or subsistence on standard courses at further or higher education institutions. Awards are not normally available to overseas students studying in the UK.

Applications

Applications should be made in writing to the correspondent, through an organisation such as a college or university. Applications are normally considered quarterly.

Other information

Grants are also given to organisations and individuals who are members of the Goldsmiths' Company for various charitable purposes. In 2013/14 Goldsmith's Craft and Design Council received a grant of £34,000.

The latest annual report states:

> The objective of the Goldsmiths Arts Trust Fund, as laid down in the Trust Deed, is to promote, maintain, improve and advance education particularly by the encouragement of the art of design and good craftsmanship. In seeking to achieve this objective, the Trustee's aim is to ensure that the associated grant making is targeted effectively.

The Doctor Dorothy Jordan Lloyd Memorial Fund

£1,000

Correspondent: Kerry Senior, Leather Trade House, Kings Park Road, Northampton NN3 6JD (01604 679955; email: info@uklf.org)

CC number: 313933

Eligibility

People under the age of 40 working in the leather industry, studying or doing a research on related subjects, and scientist developing the leather production technology. Grants are available to both UK and overseas students (who are required to be fluent in English and intend to return to work in their home country).

Types of grants

Grants are available for travel overseas to study the leather science and technology or work on related projects. The support is not intended for students in full/part-time courses rather to encourage short and focused visits.

Annual grant total

In 2013/14 the fund had an income of £5,500 and an expenditure of £1,500. We have estimated the annual total amount of grants awarded to be around £1,000.

Exclusions

Our research shows that the fellowship may not be offered to an applicant resident in, or a citizen of, a country which restricts free trade in hides, skins or leather.

Applications

Apply in writing to the correspondent. Applications can be submitted directly by the individual for consideration at any time.

Norton Folgate Trust

£237,000 (78 grants)

Correspondent: The Craft and Charities Administrator, Carpenter's Company, Carpenter's Hall, 1 Throgmorton Avenue, London EC2N 2JJ (020 7588 7001; email: info@carpentersco.com; website: www.thecarpenterscompany.co.uk/pages/charities/norton_folgate_charitable_trust/default.aspx)

CC number: 230990

Eligibility

People in further or higher education at an institution in the UK who are studying the craft of carpentry, fine woodwork, stonemasonry, historic building conservation, any branch of the building industry or related courses.

Types of grants

Grants ranging from £500 to £7,500 can be given to help with school, college or university fees or to supplement existing grants. Support may be available to school pupils towards general educational necessities but most grants are distributed to secondary or tertiary education students, particularly to individuals at the Building Crafts College in Stratford, East London. Some funds may be given towards wood craft tools.

Annual grant total

In 2013/14 the trust had assets of £6.1 million, an income of £271,500.

Grants totalling £237,000 were made to 78 individuals, broken down as follows:

Craft education	53	£145,400
Other education	15	£48,500
Liverymen, Freemen, retirees and their dependants	10	£43,000
Total	**78**	**£237,000**

Exclusions

Grants are not made retrospectively.

Applications

Application forms are available on the trust's website and have to be submitted by June for the academic year beginning in September. Applicants will be notified of a decision in August.

Students at the Building Crafts College should apply to the following address before May (applicants will be notified of a decision in June): The Bursar, Building Crafts College, Kennard Road, Stratford, London E15 1AH.

People applying for grants for wood craft tools should write to the correspondent.

The Queen Elizabeth Scholarship Trust

£356,500 (46 grants)

Correspondent: Lyanne Nicholl, Secretary, 1 Buckingham Place, London SW1E 6HR (020 7798 1533; email: info@qest.org.uk; website: www.qest.org.uk)

CC number: 802557

Eligibility

▶ You must be over the age of 17 to apply and there is no upper age limit
▶ You need to demonstrate you already have a high level of skill and are firmly committed to your craft or trade
▶ Only those who live and work permanently in the UK are eligible for a scholarship
▶ It is not necessary to be connected with companies or individuals holding Royal Warrants of Appointment

Types of grants

One-off and staged scholarships over a maximum of four years, each worth between £1,000 and £18,000. Support can be given for further education, such as work experience and training, related travel costs, research visits, special courses and other projects.

Previous grant recipients have included antiques restorers, calligraphers, book conservators, potters, silversmiths, upholsterers, designers and so on.

Annual grant total

In 2013 the trust had assets of £5 million and an income of £187,500. A total of £356,500 was awarded in 46

scholarships. At the time of writing (October 2015) the information provided was the latest available.

Exclusions

Grants are not made for tools, equipment, materials, leasing studios/workshops, staging exhibitions, business start-up or for general further education unrelated to a craft skill.

Applications

Application forms are available on the trust's website. See the trust's website for application deadlines.

The Wine Guild Charitable Trust

£3,000

Correspondent: Joseph Ferris Lulham, Correspondent, 1 Icklingham Road, Cobham, Surrey KT11 2NG (01932 869557; email: jrf.lulham@virgin.net; website: wineguilduk.org/the-charity.php)

CC number: 1105374

Eligibility

Young people wishing to further their studies in the wine making industry.

Types of grants

Grants, loans or bursaries. The trust's website states: 'The Trustees would be pleased to hear of any young person who might be in need of financial support for his or her studies in the wine industry.'

Annual grant total

In 2014 the trust had an income of £12,400 and a total expenditure of £6,100. We estimate that educational grants to individuals totalled about £3,000.

Applications

Applications should be made in writing to the Council Secretary, Jane Grey-Edwards (tel: 01798 345262; email: jgrey-edwards@tiscali.co.uk) at Christmas Cottage, North Street, Petworth GU28 0DF.

Other information

The trust also helps to arrange meetings, lectures and conferences with the aim of sharing knowledge and appreciation of wine with the general public.

Social sciences

The Airey Neave Trust

£45,000

Correspondent: Sophie Butler, Administrator, PO Box 111, Leominster HR6 6BP (email: aireyneavetrust@gmail.com; website: www.aireyneavetrust.org.uk)

CC number: 297269

Eligibility

People engaged in research projects looking into 'issues related to personal freedom under democratic law against the threat of political violence'. Funding has also been provided towards conferences and seminars on anti-terrorism issues.

Types of grants

Grants for research projects or seminars. For example, previously support has been given for a seminar on counter-terrorism policy and for a project on territorial motivations of terrorist organisations. The trust stresses that only modest funds are available.

Annual grant total

In 2013/14 the trust had an income of £26,000 and an expenditure of £61,000. Previously around £45,000 has been awarded for research purposes.

Exclusions

Financial assistance to refugees is no longer provided.

Applications

Apply in writing to the correspondent.

Other information

The trust has stopped funding for refugees in order to focus all of its funds on research grants.

The Barry Amiel and Norman Melburn Trust

£35,500

Correspondent: Millie Burton, Administrative Officer, 34, Claverdale Road SW2 2DP (07949716043; email: millie.burton@outlook.com; website: www.amielandmelburn.org.uk)

CC number: 281239

Eligibility

Groups and individuals working to advance public education in the philosophy of Marxism, the history of socialism, and the working class movement.

Types of grants

Grants to individuals and organisations normally range from £200 to £7,000 and are paid for a range of archiving, research, printing, publishing and conference costs.

Previously funded projects have included the organisation of lectures, discussions, seminars and workshops; the carrying out of research, written work and publications; and the maintenance of libraries and archive material.

Annual grant total

In 2013/14 the trust had assets of £2.9 million an income of £64,000 and a charitable expenditure of £97,500. Grants awarded for research and archiving totalled £35,500.

Exclusions

The trust does not award funds to subsidise the continuation or running of university/college courses; to cover transport costs to or from conferences; or to subsidise fees/maintenance for undergraduate/postgraduate students.

Applications

Application forms are available from the correspondent which must be returned in hard copy. Application guidelines are available to download from the website. Closing dates for applications are noted on the website. The trustees meet twice a year to consider applications, usually in January and June; however, applications for major grants (of more than £6,000) are only considered once a year at the January meeting.

Gilbert Murray Trust – International Studies Committee

£6,500

Correspondent: Professor Richard Alston, Classics Department, Royal Holloway University of London, Egham, Surrey TW20 0EX (0447786543925; email: r.alston@rhul.ac.uk; website: www.gilbertmurraytrust.org.uk)

CC number: 212244

Eligibility

People under the age of 25 who are studying, or have studied, international relations (including international law, security, peace, development studies, global governance) at an institution of higher education in the UK. Applicants above the age of 25 could be considered if there are specific reasons for a delay in their education, such as ill health or financial problems.

Types of grants

Grants of up to £1,000 are available towards a specific project relevant to the work and purposes of the United Nations (for example, research-related visits to a specific country/headquarters of an international organisation, or a short course at an institution abroad) which will directly contribute towards the applicant's studies.

Annual grant total

In 2014/15 the charity had an income of £25,500 and a charitable expenditure of £7,500. A total of £6,500 was awarded in grants.

Exclusions

Grants are not intended to support international affair students with general educational expenses and needs.

Applications

Apply in writing to the correspondent. Applications should include a brief CV, a short statement of career intentions, detailed description of the project with associated costs and sources of additional funding (if required), an assessment by a person 'in a position to judge the applicant in his or her suitability for the award' and, if relevant, reasons for delayed education.

Applications and all the relevant information should be provided in five copies and submitted no later than 2 April.

Other information

The charity's Classical Committee also offers recurring support and awards for various projects and initiatives which seek to promote the studies of ancient Greek civilisation, culture and language. The Secretary of the Classical Committee is Prof. Michael Trapp (email: michael.trapp@kcl.ac.uk) at Department of Classics, King's College, Strand, London WC2R 2LS.

Organisations can also be supported.

Society of Antiquaries of London
See entry on page 54

Archaeology

The British Institute of Archaeology at Ankara (British Institute at Ankara)

£130,000

Correspondent: Claire McCafferty, Administrator, 10 Carlton House Terrace, London SW1Y 5AH (020 7969 5204; fax: 020 7969 5401; email: biaa@britac.ac.uk; website: www.biaa.ac.uk)

CC number: 313940

Eligibility

British undergraduates and postgraduates studying the Turkish and Black Sea littoral in academic disciplines within the arts, humanities and social sciences, particularly the archaeology of Turkey. Applicants must be based at a UK university or academic institution.

Scholars from Turkey and the countries surrounding the Black Sea who are studying in the UK can also be supported.

Types of grants

The grants are given for the following purposes:

- Study grants – of up to £2,000 towards travel and subsistence expenses for individuals carrying out doctoral or postdoctoral research
- Fieldwork grants – check the website for latest criteria
- Project funding – up to £5,000 a year for a maximum of three years. Applications are invited for advanced research within one of the strategic research initiatives currently sponsored by the institution (see the website for details)

The institute also offers funding for an annual postdoctoral research fellowship and a research scholarship based at the Institute in Ankara, and also provides scholarships to enable students from Turkey and the Black Sea region to travel to the UK.

Annual grant total

In 2013/14 the institute had assets of £423,000 and an income of £701,500. Grants to individuals were made totalling around £130,000.

Applications

Application forms are available from the institute's website or upon request from the correspondent. The institute notes that 'applications are judged on their academic merit through a stringent process of peer review by appropriate experts'. The deadline for applications is 1 April.

Other information

In 2013/14 the institute also supported institutions (£48,000) and academics from Turkey through the Turkish scholars fund (£2,500).

The institute runs a number of schemes solely for postgraduates, as well as overseeing a number of other funds. See the website for further details.

Cultural studies

The British Institute for the Study of Iraq (Gertrude Bell Memorial)

See entry on page 31

The Hellenic Foundation

£13,500

Correspondent: The Trustees, 150 Aldersgate Street, London EC1A 4AB (020 7251 5100)

CC number: 326301

Eligibility

Students studying the culture, tradition and heritage of Greece, particularly in the subjects involving education, research, music, theatre productions, exhibitions and concerts.

Types of grants

One-off and recurrent grants for projects involving education, research, music and dance, books and library facilities and university symposia.

Annual grant total

In 2013 the foundation had an income of £19,400 and a total charitable expenditure of £14,000. We estimate that grants totalled £13,500.

The information provided was the latest available at the time of writing (October 2015)

Applications

Apply in writing to the correspondent.

Il Circolo Italian Cultural Association Ltd

£7,800

Correspondent: Colin Angwin, Secretary, Flat 7, Farley Court, Melbury Road, London W14 8LJ (02076032364; email: grants@ilcircolo.org.uk; website: www.ilcircolo.org.uk)

CC number: 1108894

Eligibility

Students who have been accepted onto a course at a British higher education institution, either at undergraduate or postgraduate level, pursuing studies, training or research relating to Italian culture (humanities, arts and crafts, sciences and performing arts).

Types of grants

Scholarships for students who wish to further their education in the field of Italian and related studies.

Annual grant total

In 2014 the association had assets of £51,500 and an income of £56,500. Grants to students totalled £7,800. Charitable organisations received a further £13,800.

Applications

Apply in writing to the correspondent. Selected candidates will be interviewed, usually in May.

Turath Scholarship Fund

£2,000

Correspondent: Dr Imran Satia, Trustee, 4 West Park Road, Blackburn BB2 6DG (07825346320; email: scholarship@turath.co.uk; website: www.turath.co.uk/front/turath-scholarship-fund)

CC number: 1138153

Eligibility

To be eligible for a grant you must: be a UK citizen; be between the ages of 18 and 24; preferably hold a degree from a good UK university with at least a 2.1 grading; be committed to studying your chosen discipline for a prolonged period of time; and demonstrate some teaching experience.

Types of grants

Grants are available individuals hoping to study any aspect of the Islamic Sciences outside their university degree. Grants can be used to pay for training or tuition including fees and travel.

Annual grant total

In 2014/15 the fund had both an income and an expenditure of £6,000. We estimate that around £2,000 was distributed in grants to individuals.

Applications

Application forms are available from the website and should be returned by email.

Geography

Royal Geographical Society (with the Institute of British Geographers)

£68,000

Correspondent: Grants Office, 1 Kensington Gore, London SW7 2AR (020 7591 3073; fax: 020 7591 3001; email: grants@rgs.org; website: www.rgs. org)

CC number: 208791

Eligibility

People over the age of 16 who are carrying out geographical research and projects. Teachers, undergraduate and postgraduate students, scientists, also non-academics (for example independent travellers) are all eligible.

The society has previously stated that its grants programme aims to promote geographical research and a wider understanding of the world and, therefore, applicants are not required to have a geography degree, work in a geography department or define themselves as a geographer, but must share the society's interest in the world, people and environment.

Note: Some grants are only open to fellows of the society.

Types of grants

The society administers a large number of grants, each with separate eligibility criteria and application process. The awards are broken down into the following categories: established researchers; early career researchers; postgraduate; undergraduate; expeditions, fieldwork and independent travel; teaching. For full details of each award see the society's website.

Support can be given for work both in the UK and overseas in the range of £250–£30,000.

Annual grant total

In 2014 the society had assets of £15.8 million, an income of £7.1 million and made grants totalling £206,000. Of that sum, £68,000 was awarded to individuals and consisted of support for expeditions and fieldwork (£65,000) and education and teaching (£3,000).

Exclusions

Grants are not made retrospectively or given for fees/living costs associated with degrees.

Applications

All grant details, guidelines, application forms and specific deadlines can be obtained from the society's website.

Generally, the application process lasts between three and four months. All candidates are informed about the outcome of their application.

Other information

The society also supports institutions and offers information, advice, resources and training to support anyone planning a fieldwork or scientific expedition.

National charities classified by occupation/parent's occupation

Armed forces

ABF The Soldiers' Charity (also known as The Army Benevolent Fund)

£1.3 million

Correspondent: The Welfare Team, Mountbarrow House, 6–20 Elizabeth Street, London SW1W 9RB (020 7901 8900; fax: 020 7901 8901; email: info@soldierscharity.org; website: www.soldierscharity.org)

CC number: 211645

Eligibility

Members and ex-members of the British Regular Army and the Reserve Army (Territorial Army) and their dependants who are in need. Serving TA soldiers must have completed at least one year's satisfactory service, and former TA soldiers should have completed at least three years' satisfactory service.

Types of grants

Funding is given:
- To training colleges helping to retrain soldiers with disabilities and towards training course fees and essential equipment for individual soldiers
- To support ex-soldiers taking higher education courses to start on new careers after leaving the army
- To help the continuing education of children of soldiers who have died or have got a severe disability while serving

Annual grant total

In 2013/14 the charity had assets of £45.6 million and an income of £14.5 million. Grants totalled £7.9 million, of which £5 million was awarded to individuals. We estimate that the amount of grants given to individuals for social welfare purposes were given in the form of routine grants totalling £3.4 million, and from the Quick Reaction Fund totalling £279,000. This leaves £1.3 million that we believe was given to individuals for educational and training purposes, £847,000 given for specialist employment consultants and £460,000 awarded in Individual Recovery Plan grants.

Applications

The charity does not deal directly with individual cases. Soldiers who are still serving should contact their regimental or corps association, who will then approach the fund on their behalf. Former soldiers should first contact SSAFA or The Royal British Legion. Applications are considered at any time, but all are reviewed annually in July.

Enquiries may be made directly to the fund to determine the appropriate corps or regimental association.

Other information

As well as making grants to individuals for social welfare purposes, ABF makes grants to other charities working to support service and ex-service people. In 2013/14 there was a focus on the following areas: care for older people; mental health and respite care; homelessness; supported housing; and education, training for employment and welfare support.

Help for Heroes

£450,000

Correspondent: Grants Team, 14 Parker's Close, Downton Business Park, Downton, Salisbury, Wiltshire SP5 3RB (01980 844354; email: grants@helpforheroes.org.uk; website: www.helpforheroes.org.uk)

CC number: 1120920, SC044984

Eligibility

Current and former members of the armed forces who have suffered a life-changing injury or illness while serving, or as a result of their service, and their dependants.

Types of grants

Grants towards equipment, facilities or services to assist individuals' rehabilitation. Individuals are supported through Quick Reaction Fund (QRF). Assistance can be given towards academic and (re)training courses, vocational or employment opportunities and associated needs, such as educational necessities or specialist equipment. In urgent cases, QRF support is aimed to be provided within 72 hours.

Annual grant total

In 2013/14 the charity had assets of £111.3 million and an income of £37.2 million. The annual report and accounts for 2013/14 state: 'In 2014 Help for Heroes gave 936 grants to individuals with awards totalling £0.9m, and granted over £4 million in 2014 to other charities and organisations that work alongside us to support our beneficiaries.' We estimate grants for educational and training needs to have totalled around £450,000.

Applications

Candidates are encouraged to contact the correspondent to discuss their needs and the application procedure.

Other information

Help for Heroes runs the H4H Career Recovery service to help individuals with their new futures outside the armed forces. For more information, visit the website or contact the Career Recovery team by email (career.recovery@helpforheroes.org.uk) or by telephone (01980 844257).

The charity works with the armed forces and other military charities. Funding is also given to individuals for general welfare needs and organisations working for the benefit of members of the armed forces.

Individuals and their families or carers are also welcomed to visit one of the 'support hubs' to receive further advice and support on a range of welfare issues. For more details and contact information of the recovery centres see the website.

Lloyd's Patriotic Fund

£7,500 (7 grants)

Correspondent: The Secretary, Lloyd's Patriotic Fund, Lloyd's, One Lime Street, London EC3M 7HA (020 7327 6144; email: communityaffairs@lloyds.com; website: www.lloyds.com/lpf)

CC number: 210173

Eligibility

Children of officers and ex-officers of the Royal Navy, the Army, Royal Marines and Royal Air Force. Preference may be given to schoolchildren with serious family difficulties where the child has to be educated away from home and to people with special educational needs.

Types of grants

Bursaries ranging from around £800 to £1,500 per year are given for school fees.

Annual grant total

In 2013/14 the fund had assets of £3 million and an income of £399,500. During the year, educational grants totalled £7,500 and were distributed in seven bursaries through The Royal Navy and Royal

Marines Children's Fund and The Royal Navy Officer's Charity. Educational grants account only for a small proportion of the charitable activities.

Applications

Grants are awarded through The Royal Navy and Royal Marines Children's Fund and The Royal Naval Scholarship Fund. All applications should be made through these organisations.

Other information

The fund works with SSAFA and other partners through which funds are administered. Various military organisations are supported, with a particular focus on those helping people who have disabilities or individuals facing poverty, illness and hardship.

The Dr Thomas Lyon Bequest

£700

Correspondent: Gregor Murray, Secretary and Chamberlain, The Merchant Company, The Merchant Hall, 22 Hanover Street, Edinburgh EH2 2EP (0131 220 9284; email: gregor.murray@mcoe.org.uk; website: www.mcoe.org.uk/charities)

OSCR number: SC010284

Eligibility

Scottish orphans of members of Her Majesty's Forces and of the Mercantile Marine. Applicants should be between the ages of 5 and 18 and require financial assistance.

Types of grants

Grants ranging from £500 to £1,500 are offered to children in primary and secondary education towards the costs of clothing and school uniforms, books, educational outings and school fees.

Annual grant total

In 2013/14 the charity had an income of £7,500 and a total expenditure of £1,700. We estimate that about £700 was given in grants to individuals.

Applications

Applications may be made in writing to the correspondent. They should state the individual's total income and the regiment/service of their parent as well as the cause and date of their death.

Poppyscotland (The Earl Haig Fund Scotland)

£30,000

Correspondent: The Trustees, New Haig House, Logie Green Road, Edinburgh

EH7 4HR (0131 557 2782; fax: 0131 557 5819; email: enquiries@poppyscotland. org.uk; website: www.poppyscotland.org. uk)

OSCR number: SC014096

Eligibility

People in Scotland of working-age who have served in the UK Armed Forces (regular or reserve) and are now unemployed, low-skilled or in low-paid employment.

Types of grants

Poppyscotland makes grants for a wide range of purposes. They include Employment Support Grants of up to £2,000 for individuals who are leaving the armed forces to allow them to undertake vocational training and qualifications which will have a 'strong likelihood of leading to sustainable employment'. See the website for more information.

Annual grant total

In 2013/14 the fund had an income of £4.3 million and a total expenditure of £4.7 million. Grants made totalled around £1.4 million. Previously grants for educational purposes to individuals have totalled approximately £30,000.

Applications

Apply in writing to the correspondent.

Other information

Poppyscotland is in many respects the Scottish equivalent of the benevolence department of The Royal British Legion in the rest of Britain. Like the legion, it runs the Poppy Appeal, which is a major source of income to help those in need. There is, however, a The Royal British Legion Scotland, which has a separate entry in this guide. The two organisations share the same premises and work together.

In 2006 the Earl Haig Fund Scotland launched a new identity – Poppyscotland – and is now generally known by this name.

The Royal British Legion Women's Section President's Award Scheme

£28,000

Correspondent: Welfare Team, The Royal British Legion, 199 Borough High Street, London SE1 1AA (020 3207 2183; email: wswelfare@britishlegion.org.uk; website: www.rblws.org.uk/how-we-help/president-s-award-scheme)

CC number: 219279

Eligibility

Serving or ex-service personnel, their spouses and dependants who are in need. This includes widows and divorced spouses/partners who have not re-married and are not in another cohabiting relationship.

Dependent children applying for scholarships must be under the age of 21.

Types of grants

The scheme offers:

▶ Educational scholarships – awards of £1,500 per year (or for a term) for a first degree course towards fees, books, travel costs, living/maintenance expenses and other course-related needs

▶ Educational grants – of up to £500 towards educational courses or retraining (people training for a new career can receive small grants towards course costs, books and travel expenses)

Annual grant total

In 2013/14 the Royal Legion Women's Section had assets of £5.2 million, an income of £1 million and expenditure of £1.1 million. Financial information on grant-making was not available but in previous years grants of around £28,000 have been awarded for educational purposes.

Exclusions

Scholarships are not given for postgraduate studies.

Applications

Initial enquiries should be made to the correspondent by telephone or in writing. Applicants will be visited by a welfare team officer who will submit an application form and financial statements. Grants are considered on a regular basis. The correspondent has informed us that all applications are put to a committee for approval and it is the members who decide on the amount to be awarded.

Other information

Grants are made through the Women's Section which is an autonomous organisation within The Royal British Legion, concentrating on the needs of widows and ex-servicewomen and dependent children of ex-service personnel. It works in close association with the Legion but has its own funds and its own local welfare visitors.

This scheme also helps with the costs of a welfare break. The Royal British Legion and the Women's section have many grants available for welfare purposes and the charity's website also notes that where they are unable to assist the welfare team will signpost the applicants to other agencies who may help.

The Royal Caledonian Education Trust

£316,500 (300 grants)

Correspondent: James MacBain, Chief Executive, Queen Elizabeth House, 4 St Dunstan's Hill, London EC3R 8AD (020 7463 9232; fax: 020 7463 9241; email: admin@rcst.org.uk; website: www.rcst.org.uk)

CC number: 310952

Eligibility

Children of Scottish people who have served or are serving in the armed forces. Priority is given to 'families who are facing particular and challenging financial circumstances, health problems and other difficulties at home'. Support may also be given to the children of Scottish people in financial need living in London who are not entitled to parochial relief.

Types of grants

The trust's website states:

The Trust has two major areas of activity. We make grants to the children of Scots who are serving or have served in the British Armed Forces. We make around 300 individual grants a year. We also work through our Education Programme in Scotland with schools, local authorities, Armed Forces charities and the military on initiatives to support Armed Forces Children, their teachers and their families in the school environment.

We provide support in several ways: We provide educational grants to help pay for school clothing, school trips and after school activities like swimming and football, where qualifying families have difficulty in funding these themselves. We support those who want to continue their education beyond school by assisting with their living expenses while in higher education or vocational training, especially where financial circumstances might otherwise prevent them from taking up a course. We provide charitable funds and resources to selected schools and local authorities in Scotland to improve support for Armed Forces children and their families particularly prior to, during and after the deployment of a close family member. We also actively promote best practice in dealing with such matters through our Education Programme in Scotland.

Annual grant total

In 2013/14 the trust had assets of £4.4 million, an income of £250,000 and a charitable expenditure of £500,000. The amount of grants given to individuals totalled £316,500.

The trustees' annual report for 2013/14 states that currently between 250 and 300 grants are made a year.

Exclusions

The trust will not provide funding where the need should be met by statutory provisions.

Applications

Application forms are available from the trust's website or can be requested from the correspondent. The grants committee meets in January, March, June and October to consider the applications.

Other information

In addition to making grants to individuals, the trust also works through its Education Programme with schools, local authorities, armed forces charities and military communities to support the armed forces children, teachers and families in the school environment, especially in relation to childrens' emotional well-being. During the year around £125,500 was spent in the Education Programme.

The Kathryn Turner Trust (Whitton's Wishes)
See entry on page 248

Army

The Black Watch Association

£75,000

Correspondent: The Trustees, Balhousie Castle, Hay Street, Perth PH1 5HR (01738 623214; email: bwassociation@btconnect.com; website: theblackwatch.co.uk/regimental-association)

OSCR number: SC016423

Eligibility

Serving and retired Black Watch soldiers, their wives, widows and children.

Types of grants

One-off grants, usually ranging from £250 to £500. Grants can be made to schoolchildren, people starting work and students in further/higher education for equipment/instruments, fees, books and maintenance/living expenses.

Annual grant total

In 2014 the association had an income of £151,500 and a total expenditure of £214,000. According to our research, educational grants amount to about £75,000 each year.

Exclusions

Our research suggests that no grants are given towards council tax arrears, loans or large debts.

Applications

The website states: 'Financial assistance is given when a report, prepared by SSAFA Forces Help, indicates a genuine need. Any grant given is authorised by an experienced Welfare Committee (who meet monthly) and is then paid to SSAFA Forces Help who administer the expenditure.' The contact details of local SSAFA branches can be found on the SSAFA website (www.ssafa.org.uk). Alternatively, SSAFA's Forcesline telephone service can be contacted from the UK by calling 0800 731 4880.

Royal Artillery Charitable Fund

£43,000

Correspondent: Lt. Col. I. A. Vere Nicoll, Secretary, Artillery House, Royal Artillery Barracks, Larkhill, Salisbury, Wiltshire SP4 8QT (01980 634309 or 01980 845698; email: rarhq-racf-welfaremailbox@mod.uk; website: www.theraa.co.uk/how-can-we-help/ra-charitable-fund)

CC number: 210202

Eligibility

Current or former members of the Royal Artillery and their dependants who are in need.

Types of grants

This is mainly a relief-in-need charity, which as part of its welfare work supports the children of its members who have started private education before the family's breadwinner became unable to earn and, therefore, is unable to help them continue their education. It also supports specialist clothing and fees for mature students and people starting work.

Annual grant total

In 2014 the fund had assets of £16.2 million and an income of £1.2 million. Individual grants totalled £643,000 and were distributed to 1,443 people. Most of the assistance is given for general welfare, although educational costs are also supported. We estimate that educational grants amounted to around £43,000.

Exclusions

Grants are not given towards income tax, loans, credit card debts, telephone bills, legal fees or private medical treatment.

Applications

Applications should be made through SSAFA (details of local branches can be found on SSAFA's website, telephone directories or from Citizens Advice) or other organisations, such as The Royal British Legion or Poppyscotland (see a

separate entry on page 98), Officers Association, Royal Artillery Association or other regimental charities. Applications can be considered at any time.

Other information

Grants are mostly given for relief-in-need purposes and are also awarded to organisations (£279,500 in 2014).

The fund is the sole corporate trustee of the Royal Artillery Charitable Fund (Permanent Endowment), the Royal Artillery Benevolent Fund, the Royal Artillery Association and the Kelly Holdsworth Artillery Trust.

Royal Air Force

The Royal Air Force Benevolent Fund

£291,000

Correspondent: General Welfare dept., 67 Portland Place, London W1B 1AR (0800 169 2942; email: info@rafbf.org.uk; website: www.rafbf.org)

CC number: 1081009

Eligibility

The children (aged 8 to 18) of officers and airmen who have died or got a severe disability while serving in the Royal Air Force. Additionally, help may be considered in those circumstances where the parent dies or develops a severe disability after leaving the Royal Air Force. Students studying for a first degree or equivalent qualification.

Types of grants

Grants to enable the education plans commenced or envisaged by the child's parents to be fulfilled. Assistance is given with boarding school fees and university scholarships.

Our research also indicates that children with special needs are given grants to help with schooling fees, equipment and care costs. Children in good health but where parents are in a difficult financial situation can receive grants for such things as the cost of school uniforms.

Annual grant total

In 2014 the charity had assets of £122.9 million, an income of £21.7 million and a charitable expenditure of £18.7 million. The charity's strategic report for the year stated the following: 'Over the year, the Fund proudly considered 6,150 individual cases and spent £12.6m on all forms of welfare support to the serving and ex-serving communities'. We believe educational grants amounted to £291,000 and were awarded to 29 individuals.

Exclusions

No grants are given for private medical costs or for legal fees.

Applications

Requests for assistance can be made by contacting the charity. There is an online contact form on the website. Alternatively, assistance can also be obtained through RAFA and SSAFA. The charity runs a free helpline which potential applicants are welcome to call for advice and support on the application process. Applications are considered on a continuous basis.

Other information

The charity provides advice and assistance on a range of issues including benefits, debt advice and relationships. It also can support its beneficiaries with residential and respite care and housing. See the website for more information on the services, support and financial assistance available.

Royal Navy and Marines

Greenwich Hospital

£4,000

Correspondent: Charity Administrator, Greenwich Hospital, 1 Farrington Street, London EC4M 7LG (020 7396 0150; email: enquiries@grenhosp.org.uk; website: www.grenhosp.org.uk)

Eligibility

Children and grandchildren of serving or retired officers and ratings of the Royal Navy, Royal Marines and UK Merchant Navy or children and grandchildren of other seafaring professions. A minimum of three years qualifying seafaring service is normally required. Applicants' academic performance and financial need will be taken into account.

Types of grants

The charity provides bursaries to attend the Royal Hospital School. The awards are only available upon entry and will not be made retrospectively.

Some discounts can also be offered to eligible seafarers who are successful in the January entrance examination and at the interview.

Annual grant total

Our research indicates that generally around £4,000 is awarded in bursaries.

Applications

Initial application forms can be found on the charity's website or can be requested from the admissions officer. Applications should be submitted before the closing date in December and not before 5 April in the year preceding entry to the school. Awards are usually awarded by January.

Further details are available on the website.

Other information

The charity also provides:

- University of Greenwich Undergraduate Awards – three annual bursaries of up to £3,000 for a maximum of four years available to former members of the Royal Navy or Royal Marines or the children of current or former members of the Royal Navy or Royal Marines
- University of Greenwich Postgraduate Awards – one bursary of £3,000 for a retired member of the Royal Navy or the Royal Marines for a master's degree in MA International Maritime Policy, MA by Research: Maritime Studies, MA International Maritime Policy or MPhil programmes
- Bursaries to study at the Trinity Laban Conservatoire of Music and Dance – to the children of current or former members of the Royal Navy or Royal Marines for a maximum of three years

The Royal Naval Benevolent Trust

£16,000

Correspondent: The Grants Administrator, Castaway House, 311 Twyford Avenue, Portsmouth PO2 8RN (023 9269 0112; fax: 023 9266 0852; email: rnbt@rnbt.org.uk; website: www.rnbt.org.uk)

CC number: 206243

Eligibility

Members of 'The RNBT Family': serving and former Royal Navy ratings and Royal Marines other ranks, and their dependants, who are in need.

Types of grants

Educational grants are available to schoolchildren and people wishing to change their careers. This is a welfare charity and educational grants are made as part of its wider work.

Annual grant total

In 2013/14 the trust had assets of £35.1 million and an income of £5.25 million. The amount of grants given to individuals totalled £2.3 million, the vast majority of which, we believe, was given for social welfare purposes. In previous years, grants for educational purposes have totalled around £16,000.

Applications

Contact the RNBT by telephone, email or letter and it will arrange for a caseworker to visit you to complete an application form.

Other information

Amongst its activities, RNBT runs a residential and nursing home for older ex-naval men (not women) namely, Pembroke House in Gillingham.

The trust has an informative website.

The Royal Naval Reserve (V) Benevolent Fund

£3,500

Correspondent: Lieutenant Yasmin Tortelli, Correspondent, M.P. 3.4, NCHQ, Leach Building, Whale Island, Portsmouth PO2 8BY (023 9262 3570)

CC number: 266380

Eligibility

The children of members or former members of the Royal Naval Volunteer Reserve, Women's Royal Naval Volunteer Reserve, Royal Naval Reserve and the Women's Royal Naval Reserve who are serving or who have served as non-commissioned rates.

Types of grants

One-off grants are occasionally made for schoolchildren who, because of the poverty of their families, need help with clothes, books, equipment or necessary educational visits, and, secondly, for eligible children with aptitudes or disabilities which need special provision. Grants are normally limited to a maximum of £200 for any applicant.

Annual grant total

In 2014 the fund had an income of £4,400 and a total expenditure of £7,500. We estimate that around £3,500 was distributed in grants to individuals for educational purposes.

Applications

Applications may be made in writing to the correspondent directly by the individual or through the local reserve division, The Royal British Legion, SSAFA or Royal Naval Benevolent Trust, which investigates applications.

Other information

The fund also makes grants to individuals for social welfare purposes.

The Royal Navy and Royal Marines Children's Fund

£644,000

Correspondent: Monique Bateman, Director, Castaway House, 311 Twyford Avenue, Stamshaw, Portsmouth

PO2 8RN (023 9263 9534; fax: 023 9267 7574; email: rnchildren@btconnect.com; website: www.rnrmchildrensfund.org)

CC number: 1160182

Eligibility

Dependants of serving and ex-serving members of the Royal Navy, the Royal Marines, the Queen Alexandra's Royal Naval Service or the former Women's Royal Naval Service, who are under the age of 25 and are in need.

Types of grants

One-off and recurrent grants, which in 2013/14 averaged £767 per child/young person, are made to schoolchildren, college students, undergraduates and vocational students where there is a special need. Grants are given towards school fees, the costs of extra tuition and school uniforms, for example.

Annual grant total

In 2013/14 the fund had assets of £9.4 million and an income of £1.4 million. Grants made during the year totalled £1.1 million, at least £644,000 of which was awarded for educational purposes. They were distributed in support of 1,694 children as follows:

School fees	£545,000
Childminding and respite	£206,000
Clothing and equipment	£205,000
Extra tuition fees	£99,000
Children's travel	£54,000
Holidays and birthdays	£2,100

During the year, a further £2,000 was paid towards other charity's expenditure.

Applications

Application forms are available from the correspondent or can be downloaded from the website. Applications can be submitted directly by the individual or through the individual's school/college, SSAFA, Naval Personal, social services or other third party. The fund can be contacted by telephone and can provide, where possible, assistance with the form's completion. Applications can be made at any time.

Other information

In August 2015 the charity was incorporated and it now has a new Charity Commission number.

The Royal Navy Officer's Charity

£4,000

Correspondent: Cdr Michael Goldthorpe, Director, 70 Porchester Terrace, Bayswater, London W2 3TP (020 7402 5231; email: rnoc@arno.org.uk; website: www.arno.org.uk)

CC number: 207405

Eligibility

The children of officers and former officers of the Royal Navy, Royal Marines, QARNNS and WRNS and their reserves. Families must be experiencing an unexpected change in circumstances, such as the death of a parent, or serious illness, which would result in the child having to leave school.

Types of grants

Awards from the RN Scholarship Fund are of up to £500 per term and given for private school fees.

Annual grant total

In 2014 the charity had assets of £13.7 million and an income of £1.3 million. The amount of grants given to individuals totalled £264,000, the vast majority of which was given for social welfare purposes. Scholarships totalled £4,000.

Applications

Application forms are available from the correspondent.

The WRNS Benevolent Trust

£1,300

Correspondent: Roger Collings, Grants Administrator, Castaway House, 311 Twyford Avenue, Portsmouth, Hampshire PO2 8RN (023 9265 5301; fax: 023 9267 9040; email: grantsadmin@ wrnsbt.org.uk; website: www.wrnsbt.org. uk)

CC number: 206529

Eligibility

Ex-Wrens and female serving members of the Royal Navy (officers and ratings) who joined the service between 3 September 1939 and 1 November 1993 who are in need.

Types of grants

This charity is essentially a relief-in-need charity which offers grants for educational purposes. These are usually given to former Wrens who are mature students to help with training courses, study costs, computers, books, etc.

Annual grant total

In 2014 the trust had assets of £3.8 million and an income of £272,000. The amount of grants given to individuals totalled £318,500, the vast majority of which was for social welfare purposes. Educational grants amounted to £1,300.

Exclusions

People who deserted from the service are not eligible.

Applications

Applications can be made directly to the correspondent; however, the trust states the following on its website:

> The WRNS Benevolent Trust is a small Charity. We have no caseworkers of our own and therefore work mainly with the Royal British Legion (RBL) and the Soldiers, Sailors, Airmen and Families Association (SSAFA), and their caseworkers call on any applicant on our behalf. They are discreet and knowledgeable, and can give friendly support and advice on a wide variety of matters. They complete a report, which is then put before our Grants Committee for consideration.

Applications can be made directly by the individual or, with their consent, by a relation or friend.

Other information

The trust states the following on its informative website:

> One of our biggest problems is raising awareness; it is surprising how many former Wrens do not even know of our existence. If you ever hear of a former Wren who you think may be having difficulties, do please tell her about us or approach us on her behalf. Many are too proud to ask for help, but we always stress that we are their special charity and one which they may have contributed to during their time in the Women's Royal Naval Service.

Arts and culture

Equity Charitable Trust

£131,500 (31 grants)

Correspondent: Kaethe Cherney, Acting Secretary, Plouviez House, 19–20 Hatton Place, London EC1N 8RU (020 7831 1926; fax: 020 7242 7995; email: kaethe@ equitycharitabletrust.org.uk; website: www.equitycharitabletrust.org.uk)

CC number: 328103

Eligibility

Professional performers who are eligible for an Equity card, who have a minimum of ten years' experience as an adult.

Types of grants

Grants to enable retraining or education at recognised colleges or training centres on courses which must lead to a recognised qualification. Grants can be given to assist with some or all of the course costs (depending on the applicant's circumstances) and, in some cases, the trust has assisted with the purchase of books or essential materials.

Annual grant total

In 2013/14 the trust had assets of £10.7 million and an income of £448,000. Grants totalled £346,000, £102,500 of which was awarded to organisations. Grants made to individuals amounted to £243,000 and included £111,500 paid in welfare and benevolence grants to 122 people. Education and training grants to 40 individuals totalled £131,500.

Exclusions

The trust cannot help amateur performers, musicians or drama students. Courses for the improvement of performance skills are not eligible for funding, and assistance with short courses, courses overseas or summer schools is not usually considered.

Applications

Applications can be made using a form, which is available to download from the website or on request by emailing kaethe@equitycharitabletrust.org.uk or by calling 020 7831 1926. As part of the application, a CV showing the applicant's experience and evidence of their current financial position are required. The application form should be returned to the trust accompanied by any supporting documents. If the trust will make contact with the applicant if there are any questions about their application and, if the application is accepted, it will be considered at the next trustees' meeting.

The trust's website also notes this additional helpful information: 'If you are interested in applying, please contact Kaethe Cherney from January onwards. The Trustees usually meet between April-August to allocate the grants.'

Other information

The trust also assists professional performers who are suffering hardship through welfare and benevolence grants. As part of the application process for these grants, beneficiaries are able to speak with an experienced money advisor who can help to find other sources of funding, including state benefits.

The R. C. Sherriff Rosebriars Trust

£11,500 (3+ grants)

Correspondent: Dean Blanchard, Correspondent, Charity House, 5 Quintet, Churchfield Road, Walton-on-Thames, Surrey KT12 2TZ (01932 229996; email: arts@rcsherrifftrust.org. uk; website: www.rcsherrifftrust.org.uk)

CC number: 272527

Eligibility

Amateur and professional artists (composers, craftspeople, curators, designers, directors, film-makers, musicians, performers, producers, promoters, theatre technicians, visual artists, writers and so on) in the borough of Elmbridge.

The trust's grant-making guidelines specify that 'managers, education officers, fundraisers, marketing staff, press officers and workshop leaders may apply for individual grants towards training and personal development only'.

Types of grants

Grants and bursaries, usually of up to £500 a year for up to three years, to assist with:

- Professional development and training (including travel grants), such as short courses in specific skills, work placements with other artists or specified periods of travel and/or study
- Research and development for arts projects
- Publication or production of a specific piece of work
- Capital items (for example, equipment)

Annual grant total

In 2013 the trust had assets of £3.9 million and an income of £186,000. There were 35 grants made totalling £48,000. This included £12,000 awarded in grants of under £1,000 to institutions and individuals. There were three larger grants (above £1,000) awarded to individuals totalling £5,500. We estimate that the amount of grants given to individuals totalled around £11,500.

The trust's website states that approximately £60,000–£70,000 is available each year for distribution in awards to individuals and organisations.

At the time of writing (November 2015) the annual report and accounts for 2014 were not yet received by the Charity Commission.

Exclusions

Grants are not given:

- For arts activities or events taking place outside Elmbridge (except in the case of attendance at training courses/development opportunities for individuals)
- Activities that are not arts-related
- Fundraising events, e.g. special performances in aid of a local charity
- Activities that provide no potential benefit to the public
- Activities which have already taken place
- Goods or services that have been bought or ordered before receiving an offer letter
- Higher education courses, long-term vocational training (for example, Drama School) or ongoing training programmes (such as piano lessons or regular dance classes)

If successful, applicants can apply once a year for a maximum of three consecutive years, after which they must wait at least one complete financial year (January – December) before applying again.

Applications

Initial contact should be made with the correspondent prior to formal application to ensure that the project meets the eligibility criteria. Application forms are available to download from the trust's website. The trustees meet quarterly to consider applications. For specific deadlines see the website, although generally they are in the middle of January, April, July and October.

The application guidelines state:

> A full financial budget relating to the proposed work/purchase must be enclosed with the proposal and the budget must show the full costing for the project, and how this will be covered i.e. how much money can be raised from other funding sources and how much (the balance) you are requesting from the trust.

Other information

Grants are also made to arts organisations and for various arts projects. Part of the trust's expenditure is allocated for the publication of a magazine Art Focus and for organising and managing arts initiatives (£55,500 in 2013).

Further guidance, information and advice can also be obtained via phone.

Acting

The Actors' Children's Trust (TACT)

£148,500

Correspondent: Robert Ashby, General Secretary, 58 Bloomsbury Street, London WC1B 3QT (020 7636 7868; email: robert@tactactors.org; website: www. tactactors.org)

CC number: 206809

Eligibility

Children (aged under 21) of professional actors who are in financial need with a particular focus on children with special needs, learning disabilities or long-term illnesses or those facing family crisis.

One or both parents must be a professional actor. If the actor-parent is now doing other work, acting must still have formed the majority of the paid work in their career to date. **Note:** The trust cannot help those who have solely worked in variety, amateur dramatics or as an extra.

Types of grants

Grants have been made to help parents with the costs of: extra-curricular, after-school activities; play schemes; groups and sports clubs; music lessons; dance and drama; clothing and school uniforms; curriculum-linked school trips; extra tuition to help with dyslexia or maths; and additional therapy for children with disabilities. Grants are also made to help with childcare costs, daily essentials, such as school lunches, and in the form of gift vouchers and payments to service providers.

Maintenance grants of £1,200 per year are offered to higher education students who are children of professional actors.

Annual grant total

In 2013/14 the trust had assets of £6.8 million and an income of £697,000. Grants for educational and welfare purposes were made to 131 families, with 212 children between them. Grants were made totalling £296,500 with an average spend per child being £1,400. We estimate that about £148,500 was given for educational purposes.

Exclusions

Grants are not usually given for private school fees; however, the trust may consider making a grant if private education would be beneficial to the child i.e. due to special educational needs or family situation. TACT does not pay independent school fees.

Applications

Application forms may be filled in online, downloaded and printed from the trust's website or requested from the correspondent. Applicants are strongly advised to contact the trust to discuss their situation before making an application. Applications can be submitted at any time either by the individual or a parent. Awards are decided in July each year.

Other information

The annual report for 2013/14 states:

> The two largest areas of funding continued to be education including extra-curricular activities (music lessons and exams, dance, drama, sports, and so on) and childcare. Smaller areas of funding include school transport, holidays, crisis relief, clothing and uniform, sports kit, and performing arts kit.

Note that on 31 March 2014 the trustees the trustees closed a small related charity, TACT Education Fund, which awards student grants to the older children of actors, and transferred its activity, assets and liabilities to TACT, as a restricted endowment with its income applied for the same purposes.

Dance

The Independent Dancers Resettlement Trust (Dancers' Career Development)

£214,000 (91 grants)

Correspondent: Jennifer Curry, Director of Development, Plouviez House, 19–20 Hatton Place, London EC1N 8RU (020 7831 1449; fax: 020 7242 1462; email: jennifer@thedcd.org.uk; website: www.thedcd.org.uk)

CC number: 327747

Eligibility

Professional and independent dancers in the UK, regardless of their artistic background. All applicants must have worked as a professional dancer for a minimum of eight years and have worked a minimum of five years in the UK. In addition to that:

- **Independent dancers** must demonstrate that they have earned an income as a dancer for a minimum of 16 weeks in each year (on average)
- **Company dancers** must have spent at least five years with one or more of the following companies affiliated to the organisation: Birmingham Royal Ballet; English National Ballet; Northern Ballet; Phoenix Dance Theatre; Rambert Dance Company; Richard Alston Dance Company; Scottish Ballet; Siobhan Davies Dance; and The Royal Ballet

Dancers who had to retire due to illness or injury may still be eligible for help even if they are unable to meet the above criteria.

Professional dancers are eligible to apply for up to ten years after they cease performing professionally.

Types of grants

One-off payments and financial assistance for retraining are given to dancers at the end of their career. Support is available for course and training fees, business start-up equipment, maintenance, travel costs, childcare costs and so on.

There are certain upper limits for grants: £1,000 for computer support equipment; £5,000 for career support equipment; and a maximum of £15,000 to an individual applicant.

Annual grant total

In 2013/14 the trust had assets of £870,500 and an income of £466,500 mostly in contributions from member companies. Grants to 91 individuals amounted to £214,000.

Applications

Applications may be obtained from the Dancers Career Development website or from the correspondent. They should be submitted directly by the individual. Applications should also include a dance career CV, covering letter addressed to the trustees, information on the course or equipment and a detailed application budget. The trustees meet four times a year to consider the applications. Deadlines are also published on the DCD website and in a monthly e – newsletter. Detailed guidelines are also available on the website.

Other information

DCD offers free educational, emotional, careers advice and counselling to eligible dancers.

The DCD website contains a lot of useful information including application guidelines, sample budgets and links to organisations which may be able to help individuals who have not spent enough time dancing in the UK to qualify for help from DCD.

DCD is a founding member of the International Organisation for the Transition of Professional Dancers.

During the last accounting period there were a total of 91 new awards made to dancers from both the Company Fund (38 awards) and Independent Trust (53 awards). The total number of awards made is slightly less than the number of grants awarded in 2012/13 (104). The number of new awards from the Independent Trust remains similar (51 awards in 2012/13).

Music

Josephine Baker Trust

£20,000

Correspondent: David Munro, Trustee, Grange Cottage, Frensham, Farnham, Surrey GU10 3DS (01252 792485; email: munrodj@aol.com)

CC number: 1086222

Eligibility

People studying vocal music and young singers at the beginning of their career.

Types of grants

Grants ranging from £125 to £250 are awarded to young singers. Support is typically given for the soloist fees at selected concerts.

Annual grant total

In 2014 the trust had an income of £20,000 and a total expenditure of £23,000. Normally around £20,000 each year is awarded to individuals.

Applications

Apply in writing to the correspondent. Candidates are required to attend an audition.

Other information

The trust has established links with the Royal Academy of Music and the Royal College of Music.

The Busenhart Morgan-Evans Foundation

£5,000

Correspondent: Bev Sturdey, Trustee, Brambletye, 455 Woodham Lane, Woodham, Addlestone, Surrey KT15 3QQ (01932 344806; email: BusenhartME@aol.com)

CC number: 1062453

Eligibility

Young musicians at the start of their professional career.

Types of grants

One-off or recurrent grants towards the cost of equipment, instruments, course fees and also music scholarships.

Annual grant total

In 2013/14 the foundation had an income of £10,500 and an expenditure of £10,000. We estimate the annual total amount of grants awarded to individuals to be about £5,000.

Applications

Applications should be made through the individual's educational institution at any time.

Other information

Organisations are also supported for music, health and local community causes.

The Michael James Music Trust

£13,500

Correspondent: Edward Monds, Trustee, Garden House, Cuthburga Road, Wimborne BH21 1LH

CC number: 283943

Eligibility

Individuals engaged in any musical education, particularly in a Christian context.

Types of grants

One-off and recurrent grants are given towards tuition fees and expenses.

Annual grant total

In 2014/15 the trust had an income of £20,000 and a total expenditure of

£14,500. We estimate that grants totalled about £13,500.

Exclusions

No grants are given for the purchase of instruments or equipment.

Applications

Application forms are available from the correspondent. Applications should be received by 30 April each year.

Other information

Grants are also made to churches, universities and schools.

Business, financial services and insurance

The Bank Workers Charity

£165,500

Correspondent: The Client Advisor, Pinners Hall, 105–108 Old Broad Street, London EC2N 1EX (0800 023 4834 (helpline); email: info@bwcharity.org.uk; website: www.bwcharity.org.uk)

CC number: 313080

Eligibility

Current and ex-employees of banks in the UK, and their dependants.

Types of grants

One-off and recurrent grants for fees and other educational expenses.

Annual grant total

In 2013/14 the charity had assets of £47.7 million and an income of £1.7 million. Cash grants totalled £767,000, broken down as follows:

Families	£308,500
Retirees	£293,000
Child education	£165,500

We take the amount given as 'child education needs' to represent educational support awarded.

Exclusions

People who have worked in the insurance or stock broking industries are generally not helped.

Applications

Contact the charity' Client Advisors in the first instance to discuss making an application and learn about support available. The trustees meet quarterly to consider new cases.

Other information

The charity also provides support in three main areas – home, money and well-being. They have client advisors who offer information, advice and guidance covering a range of issue as well as offering independent and confidential counselling. The cost of service delivery and client support amounted to over £1.1 million.

The charity planned to distribute about £900,000 in grants in 2014/15.

The Chartered Institute of Management Accountants Benevolent Fund

£10,000

Correspondent: Caroline Aldred, Secretary, CIMA Benevolent Fund, The Helicon, One South Place, London EC2M 2RB (020 8849 2221; email: benevolent.fund@cimaglobal.com; website: www.cimaglobal.com)

CC number: 261114

Eligibility

Children of past and present CIMA members within and outside the UK.

Types of grants

Educational grants and loans for dependent children according to need.

Annual grant total

In 2014 the fund had assets of £2.1 million and an income of £110,000. Grants to 44 individuals totalled £109,000 (14 of these grants included funding for families with dependants), the majority of which were for social welfare purposes. The amount awarded in educational grants was not specified in the accounts. We estimate that educational grants totalled around £10,000

Applications

Applications can be made on a form available from the correspondent or to download from the website. Applications can be submitted directly by the individual or through a recognised referral agency (Citizens Advice, doctor, social worker and so on), or through a third party. Anybody wishing to discuss a possible application informally can contact the Secretary 'in complete confidence'.

Other information

The charity can also signpost people to relevant services and provide support from a welfare officer. Support is given for general welfare needs as well.

CIMA also has another charity, the General Charitable Trust Fund, which funds the advancement of education in accountancy and related topics.

The George Drexler Foundation

£74,500

Correspondent: Nicola Extance-Vaughan, Correspondent, 35–43 Lincolns Inn Fields, London WC2A 3PE (020 7869 6080; email: info@georgedrexler.org.uk; website: www.georgedrexler.org.uk)

CC number: 313278

Eligibility

UK citizens who have a direct (personal or family) link with commerce – candidates (or their parents or grandparents) must have worked in or owned a commercial business. Our research suggests that this does not include professional people, such as doctors, lawyers, dentists, architects or accountants. Selected Medical Schools and Schools of Music apply by invitation only.

Preference is given to can be given to particularly gifted or talented students who are in need of financial support. Schoolchildren with serious family difficulties so that the child has to be educated away from home and people with special educational needs may also be favoured.

Types of grants

One-off and recurrent grants of £1,000 to £10,000. Awards can be made to support individuals in full-time undergraduate or postgraduate education. The foundation seeks to 'enrich the educational experiences of younger people' and the trustees bear in mind the founder's expressed desire to benefit medical research and education.

Annual grant total

In 2013/14 the foundation had assets of nearly £6.5 million and an income of £260,000. Educational grants totalled £174,500, consisting of £74,500 given to individuals and £100,000 given to The Royal College of Surgeons of England for educational facilities and tutors. Grants to individuals to relieve poverty totalled £38,000.

Exclusions

Support is not given for:
- Overseas students
- Volunteering
- Part-time study
- Study abroad
- Medical electives
- Gap year projects
- Non-UK citizens

Applications

The foundation accepts applications between 1 January and 30 April. Applications must be submitted using an online system on the foundation's website. Outside these dates appeals are not accepted or processed. Successful and unsuccessful applicants are notified of outcome by letter/email in June.

Other information

The foundation also provides welfare grants to former employees of the Ofrex Group and their dependants (other people formerly employed in commerce and their families may be considered).

Alfred Foster Settlement

£15,500

Correspondent: Graham Prew, Correspondent, Barclays Bank Trust Co. Ltd, Executorship and Trustee Service, Osborne Court, Gadbrook Park, Rudheath, Northwich CW9 7UE (01606 313118)

CC number: 229576

Eligibility

Current and former employees of banks and their dependants who are in need. Applying students should be aged less than 28 years.

Types of grants

One-off grants of £250–£1,000, for example, to help with university fees, books, travel costs and living expenses while in further education. Support may also be given to help with the education of children; although the general policy is to support people in higher education.

Annual grant total

In 2013/14 the charity had assets of £867,500, an income of £35,500 and awarded over £31,000 in grants. Further breakdown was not given; therefore, we estimate that about £15,500 was given in educational awards.

Applications

Applications may be made in writing to the correspondent. They can be submitted directly by the individual or through the school/college or educational welfare agency.

Other information

The charity also makes grants to individuals for welfare purposes.

The Ruby and Will George Trust

£46,500

Correspondent: Damien Slattery, Administrator, 125 Cloverfield, West

Allotment, Newcastle upon Tyne NE27 0BE (0191 266 4527; email: admin@rwgt.co.uk; website: www.rwgt.co.uk)

CC number: 264042

Eligibility

The dependants of people in need who have been or who are employed in commerce. Preference is given to people who live in the North East.

Types of grants

One-off and recurrent grants of up to £2,000 towards maintenance and fees, mainly for those in secondary or further education. Grants relating to fees are usually paid directly to the educational establishment. Occasionally, assistance with maintenance, books and basic travel expenses will be awarded.

Annual grant total

In 2013/14 the trust had assets of £3.7 million and an income of £74,000. A total of 38 grants were made to individuals during the year, amounting to £61,500. The annual report and accounts state that: 'The vast majority of the income generated by the trust's assets is paid out by means of either one-off or continuing grants, these being predominantly made to those in either secondary or further education.' With this in mind, we estimate that grants for social welfare purposes totalled around £46,500.

Exclusions

Our research indicates that expeditions, study visits and student exchanges are not funded.

Applications

The trust has an online application process, although its annual report also states that 'those without access to the internet are also provided with the means to submit paper-based applications where appropriate'. Applicants will need to prove their commerce connection and their income and expenditure. Two references are required. The trust considers applications four times a year. The precise dates of these meetings, and of deadline dates for applications, can be found on the website.

The Insurance Charities

£58,000

Correspondent: Annali-Joy Thornicroft, CEO and Company Secretary, 20 Aldermanbury, London EC2V 7HY (020 7606 3763; fax: 020 7600 1170; email: info@theinsurancecharities.org.uk; website: www.theinsurancecharities.org.uk)

CC number: 206860

Eligibility

People who have been engaged in any aspect of the UK or Irish insurance industry, normally for at least five years, and their dependants.

According to the website:

> The Paul Golmick Fund is a Trust, separate from The Insurance Charities, which promotes the maintenance and education of those under the age of 24, and primarily under the age of 18, who reside in the UK or Ireland and have at least one parent/guardian in insurance.

Types of grants

Help may be given for education and training needs, including first degree students towards day-to-day expenses, there is family financial hardship. One-off and ongoing assistance is considered.

Annual grant total

In 2013/14 the charity had assets of £31.25 million and an income of nearly £1.3 million. Grants were made to 251 individuals totalling £920,000. This figure includes £58,000 – the contribution made by the Paul Golmick Fund towards grants, which we take to represent awards for educational purposes. Note that this amount may be higher where the trustees decide to use the general fund to assist with educational needs.

Applications

If you think you may qualify for help, in the first instance you should complete an initial form, which can be completed online, downloaded and emailed or printed off and post to the charity. The Grants Committee meets quarterly to consider awards.

Other information

The charity also provides loans and grants support for general social welfare purposes. Money advice service is also offered.

The Royal Pinner School Foundation

£439,000 (163 grants)

Correspondent: David Crawford, Company Secretary, 110 Old Brompton Road, South Kensington, London SW7 3RB (020 7373 6168; email: admin@royalpinner.co.uk; website: www.royalpinner.co.uk)

CC number: 1128414

Eligibility

Children of commercial travellers, travelling sales and technical representatives and manufacturer's agents, where the family has experienced adversity or hardship. Preference is given to individuals under the age of 25 and orphans.

Types of grants

One-off or recurrent grants are available to individuals at any state, private day or boarding school, college or university. Support is given towards general educational needs, maintenance costs, clothing, equipment, books, travel expenses in the UK and overseas, undertaking activities in arts and music, also assistance to people starting career/entering a profession, trade or calling.

Annual grant total

In 2013/14 the foundation had assets of £5.4 million and an income of £749,000. A total of almost £439,000 was awarded in grants to 163 individuals, broken down as follows:

Children at day and boarding schools	102	£243,000
Students at universities and colleges of higher and further education	66	£127,000
Travel, the arts, outfitting grants and special educational needs	45	£69,000

Exclusions

The foundation does not normally provide loans or support part-time education.

Applications

Apply in writing to the correspondent. The grants committee meets about five times a year.

Other information

Note that no applications can be considered except those applying for the sons and daughters of travelling sales representatives or manufacturers' agents.

Scottish Chartered Accountants' Benevolent Association

£60,000

Correspondent: Robert Linton, Correspondent, Robert Linton and Co., c/o ICAS 2nd Floor, 7 West Nile Street, Glasgow G1 2PR (0141 301 1788; email: scaba@robertlinton.co.uk; website: www.icas.com/our-charitable-work/scaba-scottish-chartered-accountants-benevolent-association)

OSCR number: SC008365

Eligibility

The dependants of members of the Institute of Chartered Accountants of Scotland who are in financial need.

Types of grants

One-off grants are given for a variety of needs. Past grants have been given for school fees, maintenance expenses and retraining.

Annual grant total

In 2014 the association had an income of £211,000 and a total expenditure of £162,500. Our research suggests that grants usually total about £120,000 each year. We estimate that about £60,000 was given for educational purposes.

Applications

An initial letter or telephone call should be made to the correspondent. A member of the fund will then make contact and arrange a visit if appropriate. Following this, an application, report and recommendation will be made to the fund's council for approval.

Education and training

IAPS Charitable Trust
See entry on page 27

The Lloyd Foundation

£102,500 (58 grants)

Correspondent: Margaret Keyte, Secretary, 1 Churchill Close, Breaston, Derbyshire DE72 3UD (01332 873772; email: keytelloyd@btintenet.com)

CC number: 314203

Eligibility

Children (aged between 5 and 25) of British citizens ordinarily living/working overseas.

Assistance is also available to 'teaching members of staff of schools outside the UK conducted in accordance with British educational principles and practice' and to people in need who 'have been employed by the former English School Cairo for at least five years or at the time of its closure'.

Types of grants

The foundation may offer scholarships, bursaries, maintenance allowances to school pupils and further/higher education students 'to obtain British type education either overseas or in the UK whilst family is living/working overseas.' Our research suggests that the grants normally range between £300 and £3,000 and can be given towards general educational purposes, including fees, books, equipment/instruments, living expenses, travel costs, study of music or the arts and so on. According to our research, grants are primarily given to attend the nearest English-medium schools and where no such school exists help can be given towards fees for a school in the UK.

Annual grant total

In 2013/14 the foundation had assets of £3.5 million, an income of £157,500 and grants totalling £102,500 were awarded to 58 beneficiaries. A further 87 applications and enquiries for awards did not meet the terms of reference of the Foundation.

Exclusions

Children under the age of five or for those taking postgraduate courses are not normally supported.

Applications

Application forms can be requested from the correspondent. Submissions can be made directly by the individual or through a third party. The trustees normally meet quarterly.

NASUWT (The Teachers' Union) Benevolent Fund

£449,000 (1,309 grants)

Correspondent: Legal and Casework Team, NASUWT, Hillscourt Education Centre, Rose Hill, Rednal, Birmingham B45 8RS (0121 453 6150 (8.30am - 5.30pm); email: legalandcasework@mail.nasuwt.org.uk; website: www.nasuwt.org.uk)

CC number: 285793

Eligibility

Members, former members and the dependants of members and former members and dependants of deceased members of NASUWT The Teachers' Union.

Types of grants

Grants of £125 for schoolchildren aged 16 and under and £150 for those 17 and over.

Annual grant total

In 2013 the fund had assets of £1.9 million and an income of £306,000. 1,309 grants were made to individuals totalling £449,000 for education and welfare purposes.

These were the latest accounts available at the time of writing (October 2015).

Exclusions

No support is given for private school fees, education courses, repayments of student loans or to assist students with general living expenses.

Applications

All applications must be submitted on behalf of the member by a Benevolence Visitor or another appropriate official of the Union. Arrangements may be made for a benevolence visitor to visit and complete the application form. Applicants must also supply information regarding their household income and expenditure.

Other information

Help is also available from this fund for welfare purposes, and they also provide money advice.

Environment and animals

The Dairy Crest and National Farmers' Union Scholarship Fund

£15,000

Correspondent: Catherine Booth, Administrator, Higher Moorlake Cottage, Moorlake, Crediton, Devon EX17 5EL (01363 776623; fax: 01363 774992; email: aba@adelabooth.co.uk)

CC number: 306598

Eligibility

Children of farmers or farm workers, ex-farmers, smallholders and ex-smallholders in Cornwall, Devon, Dorset and Somerset who are studying a dairy-related topic at tertiary level or equivalent and intend to follow a career in this field.

Types of grants

Scholarships in the range from £200 to £2,000 can be provided to people studying dairy-related topics. Support is given for books, fees, equipment, maintenance/living expenses, travel/study costs and research.

Annual grant total

In 2013/14 the fund had an income of £20,500 and an expenditure of £21,500. Around £15,000 is available for distribution in grants to individuals each year.

Applications

Application forms can be found on the AgriFood Charities Partnership website or requested from the correspondent. Applications should be submitted by 12 August each year. Eligible applicants will be invited for an interview.

Gardeners' Royal Benevolent Society (Perennial)

£61,000

Correspondent: Sheila Thomson, Director of Services, 115–117 Kingston Road, Leatherhead, Surrey KT22 7SU (0800 093 8510; email: info@perennial. org.uk; website: www.perennial.org.uk)

CC number: 1155156, SC040180

Eligibility

Horticulturalists or those training to become one, who are experiencing hardship. The dependent children of horticulturalists who are in full-time education. Eligible beneficiaries include employed, self-employed or retired gardeners and horticulturalists.

Types of grants

The charity offers one-off grants and ongoing bursaries for educational activities, training or retraining after a career change. Education is understood in its broad sense and may include training of horticulturalists, professional development needs or child schooling needs, including extra-curricular activities or after-school clubs to allow parents undertake full-time work.

The following support is available:

▶ The Lironi Training Fund – helps horticulture students and 'offers a range of training initiatives available to those who are in need of financial support unavailable from any other statutory source'
▶ Sons and daughters bursaries maximum of £1,500 per year to full-time horticultural students under the age of 40 who are themselves children of horticulturalists
▶ Hardship bursaries one-off grants of up to £1,000 to horticultural students experiencing exceptional, unforeseen hardship
▶ Support for long-term career horticulturalists who find themselves in hardship and are looking to regain satisfactory employment within the industry or elsewhere following adverse circumstance, such as an accident or ill health
▶ Grants are also available for general education for the dependent children of horticulturalists. The regional caseworker should be contacted in the first instance

Annual grant total

In 2014 the charity had assets of £46.9 million and an income of £3.5 million. The consolidated accounts state that a total of about £490,000 was spent in grants and benefit payments to beneficiaries, including restricted income funds and designated funds (this appears to include support and administration costs).

The notes on Designated Funds mark that grants and benefit payments from The Lironi Training Fund totalled £61,000, from The Good Samaritan Welfare Fund – £186,000, and from 1839 Regular Beneficiary Fund – £183,000.

The notes on Restricted Funds show that grants and benefit payments from The Children's Fund totalled £51,000 and from the Clients Grants Fund – £9,000.

The 'Our Financial Assistance & Special Circumstances' section in the accounts note that £176,000 was paid from The Regular Beneficiary Fund, £167,000 from The Good Samaritan Welfare Fund and over £41,000 from The Lironi Training Fund. The Children's Fund was established to provide both educational and welfare support; therefore, we add half of this amount towards the educational expenditure. We calculate the annual total amount of grants awarded for educational purposes to be around £61,000.

The biggest part of the charity's expenditure is spent in providing advice and advocacy services, including debt advice (£959,000 in 2014).

Applications

Applicants are advised to check the website for the application advice relating to separate schemes. Individuals are encouraged to get in touch with the charity to discuss their eligibility and support available.

The charity's website notes: 'When someone gets in touch with us, we aim to make telephone contact with them within three working days of receiving their contact details. This is usually followed up with a home visit from a caseworker or debt adviser within two weeks.'

Other information

In 2010 this charity merged with the Royal Fund for Gardeners' Children. From 2014 the charity had a change in its legal status – became a company limited by guarantee and was registered with the Charity Commission. It continues to be registered with the Office of the Scottish Charity Regulator.

The charity's website notes: 'Perennial provides free and confidential advice, support and financial assistance to people of all ages working in, or retired from horticulture. This help extends to spouses, partners and children.'

To access help get in touch with the charity via email or phone: general advice at 0800 093 8543, services@perennial.org.uk (educational activities at training@perennial.org.uk); debt advice at 0800 093 8546.

Grants are also available to individuals for welfare purposes.

RSABI (Royal Scottish Agricultural Benevolent Institution)

£20,000

Correspondent: The Welfare Team, The Rural Centre, West Mains of Ingliston, Newbridge, Midlothian EH28 8LT (0300 111 4166 (helpline); fax: 0131 472 4156;

email: rsabi@rsabi.org.uk; website: www.rsabi.org.uk)

OSCR number: SC009828

Eligibility

People who have been engaged for at least ten years, full-time in a land-based occupation in Scotland, and their dependants. Applicants should be either retired or unable to work, on a low income (RSABI does not include non-means-tested disability benefits when calculating qualifying income) and have limited savings (£12,000 for a single applicant, £16,000 for couples) or be facing a crisis due to ill health, accident or bereavement, for example.

Qualifying occupations include: agriculture, aquaculture, crofting, forestry, fish-farming, gamekeeping, horticulture, rural estate work and other jobs that depend on the provision of services directly to these industries.

Types of grants

One-off grants towards skills training or accreditation, where it will help address the hardship.

Annual grant total

In 2013/14 the charity had assets of £10.7 million (which includes restricted and endowment funds) and an income of £1.3 million.

The amount of grants given to individuals totalled around £526,000. The annual report for 2013/14 further specifies that 1563 payments were processed to 498 distinct beneficiaries. From the total, £356,000 was made in Basic Benefit Grants and £170,000 was paid in Single Grants to 46 individuals, of which £90,000 was paid through the designated Weather 2012 Fund (covering 28 families) and £8,200 through Centenary Fund.

The support was allocated as follows:

Annual beneficiaries	£341,000
Weather 2012	£89,000
Single grants	£78,000
TV licences	£13,000
Centenary and Christmas grants	£5,000

The amount awarded for educational purposes was not specified in the accounts; therefore, we estimate that it could have totalled around £20,000.

Exclusions

Grants are not made to help with:
- Business expenses
- Repayment of loans, overdrafts or credit facilities
- Setting up any debt arrangement

Applications

Preliminary application forms are available from the correspondent or can be downloaded from the website. They can be submitted directly by the individual or through a third party (such as a social worker or Citizens Advice)

and are considered at any time. The charity's website states:

> We will let you know as soon as possible after receiving the Form whether or not we may be able to help you. If we can, one of our Welfare Officers will arrange to visit at a suitable time and will help you to complete our formal Application for Assistance Form and discuss how RSABI may best be able to help.

Candidates are also encouraged to contact the charity to discuss their application.

Other information

The trustees' annual report for 2013/14 notes that while welfare support and guidance 'remain the trustees principal focus, consideration is, and will be, given to educational or training-related activities..., particularly where these might help raise awareness of the charity'.

RSABI also offers advice on benefits, support available from other organisations, provide guidance through key life events, such as bereavement, serious illness, redundancy or retirement, and offer home visits by welfare officers to provide ongoing support and friendship. A confidential listening and support service for Scotland's farming and land-based community – GATEPOST – is operated by the charity. Call 0300 111 4166 – Monday–Friday, 9am–5pm.

Hospitality and retail

The Fashion and Textile Children's Trust
See entry on page 111

Information and communication

The Book Trade Charity

£1,800

Correspondent: David Hicks, Chief Executive, The Foyle Centre, The Retreat, Abbots Road, Kings Langley, Hertfordshire WD4 8LT (01923 263128 or 01329848731; fax: 01923 270732; email: david@btbs.org or info@booktradecharity.org; website: www.booktradecharity.org)

CC number: 1128129

Eligibility

People in need who have worked in the book trade in the UK for at least one year (normally publishing/distribution/book-selling), and their dependants.

Types of grants

One-off grants of up to £1,000 are given to help retrain people from the book trade who have been made redundant. These grants are given to eligible mature students where a welfare need is evident. Training grants of up to £1,000 are also made and, whilst these awards are predominantly aimed at those who are currently unemployed in the book trade or facing redundancy, the charity will also consider assisting, where there is a demonstrable financial need, individuals who are employed elsewhere but seeking to return to the book trade or those who need to improve or update their skills in order to progress within the trade.

The society is predominantly a relief-in-need charity and retraining is only a small part of its work. Therefore, general educational grants are not usually made.

Annual grant total

In 2014 the charity had assets of nearly £5.7 million consisting for the most part of land and buildings and, therefore, not available for grant-giving, and an income of £543,000. Grants were made totalling £130,000, of which £1,800 was given to support people in training, retraining and education.

The remaining £128,000 given in grants was awarded for social welfare purposes (including £7,000 in medical costs).

Applications

Application forms are available from the correspondent or the charity's website. They can be submitted by the individual or through a recognised referral agency (a social worker, Citizens Advice, doctor and so on). They are considered as they arrive.

The Chartered Institute of Journalists Orphan Fund

£9,700

Correspondent: Dominic Cooper, Trustee, Institute of Journalists, 2 Dock Offices, Surrey Quays Road, London SE16 2XU (020 7252 1187; email: memberservices@cioj.co.uk)

CC number: 208176

Eligibility

Orphaned children of institute members who are in need, aged between 5 and 22 and in full-time education.

Types of grants

Grants are given to schoolchildren towards the cost of school clothing, books, instruments, educational outings and school fees. Grants are also given to students who are in further or higher education towards the cost of books, help with fees/living expenses and study or travel abroad.

Annual grant total

In 2014 the fund had assets of £2.4 million and an income of £100,500. The amount of grants given to individuals totalled £19,400 for both welfare and education. We estimate that the amount of grants given to individuals for educational purposes totalled around £9,700

Applications

Applications should be submitted in writing by the child's surviving parent or another third party. They are considered quarterly.

The Grace Wyndham Goldie (BBC) Trust Fund

£26,500 (18 grants)

Correspondent: Cheryl Miles, Secretary, BBC, Room M1017, Broadcasting House, Cardiff CF5 2YQ (029 2032 2000; website: www.bbc.co.uk/charityappeals/about/grants/grace-wyndham-goldie)

CC number: 212146

Eligibility

Individuals currently or previously engaged in broadcasting, and their dependants.

Types of grants

One-off grants are given to help with educational costs such as school or college fees, travelling expenses, school uniforms, books and equipment, living expenses or to supplement existing educational awards.

Annual grant total

In 2014 the fund had assets of £1.3 million and an income of £52,500. It made 18 grants for educational purposes, totalling £26,500. Two welfare grants, amounting to £3,300, were also given.

Exclusions

Grants are not made on an ongoing basis.

Applications

Application forms are available to download from the fund's page on the BBC website. Applicants are asked to provide full information about the circumstances supporting their application. All applications are considered in confidence. Completed forms should be returned to: Trustees, Grace Wyndham Goldie (BBC) Trust Fund, BBC Pension and Benefits Centre, Broadcasting House, Cardiff CF5 2YQ.

The Walter Hazell Charitable and Educational Trust Fund

£8,500

Correspondent: Rodney Dunkley, Trustee, 20 Aviemore Gardens, Northampton NN4 9XJ (01604 765925; email: roddunkley@yahoo.co.uk)

CC number: 1059707

Eligibility

Employees and past employees of the printing trade in Buckinghamshire and Berkshire. Spouses, widows, widowers and children and any other financial dependants can also be supported.

Types of grants

One-off and recurrent grants are given to further/higher education students towards the cost of books, necessities, equipment/instruments or other course-related expenses.

Annual grant total

In 2013/14 the fund had an income of £17,500 and an expenditure of £17,500. We estimate the annual total amount of grants awarded to individuals to be around £8,500.

Exclusions

According to our research, grants are not made towards the course fees.

Applications

Apply in writing to the correspondent.

Other information

This fund also awards Christmas payments to ex-employee pensioners of BPC Hazells.

The Newspaper Press Fund (Journalists' Charity)

£10,000

Correspondent: David Ilott, Director, Dickens House, 35 Wathen Road, Dorking, Surrey RH4 1JY (01306 887511; fax: 01306 888212; email: enquiries@journalistscharity.org.uk; website: www.journalistscharity.org.uk)

CC number: 208215

Eligibility

Practising and former journalists and their dependants who are in need because of sickness, accident or other unforeseen circumstances. There are no age restrictions.

Types of grants

One-off and recurrent grants are given. This fund mainly supports welfare causes, although there is some crossover with the educational purposes. Help with school, college or university fees is only given in exceptional circumstances.

Annual grant total

In 2014 the charity had assets of £11.4 million and an income of £1.6 million. It would appear that full accounts were not able to view. Our research indicates that, normally, around 150–200 awards are made each year totalling around £300,000. The majority of support is given for welfare purposes. We estimate that educational grants for individuals total around £10,000.

Exclusions

The charity states that their 'aim is to give financial support in times of need however [they] cannot subsidise those who, in the long term, find it difficult to make a living from journalism unless through illness or other misfortune'. Grants are not offered to subsidise an existing lifestyle.

Applications

Application forms can be requested from the correspondent using an online form on the charity's website. They can be submitted directly by the individual or a family member. Applications should include details of the career in journalism and are considered monthly. The consideration process may take two to six weeks.

Other information

The fund also runs residential and care homes in Dorking.

The Printing Charity

£46,000

Correspondent: Henry Smith, Grants Officer, First Floor, Underwood House, 235 Three Bridges Road, Crawley, West Sussex RH10 1LS (01293 542820; fax: 01293 542826; email: info@theprintingcharity.org.uk; website: www.theprintingcharity.org.uk)

CC number: 208882

Eligibility

People who have worked for at least three years in the printing profession, graphic arts or allied trades who are in need. A list of eligible trades can be found on the charity's website.

Types of grants

Training grants, which are usually up to £750, are given to help with costs associated with:

- Occupational training and related expenses such as travel, buying computers and course books
- Access to training
- Redundancy support
- Apprenticeships
- Learning support/college top-up fees

The website explains: 'We have, for example, helped a litho printer undertake training in digital print, another to retrain as a tiler and one to train for a career in conservation.'

For more information on educational support given by the charity, see the website.

Annual grant total

In 2014 the charity had assets of £36.8 million and an income of £1.7 million. Educational bursaries totalled £46,000.

The charity also continued its work through the Future Proposals scheme and its partnership with the Prince's Trust which are aimed at assisting younger people with education and employment. Grants are also given for welfare needs and a great part of the overall charitable expenditure is spent in the provision of specifically sheltered accommodation for older people.

Applications

Application forms and guidelines are available from the charity's website. Further information on the application process can also be received by contacting the correspondent. Assistance is means-tested so applicants should be prepared to make a full declaration of their finances, including state benefits and funding from other charitable sources. Applications can be made by individuals directly or through a welfare agency. The charity advises potential applicants to contact the correspondent before submitting an application. The Grants Officer's direct contacts are: 01293 649368, henry@theprintingcharity.org.uk.

Other information

The Print Futures Awards

In conjunction with partners (British Printing Industries Federation – BPIF, The John Crosfield Foundation, St Bride Foundation and Unite the Union GPM Sector) the charity supports The Print Futures Awards to assist people between the ages of 16 and 30 with costs associated with a relevant training course in printing, publishing or graphic arts. Cash grants of up to £1,500 are awarded.

Individuals between the ages of 16 and 30 who live in the UK may apply for the awards if they: already work in printing, publishing or graphic arts; or intend to study or are already studying for a career in printing, publishing or graphic arts.

See the charity's website for more information.

Applications for The Print Futures awards are open in January each year, with shortlisted applicants interviewed in London in June, and awards presented in July. For more information, contact the Awards Secretary, Terry Ulrick: 07850 105 027, terryulrick@tucommunications.co.uk. Alternatively, visit the website: www.printfuturesawards.co.uk.

Legal professions

The Barristers' Benevolent Association

£89,500

Correspondent: Susan Eldridge, The Secretary, 14 Gray's Inn Square, London WC1R 5JP (020 7242 4761; fax: 020 7831 5366; email: susan@the-bba.com; website: www.the-bba.com)

CC number: 1106768

Eligibility

Past or present practising members of the Bar in England and Wales, and their dependants, who are in need.

Types of grants

Educational grants for dependants are only given in the most exceptional circumstances, for example where the death or disability of a barrister leaves his or her children stranded in mid-education. Grants or loans are given to schoolchildren towards books, educational outings, maintenance or school uniforms or clothing; students in further/higher education for help with books, fees and living expenses; mature students for books, travel, fees or childcare; and people starting work for books, equipment, clothing and travel.

Annual grant total

In 2014 the association had assets of £10.4 million and an income of £590,000. Grants totalled £178,500 and are awarded both for social welfare and educational purposes. We estimate that educational grants amounted to £89,500.

Exclusions

School fees are only paid in exceptional circumstances such as if the student is facing imminent examinations.

Applications

Applications are available to download from the website.

The Incorporated Benevolent Association of the Chartered Institute of Patent Attorneys

£0

Correspondent: Derek Chandler, Secretary, 3rd Floor, 95 Chancery Lane, London WC2A 1DT

CC number: 219666

Eligibility

British members and former members of the institute, and their dependants.

Types of grants

One-off and recurrent grants or loans according to need.

Annual grant total

In 2013/14 the association had assets of £1 million and an income of £85,000. The amount of grants given to individuals totalled £22,000 and was given for social welfare purposes only. Based on the annual reports and accounts available to view from the Charity Commission, it would appear that there have been no grants of an educational nature made for some time.

Applications

Apply in writing to the correspondent, marked 'Private and Confidential'. Applications can be submitted at any time. Where possible, grants are provided via a third party.

Manufac-turing

The Fashion and Textile Children's Trust

£288,500

Correspondent: Grants Co-ordinator, Office 1 and 2, J411/412 The Biscuit Factory, 100 Clements Road, London SE16 4DG (0300 123 9002; fax: 020 7691 9356; email: grants@ftct.org.uk; website: www.ftct.org.uk)

CC number: 257136

Eligibility

Children and young people under 18 years old whose parents or full-time carer work or have worked (within the last nine years) in the UK fashion and textile retailing and manufacturing industry.

Types of grants

Grants are given to support the educational needs of children who are facing 'significant health, emotional, social or family difficulties'. They can be used to provide funding for things such as: specialist tutorial support; learning tools (e.g. specialist tools, books and course equipment); school necessities (e.g. uniform and sports equipment); and transport fees. School fees are considered where the state education system has been unable to meet a young person's needs. The website also states: 'In exceptional cases, applications for support will be considered where the child is in a critical phase of their education (GSCEs) and the family are unable to self-fund due to unexpected circumstances e.g. redundancy, bereavement, divorce or personal illness.'

Annual grant total

In 2013/14 the trust had assets of £8.5 million and an income of £591,500. Grants to children in support of their education totalled £288,500.

Exclusions

Our research indicates that no grants are given towards childcare; study/travel abroad; overseas students studying in Britain; student exchange; or people starting work. No grants are available for those in higher education.

Applications

Initially contact the Grants Co-ordinator by telephone or by using the online enquiry form to discuss your child's needs and to see if the trust may be able to assist. You should have evidence of your connection to the trade to hand (P45/P60/an employer's letter/an NI letter). If the Grants Co-ordinator feels that the trust may be able to help, an application form will be sent to you. It may be returned at any time and the trust can offer assistance with completing it. Supporting evidence, which must be provided, is listed on the website.

Other information

Some grants are also made in support of children's well-being.

Mariners

The Marine Society and Sea Cadets

£607,000

Correspondent: Claire Barnett, Company Secretary, 202 Lambeth Road, London SE1 7JW (020 7654 7011; fax: 020 7928 8914; email: info@ms-sc.org; website: www.ms-sc.org)

CC number: 313013/SC037808

Eligibility

Professional seafarers, active or retired, serving in the Royal Navy, the British Merchant Navy or fishing fleets or any other maritime career persons who are serving in the navies, merchant navies or fishing fleets, members of the Sea Cadet Corps, and any other young people considering a maritime career.

Types of grants

It is the society's policy to help where financial hardship is evident. If the applicant is likely to be employed or re-employed then interest-free loans may be given rather than grants. The award of a loan or grant is usually made to an applicant who is attempting to improve his career prospects, or who has to change his career due to unforeseen circumstances. Loans are normally up to £2,000 repayable over the period of two years (starting four months after completion of the course of study) and are aimed to help 'professional seafarers to help offset the costs of attending vocational courses or studying at colleges for professional advancement'.

The society also offers scholarship schemes for seafarers or prospective seafarers – Slater scholarships (up to £17,500 for four years to serving Merchant Navy ratings over the age of 20 considering career progression through any approved UK nautical college) and Worcester scholarships (to 'UK officers embarking upon qualifications that will help prepare for a broader career in the maritime sector'.

Annual grant total

In 2013/14 the charity had assets of £23.7 million and an income of £15.3 million. Grants totalled £3.8 million and consisted of £2.6 million given to organisations and £1.2 million to individuals. Note that the charity states that 'individual grants given are small and not material within the overall total'. As the accounts did not specify the proportion of awards given for educational and for welfare purposes we have divided the £1.2 million figure between the two.

Exclusions

Recurrent grants are not made.

Applications

Application forms are available from the correspondent and are considered as they arrive.

Other information

Grants are also made to sea cadet units and support can be given to 'nautical or other schools or training establishments which are charities or to other organisations established for charitable purposes'. In addition grants are provided to volunteers to allow upkeep or purchase of uniforms on promotion or for wear and tear during the year.

The Royal Liverpool Seamen's Orphan Institution (RLSOI)

£112,500

Correspondent: Linda Cotton, Secretary, 2nd Floor, Tower Building, 22 Water Street, Liverpool L2 1BA (0151 227 3417 or 07747 607062 (mobile); email: enquiries@rlsoi-uk.org; website: www.rlsoi-uk.org)

CC number: 526379

Eligibility

Children of deceased British merchant seafarers and fishermen. Applicants may be of pre-school age or in full-time education (including further and higher education). Help may also be given to seafarers who are at home caring for their family alone.

Types of grants

Discretionary awards are available to help with education costs and monthly maintenance. Annual clothing grants and support for school fees are available. Grants can be provided throughout the child's education.

Annual grant total

In 2014 the charity had assets of £2.8 million and an income of £222,500. The amount of grants given to individuals totalled £225,500 for both welfare and educational purposes. During the year a total of 80 individuals were supported, including 16 new beneficiaries. The breakdown between educational and welfare support was not specified; therefore, we estimate that about £112,500 was awarded for educational needs.

Applications

Application forms are available from the correspondent and can be submitted at any time. They should also be downloadable from the charity's website. At the time of writing (August 2015) forms were being revised and not accessible online. Each application is considered on its own merits.

Other information

Support is given to both educational and welfare causes. While the proportions given for each cause were not specified, all grants are given to children and young people who are in attendance at school and further or higher education institutions. The charity's website also provides links to other organisations helping seafarers.

In 2013 the charity came to an arrangement with the Royal Merchant Navy Education Foundation whereby they would in future take over the support of beneficiaries in further education. In 2014 two students have been transferred following the agreement.

The Royal Merchant Navy Education Foundation

£101,000 (30 grants)

Correspondent: Commander Charles Heron-Watson, Secretary, Mole Lodge, Mole Road, Sindlesham, Wokingham, Berkshire RG41 5DB (0118 997 7700; email: office@rmnef.orh.uk; website: www.rmnef.org.uk)

CC number: 1153323

Eligibility

Children in need at any stage of education who have a parent who has served or is serving as a seaman of any grade in the British Merchant Navy. This parent must either have died whilst on duty, or have left the sea because of illness (in which case the child must have been born before the parent left the sea), or be unable to provide fully for the education, maintenance and upbringing of the child.

Types of grants

One–off and recurrent grants are made towards school and university fees, educational extras, school uniforms, some travel to and from the school, equipment and instruments, educational outings, books; some university expenses may be covered. Career and personal development endeavours such as Outward Bound courses, apprenticeships, career training or pre-school level education are also supported. Grants are tailored to meet the needs of each individual and are usually paid directly to institutions.

The trustees understand that 'if the need for fee-paying education is established, the families will usually be unable to meet a large percentage of the costs'; therefore, the foundation 'makes quite large awards in order to meet the needs of individuals'. Families will be expected to make contributions towards the expenses within their means.

Annual grant total

In 2013/14 the foundation had assets of £13.2 million and an income of £497,500. It had 36 beneficiaries at a secondary education level or beyond and made grants totalling almost £101,000.

Applications

Initial contact should be made with the correspondent via letter or email. Phone enquiries to discuss individual circumstances are also welcomed.

Application forms will then be provided to eligible applicants. Candidates will be paid a home visit and may be required to provide an assessment by a relevant professional. Information about the parents' employment and financial situation will also be required.

Other information

Previously known as the Royal Merchant Navy School Foundation (Charity Commission no. 309047), the assets and liabilities of the foundation were transferred to the Royal Merchant Navy Education Foundation, a charitable incorporated organisation, in 2013.

Foundation also assists beneficiaries over the age of 18 who have previously been supported by the Royal Liverpool Seamen's Orphan's Institution.

Sailors' Children's Society

£38,000

Correspondent: Deanne Thomas, Chief Officer, Francis Reckitt House, Newland, Cottingham Road, Hull HU6 7RJ (01482 342331; fax: 01482 447868; email: info@sailorschildren.org.uk; website: www.sailorschildren.org.uk)

CC number: 224505

Eligibility

Seafarers' children (generally under the age of 18 – see 'Types of grants' for exceptions) who are in full-time education and the families are in severe financial difficulties. One of the child's parents must have served in the Royal or Merchant Navy or in the fishing fleets, including on ferries, tankers, cruise ships or cargo boats.

Applicants must be in receipt of Housing Benefit or Council Tax Benefit (other than single person's 25% discount or disability reduction), with the following information given on the website: 'All the families we help are on a means tested benefit which ensures we only help those in most need.'

Types of grants

The charity supports children's education in a number of ways. These include:

- Clothing grants – payable per child twice a year to help children start off the new school year and, secondly, to buy a new winter coat and shoes
- Student Support Scheme – if a young person is over the age of 18 and currently supported on the Child Support Scheme, the charity can continue its support with a welfare grant to help with their ongoing studies at university or college

- Vouchers can be given to support days out for families during the school holidays

Annual grant total

In 2014/15 the charity had assets of £2.1 million and an income of £762,000. Grants totalled £396,500, the majority of which was given for social welfare purposes. At least £38,000 was given in grants for home computers. We were unable to determine the total amount of grants awarded for other educational expenditure such as school clothing, school holidays or student support.

Applications

Application forms are available from the correspondent and require details about children and the family's income and expenditure. Copies of relevant certificates, for example birth certificates and proof of seafaring service, should also be provided. Applications can be submitted directly by the individual or through a social worker, Citizens Advice, other welfare agency, or through seafaring organisations. Applications are considered every other month, beginning in February.

Other information

The charity, which was previously known as Sailors' Families' Society, has an informative website where more details can be found.

The charity notes that even if it is unable to help an individual directly, it may be able to direct them to another organisation that may be able to assist.

Medicine and health

The Birmingham and Three Counties Trust for Nurses

£4,800

Correspondent: David Airston, 16 Haddon Croft, Halesowen B63 1JQ (0121 602 0389; email: ruthmadams_45@msn.com)

CC number: 217991

Eligibility

Nurses on any statutory register, who have practiced or practice in the City of Birmingham and the counties of Staffordshire, Warwickshire and Worcestershire.

Types of grants

One-off grants, usually up to £300 per annum, to nurses taking post-registration or enrolment courses (post-basic nurse training or back-to-nursing course). Grants are made towards books, travel and/or fees.

Annual grant total

In 2013/14 the trust had an income of £8,700 and a total expenditure of £16,000. Assistance in previous years has mostly been given for welfare purposes. We estimate that educational grants totalled around £4,800.

Applications

Applications can be made on a form available from the correspondent. They should be submitted directly by the individual. Applications are considered at any time.

The Cameron Fund

£115,000

Correspondent: David Harris, Company Secretary, BMA House, Tavistock Square, London WC1H 9HR (020 7388 0796; email: info@cameronfund.org.uk; website: www.cameronfund.org.uk)

CC number: 261993

Eligibility

Current and former registered general practitioners and their dependants. Doctors on postgraduate specialty training who have successfully completed the training or those who only completed it partially, due to unforeseen circumstances, are also considered.

There is a specific scheme to assist the children of existing and former beneficiaries with expenses relating to studying and training. Applicant for student grants should be over the age of 18.

Types of grants

Grants to GPs' dependent children in education or training and to support retraining of GPs who are trying to enter new or re-establish their previous careers.

Assistance may include funding for living expenses while on training, children's extra-curricular activities and after school clubs, school fees (in certain circumstances), travel to school, school uniforms and so on. Private education costs can be assisted during an examination year or for a short period before a child joins or re-enters the state system. Student grants, made to dependants of current or former beneficiaries, can be towards living expenses while undertaking first degree or vocational training.

Our research suggests that grants are generally of up to £3,000. Interest-free loans are also available.

Annual grant total

In 2014 the charity had assets of £5.8 million and an income of £349,000.

The trustees' annual report notes that new applications for assistance were received from 139 individuals and grants and loans, including Money Advice, were authorised totalling £319,500 to 191 beneficiaries. Grants totalled around £229,500. The accounts did not specify how much was given in support of educational needs; therefore, we estimate that educational assistance totalled around £115,000.

Exclusions

Grants cannot be made towards items which should be provided through statutory sources. Student grants are only given to families previously supported by the charity.

Applications

Student application forms can be found on the charity's website or requested from the correspondent. Applications can be made directly by individuals or on their behalf. Referrals from Local Medical Committees and other organisations or individuals who may know of someone who might benefit from support from the charity are also welcome. Applicants are invited to get in touch with the correspondent if they are unsure about the eligibility or the application procedure.

Further information, such as copies of confirmation of acceptance on a course and financial notifications of tuition fees, maintenance loan, supplementary grants, and any other documentation which illustrates the financial circumstances of the applicant are requested and references may be required. A trustee may visit the applicant before agreeing a grant. Applicants should have started the process of claiming state and/or local authority benefits.

Applicants must ensure that they have begun the process of claiming state and local authority benefits.

Note: Signed application forms can be returned in an unstamped envelope addressed to FREEPOST CAMERON.

Other information

Grants are also made for welfare purposes. Financial, legal, career advice and counselling are also offered.

The trustees' annual report for 2014 notes: 'Close relations are fostered with other medical benevolent funds and with BMA Charities, which enables a more concerted and appropriate response to be made to those applicants who may be eligible for assistance from other charities.'

It is further specified: 'The potential beneficiaries who are eligible to be considered for support comprise over 39,000 general medical practitioners in the United Kingdom and their

dependants, together with GP trainees and retired GPs.'

The Dain Fund

£18,000 (34 grants)

Correspondent: Marian Flint, Administrator, BMA Charities, BMA House, Tavistock Square, London WC1H 9JP (020 7383 6142; fax: 020 7554 6334; email: info.bmacharities@ bma.org.uk; website: bma.org.uk/about-the-bma/who-we-are/charities)

CC number: 313108

Eligibility

Children of doctors or deceased doctors (not nurses or physiotherapists and so on) in state, private or higher education and whose families have experienced an unexpected change in financial circumstances following crises such as unemployment, family breakdown or serious illness of a parent or guardian. The fund has also undertaken outreach work to support the children of refugee doctors.

Types of grants

Most grants relate to educational expenses such as school uniforms and study trips for children in state schools where the family is on a low income. Grants are sometimes made for short-term interventions in which school fees are paid for a few terms either until the child finishes GCSEs or A-levels or the child is found a place in the state education system. Occasionally grants are made to students in tertiary education.

Annual grant total

In 2014 the fund had assets of almost £1.6 million and an income of £51,500. Grants were made totalling £18,000 to the benefit of 34 children.

Applications

Application forms are available from the correspondent.

Other information

This fund is designed to help families in an emergency and is not a scholarship provider.

The RCN Foundation

£180,000 (97 grants)

Correspondent: Grants Manager (Hardship or Educational), 20 Cavendish Square, London W1G 0RN (020 7647 3645; email: rcnfoundation@rcn.org.uk; website: www.rcnfoundation.org.uk)

CC number: 1134606

Eligibility

Registered nurses, midwives, health practitioners, health-care assistants and people training for these professions.

Types of grants

Scholarships, bursaries and grants for a range of learning, development and research opportunities.

Annual grant total

In 2014 the foundation had assets of £29.4 million and an income of £1 million. Grants during the year amounted to £466,000, with organisations receiving £94,000, and benevolent grants to individuals totalling £216,000. Educational bursaries were awarded to 97 individuals totalling £180,000, of which £24,000 was written back to the foundation.

Applications

There is a list of available bursaries, together with opening and closing dates for applications, listed on the website. Full eligibility criteria and application forms are also available to download.

Other information

Previously known as The Royal College of Nursing Benevolent Fund, the purpose of the foundation is to enable nurses and nursing to improve the health and well-being of the public through:

- Benevolent funding
- Education and training bursaries
- Supporting the development of clinical practice and the improvement of care
- Developing practice to enable people and communities to make positive choices about their own health and well-being
- Promoting research.

The Royal Medical Benevolent Fund (RMBF)

£360,500 (At least 80 grants)

Correspondent: The Casework Department, 24 King's Road, Wimbledon, London SW19 8QN (020 8540 9194; email: help@rmbf.org; website: www.rmbf.org)

CC number: 207275

Eligibility

Doctors who have held GMC Registration, and their dependants, who are on a low income and unable to support themselves due to illness, disability, bereavement or being over state retirement age. Medical students experiencing unforeseen financial hardship, and their dependants. Refugee doctors practising in the UK.

Types of grants

Help provided can range 'from financial assistance in the form of grants and interest-free loans to a telephone befriending scheme for those who may be isolated and in need of support'. Assistance is tailored to the individual's needs. Support includes:

- Regular monthly grants towards day-to-day living costs
- Back-to-work awards for those returning to work following a period of illness (including retraining costs, professional fees and occasionally childcare costs)
- Other awards towards specialist equipment, car and home adaptations
- Top-ups for residential care fees, extra care costs
- Secured loans, where the beneficiary has significant equity in property
- Specialist money and debt management advice to renegotiate debts and secure all eligible state benefits
- Support for medical students in exceptional financial hardship
- Support for refugee doctors retraining in the UK

The Medical Student Programme 'aims to help medical students who are facing exceptional hardship to finalise their studies, qualify as doctors and complete their foundation years'. Students must intend to remain in the UK after qualification, be in the final two years of their training, demonstrate exceptional hardship and have exhausted other sources of support.

The charity aims to help its beneficiaries to 'become more independent and self-sufficient again wherever possible, whilst maintaining longer term support for those for whom this is needed'.

For full details on eligibility for financial help check the financial support section of the charity's helpful website or get in touch with the caseworkers.

Annual grant total

In 2013/14 the charity had assets of £28.8 million and an income of £1.5 million. Amounts paid to individuals totalled £721,500. The breakdown between educational and welfare support was not given; therefore, we estimate that about £360,500 was given for educational purposes.

During the year 19 beneficiaries were supported during their return to work, 16 beneficiaries were helped to remain in work, 26 beneficiaries were assisted with training with the aim of securing employment and also 19 students (who were dependants of doctors) were helped financially while undertaking the undergraduate degree.

The charity aims to provide a total of at least £720,000 each year to its beneficiaries. The key objective to March 2015 was to provide about £750,000 in financial support.

Exclusions

The following are excluded:

- Private healthcare and medical insurance
- Private education
- Legal fees
- HMRC payments
- Debts to relatives or friends

Applications

For an application pack and further information, get in touch with the correspondent via email or phone. Applications can be submitted either directly by the individual or through a third party, for example a social worker, Citizens Advice, other welfare agency, medical colleague or other medical and general charities.

Two references are required (at least one of which should be from a medical practitioner). All applicants are visited before a report is submitted to the Case Committee, which meets on a two month basis (although emergency assistance may be given). The income/capital and expenditure are fully investigated, with similar rules applying as for those receiving Income Support.

Other information

The latest annual report for 2013/14 notes that 'a formal review of the Medical Students Programme is underway and a review of the pilot Mentoring Programme will follow later in the year'.

The charity has an informative website where further details can be found. Both educational and welfare needs are assisted.

Additionally specialist information and advice for doctors through the Support4Doctors website (www.support4doctors.org) are provided on a range of areas, including career, health, employment, money management and practical issues.

There are the following restricted funds: Late Dr S.H. Kutar Trust which seeks to 'make grants to students under the age of 35 who are children of medical graduates to assist with their education when there are limited financial resources'; The Job Trust which aims 'to assist the daughters of doctors with professional or vocational education'; The Masina-Hele Memorial Donation 'to support eligible beneficiaries in the furtherance of their medical education'; and The British Humane Association which helps 'medical students who have fallen on hard times through no fault of their own'.

The Royal Medical Foundation of Epsom College

£74,500 (13 grants)

Correspondent: Helen Jones, Caseworker, RMF Office, Epsom College, College Road, Epsom, Surrey KT17 4JQ (01372 821010; email: rmf-caseworker@epsomcollege.org.uk; website: www.royalmedicalfoundation.org)

CC number: 312046

Eligibility

Dependants, aged up to 18, of current or former medical practitioners (GMC registered) who are in need.

Types of grants

Grants are given to schoolchildren and college students towards fees. Preference is given to pupils with family difficulties so that they have to be educated away from home, pupils with special educational needs and medical students.

The Epsom College awards bursaries, the average of which is of £18,600 per annum.

Annual grant total

In 2013/14 the foundation made 42 grants totalling £122,000. This included educational grants amounting to £74,500 for 13 individuals. Grants were distributed as follows:

Financial assistance with educational expenses	12	£48,000
Short-term payments or one-off grants where urgent assistance is required	23	£30,000
Financial assistance with educational expenses at Epsom College	1	£27,000
Regular payments to medical practitioners and their widows/widowers	4	£16,900
Other grants	2	£700

Applications

There is an online financial assistance request form on the foundation's website. For more information contact the correspondent. Applicants must have applied for any state benefits to which they may be entitled before an application can be considered and will be visited by the caseworker as part of the application process. The foundation's board meets quarterly, in January, April, July and October and applications should be submitted well in advance (specific dates are listed on the website).

Other information

The Royal Medical Foundation is a charity founded by Dr John Propert in 1855 and administered by Act of Parliament. Its original objects were to provide an asylum for qualified medical practitioners and their spouses and to found a school for their sons. Today, the foundation's aims and objectives are to assist registered doctors and their families who are in financial hardship. Practical assistance is given in three ways:

▸ Provision of regular payments to their widows, widowers and their children
▸ Provision of one-off grants when emergency help is required and
▸ In exceptional circumstances, assistance with school fees for sons or daughters of registered doctors enabling them to maintain educational stability at times of distress caused by illness, bereavement or financial need in their family

The foundation is managed by a board of directors drawn from various professions and is located at Epsom College.

The Society for Relief of Widows and Orphans of Medical Men (The Widows and Orphans)

£50,000 (6 grants)

Correspondent: Charlotte Farrar, Secretary, Lettsom House, 11 Chandos Street, Cavendish Square, London W1G 9EB (01837 83022; email: info@widowsandorphans.org.uk; website: www.widowsandorphans.org.uk)

CC number: 207473

Eligibility

Support is given in the following order of priority:

▸ Necessitous dependants of deceased members of the society
▸ Necessitous members of the society
▸ Necessitous dependants of members of the society
▸ Necessitous medical practitioners not being members of the society and their dependants

Types of grants

Our research suggests that one-off and recurrent grants from £500 to £3,000 are available to college students, undergraduates, vocational and mature students for fees, books, maintenance/living expenses, instruments/equipment and clothing (not to mature students). Support is also given to schoolchildren and people starting work for maintenance/living expenses. The society has given help to former doctors for retraining and specific extra costs involved in further education to help them re-enter employment.

Clinical medical students receive higher awards more because of the shorter holidays and the lack of opportunity for supplementing their income through holiday jobs.

Annual grant total

In 2014 the society had assets of £5.9 million and an income of £169,000. The amount of grants given to individuals totalled £105,000. The trustees' annual report specifies that six students received awards. We estimate that around £50,000 was awarded in educational support.

Exclusions

Grants are not normally given for second degrees.

Applications

Application forms (separate for different types of applicants) can be found on the society's website or requested from the correspondent. They can be submitted directly by the individual or a family member and are usually considered in February, May, August and November. Note that applications must be submitted via post.

Other information

Support is also given for welfare needs.

Mining and quarrying

Miners' Welfare National Educational Fund (MWNEF)

£92,500 (177 grants)

Correspondent: V. O. S. Jones, Secretary, The Old Rectory, Rectory Drive, Whiston, Rotherham, South Yorkshire S60 4JG (01709 728115; fax: 01709 839164; email: mwnef@ciswo.org.uk; website: ciswo.org/index.php/education)

CC number: 313246, SC038771

Eligibility

People who are or have been employed in the coal mining industry of Great Britain (including any activity conducted by British Coal) and have not undertaken full-time permanent employment since. Individuals who are the dependants of such employees or former employees are also eligible. Applicants must be at least 17 years old.

Types of grants

Grants of not more than £500 a year are given towards higher and further education. Any full-time courses of education for which LEA or SAAS support is available are eligible, including undergraduate degrees, Open University courses, full- and part-time education. Some postgraduate courses may be considered where they are related to and taken directly after a first degree or considered essential for an entry into a profession. Other postgraduate courses of not more than two years in duration, where candidates have achieved at least an upper second class honours degree (at first degree level) can be considered.

Annual grant total

In 2013/14 the fund had assets of £861,500 and an income of £47,000. A total of around £92,500 was awarded in 177 grants, broken down as follows:

North Yorkshire	68	£31,000
South Yorkshire	31	£17,000
Nottinghamshire	37	£16,000
Scotland	15	£8,000
South Wales	13	£7,000
Central	12	£6,000
HQ and others	9	£5,000
Western	4	£2,000
North East	2	£1,000
Telegraph awards	7	£300

Applications

Application forms are available from the correspondent, normally between late August and March. Candidates are required to provide a referee's report from educational institution, give full personal details and academic achievements, include a confirmation of A-level results and of award of student support. Family or financial circumstances relevant to the application can also be outlined. Grants are considered two or three times a year.

Other information

Applicants must re-apply in each academic year of an eligible course.

The trustees' annual report from 2013/14 states:

> During the 2013/14 academic year, a total of 15 applications were received from Scottish students. Requests for application forms have been received directly from employees of the coal mining industry in Scotland (Scottish Resources Group including The Scottish Coal Co. Ltd.) or from referrals generated through the staff based at the CISWO Regional Office in Bathgate, West Lothian.

North East Area Miners' Social Welfare Trust Fund

£5,000

Correspondent: Vincent Clements, Secretary, Coal Industry Social Welfare Organisation, 6 Bewick Road, Gateshead, Tyne and Wear NE8 4DP (0191 477 7242; email: vincent.clements@ciswo.org.uk; website: www.ciswo.org.uk)

CC number: 504178

Eligibility

People in need living in Durham, Northumberland and Tyne and Wear who are or have been employed by the coal industry, and their dependants.

Types of grants

One-off grants according to need. The fund aims to improve beneficiaries' health, social well-being and conditions of living.

Annual grant total

In 2013/14 the fund had assets of £3.25 million and an income of £309,500. Grants were made totalling £46,500. Of this sum a total of £25,500 was given to individuals (including £700 approved and paid in 2015). We estimate that about £5,000 was given for educational and training needs.

The fund continued to help miners and people from former mining communities to afford convalescent holidays spending £155,500 to assist individuals in the year.

Applications

Applications may be made in writing to the correspondent. They can be submitted directly by the individual or through a social worker, Citizens Advice or other welfare agency. Requests are usually considered four times a year.

Other information

The fund also makes grants to mining charities. It also provides group holidays for its beneficiaries and revenue/capital costs relating to the day-to-day running of the Sam Watson Rest Home. It would appear that most support is given for general welfare needs.

Public and government sector

The Gurney Fund for Police Orphans

£414,500

Correspondent: Christine McNicol, Director, 9 Bath Road, Worthing, West Sussex BN11 3NU (01903 237256; email: gurneyfund@btconnect.com; website: www.gurneyfund.org)

CC number: 1156903-1/261319

Eligibility

Children under the age of 18 of deceased or incapacitated police officers from 22 subscribing forces in England and Wales. The list of subscribing forces can be found on the fund's website.

Types of grants

Support is available for long periods of time (up to 20 years). Grants are given for general educational needs, including uniforms, sports kits, school activities, music tuition and instruments, books, equipment, extra-curricular activities and educational travel or school trips. Grants can be both one-off of up to £2,500 or recurrent in the range of £10–£60 per week.

Annual grant total

In 2013/14 the fund had assets of £8.2 million, an income of £485,500 and a total charitable expenditure of £497,500. Weekly allowances and grants to children totalled £414,500.

During the year there were a total of 189 beneficiaries on the register receiving basic weekly allowances.

Exclusions

Grants are not made to beneficiaries who go on to higher education but the fund may consider assisting with the payment of annual tuition fees and the cost of books and ancillary equipment.

Funding is not normally given for skiing holidays and school fees (here exceptions can be made for children with special educational needs).

Applications

Applications can be made through the force welfare officers, local representatives or the subscribing forces directly. They can be made at any time and are normally considered in February, May, August and November. A copy of the child's birth certificate will have to be provided. Successful candidates will be asked to complete an income and expenditure form and produce receipts if assistance is requested for specific expenditure.

Other information

The fund also awards Christmas gift cheques to all children aged 18 or under and arranges holidays for the beneficiaries. Christmas gifts were awarded totalling £24,000 in 2013/14.

This fund is linked to The Gurney Fund (Charity Commission no. 1156903). Grants are also made through The Gurney Benevolent Fund.

Emergency services

St George's Police Children Trust (formerly St George's Police Trust)

£102,000 (At least 68 grants)

Correspondent: The Trust Administrator, St Andrews, Harlow Moor Road, Harrogate, North Yorkshire HG2 0AD (01423 504448; email: enquiries@thepolicetreatmentcentres.org; website: www.stgeorgespolicechildrentrust.org)

CC number: 1147445/SC043652

Eligibility

Children and young people in full-time education of serving or retired officers who were members of a police force covered by the trust (see 'Other information'), and who are now deceased or have been incapacitated whilst on duty and can no longer work. Young people not in full-time education who have lost a police officer parent, but who are unable to earn their own living as a result of having special needs, may also be eligible.

Note: Usually, to be eligible, the police officer parent must have donated to the trust whilst serving.

Types of grants

One-off and recurrent grants. The amount awarded is dependent upon the household income and the potential need or hardship. Registration grant of £100 is given to all eligible applicants, before the full consideration at the trustees' meeting.

The trust offers:

- **Further Education Grants** – £1,500 a year to eligible beneficiaries aged 18–25 for any form of further education, including first degree, HNC, HND or NVQ Level 4 (a course can be supported up to a maximum of four years)
- **Special Needs Grants** – to children who are deemed to be classed as having a special need, i.e. are in receipt of the 'children's award' as defined in the police pensions regulations (poof of receipt will be required)
- **Ex-Gratia Grants** – to children and young people in full-time education and school leaving age towards trade tools when leaving school to start work, musical instruments and necessary text books, amongst other things
- **St George's Police Children Trust Grants** – available to eligible beneficiaries in full-time education to statutory school leaving age, or up to the end of the school year in which they turn 19 years of age
- **Weekly Support Allowances** – to children satisfying the eligibility criteria
- **Seasonal Gifts** – awarded twice yearly in summer and at Christmas

The website informs:

Weekly maintenance allowances and grants approved by the Trustees will be back dated to the date of the event giving rise to the application, or where the date of the event giving rise to the application is more than twelve months previously, to a maximum of twelve months preceding the date of the application.

Annual grant total

In 2014 the trust had assets of over £12 million and an income of £908,000. Grants were made totalling £247,000, including awards to 2,231 children in full-time education and further 68 individuals undertaking further education. We estimate that educational support totalled at least £102,000.

Exclusions

People in education beyond first degree level cannot be assisted. Grants are not made for gap year activities. If you are applying for a Further Education Grant after a gap year, note that application can only be considered after a single gap period from education of not more than one year. The trust does not pay allowances or grants where the beneficiary is in work and earning money.

Applications

Application forms are available to download from the website or can be requested from Police Federation representatives or Police Force Benevolent Funds. They have to be submitted via the police force in which the parent served and **not** directly to the trust. This is usually done through the police federation office, the occupational health and welfare department or occasionally the force benevolent fund. Request should be accompanied by relevant documentation. Applications are considered on a quarterly basis in February, May, August and November.

Other information

Both educational and general welfare needs can be assisted. The trust also provides one-week respite holidays at the trust's holiday home in Harrogate available to all current and future beneficiaries.

The website notes that the foundation for The St George's Police Children Trust was laid by Catherine Gurney who opened Northern Police Orphanage in 1898 'for the care and welfare of Northern Police Force children who had lost one or both parents'. In the second half of the 20th century the orphanage was closed and St George's Fund and the Northern Police Orphans Trust, both providing grants to police officers' children, were formed. The two charities merged in 2006 to form St George's Police Trust.

In 2013 the trade and assets not restricted by permanent endowment of the St George's Police Trust were transferred to the St George's Police Children Trust which has been granted a linking order between the two charities. The St George's Police Children Trust acts as the corporate trustee of the St George's Police Trust, which remains registered with the Charity Commission (Charity Commission no. 1147445–1).

The trust covers the following police forces: Cheshire; Cleveland; Cumbria; Derbyshire; Durham; Greater Manchester Police; Humberside; Lancashire; Lincolnshire; Merseyside; Northumbria; North Wales; North Yorkshire; Nottinghamshire; Police Service of Scotland; South Yorkshire; Staffordshire; West Mercia; West Yorkshire. The accounts state that 'the number of serving police officers in this catchment area is now approximately 63,000 and the number of police officers making the voluntary donation is around 37,000 (the number of retired police officers is likely to be similar)'.

The National Police Fund

£35,000 (35 grants)

Correspondent: Gill Scott-Moore, CEO, Police Dependants' Trust, 3 Mount Mews, High Street, Hampton, Middlesex TW12 2SH (020 8041 6907; fax: 020 8979 4323; email: office@pdtrust.org; website: www.pdtrust.org)

CC number: 207608

Eligibility

Dependants of serving, injured, retired or deceased members of police forces in England, Wales and Scotland who are over the age of 16. The annual household income of the candidate's family should be less than £30,000.

Types of grants

One-off grants generally of up to £1,000. Support is given for general needs (such as accommodation, learning equipment, books and so on) to students on further/higher education courses (at least one year in duration) or vocational training. Occasionally, albeit rarely, awards may be given to mature students or younger children.

Grants can be renewed only upon further recommendation in favour of renewal by the chief officer.

Annual grant total

In 2014/15 the fund had assets of £3.6 million and an income of £159,500. Grants to 35 individuals totalled £35,000.

Exclusions

Grants are not given for A-levels and where support should be obtained from statutory sources.

Applications

Application forms and further information can be requested from the correspondent or obtained from the welfare officer of the police force where the officer is serving or has served. Applications can be made by individuals but must be forwarded by the chief officer. They should be submitted by September. A reference from the student's college or university should be included together with the applicant's up-to-date weekly expenditure and income, details of any benefits received and evidence of academic attainment.

Other information

The fund is administered by The Police Dependants' Trust (Charity Commission no. 251021). Support from this fund can also be given for general welfare needs.

There is also a restricted Mary Holt fund awarding grants in exceptional cases of distress to widows or orphans of policemen below inspector level at retirement or death. Applications have to be forwarded by the chief constable for approval by the board.

The Police Dependants' Trust Ltd

£25,000 (9 grants)

Correspondent: Gill Scott-Moore, Chief Executive Officer, 3 Mount Mews, High Street, Hampton, Middlesex TW12 2SH (020 8941 6907; fax: 020 8979 4323; email: office@pdtrust.org; website: www. pdtrust.org)

CC number: 1151322

Eligibility

Dependants of current or former police officers who have died from injuries received in the execution of duty, and current or former police officers incapacitated as a result of injury received in the execution of duty, or their dependants. Eligible officers include:

- Members of the British Transport Police
- Members of the Civil Nuclear Constabulary
- People performing temporary overseas or central police force who enjoy a statutory right of reversion to such a police force

- Special Constables appointed for any such police area
- Police cadets appointed to undergo training with a view to becoming members of such police forces

Grants are **not restricted** to those individuals who are living in the UK – if you have moved but would otherwise be eligible you can still apply.

Types of grants

One-off grants ranging from around £200 to £9,000. Grants are available for retraining or new career opportunities and to the children of police officers who are at school or university. The annual report for 2013/14 states that educational grants are 'not just to cover essentials such as clothing but also for the purchase of sports or computer equipment, musical instruments or other educational facilities'. Extra-curricular activities are also assisted.

There is an education bursary to help young people under the age of 25 with living costs while undertaking full-time higher education, further education or vocational training (up to £1,000 per year).

Note that this is primarily a relief-in-need charity, so most of the grants will be given for welfare rather than educational purposes.

Annual grant total

In 2013/14 the trust had assets of £25.6 million and an income of over £1.4 million. There were 117 grants made totalling £327,000, of which nine awards were educational grants. Support was allocated as follows:

Special purpose grants	£315,500
Children support grants	£11,500

Assistance grants	73
Special purpose grants	34
Education grants	9
Other (bereavement, residential care)	1

There was no breakdown given of the amounts given in educational grants and welfare grants. We have estimated the educational grants to be around £25,000.

During the year the Management Committee considered a total of 246 applications for assistance, including 53 new applications and five urgent appeals (dealt with immediately).

Exclusions

Cash is not normally given (unless in exceptional circumstances and at the discretion of trustees).

Grants are not normally awarded to individuals to:

- Help where state assistance or statutory services are available
- Repay debts
- Cover legal expenses such as county court costs and solicitors' fees
- Help in the form of a loan

- Assist with medical care
- Help where the impact of an injury was temporary (unless exceptional circumstances apply)

Applications

Application forms are available on the trust's website or from the correspondent. They can be submitted at any time but all applicants must first register with the trust. Supporting materials may be required. Applications are generally considered every two months although urgent cases can be addressed between meetings. Generally applications are received, processed and concluded within twelve weeks.

Other information

The Police Dependants' Trust was founded in 1966 as a response to the deaths of three police officers who were shot while on duty in London. An anonymous donation of £100,000 was offered to a Home Office Minister to establish a permanent trust. It offers support to both welfare and educational needs.

The trust's activities have been transferred to The Police Dependants' Trust Ltd (Charity Commission no. 1151322), registered in March 2013. It has previously operated as Police Dependants' Trust (Charity Commission no. 251021). The new entity maintains the same objectives.

The website notes that the trust 'also administers the National Police Fund, which shares broadly the same eligibility criteria i.e. financial support is provided to the families/dependants of police officers who have been killed or injured on duty, and this support is provided on the basis of need'. The National Police Fund provides grants to:

- Police dependants who are in further education (university degree or vocational qualification)
- Widows and orphans of police officers who were below inspector level at the time of their death or medical retirement (through the Mary Holt Fund)
- Police benevolent funds or sports/social clubs
- Police charities and other bodies which assist the police services

The Royal Ulster Constabulary – Police Service of Northern Ireland Benevolent Fund

See entry on page 134

Religion

Children of the Clergy Trust

£2,300

Correspondent: The Revd I. Thomson, Trustee, 4 Keirhill Gardens, Westhill, Aberdeenshire AB32 6AX

OSCR number: SC001845

Eligibility

Children of deceased ministers of the Church of Scotland.

Types of grants

One-off or recurrent grants according to need. Our research tells us that grants in previous years have ranged from £500 to £1,000 for any educational need.

Annual grant total

In 2014 the trust had an income of £5,000 and a total expenditure of £4,700. We estimate that educational grants to individuals totalled around £2,300, with grants also awarded to individuals for social welfare purposes.

Applications

Apply in writing to the correspondent. Applications should be submitted directly by the individual and should include information about the applicant's ministerial parent, general family circumstances and other relevant information.

Other information

The trust is also known as Synod of Grampian Children of the Clergy Trust.

Lord Crewe's Charity

£173,000 (118 grants)

Correspondent: Clive Smithers, Clerk Manager, Rivergreen Centre, Aykley Heads, Durham DH1 5TS (0191 383 7398; email: enquiries@ lordcrewescharity.co.uk; website: www. lordcrewescharity.org.uk)

CC number: 1155101

Eligibility

Church of England clergy and their dependants who live in the dioceses of Durham and Newcastle and are in need. Grants may be given more generally to people in need who live in the area of benefit, with preference to people resident in parishes where the charity owns land or has the right of presentation to the benefice.

Types of grants

Grants are given for a whole range of education needs up to and including first degrees.

Annual grant total

In 2014 the charity had assets of £39 million and an income of £38.1 million (which includes a transfer of assets, liabilities and undertakings of the old charity worth £36.9 million). There were 118 educational grants made totalling £173,000 (note that this relates to two educational years – second instalments of grants for 2013–14 and first instalments of grants for 2014–15). A further £28,500 was paid in support of clergy in need and an additional £15,900 was spent as 'miscellaneous charitable giving'.

The accounts for 2014 note that 'educational grants awarded for 2014–15 for the first time contained an element of scaling, to ensure those on the lowest incomes within the family income threshold of £46,440 received proportionately larger grants than those at the higher end of the scale'.

Exclusions

Applicants who are not members of clergy are not supported and the trustees ask not to be contacted by people who do not fit the criteria.

Applications for church buildings and church projects are not assisted (except in the very small number of parishes in which the charity holds property or has rights of presentation).

Applications

The charity's website states that there is no 'application form or an open application procedure for grants' and instead 'the charity works directly with its beneficiaries and with a number of partner organisations'. The application round opens in March and continues until July. Grants are considered in the first two weeks of August and the outcome is communicated to the applicant by the end of the month. Consult the website for the latest updates on awards available.

Other information

From 2014 the charity has become a charitable incorporated organisation and changed its registered charity number (previously 230347).

Small annual grants are made to organisations (annual sums specified in the trust deed totalling £7,000 were paid in 2014) and support is also given for welfare purposes. Payments are made to Lincoln College of Oxford to be applied in scholarships, fellowships and hardship grants (£157,000 in 2014, consisting of 11 undergraduate scholarships, 12 graduate scholarships, a postdoctoral fellowship, and the provision of hardship funds for undergraduates). No other institution can be supported in the same way. During the year an award of £120,000 was also made to the Diocese of Newcastle. The charity's website further specifies that the grant was:

> For a package of approved projects to support clergy through services including pastoral care and counselling, mentoring, continuing ministerial development, support for engagement in parishes in areas of high deprivation, and the replacement of inefficient boilers and improvement of central heating systems control in clergy housing with higher than average fuel costs.

A linked charity, Lord Crewe's Library and Archives Trust (Charity Commission no. 1155101–2), has been established to own the libraries and archives collections currently held at Durham Cathedral, Durham University, the North East Religious Learning Resource Centre, and the Northumberland Records Office.

In 2014 the trustees continued the previously set grants programme for another year while undertaking a full evaluation of activities undertaken. The evaluation will then inform the trustees' consideration of whether to operate any further three year programme, and if so what its contents should be.

The EAC Educational Trust

See entry on page 10

The Silcock Trust

£18,000

Correspondent: Claire Tallis, Trustee, 49 Hereford Road, London W2 5BB (07880831473; email: claire.tallis@gmail. com)

CC number: 272587

Eligibility

Mainly children of clergy of the Church of England. Preference may be given to those with learning and/or other difficulties.

Types of grants

Our research indicates that help is available towards the maintenance costs and fees for schoolchildren. Preference will be given to children with serious family difficulties and/or special educational needs. Grants can range from £250 to £2,000.

Annual grant total

In 2014 the trust had an income of £15,300 and a total expenditure of £18,200. We estimate that the annual total amount of grants awarded was around £18,000.

Applications

Apply in writing to the correspondent.

Society for the Benefit of Sons and Daughters of the Clergy of the Church of Scotland

£15,000 (25 grants)

Correspondent: Fiona Watson, Administrator, Scott-Moncrieff, Exchange Place 3, Semple Street, Edinburgh EH3 8BL (website: www. scott-moncrieff.com/services/charities/charitable-trusts/society-for-the-benefit-of-sons-and-daughters)

OSCR number: SC008760

Eligibility

Children of ministers of the Church of Scotland aged between 12 and 25. Preference is given to families on a low income.

Types of grants

Grants are in the range from £100 to £1,800 towards general educational purposes. Grants are made for one year only but renewals may be granted following a fresh application.

Annual grant total

In 2014 the society had an income of £29,000 and an expenditure of £49,000. The charity administrators' website states that normally around £15,000 is available for educational grants.

Applications

Application forms can be downloaded from the Scott-Moncrieff website and should be posted to the correspondent. Applications should provide full details of the family income and need to be submitted by a parent/guardian before 31 May each year. Grants are distributed by early September.

Other information

The society co-operates with the Glasgow Society of Sons and Daughters of Ministers of the Church of Scotland and the Esdaile Trust in the distribution of grants for the benefit of students.

Other limited funds offering support to dependants are: the John Lang Macfarlane Fund for unmarried and widowed daughters of ministers (with £6,000 available for distribution each year) and the Robertson Chaplin Fund for unmarried sisters over 40 of ordained ministers, with preference given to the aged and infirm (£1,000 available annually).

Sons and Friends of the Clergy

£817,000

Correspondent: The Rt Revd Graeme Knowles, Registrar, 1 Dean Trench Street, Westminster, London SW1P 3HB (020 7799 3696; email: enquiries@ clergycharities.org.uk; website: www. clergycharities.org.uk)

CC number: 207736

Eligibility

Our previous research suggests that grants can be made to children of clergy who are under the age of 25, unmarried and in full-time pre-graduation education towards various educational costs in both maintained and independent sectors.

Types of grants

See 'Applications' information. In the past, assistance has been given with: school uniforms; travel costs; school trips/language exchanges; music lessons; musical instruments; art/sporting activities; computers (including related software); school fee grants for children attending independent schools; and grants for children continuing in education after leaving school.

Annual grant total

In 2014 the charity had assets of £89.1 million and an income of £4 million. During the year, 1,332 grants were awarded to individuals and four to organisations totalling £2.1 million. Grants for educational purposes amounted to £817,000 and were distributed as follows:

University maintenance	£266,500
Other education expenses	£244,500
School fees	£146,000
School clothing	£85,000
Ordinand book grants	£75,000

The figures in this table may also include funding awarded to organisations.

An additional £1.3 million was given for social welfare purposes.

Exclusions

Exclusions are usually described on the charity's website. Contact the correspondent for more information.

Applications

At the time of writing (November 2015) the charity was in the process of updating its website. A message posted on 2 March 2015 read: 'We are currently in the process of updating our website. For information about grants please telephone (020 7799 3696) or email (enquiries@clergycharities.org.uk)'.

Other information

The information in this entry is taken from the charity's website:

The charity now known as the Corporation of the Sons of the Clergy was founded in 1655 by a group of merchants in the City of London and clergymen who were all sons of the cloth. During the Commonwealth, persecution of clergy who had remained loyal to the Crown was widespread and many who had been deprived of their livings by Cromwell were destitute. The charity's foundation dates from a recognition by a body of sons of clergymen that action was required to meet a pressing need among clergy families for charitable help. The charity's present name is often felt to be a misleading one, but it is in fact an accurate description of its founding fathers.

Sciences and technology

Royal Society of Chemistry Benevolent Fund

£76,500

Correspondent: Benevolent Fund Team, Thomas Graham House, Science Park, Milton Road, Cambridge CB4 0WF (01223 432227; website: www.rsc.org/awards-funding/funding/benevolent-fund)

CC number: 207890

Eligibility

People who have been members of the society for the last three years, or ex-members who were in the society for at least ten years, and their dependants, who are in need.

Society members who have at least two years of membership and have completed all planned study (and within 18 months of this study being completed) may apply for a Breathing Space Grant. To be eligible the individual must be seeking, or have secured, paid employment. Other household and financial circumstances are considered as part of the application.

Types of grants

This fund is essentially a relief-in-need charity which also makes grants for education. It offers regular allowances, one-off grants and loans towards needs such as school uniforms and educational trips.

The fund also makes Breathing Space Grants of up to £300 to recent graduates who are seeking their first job.

Annual grant total

In 2014 the fund had an expenditure of £153,000 and grants were made for both social welfare and educational purposes.

We estimate that educational grants to individuals totalled £76,500.

Exclusions

Anything which should be provided by the government or local authority is ineligible for funding. Retrospective funding cannot be given.

Applications

Individuals should, in the first instance, contact the correspondent to discuss their situation. An application form will then be sent. The fund's webpage states: 'As part of assessing and supporting your application, we will ask that all sources of relevant state benefits have been explored.' The fund may also be able to signpost to other sources of potential support. Applications can be submitted by post or electronically and require information on the individual's personal and financial circumstances. If there are difficulties in completing an application form, the benevolent fund team can be contacted for assistance. The fund's advisor reviews applications to ensure all relevant information has been gathered and as a final check for eligibility. Following this, applications are presented to the Grants Committee, which meets four times a year.

Other information

The society also provides advice and guidance services.

Secretarial and administration

The Worshipful Company of Chartered Secretaries and Administrators Charitable Trust

£5,500

Correspondent: Erica Lee, Secretary, WCCSA Charitable Trust, 3rd Floor, Saddlers Hall, 40 Gutter Lane, London EC2V 6BR (020 7726 2955; email: assistant.clerk@wccsa.org.uk; website: www.wccsa.org.uk/Education.html)

CC number: 288487

Eligibility

Chartered secretaries and administrators studying commercial courses in various universities and the apprentices of the Worshipful Company of Chartered Secretaries and Administrators.

Types of grants

The trust awards prizes of up to £500 for success in the examinations of the Institute of Chartered Secretaries and Administrators (ICSA) and in collaborative courses between ICSA and various universities. Support is also available to apprentices of the Worshipful Company of Chartered Secretaries and Administrators.

Annual grant total

In 2013/14 the trust had assets of £1.4 million, an income of £60,000 and a total charitable expenditure of about £34,500. Grants to individuals for educational purposes totalled around £5,500, distributed through prizes and awards.

Applications

Apply in writing to the correspondent. Our research suggests that grants are normally considered every three months, usually January, April, July and October.

Skilled crafts and trades

The GPM Charitable Trust

£5,000

Correspondent: Keith Keys, c/o 43 Spriggs Close, Clapham, Bedford MK41 6GD (07733 262991; email: gpmcharitabletrust@tiscali.co.uk; website: www.gpmtrust.org)

CC number: 227177

Eligibility

Workers, former workers and their dependants in the printing, graphical, papermaking and media industries.

Types of grants

Grants for retraining, skills enhancement, educational requirement especially following redundancy or other reduction in income.

Annual grant total

In 2013/14 the trust had an income of £7,700 and a total expenditure of £23,500. Grants are made to individuals and organisations for both social welfare and educational purposes. We estimate that educational grants to individuals totalled £5,000.

During the year, the trust continued working with the Bookbinders Charitable Society on a refurbishment project for applicants in sheltered accommodation.

Applications

An application form can be downloaded from the website or requested from the correspondent. It must be printed, completed in black ink and returned to the trust. The dates of application deadlines for subsequent trustees' meetings are listed on the website.

Other information

Formed in 2001, the trust brought together the former Lloyd Memorial and NATSOPA (National Society of Operative Printers and Assistants) trusts. The Sheridan Trust, a Manchester-based printing charity, joined in 2010.

Johnson Matthey Public Ltd Company Educational Trust

£80,000

Correspondent: Stephanie Hamilton, Administrator, Johnson Matthey plc, 25 Farringdon Street, London EC4A 4AB (020 7269 8400; email: group.hr@ matthey.com)

CC number: 313576

Eligibility

UK students over the age of 16 who have a parent or grandparent employed by Johnson Matthey or associated with the precious metals industry, and who are studying a scientific or technical subject.

Types of grants

Grants are awarded to college students and undergraduates for fees, books, equipment and maintenance/living expenses. Our research suggests that grants are usually between £400 and £500.

Annual grant total

In 2013/14 the trust and an income of £6,000 and an expenditure of £82,500. We estimate that the amount of grants given to individuals totalled £80,000.

Exclusions

Grants are not normally made to students studying second degrees or mature students.

Applications

Apply in writing to the correspondent. If possible, applications should be submitted by the relevant partner or grandparent on behalf of the individual. Applications are normally invited in October, for considerations in December.

Other information

The trust was set up in 1967 to commemorate the 150th anniversary of the founding of the company. It is also concerned with promoting research and establishing professorships, lectureships or other teaching posts.

Sports

National Trainers' Federation Charitable Trust (N. T. F. Charitable Trust)

£2,000

Correspondent: Janet Byrd, Racing Welfare, 20B Park Lane, Newmarket, Suffolk CB8 8QD (01638 560763; email: info@racingwelfare.co.uk; website: www. racingwelfare.co.uk)

CC number: 1004308

Eligibility

Individuals who work or have worked in the British thoroughbred horseracing and breeding industry who have had an accident/been injured in the course of their employment in racing and, therefore, cannot return to work or perform it in the same capacity. The dependants of such people are also eligible.

Types of grants

Grants are provided for retraining. Individuals can either aim for employment within the racing industry but in different capacity or enter a new industry altogether. Some examples of courses supported include: plastering; nursing; driving instructing; HGV driving; racing secretary; secretarial and accountancy courses.

Annual grant total

In 2013/14 the trust had an income of £21,000 and an expenditure of £9,000. We estimate the annual total amount of grants available for education to be around £2,000. Note that this was a 21-month accounting period.

Applications

Application forms can be requested from the correspondent. The trust invites applicants to seek advice of a local welfare officer when completing the application. Candidates should provide a doctor's report stating the reasons why the applicant is no longer suited to work in their present capacity as well as details of the course they are intending to take.

Other information

The trust also supports organisations.

Professional Footballers' Association Educational Fund

£1.2 million

Correspondent: Darren Wilson, Trustee, 20 Oxford Court, Bishopsgate, Manchester M2 3WQ (0161 236 0575; email: info@thepfa.co.uk; website: www. thepfa.com/education/funding)

CC number: 306087

Eligibility

Current and former members of the Professional Footballers' Association who wish to retrain in order to continue employment once their football careers have ceased. The fund notes that members who have only ever played at a non-league level are unlikely to receive a grant.

Types of grants

Grants can be given towards a wide variety of educational courses and vocational training, including tuition, exam, registration fees or books. Awards are of up to £1,500 a year, covering up to 50% of the study costs. The funding is capped at £5,000 for each member and a maximum lifetime grant towards book costs is £300.

Annual grant total

In 2013/14 the fund had an income of £5.4 million and a total expenditure of £16.4 million. Full accounts were not available to view on the Charity Commission website at the time of writing (November 2015). We estimate that educational and vocational grants totalled around £1.2 million.

Exclusions

The fund is unable to provide money for:

- Postgraduate/master's degrees
- Purchase of computers
- Medical costs
- Travel and parking expenses
- Accommodation
- Membership fees
- Kits and uniforms
- Tools and equipment
- Postage fees

Applications

Application forms can be obtained from the fund's website or requested from the correspondent. Applications for undergraduate grants should be made at the end of the academic year and for open learning courses at the end of the module. Note that the fund is unable to make up-front payments and grants are only paid upon receiving proof of completion of the course and receipts for the books purchased. Applicants should

have paid for the course or training in full themselves before receiving the grant.

Be aware that grants can only be claimed within a year of the delivery and retrospective claims will not be considered.

Other information

The fund also gives grants to organisations to advance the public knowledge of the history and social significance of football, to promote good community and race relations at football events and towards medical initiatives that promote the health of beneficiaries.

Note: Members taking out student loans to pay for tuition fees will not receive a grant unless one third (or the maximum of £1,000) is paid back to the Student Loan Company and a confirmation receipt is provided. Individuals receiving a full scholarship covering their tuition fees whilst studying in America, will not be eligible to apply for funding from the fund. A grant will be available in the case of candidates having to make a contribution towards their tuition fees, subject to providing appropriate detailed receipts.

The RFL Benevolent Fund (Try Assist)

£12,500

Correspondent: Steve Ball, General Manager, Red Hall, Red Hall Lane, Leeds, West Yorkshire LS17 8NB (0844 477 7113; email: info@tryassist.co.uk; website: www.rflbenevolentfund.co.uk)

CC number: 1109858

Eligibility

People who play or assist, or who have played or assisted, in the game of Rugby League in the UK or for a team affiliated to an association primarily based in the UK and their dependants. Beneficiaries should be in hardship or distress, in particular, as a result of injury through playing or training, or when travelling to or from a game or training session.

Types of grants

Assistance is given with educational courses, career guidance and computer equipment.

Annual grant total

In 2014 the fund had assets of £521,500 and an income of £224,000. We believe grants for educational purposes to have totalled around £12,500.

Applications

In the first instance, contact the correspondent.

Other information

Grants are also made for welfare purposes, including those towards special vehicles and repairs, home improvements, furniture, wheelchairs, gym equipment, computers, hotel accommodation, travel, physiotherapy, home appliances and Christmas presents.

Transport and storage

The Air Pilots Benevolent Fund

£34,500

Correspondent: Chris Spurrier, Trustee, Cobham House, 9 Warwick Court, Gray's Inn, London WC1R 5DJ (020 7404 4032; fax: 020 7404 4035; email: office@airpilots.org; website: www. airpilots.org)

CC number: 212952

Eligibility

Members of The Honourable Company of Air Pilots and those who have been engaged professionally as air pilots or air navigators in commercial aviation, and their dependants.

People who want to become pilots or wish to gain further qualifications in the aviation industry are supported by The Honourable Company of Air Pilots.

Types of grants

Scholarships and bursaries, including those to flying instructors. Academic bursaries are awarded at City University to students in one of the three specific MSc courses. Awards towards general educational needs to the dependants of aviators.

Annual grant total

In 2013/14 the fund had assets of £748,000 and an income of £57,000. Grants were made totalling £44,500 and consisted of:

PPL scholarship via Air Pilots Trust	£9,000
Occasional grants	£8,800
Flying instructor development bursaries via E&TC	£7,800
Flying scholarship for people with disability	£7,000
Ray Jeffs gliding scholarships	£4,000
Inner London schools gliding	£3,900
City University bursary via Air Safety Trust	£3,000
Regular grants	£1,100

Educational support totalled at least £34,500; we take it that regular and occasional grants included more social welfare-related requests.

Exclusions

The fund cannot give 'grant or loan money for the repayment of debts or long-term expenses such as school fees, prolonged medical care or for obtaining professional pilots' licences and ratings'.

Applications

Requests for support should be made on the 'Application for Financial Assistance' form. Appeals are reviewed at the quarterly meetings, although immediate grants may be made (the fund's office should be contacted directly if there is such an urgent need).

Scholarship and bursary forms are available from the fund's website. Details of individual criteria and dates relating to each scholarship are included in the application form.

The fund works closely with the other aviation charities for individuals (both military and civilian). If an applicant has approached another such charity, they should say so in their application to the fund.

Other information

The charity was previously called The Guild of Air Pilots Benevolent Fund and provides both educational and welfare support.

The fund is administered by The Honourable Company of Air Pilots which is also managing Air Safety Trust and Air Pilots Trust (see a separate entry on page 67).

The BMTA Trust Ltd
See entry on page 26

The British Airline Pilots' Association Benevolent Fund (BALPA)

£23,500

Correspondent: Antoinette Girdler, BALPA House, 5 Heathrow Boulevard, 278 Bath Road, West Drayton UB7 0DQ (020 8476 4029; email: tonigirdler@ balpa.org)

CC number: 229957

Eligibility

Dependants of current or retired British commercial airline pilots, flight engineers and winchmen.

Types of grants

Grants are made towards the cost of books, uniforms and associated educational expenses.

Annual grant total

In 2013/14 the charity had assets of £1.6 million and an income of £34,000.

Grants totalled £47,000 and interest-free loans were made to the sum of £12,000. We estimate that grants for educational purposes totalled around £23,500.

Exclusions

Grants are not given for school fees.

Applications

Application forms can be requested from the correspondent. Requests are considered quarterly.

The Railway Benefit Fund

£4,400 (7 grants)

Correspondent: Abigail Smith, Executive Director, Electra Way, Crewe, Cheshire CW1 6HS (01270 251316; email: info@ railwaybenefitfund.org.uk; website: www. railwaybenefitfund.org.uk)

CC number: 206312

Eligibility

Current and former railway staff, and their dependants, who are in need.

Types of grants

One-off grants to help the parents of dependent children with the costs of clothing and footwear, school projects and the initial costs of beginning higher education. In 2014 the average grant was £635.

Annual grant total

In 2014 the fund had assets of £3.5 million and an income of £484,500. Grants totalled £328,500, the majority of which were given for welfare purposes. Grants for educational purposes were awarded to seven families, amounting to £4,400.

Applications

Applications are available to download from the website, or can be requested by telephone, via the 'Contact us' form on the website, or by emailing welfare@railwaybenefitfund.org.uk. The form should be completed and returned to the charity, along with evidence of railway employment and the relevant documents detailed on the form, to the following address: FREEPOST, RRBA-KSXA-RYAE, RBF, Electra Way, Crewe CW1 6HS. Applications can be submitted directly by the individual or by another person and are reviewed by the Benefits Committee monthly.

Other information

This is primarily a welfare charity, and educational grants are part of its wider welfare work.

Livery companies, orders and membership organisations

The Grand Lodge of Antient, Free and Accepted Masons of Scotland

Correspondent: The Trustees, c/o Freemasons Hall, 96 George Street, Edinburgh EH2 3DH (0131 225 5577; fax: 0131 225 3953; email: curator@grandlodgescotland.org; website: www.grandlodgescotland.com)

OSCR number: SC001996

Eligibility
Children of members and deceased members.

Types of grants
Grants for people entering further education.

Annual grant total
In 2013/14 the charity had an income of £659,500 and a total expenditure of £410,500. Our research indicates that educational grants usually total around £25,000; however, considering that the figures for the year's income and expenditure were unusually low, the actual sum of these grants may have also been lower.

Applications
Application forms are available from the correspondent, or by direct approach to the local lodge.

Other information
The charity also makes benevolence grants to individuals, as well as grants to organisations, and runs care homes for older people.

The Journal Children's Fund (in conjunction with the Royal Antediluvian Order of Buffaloes)

£18,000

Correspondent: C. McMahon, Administrator, RAOB GLE Trust Corporation, Grove House, Skipton Road, Harrogate, North Yorkshire HG1 4LA (01423 502438; email: hq@raobgle.org.uk; website: www.raobgle.org.uk)

CC number: 529575

Eligibility
The charity's objectives are: 'The education and preferment of orphan or necessitous children of deceased members of the Royal Antediluvian Order of Buffaloes Grand Lodge of England.' The fund's activities extend worldwide.

Types of grants
Help with the cost of books, clothing and other essentials for schoolchildren. Grants may also be available for those at college or university who are eligible.

Annual grant total
In 2013/14 the fund had assets of £411,000 an income of £46,500. Grants were made to individuals for education totalling £18,000.

Applications
Initial enquiries regarding assistance can only be made through the individual's branch of attendance.

The Merchant Taylors' Company Charities Fund (Livery and Freemen Fund)

£13,500

Correspondent: David Atkinson, Merchant Taylors' Hall, 30 Threadneedle Street, London EC2R 8JB (020 7450 4441; email: charities@merchant-taylors.co.uk; website: www.merchant-taylors.co.uk)

CC number: 1069124

Eligibility
People who attend one of the Merchant Taylors' supported schools or who have some association with the company. Preference may be given to beneficiaries in the inner city London, particularly boroughs of Lewisham, Southwark, Tower Hamlets, Hackney, and their environs.

Types of grants

Loans and grants to cover direct educational costs of individuals in secondary and further/higher education or training.

Annual grant total

In 2014 the fund had assets of £828,000 and an income of £283,500. A total of £95,000 was given in grants. Education and training awards totalled £13,500.

Applications

The fund does not normally support individual applications. Awards are made to educational institutions; therefore, applications should be made through the individual's school or college.

Other information

Grants are also made to organisations, churches and clergy.

In 2014 the following schools were supported: Merchant Taylors' School Northwood; Merchant Taylors' School, Crosby; Wolverhampton Grammar School; Wallingford School, Oxfordshire; St Helen's School; St Paul's Cathedral Choir School; Royal School of Needlework; City and Guilds of London Art School.

The Norfolk (Le Strange) Fund

£6,300

Correspondent: Russell Carter, Trustee, Brick Kiln Farm, Cross Road, Starston, Harleston, Norfolk IP20 9NH (01379 854600; email: rcarter@carrotech.com)

CC number: 209020

Eligibility

Dependants of Freemasons of the Province of Norfolk.

Types of grants

Help with the cost of books, clothing and other essentials for schoolchildren. Grants may also be available for those at college or university. The charity will ensure that all eligible people are supported throughout their education.

Annual grant total

In 2014 the charity had an income of £13,700 and a total expenditure of £26,500. We estimate that educational grants to individuals totalled about £6,300.

Applications

Applications may be made in writing to the correspondent. They are considered every two months. The charity does not respond to unsuccessful applications that fall outside its area of interest and prefers applicants to enquire and apply by post or email, rather than by phone.

Other information

Funding is also awarded to Masonic charities and to individuals for relief-in-need purposes.

The Provincial Grand Charity

£10,500

Correspondent: Michael de-Villamar Roberts, Ingham and Co., George Stanley House, 2 West Parade Road, Scarborough, North Yorkshire YO12 5ED (01723 500209; email: mdvr@mdvr.karoo.co.uk)

CC number: 517923

Eligibility

Children (including adopted and step-children) of present and deceased Masons who live or lived in North Yorkshire and Humberside.

Types of grants

Grants for those at school, college or university towards school clothing, books, school fees and living expenses depending on the parental circumstances. Grants range from £100 to £3,000.

Annual grant total

In 2014 the charity had assets of £940,000 and an income of £47,500. The amount of grants given to individuals totalled £10,500.

Applications

Applications can be made in writing to the correspondent and are considered at quarterly meetings. Applications must be supported by the relative who is a member of the Masons.

The Royal Masonic Trust for Girls and Boys

£5 million (2,062 grants)

Correspondent: Leslie Hutchinson, Administrator, Freemasons' Hall, 60 Great Queen Street, London WC2B 5AZ (020 7405 2644; fax: 020 7831 4094; email: info@rmtgb.org; website: www.rmtgb.org)

CC number: 285836

Eligibility

Generally the dependants of Freemasons. The objects of the trust are to relieve poverty and to advance education. The trust also has power, provided sufficient funds are available, to help children who are not the connected to the Freemasons. Such assistance is usually given by way of grants to other children's charities and via the subsidiary funds.

Non-Masonic support used to be available through the Choral Bursary Scheme but the trustees' annual report from 2013 states that, 'although the support will continue be provided to existing beneficiaries, the Choral Bursary Scheme was closed to new applicants in 2013'.

Types of grants

Any necessary kind of assistance to children in any kind of educational environment, including state and private schools, colleges and universities and vocational training or apprenticeships. Help towards educational travel or extra-curricular activities is also given. Grants can be one-off or recurring and are offered towards fees, maintenance costs, computer equipment, music and sports activities, instruments, tools and any other specific and identifiable need.

Through the TalentAid scheme support can be given to individuals exceptionally gifted in music, sports or performing arts. Awards are made towards coaching, advanced lessons and fees at specialist institutions or in one-off payments towards equipment and instruments or attendance of events.

Annual grant total

At the time of writing (October 2015) the information provided was the latest available. In 2013 the trust had assets of £152.2 million and an income of £21.3 million. There were 2,062 beneficiaries supported during the year totalling around £5.9 million. Of that sum some help has been given in welfare support; therefore, we estimate that educational grants totalled around £5 million. Grants can be broken down as follows:

Amount awarded for beneficiaries	1964	£5.4 million
TalentAid	69	£393,000
Choral Bursaries	29	£197,000

Exclusions

No grants are available for student exchanges.

Support towards fees for independent schools can be considered but only in exceptional circumstances.

Applications

Applications should be made in the first instance to the nearest Masonic authority or, where that is not known, a preliminary enquiry may be addressed to the correspondent.

Applications for TalentAid support can be made on a form available on the trust's website from November to April.

Note that new applications for choral bursaries are no longer accepted.

Other information

In 2013 the Girls' and Boys' Special Funds were merged into the General Fund together with some other specific funds.

The trust has welfare and case advisers to assist families. Most of the funds are given to individuals with a Masonic connection.

Through its Stepping Stones scheme the trust also provides support to other charities working for the benefit of children and young people. Assistance is also given to Lifelitcs Charity providing technology for children's hospices. A number of subsidiary funds which offer further support to children and young people towards charitable work or educational travel overseas are also administered by the trust.

Trades Union Congress Educational Trust

£12,000

Correspondent: Basil Skeete, Administrator, Congress House, 23–28 Great Russell Street, London WC1B 3LS (020 7467 1278; email: financeoffice@tuc.org.uk; website: www.unionlearn.org.uk/resources/funding/bursaries)

CC number: 313741

Eligibility
Members of Trades Union Congress affiliated trade unions to attend courses at selected colleges and universities. Applicants should not be receiving any other grants.

Types of grants
The trust offers scholarships and bursaries to students at selected institutions:

- Keele University bursaries – ten annual bursaries of £250 for Undergraduate Certificate in Industrial Relations (open to anyone with industrial relations experience); also three annual bursaries of £1,000 for part-time postgraduate courses in industrial relations, industrial relations and employment law, industrial relations and HRM or European HRM and industrial relations
- One Year Awards – at Northern College, Coleg Harlech, Hillcroft College, Fircroft College and Newbattle Abbey College for one-year residential courses leading to a diploma in labour studies, history or social studies. These courses are financed by mandatory state grants and the TUC provides three additional bursaries of £925
- Ruskin College bursaries – three annual bursaries of £1,000 for an MA in International Labour and Trade Union Studies
- Clive Jenkins European Study Bursary – two bursaries of £800 each to cover travel and subsistence costs for a visit to a European Union country to study aspects of trade unionism, industrial relations or training and employment

Annual grant total
At the time of writing (October 2015) the latest financial information available was from 2013. In 2013 the trust had an income of £92,500 and a total charitable expenditure of £72,500. We estimate that grants awarded to individuals totalled around £12,000. In the previous year the trust awarded two Clive Jenkins European Study bursaries, one Birkbeck and three Keele University bursaries, three Ruskin College bursaries and one Harvard scholarship. Scholarships and bursaries totalled £13,800 (2012).

Full accounts were not available to view on the Charity Commission's website.

Applications
For some awards applications need to be made through an educational institution, for others application forms are available online. See the Union Learn website for more details on each of the available bursaries.

Other information
More information about the bursaries can also be obtained by contacting Liz Rees at lrees@tuc.org.uk.

Local charities

This section lists local charities that award grants to individuals for educational purposes. The information in the entries applies only to educational grants and concentrates on what the charity actually does rather than on what its governing document allows it to do.

Regional classification

We have divided the UK into 12 geographical areas, as numbered on the map on page 130. Scotland, Wales and England have been divided into unitary or local authorities, in some cases grouped in counties or regions. On page 131 you can find the list of unitary or local authorities within each county or area. (Please note: not all of these unitary authorities have a grant-making charity included in this guide.)

Northern Ireland

Unfortunately, the section for Northern Ireland remains limited, as very little information is available at present on charities based there. It is estimated that there are between 7,000 and 12,000 charities operating in Northern Ireland. The Charity Commission for Northern Ireland, therefore, expects the completion of the registration process to take several years. In the meantime, up-to-date information on the progress of registration can be found on the Charity Commission for Northern Ireland's website: www.charity commissionni.org.uk.

The Northern Ireland section has not been subdivided into smaller areas. Within the other sections, charities are ordered as follows:

Scotland

▶ First, the charities which apply to the whole of Scotland, or at least two areas in Scotland, are listed.
▶ Second, Scotland is further divided into electoral board areas, and then again into council areas.
▶ Should an entry apply to at least two council areas, it will appear in the appropriate electoral board section.

Wales

▶ First, charities which apply to the whole of Wales, or at least two areas of Wales, are listed.
▶ Second, Wales is sub-divided into four regions. The entries which apply to the whole region, or to at least two local government areas within it, appear first.
▶ Third, the remaining charities are listed under the relevant local government division.

England

▶ First, charities which apply to the whole of England, or at least two regions within it, are listed.
▶ Second, England is divided into nine regions. The entries which apply to the whole region, or to at least two counties within it, appear first.
▶ Third, the regions are divided into counties.
▶ The counties are sub-divided into relevant local government areas.

London

▶ First, the charities which apply to the whole of Greater London, or to at least two boroughs are listed.

▶ The charities serving London are further sub-divided into the relevant boroughs.

Within each geographical category, the charities are listed alphabetically.

To make sure you identify every relevant local charity, look at the entries in each relevant category in the following order:
1   Unitary or local authority (for England, Scotland and Wales) or borough (for Greater London)
2   County (for England)
3   Region (for England, Wales and, in some cases, Scotland)
4   Country (for England, Northern Ireland, Scotland and Wales)

For example, if you live in Liverpool, first establish which region Merseyside is in by looking at the map on page 130. Then, having established that Merseyside is in region on page 231, North West, look under the 'Geographical areas' list on page 131 and find the page where the entries for Merseyside begin. Firstly, look under the heading for Liverpool to see if there are any relevant charities. Then work back through the charities under Merseyside generally, the charities under North West generally, and then charities listed under England generally.

Having found grant-makers covering your area, please read any other eligibility requirements carefully. While some charities can and do give grants for any need for people in their area of benefit, most have other, more specific criteria which potential applicants must meet in order to be eligible.

Geographical areas

1. Northern Ireland 133

2. Scotland 135

General 135

Ayrshire 143

South Ayrshire

Central Scotland 144

Stirling

Dumfries and Galloway 144

Dunbartonshire and Argyll 145

West Dunbartonshire

Fife 145

Glasgow 146

Grampian 146

Aberdeen and Aberdeenshire

Highlands and Na h Eileanan Siar (Western Isles) 148

Lothian 148

East Lothian; West Lothian

Tayside 149

Angus; Perth and Kinross

3. Wales 151

General 151

Mid Wales 152

Powys

North Wales 153

Conwy; Denbighshire; Gwynedd; Isle of Anglesey; Wrexham

South East Wales 156

Cardiff; Monmouthshire; Torfaen; Vale of Glamorgan

South West Wales 157

Carmarthenshire; Pembrokeshire; Swansea

4. East Midlands 159

General 159

Derbyshire 160

Derby; Derbyshire Dales; Erewash; High Peak

Leicestershire 161

Charnwood; Harborough; Hinckley and Bosworth; Oadby and Wigston

Northamptonshire 164

Northampton; South Northamptonshire

Nottinghamshire 167

Mansfield; Newark and Sherwood; Nottingham; Rushcliffe

Rutland 169

5. West Midlands 171

General 171

Herefordshire 173

Shropshire 175

Shropshire; Telford and Wrekin

Staffordshire 176

Cannock Chase; East Staffordshire; Stafford; Tamworth

Warwickshire 178

Rugby; Stratford-on-Avon; Warwick

West Midlands 182

Birmingham; Coventry; Dudley; Sandwell; Walsall

Worcestershire 188

Malvern Hills; Worcester; Wychavon; Wyre Forest

6. East of England 191

General 191

Cambridgeshire 191

Fenland; Huntingdonshire; South Cambridgeshire

Lincolnshire 193

Boston; East Lindsey; Lincoln; North East Lincolnshire; North Lincolnshire; South Holland; West Lindsey

Norfolk 199

Breckland; North Norfolk; Norwich; South Norfolk

Suffolk 203

Mid Suffolk; Suffolk Coastal; Waveney

7. London 207

General 207

Barnet 211

Camden 212

City of London 213

City of Westminster 214

Croydon 216

Ealing 216

Enfield 217

Greenwich 217

Hackney 217

Hammersmith and Fulham 218

Harringey 218

Hillingdon 219

Hounslow 219

Islington 219

Kensington and Chelsea 220

Lambeth 221

Lewisham 221

Merton 222

Richmond upon Thames 222

Southwark 224

Tower Hamlets 225

Waltham Forest 225

8. North East 227

General 227

County Durham 228

County Durham; Hartlepool

Northumberland 229

Tyne and Wear 230

Sunderland

9. North West 231

General 231

Cheshire 231

Cheshire East; Cheshire West and Chester

Cumbria 233

Carlisle; Copeland; South Lakeland

Greater Manchester 236

Bolton; Rochdale; Salford; Stockport; Wigan

Lancashire 240

Blackburn with Darwen; Blackpool; Burnley; Chorley; Preston; West Lancashire

Merseyside 243

Liverpool; Wirral

10. South East 247

General 247

Bedfordshire 248

Bedford; Central Bedfordshire

Berkshire 250

Reading; Windsor and Maidenhead; Wokingham

Buckinghamshire 253

Aleysbury Vale; Milton Keynes; South Buckinghamshire; Wycombe

East Sussex 255

City of Brighton and Hove; Hastings

Essex 257

Braintree; Brentwood; City of Chelmsford; Epping Forest

Hampshire 260

Basingstoke and Dean; Fareham; Gosport; Portsmouth; Test Valley

Hertfordshire 262

Broxbourne; Dacorum; East Hertfordshire; Hertsmere; North Hertfordshire; Welwyn Hatfield

Isle of Wight 267

Kent 268

Ashford; City of Canterbury; Dartford; Maidstone; Medway; Sevenoaks; Shepway; Swale

Oxfordshire 272

Cherwell; City of Oxford; South Oxfordshire; Vale of White Horse; West Oxfordshire

Surrey 276

Mole Valley; Reigate and Banstead; Runnymede; Waverley

West Sussex 279

Arun

11. South West 281

General 281

City of Bristol 282

Cornwall 284

Carrick

Devon 285

City of Exeter; City of Plymouth; East Devon; Mid Devon; North Devon; South Hams; Torridge

Dorset 289

North Dorset; Purbeck; Weymouth and Portland

Gloucestershire 292

Cheltenham; Cotswold; South Gloucestershire; Stroud

Somerset 295

Bath and North East Somerset; North Somerset; South Somerset; Taunton Deane

Wiltshire 298

Swindon; Wiltshire

12. Yorkshire 301

General 301

East Riding of Yorkshire 301

East Riding of Yorkshire

North Yorkshire 305

Hambleton; Scarborough; York

South Yorkshire 307

Barnsley; Sheffield

West Yorkshire 310

Calderdale; Kirklees; Leeds; Wakefield

Northern Ireland

Belfast Association for the Blind

£8,000

Correspondent: R. Gillespie, Hon. Secretary, 30 Glenwell Crescent, Newtownabbey, County Antrim BT36 7TF (028 9083 6407)

IR number: XN45086

Eligibility
People in Northern Ireland who are registered as blind. Consideration may also be given to those registered as partially sighted.

Types of grants
One-off grants (generally up to £350) for educational needs, such as computers, course fees and so on.

Annual grant total
We have no current information for this charity. Previously around £16,000 has been given in grants to individuals for both educational and social welfare purposes.

Applications
Applications may be made in writing to the correspondent, through a social worker. Requests can be considered throughout the year.

Other information
Grants can also be made to organisations and to individuals for welfare purposes. The association can also assist the research of causes and cure and prevention of blindness.

The Thomas Devlin Fund

£5,500 (6 grants)

Correspondent: Barbara Woods, Community Foundation for Northern Ireland, Community House, Citylink Business Park, Albert Street, Belfast BT12 4HQ (028 9024 5927; email: bwoods@communityfoundationni.org; website: www.communityfoundationni. org/Grants/Thomas-Devlin-Fund)

Eligibility
Young people in Northern Ireland between the ages of 15 and 19 who are aiming to pursue a career in the arts and require a small amount of financial assistance to undertake an opportunity or training.

Types of grants
Bursaries of up to £1,750 for specific opportunities and activities which will help to develop young people's skills in music and arts.

Annual grant total
In 2013 the fund received a total of 14 applications, of which six were successful. We have estimated that the annual total amount of grants awarded to individuals was around £5,500. Normally the fund can support up to ten individuals awarding a total of around £4,000–£6,000 each year. At the time of writing (October 2015) the information provided was the latest available.

Exclusions
Due to high demand, lessons or exam fees are not normally supported and assistance can only be given in exceptional circumstances.

Applications
Application forms can be downloaded from the fund's website and will need to be completed by individuals together with their tutor/teacher. Applicants have to outline how the award would improve their performance and what positive impact it would have on others.

The fund normally opens in early spring; however, the application deadlines are likely to change – consult the website for the latest updates.

Other information
This fund was set up in memory of Belfast teenager Thomas Devlin and has its own website www.thomasdevlin.com. The fund is administered by the Community Foundation for Northern Ireland which also administers a number of funds for organisations. The fund is intended to be awarding grants until 2066.

The Fermanagh Recreational Trust

Correspondent: The Secretary, Fermanagh Recreational Trust, Fermanagh House, Broadmeadow Place, Enniskillen BT74 7HR (02866320 210; email: info@fermanaghtrust.org; website: www.fermanaghtrust.org)

CC number: XR 22580

Eligibility
Individuals based in County Fermanagh.

Types of grants
Grants can be given towards equipment and in educational bursaries for training or other activities which will help individuals to develop their potential, particularly through recreation and sport.

Annual grant total
The total amount of grants awarded was not specified.

Exclusions
Grants are not considered retrospectively.

Applications
Application forms are available to download from the trust's website. They should be submitted by the end of February or August. Two independent references must also be included (this requirement is only waived in exceptional circumstances).

Other information
This fund is administered by the Fermanagh Trust which also administers funds for organisations for a variety of purposes in Fermanagh, particularly involving young people and youth development.

Some of the funds administered by the Fermanagh Trust offer support to individuals, including awards for voluntary work overseas and bursaries for sport, arts or community service activities. Details of grants available are given on the Fermanagh Trust website.

NIACRO
See entry on page 44

The Presbyterian Orphan and Children's Society

£289,000

Correspondent: Dr Paul Gray, Executive Secretary, Glengall Exchange, 3 Glengall Street, Belfast BT12 5AB (028 9032 3737; email: paulgray1866@gmail.com; website: www. presbyterianorphanandchildrenssociety. org)

CC number: NIC101444

Eligibility
Children aged 23 or under who are in full- or part-time education, living in Northern Ireland and Republic of Ireland, usually in single parent families. One parent must be a Presbyterian.

Types of grants
One-off 'exceptional' grants of up to £300 (up to £500 in very exceptional circumstances) are made to assist with educational expenses. Regular grants are also given to families.

Annual grant total
In 2014 the charity had assets of £10.4 million and an income of £786,500. Grants to children amounted to £578,000 and were given for both social welfare and educational purposes. We estimate educational grants to have totalled around £289,000.

The annual report and accounts included the following information: 'Around 730 children in 389 families were helped through regular grants' and '124 exceptional grants (the highest number for some time) were paid at an average value of £437.'

Applications
Applications should be made by Presbyterian clergy. Application forms are available from the correspondent or can be downloaded from the website.

The Royal Ulster Constabulary – Police Service of Northern Ireland Benevolent Fund

£400,000

Correspondent: Fund Administrator, Police Federation for Northern Ireland, 77–79 Garnerville Road, Belfast BT4 2NX (028 9076 4215; email: benevolentfund@policefedni.com; website: www.rucgc-psnibenevolentfund. com)

IR number: XN 48380

Eligibility
Members and former members of the Royal Ulster Constabulary, and their dependants. The main objectives of the charity are to look after serving PSNI officers, widows/widowers, other dependants, injured officers and those with disabilities, pensioners and former members who are not pensionable and parents of deceased officers, all experiencing financial hardship or difficulties. Eligibility relates to financial hardship but 'the bottom line is simply that a case of need must be identified'.

Types of grants
Support can be given in grants and loans to people in education, including schoolchildren, college students, undergraduates, mature students and individuals with special educational needs. Help can be given towards general educational needs. Interest-free loans are also offered.

Annual grant total
Previously about £800,000 has been spent supporting the beneficiaries. We divide this figure between educational and welfare causes as no further details were available.

Exclusions
Our research suggests that loans for debt cases cannot be supported.

Applications
Initial contact should be made in writing to the charity. Eligible applicants will then be advised on further application process. Candidates are visited by the representatives of the charity who then present the case to the Management Committee, which meets on the first Wednesday of each month. Each Regional Board has an appointed Benevolent Fund Representative. Applicants will be required to provide full financial breakdown and quotes where possible.

Other information
The charity also supports beneficiaries for welfare causes and maintains eight apartments in Portrush and eight holiday cottages in Kesh, allowing beneficiaries to 'enjoy a short break away from the difficulties imposed on them by their own circumstances or environment'. Convalescent support and therapy are also available for serving and former members.

Note that the administration of all Police Dependant's Trust applications from Northern Ireland are also administered by the charity.

Additional help is offered by a number of other organisations, details of which can be found on the Northern Ireland Police Family Assistance website (www. northernirelandpolicefamilyassistance. org.uk).

Scotland

General

Arts Trust of Scotland

£40,000 (About 10 grants)

Correspondent: The Trustees of Art Trust of Scotland, Waverley Gate, 2–4 Waterloo Place, Edinburgh EH1 3EG (email: arts.trust@creativescotland.com; website: www.artstrustscotland.org.uk)

Eligibility
Emerging artists in Scotland. Applicants must either be in full-time art education (including mature students) or have been out of it for no more than five years.

Types of grants
Awards (in the range of £500–£2,000) are made for artistic projects, especially those that are 'falling through the cracks of mainstream funding'. Art in any form may be supported. The website states:

> So you've got a great idea – a sculpture, an installation, a painting, a play, a book, a screenplay or maybe something else – but you need a little money to take your idea from blank page to reality. Well, we're here to help. We arrange grants and funding for all kinds of arts projects.

Examples can include (but are by no means limited to): 'first publication, CD or CD-ROM or DVD; first solo exhibition or performance (or collective duo) rather than group show; equipment or instrument purchase'. Examples of previous grant recipients are also given on the website.

Annual grant total
In 2013/14 the trust had an income of £44,500 and a total expenditure of £55,000. The website states that about £40,000 is allocated for grant-making annually. About ten individuals can be assisted each year.

Exclusions
The following is not funded:
- Individuals seeking funding for full-time courses of study
- General fundraising drives
- Projects outside the arts
- Organisations applying on behalf of individuals (i.e. the trustees will not fund bursaries awarded through organisations – only directly to individuals)

Applications
Application forms can be accessed on the trust's website when the application round is open. The latest round was in October 2014. Very specific guidelines on what needs to be stated and included in the application are given on the website.

Other information
The trust is an independent charity, although it 'draws on Creative Scotland for assistance in administration to ensure running costs are kept to a minimum'. It shares the address with Creative Scotland and has the applications administered through the organisation; however, it appears that funds are kept separately. We have included a separate entry because the trust has its own OSCR number and charitable objectives. The trust's website states: '[The trust] makes use of the expertise which already exists within Creative Scotland, but final decisions on what is funded rests with the trustees.'

The Avenel Trust

£3,100

Correspondent: The Trustees, 77 Comiston Drive, Edinburgh EH10 5QT

OSCR number: SC014280

Eligibility
Children in need under 18 and students of nursery nursing living in Scotland.

Types of grants
One-off grants.

Annual grant total
In 2013/14 the trust had an income of £25,000 and a total expenditure of £26,500. Grants are made to individuals and organisations, it would appear, mainly for social welfare purposes. We estimate that educational grants to individuals totalled £3,100.

Exclusions
Grants are not given for holidays or household furnishings.

Applications
Applications are considered every two months and should be submitted through a tutor or third party such as a social worker, health visitor or teacher. Applicants are encouraged to provide as much information about their family or individual circumstances and needs as possible in their applications. Applications can only be accepted from people currently residing in Scotland.

Ayrshire Educational Trust

£2,500

Correspondent: Catherine Martin, Principal Administration Officer, East Ayrshire Council, Council Headquarters, London Road, Kilmarnock KA3 7BU (01563 576123; fax: 01563 576269; email: CLDEnquires@east-ayrshire.co.uk; website: www.east-ayrshire.gov.uk)

OSCR number: SC018195

Eligibility
Individuals who live in the former county of Ayrshire.

Types of grants
Grants are awarded to schoolchildren and further/higher education students. Support is given towards study/travel abroad or in the UK in pursuance of education, equipment for students with special educational needs, educational outings/visits and excursions, also holiday travel for school pupils.

Annual grant total
In 2013/14 the trust had an income of £55,500 and an expenditure of £2,900. We estimate that the annual total amount of grants awarded to individuals was around £2,500.

Exclusions
The trust will not support people who are studying for a second qualification and will not assist with the cost of uniforms or instruments.

Applications

Application forms can be requested from the correspondent. Applications are normally considered four times a year and can be made directly by individuals.

Other information

The trust also supports organisations, groups, clubs or societies, which benefit young people in Ayrshire.

Dr John Calder Trust

£7,000

Correspondent: Clive Phillips, Administrator, St Machar's Cathedral, 18 The Chanonry, Aberdeen AB24 1RQ

OSCR number: SC004299

Eligibility

People in need who live in the parish of Machar or within the city of Aberdeen. Individuals who are only resident in the area for their education and people from the area studying elsewhere are both eligible.

Types of grants

Grants are usually of up to £500 and can be given for general educational needs.

Annual grant total

In 2013/14 the trust had an income of £17,300 and a total expenditure of £16,900. The trust mainly gives grants to individuals and organisations for educational purposes. We estimate that educational grants to individuals totalled £7,000.

Applications

Previously the trust has stated that funds were fully committed and that this situation was likely to remain so for the medium to long term.

Other information

A smaller proportion of charitable expenditure is given to individuals for welfare needs. Organisations may also be supported.

The Carnegie Trust for the Universities of Scotland

£2.4 million

Correspondent: Professor Andy Walker, Secretary and Treasurer, Andrew Carnegie House, Pittencrieff Street, Dunfermline, Fife KY12 8AW (01383 724990; fax: 01383 749799; email: jgray@carnegie-trust.org; website: www.carnegie-trust.org)

OSCR number: SC015600

Eligibility

The trust supports undergraduate or postgraduate students and academic staff at the fifteen Scottish universities (Aberdeen, Abertay, Dundee, Edinburgh, Edinburgh Napier, Glasgow, Glasgow Caledonian, Heriot-Watt, Queen Margaret, Robert Gordon, St Andrews, Stirling, Strathclyde, UHI and West of Scotland).

More specific eligibility requirements apply to different categories (very detailed guidelines are available on the trust's website).

Types of grants

The trust offers support through the following awards:

- Fee assistance – help with the tuition fees for a first degree course at a Scottish university to individuals who lack financial means to attend the course
- Vacation Scholarships – £175 per week to undergraduate degree students at a Scottish university demonstrating exceptional merit to undertake a specific programme of independent research over the summer vacation (two to six weeks in length). Projects should be of direct benefit to the applicant's academic work
- Carnegie-Caledonian PhD Scholarships – the value for the 2013/14 academic year was £15,400 (this figure is expected to rise in future academic years in line with awards funded by the research councils). First Class Honours undergraduate degree is a pre-requisite
- St Andrew's Society of New York Scholarships – awarded by the St Andrew's Society for the State of New York. Awards are given to Scottish students towards a year of study in the United States, mainly covering accommodation and travel expenses. Preference is given to individuals who 'have no previous experience of the United States and for whom a period of study there can be expected to be a life-changing experience'
- Research Incentive Grants – from £500 to £7,500 to academics employed by a Scottish university to undertake a short research project. Early career researchers are encouraged and special consideration is given to applicants who are within five years (excluding breaks) of starting their independent academic career
- Carnegie Centenary Professorship – a maximum of two awards each year of up to £40,000 for a period of three to six months to visiting world class scholars who have been nominated. Professorships are tenable at any of the fifteen Scottish universities
- Collaborative Research Grants – of up to £50,000 for a joint research project (researchers from more than one Scottish university) lasting one to two years

Annual grant total

In 2013/14 the trust had assets of £73.6 million and an income of £2.8 million. Grants and awards totalled £2.4 million distributed as follows:

Scholarships	60	£903,000
Research grants	258	£810,000
Post-Grad taught Bursaries	100	£367,500
Fee assistance	74	£150,000
Vacation scholarships	86	£93,000
Carnegie professorships	5	£79,000
Expeditions	14	£28,000

Exclusions

Undergraduates who receive government funding towards the costs of their tuition fees (SAAS support) are not eligible. Courses at the Scottish Higher Education Institute delivered and validated by a university outside Scotland, Open University courses, HNC and HND diploma courses, access courses, accelerated degree courses with a graduate entry, Continuing Professional Development courses, university courses below degree level (diploma or certificate courses) and second degrees are not supported towards the tuition fees.

Applications

Some applications may be made online on the trust's website, some may need an academic referral or nomination and Vacation Scholarships **must** be applied for via the university. For specific details of each of the awards see the trust's website. A preliminary telephone call may be helpful.

Applications are considered as follows:

- Fee assistance: applications are considered from 15 May to 1 December for assistance with fees for the following academic year
- Carnegie-Caledonian PhD Scholarships: end of February
- Vacation Scholarships: applications must be received by 15 March
- St Andrew's Society of New York Scholarships: universities should send applications for the nominated candidates by 15 March
- Research Incentive Grants: 15 September and 15 March
- Carnegie Centenary Professorships: 15 July
- Collaborative Research Grants: 31 January

Other information

Carnegie-Cameron Bursaries are made available to support fees for one-year taught postgraduate degree courses and are awarded through the Universities.

The Henry Dryerre scholarship which supports students wishing to undertake a PhD in medical or veterinary physiology is offered every three years. The scheme is administered in the same way as the Carnegie/Caledonian scholarships. It will next be offered in 2017.

Churchill University Scholarships Trust for Scotland
See entry on page 33

Creative Scotland

£600,000 (80+ grants)

Correspondent: Charity Administrator, Waverley Gate, 2–4 Waterloo Place, Edinburgh EH1 3EG (0845 603 6000; email: enquiries@creativescotland.com; website: www.creativescotland.com)

Eligibility
People working at a professional level in the arts, screen and creative industries based in Scotland.

Types of grants
A number of funding programmes are available:

Open Project funding
This fund supports the arts, screen and creative industries, with projects that help them explore, realise and develop their creative potential, widen access to their work in duration. It is open to both individuals and organisations. The website notes: 'You can apply for funding from £1,000 to £100,000. We will also consider applications up to £150,000.'

Regular funding
Regular funding provides support for a range of arts and creative organisations and sustainable environments through which artists and creative people can deepen and deliver their work. Three-year funding for organisations is given.

Targeted funding
Targeted funding addresses specific activities and development needs in a sector, specialism, and/or geographic area. Funding can be shaped in response to sectoral reviews, strategic planning or consultation with external partners.

Annual grant total
From January to March 2015 a total of around £600,000 was awarded to over 80 individuals, mainly through Open Project Funding and Targeted Funding.

Exclusions
Awards are not generally made to students. Most funding is not available to architects/designers, academics, amateur companies, individuals in permanent employment within foundation organisations, flexibly funded organisations or national companies and collections.

For specific exceptions for each of the funds see the guidelines on the website.

Applications
Application forms, guidelines and deadlines for different funding programmes are available from the Creative Scotland's website.

Other information
Creative Scotland is a 'public body that supports the arts, screen and creative industries across all parts of Scotland on behalf of everyone who lives, works or visits here'. Funding is distributed from the Scottish Government and The National Lottery.

The Cross Trust

£85,000

Correspondent: Kathleen Carnegie, Secretary, McCash and Hunter LLP, Solicitors, 25 South Methven Street, Perth PH1 5ES (01738 620451; fax: 01738 631155; email: kathleencarnegie@mccash.co.uk; website: www.thecrosstrust.org.uk)

OSCR number: SC008620

Eligibility
People aged 16 to 30 who are of Scottish birth or parentage proposing 'a study or project that will extend the boundaries of their knowledge of human life'. Applicants must be in genuine financial need.

Types of grants
The trust offers support from £200 to £2,000 through the following:
- Awards for university or college (including music and art schools) students who can demonstrate outstanding academic achievements and who have taken full advantage of support available from local authorities, student loan opportunities and so on. Second degree and postgraduate studies are only considered in exceptional circumstances. Grants are made towards university or college costs, study/travel overseas, study visits and projects. Attendance at conferences, symposia, extra-curricular courses, voluntary work and gap year opportunities can also be considered
- Assistance towards projects and expeditions which do not form part of a degree. Candidates are required to provide evidence of efforts to secure funding elsewhere
- Awards for vacation studies in the arts (in its broad sense). The awards are designed 'to enable students of the highest academic merit and limited financial circumstances to attend conferences, symposia, workshops or master classes or to visit libraries, museums, galleries, concerts or centres of excellence in direct and demonstrable connection with their studies.' Around 15–20 awards can be made each year to people studying at Scottish universities
- Awards for medical electives studies abroad (20 awards each year)
- The John Fife Travel Award to people (normally under the age of 30, but in exceptional cases up to 40 years old) studying or working in horticulture. The award is generally up to £500 but a maximum of £1,000 can be awarded in exceptional circumstances

Annual grant total
In 2013/14 the trust had an income of £203,000 and a total expenditure of £199,000. The trust notes that, although both individuals and organisations can be supported, most of its funding is given to individuals. We estimate that the amount of grants given to individuals totalled around £85,000. In the previous year the trust made awards to 46 individuals.

Exclusions
The trust reminds that 'students who have already received support from the trust for a period of elective study abroad are not eligible for further support'.

Applications
Application forms for each of the awards can be found on the trust's website. Applicants are required to provide full information on their financial circumstances, attach a passport photo, provide an academic reference and details of applications for other funding. Further guidance and closing deadlines for applications for each of the awards can be found on the website.

The trustees normally meet four times a year, in March, February, June and November.

City of Dundee Educational Trust Scheme

£19,000

Correspondent: Jeffrey Hope, Administrator, Miller Hendry Solicitors, 13 Ward Road, Dundee DD1 1LU (01382 200000; email: JeffreyHope@millerhendry.co.uk)

OSCR number: SC015820

Eligibility
Further/higher education students in, or with a strong connection to, Dundee. Priority is given to those who do not receive any statutory awards.

Types of grants

One-off grants ranging from £200 to £300 towards general educational costs.

Annual grant total

In 2014 the trust had an income of £17,000 and an expenditure of £19,300. We estimate that around £19,000 was awarded in grants to individuals.

Applications

Application forms can be requested from the correspondent. Applications, together with a CV, should be submitted at least two weeks before the trustees' quarterly meetings. The meetings are held in March, June, September and December.

East Lothian Educational Trust

£22,000

Correspondent: J. Morrison, Administrator, Department of Corporate Resources, John Muir House, Haddington, East Lothian EH41 3HA (01620 827273; email: eleducationaltrust@eastlothian.gov.uk; website: www.eastlothian.gov.uk/info/828/activities_and_support_for_young_people/1496/east_lothian_educational_trust)

OSCR number: SC010587

Eligibility

People in education or training who live in the area covered by East Lothian Council (former county of East Lothian).

Types of grants

Support is available to people 'undertaking studies, courses or projects of an educational nature, including scholarships abroad and educational travel'. Grants are normally one-off and means-tested. According to our research they range from around £100 to £700 and can be awarded to schoolchildren, further/higher education students (including mature students and postgraduates), people in training, and individuals with special educational needs. Assistance is available for a wide range of educational needs, including uniforms/clothing, fees, study/travel abroad, books, equipment/instruments, maintenance/living expenses, research, accommodation and excursions.

Annual grant total

In 2013/14 the trust had an income of £60,000 and an expenditure of £49,500. We estimate that around £22,000 was given in grants to individuals.

Exclusions

Residents of Musselburgh, Wallyford and Whitecraig are not included. Grants are intended to be supplementary only.

Applications

Application forms can be downloaded from the trust's website or requested from the correspondent. Applicants should provide full costs of the course and associated expenses (such as fees, accommodation, travel, necessities, maintenance, special equipment) and give details of their household income. Applications can be submitted directly by the individual or through a parent/guardian. The trustees meet four times a year, usually in February, May, August and November.

Other information

Grants are also available to clubs and organisations for various studies or projects of educational nature.

Esdaile Trust Scheme 1968

£28,000 (60 grants)

Correspondent: Fiona Watson, Administrator, Exchange Place 3, Semple Street, Edinburgh EH3 8BL (0131 473 3500; fax: 0131 473 3535; email: fiona.watson@scott-moncrieff.com; website: www.scott-moncrieff.com/services/charities/charitable-trusts/esdaile-trust)

OSCR number: SC006938

Eligibility

Daughters of ministers of the Church of Scotland, daughters of missionaries appointed or nominated by the Overseas Council of the Church of Scotland, and daughters of widowed deaconesses. Applicants must be between the ages of 12 and 25. Preference is given to families with a low income.

Types of grants

Annual grants towards general educational costs, ranging between £150 and £800.

Annual grant total

In 2013/14 the trust had an income of £26,500 and an expenditure of £34,000. Around £28,000 is available for distribution each year. Previously about 60 grants have been made annually.

Applications

Application forms can be obtained from the trust's website and should be completed by a parent/guardian. Applications should be submitted to the correspondent no later than 31 May each year. Grants are distributed by early September.

Other information

The trust also co-operates with the Society for the Benefit of Sons and Daughters of Ministers of the Church of Scotland and the Glasgow Society of the Sons and Daughters of Ministers of the Church of Scotland in the distribution of student grants. The societies can support both boys and girls.

Fife Educational Trust

£25,000

Correspondent: Education Services, Finance and Procurement, Fife Council, Rothesay House, Glenrothes KY7 5PQ

OSCR number: SC004325

Eligibility

People who have a permanent address within the Fife council area and who attended a secondary or primary school there.

Types of grants

Support for individuals below postgraduate level is usually restricted to travel grants where this is an integral part of the course of study; however, assistance can also be given for music, drama and visual arts. Grants range from £50 to about £75.

Annual grant total

In 2013/14 the trust had an income of £71,500 and a total expenditure of £50,000. We estimate that the total amount of grants awarded to individuals was approximately £25,000 as the trust also awards grants to organisations.

Applications

Apply in writing to the correspondent. Applicants must give their permanent address, details of schools they attended within Fife with dates of attendance, and details of other money available. Applications are considered in March.

The Caroline Fitzmaurice Trust

£16,000

Correspondent: The Secretaries, 106 South Street, St Andrews KY16 9QD (01334 468604; email: elcalderwood@pagan.co.uk; website: www.carolinefitzmaurice.org.uk)

OSCR number: SC00518

Eligibility

Girls and young women under the age of 23 who live in the geographical area of the Diocese of St Andrews, Dunkeld and Dunblane. The trustees will require successful applicants to make an effort in raising funds elsewhere through their own personal attempts and to subsequently contribute to the community wherever they may settle. Applicants must demonstrate a specific financial need and evidence of high promise in educational, social or cultural background.

Types of grants

Grants of between £200 and £5,000 are given if there is a specific need.

Annual grant total

In 2013/14 the trust had an income of £22,500 and an expenditure of £16,500. We estimate that the annual total amount of grants awarded was around £16,000.

Exclusions

The application guidelines on the trust's website note that 'the trustees will not approve applications which are based on solely financial need, and will require evidence of high promise. They will fund only a proportion of the total costs.'

Applications

Application forms can be obtained from the correspondent and are considered only once a year, usually in early June. The closing date for applications is 30 April annually. Written report from the applicant's referee is required and applicants who are under the age of 18 at the time of the application are additionally asked to provide full information on both parents' financial circumstances.

Other information

Successful applicants are required to provide a written report to the trustees as soon as practicable after the end of each period of funding.

Glasgow Educational and Marshall Trust

£50,000 (60 grants)

Correspondent: Avril Sloane, Secretary and Treasurer, Merchants House of Glasgow, 7 West George Street, Glasgow G2 1BA (0141 433 4449; fax: 0141 424 1731; email: enquiries@gemt.org.uk; website: www.gemt.org.uk)

OSCR number: SC012582

Eligibility

People, normally over 18 years old, who are in need and who have lived in the city of Glasgow (as at the re-organisation in 1975) for a minimum of five years (excluding time spent studying in the city with a home address elsewhere). The trust holds a list of the postcodes which qualify for support and can provide it upon request.

The trust states that awards to undergraduate students are made only in exceptional circumstances.

Types of grants

One-off and recurrent grants ranging from £100 to £1,000, although in exceptional cases higher awards have been made. Support can be given to mature students, postgraduates, people

in further/higher education and vocational training. Travel expenses, school excursions, books, course fees, living expenses, study/travel abroad, equipment/instruments, childcare for mature students can all be funded.

Grants are normally given for courses where a Students Awards Agency for Scotland grant is not available or where such grants do not cover the total costs.

Annual grant total

In 2013/14 the trust had an income of £98,500 and a total expenditure of £87,000. Previously about 60 awards have been made annually totalling around £50,000.

Exclusions

Retrospective awards are not made and courses run by privately owned institutions are not supported.

Applications

Application forms and full guidelines are available on the trust's website and can be submitted directly by the individual together with two written references. The trustees meet on the first Wednesday of March, June, September and December. Applications for grants for university courses which start in September/October must be received by 31 July.

Candidates are expected to apply for any loans available through the Student Loans Company and should show evidence of savings and other fundraising activity.

Other information

The trust also makes grants to organisations.

The Glasgow Highland Society

£5,500

Correspondent: The Secretaries, Alexander Sloan, 38 Cadogan Street, Glasgow G2 7HF (0141 354 0354; email: kt@alexandersloan.co.uk; website: www.alexandersloan.co.uk/ghs)

OSCR number: SC015479

Eligibility

Students who have a connection with the Highlands (for example, lived or went to school there) and who are now studying in Glasgow. Grants are normally given for first degrees only, unless postgraduate studies are a natural progression of the degree.

Types of grants

Grants of around £75 help with fees for people at college or university or who are in vocational training (including mature students). Grants may also be given for Gaelic research projects and apprenticeships.

Annual grant total

In 2013 the charity had an income of £5,500 and an expenditure of £6,100. We estimate that grants made to individuals for education totalled around £5,500.

The 2013 accounts are the latest available at the time of writing (November 2015).

Applications

Application forms are available from the correspondent. Applications should be submitted directly by the individual by 6 November and are considered in December.

Other information

The correspondent has informed us that the trust may be winding down; however, a decision has not been made yet. Applications are still being accepted.

The Glasgow Society of the Sons and Daughters of Ministers of the Church of Scotland

£15,200

Correspondent: Fiona Watson, Charity Accounting Services, Scott-Moncrieff, Exchange Place, 3 Semple Street, Edinburgh EH3 9BL (0131 473 3500; email: fiona.watson@scott-moncrieff.com; website: www.scott-moncrieff.com/services/charities/charitable-trusts/glasgow-society-of-the-sons-and-daughters)

OSCR number: SC010281

Eligibility

Children of Ministers of the Church of Scotland, with a preference for those children who are training for the ministry or mission work of the Church of Scotland.

Types of grants

Grants to support the costs of attending university or postgraduate training.

Annual grant total

In 2013/14 the charity had an income of £57,500 and a total expenditure of £68,500.

The charity is administered by Scott-Moncrieff, whose website stated the following:

£45,000 is available for distribution during the year. Last year, 15 children of deceased Ministers were supported, each receiving between £1,075 and £2,310. Eight grants were made in connection with educational and training ranging from £1,350 to £2,030 per annum. One grant was also made out of a separate fund in connection with applications which fell out with the criteria indicated above but were nevertheless for educational purposes.

We estimate that grants for educational purposes totalled around £15,200.

Applications

Application forms are available from the correspondent or can be downloaded from the website. Applications should be sent in no later than 31 May each year and grants are distributed by early September.

The Guildry Incorporation of Perth

£20,000

Correspondent: Lorna Peacock, Secretary, 42 George Street, Perth PH1 5JL (01738 623195; email: guildryperth@btconnect.com; website: www.perthguildry.org.uk)

OSCR number: SC008072

Eligibility

Young people aged 17 to 25 who are in need, living in Perth or Guildtown and following a course of further or higher education in the UK. The charity also supports young people taking part in Raleigh International, Link Overseas Exchange Projects and similar activities.

Types of grants

Grants of up to £800.

Annual grant total

In 2014/15 the charity had an income of £209,000. Our research shows that grants to individuals have previously totalled around £80,000, with approximately £20,000 given for educational purposes.

Applications

Application forms can be requested from the correspondent. They are considered at the trustees' meetings on the last Tuesday of every month. Applicants are required to write a short covering letter of around 250 words explaining why they require funding and how the grant they receive could help their local community.

Highlands and Islands Educational Trust Scheme

£11,000

Correspondent: Charity Administrator, Shepherd and Wedderburn LLP, 1 Exchange Crescent, Conference Square, Edinburgh

OSCR number: SC014655

Eligibility

Students who live in the counties of Argyll, Bute, Caithness, Inverness, Orkney, Ross and Cromarty, Sutherland or Shetland and are of the Protestant faith. Candidates have to be in the fifth/sixth form at school and preparing to go on to higher/further education. Preference is given to Gaelic speakers.

Types of grants

One-off grants in the range of £120 to £160 are available towards the cost of books and maintenance/living expenses to people who are about to start their first degree course at university or college. Applicants' academic results and financial means are taken into account.

Annual grant total

In 2014/15 the charity had an income of £12,900 and a total expenditure of £11,200. We estimate the annual total amount of grants awarded to be around £11,000.

Applications

Apply in writing to the correspondent. Applications should be submitted through the individual's school and include confirmation of the applicant's faith, details of the occupation and income of parents/guardians, ability at Gaelic (if applicable), information on the course to be undertaken and intended career plans. Applications should be made between March and June for consideration within the following three months.

The Lethendy Trust

£8,600 (18 grants)

Correspondent: George Hay, Trust Administrator, Henderson Loggie, The Vision Building, 20 Greenmarket, Dundee DD1 4QB (01382 200055; fax: 01382 221240; email: ghay@hlca.co.uk)

OSCR number: SC003428

Eligibility

Young people with a strong connection to the Tayside or North Fife areas.

Types of grants

Educational and development activities are supported. Our research suggests that grants of £150 to £400 are available. They are given to young people who are taking part in character building charitable activities, such as Project Trust, or are travelling abroad with charitable organisations to carry out charitable activities, for example.

Annual grant total

In 2014/15 the trust had an income of £76,000 and a total expenditure of £87,000. The trust has informed us that a total of nearly £8,600 was given to 18 individuals. Note that this figure is higher than in the previous few years.

Exclusions

Support is not given to individuals for school/college fees. The correspondent has informed us that the trust 'does not currently support purely academic funding requests from individuals and any requests from individuals for any purpose who do not have a strong connection with Tayside or north Fife'.

Applications

Applications may be made in writing to the correspondent. The trust states that there are regular meetings throughout the year to consider applications.

Other information

The trust also supports organisations.

The Logan and Johnstone School Scheme

£5,000

Correspondent: Deputy Director of Education, Education Services, Wheatley House, 25 Cochrane Street, Merchant City, Glasgow G1 1HL

Eligibility

Students in further and higher education (including mature students, people starting work, undertaking apprenticeships and postgraduates) who live in the former Strathclyde region.

Types of grants

One-off grants are available for books, equipment, instruments and fees. Awards usually range from £200 to £700.

Annual grant total

Our research suggests that about £5,000 is normally given a year.

Exclusions

Grants are not made towards living costs or travel expenses.

Applications

Application forms are available from the correspondent. They should be submitted directly by the individual between April and June for consideration in August.

Mathew Trust

£10,000

Correspondent: Fiona Bullions, Administrator, Henderson Loggie, Chartered Accountants, Royal Exchange, Panmure Street, Dundee DD1 1DZ (01382 201234; fax: 01382 221240; email: fiona.bullions@hendersonloggie.co.uk)

OSCR number: SC016284

Eligibility

People in need who live in the local government areas of the City of Dundee, Angus, Perth and Kinross and Fife.

Types of grants

One-off grants for fees and study/travel abroad are available to college/university students (including mature students), people in vocational or professional training/retraining, people starting work, people struggling to secure employment, also overseas students and people with special educational needs. Awards are usually up to £400 but greater sums may be awarded.

Annual grant total

In 2013/14 the trust had an income of £262,000 and a total expenditure of £265,500. According to our research about £10,000 is given to individuals each year.

Applications

Apply in writing to the correspondent. Applications can be submitted directly by the individual for consideration every two months.

Other information

Grants are also made to organisations.

Maxton Bequest

Correspondent: Donna Cessford, Support Assistant, Education and Learning Service, 4th Floor, Rothesay House, Rothesay Place, Glenrothes KY7 5PQ (03451 55 55 55 + Ext 44 19 98; email: donna.cessford@fife.gov.uk)

Eligibility

People above school age who are 'engaged in study at any continuation class, secondary school, further education college or university or engaged in training or serving apprenticeship to any trade or profession'. Applicants must ordinarily reside (or have parents resident) in Crieff or Kirkcaldy and be in need.

Types of grants

Our research suggests that grants are of around £100 and available for clothing, books, equipment, educational outings in the UK, fees or living expenses.

Annual grant total

We were unable to determine the amount awarded through the fund.

Applications

Application forms and further guidelines can be requested from the correspondent. The application deadlines vary each year but usually are around October/November.

Other information

The charity's funds form part of the Fife Educational Trust. The fund does not have a registered charity number.

The McGlashan Charitable Trust

£10,000

Correspondent: Gordon Armour, Administrator, 66 Octavia Terrace, Greenock PA16 7PY (email: gordon. armour66@btinternet.com)

OSCR number: SC020930

Eligibility

Grants are made in a very wide range of subjects to postgraduate students who are aged under 30 and were either born in Scotland or were born elsewhere and are studying in Scotland.

Types of grants

Grants tend to be in the range of £500 to £1,000.

Annual grant total

The trust has informed us that it is fairly small and grants to students vary from year to year but the total expenditure on postgraduate students tends to be around £10,000 per annum.

Applications

Applications can be made via email to the correspondent during April (those arriving earlier or later will be ineligible) and must clearly state a need for financial support. Awards are made during July.

Other information

A few substantial grants are made to major Scottish charities, mainly those active in the arts. These applications may be made at any time of year.

Moray and Nairn Educational Trust

£5,000

Correspondent: Jean-Anne Goodbrand, Administrative Officer, Grants and Bursaries, Council Office, High Street, Elgin IV30 1BX (01343 551374; fax: 01343 563478; email: jeananne. goodbrand@moray.gov.uk or educationalservices@moray.gov.uk; website: www.moray.gov.uk/moray_standard/page_43905.html)

OSCR number: SC019017

Eligibility

People who or whose parents have lived in the former combined county of Moray and Nairn for at least five years and schoolchildren/young people attending Moray and Nairn schools or further education centres. Applicants' household earnings must be below £34,000 a year plus an allowance for dependent children.

Types of grants

Bursaries are available to students (including mature and postgraduate) in Scottish universities and people pursuing education at a Scottish Central Institution or Training College. Financial support can also be given for study/travel overseas and to school pupils for educational outings and visits. Adult education is also assisted. Grants are normally one-off and can reach up to £200.

Annual grant total

In 2013/14 the trust had an income of £15,000 and a total expenditure of £10,200. We estimate that about £5,000 was given in grants to individuals.

The website notes that the amount available to disburse in the financial year 2015/16 is £11,300.

Applications

Application forms can be found on the trust's website and should be submitted before 30 September annually. Note that current guidelines and application forms are subject to change – for latest updates you should consult the website.

Other information

Grants can also be made to local schools, further education centres or clubs and organisations operating in the area of benefit for facilities, special equipment or promotion of adult education.

Renfrewshire Educational Trust

£30,000

Correspondent: The Administrator of Renfrewshire Educational Trust, Finance and Corporate Services, Renfrewshire House, Cotton Street, Paisley PA1 1TR (0141 618 7104; email: sarah.white@renfrewshire.gov.uk; website: www.renfrewshire.gov.uk)

OSCR number: SC008876

Eligibility

People who live, or have lived for a consecutive period of at least three years in the last ten years, in the Inverclyde, Renfrewshire or East Renfrewshire local authority areas. Applicants' household income must not exceed £34,000 per annum.

In order to qualify for a taught master's award applicants must intend to study on a course which does not attract Student Awards Agency for Scotland (SAAS) funding. Candidates must be in their final year of an undergraduate degree or have graduated in the previous year from either Glasgow Caledonian University, Glasgow School of Art, the University of Strathclyde, the Royal Conservatoire of Scotland, the University of Glasgow or the University of the West of Scotland.

Types of grants

Support is given in three categories:

- School excursions – grants for educational outings to pupils who receive free school meals
- Further and higher education/ performing arts/travel grants – awards ranging from £200 to £400 are given towards the fees of higher education courses to exceptional students in music, drama or visual arts and for travel abroad for educational purposes
- Taught master's awards – one grant worth £3,400 is awarded each year to a student on a one year taught master's degree in the UK (the award is paid to the university directly)

Annual grant total

In 2013/14 the trust had both an income and a total charitable expenditure of £34,000. We estimate the annual total amount of grants awarded to individuals to be around £30,000.

Exclusions

Applicants from households with annual income above £34,000 are not eligible. Support is not available to people who are already in receipt of some kind of award or bursary, including SAAS loan (note that an award from the trust would allow the successful student not to have to take a student loan to cover the cost of fees).

Applications

Application forms for each category are available on the trust's website or can be requested from the correspondent. Application deadline for the taught master's degree award is normally 30 June each year, for school excursions in January and for educational/ performing arts/travel grants by the end of January, April, July or October.

Charities Administered by Scottish Borders Council

£10,000

Correspondent: Charity Administrator, Community Services Council, Newtown St Boswells, Melrose, Roxburghshire TD6 0SA (01835 825020; website: www. scotborders.gov.uk/directory/23/ education_trusts)

Eligibility

The Scottish Borders Council administers four educational funds corresponding to the four former counties of Berwickshire, Peeblesshire, Roxburghshire and Selkirkshire.

Applicants should either live in these areas or have family resident there.

Types of grants

Small grants can be given for educational outings and travel, adult education, studies of drama, music and visual arts, research, special equipment/instruments and postgraduate studies. Consult the charity's website for specific details. Grants are usually from £20 to £250.

Annual grant total

Our research suggests that the annual budget for grants is normally about £10,000.

Applications

Application forms for each of the funds can be found on the Scottish Borders Council website or requested from the correspondent. Applications can be made at any time.

Other information

Awards are made on a first come first served basis. Support can also be given to local clubs.

Scottish International Education Trust

£30,000

Correspondent: Dr Michael Ewart, Director, Turcan Connell, Princes Exchange, 1 Earl Grey Street, Edinburgh EH3 9EE (email: siet@turcanconnell. com; website: www.scotinted.org.uk)

OSCR number: SC009207

Eligibility

Scottish people (by birth or upbringing) who wish to take their studies or training further in order to start a career. The trust looks for individuals who have ability and promise, generally with a good first degree (first class honours or close to it) or an equivalent. Grants are rarely made to undergraduates and priority is given to postgraduate students, especially if assistance from public funds is not available (for example, if the course is at an overseas institution).

Types of grants

One-off and recurrent grants of up to £2,000 for educational expenses, such as fees, books/equipment, research or travel.

In the past grants included those in the areas of: international affairs; history; drama, dance and ballet; music; law; film-making, cinematography; science, engineering and technology.

Annual grant total

In 2013/14 the trust had an income of £46,000 and an expenditure of £81,000.

Further financial information was not available; however, the website notes that 'the trust makes grants amounting generally to about £30,000 annually' and that 'these are normally made up of grants to individual students who apply direct to the trust'. We use this figure as an indication of support available to individuals.

Exclusions

The trust does not normally make grants for:

- Courses leading to qualifications required for entry into a profession (e.g. teaching, legal practice)
- Purchase of musical instruments
- Undergraduate courses or courses below degree level

The trust's website notes: 'Regrettably we cannot accept applications based purely on acute financial need.'

Applications

Applications should be made in writing via post or email to the correspondent including: a CV; details of the course; a statement of aims; the amount sought; two references. Full details of information required can be found on the website. Applications may be submitted at any time and will be assessed when received.

The website notes:

> Applicants who pass the initial assessment may be awarded a grant at that stage, or may be submitted to the full board of trustees for a second assessment. Trustees meet for second assessments of applications normally in late March and early September; papers for each meeting are drawn up about a month beforehand; so if the timing is critical to you, you should aim to get an application in as soon as possible and in any event not later than 7th February (for the March meeting) or 7th August (for the September meeting) to allow time for the initial assessment and a possible second assessment.

Other information

The trust can also support organisations or corporate projects; however, note the following stated on the trust's website: 'As the Trust has a particular focus on supporting individuals, grants to organisations or corporate projects are occasionally reduced in number to only one or two projects per year.'

It is further noted: 'Our resources are limited, and when bids for help exceed the funds available – as they regularly do – we have to prioritise. So if you apply to us you should expect competition.'

Charles and Barbara Tyre Trust

£35,000

Correspondent: Christine Heads, Clerk to the Governors, William Duncan and Co., Loch Awe House, Barmore Road, Tarbert, Argyll PA29 6TW (01880 820227; email: christine@ williamduncantarbert.co.uk; website: www.charlesandbarbaratyretrust.org.uk)

OSCR number: SC031378

Eligibility

Children and young people between the ages of 18 and 25 who live within the former county of Argyll (which includes Kinlochleven but excludes Helensburgh and the Island of Bute), have completed their school education and are of the Protestant faith.

Types of grants

Grants are given to improve individual's qualifications or for retraining. Support can be offered towards further/higher education, Open University courses, training and development courses which are additional to the applicant's existing degree or qualification. Funding can be given for gaining new skills, leadership and initiative development and similar educational activities.

People with physical or mental disability (whether temporary or permanent) are also entitled to apply for re-creative holidays.

Annual grant total

In 2013/14 the trust had an income of £32,500 and an expenditure of £39,500. We estimate the annual total amount of grants awarded to individuals for educational purposes to be around £35,000.

Applications

Application forms can be downloaded from the trust's website and should be emailed to the correspondent by 31 May annually. Successful applicants will be notified by the end of August. Applications received after the closing date are not considered, unless in exceptional circumstances.

John Watson's Trust

£90,500 (70 grants)

Correspondent: Laura Campbell, Trust Administrator, The Signet Library, Parliament Square, Edinburgh EH1 1RF (0131 225 0658; email: lcampbell@ wssociety.co.uk; website: www. thewssociety.co.uk/index.asp?pg=145)

OSCR number: SC014004

Eligibility

Children and young people under the age of 21 who have a physical/learning disability or are socially disadvantaged and live in Scotland. Preference is given to people living in or connected with Edinburgh or the Lothian region.

Orphans, children from a single parent family or individuals who are burdened with some other special family difficulty, which is not purely financial, can also be supported towards boarding school costs.

Types of grants

Grants in the range of £30–£2,000 are given towards special tuition, educational trips, computers (especially for people with special educational needs), laptops, books, uniforms, tools, equipment, expenses for further training and education, travel and other activities contributing to education and advancement in life.

School boarding fees may be partially covered but usually in exceptional circumstances, where personal situation makes boarding a necessary option.

Annual grant total

In 2014 the trust had an income of £162,000 and a total expenditure of £212,500. Approximately £150,000 is allocated for distribution in grants each year.

Exclusions

Grants are not available for day school or university fees.

Applications

Application forms and full guidelines can be found on the WS Society's website or requested from the correspondent. They can be submitted directly by the individual, or through a third party, for example, a social worker, Citizens Advice, other welfare agency, if applicable. Applications must include details of the candidate's household income, specify the support required and provide references.

The grants committee meets approximately five or six times each year and the application deadlines are available on the website.

Applications for school trips to outdoor residential centres must be made by the school, not the individual.

Other information

Grants are also made to organisations and groups working with disadvantaged children or young individuals with physical/learning disabilities.

Ayrshire

The Spiers Trust

£2,000

Correspondent: The Executive Director (Economies and Communities), North Ayrshire Council, Cunninghame House, Irvine KA12 8EE (01294 324428; website: www.north-ayrshire.gov.uk)

Eligibility

Children and young people who live in the parishes of Beith, Dalry, Dunlop, Kilbirnie, Lochwinnoch or Neilston and who attend secondary education there. Preference will be given to students from families with financial difficulties.

Types of grants

Grants ranging between £50 and £200 are available to secondary school and further/higher education students towards the cost of course fees and special tuition in academic, artistic, scientific or technological subject, also travel costs or educational necessities.

Annual grant total

According to our research, the trust gives around £2,000 a year in grants.

Applications

Application forms can be requested from the correspondent and should normally be returned by October. Applicants may be requested to provide some evidence of need.

Other information

The trust generates its income from investments and the rent derived from letting the land adjacent to former school grounds for grazing.

South Ayrshire

The C. K. Marr Educational Trust Scheme

£201,000

Correspondent: Alan Stewart, Clerk, 1 Howard Street, Kilmarnock KA1 2BW (01563 572727; fax: 01563 527901)

OSCR number: SC016730

Eligibility

Students in tertiary education who live in Troon or the Troon electoral wards.

Types of grants

Bursaries, scholarships and educational travel grants to people at college or university, support towards postgraduate research and assistance to individuals with disability.

Annual grant total

In 2013/14 the charity had an income of £337,000 and a total expenditure of £461,000. We estimate that the amount of grants given to individuals totalled £201,000.

Applications

Apply in writing to the correspondent. Applications can be made either directly by the individual or through a third party, such as a university/college or an educational welfare agency, if applicable.

Other information

The charity also makes grants to organisations.

Central Scotland

Stirling

Stirlingshire Educational Trust

£85,000

Correspondent: Iain Flett, Administrator, 68 Port Street, Stirling FK8 2LJ (01786 474956; fax: 01786 474956; email: stgedtrust@btconnect. com; website: www. stirlingeducationaltrust.org.uk)

OSCR number: SC007528

Eligibility

People in need who live, or have lived in the past for a period of at least five consecutive years, in Stirlingshire (including Denny/Bonnybridge, Falkirk, Grangemouth, Kilsyth, Polmont, Stirling and environs).

Types of grants

The trust offers:
- Travel post-graduation scholarships – for research work or advanced/special study to postgraduates
- Travel scholarships – for travel within the UK or abroad for educational purposes
- Special grants – to mature students (over the age of 21) for obtaining the necessary educational qualifications to enter university or an institute of further education

Support can be given towards fees, books, travel expenses, equipment/ instruments or other educational necessities and is normally in the range of £150 to £500.

Annual grant total

In 2014/15 the trust had an income of £122,500 and a total expenditure of £118,500. Usually around £85,000 a year is distributed in educational grants.

Applications

Applications can be made online on the trust's website. An acknowledgement will be sent by email following the application providing further information.

Other information

Organisations can also be supported.

Dumfries and Galloway

The Dumfriesshire Educational Trust

£18,000

Correspondent: Janice Thom, Area Committee Administrator, Municipal Chambers, Buccleuch Street, Dumfries DG1 2AD

OSCR number: SC003411

Eligibility

People normally living in Dumfriesshire who have had at least five years of education in Dumfriesshire.

Types of grants

Grants of up to £60, usually recurrent, are given to:
- Schoolchildren towards educational outings
- Students in further/higher education for books, fees/living expenses, study/ travel abroad and student exchanges
- Mature students towards books and travel

Annual grant total

In 2013 the trust had an income of £48,500 and a total expenditure of £52,000. Our research tells us that grants to individuals usually total around £18,000 a year.

At the time of writing (October 2015) this was the most recent information available for the trust.

Exclusions

Grants are not available for childcare to mature students or to foreign students studying in the UK.

Applications

Application forms are available from the Education Offices at Woodbank or from schools. They are considered quarterly, usually in March, June, September or December, and closing dates are stated on the form. Applications can be submitted directly by the individual, through the relevant school/college/ educational welfare agency or through another third party. The form should be signed by the applicant. For recurrent grants, applicants must re-apply each academic year.

The Holywood Trust

£26,000

Correspondent: Richard Lye, Trust Administrator, Hestan House, Crichton Business Park, Bankend Road, Dumfries DG1 4TA (01387 269176; fax: 01387 269175; email: funds@holywood-trust. org.uk; website: www.holywood-trust. org.uk)

OSCR number: SC009942

Eligibility

Primarily young people aged 15 to 25 living in the Dumfries and Galloway region, with a preference for those who are mentally, physically or socially disadvantaged.

The trust's website further states:

> Our focus is primarily on young people aged 15 – 25 years, however we will consider grants for younger vulnerable children if they are preventative measures in relation to health or social disadvantage, or if a child has an exceptional talent and requires funding to further this.

Types of grants

One-off and recurrent grants of £50 to £500 are given towards, for example: college and university expenses; participation at regional, national and international sporting and cultural events; and to purchase musical instruments or sporting equipment. The average award is around £200.

Annual grant total

In 2014/15 the trust had an income of £2 million and a total expenditure of £2.5 million. The trust's annual report and accounts for the year were not available to view at the time of writing (November 2015) and so we were unable to determine how much was distributed in grants for educational purposes. Our research suggests that educational grants have previously totalled around £26,000.

Exclusions

No grants are given towards carpets or accommodation deposits. Retrospective (backdated) awards are not made.

Applications

Application forms can be downloaded from the website (where a helpful application Q&A can also be found), or requested from the correspondent. The application guidelines provide the following advice: 'It will always be helpful to have a supporting letter from a third-party who knows you in a formal capacity. Depending on your circumstances the third-party could be a Social Worker, support worker, college tutor, sports coach, etc.' At least four weeks should be allowed for an application to be processed. Normally only one grant is made per beneficiary per year.

Other Information

The trust also supports individuals with welfare needs and group and project applications which benefit young people.

John Primrose Trust

£2,600

Correspondent: The Trustees, 1 Newall Terrace, Dumfries DG1 1LN

OSCR number: SC009173

Eligibility

Young people in need who live in Dumfries and Maxwelltown or have a connection with these places by parentage.

Types of grants

Grants may be given to students to help with educational needs or to help people starting work or undertaking apprenticeships.

Annual grant total

In 2014/15 the trust had an income of £16,400 and a total expenditure of £10,600. We estimate that the amount of grants given to individuals for educational purposes totalled around £2,600.

Applications

Application forms are available from the correspondent. They are generally considered in June and December.

Other information

The trust awards grants to both individuals and organisations for educational and social welfare purposes.

John Wallace Trust Scheme

£11,500

Correspondent: Joanne Dalgleish, Senior Administrator, The Director of Education Services, Woodbank, 30 Edinburgh Road, Dumfries DG1 1NW (01387 260493; fax: 01387 260453; email: Joanne.dalgleish@dumgal. gov.uk; website: www.dumgal.gov.uk/ index.aspx?articleid=10758)

OSCR number: SC011640

Eligibility

Young people living in the following areas: the electoral wards of Crichton, Douglas, that part of Dalswinton lying outside the parish of Dumfries, Kirkland, Kello and Morton – all in the local government area of Nithsdale District.

Types of grants

The trust provides the following:

- Supplementary Bursaries – to further/ higher education students, including Open University students, for general educational costs
- Travel Grants – for educational visits either within Great Britain or abroad
- Agricultural Bursaries – to students at Barony College Parkgate or other institution specialising in agriculture and allied sciences

Financial assistance can be renewed for up to five years.

Annual grant total

In 2013/14 the trust had an income of £9,400 and an expenditure of £11,800. We estimate that about £11,500 was given in grants, as it appears that the main focus of charitable giving is on individuals.

Applications

Application forms for bursaries can be obtained from the correspondent. The closing date for applications is 31 December.

People applying for travel grants are requested to do so in writing providing a statement of purpose for the journey, places to be visited, anticipated length and costs of the trip.

Other information

The trust also provides money to the Rector of Wallace Hall Academy for distribution of annual Ferguson Prizes to students following courses in agriculture or allied sciences.

Schools can also apply for travel grants.

Dunbartonshire and Argyll

West Dunbartonshire

West Dunbartonshire Trusts

£0

Correspondent: Charity Administrator, West Dunbartonshire Council, Council Offices, Garshake Road, Dumbarton G82 3PU

OSCR number: SC025070

Eligibility

People who live in the old county area of Dumbarton district and are aged 16 or over. Preference may be given to people who come from deprived areas or those who are otherwise disadvantaged.

Types of grants

Grants are of around £50–£100, larger awards are only made in exceptional circumstances. Our research suggests that previously support has been given in different categories, such as: supplementary bursaries for higher education students; to people entering a profession/vocational training; educational excursions; travel awards; specialist equipment; sports facilities; adult education; assistance to various clubs and groups; education in music, drama and visual arts.

Under the West Dunbartonshire Trusts heading fall:

- Dunbartonshire Educational Trust Scheme 1962 awarding educational prizes and bursaries
- McAuley Prize for Mathematics for students of mathematics and computing
- Halkett Memorial Trust for young writers and painting competition
- UIE Award for students studying apprenticeships or training in industry

Annual grant total

In 2014/15 the funds had an income of £4,300 and an expenditure of £1,500. It would appear that this was given to organisations rather than individuals. Our research suggests that in the past grants have totalled about £3,000.

Applications

Application forms are available from the correspondent. They are considered throughout the year, but students usually apply before the start of their course.

Other information

The funds are administered by the Dunbartonshire Council.

Fife

New St Andrews Japan Golf Trust

£4,000

Correspondent: M. Rigg, 7 Pilmour Links, St Andrews, Fife KY16 9JG

OSCR number: SC005668

Eligibility

Children and young people in need who live in the county of Fife and are undertaking sports and recreational activities with a preference for golf.

Types of grants

One-off and recurrent grants ranging from £200 to £1,500 are offered for sports equipment, travel costs, student exchange, accommodation expenses, coaching assistance, university fees or sports scholarships.

Annual grant total

In 2014/15 the trust had an income of £6,500 and a total charitable expenditure of £8,000. We estimate that the amount of grants given to individuals totalled about £4,000.

Applications

Apply in writing to the correspondent. Contact details of two referees are required.

Other information

The trust supports both individuals and organisations.

Glasgow

James T. Howat Charitable Trust

£11,000

Correspondent: Trust Administrator, Harper Macleod LLP, The Ca'd'oro, 45 Gordon Street, Glasgow G1 3PE

OSCR number: SC000201

Eligibility

People who live in Glasgow and are undertaking education which is aimed at addressing unmet local cultural and social needs, other than in municipal, governmental or religious areas.

Types of grants

One-off grants ranging from £100 to £1,000 can be awarded to schoolchildren and further/higher education students. Mature and overseas students can also be assisted. Support can be given towards books, equipment/instruments, course fees, maintenance expenses or study/travel overseas. Mature students can also get help for the childcare costs and people with special educational needs can receive assistance for educational outings/excursions.

Annual grant total

In 2013/14 the trust had an income of £285,000 and an expenditure of £269,500. Most of the trust's funding is directed to organisations. Previously grants to individuals have totalled around £11,000.

Exclusions

Support is not normally given for medical electives, second or further qualifications, payments of school fees or costs incurred at tertiary educational establishments.

People studying at Glasgow University, Strathclyde University or Royal Scottish Academy of Music and Dance are not

likely to be supported, because the trust already makes block payments to the hardship funds of these institutions.

Applications

Applications should be made in writing to the correspondent outlining why the assistance is required and what kind of support is needed. The trustees meet four times a year, normally in March, June, September and December. Applications should be submitted at least a month prior to the meeting.

Other information

The trust mainly supports organisations.

The Trades House of Glasgow

£19,800

Correspondent: The Clerk, Administration Centre, North Gallery – Trades Hall, 85 Glassford Street, Glasgow G1 1UH (0141 553 1605; email: info@tradeshouse.org.uk; website: www.tradeshouse.org.uk)

OSCR number: SC040548

Eligibility

People in need who live in Glasgow.

Types of grants

Grants are given to encourage promising young people in university or colleges.

Annual grant total

In 2013/14 the charity had assets of £22 million and an income of £1.1 million. The amount of grants given to individuals totalled £219,000, of which £199,000 was given for social welfare purposes. Bursaries and educational grants to individuals totalled £19,800.

Applications

Apply in writing to the correspondent.

Other information

Guilds and Craft Incorporations are the Scottish equivalent of the craft guilds or livery companies, which developed in most of the great cities of Europe in the Middle Ages. Over the years many of the House's political and legal duties have been transferred to other bodies, but the charitable functions and concern for the future of Glasgow remain. The assistance of the needy, the encouragement of youth and support for education, particularly of schools and further education colleges in developing craft standards, are now its chief objects.

The Trades House also operates the Drapers Fund which distributes £50,000 annually to children in need who are under the age of seventeen. The fund has its own application form, which is available to download from the charity's website.

Grampian

Banffshire Educational Trust

£10,000 (50 grants)

Correspondent: Jean-Anne Goodbrand, Admin Officer, Education and Social Care, The Moray Council, High Street, Elgin, Moray IV30 1BX (01343 551374; fax: 01343 563478; email: jeananne.goodbrand@moray.gov.uk; website: www.moray.gov.uk)

Eligibility

People who/whose parents live in the former county of Banffshire or who attend schools or further education centres there. Applicants' household earning should be below £34,000 a year.

Types of grants

The trust offers postgraduate scholarships for research work or an advanced/special study; bursaries for further/higher education students, including Open University and second/subsequent degrees; grants to mature students to enable them to achieve necessary qualifications to enter university or other institution of further/higher education; financial support towards books, instruments, tools, kits, personal equipment and so on to people undertaking apprenticeships or training; assistance towards study/travel abroad, including fees, books or equipment/instruments; funds for educational outings and visits to schoolchildren and young people attending further education centres; grants for any courses of adult education; and support for research and educational experiments which would be beneficial to the Banffshire county people.

Annual grant total

According to our research, grants totalling around £10,000 are made to about 50 individuals each year.

Applications

Separate application forms for each category and detailed guidelines are available on the trust's website or can be requested from the correspondent. Applications should be submitted by 30 September for consideration in December.

The equal opportunities form should be sent in a separate envelope marked 'private and confidential' to: Alan Taylor, Admin Assistant, Education and Social Care, The Moray Council, High Street, ELGIN, Moray IV30 1BX.

Other information

Support is also given to schools, further education centres, clubs and organisations which operate for the benefit of the people of Banffshire.

Aberdeen and Aberdeenshire

Aberdeen Endowments Trust

£649,000

Correspondent: David Murdoch, Clerk to the Trust, 19 Albert Street, Aberdeen AB25 1QF (01224 640194; fax: 01224 643918; email: aet1909@btopenworld.com; website: www.aberdeenendowmentstrust.co.uk)

OSCR number: SC010507

Eligibility

People of any age who were born and brought up in Aberdeen, as constituted in 1967. Secondary school pupils in the former Grampian region can be supported according to need and academic performance.

Types of grants

Most of the trust's funding is spent in providing free places at Robert Gordon's Secondary College to pupils who otherwise would not be able to attend it. The trust supports around 60 pupils at Robert Gordon's College.

Educational travel:
More than 100 pupils at city primary and secondary schools are given help to participate in school trips each year. Applications can be made at any time of year, using forms available from the trust. The trips should have a clear education content and the means-tested awards are paid directly to the school, typically comprising 50% of the trip costs. The trustees are happy to consider applications for group travel.

Secondary School bursaries:
Bursaries are awarded in September each year to help disadvantaged families. The awards can be made for up to four years, subject to satisfactory school reports on attendance and progress. 30 new bursaries were awarded in September 2014 for pupils at secondary schools in North East Scotland. Annual payments for these awards range from £160 to £500 per child. Application forms are available from the trust each year and are sent to the headteachers of all North East primary schools.

Further education grants:
The trust provides grants to people progressing to further education at college, university or other institutions. Each year around 20 grants are made to students from the city ranging up to £1,000.

Foreign language education grants:
Grants are available to help pupils develop their skills in modern languages through travel or a course of study. Application forms are available from the trust and are sent each year to principal teachers of modern languages in city schools. Applications can be considered at any time. Grants since 2012 have typically been around £300 per pupil.

Annual grant total

In 2014 the trust had an income of £1 million and a total expenditure of £1.1 million. Grants were made totalling £649,000.

Applications

Application forms can be requested from the correspondent. They are normally considered monthly, except in January, July and August.

Other information

Occasionally grants can be made to organisations.

Aberdeenshire Educational Trust

£17,000

Correspondent: Maureen Adamson, Administrator, Trust Section, Aberdeenshire Council, St Leonards, Sandyhill Road, Banff AB45 1BH (01261 813336; email: maureen.adamson@aberdeenshire.gov.uk)

OSCR number: SC028382

Eligibility

Schoolchildren and students who, or whose immediate family, are resident in the former county of Aberdeenshire. Applicants' household income should not exceed £20,525.

Types of grants

Grants of £200, to further education students for travel, fees, books, equipment and school trips. Support is also given for starting work or apprenticeships.

Annual grant total

In 2014/15 the trust had assets of £3.4 million and an income of £117,000. A total of £35,000 was spent in grants and donations, broken down as follows:

Travel grants	£26,000
Educational excursions	£4,000
Preference grants	£4,000
Prizes	£1,000

The amount awarded in grants to individuals was not specified in the accounts. We estimate that around £17,000 was given to individual beneficiaries.

Applications

Application forms are available from the correspondent. Grants are considered throughout the year. All applications are means-tested; therefore, applicants are required to provide documentary evidence of their income from the last tax year.

Other information

Grants are also made to schools, clubs and educational groups. Annual school prizes and preference grants are also awarded.

Huntly Educational Trust 1997

£7,000

Correspondent: A. Mitchell, Secretary, Peterkins, 3 The Square, Huntly, Aberdeenshire AB54 8AE (01466 792101)

OSCR number: SC026920

Eligibility

Primarily people living in the district of Huntly. Applicants from elsewhere in Scotland may also be supported if there are remaining funds and at the trustees' discretion.

Types of grants

Grants are given towards education and training, including vocational courses. General educational needs can be addressed, including books, equipment, tools, clothing and so on. Awards are of around £200 on average.

Annual grant total

In 2013/14 the trust had an income of £15,500 and an expenditure of £14,000. We estimate that the amount of grants given to individuals totalled around £7,000.

Applications

Application forms can be requested from the correspondent or downloaded from The Gordon Schools' website (gordonschools.aberdeenshire.sch.uk/finance-grants). Grants are normally considered at monthly meetings.

Other information

The trust also makes grants to local schools, colleges and other educational establishments.

Highlands and Na h Eileanan Siar (Western Isles)

The Highland Children's Trust

£10,000

Correspondent: Trust Administrator, 105A Castle Street, Inverness IV2 3EA (01463 243872; email: info@hctrust.co.uk; website: www.hctrust.co.uk)

OSCR number: SC006008

Eligibility

Children and young people in need who are under 25 and live in the Highlands.

Types of grants

One-off grants of £50 to £500 are available for the following purposes:

- Student hardship funding – small grants to assist students at college or university who are finding it hard to manage financially
- School or educational trips – for children attending Highland schools who cannot afford the whole cost of a trip
- Family holidays – for families who would not normally be able to go on holiday, the trust runs a scheme which enables the children of a family to have a holiday accompanied by an adult. A copy of the current holiday scheme can be obtained by application to the administrator
- Educational items for children with special educational needs – help can be given in certain circumstances to help with the cost of educational equipment

Annual grant total

Our research indicates that this trust awards around £20,000 a year for both education and welfare purposes. We estimate that around £10,000 is given for educational purposes.

Exclusions

Grants are not given: for postgraduate study; to pay off debts; or to purchase clothing, footwear, food, furniture, cars, etc. Holidays abroad are not considered for the holiday scheme.

Applications

Application forms can be requested from the correspondent in writing or by email, or can be downloaded from the website, where guidelines are also given. Requests can be submitted at any time either directly by the individual or through a social worker, Citizens Advice or other welfare agency. Applicants under the age of 18 must have their form counter-signed by their parent or guardian.

Ross and Cromarty Educational Trust

£5,000

Correspondent: Catriona Maciver, Department of Education and Children's Services, Comhairle Nan Eilean Siar, Sandwick Road, Stornoway HS1 2BW (01851 709546; email: catriona-maciver@cne-siar.gov.uk; website: www.cne-siar.gov.uk/education)

Eligibility

People who live on the Isle of Lewis. The area is defined by postal codes HS1 and HS2 (sector 0 and sector 9).

Types of grants

Grants in the range of £30 to £200 are available for general educational expenses and various social, cultural and recreational purposes. Schoolchildren can be assisted towards educational outings and excursions; people entering a trade or a vocational occupation towards equipment/instruments and clothing; higher education students (including postgraduates) may be awarded scholarships. Visual arts, drama, music, dance studies and adult education can also be supported. Application guidelines provide a list of specific sections, where assistance can be requested.

Annual grant total

Our research suggests that the trust normally has an income of about £10,000 each year, all of which is distributed for charitable purposes. We estimate the annual total amount of grants awarded to individuals to be about £5,000.

Applications

Application forms can be found on the Comhairle Nan Eilean Siar website or requested from the correspondent. Applicants should only apply for one specific cause at a time and provide the details of estimated costs of their activities.

Other information

Local schools, educational establishments and other organisations or clubs can be supported towards the cost of special equipment, facilities, sports equipment and so forth.

Since 1975, Comhairle Nan Eilean Siar local government council operates the sections of the Ross and Cromarty Educational Trust Scheme which relate specifically to the Isle of Lewis. These sections are operated in agreement with Highland Council, which is responsible for the capital of the trust fund.

Lothian

East Lothian

The Red House Home Trust

£10,000 (31 grants)

Correspondent: Fiona Watson, Administrator, Scott-Moncrieff, Exchange Place 3, Semple Street, Edinburgh EH3 8BL (0131 473 3500; fax: 0131 473 3500; email: fiona.watson@scott-moncrieff.com; website: www.scott-moncrieff.com/services/charities/charitable-trusts/red-house-home-trust)

OSCR number: SC015748

Eligibility

Young people under the age of 22 who live in East Lothian and are in need of care, live in deprived circumstances or are adjusting to independent living.

Types of grants

Grants in the range of £150 to £1,000 are given for general needs relating to education and training.

Annual grant total

In 2014 the trust had an income of £21,500 and an expenditure of £25,500. The trust's website notes that about £10,000 is available for distribution each year.

The trust's website states:

'Last year 31 grants were made ranging from £150 to £1,000.'

Applications

Application forms are available from the Scott-Moncrieff website or can be requested from the correspondent. They should be returned by post to the correspondent. The trustees normally meet three times a year to review applications and award grants.

West Lothian

West Lothian Educational Trust

£4,500

Correspondent: Fiona Watson, Scott-Moncrieff, Exchange Place 3, Semple Street, Edinburgh EH3 8BL (0131 473 3500; fax: 0131 473 3535; email: fiona.watson@scott-moncrieff.com; website: www.scott-moncrieff.com/services/charities/charitable-trusts/west-lothian-educational-trust)

Eligibility
People who were born in West Lothian or have lived there for the last two years.

Types of grants
Normally, one-off grants from £100 to £300 are given; however, recurrent grants may be considered for a training course lasting over a year. Financial support is available for undergraduate and postgraduate studies, apprentices, people entering a trade, travel/study costs within and outside Scotland or for educational outings. Adult education, visual arts, music, drama or educational experiments and research can also be supported.

Annual grant total
The trust's website states that normally, 'after various prize monies and bursaries have been paid, about £4,500 is available for distribution each year'. Previously two awards were made during the year. In 2013/14 the trust had an income of £11,000 and a total expenditure of £15,500.

Applications
Application forms are available from the trust's website or can be requested from the correspondent. Applications must be received by 1 February, 1 May and 1 September each year.

It is advised to provide as much information on applicants' financial and personal circumstances as possible, but please **do not** send any additional documentation (such as CVs, references or statements).

Other information
Schools and colleges can be supported towards the cost of special equipment, sports facilities and clubs can be supported for activities of educational nature.

Tayside

The Anne Herd Memorial Trust

£12,500

Correspondent: The Trustees, 27 Bank Street, Dundee DD1 1RP
OSCR number: SC014198

Eligibility
People who are blind or partially sighted who live in Broughty Ferry. Applicants from the City of Dundee, region of Tayside or those who have connections with these areas and reside in Scotland will also be considered.

Types of grants
Grants are given for educational equipment such as computers and books. Grants are usually at least £50.

Annual grant total
In 2013/14 the trust's income (£120,500) and expenditure (£122,500) were both unusually high. Our research suggests that the trust usually gives approximately £25,000 a year in grants for education and welfare. We estimate that grants for educational purposes total around £12,500.

Applications
Applications can be made in writing to the correspondent. They can be submitted directly by the individual in March/April for consideration in June.

The Morgan Trust Scheme 1982

£11,500

Correspondent: The Clerk, Miller Hendry Solicitors, 13 Ward Road, Dundee DD1 1LU (01382 200000; fax: 01382 200098; email: info@millerhendry.co.uk)
OSCR number: SC010527

Eligibility
Children whose parents were either born/educated in the former royal burghs of Dundee, Forfar, Arbroath and Montrose, or have been resident in any of these areas for five years immediately prior to the application (or immediately before their death).

Types of grants
The trust offers maintenance grants to pupils according to need and school scholarships to promising children in day or boarding fee paying schools. Emergency grants may also be awarded to schoolchildren whose parent/guardian dies or suffers a serious loss of income and can no longer support the child's education (such support is continued until the beneficiary finishes school or assistance is deemed no longer necessary). Grants are generally in the range of £200.

Annual grant total
In 2014 the trust had an income of £11,900 and an expenditure of £11,700. We have estimated that the annual total amount of grants awarded was around £11,500.

Exclusions
According to our research, grants are not given to people with an income of more than £10,000, unless there are exceptional circumstances.

Applications
Application forms are available from the correspondent. They should be completed by a third party on behalf of the applicant providing full details of their financial situation. Awards are usually considered in May and November.

Other information
In addition to the above the trust gives Tom's Prizes awarded by competition or merit and progress in school.

Angus

Angus Educational Trust

£17,000

Correspondent: Trust Administrator, People Directorate, Angus House, Orchardbank Business Park, Forfar DD8 1AE (01307 476339; fax: 01307 461848; website: www.angus.gov.uk/services/view_service_detail.cfm?serviceid=1362)
OSCR number: SC015826

Eligibility
People in need residing in the Angus council area who are attending or entering full/part-time undergraduate courses in universities. **Note:** Any student entitled to apply for a loan under the Student Loans Scheme must have taken up this option before an application to the trust will be considered.

Types of grants
The trust provides financial assistance towards undergraduate university courses and offers travel grants for those studying on higher education courses outside Scotland. Young people travelling abroad for other educational purposes can also be supported. Awards are means-tested and are intended to supplement existing grants.

Annual grant total

In 2013/14 the trust had an income of
£23,500 and a total expenditure of
£34,000. The trust also supports
organisations; therefore, we estimate that
the amount of grants given to
individuals totalled around £17,000.

Exclusions

Postgraduate studies and students at
colleges are not supported.

Applications

Application forms can be downloaded
from the trust's website or requested
from the correspondent. Applicants must
state full details of their financial
situation, provide copies of P60 forms
(for those employed) and enclose a copy
of the letter from the awarding authority
allocating or rejecting their grant/bursary
application. The trustees meet twice a
year normally in March and September
to consider applications and can take
three to four months to come to a
decision.

Other information

Grants are also available to various local
clubs, groups working to improve
educational opportunities and learning
in Angus and rural primary schools for
educational excursions.

Perth and Kinross

Perth and Kinross Educational Trust

£8,000

Correspondent: Trust Administrator,
Perth and Kinross Council, Chief
Executive's Service, 2 High Street, Perth
PH1 5PH (01738 476200; email:
ECSFST@pkc.gov.uk)

OSCR number: SC012378

Eligibility

Students in further or higher education
who were born or attended school in
Perth and Kinross. Mature students,
postgraduates and people undertaking
apprenticeships are all eligible.

Types of grants

Grants of up to £150 can be awarded
towards books, fees, living expenses and
study/travel abroad.

Annual grant total

In 2013/14 the trust had an income of
£42,500 and an expenditure of around
£45,000. According to our research,
previously about £8,000 a year has been
given to individuals.

Applications

Application forms can be obtained from
the Perth and Kinross Council.
Applications should normally be
submitted by mid-May for consideration
in June. The exact closing date can be
found on the application form. Late
applications are not considered.

Other information

Organisations may also be supported.

Wales

General

Cambrian Educational Foundation for Deaf Children in Wales

£16,000

Correspondent: Pamela Brown, Clerk to the Trustees, Montreux, 30 Lon Cedwyn, Sketty, Swansea SA2 0TH (01792 207628; email: pam-brown@homecall.co.uk)

CC number: 515848

Eligibility

People who are deaf or have partial hearing, are aged under 25, and who/whose parents live in Wales. Beneficiaries include people in special classes (units) in ordinary and special schools in Wales, students in further education and people entering employment.

Types of grants

One-off and occasional annual grants of up to a maximum of £500. Grants have been provided for computers, software, school uniforms, tools/equipment, instruments, books, occasionally for educational outings in the UK and for study or travel abroad. Support has also been given to people starting work and to further and higher education students for books.

Annual grant total

In 2014 the foundation had an income of £22,500 and a total expenditure of £22,700. We estimate that the amount of grants given to individuals totalled £16,000.

Exclusions

Grants are not given for leisure trips.

Applications

Applications are available to download from the foundation's website. If the applicant is under the age of 18, the form should be completed by a parent/guardian or another authorised person. Applications should be supported in writing by the applicant's teacher or tutor. They are considered throughout the year.

The Gane Charitable Trust

£15,000

Correspondent: Ken Stradling, Administrator, c/o Bristol Guild of Applied Art, 68–70 Park Street, Bristol BS1 5JY (0117 926 5548)

CC number: 211515

Eligibility

Students of arts and crafts, or design and social welfare. There is a preference for applicants from Bristol and South Wales and those in further education.

Types of grants

Grants are available to help meet the educational costs of college students, vocational students and mature students and their children. Grants are given towards fees, books and equipment/instruments, range from £200 to £500 and are normally one-off.

Annual grant total

In 2014 the trust had assets of £907,000 and an income of £31,000. Expenditure totalled £36,000 and we estimate that grants made to individuals for education totalled around £15,000.

Applications

Application forms are available from the correspondent.

Other information

The trust also makes grants to individuals for social welfare purposes and to organisations.

The Glamorgan Further Education Trust Fund

£32,000

Correspondent: Naomi Davies, Administrator, 1st Floor Aberafan House, Education Finance, Port Talbot Civic Centre, Port Talbot, West Glamorgan SA13 1PJ (01639 763553; email: n.davies11@npt.gov.uk)

CC number: 525509

Eligibility

Pupils who attend a county secondary school in Glamorgan and female pupils who attend a maintained primary schools in the parishes of Llantrisant, Pontypridd, Pentyrch, Llanfabon, Llantwit Fardre, Eglwysilan and that part of the parish of Llanwonno comprising the former Ynysybwl ward of the former Mountain Ash urban district.

Types of grants

Cash grants tenable at any teacher training college, university or other institution of further education (including professional and technical) approved by the council and governed by rules made by the council. Financial assistance can be given for outfits, clothing, tools, instruments or books to assist those leaving school, university or other educational establishments to prepare for or enter a profession, trade or calling.

Annual grant total

In 2013/14 the fund had an income of £70,000 and a total expenditure of £45,500. Grants totalled £32,000 given in scholarships and awards.

Exclusions

Applicants are not eligible for assistance if they are in receipt of a central government bursary or a mandatory or discretionary award, or are exempt from the payment of the tuition fee.

Applications

Application forms are available from the correspondent. Applications should be submitted before 31 May each year for consideration in July/August.

The Geoffrey Jones (Penreithin) Scholarship Fund

£9,000

Correspondent: Keith Butler, Trustee, Marchant Harries, 17–19 Cardiff Street, Aberdare CF44 7DP (01685 885500; email: keithbutler@marchantharries.co.uk)

CC number: 501964

Eligibility

Students who have been resident in the parishes or districts of Penderyn, Ystradfellte Vaynor or Taff Fechan Valley, Merthyr Tydfil for at least 12 months.

Types of grants

Assistance with the cost of books, fees, maintenance/living expenses and study/travel abroad is available to students in further or higher education.

Annual grant total

In 2014/15 the fund had both an income of £6,000 and a total expenditure of £9,500. We estimate that the annual total amount of grants awarded was around £9,000. Our research shows that about 25 grants are made each year.

Applications

Apply in writing to the correspondent.

Elizabeth Jones' Scholarships for Boys and Girls of Aberavon and Margam (Elizabeth Jones' Trust)

£7,000

Correspondent: David Scott, Trustee, 28 Wildbrook, Port Talbot SA13 2UN (01639 887953; email: scott-david11@sky.com)

CC number: 525517

Eligibility

Young people aged between 16 and 25 who/whose parents live in the borough of Port Talbot and who have attended a county or voluntary school in/around the area of benefit for at least two years. Also students at the Margam College of Further Education.

Types of grants

According to our research, one-off grants ranging from £50 to £400 are available towards general educational costs, including books, equipment/instruments, travel costs and other necessities.

Annual grant total

In 2013/14 the charity had an income of £2,500 and an expenditure of £7,500. We estimate the annual total amount of grants to be around £7,000.

Applications

Apply in writing to the correspondent.

The Peter Saunders Trust

£10,000

Correspondent: Peter Saunders, Trustee, c/o The Sure Chill Company, Pendre, Tywyn, Gwynedd LL36 6AH (01654713939; email: enquiries@petersaunderstrust.co.uk; website: www.petersaunderstrust.co.uk)

CC number: 1108153

Eligibility

People throughout Wales (and particularly living in rural Wales between the Dyfi and the Mawddach rivers) who are in need of financial assistance towards their projects.

The trust's website states that 'the trust aims to promote excellence and favours projects which show endeavour, a measure of self-reliance and spirit of enterprise' and will prefer projects 'that others might find hard to support, perhaps because they break new ground, involve risk or lack popular appeal'. The trust may initiate projects when 'new thinking is required or when it believes that an opportunity is being missed'.

Types of grants

Grants are made towards entrepreneurial projects which provide opportunities and learning experiences.

Annual grant total

In 2014/15 the trust had an income of £1,400 and an expenditure of £41,000. We estimate that about £10,000 could have been given in grants to individuals. Note that charitable giving is currently suspended.

Exclusions

Grants are not available for university education, either at undergraduate or postgraduate level.

Applications

See the trust's website to know when it resumes charitable giving and what the application procedure is.

Other information

Note the following stated on the website: 'The Trust is taking a break now and not considering any new applications at this time. A review is being made of not only the impact of the work of the Trust to date, but also its strategy for the future and the impact the Trust might have in new areas.'

The trust's website defines their beneficial area as Wales, with particular focus on 'rural Wales between the Dyfi and the Mawddach rivers'.

The trust has helped both individuals and organisations supporting a number of projects and has assisted Atlantic College and Tring School for the Performing Arts with bursaries.

Yr Ymddiriedolaeth Ddarlledu Gymreig (The Welsh Broadcasting Trust)

See entry on page 80

Mid Wales

The Thomas John Jones Memorial Fund for Scholarships and Exhibitions

£67,000 (36 grants)

Correspondent: David Meredith, Clerk to the Trustees, Cilmery, The Avenue, Brecon, Powys LD3 9BG (01874 623373; email: davidwm@hotmail.co.uk)

CC number: 525281

Eligibility

People under the age of 26 pursuing education and training for a higher post in industry who have both been resident and attended secondary school in the former county of Breconshire. Preference is given to applicants undertaking courses of advanced technical education.

Postgraduate applicants must have gained an upper second class degree or above (except in exceptional circumstances).

Types of grants

Exhibitions of £1,500 per year for the duration of the course. Scholarships of up to £2,300 (plus £500 for full-time courses) to postgraduate students to cover the tuition fees are available for up to three years. Postgraduate non-technical studies are only supported for one year. Renewals of the award are subject to annual review.

Bursaries have been suspended.

Annual grant total

In 2013/14 the fund had assets of £1.7 million, an income of £59,500 and awarded educational grants totalling £67,000 to 36 individuals.

Applications

Apply in writing to the correspondent. The trustees meet at least once a year and as required. Applications should include full details of the nature, location, type (full/part-time) and duration of the study and the qualification aimed at. Usually they must be returned to the correspondent by 31 August annually.

Powys

Edmund Jones' Charity

£4,500

Correspondent: Ruth Jefferies, Administrator, Steeple House, Brecon, Powys LD3 7DJ (01874 638024; email: edmundjonescharity@gmail.com)

CC number: 525315

Eligibility

People under the age of 25 who live or work within the town of Brecon.

Types of grants

Grants are available to people undertaking apprenticeships and starting work, mainly towards tools; to college students towards equipment; and to university students towards books. Awards usually range from £50 to £300.

Annual grant total

In 2014 the charity had assets of £440,500 and an income of £39,000. Grants totalled £9,500. The proportion of grants to individuals and organisations was not specified in the accounts; therefore, we estimate that grants to individual students totalled around £4,500.

Applications

Applications should be made in writing to the correspondent, giving details of the college/course/apprenticeship and the anticipated costs, together with the information on any other grants received or applied for. Applications may be submitted by individuals, through their parents or via college. According to our research, applications are mainly considered in October.

Other information

Schools and colleges located in the area of benefit may also be assisted.

Llanidloes Relief-in-Need Charity

£1,300

Correspondent: Elaine Lloyd, Correspondent, Woodcroft, Woodlands Road, Llanidloes, Powys SY18 6HX

(01686 413045; email: elainellloyd@gmail.com)

CC number: 259955

Eligibility

Students who live in the communities of Llanidloes and Llanidloes Without.

Types of grants

Our research suggests that grants can be given to help with the cost of books, living expenses and other essential items for those at college or university.

Annual grant total

In 2014/15 the charity had an income of £440 and a total expenditure of £1,600. We estimate that about £700 was given in educational grants.

Exclusions

Support cannot be given to students not living within three miles of the town or to foreign students studying in the area.

Applications

Applications may be made in writing to the correspondent.

Other information

Relief-in-need grants are also given.

North Wales

The Educational Charity of John Matthews

£13,500

Correspondent: Mr P. Smith, Administrator, Lyndhurst, 6 Vernon Avenue, Hooton, Ellesmere Port, Cheshire CH66 6AL (0151 327 6103; email: pbsberlian@aol.com; website: www.johnmathewscharity.co.uk)

CC number: 525553

Eligibility

People under the age of 25 who are descendants of the founder of the charity (John Matthew) or are resident in the North Wales areas comprising Chirk, district of Glyndwr, Llanarmon-yn-Ial, Llandegla, Llangollen Rural, Llantysilio, the borough of Wrexham Maelor and the borough of Oswestry, in Shropshire.

Types of grants

Grants of £250 to £2,000 are awarded to young people 'seeking to build upon their talents and improve their educational and career prospects'. Grants have been given to a wide range of applicants, for example musicians, actors, journalists, tree surgeons, medical students and so on. Support can be provided towards specialist equipment, course fees, books, tools and other necessities.

The charity can support undergraduate, postgraduate, second degree students (particularly on courses with a vocational element), people starting work and individuals undertaking apprenticeships. Those who are not able to get other financial support and can demonstrate exceptional talent and passion are favoured.

Annual grant total

In 2014 the charity had an income of £17,000 and an expenditure of £14,000. We estimate that the amount of grants given to individuals totalled around £13,500.

Exclusions

Financial assistance towards ongoing education within the state or private education system can only be considered in exceptional circumstances.

Applications

Application forms and further guidelines can be found on the charity's website. They should be submitted along with a covering letter giving as much information as possible about the course and the applicant's career aspirations as well as financial and personal circumstances (including proof of identity and residence). The trustees usually meet twice a year, in May and November, but considerations can be made more frequently if needed.

People applying as the descendants of the founder will be required to provide extensive supporting documentation.

Other information

The charity welcomes informal contact prior to the application.

The following is taken from the charity's website:

> John Mathews left his estate in Trust in his Will on 27 October 1630 so that young people should be able to nurture their talents and overcome financial barriers that may stand in their way. Today the charity of John Mathews follows the same ethos and encourages applications from young people seeking to build upon their talents and improve their educational and career prospects.

Conwy

The Sir John Henry Morris-Jones Trust Fund

£5,000

Correspondent: Mrs C. Earley, Clerk to the Trustees, The Bay of Colwyn Town Council, Town Hall, 7 Rhiw Road, Colwyn Bay, Conwy LL29 7TE (01492 532248; email: info@colwyn-tc.gov.uk;

website: www.colwyn-tc.gov.uk/town-council/grants-available-and-local-trusts)

CC number: 504313

Eligibility

People under the age of 19 who are resident in the area of the former borough of Colwyn Bay, as existing on 31 March 1974 (Colwyn Bay, Llysfaen, Mochdre, Old Colwyn and Rhos on Sea). People undertaking full-time education outside the borough but normally resident there are eligible.

Types of grants

One-off scholarships to individuals who demonstrate excellence in one of the following fields: arts, crafts and music; sport; academic and research; commerce and business; science and technology; any other field which would satisfy the trustees.

Annual grant total

In 2014/15 the charity had an income of £5,200 and an expenditure of £5,200. We estimate the annual total amount of grants awarded to individuals to be around £5,000.

Exclusions

Applications for courses at higher or further education levels are not considered.

Applications

Application forms are available on the charity's website or from the correspondent. They should be submitted by 31 March. Applicants are invited for an interview in May.

Denbighshire

Freeman Evans St David's Day Denbigh Charity

£1,200 (2 grants)

Correspondent: Medwyn Jones, Town Clerk, Denbigh Town Council, Town Hall, Crown Square, Denbigh LL16 3TB (01745 815984; email: townclerk@ denbightowncouncil.gov.uk)

CC number: 518033

Eligibility

People in need who live in Denbigh and Henllan. Particularly those who are older, have disabilities or an illness.

Types of grants

One-off grants towards the cost of volunteer programmes overseas, educational equipment and so on. In 2013/14 awards were made for computer equipment and in the past a grant has been given towards the fees of a dyslexia assessment. The charity appears to pay to service/item providers rather than making direct cash payments to individuals.

Annual grant total

In 2013/14 the charity had assets of £155,500, an income of £34,000 and a total expenditure of almost £100,000. Grants were made totalling £97,000 and consisted of 32 awards. We believe that two educational grants to individuals totalled £1,200.

Applications

Applications may be made in writing to the correspondent, either directly by the individual or through a third party, such as a social worker, Citizens Advice or other welfare agency. The trustees meet regularly throughout the year to consider applications.

Other information

Organisations are also supported and assistance is given to individuals for social welfare purposes.

The Robert David Hughes Scholarship Foundation

£16,500

Correspondent: Peter Bowler, Trustee, McLintocks, 46 Hamilton Square, Birkenhead, Wirral CH41 5AR (0151 647 9581)

CC number: 525404

Eligibility

University students who have connections with the community of former borough of Denbigh. Applicants should either be born in the community of Denbigh or have a parent or parents who have been resident in the area for at least ten years. Full documentary evidence is requested.

Types of grants

One-off and recurrent grants are offered to university students according to need.

Annual grant total

In 2013/14 the foundation had an income of £18,000 and an expenditure of £17,000. We estimate the annual total amount of grants awarded to individuals to be around £16,500.

Exclusions

Students in colleges of further education are not normally supported.

Applications

Apply in writing to the correspondent. Our research suggests that applications should be submitted by 30 September for consideration in November. Grants are awarded each term upon receipt of completed certificates of attendance, signed by the principal or registrar of the university. Normally, the grant recipients are automatically sent application forms for subsequent years.

Gwynedd

Dr Daniel William's Educational Fund

£59,000 (204 grants)

Correspondent: Dwyryd Williams, Clerk to the Trust, Bryn Golau, Pencefn, Dolgellau, Gwynedd LL40 2YP (email: dwyryd@pencefn.freeserve.co.uk)

CC number: 525756

Eligibility

People under the age of 25 in further/ higher education or training. Priority will be given to former pupils of Dr Williams' School, or their descendants, and people who are resident, or whose parents are resident, in the former administrative district of Meirionnydd.

Types of grants

One-off or recurrent grants can be awarded towards the costs of clothing, uniforms, equipment/instruments, books and other necessities to people entering a trade/starting work; for study/travel overseas; towards the study of music and other arts; for general educational costs to further/higher education students and people in training. Grants usually reach up to a maximum of £500.

Annual grant total

In 2012/13 the fund had assets of £1.2 million, an income of £54,000 and awarded grants to 204 individuals totalling £59,000. The grants were distributed in the following categories:

Course fees	58
Music tuition	39
Educational trips	77
Books, clothing and equipment	6
IT equipment	6
Sports tuition	6
Additional training	3
Musical instruments	3
Travelling expenses	3
Additional learning needs	2
Dance and drama tuition	1

At the time of writing (November 2015), this was the latest financial information available for the fund.

Applications

Application forms can be requested from the correspondent.

Isle of Anglesey

Owen Lloyd Educational Foundation

£5,000

Correspondent: Emlyn Evans, Correspondent, Nant Bychan Farm, Moelfre, Gwynedd LL72 8HF (01248 410269)

CC number: 525253

Eligibility

People between the ages of 16 and 25 in further/higher education who live in Penrhoslligwy and neighbouring parishes.

Larger grants may be given to residents of Penrhoslligwy, as this was the original area covered by the trust deed.

Types of grants

Grants are given to help with the cost of books, fees, living expenses, travel costs (but not for study/travel abroad) and tools/equipment. People starting work and apprentices can be supported towards the cost of books, equipment, clothing, travel and so on.

Annual grant total

In 2013/14 the foundation had an income of £9,500 and an expenditure of £10,600. We estimate the annual total amount of grants awarded to individuals to be around £5,000.

Applications

Application forms can be requested from the correspondent. They should include details of the applicant's financial situation. Applications are normally considered in October with grants being awarded in June.

Other information

Grants are also given to organisations and educational establishments.

Wrexham

Dame Dorothy Jeffreys Educational Foundation

£4,600

Correspondent: Frieda Leech, Administrator, Holly Chase, Pen Y Palmant Road, Minera, Wrexham LL11 3YW (01978 754152; email: clerk. wpef@gmail.com)

CC number: 525430

Eligibility

People in need aged between 16 and 25 who live or have attended school in the former borough of Wrexham or the communities of Abenbury, Bersham, Broughton, Bieston, Brymbo, Esclusham Above, Esculsham Below, Gresford, Gwersyllt and Minera.

Types of grants

Grants are of at least £50. Grants for general education purposes are given to schoolchildren, further/higher education students, people starting work and vocational students. Mature students up to the age of 25 can also receive grants.

Annual grant total

In 2014 the foundation had an income of £3,800 and an expenditure of £4,800. We estimate that grants totalled £4,600.

Applications

Application forms are available from the correspondent to be submitted directly by the individual. Applications are usually considered in November/December and should be submitted by 1 October.

Ruabon and District Relief-in-Need Charity

£800

Correspondent: James Fenner, 65 Albert Grove, Ruabon, Wrexham LL14 6AF (01978 820102; email: jamesrfenner65@tiscali.co.uk)

CC number: 212817

Eligibility

People in need who live in the county borough of Wrexham, which covers the community council districts of Cefn Mawr, Penycae, Rhosllanerchrugog (including Johnstown) and Ruabon.

Types of grants

One-off and occasionally recurrent grants of up to £200. Grants are given to schoolchildren towards uniforms/clothing, equipment/instruments and educational visits/excursions.

Annual grant total

In 2014 the charity had an income of £3,100 and an expenditure of £1,700. The accounts were not required to be submitted to the Charity Commission because of the low income. We estimate that grants for education totalled approximately £800.

Exclusions

Loans and grants to investigate bankruptcy proceedings are not made.

Applications

Apply in writing to the correspondent either directly by the individual or a family member, through a third party such as a social worker or teacher, or through an organisation such as Citizens Advice or a school. Applications are considered on an ongoing basis.

The Wrexham (Parochial) Educational Foundation

£31,500 (61 grants)

Correspondent: Frieda Leech, Clerk to the Trustees, Holly Chase, Pen Y Palmant Road, Minera, Wrexham LL11 3YW (01978 754152; email: clerk. wpef@gmail.com)

CC number: 525414

Eligibility

People between the ages of 16 and 25 who live in the county borough of Wrexham and who are former pupils of one of the following schools: Brymbo and Minera Voluntary Aided Schools, St Giles Voluntary Controlled School and St Joseph's Catholic and Anglican High School.

Types of grants

The foundation provides scholarships, money towards clothing/uniforms, books and equipment/tools, also for travel expenses in the UK and abroad. Help is offered to students in secondary and further/higher education and people starting an apprenticeship or training. Previously grants have included supporting a student with disabilities who was living at home and unable to receive a statutory grant.

Annual grant total

In 2014 the foundation had assets of £12.2 million, an income of £422,500 and a total charitable expenditure of £280,000. A total of £31,500 was awarded in 61 educational grants.

Applications

Application forms can be requested from the correspondent, preferably by email. Applications can be made by individuals directly and should be submitted by 1 October.

Other information

The foundation provides grants to schools within the area of benefit towards equipment/services and also promotes religious education.

South East Wales

The Roger Edwards Educational Trust (formerly the Monmouthshire Further Education Trust Fund)

£7,900 (13 grants)

Correspondent: Mr R. Morse, Trustee, 4 Chepstow Road, USK NP15 1BL (01291673233; email: rogeredwardstrust@yahoo.co.uk)

CC number: 525638

Eligibility

Further or higher education students who have attended a local comprehensive/secondary school and have lived in the Greater Gwent area, except Newport, that is, the council areas of Caerphilly (part), Torfaen, Blaenau Gwent and Monmouthshire.

Types of grants

One-off grants, although students can re-apply in subsequent years, towards books, fees, living costs, travel and equipment. Grants range between £60 and £360, depending on the student's circumstances. Full-time students receiving funding from another source are not funded.

Annual grant total

In 2013/14 the trust had assets of £2.2 million and an income of £68,500. Charitable expenditure totalled £52,000 and grants were made to 13 individual students totalling £7,900.

Applications

Application forms are available from the correspondent. They are considered throughout the year.

Other information

Grants include awards to Usk Church in Wales Primary School totalling £1,600. A further £42,000 was awarded to other educational bodies.

Cardiff

Cardiff Further Education Trust Fund

£400,000

Correspondent: Mrs N. Griffiths, Administrator, Cardiff City Council, City Hall, King Edward VII Avenue, Cardiff CF10 3ND

CC number: 525512

Eligibility

Young people in need who are over the age of 16, resident in city and borough of Cardiff and have attended a secondary school there for at least two years.

Types of grants

Grants to enable individuals to undertake further education or vocational training. Support towards travel and attendance of special educational courses may also be provided.

Annual grant total

In 2013/14 the fund had an income of £145,500 and an expenditure of £500,500. We estimate that the amount of grants given to individuals totalled £400,000. At the time of writing (August 2015) full accounts were not available to view on the Charity Commission's website.

Applications

Apply in writing to the correspondent.

Monmouthshire

Monmouth Charity

£2,500

Correspondent: Andrew Pirie, Trustee, Pen-y-Bryn, Oakfield Road, Monmouth NP25 3JJ (01600 716202; email: carol@pirie.info)

CC number: 700759

Eligibility

Students who are in further education and live within a ten-mile radius of Monmouth.

Types of grants

One-off grants usually up to a maximum of £500.

Annual grant total

In 2013/14 the charity had an income of £10,200 and a total expenditure of £11,000. Grants are made to individuals and organisations for a wide range of charitable purposes, including for the relief of poverty or disability and educational needs. We estimate that educational grants to individuals totalled £2,900.

Applications

The fund advertises in the local press each September/October and applications should be made in response to this advertisement for consideration in November. Emergency grants can be considered at any time. There is no application form. Applications can be submitted directly by the individual or through a social worker, Citizens Advice or other welfare agency.

The Monmouthshire County Council Welsh Church Act Fund

£600

Correspondent: Joy Robson, Head of Finance, Monmouthshire County Council, Innovation House, PO Box 106, Magor, Caldicot (01633 644657; email: davejarrett@monmouthshire.gov.uk; website: www.monmouthshire.gov.uk)

CC number: 507094

Eligibility

People of any age studying at school, university or any other place of study, who live in the boundaries of Monmouthshire County Council (and their dependants). Grants are also made to people starting work.

Types of grants

Applications will be considered from individuals for aid towards a specific activity. The normal level of support to individuals is between £50 and £150.

Annual grant total

In 2013/14 the fund had assets of £4.7 million and an income of £166,000. Grants to individuals for the advancement of their education totalled £600.

Applications

Application forms are available from the correspondent at any time. Applications can be made either directly by the individual, or through his or her school, and must be signed by a county councillor. They are usually considered quarterly.

Other information

The fund also makes grants to organisations.

The Monmouthshire Further Education Trust Fund

£10,000

Correspondent: The Trustees, The Community Foundation in Wales, St Andrew's House, 24 St Andrew's Crescent, Cardiff CF10 3DD (029 2037 9580; email: mail@cfiw.org.uk; website: www.cfiw.org.uk/eng/grants/25-monmouthshire-further-education-trustfund)

Eligibility

Grants of up to £500 are available to provide financial support to individuals under the age of 25 who are pursuing further/higher education or training and who reside in the Gwent area (specifically the County of

Monmouthshire as it existed in 1956), excluding Newport.

Types of grants

Applicants can apply for grants ranging between £50 and £500. Successful applicants will be paid upon receipt of the proof of enrolment on the stated course and/or quotes/invoices for items.

Annual grant total

About £10,000 each year is available for distribution in grants to individuals.

Applications

Application forms are available from the website.

The fund welcomes informal contact prior to applications being formally made. The closing date for applications is 31 August.

Torfaen

The Cwmbran Trust

£2,500

Correspondent: Kenneth Maddox, Secretary, c/o Meritor HVBS (UK) Ltd, Grange Road, Cwmbran, Gwent NP44 3XU (01633 834040; email: cwmbrantrust@meritor.com)

CC number: 505855

Eligibility

People in need living in the town of Cwmbran, Gwent.

Types of grants

The trust gives one-off and recurrent grants for a wide variety of purposes. Previous grants of educational nature have included funding for home study courses and IT equipment. Grants usually range between £125 and £2,500.

Annual grant total

In 2014 the trust had assets of £2.35 million and an income of £98,500. Grants were made to 33 individuals totalling £19,500 for educational and welfare purposes. The majority of funding for individuals is given for social welfare purposes with some of those being of educational nature.

Applications

Applications may be made in writing to the correspondent. They can be submitted directly by the individual or through a social worker, Citizens Advice, welfare agency or other third party. Applications are usually considered in March, May, July, October and December.

Other information

The trust also makes grants to organisations (£59,500 to 18 organisations in 2014).

Vale of Glamorgan

The Cowbridge with Llanblethian United Charities

£400

Correspondent: Clerk to the Trustees, 66 Broadway, Llanblethian, Cowbridge CF71 7EW (01446 773287; email: h.phillips730@btinternet.com)

CC number: 1014580

Eligibility

People in need who live in the town of Cowbridge with Llanblethian.

Types of grants

Grants are made towards clothing, fees, travel and maintenance for people in further, higher or vocational education.

Annual grant total

In 2013/14 the charity had an income of £30,000 and a total expenditure of £22,500. Grants totalled £20,000, of which £400 was awarded to students. The majority of grants (£19,200) were given to individuals for social welfare purposes and a further £500, which, we believe, was received by organisations, was given for the general benefit of the Cowbridge area.

Applications

Apply in writing to the correspondent. Applications can be submitted directly by the individual or through a school/college or educational welfare agency.

South West Wales

Carmarthenshire

Minnie Morgan's Scholarship

£17,000

Correspondent: Chris Moore, Head of Financial Services, Carmarthenshire County Council, County Hall, Carmarthen SA31 1JP (01267 234567)

CC number: 504980

Eligibility

People under the age of 25 who have attended any of the secondary schools in Llanelli and who are studying drama or dramatic art at the University of Wales or any school of dramatic art approved by the trustees.

Types of grants

One-off grants, usually around £1,000.

Annual grant total

In 2013/14 the charity had an income of £13,000 and an expenditure of £17,000. We estimate that grants totalled £17,000.

Applications

Apply in writing to the correspondent. Applications should be submitted by 31 October each year.

Pembrokeshire

The Charity of Doctor Jones

£3,500

Correspondent: Malcolm Crossman, Trustee, Guinea Hill House, Norgans Hill, Pembroke, Dyfed SA71 5EP (01646 622257)

CC number: 241351

Eligibility

Young people between the ages of 16 and 25 who/whose parents live in Pembroke or the previous Pembroke borough.

Types of grants

Grants are given to further/higher education students, people in training and those undertaking apprenticeships. Support is available towards general costs associated with the course or training, including outfits, tools, equipment, books, travel expenses, maintenance costs and fees.

Annual grant total

In 2013 the charity had an income of £41,000 and an expenditure of £38,000. We estimate that the amount of grants given to individuals totalled around £3,500.

The 2013 accounts were the latest available at the time of writing (November 2015).

Applications

Application forms can be requested from the correspondent.

Other information

Our research indicates that the charity advertises locally when grants are available, usually twice a year.

Support can also be given to local people for welfare needs. Organisations may be supported but the trustees prioritise helping individuals. The charity also maintains a number of properties in the area and assists the tenants with maintenance and repairs.

Milford Haven Port Authority Scholarships

£6,000 (4 grants)

Correspondent: Scholarship Scheme Administrator, Gorsewood Drive, Milford Haven, Pembrokeshire SA73 3EP (01646 696100; fax: 01646 696125; email: communications@mhpa. co.uk; website: www.mhpa.co.uk)

Eligibility

Undergraduate students at British universities who have completed most of their secondary education in Pembrokeshire or nearby county.

Types of grants

The charity offers one-off undergraduate scholarships of £1,500 and a placement at the Port of Milford Haven during the summer.

Annual grant total

Four scholarships of £1,500 are awarded every year.

Applications

Application forms can be accessed from the charity's website or requested from the correspondent, when the scheme is open. For the scheme opening dates and application deadlines, consult the website. Our research indicates that all communication should be marked 'Scholarship Scheme'.

Narberth Educational Charity

£1,500

Correspondent: Ann Handley, Administrator, Pembrokeshire County Council, County Hall, Freemens Way, Haverfordwest, Dyfed SA61 1TP (01437 775039; email: ann.handley@ pembrokeshire.gov.uk; website: pembrokeshire.gov.uk/ content.asp?nav=&id=5606&Positioning_Article_ID=)

CC number: 1013669

Eligibility

People who live in the community council areas of Narberth, Llawhaden, Llanddewi Velfrey, Lampeter Velfrey (including Tavernspite and Ludchurch), Templeton, Martletwy (including Lawrenny), Begelly, part of Jeffreyston, Minwere and Reynalton. Applicants should have lived there for at least two years and be aged under 25.

Types of grants

Grants, normally ranging from £100 to £150, to help those at school and those transferring to a recognised course or further or higher education.

Annual grant total

In 2013/14 the charity had an income of £3,000 and a total expenditure of £3,300. We estimate that the amount of grants given to individuals for educational purposes totalled around £1,500.

Applications

Application forms are available from Student Support, North Wing Reception, Haverfordwest from August onwards and should be returned to the office by 8 October.

Other information

The charity also provides financial assistance for local organisations engaged in youth activities and the promotion of education for young people/children living in the catchment area.

Swansea

The Swansea Foundation

£27,000

Correspondent: Jacqueline Shoemaker, Administrator, Council of City County of Swansea, Legal Department, Civic Centre, Oystermouth Road, Swansea SA1 3SN (01792 636704; email: jackie. shoemark@swansea.gov.uk)

CC number: 1086884

Eligibility

People in education who are under the age of 25 and live in the city or county of Swansea. Preference is given to people who have attended one of the following schools or colleges: Bishop Gore Comprehensive School, Dynevor Comprehensive School, Swansea College and Swansea Institute of Higher Education.

Types of grants

One-off and recurrent grants are given according to need.

Annual grant total

In 2013/14 the foundation had an income of £1,100 and an expenditure of £27,500. We estimate that grants totalled about £27,000.

Applications

Apply in writing to the correspondent.

Other information

Note the following information taken from the Swansea council's website: 'The Swansea Further Education and Foundation Trust Funds are currently not available due to the ratification of the funds taking longer than usual.'

East Midlands

General

Babington's Charity

£9,500

Correspondent: Helen McCague, Trustee, 14 Main Street, Cossington, Leicester, Leicestershire LE7 4UU (01509 812271)

CC number: 220069

Eligibility

People in need in the parish of Cossington, Leicestershire.

Types of grants

Grants for equipment, clothing, fees, books and other necessities, computer equipment, travel costs or maintenance expenses to people under the age of 25 to help with tertiary education costs, vocational training or entering a trade. One-off or recurrent support towards other educational needs may also be given, according to need. Mature students have been supported for retraining following a redundancy.

Annual grant total

In 2014 the charity had an income of £40,500 and a total expenditure of £40,000. In previous years grants have on average amounted to about 61% of the charity's total expenditure and on average about 78% of the overall grant-making was made to students and individuals. We estimate that about £19,000 was given to individuals, of which about £9,500 for educational needs.

At the time of writing (September 2015) the latest accounts were not available to view on the Charity Commission's website.

Applications

Applications may be made in writing to the correspondent. The trustees meet at least twice a year.

Other information

The charity gives to individuals and organisations for both educational and social welfare purposes.

The Francis Bernard Caunt Education Trust

£43,500

Correspondent: James Kitchen, Trustee, Larken and Co., 10 Lombard Street, Newark NG24 1XE (01636 703333; email: info@larken.co.uk; website: www. larken.co.uk)

CC number: 1108858

Eligibility

People aged between 16 and 25 who are, or whose parents or guardians are, resident within a 12-mile radius of Newark on Trent Parish Church.

Applicants should have attended or attend Newark schools or colleges or Southwell or Tuxford schools in the previous eight years for at least two years and be intending to study part time or full time for at least one year on a recognised academic or vocational course.

Types of grants

Grants and loans of £500–£2,000.

Annual grant total

In 2013/14 the trust had assets of £1.4 million, an income of £49,000 and made grants totalling £43,500.

Applications

Applications should be made using an application form available from the website and providing a letter of reference from a headteacher, employer or other appropriate person such as a career adviser.

Thomas Monke

£2,000

Correspondent: Christopher Kitto, Correspondent, 29 Blacksmiths Lane, Newton Solney, Burton-on-Trent, Staffordshire DE15 0SD (01283 702129; email: chriskitto@ btinternet.com)

CC number: 214783

Eligibility

Young people under the age of 25 who live in Austrey, Measham, Shenton and Whitwick.

Types of grants

One-off and recurrent modest grants (up to the maximum of £200) towards the cost of goods, tools, books, fees and travelling expenses for educational purposes, including vocational training.

Annual grant total

In 2014 the charity had an income of £4,000 and an expenditure of £4,400. We estimate that the amount of grants given to individuals for educational purposes totalled around £2,000.

Exclusions

Expeditions, scholarships and university course fees are not funded.

Applications

Application forms are available from the correspondent and should be submitted directly by the individual before 31 March, in time for the trustees' yearly meeting held in April.

Other information

The charity can also support individuals for social welfare purposes and organisations. Educational support is, however, the primary concern.

Scargill's Educational Foundation

£9,000

Correspondent: Stephen Marshall, Administrator, Robinsons Solicitors, 10–11 James Court, Friar Gate, Derby DE1 1BT (01332 254105; email: stephen. marshall@geldards.com)

CC number: 527012

Eligibility

People under the age of 25 who live in the parishes of West Hallam, Dale Abbey, Mapperley and Stanley (including Stanley Common).

Types of grants

The main beneficiary of the charity is Scargill Church of England Primary School. Priority is also given to three other schools in the area. After that, help is available for groups and also for individuals for the following purposes:

▶ Grants, usually up to about £45, for sixth form pupils to help with books, equipment, clothing or travel

▶ Grants, usually up to about £175, to help with school, college or university fees or to supplement existing grants

▶ Grants to help with the cost of books and educational outings for schoolchildren

▶ For the study of music and other arts and for educational travel

Annual grant total

In 2014 the foundation had an income of £46,500 and a total expenditure of £32,500. Around £8,000 to £10,000 is given in educational grants to individuals each year.

Applications

Application forms are available from the correspondent.

Derbyshire

Dronfield Relief in Need Charity

£800

Correspondent: Dr Anthony Bethell, Trustee, Ramshaw Lodge, Crow Lane, Unstone, Dronfield, Derbyshire S18 4AL (01246 413276)

CC number: 219888

Eligibility

People in need who are under the age of 25 and live in the ecclesiastical parishes of Dronfield, Holmesfield, Unstone and West Handley.

Types of grants

One-off small grants of up to a value of £100 can be given, including those for social and physical training.

Annual grant total

In 2014 the charity had an income of £3,600 and an expenditure of £3,300. We estimate that about £800 was given to individuals for educational purposes.

Applications

Applications may be made in writing to the correspondent although a social worker, doctor, member of the clergy of any denomination, a local councillor, Citizens Advice or other welfare agency. Applicants should ensure they are receiving all practical/financial assistance they are entitled to from statutory sources.

Other information

Grants are also given to local organisations and for social welfare purposes.

Hilton Educational Foundation

£4,400

Correspondent: Sue Cornish, Administrator, 6 Willow Brook Close, Hilton, Derby DE65 5JE (01283 734110)

CC number: 527091

Eligibility

Young people under the age of 25 in further or higher education who live, or whose parents live, in the parish of Hilton.

Types of grants

One-off grants, usually of around £100–£150, are given towards travel, clothing, books and equipment needed for studies, also towards the studies of music and other arts.

Annual grant total

In 2013/14 the foundation had an income of £11,000 and an expenditure of £5,900. Previously about three quarters of the overall expenditure have been awarded in grants to individuals; therefore, we estimate the annual total amount of grants awarded to be about £4,400.

Applications

Apply in writing to the correspondent. Applications can be submitted directly by the individual. They should normally be made in March and October and are considered in the same month.

Other information

Grants are also available to schools in the local area.

Derby

The Spondon Relief-in-Need Charity

£3,100

Correspondent: Lynn Booth, Secretary and Treasurer, PO Box 5073, Spondon, Derby DE21 7JZ (01332 678533; email: info@spondonreliefinneedcharity.org; website: www. spondonreliefinneedcharity.org)

CC number: 211317

Eligibility

People who live in the ancient parish of Spondon within the City of Derby.

Types of grants

Grants are made to university students, although sixth form students can also be supported, towards books, other equipment and travel. They are also made for school uniforms and trips.

Annual grant total

In 2014 the charity had assets of £706,000 and an income of £29,500. Grants totalled £22,500, of which, we believe, £3,100 was given for educational purposes (£1,800 in student grants to four individuals and £1,300 for school uniforms).

During the year, social welfare grants to individuals amounted to around £16,000 and at least two grants of more than £1,000 were made to organisations, totalling £3,600.

Exclusions

No grants are made for the relief of rates and taxes, or any expenses usually covered by statutory sources.

Applications

The charity's website gives the following advice: 'For more details please write or email us explaining why you think we can help you. Please provide your full contact details with your enquiry.'

Derbyshire Dales

The Ernest Bailey Charity

£350

Correspondent: Ros Hession, Community Engagement Officer, Community Development Department, Derbyshire Dales District Council, Town Hall, Bank Road, Matlock DE4 3NN (01629 761302; email: ros.hession@ derbyshiredales.gov.uk; website: www. derbyshiredales.gov.uk)

CC number: 518884

Eligibility

People in need who live in Matlock and district (this includes Bonsall, Cromford, Darley Dale, Matlock and Matlock Bath, Northwood, Rowsley (part of), Starkholmes, South Darley and Tinkersley).

Types of grants

Most applications have been from local groups, but individuals in need and those with educational needs are also supported. Educational grants are one-off and generally of around £100–£200. Awards can be given to students in further/higher education towards books, fees, living expenses and study or travel abroad. Mature students can apply towards books, travel, fees or childcare. People with special educational needs are considered. Each application is considered on its merits.

Annual grant total

In 2013/14 the charity had an income of £1,900 and an expenditure of £1,600. The website notes that 'in 2014 a total of a £1,350 was awarded between 16 recipients'. We estimate that educational grants to individuals totalled about £350.

Applications

Application forms are available online or can be requested from the correspondent. They can be submitted online or via post, directly by the individual and/or can be supported by a relevant professional. Most recently the submission deadline was in October. Requests should include costings (total amount required, funds raised and funds promised). Previous beneficiaries may apply again. The charity will take into account that assistance has been given in the past.

Other information

Organisations are also supported. Social welfare grants are also given.

Erewash
Risley Educational Foundation

£14,000 (54 grants)

Correspondent: Margaret Giller, The Clerk to the Trustees, 27 The Chase, Little Eaton, Derby DE21 5AS (01332 883361; email: margaret@giller.eclipse. co.uk)

CC number: 702720

Eligibility

People under the age of 25 who are in further education and live in the parishes of Breaston, Church Wilne, Dale Abbey, Draycott, Hopwell, Risley, Sandiacre or Stanton-by-Dale.

Types of grants

Grants of about £250 are available to further education students towards the cost of books, equipment/instruments, travel for educational purposes, study of music and arts.

Annual grant total

In 2013/14 the foundation had assets of £777,500 and an income of £57,000. The total charitable expenditure reached £30,500, of which £14,000 was awarded in grants to 54 individuals.

Applications

Apply in writing to the correspondent. The trustees' annual report from 2013/14 also states that 'the charity advertises widely within the area of benefit to ensure that individuals are aware of the grants available'. According to our research, applications are normally considered on a quarterly basis.

Other information

The foundation also supports local schools allowing up to 5% of the annual income to be awarded to the Church of England Sunday schools and up to 25% to other local schools. The remainder is then allocated for grants to individuals.

In 2013/14 grants totalling £12,000 were made to seven schools for the instruction of their pupils in music and a total of £2,500 to five Sunday schools.

High Peak
The Bingham Trust

£19,500

Correspondent: Emma Marshall, Secretary, Unit 1, Tongue Lane Industrial Estate, Dew Pond Lane, Buxton SK17 7LN (01298 600591; email: binghamtrust@aol.com; website: www. binghamtrust.org.uk)

CC number: 287636

Eligibility

People in need, primarily those who live in Buxton, Derbyshire (SK17 postcode area). Most applicants from outside Buxton are rejected unless there is a Buxton connection.

Types of grants

One-off grants ranging from £200 to £1,500. Grants are made to individuals for a wide variety of needs, including further education. Grants made to individuals are usually by cheque made out to the provider of the service or goods.

Annual grant total

In 2013/14 the trust had assets of £4.45 million and an income of £191,000. During the year a total of 130 organisations and individuals were supported totalling £174,000. The amount of grants given to individuals totalled £39,000. There was no breakdown of how much was awarded in educational/social welfare grants and we estimate the total amount of educational grants to be around £19,500.

Exclusions

The trust cannot provide:

- Support for higher educational purposes – university and college level
- Grants to repay existing debts
- Grants for businesses, profit-making organisations (even if they are not actually making a profit)

In exceptional circumstances assistance may be given for people in higher education who suffer from disabilities for the purchase of specialised equipment.

Applications

Application forms are available from the website or may be requested from the correspondent and returned via post or email (with no additional attachments). Appeals by letter are also accepted but may take longer to proceed. The trust states that 'usually, applications look better if they are posted or sent by email as a letter attachment'. Individuals, not applying via an organisation or charity, must send a supporting letter from a third party, such as social worker, doctor, minister, charity or community organisation which knows their circumstances. Applications are considered during the first two weeks of January, April, July and October and should be received before the end of the previous month.

Queries can be made to the correspondent via the email address given or on 07966 378 546.

The trust's website states: 'All applications are acknowledged either by letter or email. If you do not receive an acknowledgment, you can assume that we have not received your application. If you do not hear from us within one month of our meeting, you can assume that your application has not been funded.'

Other information

The trust gives primarily to organisations. Special consideration is given to those involved with research into arthritis, anywhere within Britain.

Leicestershire
Charnwood
The Dawson and Fowler Foundation

£38,000

Correspondent: Lesley Cutler, Clerk to the Trustees, PO Box 73, Loughborough, Leicestershire LE11 0GA (07765 934117; email: dawsonfowler@fsmail.net)

CC number: 527867

Eligibility

Young people between the ages of 11 and 25 who have lived in the borough of Loughborough (including Hathern), normally for at least three years.

Types of grants

The foundation offers:

- School uniform grants – pupils in Years 7, 8, 9, 10 and 11 can apply once in every 12 months for assistance with the purchase of school uniform. Grants currently have a maximum value of £100

- 'Lump sums' are made available to the local senior schools and academies, to be used at the discretion of the headteachers to support pupils known to be in genuine need with the purchase of text books and equipment (including musical instruments) for their exclusive use. Help may also be given for educational visits, residential courses, conference attendance and interview expenses. The maximum grant per individual should not exceed £200 (for the Endowed Schools: £500) although this limit may be exceeded with the permission of the trustees
- Scholarships to the endowed schools – a grant for fees of £500 per term for one student was committed until 2015
- Other Grants – the trustees consider applications from students in higher education, apprentices, young people involved in scouting, guiding, sports activities, the Duke of Edinburgh Award Scheme, etc. in the usual way and make awards as they deem appropriate. Where these are school based, they may be funded from the lump sum. Young people who join voluntary organisations that require a uniform may also be helped with its provision

Annual grant total

In 2014 the foundation had assets of £732,000 and an income of £50,000. Grants to schools, academies and individuals totalled over £38,000 and can be broken down as follows:

Uniform grants	£31,000
Grants to state schools	£5,000
Scholarships and grants (endowed schools)	£1,500
Other grants for course	£1,000

Exclusions

Grants are not normally given for accommodation, subsistence, day-to-day travelling costs, tuition, examination fees or childcare costs. Applications from groups of students or classes of pupils cannot be considered.

Applications

Application forms are available from the correspondent or can be asked for at the applicant's school office. The trustees meet quarterly and applications should be made in advance to avoid disappointment. The school uniform sub-committee normally considers uniform applications in July or August prior to the start of the academic year.

Other information

The trustees have previously stated that they would like to encourage independent applications.

Mountsorrel Educational Fund

£71,000 (140 grants)

Correspondent: Paul Blakemore, Clerk to the Trustees, c/o KDB Accountants and Consultants Ltd, 21 Hollytree Close, Hoton, Loughborough LE12 5SE (01509 889369; email: paulblakemore@hotmail.co.uk; website: www.mountsorrelunitedcharities.com)

CC number: 527912

Eligibility

People under the age of 25 who have been (or whose parent/guardian has been) resident in the parish of Mountsorrel for at least a year or who are current or former pupils of Christ Church and St Peter's Church of England School.

Types of grants

One-off and recurrent grants in the range of £100–£1,000 towards general education and training needs, including courses, books, equipment, specialist clothing, music tuition, educational visits and training schemes or apprenticeships.

Annual grant total

In 2014 the fund had assets of £129,000 and an income of £130,500 (the fund's income is provided by Mountsorrel United Charities). The amount of grants given to individuals totalled around £71,000, broken down as follows:

Higher education and training	66	£64,000
A-level college students	29	£4,500
Music	20	£2,800
Other	25	£2,100

Exclusions

Support is not normally available where assistance should be provided by the local authorities.

Applications

Application forms can be obtained by writing to the correspondent and providing an sae. The trustees meet twice a year, in May and November, but applications need to be received in the month preceding the meeting. Further guidelines can be obtained from the correspondent.

Other information

Grants are also made to Christ Church and St Peters Church of England School (£2,600 in 2014).

This is one of the two funds, together with Mountsorrel Relief in Need Charity (Charity Commission no. 217615), administered under the Mountsorrel United Charities (Charity Commission no. 1027652) name.

The Thomas Rawlins Educational Foundation

£1,300

Correspondent: Mrs Gill Bertinat, 21 Haddon Close, Syston, Leicester LE7 1HZ (01509622800)

CC number: 527858

Eligibility

People under the age of 25 living in Barrow upon Soar, Quorn, Woodhouse and Woodhouse Eaves only.

Types of grants

Our research shows that grants normally range from £50 up to £250. Support is given to school pupils to help with books, equipment, school uniform, maintenance or fees, but not other school clothing or educational outings; to students in further and higher education to help with books, equipment, instruments, study or travel abroad or fees, but not for student exchange or for foreign students studying in the UK; also to people starting work to help with the cost of books, equipment and instruments, travel and clothing.

Annual grant total

In 2013/14 the foundation had an income of £2,400 and an expenditure of £1,500. We estimate that grants totalled around £1,300.

Applications

Application forms can be requested from the correspondent and should be submitted directly by the individuals or their parents/guardians at any time.

Harborough

The Market Harborough and The Bowdens Charity

£45,500 (32 grants)

Correspondent: James Jacobs, Steward, 10 Fairfield Road, Market Harborough, Leicestershire LE16 9QQ (01858 419128; email: admin@mhbcharity.co.uk; website: www.mhbcharity.co.uk)

CC number: 1041958

Eligibility

Disadvantaged young adults entering further/higher education (including postgraduate courses) or undertaking vocational training or apprenticeships. Applicants should normally be aged between 19 and 30 and live within Market Harborough or immediately outside the area.

Types of grants

Grants of up to £5,000 are given towards fees and maintenance/living expenses. Associated equipment costs may also be covered.

Annual grant total

In 2014 the charity had assets of £17.6 million and an income of £645,500. Grants to individuals amounted to £680,500, of which £21,500 was given for relief-in-need purposes. Grants from the educational fund to 32 individuals totalled £45,500.

Applications

Application forms for different types of grants are available on the charity's website. Applications should be supported by two suitable referees such as employers, teachers or tutors. Applications for vocational and undergraduate support should normally be submitted by mid-April with interviews taking place in June.

Other information

Grants are also given to individuals for welfare purposes, to organisations, institutions and towards preservation of historic churches in the area.

The Marc Smith Educational Charity

£7,800

Correspondent: Diana Jones, Secretary, 21 Highcroft, Husbands Bosworth, Lutterworth, Leicestershire LE17 6LF (01858 880741; email: dianajones929@ gmail.com)

CC number: 1045965

Eligibility

People under the age of 25 who live or have attended school in the ancient parishes of Claybrooke Magna, Claybrooke Parva, Ullesthorpe or Wibtoft, or whose parents live there.

Types of grants

Support is given to people in further education or training and individuals undertaking apprenticeships or starting work. Schoolchildren moving from primary to upper schools can also be supported, usually for clothing.

Annual grant total

In 2014 the charity had an income of £8,100 and an expenditure of £15,900. We estimate the annual total amount of grants awarded to individuals to be around £7,800.

Applications

According to our research, applications from pupils should be made in writing to the correspondent and are normally considered in May. Applications from further education students are normally considered in September and should be submitted at a meeting, which applicants are invited to through local advertisements near to the time of the meeting.

Other information

Grants may also be made to local schools for educational projects and to organisations, depending on the income of the charity.

Hinckley and Bosworth

The Dixie Educational Foundation

£8,500

Correspondent: Peter Dungworth, Clerk to the Trustees, 31 Oakmeadow Way, Groby, Leicester LE6 0YN (0116 291 3683; email: pdungworth@hotmail.co. uk.)

CC number: 527837

Eligibility

People under the age of 25 who or whose parents/guardians live, or have lived for at least two years, in the civil parishes of Barlestone, Cadeby, Carlton, Market Bosworth, Osbaston, Shenton, Sutton Cheney or in such civil parishes situated in the former rural district of Market Bosworth, as the trustees decide.

Types of grants

One-off grants in the range of £75 and £150 are available to further education students for general educational costs, including clothing, books, equipment/ instruments, educational outings in the UK or study/travel abroad.

The foundation also awards Sir Wolstan Dixie Exhibition scholarship for pupils 'who demonstrate academic excellence in the examination for entry into Year 7 of The Dixie Grammar School'.

Annual grant total

In 2014/15 the foundation had assets of £90,500 and an income of £107,500. A total of £52,000 was spent in charitable activities, of which £8,500 was awarded in grants to individuals.

Applications

Apply in writing to the correspondent. Applications can be submitted directly by individuals, their parents/guardians, through a school/college or educational welfare agency, if applicable. Applicants should provide their date of birth, residential qualification, brief details of educational background and present course of study or apprenticeship together with details and estimates of the required assistance. Our research suggests that applications should be received at least two weeks before each of the termly meetings which are held on the first Friday of March, June and November.

For Sir Wolstan Dixie Exhibition Scholarship the parents of candidates should contact the bursar (01455292244 or bursar@dixie.org.uk) for a declaration of income form to access the eligibility and then apply as usual.

Other information

In 2014/15 a total of £43,000 was awarded to individuals.

Thomas Herbert Smith's Trust Fund

£5,100

Correspondent: Andrew York, 6 Magnolia Close, Leicester LE2 8PS (0116 283 5345; email: andrew_york@ sky.com)

CC number: 701694

Eligibility

People who live in the parish of Groby in Leicestershire.

Types of grants

One-off and recurrent grants, usually ranging from £100 to £500.

Annual grant total

In 2013/14 the fund had an income of £17,000 and a total expenditure of £20,500. Grants are made to individuals and organisations for both social welfare and educational purposes. We estimate that the amount of grants given to individuals for educational purposes totalled £5,100.

Applications

Applications can be made using a form available from the correspondent. They can be submitted either directly by the individual, or through a social worker, Citizens Advice or other third party, and are considered throughout the year.

Stoke Golding Boy's Charity

£6,500

Correspondent: Anthony John Smith, The Middle Stores, 2 Church Walks, Stoke Golding, Nuneaton CV136HB (01455 212489)

CC number: 519728

Eligibility

Young men and boys under the age of 25 who live in Stoke Golding. Our research suggests that some preference may be given to people with special educational needs.

Types of grants

One-off grants, generally of around £200, depending on availability and circumstances. Support is given for a wide range of educational needs.

Annual grant total

In 2014 the charity had an income of £6,000 and an expenditure of £7,000. The charity normally spends the whole amount of the annual interest in grants; therefore, we estimate that around £6,500 was available for distribution in grants to individuals.

Applications

Apply in writing to the correspondent. Applications can be made directly by the individual and normally should be submitted by mid-March for consideration in April.

Oadby and Wigston

The Oadby Educational Foundation

£25,500 (245 grants)

Correspondent: Rodney Waterfield, Hon. Secretary and Treasurer, 2 Silverton Road, Oadby, Leicester LE2 4NN (0116 271 4507; email: rodatthegnomehouse@talktalk.net)

CC number: 528000

Eligibility

People under the age of 25 who are in full-time education, have a home address within the former urban district of Oadby in Leicestershire, and were educated in the parish.

Types of grants

One-off grants, usually in the range of £50–£200, are made to schoolchildren, college students and undergraduates, including those towards uniforms/clothing, study/travel abroad and equipment/instruments. People of any age can receive one-off grants towards expeditions and voluntary work such as Operation Raleigh or voluntary service overseas.

Annual grant total

In 2014 the foundation had assets of £1.3 million and an income of £49,000. Grants totalled £56,000, of which £25,500 was given in grants to students. Organisations also received funding for educational and religious purposes.

Applications

Applications can be made on a form available from the correspondent. They should be submitted either through the individual's school, college or educational welfare agency, or directly by the individual.

Other information

Grants can also be made for social welfare purposes.

Northamp-tonshire

Arnold's Educational Foundation

£6,500

Correspondent: Jane Forsyth, Administrator, 4 Grange Park Court, Roman Way, Grange Park, Northampton NN4 5EA (01604 876697; email: meaton@wilsonbrowne.co.uk)

CC number: 310590

Eligibility

People in need who are under 25 and live in the parishes of Stony Stratford, Buckinghamshire; Nether Heyford, Upper Heyford, Stowe-Nine-Churches, Weedon Bec, Northamptonshire; and the ancient parish of St Giles, Northampton. Preference can be given to members of the Church of England.

Types of grants

One-off and recurrent grants for the study of music and the arts, as well as social and physical training. Grants are made: for schoolchildren towards the cost of clothing, books, educational outings, maintenance and school fees; towards the cost of books, fees/living expenses, travel exchange and study or travel abroad for students in further or higher education; and towards books, equipment/instruments, clothing and travel for people starting work. Grants range from £200 to £500.

Annual grant total

In 2014 the foundation had an income of £12,200 and an expenditure of £6,700. We estimate that grants were made totalling £6,500.

Applications

Application forms are available from the correspondent.

Church and Town Allotment Charities and others

£6,000

Correspondent: Anne Ireson, Administrator, Kettering Borough Council, Council Offices, Bowling Green Road, Kettering NN15 7QX (01536 534398; email: anneireson@kettering.gov.uk)

CC number: 207698

Eligibility

People in further/higher education who are over the age of 16 and live in Kettering or Barton Seagrave.

Types of grants

Financial support is available towards general educational needs, including books, equipment/instruments and other necessities. People in vocational training, people starting work, mature students and individuals with special educational needs can all be assisted.

Annual grant total

In 2012/13 the charity had an income of £14,800 and an expenditure of £12,200. We estimate the annual total amount of grants awarded to individuals for educational purposes to be around £6,000.

At the time of writing (October 2015) the information provided was the latest available.

Applications

Apply in writing to the correspondent. Applications can be made by individuals directly or through their parents/guardians, educational establishment or welfare agency, if applicable. Details of the applicant's financial situation should also be included. The trustees usually meet twice a year, in February and November.

Other information

Our previous research suggests that applications from mature students are encouraged.

Support is also given to the Kettering parish church and to local retired people who live alone to help with the cost of fuel in winter.

The Charity of Hervey and Elizabeth Ekins

£12,000

Correspondent: Richard Pestell, Correspondent, 41 Thorburn Road, Northampton NN3 3DA (01604 408712; email: pestells@btinternet.com)

CC number: 309858

Eligibility

People who have lived in the borough of Northampton or the parish of Great Doddington for no less than three years, attended a state school for no less than one year, and attended a Church of England church on a regular basis.

Preference will be given to boys and girls residing in the ecclesiastical parishes of St Peter, Weston Favell, St Peter and St Paul, Abington and Emmanuel, Northampton.

Types of grants

Grants are given to schoolchildren, students in further or higher education and to people starting work towards books, equipment and educational outings in the UK and overseas.

Grants are also given for music tuition fees. Preference is given to those entering the ministry of the Church of England.

Grants average around £200, but in exceptional circumstances can be for as much as £500. Other grants are given to a school for larger projects.

Annual grant total

In 2013/14 the charity had assets of £1 million and an income of £44,500. The amount of grants given to individuals totalled £12,000, with £8,000 awarded for further and higher education and £4,000 for music and residential activities.

Exclusions

Grants are not given for school fees.

Applications

Applications can be made in writing to the correspondent directly by the individual, including details of school and church attended.

Other information

Grants of £36,000 were made to churches and a commitment was made in the year to pay grants of £10,000 to each of the three parish churches for their work with young people in the preferred area of benefit in 2014/15.

The Horne Foundation

£181,000 (91 grants)

Correspondent: Ros Harwood, Trustee, PO Box 6165, Newbury RG14 9FY (email: hornefoundation@googlemail.com)

CC number: 283751

Eligibility

Higher education students in need who live in Northamptonshire.

Types of grants

The foundation awards bursaries to higher education students towards course fees, living expenses and other educational costs. Grants are of up to of £5,000.

Annual grant total

In 2013/14 the foundation had assets of £7.2 million, an income of £186,000 and an expenditure of £202,000. Grants to 91 individuals totalled £181,000.

Applications

Bursaries to schoolchildren are made on the recommendation from schools. If the applicant is at school, he or she should apply through the headteacher of the school. Students can apply to the foundation directly, in writing. Applications are considered twice a year.

Other information

The foundation also supports organisations towards educational projects that involve new buildings and through regular smaller donations to local projects in the Northampton and Oxfordshire area.

The trustees' policy is to distribute an amount approximately equal to the investment income received.

The Dorothy Johnson Charitable Trust

£28,000

Correspondent: Zinaida Silins, Clerk to the Trust, Hybank, 12 Old Road, Walgrave, Northampton NN6 9QW (01604 780662; email: zinaida@ zinaidasilins.com)

CC number: 298499

Eligibility

People under 25 who were born and are living, have lived or were educated at some time in Northamptonshire.

Types of grants

One-off and recurrent grants in the range of £100–£500. Grants are made to schoolchildren, college students, undergraduates, vocational students, postgraduates and people with special educational needs, towards clothing/ uniforms, fees, study/travel abroad, books, equipment/instruments, maintenance/living expenses and excursions.

Annual grant total

In 2013/14 the trust had an income of £18,500 and an expenditure of £28,500. Grants totalled approximately £28,000.

Applications

Apply in writing to the correspondent. Applications are considered three times a year.

Northamptonshire Community Foundation

£10,300 (26+ grants)

Correspondent: Victoria Miles, Chief Executive, 18 Albion Place, Northampton NN1 1UD (01604 230033; email: enquiries@ncf.uk.com; website: www.ncf.uk.com)

CC number: 1094646

Eligibility

▶ Northamptonshire Champions Fund – people under the age of 25 (under the age of 35 for people with disability) who are competing/have a potential to compete within 18 months for England or Great Britain at regional or, ideally, national level. Applicants must live, train, coach or officiate in Northamptonshire. Performers from all sports recognised by Sport England (an extensive list is available online) are assisted. Athletes with disabilities over the age of 35 can still apply if they can demonstrate that they have taken up the sport for which they are applying for, within the last three years

▶ Arts and Music Fund – young people wishing to take part in Royal and Derngate Youth Theatre

Types of grants

Two funds offer help to individuals:

▶ Northamptonshire Champions Fund – bursaries are available to 'Northamptonshire's emerging sports stars' to help with the costs of sports-based activities, including travel expenses, clothing, equipment and training/coaching. Grants range between £150 and £400 in the first year and up to a maximum of £400 in subsequent years. Funding can be used to help applicants to remain in education if they are experiencing financial difficulties and to athletes on a low income generally or to athletes with disabilities who require an assister or carer in order to compete

▶ Arts and Music Fund – bursaries of up to £165 to contribute towards the cost of fees

Annual grant total

In 2013/14 the foundation had assets of £3.5 million, an income of £1.4 million and a total expenditure of £706,000. Northamptonshire Champions Fund made 26 awards totalling £8,900 and the Arts and Music Fund gave bursaries totalling £1,400.

Exclusions

Overseas travel or expeditions are not supported and help is not available where statutory or public funding should be provided.

Applications

Application forms together with detailed guidelines can be found on the foundation's website and should be submitted in **two copies,** one electronically and one by post. Applications can be made at any time and should be accompanied by an independent reference for Northamptonshire Champions Fund and an academic reference for Arts and Music Fund.

The foundation invites potential applicants to approach its staff members for an informal advice or feedback on applications prior to final submission. Applicants are reminded that the funds may open and close at short notice and are asked to check the website for any changes before applying.

Other information

The foundation manages a number of funds the majority of which are supporting organisations.

The Wilson Foundation

£13,500 (38 grants)

Correspondent: Pollyanna Wilson, Trustee, The Maltings, Tithe Farm, Moulton Road, Holcot, Northamptonshire NN6 9SH (01604 782240; fax: 01604 782241; email: polly@tithefarm.com; website: www.thewilsonfoundation.co.uk)

CC number: 1074414

Eligibility

Young people (normally 10 to 21 years of age) who were born or have lived in Northamptonshire for at least a year, particularly those who are disadvantaged or underprivileged.

Types of grants

Scholarships can be given for trips and expeditions or Outward Bound courses which help build the individual's character and can make a lasting impact on his/her life. Support can also be given towards educational necessities, such as school uniforms and clothing, equipment or books.

Grants can range from £100 to about £3,000 with an average grant of around £200.

Annual grant total

In 2013/14 the foundation had assets of £5.3 million, an income of £110,000 and a total charitable expenditure of £178,500. During the year £13,500 was awarded in grants to 38 individuals.

Applications

Application forms can be downloaded from the foundation's website and once completed should be sent to the correspondent. At least one reference must be supplied. The trustees meet at least twice a year.

Northampton

Beckett's and Sergeant's Educational Foundation

£118,000 (150 grants)

Correspondent: Angela Moon, Administrator, Hewitsons LLP, Elgin House, Billing Road, Northampton NN1 5AU (01604 233233; fax: 01604 627941; email: angelamoon@hewitsons.com)

CC number: 309766

Eligibility

People under the age of 25 who either live in the borough of Northampton, or are attending/have attended for at least two years All Saints CEVA Primary School, or who are attending schools or further/higher education institutions within the borough.

The trustees have discretion to award grants to further/higher education students ordinarily resident in but undertaking courses beyond the borough of Northampton.

Types of grants

Grants are of up to £1,000 and can be given for a wide range of educational and training purposes, including educational trips, books, equipment, study of music or other arts and supplementing existing grants.

Annual grant total

In 2014 the foundation had assets of £3 million, an income of £190,000 and gave grants to 150 individuals totalling £118,000.

Applications

Application forms can be requested from the correspondent in writing. Awards are normally considered four times a year.

Other information

In 2014 a total of £6,000 was awarded to institutions.

Blue Coat Educational Charity

£7,000

Correspondent: Richard Pestell, Trustee, 41 Thorburn Road, Northampton NN3 3DA (01604 401237; email: pestells@btinternet.com)

CC number: 309764

Eligibility

Schoolchildren, students and people entering work who are under the age of 25 and live in the borough of Northampton.

Types of grants

One-off and recurrent grants for general educational purposes, including the costs of clothing, educational outings, books, fees, study/travel abroad or student exchange, equipment/instruments and tools. Grants can reach up to £500 per individual.

Annual grant total

In 2014/15 the charity had an income of £9,000 and an expenditure of £15,000. It also supports local schools; therefore, we estimate that the total amount of grants awarded to individuals was around £7,000.

Exclusions

Grants are not available to mature students or overseas students studying in Britain.

Applications

Apply in writing to the correspondent. Our research suggests that applications are usually considered in February, July and November.

Other information

Grants are also made to the Church of England schools in Northampton.

Sir Thomas White's Northampton Charity

£80,000

Correspondent: Angela Moon, Charities Manager, Hewitsons LLP, Elgin House, Billing Road, Northampton NN1 5AU (01604 233233; fax: 01604 627941; email: angelamoon@hewitsons.com)

CC number: 201486

Eligibility

Younger people who live within the extended borough of Northampton.

Types of grants

The charity gives assistance in two ways:

- Grants are made to young people between the ages of 16 and 25 to assist with their education
- Interest-free loans are made to people between the ages of 21 and 34

The charity was originally set up for the provision of tools for people setting up in a trade or profession.

Annual grant total

In 2014 the charity had assets of almost £3.5 million and an income of £265,500. During the year, £80,000 was awarded in grants to students. Four loans were made to individuals amounting to £12,500.

Applications

Application forms can be requested in November, following a public notice advertising the grants.

Other information

The charity was previously called Sir Thomas White's Loan Fund.

South Northamptonshire

The Brackley United Feoffee Charity

£9,200

Correspondent: Irene Bennett, 24 Broad Lane, Evenley, Brackley NN13 5SF (01280 703904; email: caryl.billingham@tesco.net)

CC number: 238067

Eligibility

People under the age of 25 who live in the ecclesiastical parish of Brackley (which consists of the town of Brackley and the village of Halse only).

Types of grants

One-off grants, usually in the range of £100–£1,000. Grants made during 2013/14 included: assistance with the travel costs of young people going on expeditions overseas; assistance to families who are in need towards the travel costs for their children to attend school trips in the UK and Europe; assistance with the purchase of school uniforms for families on low incomes.

Annual grant total

In 2013/14 the charity had an income of £33,500 and a total expenditure of £31,500. Grants from the educational fund amounted to £9,200.

Applications

Applications can be made in writing to the correspondent either directly by the individual or through the individual's school, college or educational welfare agency. The trustees meet every three to four months.

Other information

The charity awards grants to individuals and organisations for both educational and social welfare purposes.

Middleton Cheney United Charities

£2,200

Correspondent: Linda Harvey, Administrator, 1 The Avenue, Middleton Cheney, Banbury, Oxfordshire OX17 2PE (01295712650)

CC number: 202511

Eligibility

People who live in Middleton Cheney and are in need.

Types of grants

Our research suggests that one-off grants are available to schoolchildren for equipment/instruments and to students in higher/further education (including mature students) for books and study or travel abroad. Awards are in the range of £100 to £200.

Annual grant total

In 2014 the charity had an income of £2,500 and an expenditure of £4,500. We estimate that educational support to individuals totalled around £2,200.

Applications

Apply in writing to the correspondent. Applications can be submitted directly by the individual and are considered four times a year.

Other information

Support may also be given to organisations.

Nottingham-shire

Arnold Educational Foundation

£16,000

Correspondent: Brian West, Administrator, 73 Arnot Hill Road, Arnold, Nottingham NG5 6LN (0115 920 6656; email: b.west909@btinternet.com; website: stmarysarnold.org.uk/arnold_parochial_charities.html)

CC number: 528191

Eligibility

People under the age of 25 who/whose parents live in the ancient parish of Arnold (which includes Daybrook and Woodthorpe) and who require financial assistance.

Types of grants

Mainly further/higher education students can be assisted with the cost of books, equipment/instruments, course fees or educational expeditions. According to our research, schoolchildren may only be assisted in special circumstances towards the cost of books, clothing or other essentials.

Annual grant total

In 2013/14 the foundation had an income of £16,000 and an expenditure of £16,500. We estimate the annual total amount of grants awarded to be around £16,000.

Applications

Application forms can be found on the St Mary's Arnold website or requested from the correspondent. The receipts for purchased items must be included.

Bingham United Charities 2006

£2,000

Correspondent: Susan Lockwood, 23 Douglas Road, Bingham, Nottingham NG13 8EL (01949 875453; email: lockwoodsue79@gmail.com)

CC number: 213913

Eligibility

People in need who live in the parish of Bingham.

Types of grants

Grants can be given for a wide range of purposes.

Annual grant total

In 2014/15 the charity had an income of £9,400 and a total expenditure of £8,300. Grants can be made to individuals and organisations for both educational and social welfare purposes. We estimate that educational grants to individuals totalled £2,000.

Applications

Application forms are available from the secretary. Those applications which are supported by a professional, medical, or social care agency can often be dealt with more quickly.

Mansfield

Faith Clerkson's Exhibition Foundation

£7,500

Correspondent: Mr C. McKay, 68 Hillside Road, Beeston, Nottingham NG9 3AY (07771 978622; email: colinp.mckay@btinternet.com)

CC number: 528240

Eligibility

People going to university or entering further education who have lived in the borough Mansfield or the urban district of Mansfield Woodhouse for at least two years.

Types of grants

Small grants are available to help higher/further education students and others leaving school with general educational costs, including books, equipment, clothing and travel.

Annual grant total

In 2013/14 the foundation had an income of £3,100 and a total expenditure of £7,700. We estimate the annual total amount of grants awarded to be around £7,500.

Exclusions

According to our research, grants are not available towards course fees.

Applications

Apply in writing to the correspondent. The trustees normally meet in June and October.

Warsop United Charities

£1,600

Correspondent: Jean Simmons, Trustee, Newquay, Clumber Street, Warsop, Mansfield, Nottinghamshire NG20 0LX

CC number: 224821

Eligibility

People in need who live in the urban district of Warsop (Warsop, Church Warsop, Warsop Vale, Meden Vale, Spion Kop and Sookholme).

Types of grants

Grants for specific items to people at school, college or university.

Annual grant total

In 2014 the charity had an income of £6,000 and a total expenditure of nearly £7,000. We estimate that the amount of grants given to individuals for educational purposes totalled around £1,600.

Applications

Applications may be made in writing to the correspondent. The trustees meet three or four times a year.

Other information

Grants are also made for relief-in-need purposes. Both individuals and organisations can be supported.

Newark and Sherwood

The John and Nellie Brown Farnsfield Trust

£6,200

Correspondent: Alan Dodd, Trustee, Roan House, Crabnook Lane, Farnsfield, Newark NG22 8JY (01623 882574; email: alan@alandodd.force9.co.uk)

CC number: 1078367

Eligibility

People in need who live in Farnsfield in Nottinghamshire and the surrounding area.

Types of grants

Grants are given according to need.

Annual grant total

In 2013/14 the trust had an income of £5,000 and a total expenditure of £26,000. Grants are made to individuals and organisations for both educational

and social welfare purposes. We estimate that educational grants to individuals totalled £6,200.

Applications

Apply in writing to the correspondent.

Nottingham

Audrey Harrison Heron Memorial Fund

£3,500

Correspondent: NatWest Trust Services, Ground Floor, Eastwood House, Glebe Road, Chelmsford CM1 1RS (01245 292445; email: nwb.charities@natwest. com)

CC number: 504494

Eligibility

Girls and women under the age of 25 living in the city of Nottingham.

Types of grants

One-off and recurrent grants between £50 and £2,000 to help with the cost of books, equipment/instruments, clothing, travel in the UK and overseas, also school, college or university fees.

Annual grant total

In 2014/15 the fund had an income of £5,000 and an expenditure of £4,000. We estimate the annual total amount of grants awarded to be around £3,500.

Applications

Application forms can be requested from the correspondent. Applications can be submitted either directly by the individual or through a third party, such as school/college/educational welfare agency, if applicable. Our research shows that applications are considered all year round.

Other information

Grants can also be awarded to societies or charitable organisations which share the fund's objectives.

Nottingham Gordon Memorial Trust for Boys and Girls

£12,500

Correspondent: Anna Chandler, Charity Administrator, Cumberland Court, 80 Mount Street, Nottingham NG1 6HH (0115 901 5562; email: anna.chandler@ freeths.co.uk)

CC number: 212536

Eligibility

Children and young people under the age of 25 who are in need, hardship or distress and live in Nottingham or the

area immediately around the city. Preference can be given to individuals who are of the former Nottingham Gordon Memorial Home for Destitute Working Boys.

Types of grants

Grants are given to schoolchildren and further/higher education students. Assistance is awarded towards general education and training needs, books, equipment/instruments, tools, maintenance/living expenses, educational outings in the UK and study/travel abroad and school uniforms or other clothing.

Annual grant total

In 2014 the trust had assets of £1.2 million and an income of £47,500. A total of £35,500 was awarded to individuals. The total amount of grants included £12,000 in 'educational grants to assist a number of students with the cost of education', £6,200 'to individuals and organisations taking part in trips both in the UK and overseas', £5,400 ' to organisations in order to assist a number of individuals' and £2,800 'was awarded to Nottingham Scout Association which was distributed to 14 Explorer Scouts who had been selected to take part in the World Scout Jamboree in Japan'. We estimate that about £12,500 was given for educational purposes.

Applications

Application forms are available from the correspondent. They can be submitted through the individual's school, college, educational welfare agency, a health visitor, social worker, probation officer or similar professional. Our research suggests that individuals, supported by a reference from their school/college, can also apply directly. The trustees meet twice a year, although applications can be considered all year round.

Other information

The trust also supports organisations in the Nottingham area (£7,600 in 2014) and provides relief-in-need support for individuals.

Peveril Exhibition Endowment

£4,000

Correspondent: The Clerk to the Trustees, 5 New Road, Burton Lazars, Melton Mowbray, Leicestershire LE14 2UU (01636813532; email: peverilfund@gmail.com; website: www. peveril.org.uk)

CC number: 528242

Eligibility

Children and young people aged between 11 and 25 who/whose parents have lived in Nottingham for at least one year and who are attending, or about to attend, secondary or further education. Preference is given to people who permanently reside in Nottingham rather than on temporary or transitional basis.

Types of grants

One-off and recurrent grants are available to secondary school pupils and further/higher education students. Awards are given for general educational expenses and can reach up to £1,000.

Annual grant total

In 2014/15 the charity had an income of £6,900 and an expenditure of £4,200. We estimate that around £4,000 was given in grants to individuals.

Applications

Application forms can be requested from the correspondent and can be submitted at any time for consideration within the following six weeks. Academic references or financial details of the family may be requested and taken into account.

Rushcliffe

The Bingham Trust Scheme

£1,000

Correspondent: Gillian Bailey, Trustee, 20 Tithby Road, Bingham, Nottingham NG13 8GN (01949 838673; email: katey. cox@hemscott.net)

CC number: 513436

Eligibility

People under the age of 21 living in Bingham.

Types of grants

Grants are made in the range of £50 and £150 to help with expenses incurred in the course of education, religious and physical activities and so on. They are made in January and early July each year.

Annual grant total

In 2013/14 the charity had an income of £1,200 and a total expenditure of £1,300. Grants would seem to be made mainly for educational purposes.

Applications

Application forms are available from the correspondent. They can be submitted directly by the individual or a family member by 30 April and 31 October each year.

Other information

The charity's record on the Charity Commission's website notes that any charitable purpose can be supported, although educational support seems to be the main concern.

Rutland

The Rutland Trust

£3,500

Correspondent: Richard Adams, Clerk, 35 Trent Road, Oakham, Rutland LE15 6HE (01572 756706; email: adams@apair.wanadoo.co.uk)

CC number: 517175

Eligibility

People, usually under the age of 35, who are in need and live in Rutland. Applicants may be at any level or stage of their education.

Types of grants

One-off grants, usually ranging between £50 and £400, are made. There are no restrictions on how the grants may be spent. In the past, grants have been made towards music and school trips for needy young people, for European exchange trips, and for young people to take part in educational, missionary and life-experience programmes overseas. Grants may also be spent on books, equipment, fees, bursaries, fellowships and study visits.

Annual grant total

In 2013 the trust had an income of £20,000 and a total expenditure of £14,000. Grants are made for social welfare and educational purposes and to organisations. We estimate that grants awarded to individuals for educational purposes totalled around £3,500.

At the time of writing (November 2015) this was the most recent financial information available for the trust.

Applications

Our research suggests that an initial telephone call is recommended.

West Midlands

General

Baylies' Educational Foundation

£29,000 (Up to 100 grants)

Correspondent: David Hughes, Clerk to the Trustees, 53 The Broadway, Dudley, West Midlands DY1 4AP (01384 259277; email: bayliesfoundation@hotmail.co.uk; website: www.dudleyrotary.org.uk/baylies.html)

CC number: 527118

Eligibility

People under the age of 25 living in the area of Dudley Metropolitan Borough Council who are in need. It is necessary to demonstrate genuine financial need for a specific purpose and be unable to secure support from other sources.

Types of grants

One-off grants, usually around £200–£300, can be given to help with the university/college fees and course-related necessities (books, equipment/instruments, tools, clothing), travel expenses, educational trips abroad or in the UK, school uniforms, towards music and drama lessons or sports activities, also to unemployed people for retraining or individuals facing family difficulties to help them continue their education.

Annual grant total

In 2013/14 the foundation had assets of £1.2 million and an income of £44,000. A total of around £29,000 was awarded in grants to individuals. The trust states that during a typical year up to 100 grants are made.

Applications

Application forms are available on the foundation's website or can be requested from the correspondent.

Other information

Local schools can also be supported.

The Careswell Foundation

£9,500

Correspondent: Bridget Marshall, Administrator, 24 The Crescent, Town Walls, Shrewsbury SY1 1TJ (01743 351332; email: terri.gill@lindermyers.co.uk)

CC number: 528393

Eligibility

People under the age of 25 who live in Shropshire, the parish of Bobbington or Staffordshire and have attended any of the following schools: Adam's Grammar School (Newport), Bridgnorth Endowed School, Idsall School (Shifnal), Shrewsbury School, Thomas Adam's School (Wem) and secondary education schools for the Donnington area.

Types of grants

Grants, usually of up to about £150, are available to further/higher education students to assist with general educational expenses, including books, equipment and other necessities.

Annual grant total

In 2013/14 the foundation had an income of £11,500 and a total expenditure of £10,000. We estimate the annual total amount of grants awarded to be around £9,500.

Applications

Apply in writing to the correspondent. Our research suggests that applications should be submitted by September for consideration in October.

The W. E. Dunn Trust

£3,600 (15 grants)

Correspondent: David Corney, Chair, The Trust Office, 30 Bentley Heath Cottages, Tilehouse Green Lane, Knowle, Solihull B93 9EL (01564 773407; email: wedunn@tiscali.co.uk)

CC number: 219418

Eligibility

People who live in the West Midlands who wish to further their education, but who have special difficulties which prevent them from doing so. These can include, for example, prisoners who are using education as part of their rehabilitation, or students who have physical disabilities or who have lived through particularly difficult circumstances.

Types of grants

One-off grants usually ranging from £50 to £200.

Annual grant total

In 2013/14 the trust had assets of £4.9 million and an income of £173,500. Individuals received a total of £65,000 in 383 grants, including £3,600 paid in 15 awards for educational purposes. They were distributed as follows:

Clothing and furniture	185	£26,500
Domestic equipment	110	£22,000
Social and welfare	28	£6,000
Radio, TV and licences	40	£5,800
Education	15	£3,600
Convalescence and holidays	5	£1,000

A further £105,500 was paid in 154 grants to organisations.

Exclusions

Grants are not made to settle or reduce debts already incurred.

Applications

Apply in writing to the correspondent. Applications for educational grants from mature students should be submitted directly by the individual and other applications should be submitted through the individual's parent/guardian or school/college/educational welfare agency. They are considered two or three times a month depending on the number of applications.

The Jarvis Educational Foundation

£0

Correspondent: Rachel Jones, Correspondent, Flintsham Court, Titley, Kington HR3 3RG (07929650290)

CC number: 526881

Eligibility

People who are under the age of 25 and live the county of Hereford and Worcester, especially parishes of Staunton-on-Wye, Bredwardine and Letton.

Types of grants

In the past one-off grants ranging from £100 to £1,000 were available:

▶ To individuals at secondary school, university or college where education authority support is not available
▶ To provide outfits, clothing, tools, instruments or books to help people enter a trade, profession or calling on leaving education
▶ To enable such people to travel to pursue their education

Annual grant total

In 2014 the foundation had assets of £933,500 and an income of £28,500. Grants are not currently made – see 'Other information'.

Applications

Normally applications may be made in writing to the correspondent for consideration at any time.

Other information

The foundation also owns land and property, which are used for the purpose of a voluntary school.

Note the following stated in the annual report for 2014:

> Because of the uncertainty of the demands on the Charity with regards to selling of the old school building, grants are not being made. It is the Governors' intention to review and re-state their policy and practice on grant making once the above events are complete and the long-term financial position of the trust is clear.

It is further explained: 'In the long-term the aim is to hold the permanent endowment entirely in a broad range of investments in order to pursue the Foundation's original aim of dispensing educational and training grants.'

The James Frederick and Ethel Anne Measures Charity

£5,800

Correspondent: Laura Reid, Clerk to the Trustees, EFG Harris Allday, 33 Great Charles Street, Birmingham B3 3JN (0121 214 2340)

CC number: 266054

Eligibility

The following criteria apply:

▶ Applicants must usually originate in the West Midlands
▶ Applicants must show evidence of self-help in their application
▶ Trustees have a preference for disadvantaged people
▶ Trustees have a dislike for applications from students who have a full local authority grant and want finance for a different course or study
▶ Trustees favour grants towards the cost of equipment
▶ Applications by individuals in cases of hardship will not usually be considered unless sponsored by a local authority, health professional or other welfare agency

Types of grants

One-off or recurrent grants, usually between £50 and £500.

Annual grant total

In 2013/14 the charity had assets of £1.1 million and an income of £31,000. A total of 37 grants were made, amounting to £23,000. The charity gives to individuals and organisations for both social welfare and educational purposes. We estimate that the amount of grants given to individuals for educational purposes totalled £5,800.

Applications

Applications should be made in writing to the correspondent. No reply is given to unsuccessful applicants unless an sae is enclosed.

Perkin's Educational Foundation

£5,000

Correspondent: The Clerk to the Governors, c/o Lodders Solicitors LLP, 10 Elm Court, Arden Street, Stratford-upon-Avon, Warwickshire CV37 6PA (01789 293259; website: www.williamperkinscharity.org)

CC number: 528678

Eligibility

People aged 16 to 24 who have been living in Bidford-on-Avon, Broom, Cleeve Prior, Harvington or Salford Priors for at least two years immediately prior to their application.

Types of grants

Grants are mainly given to people entering further/higher education and to individuals undertaking vocational training or apprenticeships. Help is available towards the cost of books, equipment/instruments, clothing, other necessities, also fees, living expenses, study or travel abroad. Awards are usually of around £150–£200.

Annual grant total

In 2014 the foundation had an income of £15,000 and a total expenditure of £9,000. We estimate that the amount of grants given to individuals totalled around £5,000.

Exclusions

Awards are not usually made to students under the age of 18 doing GCSE or A-level courses, or to candidates who have reached the age of 25.

Applications

Application forms can be requested in writing from the correspondent or downloaded from the foundation's website. Applications must be signed by the applicant personally and first time applicants should provide a statement of recommendation from their headteacher, college principal or employer. Completed forms should be returned to the clerk by 15 October. Late submissions are not accepted.

The Perry Family Charitable Trust

£10,000

Correspondent: Sir Michael Perry, Trustee, Bridges Stone Mill, Alfrick Pound, Worcester WR6 5HR (01886 833290; email: perrytrust@aol.com)

CC number: 1094675

Eligibility

People in need under the age of 25 whose parents or guardians have been resident in the West Midlands for not less than three years. People starting work/entering a trade can be supported.

Types of grants

Small grants may be awarded towards travel for educational purposes in the UK or overseas, clothing, instruments, tools, books and other essentials.

Annual grant total

In 2013/14 the trust had an income of £33,000 and a total expenditure of £40,000. We estimate that the amount of grants given to individuals for educational purposes totalled around £10,000.

Applications

Apply in writing to the correspondent.

Other information

The trust also supports organisations and aims to address welfare needs of people with disabilities, the elderly, those in poor health, or suffering from poverty.

The George and Thomas Henry Salter Trust

£13,700

Correspondent: Mrs J. Styler, Lombard House, Cronehill's Linkway, West Bromwich, West Midlands B70 7PL (0121 553 3286)

CC number: 216503

Eligibility

Students in further or higher education who are in need and resident in the borough of Sandwell.

Types of grants

Grants usually range between £100 and £1,000 and are given to help students pursue their education, including general, professional, vocational or technical training, in the UK and abroad.

Annual grant total

In 2013 the trust had assets of £1.5 million and an income of £35,000. Grants amounted to £26,000, of which £11,400 was given to 15 organisations and 27 individuals for relief-in-need purposes. Education grants to local individuals at college and university totalled £13,700.

At the time of writing (November 2015) these were the most recent accounts available for the trust.

Applications

Our research indicates that individuals should initially contact the correspondent by letter. Applicants must provide full written details of their circumstances and study courses. The trustees meet regularly and will occasionally interview applicants.

The Anthony and Gwendoline Wylde Memorial Charity

£2,100

Correspondent: Kirsty McEwen, Clerk to the Trustees, c/o Higgs and Sons Solicitors, 3 Waterfront Business Park, Dudley Road, Brierley Hill, West Midlands DY5 1LX (01384327322; email: kirsty.mcewen@higgsandsons.co.uk; website: www.wyldecharity.weebly.com)

CC number: 700239

Eligibility

People in need in the areas of Dudley and Staffordshire, with a preference for residents of Stourbridge (West Midlands) and Kinver (Staffordshire) – area defined by the DY7 and DY8 postcodes.

Types of grants

Our research suggests that one-off grants, generally in the range of £50–£500, are given to college students and undergraduates for clothing, fees, books, equipment/instruments, maintenance/living expenses, voluntary work overseas and excursions.

Annual grant total

In 2013/14 the charity had assets of £876,000 and an income of £47,500. Grants were made totalling £30,500 and consisted of 25 awards to organisations totalling £26,000 and 18 awards to individuals totalling £4,300. We estimate that the amount of grants given to individuals for educational purposes totalled about £2,100.

Exclusions

The website states that 'grants are not normally made to other grant giving organisations'. Applications from areas outside the beneficial area may only be considered in exceptional circumstances. Support is not given where statutory help should be sought, towards bills or debts.

Applications

Applications should be made online on an appropriate form on the charity's website, but may also be submitted via post. Small grants (up to £750) can be dealt with quickly while larger awards (over £750) can only be approved at the trustees' meetings, which are held twice a year. There are separate forms. You will need to submit supporting documentation – a copy of a letter or email from the school/college/university, confirming the applicant is due to take a course or a copy of the course details showing the student's name (a letter addressed to the applicant is sufficient).

Other information

The charity was created by a trust deed dated 6 April 1988, in memory of Anthony and Gwendoline Wylde. It awards grants for educational and general welfare needs, and to local organisations.

The charity's website notes: 'Typically, a significant proportion of the small grants will be from individuals, and for educational purposes, and the larger grants tend to be from local organisations, although every application is considered on its merit.'

Hereford-shire

Hereford Municipal Charities

£1,500

Correspondent: Clerk to the Trustees, 147 St Owen Street, Hereford HR1 2JR (01432 354002; email: herefordmunicipal@btconnect.com)

CC number: 218738

Eligibility

People in need who live in the city of Hereford.

Types of grants

One-off grants of up to £200. Grants are given to help with the cost of education and starting work.

Annual grant total

In 2014 the charity had an income of £332,000 and a total expenditure of £252,000. At the time of writing (September 2015) the latest accounts were not available to view on the Charity Commission's website. A lot of the charity's expenditure is allocated to the running of its almshouses. In the past, grants to individuals have totalled about £32,500 on average with educational support totalling around £1,500.

Exclusions

Debts or nursery fees.

Applications

Application forms are available from the correspondent and should be submitted directly by the individual or through a relevant third party. Applications are considered five times a year but can be authorised within meetings if they are very urgent. Applicants are normally interviewed.

Other information

The charity also offers almshouse accommodation. There are two separate funds (eleemosynary and educational) administered by the Grants Committee.

The Hereford Society for Aiding the Industrious

£2,200

Correspondent: Sally Robertson, Secretary, 18 Venns Close, Bath Street, Hereford HR1 2HH (01432 274014 – Thursdays only; email: hsaialms@ talktalkbusiness.net)

CC number: 212220

Eligibility

People in need who live in Herefordshire, with preference for Hereford City and its immediate environs. Applicants may be undertaking primary, secondary, further or higher education, non-vocational training or vocational training or retraining, in most subjects.

Types of grants

Normally one-off grants ranging between £50 and £1,000 and occasionally interest-free loans. Grants can be made towards: schoolchildren for educational outings; people starting work towards books and equipment/instruments; students in further/higher education towards books, fees and living expenses; and mature students towards books, travel, fees and childcare.

Annual grant total

In 2013/14 the charity had assets of £1 million and an income of £131,000. Grants are given to individuals and organisations for both social welfare and educational purposes. During the year, grants to individuals totalled £4,500. We estimate that educational grants to individuals amounted to £2,200.

An additional £7,800 was given to organisations.

Exclusions

Grants are rarely given towards gap year travel.

Applications

Apply in writing to the correspondent. If eligible, an application form will be sent and the applicant will probably be asked to attend an interview (between 2.00pm and 4.00pm on Thursday). Grants are rarely given directly to the applicant; instead they are given to the bookseller, college and so on. The charity has stated that applications should be precise and honest. Applications are considered every month.

Other information

The charity's main areas of activity are grants and loans to individuals and maintaining almshouses. Donations are also given to Herefordshire charities for specific projects rather than for running costs.

The Herefordshire Community Foundation (known as Hereford-shire Foundation)

£2,500

Correspondent: Dave Barclay, Director, The Fred Bulmer Centre, Wall Street, Hereford HR4 9HP (01432 272550; email: info@herefordshirefoundation.org; website: www.herefordshirefoundation.org)

CC number: 1094935

Eligibility

People who are in need and live in Herefordshire.

Types of grants

One-off and recurrent grants are given according to need.

Annual grant total

In 2013/14 the foundation had assets of £3.4 million and an income of £1.8 million. The majority of grants are awarded to organisations, although a breakdown of grants made during the year was not included in the annual report and accounts. Previous research suggests that approximately £5,000 is given each year to individuals for both welfare and educational purposes.

Applications

HCF administers a number of different funds. These all have their specific application processes and criteria.

The foundation's website gives the following information:

> Applications should be addressed to 'Herefordshire Community Foundation' and if a grant is awarded the applicant will be advised of which fund (or funds) it came from it. It is rare for any of these funds to make an award of more than £1,000.
>
> Applications for under £1,000 are welcomed as a 'free-format' letter but this of course should include some standard information such as contact details, what is the grant to be used for and when, a budget/costs and why the grant is needed. Please contact us if you wish to discuss details before you apply.

The Leadership Trust Foundation

£32,500 (11 grants)

Correspondent: Robert Noble, The Leadership Trust, Weston Under Penyard, Ross-on-Wye, Herefordshire HR9 7YH (01989 767667; email: enquiries@leadership.org.uk; website: www.leadership.org.uk)

CC number: 1063916

Eligibility

Young people, primarily those aged 16 to 25, living within 25 miles of the trust's office who are undertaking activities designed to enhance their personal development and leadership training with an established and recognised charity.

Types of grants

Bursaries to enable individuals from the charitable sector to undertake training in leadership development.

Annual grant total

In 2013 the foundation had an income of £2.1 million. Bursaries made to 11 individuals to allow them to attend courses run by the foundation totalled £32,500. At the time of writing (July 2015) the 2013 accounts were the latest available.

Applications

Initially in writing to the correspondent, who will then send an application form to eligible applicants. Completed forms are considered quarterly.

Other information

The foundation provides bursaries in order to enable individuals from the charitable sector to undertake leadership development and training through attendance on the courses provided by the foundation.

Ross Educational Foundation

£3,000

Correspondent: Margaret Bickerton, Correspondent, 3 Silver Birches, Ross-on-Wye, Herefordshire HR9 7UX (01989 563260)

CC number: 527229

Eligibility

People under the age of 25 who live (or whose parents live) in the town of Ross Wye and the civil parish of Ross Rural.

Types of grants

Small, one-off and recurrent grants are available to higher education students and people in further education or vocational training. Support is given towards books, equipment and instruments, tools and other necessities or educational travel. People studying music and other arts may also apply. Grants usually range from £25 to £120.

Annual grant total

In 2014 the foundation had an income of £2,800 and an expenditure of £3,100. We estimate that the amount of grants given to individuals totalled around £3,000.

Exclusions

Our research suggests that accommodation costs and day-to-day travel expenses are not normally considered.

Applications

Applications can be made in writing to the correspondent. They can be submitted directly by the individual, normally in February and August for consideration in April and October, respectively.

Shropshire

Bowdler's Educational Foundation

£2,600

Correspondent: Mr T. Collard, Clerk to the Trustees, c/o Legal Division, Shropshire County Council, Shirehall, Abbey Foregate, Shrewsbury SY2 6ND (01743 252756; email: tim.collard@ shropshire.gov.uk)

CC number: 528366

Eligibility

People under the age of 25 who live in the county of Shropshire, with a priority for those living in the Shrewsbury area.

Types of grants

Grants, to a maximum of £100 to £200, for:

- School pupils, to help with books, equipment, clothing or travel
- Help with school, college or university fees or to supplement existing grants
- Help towards the cost of education, training, apprenticeship or equipment for those starting work

Annual grant total

In 2014 the foundation had an both an income and a total expenditure of £2,800. We estimate that grants totalled £2,600.

At the time of writing (November 2015) this was the most recent financial information available for the foundation.

Applications

Application forms are available from the correspondent.

Charity of Charles Clement Walker (The Walker Trust)

£56,500

Correspondent: Edward Hewitt, Administrator, 2 Breidden Way, Bayston Hill, Shrewsbury SY3 0LN (01743 873866; email: edward.hewitt@ btinternet.com)

CC number: 215479

Eligibility

People who live in Shropshire. Applicants should have been resident in the area for at least 12 months prior to application. Preference is given to individuals who are on low incomes or state benefits, people estranged from their families, single parents and young people leaving care.

Types of grants

Grants can be given towards further/ higher education and training courses undertaken within or outside the area of benefit, also for gap year projects, music, drama and arts costs and expeditions or travel. Individual grants range from £50 up to about £4,500.

Annual grant total

In 2013/14 the charity had assets of £6.1 million and an income of £244,000. The amount of grants given to individuals totalled over £56,500, broken down as follows:

Music and drama	£30,500
College course	£8,000
University course	£7,000
Schools and other Organisations	£5,000
Foreign Travel	£3,500
Health and disability	£2,000
Private Schools	£500

The following is taken from the trustees' annual report for 2013/14:

> In excess of 60 grants were made to individuals and organisations ranging from £50 to £4,500. Of these 9 were from single parent families, 14 from families whose only income was benefits and 2 from young people estranged from their families. Fifteen were grants for music, drama or art studies, many of which were substantial. Without the Trusts support most of these individuals would have been unable to undertake their courses.

Applications

Apply in writing to the correspondent. Applications are considered four times a year, normally in January, April, July and October. They must reach the correspondent at least one month before help is required. Decisions on urgent cases can be made between meetings.

Other information

Grants are also made to organisations (£53,500 in 2013/14).

The Shropshire Youth Foundation

£3,500

Correspondent: Karen Nixon, The Shirehall, Abbey Foregate, Shrewsbury, Shropshire SY2 6ND (01743 252724; email: karen.nixon@shropshire.gov.uk)

CC number: 522595

Eligibility

People under the age of 25 years who live in the county of Shropshire.

Types of grants

One-off grants of up to £200 can be provided towards educational leisure time activities and opportunities developing physical, mental and spiritual capacities of individuals, for example voluntary service.

Annual grant total

In 2013/14 the foundation had an income of £10,000 and an expenditure of £7,000. We have estimated the annual total of the grants to individuals to be around £3,500.

Exclusions

Financial help is not available towards course fees.

Applications

Application forms can be requested from the correspondent. The trustees meet twice a year, usually in January and June.

Other information

The main objective of the foundation is to assist youth clubs and similar organisations with specific projects benefitting local young people.

Shropshire

The Bridgnorth Parish Charity

£800

Correspondent: Elizabeth Smallman, Trustee, 37 Stourbridge Road, Bridgnorth WV15 5AZ (01746 764149; email: eeesmallman@aol.com)

CC number: 243890

Eligibility

People in need who live in the parish of Bridgnorth, including Oldbury, Quatford and Eardington.

Types of grants

Our research suggests that one-off grants are available according to need, including, for example, those towards playgroup fees or school visits.

Annual grant total

In 2014 the charity had an income of £81,000 and a total expenditure of £1,700. Note that the expenditure varies each year and in the past has fluctuated from £0 to £9,400. We estimate that the total amount of grants awarded to individuals for educational purposes was approximately £800.

Applications

Applications may be made in writing to the correspondent either directly by the individual or through a doctor, nurse, member of the local clergy, social worker, Citizens Advice or other welfare agency.

Other information

The charity also awards grants for social welfare purposes and to organisations.

The Educational Charity of John Matthews
See entry on page 153

Millington's Charity (Millington's Hospital)

£2,500 (7 grants)

Correspondent: Richard Gavin Hogg, Caradoc View Cottage, Enchmarsh, Leebotwood, Shropshire SY67JX (01743 360904; email: clerk@millingtons.org.uk)

CC number: 213371

Eligibility
Further/higher education students under the age of 25 who live or have been educated in Shropshire and who, or whose parents/guardians, are members of the Church of England.

Types of grants
One-off grants ranging from £100 to £400 are given to help people in further/higher education (including religious instruction). Support is given towards general educational expenses associated with college or university attendance, including equipment, books, maintenance/living costs, study/travel abroad. Help can also be given for a specific educational project, musical instruments or extra activities within the chosen course.

Annual grant total
In 2014 the charity had assets of £1 million and an income of £166,000. Grants to seven individuals in further education totalled £2,500.

Exclusions
Grants are not normally given towards fees.

Applications
Application forms can be obtained from the correspondent upon written request. Candidates are required to give details of their parents' income, other funding secured/applied to and provide references. Awards are made at quarterly meetings, usually in early March, June, September and December.

Telford and Wrekin
Maxell Educational Trust

£700

Correspondent: Ian Jamieson, Correspondent, Maxell Europe Ltd, Apley, Telford, Shropshire TF1 6DA (01952 522222; email: hr@maxell.eu)

CC number: 702640

Eligibility
Young people aged 9 to 25 who live, or whose family home is, in Telford, or who attend school or college there. Projects should ideally have an industrial or technological element.

Types of grants
One-off grants for schoolchildren, college students and people with special educational needs, towards books and equipment/instruments.

Annual grant total
In 2013/14 the trust had an income of £5,700 and an expenditure of £1,800. We estimate that around £700 was distributed in grants to individuals for education.

Applications
Apply in writing to the correspondent. Applications are considered throughout the year and should be submitted either by the individual or a parent/guardian, through a third party such as a teacher, or through an organisation such as a school or an educational welfare agency.

Other information
The trust was established in 1989 by Maxell Europe Ltd 'to express the company's appreciation for the support it had received from the local community'.

Staffordshire

Consolidated Charity of Burton upon Trent

£36,000 (36 grants)

Correspondent: John Southwell, Clerk, Dains LLP, 1st Floor, Gibraltar House, Crown Square, First Avenue, Burton-on-Trent DE14 2WE (01283 527067; fax: 01283 507969; email: clerk@consolidatedcharityburton.org.uk; website: www.consolidatedcharityburton.org.uk)

CC number: 239072

Eligibility
People who live in Burton upon Trent and the neighbouring parishes of Branston, Outwoods and Stretton.

Types of grants
The charity provides educational support in two forms:
- Bursaries – each year the charity awards a maximum of 30 bursaries (of £400 per annum for three years) to undergraduate students resident in the area of benefit. The schools and colleges included in the scheme are Abbot Beyne School, Burton College, The de Ferrers Academy, John Taylor High School, Paget High School and Stapenhill Sixth Form Centre
- Education and personal development grants – support is given for a range of purposes including: further education and vocational training; organised opportunities for personal development; sports activities; and arts scholarships. The maximum grant in any one year is £300, although applications may be made by individuals in subsequent years

Annual grant total
In 2014 the charity had assets of £12.7 million and an income of £457,000. Grants totalled £119,500, of which £70,500 was awarded to individuals for purposes relating to social welfare and education. During the year, 31 bursaries were taken up by individuals totalling £35,000, and five grants for education and youth development amounted to £1,400.

Exclusions
Grants are not awarded for postgraduate study.

Applications
Applications can be made using a form which is available online or to download from the charity's website. Candidates should include evidence of acceptance on the course or activity and an accompanying letter of support from a school or college. Applications for bursaries must include a personal statement and be submitted through the applicant's educational institution. Academic abilities, need and activities undertaken in the community are all taken into consideration. The trustees meet regularly to consider grants.

Other information
The charity also runs 32 almshouses and supports organisations working to the benefit of the local area.

Lady Dorothy Grey's Foundation

£25,500

Correspondent: Richard Jones, Trustee, Batfield House, Batfield Lane, Enville, Stourbridge, West Midlands DY7 5LF (01746 78350; email: enville.trusts@btopenworld.com)

CC number: 508900

Eligibility
Children and young people under the age of 25 who/whose parents live in the parishes of Bobbington, Enville or Kinver, with a preference for Enville.

Types of grants
Grants are given towards general educational expenses, including the cost of books, equipment/instruments, fees, maintenance expenses, clothing and

uniforms, educational outings or study/travel abroad. Our research suggests that one-off and recurrent grants normally range from £150 to £500 and can be given to schoolchildren or further/higher education students.

Annual grant total

In 2013/14 the foundation had assets of £62,500 and an income of £31,500. A total of £25,500 was awarded in grants to individuals.

Applications

Apply in writing to the correspondent. Applications can be made either directly by individuals or through their parents/guardians. According to our research, applications should be submitted by 31 August for consideration in October.

Maddock, Leicester and Burslem Educational Charity

£0

Correspondent: Steve Adams, Staffordshire Community Foundation, Communications House, University Court, Staffordshire Technology Park, Stafford ST18 0ES (01785 353789; email: office@staffsfoundation.org.uk; website: staffsfoundation.org.uk/maddockleicesterburslemfund)

CC number: 528586

Eligibility

Individuals resident or have parents in Stoke-on-Trent, the borough of Newcastle-under-Lyme, (post codes ST1–ST8) for a period of not less than seven years. Applicants should normally be between the ages of 15 and 21. Candidates should have achieved or be expected to achieve A or A* grades in GCSE and high grades at AS or A-level. The exception would be a pupil with learning difficulties, special needs or a very underprivileged background who had achieved substantially over and above what would be normally expected for that particular pupil.

Types of grants

Requests between £200 and £1,000 will be considered. Although there is no set limit the panel are not looking to grant considerable sums on any one applicant by paying for their education in full but to provide assistance for specific requirements of a relatively modest amount.

Annual grant total

In 2014/15 the charity had no income or expenditure. However, in previous years the charity has given around £9,000 in grants.

Exclusions

The charity will not normally consider travel costs, living expenses, running a motor vehicle, normal everyday expenditure, computer equipment, clothing or field trips.

Applications

Application forms can be requested from the correspondent and submitted by individuals directly or through their educational establishment. Our research indicates that applications should include details on what the grant is required for, what the aims of the applicant are, if any other funding is applied for/secured, and also have a comment from the school/college/university. The funding is publicised in over 20 local schools.

The Strasser Foundation

£3,800

Correspondent: The Trustees, c/o Knights Solicitors, The Brampton, Newcastle-under-Lyme, Staffordshire ST5 0QW (01782 619225; email: afhjb@fsmail.net)

CC number: 511703

Eligibility

Schoolchildren and students in the local area of Stoke-on-Trent and Newcastle-under-Lyme, with a preference for North Staffordshire.

Types of grants

Usually one-off grants for books, equipment and other specific causes or needs for educational purposes.

Annual grant total

In 2014/15 the foundation had an income of £10,100 and a total expenditure of £16,000. We estimate that the amount of grants given to individuals for educational purposes totalled around £3,800.

Exclusions

Grants are rarely made to people at doctoral level.

Applications

Applications may be made in writing to the correspondent. The trustees meet quarterly. Applications are only acknowledged if an sae is sent.

Other information

The foundation also makes grants to organisations and individuals for social welfare purposes.

Cannock Chase

The Rugeley Educational Endowment

£47,000

Correspondent: Financial Directorate, Staffordshire County Council, Finance Directorate, Wedgwood Buildings, Tipping Street, Stafford ST16 2DH (01785 276332; email: john.wood@staffordshire.gov.uk)

CC number: 528603

Eligibility

People in need who are under the age of 25 and live in the former urban district of Rugeley as constituted on 31 March 1974. Beneficiaries must have attended any comprehensive school in the area of benefit for at least two years.

Types of grants

According to our research, one-off grants of up to a maximum of £100 can be given towards the cost of school and work-related clothing, books, educational outings and projects, travel costs in the UK or abroad in pursuance of education, study of music or other arts, sports activities and for equipment/instruments or tools. Support is given to schoolchildren, students in higher or further education and to people preparing to enter a trade/start work.

Annual grant total

In 2014/15 the charity had an income of £77,000 and a total expenditure of £95,500. We estimate that the annual total amount of grants awarded to individuals was around £47,000.

Applications

Our research suggests that applications should be made through the headteacher of the school attended.

Other information

The charity has specific funds awarding prizes to pupils attending The Fair Oak Comprehensive School in Rugeley. The remainder of the endowment is used to provide educational grants.

East Staffordshire

The Tutbury General Charities

£1,300

Correspondent: Jeanne Minchin, 66 Redhill Lane, Tutbury, Burton-on-Trent, Staffordshire DE13 9JW (01283 813310)

CC number: 215140

Eligibility

People who are attending further education (college or apprenticeships) and live in the parish of Tutbury.

Types of grants

One-off grants are given, usually in the range of £40 and £80.

Annual grant total

In 2013/14 the charity had an income of £9,200 and a total expenditure of £5,600. Grants are made to individuals and organisations for social welfare and educational purposes. We estimate that educational grants to individuals totalled £1,300.

Applications

The charity has application forms, available from the correspondent, which should be returned by 1 October for consideration in November. A letter of acceptance from the place of education is required.

Other information

The Clerk has stated that details of the charity are well publicised within the village.

Stafford

The Stafford Educational Endowment Charity

£10,000

Correspondent: Financial Directorate, Staffordshire County Council, Wedgwood Buildings, Tipping Street, Stafford ST16 2DH (01785 276333; email: john.wood@staffordshire.gov.uk)

CC number: 517345

Eligibility

Pupils and former pupils of secondary schools in Stafford, who are under 25 years of age and are in need.

Types of grants

Small, one-off grants for books, travel, educational outings, educational equipment and similar expenses incurred by schoolchildren, students and people starting work. There is a preference to award grants for benefits not normally provided for by the LEA.

Annual grant total

In 2014/15 the charity had an income of £16,000 and a total expenditure of £17,000. Our research tells us that, in previous years, grants to individuals have totalled around £10,000. Funding is also awarded to secondary schools in Stafford.

Exclusions

Grants are unlikely to be given for course fees or the ordinary living costs of students.

Applications

Applications should be made through the headteacher of the secondary school attended.

Tamworth

The Rawlet Trust

£6,000

Correspondent: Christine Gilbert, 47 Hedging Lane, Wilnecote, Tamworth B77 5EX (01827 288614; email: christine.gilbert@mail.com)

CC number: 221732

Eligibility

Young people under the age of 25 who are in need and live, or have parents living, in Tamworth.

Types of grants

One-off grants ranging between £30 and £200 towards the cost of books, fees, living expenses, student exchange and study or travel abroad. Grants have also been made for equipment, instruments, clothing or travel for people starting work.

Annual grant total

In 2014/15 the trust had an income of £24,500 and a total expenditure of £25,500. Grants are made to individuals and organisations for both social welfare and educational purposes. We estimate that educational grants to individuals totalled £6,000.

Applications

Application forms are available from the correspondent. Applications should be submitted either directly by the individual or through a third party such as a social worker or Citizens Advice.

The clerk or one of the trustees will follow up applications if any further information is needed. The trustees meet in January, April, July and October to consider applications.

Warwickshire

Arlidge's Charity

£3,000

Correspondent: Colin Ritchie, Trustee, 10 Inverary Close, Kenilworth, Warwickshire CV82NZ (01926 512507; email: cjritchie3@hotmail.co.uk)

CC number: 528758

Eligibility

People under the age of 25 who live in the county of Warwick (preference is given to residents of Kenilworth) and who are, or one of whose parents are, members of Congregational Church or the United Reformed Church.

Types of grants

Help to students in further/higher education towards the cost of books, fees and travel or study abroad. Grants may be recurrent.

Annual grant total

In 2013/14 the charity had an income of £2,400 and an expenditure of £3,100. We estimate the annual total amount of grants awarded to be around £3,000.

Exclusions

According to our research, schoolchildren and people entering work are not normally supported.

Applications

Apply in writing to the correspondent. Applications should include details of the course to be taken and information of any other funding secured or applied to. Grants are normally considered in October.

Other information

The Charity Commission's record on the charity specifies that:

1/7th of the yearly income of the charity is dedicated to the current Minister of the Abbey Hill United Reformed Church either for application by him in furthering the religious and other charitable work of the congregation meeting for religious worship at the said church or in augmentation of his stipend.

The Exhall Educational Foundation

£4,000

Correspondent: Carol Gough, 53 Tewkesbury Drive, Bedworth, Warwickshire CV12 9ST (024 7636 5258; email: cagough@sky.com; website: exhalleducationalfoundation.blogspot.co.uk)

CC number: 528663

Eligibility

People under the age of 25 who live, or whose parents live, in the parish of Exhall or Keresley End.

Types of grants

One-off and recurrent grants for specific educational purposes (for example, courses, activities, materials or travel). The average award is of £200. The foundation can cover full costs or, in more expensive cases, offer supplementary assistance. Previously grants have been awarded for books, dance classes, music tuition, field trips, educational outings, expeditions, travel costs and so on.

Annual grant total

In 2014 the foundation had an income of £1,700 and an expenditure of £4,400. We estimate the annual total amount of grants awarded to individuals to be around £4,000.

Applications

Application forms are available from the foundation's website or can be requested from the correspondent. Applications are considered twice a year, in mid-March and mid-October. They can be submitted by post or by email in advance of the trustees' meeting.

Other information

Schools in the area of benefit are eligible to apply for support.

The area of benefit comprises: Ash Green, Black Bank, Exhall, Goodyers End, Keresley End, Little Bedworth Heath, Neals Green and Wagon Overthrow. The trustees encourage potential applicants to get in touch if in doubt about their geographical eligibility.

Hatton Consolidated Fund (Hatton Charities)

£2,200

Correspondent: Mrs M. Sparks, Clerk, Weare Giffard, 32 Shrewley Common, Shrewley, Warwick CV35 7AP (01926 842533; email: bsparks1@talktalk.net)

CC number: 250572

Eligibility

People in need who live in the parishes of Hatton, Beausale and Shrewley. Applications from outside these areas will not be considered.

Types of grants

One-off grants, usually in the range of £50–£500. Grants have been given to college students, undergraduates, vocational and mature students towards books, clothing, equipment and instruments. People with special educational needs have also been supported. Fees and travel expenses may also be covered. Loans may be available.

Annual grant total

In 2013/14 the fund had an income of £10,100 and a total expenditure of £8,800. We estimate that grants awarded to individuals for education totalled around £2,200.

Exclusions

Our research suggests that grants are not given to schoolchildren. Support is not made to cover taxes or where public funds should be sought first.

Applications

Applications may be made in writing to the trustees or the correspondent, directly by the individual or a family member. Applications should include details of the course and envisaged expenditure.

Other information

Grants are given to both organisations and individuals for educational and social welfare purposes.

The Watson Scholarship for Chemistry

£2,000

Correspondent: Ruth Waterman, School Partnerships Support Officer, Learning and Achievement, Saltisford Office Park, Ansell Way, Warwick CV34 4UL (01926 742075; email: ruthwaterman@warwickshire.gov.uk)

Eligibility

People who have a home address in Warwickshire, an A grade A-level in chemistry and a confirmed place on a first degree course in chemistry or one in which chemistry is the main subject.

Types of grants

Grants of up to £200, to be paid in the second semester of the first year of the course, after the university has confirmed the satisfactory progress of the student.

Annual grant total

In 2013/14 around £2,000 was given in grants to individuals. Not all those that applied were supported.

Exclusions

Students doing pharmacy or medicine will not be supported unless their main subject is chemistry.

Applications

Application forms are sent to schools/colleges in the area in September/October, or they are available from the correspondent. Forms must be signed by the headteacher of their school/college. The closing date for applications is changeable so contact the correspondent for details.

Other information

The scholarship has been running since 1918.

Rugby

The Bilton Poor's Land and Other Charities

£0

Correspondent: Robin Walls, Trustee, 6 Scotts Close, Rugby CV22 7QY (email: biltoncharities@outlook.com)

CC number: 215833

Eligibility

People in need who live in the ancient parish of Bilton (now part of Rugby).

Types of grants

This charity is not primarily an educational charity, concentrating rather on the relief of need. However, some grants are made for books, fees and other costs.

Annual grant total

In 2014/15 the charity had assets of £595,500 and an income of £64,500. Grants totalled £11,200 and were made to 198 individuals and organisations, including schools. We estimate that the amount of grants given to individuals amounted to £5,600 and believe that the awards were given only for social welfare purposes.

Applications

Applications can be made in writing to the correspondent, by the individual or through a relevant third party such as a minister, although often applications are forwarded by social services. The trustees meet three times a year.

Stratford-on-Avon

Shipston-on-Stour Educational Charity

£1,800

Correspondent: Mr D. Squires, Administrator, Pinnegar House, 49 Telegraph Street, Shipston-on-Stour CV36 4DA (email: ds@pinnegards.com)

CC number: 507400

Eligibility

People under 25 who live, or whose parents live, in the parish of Shipston-on-Stour.

Types of grants

One-off grants, ranging from £30 to £120, are given to students undertaking further and higher education, postgraduates and apprenticeships. Support can be given for uniforms/clothing, books, tools, instruments/equipment, educational outings in the UK or study or travel abroad.

Annual grant total

In 2013 the charity had an income of £3,200 and a total expenditure of £2,000. We estimate that grants totalled £1,800.

At the time of writing (November 2015) this was the most recent financial information available for the charity.

Applications

Application forms are available from correspondent. Applications should be submitted directly by the individual by the first week of September for consideration at the end of that month.

Municipal Charities of Stratford-upon-Avon – Relief in Need

£900

Correspondent: Ros Dobson, Clerk to the Trustees, c/o 6 Guild Cottages, Church Street, Stratford-upon-Avon, Warwickshire CV37 6HD (01789 293749; email: municharities@yahoo.co.uk or municharities@btinternet.com; website: www.municipal-charities-stratforduponavon.org.uk)

CC number: 214958

Eligibility

People who are in need and live in the town of Stratford-upon-Avon.

Types of grants

Occasionally, one-off grants of up to £500 are given towards the cost of:

- School uniforms, other school clothing, books, maintenance and school fees for schoolchildren
- Books for students in further and higher education
- Books, equipment and instruments for people starting work

Annual grant total

In 2014 the fund had assets of £80,500 and an income of £52,500 (including a £51,500 transfer from Charity of William Tyler). Grants from the relief-in-need fund totalled £99,500, including £45,000 given to almshouses. A total of £900 was given in educational grants.

Applications

Application forms are available from the correspondent. They should include details of the course costs and the financial circumstances of the applicant and parent(s) if appropriate. Applications for schoolchildren must be made through the school.

Warwick

Austin Edwards Charity

£2,600

Correspondent: Jackie Newton, Receiver, 26 Mountford Close, Wellesbourne, Warwick CV35 9QQ (01789 840135; website: www.austinedwards.org.uk)

CC number: 225859

Eligibility

People living in the old borough of Warwick (generally the CV34 postcode).

Types of grants

Grants are generally of no more than £300. Our research indicates that support is normally provided to students at college or university (including mature students) or people starting work. Grants are given towards the expenses for clothing, equipment, books, travel, course fees and study/travel overseas.

Annual grant total

In 2014/15 the charity had both an income and a total expenditure of £10,800. Grants are made to individuals and organisations for both social welfare and educational purposes. We estimate that educational grants to individuals totalled £2,600.

Exclusions

Grants cannot be provided for follow-on courses, postgraduate courses or additional degrees. The charity's website also reminds that 'where grants are applied for in respect of study courses, the trustees will only consider providing funding for one course per applicant'.

Applications

Apply in writing to the correspondent stating the purpose of the grant and the amount required, as well as details of any other charities approached with the same request. The individual's name and address must be supplied with the application. The trustees usually hold one meeting annually in July but will consider applications throughout the year.

Other information

The charity was named after Mr Austin Edwards who lived and worked in Warwick as a photographic manufacturer in the early years of the twentieth century. As a councillor of the borough of Warwick, he remained deeply interested in Warwickians and Warwick affairs generally. He gave generously to the Corporation of Warwick throughout his life.

William Edwards Educational Charity

£37,000 (114 grants)

Correspondent: John Hathaway, Clerk to the Trustees, Heath and Blenkinsop Solicitors, 42 Brook Street, Warwick CV34 4BL (01926 492407; email: law@heathandblenkinsop.com)

CC number: 528714

Eligibility

People under the age of 25 who/whose parents have lived in the town of Kenilworth, or those who have attended a school in the town.

Types of grants

Grants are given for school uniforms, school trips, other educational needs and in bursaries for postgraduate students and people on vocational courses.

Annual grant total

In 2013/14 the charity had assets of £6.7 million, an income of £249,500 and an expenditure of £113,500. The amount of grants given to individuals totalled £37,000. A total of 114 awards were made to assist with school uniforms, school trips and similar needs.

Applications

Apply in writing to the correspondent.

Other information

The trustees' annual report for 2013/14 states:

> The Trustees considered one hundred and thirty-five applications received by the Charity for assistance from individuals, or on behalf of individuals, under twenty-five years of age (excluding bursary applications). One hundred and fourteen awards had been made to assist with school uniforms, school trips and similar needs, the amount being awarded totalling £37,159. The Charity continued its annual bursary scheme. After interviews, three bursaries were awarded to the value

of £30,000 to assist postgraduate applicants in respect of tuition fees and living accommodation.

In 2013/14 the trust also made grants to schools totalling £9,700.

The King Henry VIII Endowed Trust – Warwick

£1,000 (1 grant)

Correspondent: Jonathan Wassall, Clerk and Receiver, 12 High Street, Warwick CV34 4AP (01926 495533; email: jwassall@kinghenryviii.org.uk; website: www.kinghenryviii.org.uk)

CC number: 232862

Eligibility

People who live in the former borough of Warwick. The area of benefit is roughly the CV34 postcode but exceptions apply so see the full list of eligible areas within the guidelines or contact the correspondent for clarification.

Types of grants

Grants can be given to schoolchildren for excursions and educational outings. College and university students may be supported for study/travel overseas and vocational students for fees (although normally students are referred to the Warwick Apprenticing Charities).

Grants are intended to be supplementary and applicants are expected to raise additional funds themselves. Payments are normally made upon submission of receipts.

Annual grant total

In 2014 the trust had assets of £28.8 million and an income of £1.37 million. Two grants to individuals totalled £2,100, one of which we estimate to be educational. The money for charitable activities is generated from the permanent endowment.

Exclusions

Grants are not made where support should be provided by the local or central government. Funding is not given retrospectively.

Applications

Application forms are available from the correspondent or from the trust's website. Applications should provide full details of the costs involved and the time schedule of the activity, where relevant. Awards are considered on a quarterly basis, usually in March, June, September and December. The closing dates for applications are the beginning of March/

June and the second half of August/ November. You will normally hear the outcome of your application within a week of the relevant meeting. In urgent cases applications can be 'fast-tracked' (the emergency should be specified in the application).

Other information

The income is distributed to the historic Anglican churches in Warwick (50%), Warwick Independent Schools Foundation for allocation in scholarships and bursaries (30%), and to organisations and individuals in the town (20%). Town grants to 33 organisations totalled £195,000, the foundation received £335,500 and the churches were awarded £544,000 in 2014.

Note the following stated in the application guidelines:

> Where the trust believes that there are more suitable charities within the town to assess applications it will either forward the application directly to another charity or recommend that the applicant approaches them directly. Young people under 24 years old applying for support at university or college will be referred directly to the Warwick Apprenticing Charities.

For Warwick Apprenticing Charities see a separate entry on page 182.

The Leigh Educational Foundation

£35,000

Correspondent: James Johnson, Clerk to the Trustees, 3 Barford Woods, Barford Road, Warwick CV34 6SZ (01926 419300; email: johnson.jf@virgin.net)

CC number: 701462

Eligibility

People in need who are under the age of 25 and who (or whose parents) are resident in the parishes of Stoneleigh, Ashow, Leek Wootton and Burton Green.

Types of grants

One-off or recurrent grants according to need, normally ranging from £100 to £1,000. Grants are given to schoolchildren, college students, undergraduates, vocational students and people starting work. Support is offered towards general educational needs, including uniforms/clothing, fees, study/ travel abroad, books, equipment/ instruments and maintenance/living expenses.

Annual grant total

In 2014 the foundation had assets of £961,500 and an income of £37,500. A total of £38,000 was spent in charitable expenditure. Previously most of the

funding was allocated to individuals; therefore, we estimate that grants to individuals totalled around £35,000.

Applications

Application forms and full guidelines are available from the correspondent (in hard copy or electronic format). Applications can be submitted directly by the individual. They are considered four times a year, in February, May, August and November.

Other information

Institutions are also eligible to apply.

The Lucy Price Relief-in-Need Charity

£16,500

Correspondent: Delia Thomas, Clerk, 13 Holly Walk, Baginton, Coventry CV8 3AE (07884 182904)

CC number: 516967

Eligibility

Only people in need who are between the ages of 5 and 25 and live in the parish of Baginton, Warwickshire.

Types of grants

Grants are made for: (i) attendance at university, living away from home; (ii) attendance at university or colleges of further education, living at home; (iii) attendance at local schools or sixth form college or A-level courses; (iv) school uniforms; (v) travel or visits of an educational nature at home or abroad organised by school or university; (vi) occasionally for equipment, instruments or books specially required for people starting work; and (vii) special educational needs requiring special courses or equipment. Grants made under (i), (ii) and (iii) are for the academic year and are paid in three equal instalments. Grants made under (iv), (v), (vi) and (vii) may be applied for at any time.

Annual grant total

In 2014 the charity had an income of £4,500 and a total expenditure of £34,000. We estimate that educational grants to individuals totalled £16,500. Grants are also given for welfare purposes.

Applications

Application forms can be obtained from the correspondent either directly by the individual or by the applicant's parents if they are under 16 years old.

Warwick Apprenticing Charities

£75,000 (64 grants)

Correspondent: C. E. R. Houghton, Clerk, Moore and Tibbits Solicitors, 34 High Street, Warwick CV34 4BE (01926 491181; email: commercial@moore-tibbits.co.uk; website: www.warwickapprenticingcharities.org.uk)

CC number: 528745

Eligibility

People under the age of 25 who have finished school and live within the town of Warwick. Residents of Warwick aged 16 to 18 who are still at school can apply for assistance in attending Outward Bound courses.

Types of grants

One-off 'advancement in life' grants are available to people undertaking apprenticeships, further/higher education students or those undertaking any other form of training which will help to advance their career. Support is given towards general educational needs, including fees, maintenance expenses, books, equipment/instruments, materials, special clothing, travel costs and so on.

Annual grant total

In 2013/14 the charity had assets of £1 million and an income of £80,500. Grants totalled £75,000 and consisted of 64 'advancement in life' awards totalling £60,000 and paid for Outward Bound places totalling £15,000.

Applications

Applications are available from the charity's website or can be requested from the correspondent. Candidates are asked to attend an interview. The trustees meet twice a year.

Charity of Sir Thomas White, Warwick

£39,500

Correspondent: Belinda Shuttleworth, Clerk and Receiver, 12 High Street, Warwick CV34 4AP (01926 350555; email: connect@sirthomaswhite.org.uk; website: www.sirthomaswhite.org.uk)

CC number: 1073331

Eligibility

People between the ages of 18 and 35 who are ordinarily resident in the town of Warwick who are establishing a business or undertaking tertiary education.

Types of grants

Interest-free loans to young people wishing to establish themselves in business, or assist them to improve their existing business in the town of Warwick. These interest-free loans are available up to £10,000 (for five years). The charity also provides for making interest-free loans to young people who or whose parents are ordinarily resident in the town of Warwick, towards the cost to them of undertaking further education or vocational training. These interest-free loans are available up to £1,500 per year for each year of their course.

Annual grant total

In 2014 the charity had assets of £389,000 and an income of £213,000. Interest-free loans during the year totalled £39,500.

Applications

Application forms are available from the correspondent or from the charity's website.

- Applications for educational loans should include details of the course to be undertaken and the applicant's financial requirements for the duration of the course. An interview with a small panel of trustees will be arranged and applications must be received by the charity at least three weeks prior to the interview date. Successful applicants are required to sign a loan agreement and two adults are required to guarantee repayment of the loan
- Applications for business loans should be submitted along with a business plan. An interview will be arranged with a small panel of trustees to discuss the business idea and applications must be received by the charity at least three weeks prior to the interview date. Successful applicants must sign a joint and several bond, as must their sureties. The number of sureties required ranges from two to four, depending on the amount requested

West Midlands

Grantham Yorke Trust

£6,800

Correspondent: Christine Norgrove, Charities Administrator, SGH Martineau, 1 Colmore Square, Birmingham B4 6AA (email: christine.norgrove@sghmartineau.com)

CC number: 228466

Eligibility

People under 25 who were born in what was the old West Midlands Metropolitan County area (basically: Birmingham, Coventry, Dudley, Redditch, Sandwell, Solihull, Tamworth, Walsall or Wolverhampton).

Types of grants

One-off grants are given to:

- Schoolchildren and students for uniforms and other school clothing, books, equipment, instruments, fees, maintenance and living expenses, childcare, educational outings in the UK, study or travel overseas and student exchange
- Students leaving school or further education for equipment and clothing, which will help them enter, or prepare for, their chosen profession or trade
- People starting work for maintenance and living expenses and childcare
- Education focused on preventing unplanned pregnancy, drug, alcohol and gambling abuse, child abuse or youth offending

Annual grant total

In 2013/14 the trust had assets of £6.8 million and an income of £249,500. Grants totalled £183,000, of which £169,500 was given to organisations. A total of 38 grants were awarded to individuals, for both social welfare and educational needs, amounting to £13,600. We estimate that educational grants to individuals totalled £6,800.

Applications

Applications can be made on a form available from the correspondent. Applications can be submitted either directly by the individual or a relevant third party; or through the individual's school, college or educational welfare agency.

The Newfield Charitable Trust

£800 (2 grants)

Correspondent: Mary Allanson, Clerk, Rotherham and Co. Solicitors, 8–9 The Quadrant, Coventry CV1 2EG (024 7622 7331; fax: 024 7622 1293; email: m.allanson@rotherham-solicitors.co.uk)

CC number: 221440

Eligibility

Girls and women (under the age of 30) who are in need of care and assistance and live in Coventry or Leamington Spa.

Types of grants

Grants are given towards school uniforms and other school clothing, educational trips, college fees, textbooks and equipment. Most grants are of less than £500.

Annual grant total

In 2014/15 the trust had assets of £1.6 million and an income of £58,000. Grants totalled £33,000, of which £32,000 was awarded to individuals for social welfare purposes. Two grants were made for educational needs, amounting to £800.

Exclusions

Grants are not made for postgraduate education.

Applications

Our research indicates that applicants should write to the correspondent to request an application form. Applications are accepted from individuals or third parties e.g. social services, Citizens Advice, school/college, etc. A letter of support/reference from someone who is not a friend or relative of the applicant (i.e. school, social services, etc.) is always required. Details of the applicant's income/expenditure and personal circumstances should also be given. Applications are considered eight times a year.

The Norton Foundation

£1,600 (22 grants)

Correspondent: Richard Perkins and Company, Administrator, 50 Brookfield Close, Hunt End, Redditch B97 5LL (01527 544446; email: correspondent@nortonfoundation.org; website: www.nortonfoundation.org)

CC number: 702638

Eligibility

Young people aged under 25 who live in Birmingham, Solihull, Coventry and Warwickshire. Applicants must be 'in need through some aspect of disadvantage defined as: in care or in need of rehabilitation, lapsing into delinquency, suffering from maltreatment or neglect, or whose potential is not yet realised due to circumstances beyond their control'.

Types of grants

One-off grants are available to schoolchildren and further and higher education students for school clothing, books, equipment, instruments, fees, maintenance and living expenses and educational outings in the UK. Grants of up to £500 can be made, although they usually range between £50 and £250.

Annual grant total

In 2013/14 the foundation had assets of £4.9 million and an income of £154,500. Grants totalled £88,500, of which £55,000 was awarded to organisations. A total of 161 grants were made directly to individuals totalling £12,000. They were distributed as follows:

Household	106	£8,100
Clothing	32	£2,200
Education and training	22	£1,600
Holidays	1	£75

In addition, £22,000 was paid in block discretionary grants to 19 sponsors for redistribution to individuals. Sponsors included South Birmingham Young Homeless Project (£14,000), St Basil's Centre (£4,000) and Action for Children (£1,000).

Applications

Applications should be made in writing and contain all the information described in the guidance notes, which are available from the website. Applications must be submitted through a social worker, Citizens Advice, probation service, school or other welfare agency, and should be typed or printed, if possible. They are considered on a monthly basis.

Note: The foundation's website gives the following helpful tips on making applications:

What are the trustees looking for in ALL applications?

- information should be specific and to the point
- evidence on the causes of the current situation or need
- what other efforts are being made to solve the problem
- a clear indication of what difference the grant will make

Other information

The foundation's website also lists helpful information on why applications fail:

- the trustees are not convinced by the case being presented
- too many assumptions and unrealistic aspirations
- the amount requested is outside the range for the grant being applied for
- the bid was to fund long-term commitments
- financial information was insufficient and inadequate
- the contact details were insufficient for the trustees to obtain further information

Birmingham

Birmingham Bodenham Trust

£12,000

Correspondent: Jackie Crowley, Administrator, Finance (WS), PO Box 16306, Birmingham B2 2XR (0121 464 3928; email: jackie.crowley@birmingham.gov.uk)

CC number: 528902

Eligibility

Young people under the age of 19 who have special educational needs. Preference may be given to people in Birmingham area.

Types of grants

Grants are given for special equipment and facilities which would advance the individual's education and training, including recreation and leisure. Support can be given towards holidays and trips, course fees, books, toys, IT equipment, summer schools and so on.

Annual grant total

In 2013/14 the trust had an income of £22,000 and an expenditure of £24,500. We estimate the annual total amount of grants awarded to individuals to be around £12,000.

Applications

Apply in writing to the correspondent. Applications are considered at quarterly meetings.

Other information

Support can also be given to individuals and organisations engaged in innovative projects on education, training, recreation or medical care of young people with special needs.

The King's Norton United Charities

£2,500

Correspondent: Canon Rob Morris, Trustee, The Parish Office, 81 The Green, Kings Norton, Birmingham B38 8RU (0121 458 3289; email: parishoffice@kingsnorton.org.uk; website: www.knuc.org.uk)

CC number: 202225

Eligibility

The charity is able to assist only those who live within the boundary of the ancient parish of Kings Norton, formerly in Warwickshire and Worcestershire, now in Warwickshire and the West Midlands. This area includes the current Church of England Parishes of Kings Norton, Cotteridge, Stirchley, parts of Bournville, Balsall Heath, Kings Heath, Moseley (St Anne's and St Mary's), Brandwood, Hazelwell, Highters Heath, Wythall, West Heath, Longbridge, Rubery and Rednal.

Types of grants

The charity's annual report states that grants are usually of between £50 and £350 and are typically for one-off purchases of essential household items, for short-term bridging support or for educational needs such as help with fees or to cover unforeseen expenses. The trustees may consider making larger grants in specific cases.

Annual grant total

Our research indicates that educational grants usually total around £2,500, with funding also awarded for social welfare purposes. At the time of writing (November 2015) the charity's 2013 annual report and accounts were the most recent available.

Applications

The trustees prefer to receive requests for grants through organisations or agencies working on behalf of families or individuals in need. An organisation or individual applying on another's behalf will then be expected to take responsibility and to account for the correct use of the grant.

The trustees meet twice each year to consider grant requests and to distribute regular amounts to the discretionary funds of the incumbents of member parishes. Other selected organisations or agencies, based within the ancient parish of King's Norton and who assist in relieving genuine poverty or hardship, may also be awarded discretionary grants. Grant applications for smaller amounts (currently up to £250) may also be agreed and paid by the chair, vice-chair and treasurer on behalf of the main meeting.

Sir Josiah Mason's Relief in Need and Educational Charity

£0

Correspondent: Edward Kuczerawy, Financial Controller, Mason Court, Hillborough Road, Birmingham B27 6PF (0121 245 1001; email: enquiries@sjmt. org.uk; website: www.sjmt.org.uk)

CC number: 1073756

Eligibility

People under 25 who live or study in the West Midlands area and are in genuine financial hardship.

Types of grants

One-off grants of up to £500 for exam or tuition fees, study materials, books and equipment or tools for training or apprenticeships.

Annual grant total

In 2013/14 the charity had assets of £4.1 million and an income of £95,500. There were no grants made to individuals during the year but previously grants have totalled around £2,000. Grants to organisations totalled £33,000.

Exclusions

No grants are given for living costs.

Applications

Application forms are available from the website or from the correspondent and can be returned by email or post.

The Mitchells & Butlers Charitable Trusts

£13,000 (33 grants)

Correspondent: Ms H. Woodall, Administrator, Mitchells & Butlers, 27 Fleet Street, Birmingham B3 1JP (0121 498 4129; website: www.mbtrusts. org.uk)

CC number: 528922

Eligibility

Students resident in the UK who are over the age of 11 and who live in the city of Birmingham and Smethwick. Preference may be given to the employees and children of the employees of Mitchells & Butlers and successors in business of the company. External applicants are invited to apply, provided they can demonstrate financial hardship. Applicants from low income households are favoured.

Types of grants

The charity's Welfare Fund offers support to schoolchildren and further/higher education students, including mature students and individuals with special educational needs. Financial assistance is available towards the course fees, living expenses, course-related necessities and expenses, such as books, equipment, clothing and uniforms, travel costs and so forth.

The charity's Scholarship Fund can assist students in courses relating to brewing industry, licensed retailing, catering and hotel management. Support can be given towards general educational expenses, including books or the cost of equipment. Previously students in Leeds Metropolitan University and University College Birmingham have been supported.

Annual grant total

In 2013/14 the charity had assets of £3.5 million and an income of £114,500. Charitable expenditure totalled £68,500 and a total of £13,000 was awarded from the Welfare Fund in educational grants to 33 individuals.

Applications

Application forms for the Welfare Fund can be found on the charity's website and should be submitted a month in advance of the trustees' meeting which is normally held in July. Inclusion of a letter of support from a teacher, educational welfare officer or other professional would benefit the application

Applications for the Scholarship Fund should be made through a relevant university and can be found on the charity's website. The annual Scholarship Fund Committee meeting takes place in early September.

Other information

Educational grants to institutions totalled £22,500 in 2013/14.

Joseph Scott's Educational Foundation

£2,200

Correspondent: Derek Duffield, Trustee, 29 Jasmin Croft, Birmingham B14 5AX (0121 444 5479; email: JSEF@gmail.com)

CC number: 528919

Eligibility

Young people who live 'and have been educated for at least 2 years at a school provided by the Birmingham education authority or at a legally designated academy or free school within the boundaries, for the time being, of the city of Birmingham'.

Types of grants

One-off grants are given to students in further/higher education and mature students towards books and fees/living expenses.

Annual grant total

In 2014/15 the foundation had an income of £1,900 and a total expenditure of £2,600. We estimate that educational grants to individuals totalled £2,200.

Exclusions

No grants are given to postgraduates.

Applications

Application forms are available from the correspondent. Applications are considered quarterly, usually in March, June, September and November.

Sutton Coldfield Municipal Charities

£22,500 (276 grants)

Correspondent: John Hemming, Grants Manager, Lingard House, Fox Hollies Road, Sutton Coldfield, West Midlands B76 2RJ (0121 351 2262 (Tuesday to Thursday, 9am to 4pm); fax: 0121 313 0651; email: info@suttoncharitabletrust. org; website: www. suttoncoldfieldcharitabletrust.com)

CC number: 218627

Eligibility

People who are in need and have lived in the four electoral wards of Sutton Coldfield (New Hall, Four Oaks, Trinity and almost all of Vesey) for at least five years. Our research indicates that educational assistance is mainly given to people under the age of 25.

School uniform grants: Parents/ guardians of primary and secondary school pupils who are permanently resident in one of the four electoral wards of Sutton Coldfield (New Hall, Vesey, Trinity and Four Oaks) and are in receipt of any one of the following: income support; Child Tax Credit; Working Tax Credit (maximum income levels may apply); Job Seeker's Allowance; guarantee element of state pension credit; Employment and Support Allowance.

Types of grants

Almost all educational grants are given to assist with the costs of school uniforms. At the time of writing (August 2015) the value of the grant was £75 per child. A maximum of four children per family can be assisted. Payment is made in the form of vouchers for use at BHS, Gracechurch Centre, Sutton Coldfield and/or Clive Mark Schoolwear, Wylde Green. Grants are also made for other educational needs, including to assist with the costs of education after formal schooling.

Annual grant total

In 2013/14 the charity had assets of almost £48.8 million and an income of £1.8 million. Grants totalled £1.6 million, the vast majority of which was awarded to organisations. Grants were made to individuals totalling £45,500, of which £22,500 was given in 276 grants for purposes related to education (£20,500 in 273 grants for school uniforms and £2,100 in three grants for educational and personal needs).

Applications

Applications for school uniform grants can be made using a form, which is available to download from the website or directly from schools in Sutton Coldfield or the correspondent. They can be made from the start of the summer term and must be submitted by 30 November.

Contact the correspondent for information on how to apply for assistance with other educational needs.

Other information

The principal objective of the charity, which is also known as the Sutton Coldfield Charitable Trust, is the provision of almshouses, the distribution of funds and other measures for the alleviation of poverty and other needs for inhabitants and other organisations within the boundaries of the former borough of Sutton Coldfield.

Yardley Educational Foundation

£118,500

Correspondent: Derek Hackett, Clerk to the Trustees, Edzell House, 121 Chester Road, Castle Bromwich, Birmingham B36 0AE (01212463625; email: enquiries@yardleyeducationalfoundation. org; website: www. yardleyeducationfoundation.org)

CC number: 528918

Eligibility

Children and young people in need between the ages of 11 and 19 who have lived in the ancient parish of Yardley for at least two years. For the specific geographical area covered by the foundation, see the map on the website. The applicant's family income must be below £16,000 per year (including maximum Tax Credits).

Types of grants

Secondary school pupils aged 11–16 can be supported towards school uniforms, school clothing, sports equipment grants, educational outings in the UK and study or travel overseas. Awards are generally in the region of £80 per year.

Young adults aged 16–19 can be assisted towards further vocational training and apprenticeships.

The foundation also provides book vouchers of £25 to students at secondary school redeemable at Waterstones.

Applications for different types of grants can also be considered. These include adventure trips, Duke of Edinburgh Award, Operation Raleigh, purchase of musical instruments, student exchange programmes or cost of attending interviews at universities.

The foundation's website states: 'We have flexibility with our grants and support many other causes for pupils residing in the ancient parish of Yardley.'

Annual grant total

In 2014/15 the foundation had assets of nearly £4.3 million and an income of £183,000. During the year the foundation received more than 1,227 applications for help. A total of around £105,500 was given in grants for clothing, sports equipment, school trips, apprenticeships and other support. A further £13,300 was given in book vouchers.

Applications

Application forms are available from the correspondent and should be submitted through the individual's school or college, usually in May or June for consideration in July and August.

Other information

The foundation also states that 'the clerk to the trustees has close liaison with the secondary schools throughout the parish and is in constant touch with them to ascertain their needs'.

According to its website, the foundation 'has its roots dating back to 1347 when the monks at Maxstoke Priory, which then had Yardley Parish as an appendage, ran the church school'.

Coventry

The Children's Boot Fund

£4,500

Correspondent: Janet McConkey, Chair, 123A Birmingham Road, Coventry CV5 9GR (024 7640 2837; email: martin_harban@btconnect.com)

CC number: 214524

Eligibility

Schoolchildren in the city of Coventry between the ages of 4 and 16 who are in need.

Types of grants

Grants are given for school footwear for children in need. No other type of award is given. Grants are made directly to footwear suppliers in the form of vouchers. Normally one child per family can be supported within one year, but exceptions may be made for families in difficult circumstances. Twins are usually given an award each. People leaving school may receive a grant for shoes to attend interviews.

Annual grant total

In 2013/14 the fund had assets of £49,500 and an income of £33,500. A total of around £4,500 was spent in direct charitable expenditure. Grants are only made for school footwear.

Applications

Application forms are available from schools in the area. They should be made by the parents/guardians and supported by the headteacher of the child's school. Applications from social care services are also considered. Applicants are required to list their benefits and income. Requests are considered four times a year.

General Charity (Coventry)

£135,500 (147 grants)

Correspondent: Victoria Tosh, Clerk to the Trustees, General Charities Office, Old Bablake, Hill Street, Coventry CV1 4AN (024 7622 2769; email: cov. genchar@btconnect.com)

CC number: 216235

Eligibility

Children and young people under the age of 25 who are in need and live in the city of Coventry. Preference may be given to children of the freemen of the city.

Types of grants

Grants are given towards school fees, books or specialised equipment and also to support music education.

Annual grant total

In 2014 the charity had assets of £9.7 million and an income of £1.5 million, of which £542,500 was in restricted funds. Grants totalled £1.3 million and, of this amount, educational grants to individuals totalled £55,500. They were distributed as follows:

School fees	13	£35,500
Books and equipment	129	£15,000
Music Award	1	£5,000

Support, totalling £80,000, was also given to four PhD students at the Department of Biological Sciences, University of Warwick.

Exclusions

Our research suggests that maintenance costs are not supported. Cash grants are not given.

Applications

Application forms can be requested from the correspondent, normally in late August/early September. They should be submitted for consideration in November. The outcome of the application is communicated in December.

Other information

The charity consists of the charities formerly known as The Relief in Need Charity, Sir Thomas White's Pension Fund and Sir Thomas White's Educational Foundation. The trustees are also responsible for the administration of Lady Herbert's Homes and Eventide Homes Ltd, providing accommodation for the elderly in the city of Coventry.

Grants are also made for welfare purposes and in pensions to people over the age of 60 in the city of Coventry. Most of the charity's assistance is given to organisations. An annual payment is made to the Coventry School Foundation.

The Andrew Robinson Young People's Trust

£10,000

Correspondent: Clive Robinson, Trustee, 31 Daventry Road, Coventry CV3 5DJ (024 7650 1579; email: ARYPT@googlemail.com)

CC number: 1094029

Eligibility

Young people who live in Coventry, particularly those who are facing social or economic disadvantages, or suffer from ill health.

Types of grants

One-off and recurrent grants to advance the religious education of young people and their faith within the Catholic Church. The support is also given to assist individuals in their personal development through various leisure activities and trips related to the Catholic faith.

Annual grant total

In 2014 the trust had an income of £19,000 and an expenditure of £21,500. We estimate the annual total amount of grants awarded to individuals to be around £10,000.

Applications

Apply in writing to the correspondent.

Other information

The trust also makes grants to organisations and provides support to relieve poverty.

Soothern and Craner Educational Foundation

£9,500

Correspondent: Gillian Waddilove, Trustee, The Hollies, Priory Road, Wolston, Coventry CV8 3FX (024 7654 4255; email: admin@soothernandcraner. org.uk; website: www.soothernandcraner. org.uk)

CC number: 528838

Eligibility

Girls and young women who live in Coventry or who are Quakers connected to Coventry Quaker Meeting. Studies may be undertaken away from Coventry but the connection with the city is crucial.

Types of grants

Grants are mainly given to further education students and people in vocational training for general educational costs, including equipment/ instruments, outfits, books and so on.

Our research indicates that support is intended to supplement existing grants or where no mandatory award is available.

Annual grant total

In 2014 the foundation had an income of £12,500 and a total expenditure of £10,000. We estimate the annual total amount of grants awarded to individuals to be around £9,500.

Exclusions

Support will rarely be given to people studying at or above first degree level.

Applications

The foundation's website provides two application forms – for those still in school and for school leavers. Applicants should have two references available. Applications can also be made on behalf of groups (by a teacher or group leader) for educational activities. The trustees request the applicants to use ordinary post rather than recorded delivery in order to avoid delays. The trustees meet in July each year with additional meetings held as required.

Dudley

The Palmer and Seabright Charity

£7,100

Correspondent: Susannah Griffiths, Clerk to the Trustees, c/o Wall James Chappell, 15–23 Hagley Road, Stourbridge, West Midlands DY8 1QW (01384 371622; email: sgriffiths@wjclaw. co.uk)

CC number: 200692

Eligibility

People under the age of 25 who live in the borough of Stourbridge.

Types of grants

One-off and recurrent grants are made to college students and undergraduates for fees, books, equipment/instruments and maintenance/living expenses. Grants are also given to schoolchildren for fees.

Annual grant total

In 2014 the charity had assets of £278,500 and an income of £39,500. Grants were made totalling £16,700 (including £2,600 in Christmas grants). We estimate that educational grants to individuals amounted to £7,100.

Applications

Applications can be made on a form available from the correspondent. Applications can be submitted either directly by the individual or a family member, through a third party such as a social worker or teacher, or through an organisation such as Citizens Advice or a school.

Daniel Parsons Educational Charity

£5,000

Correspondent: David Hughes, Trustee, 53 The Broadway, Dudley, West Midlands DY1 4AP (01384 259277; email: parsonscharity@hotmail.com)

CC number: 1068492

Eligibility

People under the age of 25 who/whose parents live in Dudley and its neighbourhood or who have attended school in that area.

Types of grants

One-off grants in the range of £200 to £500 towards education and training.

Annual grant total

In 2014 the charity had an income of £10,500 and an expenditure of £5,500. We estimate that the annual grants total was around £5,000.

Applications

Application forms can be requested from the correspondent or downloaded from Rotary Club of Dudley website. They can be submitted to the correspondent at any time.

The Sedgley Educational Trust

£1,100

Correspondent: Chris Williams, Administrator, 12 Larkswood Drive, Dudley DY3 3UQ (01902 672880)

CC number: 1091563

Eligibility

People in need who live in the ecclesiastical parishes of All Saints Sedgley, St Chad Coseley and St Mary the Virgin Sedgley.

Types of grants

One-off and recurrent grants are given according to need are available to people in education, including religious education in accordance with the doctrines of the Church of England.

Annual grant total

In 2013/14 the trust had an income of £2,700 and an expenditure of £1,300. We have estimated that the annual total amount of grants awarded was around £1,100.

Applications

Apply in writing to the correspondent.

Sandwell

The Chance Trust

£1,300

Correspondent: Revd Ian Shelton, Trustee, 192 Hanover Road, Rowley Regis B65 9EQ (0121 559 1251; email: ianshelton232@hotmail.co.uk; website: www.warleydeanery.co.uk)

CC number: 702647

Eligibility

People in need in the rural deaneries of Warley and West Bromwich (the area covered by the southern parts of Sandwell borough).

Types of grants

One-off grants, usually ranging from £50 to £400, can be given to help access the education. Our research suggests that support can occasionally be made to university students for up to three years.

Annual grant total

In 2013/14 the trust had an income of £2,800 and a total expenditure of £2,700. Grants are made to individuals for educational and social welfare purposes. We estimate that educational grants to individuals totalled £1,300.

Exclusions

Grants are not normally provided where statutory funding is available.

Applications

Apply in writing to the correspondent. Applications should specify the need and the amount required. They are usually considered in January and July.

The Mackmillan Educational Foundation

£1,600

Correspondent: Mr V. Westwood, Administrator, 18 Westdean Close, Halesowen, West Midlands B62 8UA (0121 602 2484; email: vicwestw@blueyonder.co.uk)

CC number: 529043

Eligibility

People under 25 who live in the ancient parish of Rowley Regis.

Types of grants

Grants are made to support students at school and college.

Annual grant total

In 2014/15 the foundation had an income of £1,400 and a total expenditure of £1,900. We estimate that grants made to individuals for education totalled around £1,600.

Applications

Apply in writing to the correspondent.

The Oldbury Educational Foundation (The Oldbury Charity)

£6,000

Correspondent: Ronald Kay, 43 Lee Crescent, Birmingham B15 2BJ (0121 440 7755; email: rolandkay@tiscali.co.uk)

CC number: 527468

Eligibility

Schoolchildren in the borough of Oldbury.

Types of grants

Small grants are available to help with general educational costs, including books, clothing, equipment/instruments and travel expenses. Our research suggests that most grants are awarded to pupils at Warley High School, but pupils at other schools in Oldbury can also apply.

Annual grant total

In 2013/14 the foundation had an income of £7,000 and an expenditure of £6,500. We estimate the annual total amount of grants awarded to be around £6,000.

Applications

Apply in writing to the correspondent.

Palmer Educational Charity (The Palmer Trust)

£6,500

Correspondent: David Flint, Administrator, Birmingham Diocesan Offices, 175 Harborne Park Road, Birmingham B17 0BH (0121 426 0400)

CC number: 508226

Eligibility

Children and young people under the age of 25 who live in the Warley Deanery.

Types of grants

Grants are available to schoolchildren and further/higher education students. Our research suggests that support can mainly be given towards the cost of books directly related to Christianity and religious education.

Annual grant total

In 2013 the charity had an income of £8,400 and an expenditure of £6,800. We estimate the annual total amount of grants awarded to be around £6,500.

At the time of writing (October 2015) this was the most recent financial information available.

Applications

Apply in writing to the correspondent. According to our research, applications should be submitted through the Parochial Church Council or clergy of Warley Deanery and are normally considered in March and October.

Other information

Grants are primarily made to the Church of England schools in the Warley Deanery. Local churches and organisations may also be supported.

Walsall

The Fishley Educational and Apprenticing Foundation

£19,000

Correspondent: Neil Picken, Clerk to the Trustees, Constitutional Services, Walsall Council, The Civic Centre, Darwall Street, Walsall WS1 1TP (01922 654369; email: charities@walsall.gov.uk; website: cms.walsall.gov.uk/charities)

CC number: 529010

Eligibility

Young people in need who are under the age of 25 and live, work or study in Walsall.

Types of grants

Grants are available towards general educational needs, including tuition fees, specialist equipment, books, clothing, field trips, study of music and arts, study/travel overseas and so on. Pupils and further/higher education students are supported.

Annual grant total

In 2013/14 the foundation had an income and a total expenditure of £19,500. We estimate that £19,000 was awarded in grants.

Applications

Application forms can be accessed from the foundation's website or requested from the correspondent via phone. Grants are considered at least twice a year. Applications must be supported by a member of teaching staff. You will need to provide a declaration and proof of your parental income.

Note that applications for grants towards educational trips should be made through the educational establishment.

C. C. Walker Charity

£25,000

Correspondent: Neil Picken, Clerk to the Trustees, Constitutional Services, Walsall Council, The Civic Centre, Darwall Street, Walsall WS1 1TP (01922 654369; email: charities@walsall.gov.uk; website: cms.walsall.gov.uk/charities)

CC number: 528898

Eligibility

People who are under the age of 25 and live or study in the borough of Walsall. Preference is given to those people whose parent/parents have died and who were born in Walsall and/or whose parents or surviving parent have lived there at any time since the birth of the applicant.

Types of grants

Grants according to need for any educational purpose. Grants have been given towards clothing for schoolchildren and books, fees, living expenses and equipment for students in further/higher education.

Annual grant total

In 2014/15 the charity had an income of £21,500 and an unusually high expenditure of £33,900. We estimate that the annual total amount of grants awarded was about £25,000.

Applications

Application forms are available to download from the charity's website or can be requested from the correspondent. The trustees meet at least twice a year. Grants are normally considered in January, June and October.

Walsall Wood (Former Allotment) Charity

£9,200

Correspondent: Craig Goodall, Democratic Services, Walsall Council, Council House, Lichfield Street, Walsall WS1 1TW (01922 654765; email: goodallc@walsall.gov.uk; website: www.walsall.gov.uk/charities)

CC number: 510627

Eligibility

Residents of the borough of Walsall who are in need.

Types of grants

Grants for school uniforms and clothing, including footwear.

Annual grant total

In 2013/14 the charity had an income of £22,500 and a total expenditure of £18,700. We estimate that the amount of grants given to individuals for educational purposes totalled around £9,200.

Exclusions

Grants are not made for the relief of taxes, public funds, rent arrears or utility bills.

Applications

An application form is available to download from the council's website and can also be requested from the correspondent by telephone. It is helpful, but not essential, to submit supporting evidence along with an application. This can include proof of the applicant's income, such as a wage slip, benefit letter or bank statement, or a supporting letter from a professional familiar with the applicant's case. The trustees meet around six times a year.

Other information

The charity is administered by the Walsall Council Democratic Services team, which also administers a number of other funds.

Worcestershire

The Alvechurch Grammar School Endowment

£19,000 (30+ grants)

Correspondent: David Gardiner, Administrator, 18 Tanglewood Close, Blackwell, Bromsgrove, Worcestershire B60 1BU (0121 445 3522; email: enquiries@alvechurchgst.org.uk; website: www.alvechurchgst.org.uk/index.htm)

CC number: 527440

Eligibility

Children and young people under the age of 25 who/whose parents are resident in the old parish of Alvechurch (Hopwood, Rowney Green, Bordesley and parts of Barnt Green) and who require financial assistance.

Types of grants

Scholarships, exhibitions, bursaries and maintenance allowances ranging from £50 to about £750. Support may be given for specific expenses or purchases, such as outfits/clothing, school uniforms, tools, equipment/instruments, books or travel in pursuance of education, or educational outings both in the UK and abroad. Applications are invited form people in further/higher education and training but schoolchildren and people starting work can also be supported. The charity is willing to sponsor a wide range of educational activities including various projects, personal development, training, language courses, sports, volunteering experience and so on.

Annual grant total

In 2014/15 the charity had an income of £23,000 and an expenditure of £20,500. We estimate the annual total amount of grants awarded to individuals to be around £19,000.

The charity's website states: 'In the past 12 months the trust has made more than 30 awards'

Exclusions

Assistance is only available where support cannot be received from the local authority.

Applications

Application forms can be found on the charity's website or requested from the correspondent. Applications should be submitted by 1 January, 1 May and 1 September each year.

Other information

Grants are also given to local youth organisations.

Malvern Hills

Walwyn's Educational Foundation

£4,200

Correspondent: Charles Walker, Correspondent, 29 Brookmill Close, Colwall, Malvern WR13 6HY (01684 541995; email: cdw1810@btinternet.com)

CC number: 527152

Eligibility

Young people aged 16 and over who live in the parishes of Colwall and Little Malvern and are pursuing approved courses in tertiary education up to first degree level (including vocational training). Grants may be available for secondary school, training college and higher education students, also people starting work/entering a trade. Professions insisting on qualifications beyond first degree (for example, teaching profession) will be considered on their merits.

Types of grants

Small grants, usually around £150, are available towards general educational expenses, including the cost of books, fees, equipment/instruments, living expenses and study or travel abroad.

Annual grant total

In 2014/15 the foundation had an income of £4,200 and an expenditure of £4,500. We estimate that about £4,200 was given in grants.

Exclusions

Mature students are not supported.

Applications

Application forms can be requested from the correspondent. They are considered in September and can be submitted directly by the individual.

Worcester

Worcester Municipal Exhibitions Foundation (Worcester Municipal Charities)

£8,300 (12 grants)

Correspondent: Adrian Robinson, Kateryn Heywood House, Berkeley Court, The Foregate, Worcester WR1 3QG (01905 317117; fax: 01905 619979; email: admin@wmcharities.org.uk; website: www.wmcharities.org.uk)

CC number: 527570

Eligibility

People of any age in financial hardship who are resident or have been educated in the city of Worcester and the parishes of Bransford, Leigh, Powick and Rushwick for at least two years.

Types of grants

One-off grants are given to schoolchildren, people starting work, further and higher education students (including mature students), apprentices and people entering a trade/profession. Support can be given for fees, books, equipment/instruments, educational outings in the UK, also for clothing to people starting work and for schoolchildren (excluding uniforms).

Grants are normally in the range of £20–£1,000, but can reach up to around £1,500.

Annual grant total

In 2014 the foundation had assets of £1.15 million and an income of £113,000. Educational grants to 12 individuals totalled £8,300, half of the grants being for sums over £1,000.

Exclusions

Grants are not given:

- To people outside the area of benefit
- To those attending private or fee-paying institutions unless there is no reasonable public alternative
- For travel abroad
- Beyond first degree level

The foundation no longer assists with the cost of school uniforms and related enquiries should be made directly to the individual's school. However, note that clothing grants are made through the Worcester Consolidated Municipal

Charity (Charity Commission no. 205299) for schoolchildren, based on the family's income and expenditure and their clothing needs.

Applications

Application forms and guidelines can be found on the foundation's website. They can be submitted by the individual or through a school, college or educational welfare agency, if applicable. Grants are considered monthly. The deadline for applications is 12 noon the Thursday before each monthly meeting – exact dates of these are posted on the website. Note that handwritten applications are no longer accepted.

Other information

Grants are also given to schools and educational organisations. In 2014 a total of about £47,000 was awarded in six grants to organisations which provide educational facilities within the area of benefit.

The same body of trustees administers Worcester Municipal Exhibitions Foundation (Charity Commission no. 527570) and Worcester Consolidated Municipal Charity (Charity Commission no. 205299), which provides support to individuals and organisations for welfare purposes.

Wychavon

John Martin's Charity

£257,500

Correspondent: John Daniels, The Clerk to the Trustees, 16 Queen's Road, Evesham, Worcester WR11 4JN (01386 765440; email: enquires@johnmartins.org.uk; website: www.johnmartins.org.uk)

CC number: 527473

Eligibility

People resident in Evesham, Worcestershire.

Types of grants

Individual students, between the age of 16 and state retirement age, may apply for educational grants to support study in a wide variety of courses at local colleges in addition to universities and colleges throughout the country and the Open University. Qualifying courses include HND, degree, postgraduate and part-time vocational courses. Applicants must have been a permanent resident or (if living away from home during term time) have maintained a residential address in the town for a minimum of twelve months immediately prior to 1 September in the year of application.

The charity also makes grants for:

- School uniform costs – grants may be available to assist with the cost of school uniforms for children aged 4–18 who live with a parent/guardian in Evesham
- Educational visits and music, arts and sports activities (Miscellaneous Education Grant) – grants of up to £140 may be available to students aged 4–18 for activities including school trips, music lessons/instrument hire and sporting activities. Applications are assessed based on the number of children and adults in household, and housing costs are also taken into consideration. There is an easy-to-use eligibility calculator on the website
- Standards of Excellence Awards – grants for students aged 4–18 for achieving a standard of excellence in a sporting or arts/music area. Applications are not subject to a financial assessment; however, suitable evidence of the achievement must be provided

Annual grant total

In 2014/15 the charity had assets of £22.3 million and an income of £743,500. Grants were made to individuals and organisations totalling £657,500 and were distributed as follows:

Purpose	Grants to individuals	Grants to organisations
Promotion of education	£257,500	£75,000
Relief in need	£111,500	£99,000
Health and other charitable purposes	£9,600	£29,000
Religious support	£8,200	£67,000

Exclusions

The charity does not currently provide grants for full-time courses below HND/ degree level.

Applications

Application forms are available from the correspondent or as a download from the website, where eligibility criteria is also posted, along with the grants on offer. Applications are usually accepted from July to September for further and higher education grants. Grants for part-time vocational courses are available throughout the year. Original documentation as proof of residency in Evesham must be provided and grants will not be considered without this evidence. Applications from those over 25 are financially assessed.

Application forms for Miscellaneous Education Grants and Standards of Excellence Awards are available to download from the charity's website, where eligibility criteria is also available. Application forms for school uniforms can be downloaded from the 'families and individuals' page on the website.

Other information

Grants are also made to organisations and to individuals for welfare purposes. The charity has an informative website.

Wyre Forest

The Bewdley Old Grammar School Foundation

£7,000

Correspondent: Shana Kent, Bewdley Old Grammar School Foundation, Bewdley High School, Stourport Road, Bewdley DY12 1BL (01299 403277; email: office@bewdley.worcs.sch.uk)

CC number: 527429

Eligibility

People under the age of 25 living in Bewdley, the parish of Rock and Ribbesford and Stourport-on-Severn.

Types of grants

Grants are available to schoolchildren and further/higher education students to help with general educational costs, including books, uniforms/clothing, necessities and maintenance. Music and arts studies are also supported.

Annual grant total

In 2014 the foundation had an income of £8,500 and an expenditure of £7,500. We have estimated the annual total amount of grants awarded to be around £7,000.

Applications

Apply in writing to the correspondent. Applications should be made by the individual directly or through a referral agency, if applicable.

East of England

General

Nichol-Young Foundation

£8,500

Correspondent: Foundation Administrator, Bates Wells and Braithwaite, 27 Friars Street, Sudbury, Suffolk CO10 2AD (01787 880440)

CC number: 259994

Eligibility

Individuals in need who are in full-time education, with a preference for those who live in East Anglia.

Types of grants

One-off and recurrent grants, generally of around £500, to those 'who perhaps feel marginalised by society or who wish to improve their life skills so that they in turn can then be of benefit to others'. Awards are given for general educational needs, educational trips, medical electives and other such projects undertaken by individuals. Grants may also be given for computers, equipment and tools.

Annual grant total

In 2014 the foundation had an income of £33,500 and a charitable expenditure of £23,000. Grants awarded to individuals in education totalled £8,500.

Applications

Apply in writing to the correspondent. Applications are normally considered on a quarterly basis. Unsuccessful applicants will only be contacted if an sae is provided. Where possible, payments are paid through an educational institution.

Other information

The foundation also provides grants to small organisations, clergy/Christian centres, community projects and activities aimed at children and young people. In 2014 a total of £14,300 was awarded for causes other than education, including grants to organisations, several awards to young individuals (such as support for adventure activities) and one welfare grant to an individual.

Note: The foundation has previously noted that telephone enquiries are not welcomed.

Cambridgeshire

Bishop Laney's Charity

£26,500 (111 grants)

Correspondent: Richard Tyler, Secretary, 8 Barton Close, Witchford, Ely, Cambridgeshire CB6 2HS (01353 662813; email: richard_i_tyler@hotmail.com; website: www.whitingandpartners.co.uk/Bishop-Laney-Charity-Vocation)

CC number: 311306

Eligibility

People in need under the age of 25 who live in the parishes of Soham and Ely. Consideration might be given to people under 25 who live in other parts of Cambridgeshire where funds permit.

Types of grants

Grants are given towards education and training, especially apprentices and people starting work. Where possible awards are recurrent and can be given towards uniforms/clothing, books and equipment/instruments, also study or travel abroad, excursions in the UK and maintenance/living expenses. Grants to individuals are of around £150–£250.

Annual grant total

In 2014/15 the charity had assets of £3.3 million and an income of £113,500. A total of £26,500 was awarded in 111 grants to individuals.

Applications

Application forms are available from the trust's website or can be requested from the correspondent. They can be submitted directly by the individual. Applications should include a copy of the applicant's birth certificate, proof of attendance at college/university/training and details of the items needed.

Other information

The charity can also give grants to educational establishments.

The Henry Morris Memorial Trust

£3,900

Correspondent: Peter Hains, Trustee, 24 Barton Road, Haslingfield, Cambridge CB23 1LL (email: mail@henrymorris.plus.com; website: www.henrymorris.plus.com)

CC number: 311419

Eligibility

Young people between the ages of 13 and 19 who live or attend/have attended school or college in Cambridge/Cambridgeshire. The trust's website states: 'Applicants who can demonstrate the strength of their interest, and evidence of planning, stand the best chances.'

Types of grants

The trust is offering grants for short travel expeditions with specific purposes and to help with the cost of materials and running expenses for a project not involving travel.

Some examples of previously supported activities include: making a video diary of the village shop; constructing a wildlife garden pond; investigating local wartime airfields; comparing two local windmills (home-based projects); a journey to learn about the Romans in Britain at Hadrian's Wall; a visit to a famous harpist in Dresden to listen and learn; a journey to investigate the history of the piano at the Paris Museum of Music; and an enquiry into the story surrounding the fate of the 44 Jewish children of Izieu (travel awards).

Grants are from £20 to £200. Candidates are encouraged to fundraise towards their goal themselves.

Annual grant total

In 2014 the trust had an income of £4,500 and an expenditure of £4,100. We estimate that the annual total amount of grants awarded was around £3,900.

Exclusions

Grants will not normally be made towards the full cost of a gap year project, foreign exchange, school coursework, a holiday or a project planned and managed by a school/other organisation (for example, Raleigh International). The cost of permanent equipment is not usually covered. The trust's website notes: 'In general, the trust is looking to help with expeditions or enterprises substantially planned by you.'

Applications

Application forms are available from local schools or from the trust's website. They can be submitted directly by the individual by 31 January for consideration in February/March. Candidates under the age of 18 will need a full approval from a parent/guardian. Potential grant recipients are invited for an interview in Cambridge.

Other information

The trustees are looking for independently planned and managed projects and particularly seek to encourage 'individual candidates wishing to pursue topics of particular fascination to them'. All travel and accommodation arrangements have to be made by the applicants themselves.

Applications may be made by individuals, with a friend or in a small group.

Elizabeth Wright's Charity

£4,000

Correspondent: Dr Iain Mason, Trustee, 13 Tavistock Road, Wisbech, Cambridgeshire PE13 2DY (01945 588646; email: i.h.mason60@gmail.com)

CC number: 203896

Eligibility

People who live in the parishes of St Peter and Paul and St Augustine, Cambridgeshire.

Types of grants

Grants for students of music and other arts and towards vocational education or training amongst other areas. Primary, secondary and further education students can receive grants for projects in the areas of RE, citizenship, arts, music and drama or Christian and youth work.

Annual grant total

In 2014 the charity had assets of £1 million and an income of £41,000. Grants to individuals for educational purposes totalled around £4,000.

Exclusions

Grants are not given for people starting work.

Applications

Apply in writing to the correspondent. Applications can be submitted directly by the individual at any time.

Other information

The charity also makes grants to schools and organisations and supports individuals for welfare purposes.

Fenland

Town Lands Educational Foundation

£10,000

Correspondent: Rosemary Gagen, Clerk to the Trustees, 78 High Road, Gorefield, Wisbech, Cambridgeshire PE13 4NB (01945 870454; email: leveoffees@aol.com)

CC number: 311325

Eligibility

Schoolchildren and people in further/higher education who live in Leverington, Parson Drove and Gorefield.

Types of grants

One-off grants according to need.

Annual grant total

In 2013/14 the foundation had an income of £23,500 and expenditure of £22,500. We estimate that around £10,000 was distributed in grants to individuals for education.

Applications

Application forms are available from the correspondent for consideration in September.

Other information

Grants are also made to local schools.

Huntingdonshire

Huntingdon Freemen's Trust

£153,500

Correspondent: Karen Clark, Grants Officer, 37 High Street, Huntingdon, Cambridgeshire PE29 3AQ (01480 414909; email: info@huntingdonfreemen. org.uk; website: www. huntingdonfreemen.org.uk)

CC number: 1044573

Eligibility

People in need resident in Huntingdon (normally for at least one year). See 'Other information' for specific details.

Types of grants

Grants are given to students for half of their accommodation fees while at university or college and help is also available for school equipment and educational activities. Support can be given both in the early years and in further/higher education, including vocational training.

The annual report notes:

> Local pupils benefit from grants to nursery and primary schools in the town to supplement local education authority provision, maintained at a rate of £19 per pupil. Post 16 students taking vocational courses in local colleges are assisted with course fees and some equipment costs. Students going away to university/college are helped with accommodation costs, where we have normally paid up to 50% of their annual rent.

Grants to students have been capped at £1,000 per student per year.

Annual grant total

In 2013/14 the trust had assets of £15.8 million and an income of about £438,500. The accounts state that educational grants were made totalling £153,500. Student grants for accommodation were made totalling £124,500 and school grants were awarded totalling £34,500. These figures 'include some commitments where payments are made in future years and do not therefore equate to accounts figures'.

Exclusions

The trust cannot substitute services that should be provided by the state but may supplement them.

Applications

Student application forms are available online. Potential applicants are invited to get in touch with the trust or drop by to discuss their needs. The trust's website states: 'We are always open to suggestions of how we could provide more help, so if you have an idea drop in for a chat!'

Most applications will involve visiting the applicants' homes to assess their needs and financial circumstances. If you have a support worker, it would be helpful if they liaised with the trust. If you are applying for help with accommodation costs, either a copy of the University/College fees for the Halls of Residence or a copy of your lease or rental agreement at an alternative rented accommodation, will be required.

Applications are considered at monthly meetings.

Other information

Applications can only be considered 'from individuals, groups and organisations who live or are based within the area covered by Huntingdon Town Council and have a postcode starting with PE'. This includes Oxmoor, Hartford, Sapley, Stukeley Meadows and Hinchingbrooke Park.

Organisations are supported and individuals can also receive relief-in-need grants.

South Cambridgeshire

John Huntingdon's Charity

£10,600

Correspondent: Jill Hayden, Charity Manager, John Huntingdon House, Tannery Road, Sawston, Cambridge CB2 3UW (01223 492492; email: office@ johnhuntingdon.org.uk; website: www. johnhuntingdon.org.uk)

CC number: 1118574

Eligibility

People who are in need and live in the parish of Sawston in Cambridgeshire.

Types of grants

One-off grants, usually ranging from £25 to £250, are given to help with the costs of school trips, school uniforms and, sometimes, with nursery or playgroup fees.

Annual grant total

In 2014 the charity had assets of £8.6 million and an income of £393,000. The amount of grants given to individuals totalled £21,000. Awards are given for both social welfare and educational purposes, although a breakdown of distributions was not included in the annual report and accounts. We estimate that educational grants to individuals totalled £10,600.

Applications

In the first instance, call the charity's office to arrange an appointment with one of its support workers.

Other information

The charity is proactive in supporting the community in Sawston and documents its activities in its informative annual report. Amongst its activities, the charity provides advice and housing services, sometimes in partnership with other local organisations. More details are available on the website or by contacting the charity's office.

Lincolnshire

The Alenson and Erskine Educational Foundation

£4,200

Correspondent: Edwina Arnold, Correspondent, Crooks Cottage, Wrangle Bank, Wrangle, Boston PE22 9DL (01205 270352; email: wranglepc@aol.com)

CC number: 527671

Eligibility

People under the age of 25 who live in the parishes of Old Leake, New Leake and Wrangle. Preference is given to people who have attended county or voluntary school for at least two years. Candidates should normally have been resident in the area of benefit for at least five years.

Types of grants

Grants can be given to further/higher education students towards educational necessities and fees, or to school leavers entering a trade/profession to help with the cost of books, equipment, clothing or travel.

Annual grant total

In 2014 the foundation had an income of £3,800 and an expenditure of £4,400. We estimate the annual total amount of grants awarded to be around £4,200.

Exclusions

Grants are not given for A-levels. According to our research, schoolchildren (other than those with special educational needs) are only considered if family difficulties are serious.

Applications

Application forms can be requested from the correspondent. They can be submitted by individuals directly via post or email and are usually considered in October/November. Applicants can only claim for what they have bought and not what they would like to buy and must submit receipts with their application.

Allen's Charity (Apprenticing Branch)

£4,500

Correspondent: Keith Savage, Correspondent, Lenton Lodge, 94 Wignals Gate, Holbeach, Spalding PE12 7HR (01406 490157)

CC number: 213842–1

Eligibility

Children and young people in need who live in the parish of Long Sutton. Higher education students between the ages of 18 and 25 are also supported.

Types of grants

Grants towards apprenticeships and related costs. Students can be assisted with general educational necessities.

Annual grant total

In the past the charity has made grants totalling around £4,500.

Applications

Application forms can be requested from the correspondent. The scheme is normally advertised in the local press and promoted by local employers.

Other information

This charity is linked to Allen's Charity (Charity Commission no. 213842).

Christ's Hospital Endowment at Potterhanworth

£12,000

Correspondent: Yvonne Woodcock, Clerk to the Governors, The Conifers, Barff Road, Potterhanworth, Lincoln LN4 2DU (01522 790942)

CC number: 527669

Eligibility

People under the age of 25 who live, or whose parents live, in the parish of Potterhanworth, Lincolnshire.

Types of grants

Grants are available to schoolchildren towards the cost of educational visits and extra-curricular activities such as music, arts, sports and other social and physical training. Further education students and people in vocational training, including apprentices, can be supported for general educational needs. Further education awards were of about £100 each.

Annual grant total

In 2014 the charity had an income of £70,000 and grants totalled around £12,000, broken down as follows:

Educational visits and tuition fees, etc.	£10,200
Further education students	£600
School, pre-school, autumn festival	£850
Primary school leavers	£350

Exclusions

Grants are not normally given to cover the cost of school fees or school books.

Applications

Apply in writing to the correspondent. Applications can be made either directly by the individual or through a third party, for example a parent/guardian or the individual's educational institution. Applications are normally considered once a year in November and should be received before 31 October. Where applicable, valid receipts for the items/ services purchased must be included.

Other information

The charity also supports local schools and nurseries.

Cowell and Porrill

£7,500

Correspondent: Roger Hooton, Clerk, 33 Glen Drive, Boston, Lincolnshire PE21 7QB (01205 310088)

CC number: 240438

Eligibility

People under the age of 25 who live, or whose parents live, in the parishes of Benington and Leverton.

Types of grants

Awards are usually in the range of £250 and £600. Support is given for general educational needs to people at any level or stage of their education and undertaking the study of any subject.

Annual grant total

In 2014 the charity had an income of £15,500 and an expenditure of £15,000. We estimate that the annual total amount of grants awarded to individuals was around £7,500.

Applications

Apply in writing to the correspondent. Our research shows that applications can be submitted directly by the individual by the end of July for consideration in September.

Other information

The charity also provides almshouses for the poor residents of Benington and Leverton and can support local schools, where assistance is not already provided by the local authorities.

Deeping St James United Charities

£6,100

Correspondent: Julie Banks, Clerk, The Institute, 38 Church Street, Deeping St James, Peterborough PE6 8HD (01778 344707 (Tues/Thurs 9am–12pm); email: dsjunitedcharities@btconnect.com; website: www.dsjunitedcharities.org.uk)

CC number: 248848

Eligibility

School pupils, college/university students and people in training under the age of

25 in the parish of Deeping St James (including Frognall).

Types of grants

Schoolchildren in the three local schools are assisted to enable them to take part in additional educational activities and opportunities, such as school trips or educational outings in the UK. Grants can also be made towards the expense of school uniforms.

University/college (or equivalent) students generally aged 18–25 who are undertaking their first degree/college qualification can be supported each year for three years of their course. Grants can assist with the costs of books or equipment needed for their study (e.g. scissors for hairdressers).

Annual grant total

In 2014 the charity had assets of £2.7 million and an income of £98,000. Educational grants totalled £6,100.

The 2014 annual report and accounts describe how the grants were distributed:

> A total of £4,650 was given in book grants for educational purposes in 2014. In addition a small number of grants have been given to subsidise educational trips for young people and to provide music lessons. A sum of £650 was granted to one young man in order that he could continue his A level studies online and singing lessons have been provided for a young girl who will benefit socially.

Exclusions

The charity's annual report from 2013 stated that 'the trustees decided in 2012 that, in future, it may not be possible to continue giving grants for educational trips abroad'. In 2014 no such grants were made.

Applications

Applications for grants for schoolchildren should generally be directed to the school.

Application forms for university/college students are available online or can be requested from the correspondent. They should be submitted as soon as a place on the course has been granted.

Other information

The charity is an amalgamation of a number of small charities from the local area. This charity also gives grants to individuals for welfare purposes and local organisations, groups, clubs or societies. Regular support is given to all three schools in Deeping St James for the benefit of their pupils.

Applicants are encouraged to get in touch with the charity via phone, email or by calling in to the office if they have any questions or need further assistance.

The charity is also funding counselling sessions with Citizens Advice for local residents. The sessions are held on a

fortnightly basis at the Institute (to book an appointment call: 01780 763051).

Farmer Educational Foundation

£19,000

Correspondent: Michael Griffin, Administrator, 39 Church Street, Warmington, Peterborough PE8 6TE (01832 281076; email: griffin325@ btinternet.com)

CC number: 527636

Eligibility

Children and young people who live in the parish of Holbeach, South Lincolnshire.

Types of grants

Grants are given up to £150 to help schools in higher/further education and sometimes to assist schools serving Holbeach with projects.

Annual grant total

In 2013/14 the foundation had an income of £32,000 and an expenditure of £25,000. Grants made to individuals totalled approximately £19,000.

Applications

Application forms are available from Holbeach Library, to be submitted by the individual at the end of August. Applications are considered in September.

Frampton Educational Foundation

£3,000

Correspondent: Mark Hildred, Correspondent, Moore Thompson, Bank House, Broad Street, Spalding PE11 1TB (01775 711333)

CC number: 527784

Eligibility

People who have lived in the ancient parish of Frampton for at least five years (generally above elementary education).

Types of grants

One-off and recurrent grants are given according to need.

Annual grant total

In 2013/14 the foundation had an income of £5,500 and an expenditure of £6,400. We estimate that about £3,000 was given in grants to individuals.

Applications

Applications may be made in writing to the correspondent. Requests are considered in early October and students must re-apply each year.

Other information

Grants are also given to local schools.

Gainsborough Educational Charity

£3,000

Correspondent: Maria Bradley, Clerk to the Trustees, c/o Burton and Dyson Solicitors, 22 Market Place, Gainsborough DN21 2BZ (01427 610761; email: law@burtondyson.com; website: www.burtondyson.com/about-burton-and-dyson/corporate-social-responsibility/gainsborough-educational-charity)

CC number: 527299

Eligibility

Children and young people between the ages of 11 and 25 who live, or whose parents live, in Gainsborough, Lea, Morton or Thonock.

Types of grants

The charity provides grants, bursaries, allowances to help with the cost of uniforms and specialist clothing, fees, books, equipment/instruments and other necessities to schoolchildren, further/higher education students and people starting work. Travel costs in the UK and abroad for educational purposes and music/arts studies are also supported.

Annual grant total

In 2013/14 the charity had an income of £5,300 and a total expenditure of £4,300. We estimate the annual total amount of grants awarded to individuals to be around £3,000. A local school is also supported.

Exclusions

Grants are not given towards the purchase of computers.

Applications

Application forms can be downloaded from Burton and Dyson Solicitor's website or requested from the correspondent. A completed application form, together with a reference from an academic tutor, can be submitted directly by the individual in advance of the trustees' meetings, which are held twice a year, normally in March and November.

Other information

One quarter of the charity's annual income is given to the Queen Elizabeth Grammar School at Gainsborough, for needs that are not supported by the local authority.

The Hesslewood Children's Trust (Hull Seamen's and General Orphanage)

See entry on page 302

George Jobson's Trust

£11,000

Correspondent: Sarah Steel, Correspondent, c/o Chattertons Solicitors, 5 South Street, Horncastle LN9 6DS (01507 522456; email: alistair.thomson@chattertons.com)

CC number: 213875

Eligibility

Children and young people in need who live or attend/have attended school in the parish of Horncastle.

Types of grants

Recurrent grants between £50 and £500 to people in education and training for general educational needs, including books, courses, equipment/instruments and various projects.

Annual grant total

In 2013/14 the trust had an income of £24,500 and a total expenditure of £23,000. We estimate that the amount of grants given to individuals totalled about £11,000.

Exclusions

Our research suggests that grants are not normally awarded to postgraduate students.

Applications

Application forms can be requested from the correspondent and submitted directly by the individual or through a social worker/welfare agency, if applicable.

Other information

Most of the trust's funding goes to schools, youth organisations and students at college.

The Kesteven Children in Need

£500

Correspondent: Alexandra Howard, Trustee, Nocton Rise, Lincoln LN4 2AF (01522 791217; email: enquiries@kcin.org; website: www.kcin.org)

CC number: 700008

Eligibility

Children/young people up to the age of 16 who live in Kesteven.

Types of grants

Grants of up to £500 towards books, clothing and educational outings.

Annual grant total

In 2014, the charity had an income of £15,100 and a total expenditure of £11,000. The majority of grants are usually awarded for welfare purposes, so we estimate that approximately £500 was awarded for educational purposes.

Applications

Generally applications should be made through local social workers, health visitors, teachers and education officers. Information should include the family situation, the age of the child and his/her special needs. Applications are considered throughout the year.

Kirton-in-Lindsey Exhibition Foundation

£4,200

Correspondent: Julia Melling, Correspondent, 7 Darwin Street, Kirton Lindsey, Gainsborough, Lincolnshire DN21 4BZ (01652 649425; email: julia.melling@btinternet.com)

CC number: 529749

Eligibility

People who live in the parishes of Blyborough, Grayingham, Hibaldstow, Kirton-in-Lindsey, Manton, Northorpe, Redbourne, Scotter, Scotton or Waddingham and who have attended one of the following primary schools for at least two years: Hibaldstow; Kirton-in-Lindsey; Messingham; Scotter; or Waddingham.

Types of grants

Grants are given to higher education students towards the cost of books.

The foundation's record on the Charity Commission's website notes that it offers the awards of Junior and Senior Exhibitions. The Junior ones are available to secondary school pupils and the Senior ones are given to higher education students. Awards are also available to students 'at any institution of technical, industrial or professional instruction'. Additional support given to children resident in the beneficial area to continue their education at evening schools, day or evening classes.

Annual grant total

In 2014/15 the foundation had an income of £3,800 and an expenditure of £4,500. We have estimated that the annual total amount of grants awarded to individuals was around £4,200.

Applications

Application forms are available from the correspondent.

Other information

The foundation also provides books or fittings for a school library in the parish of Kirton-in-Lindsey for the use of scholars.

The Kochan Trust

£24,000

Correspondent: Revd Roger Massingberd-Mundy, Honorary Secretary, The Old Post Office, The Street, West Raynham, Fakenham, Norfolk NR21 7AD (01328 838611; fax: 01328 838698; email: roger_mundy@btconnect.com)

CC number: 1052976

Eligibility

People studying veterinary science or creative arts, music and performance who live in Lincolnshire and are in need of financial assistance.

Types of grants

One-off grants are given according to need. Support can be given for tuition fees, purchase of an instrument, research of veterinary science or other educational expenses.

Annual grant total

In 2014 the trust had an income of £28,500 and an expenditure of £31,000. We estimate that grants were made totalling £24,000 (at the time of writing in August 2015 the accounts for 2014 had not been submitted).

Applications

Apply in writing to the correspondent. The trustees meet four times a year, usually in January, April, July and November. Applications should give some details about the candidate and state what the grant is needed for. They can be made by individuals directly or through a third party, such as a school/college or educational welfare agency, if applicable.

Lincolnshire Community Foundation

£1,600

Correspondent: Sue Fortune, Grants Manager, 4 Mill House, Moneys Yard, Carre Street, Sleaford, Lincolnshire NG34 7TW (01529 305825; email: lincolnshirecf@btconnect.com; website: www.lincolnshirecf.co.uk)

CC number: 1092328

Eligibility

Generally, residents of Lincolnshire who are in need; however, different funds have different eligibility criteria attached.

Types of grants

The type and amount of grant available depends on the fund being applied to. See the foundation's website for more information on open funds.

Annual grant total

In 2014/15 the foundation had assets of £5.7 million and an income of £664,500. Grants are mainly made to organisations. We estimate that around £1,600 was awarded to individuals for educational and opportunities purposes through The Colin Batts Family Trust, which also gives to individuals for social welfare purposes and to organisations. Educational grants to individuals have, in previous years, also been made from the MAST (Make-a-Start) Fund; however, in 2014/15 this fund had no expenditure.

Exclusions

Grants cannot be awarded retrospectively.

Applications

See the foundation's website for more information on the funds it operates and how to apply for assistance.

Dame Margaret Thorold's Apprenticing Charity

£4,200

Correspondent: The Trustees, c/o Tallents Solicitors, 2 Westgate, Southwell NG25 0JJ (01636 813411)

CC number: 527628

Eligibility

People aged 18 to 25 living in the ancient parishes of Sedgebrook, Marston and Cranwell who are undertaking an apprenticeship.

Types of grants

Small cash grants to assist students in further or higher education, especially vocational training. Grants may be recurrent or one-off and are towards books, fees/living expenses or study/travel abroad.

Annual grant total

In 2014 the charity had an income of £1,800 and an expenditure of £4,400. We estimate that grants made totalled approximately £4,200.

Applications

Applications should be submitted in writing by the individual or parent/guardian or through the school/college/educational welfare agency, by mid-January for consideration in February. If appropriate, a letter of support from the employer or place of training should be included with the application.

Boston

Sir Thomas Middlecott's Exhibition Foundation

£12,500

Correspondent: Frank Wilson, Administrator, 57A Bourne Road, Spalding PE11 1JR (01775 766117; email: info@middlecotttrust.org.uk; website: www.middlecotttrust.org.uk)

CC number: 527283

Eligibility

Students who live in the parishes of Algarkirk, Fosdyke, Frampton, Kirton, Sutterton and Wyberton in Lincolnshire, who are in further/higher education and are aged under 25. Applicants must have attended a maintained primary school in the area for at least two years.

Types of grants

Grants are given to students in further/higher education towards books, clothing and equipment/instruments.

Annual grant total

In 2013/14 the foundation had assets of £747,500 and an income of £35,000. Grants were made totalling £12,500.

Applications

Application forms are available from the correspondent, or from the foundation's website, to be submitted directly by the individual via post. Applications are considered in October and should be submitted by the end of September.

East Lindsey

Kitchings Educational Charity

£6,500

Correspondent: Mrs M. Sankey, Trustee, 50 Station Road, Bardney, Lincoln LN3 5UD (01526 398555)

CC number: 527707

Eligibility

Children and young people under the age of 25 who live in Bardney, Bucknall, Southrey or Tupholme and are in need of financial assistance.

Types of grants

Small grants to schoolchildren and further/higher education students to assist with the costs of books, equipment/instruments or other general educational necessities.

Annual grant total

In 2014/15 the charity had an income of £11,000 and an expenditure of £13,000.

It also supports local schools; therefore, we estimate the annual total amount of grants awarded to individuals to be about £6,500.

Exclusions

Our research suggests that support is not given to students who choose to take A-levels (or equivalent) at college when they could take the same course at their school.

Applications

Apply in writing to the correspondent enclosing an sae. Applications can be submitted directly by the individual or through the applicant's school, university/college, educational welfare agency, if applicable. Applications are normally considered in October and should be received by the end of September.

Other information

The charity also provides financial support to The Bardney Joint Church of England and Methodist Primary School or The Bucknall Primary School, where support is not already provided by the local authority.

Kitchings General Charity

£1,500

Correspondent: Mrs J. Smith, Secretary, 42 Abbey Road, Bardney, Lincoln LN3 5XA (01526 398505)

CC number: 219957

Eligibility

People living in the parish of Bardney, Southrey, Tupholme and Bucknall. Our research suggests that support is particularly given to students, especially mature, part-time, and vocational students.

Types of grants

Grants may be given for playgroup fees, books, excursions, uniforms and sports equipment. Awards are usually in the range of £200–£500 but can be of up to £1,000.

Annual grant total

In 2014 the charity had assets of £13,400 and an income of £36,500. Grants made for educational purposes totalled around £3,000 and we estimate that about £1,500 was given to individuals.

Applications

Applications may be made in writing to the correspondent and should include some background details, such as your age, the name of the educational establishment and course undertaken and a brief description of education to date. Our research indicates that

applications are normally considered in May, October and January.

Other information

Grants are also given to local schools and organisations, and to individuals for welfare purposes.

Mapletoft Scholarship Foundation

£5,400

Correspondent: Patrick Purves, Correspondent, The Old Vicarage, Church Street, Louth, Lincolnshire LN11 9DE (01507 605883; email: pmp@bmcf.co.uk)

CC number: 527649

Eligibility

People between the ages of 16 and 25 who are engaged or about to engage in higher education. Applicants must have attended primary school in the parishes of North Thoresby, Grainsby and Waithe and have been resident there for at least five years.

Types of grants

Grants of up to about £150 to help with further/higher education costs, including books, fees, living expenses or to supplement existing grants. Travel grants are also available. Grants are generally recurrent.

Annual grant total

In 2014/15 the foundation had an income of £5,000 and an expenditure of £5,600. We estimate that about £5,400 was given in grants.

Applications

Applications may be made in writing to the correspondent. They should be received no later than 30 September for consideration in November.

The Stickford Relief-in-Need Charity

£4,700

Correspondent: Katherine Bunting, Clerk, 28 Wide Bargate, Boston, Lincolnshire PE21 6RT (01205 351114; fax: 01205 356018)

CC number: 247423

Eligibility

Schoolchildren in need who live in the parish of Stickford.

Types of grants

School clothing grants. Grants are also made for welfare purposes.

Annual grant total

In 2014 the charity had an income of £16,900 and a total expenditure of

£19,600. Grants are made to both individuals and organisations for a range of purposes. We estimate that the amount of grants given to individuals for educational needs totalled £4,700.

Applications

Applications can be made in writing to the correspondent. They should be submitted directly by the individual and are considered all year.

Lincoln

Leeke Church Schools and Educational Foundation

£65,000 (117 grants)

Correspondent: Anne Young, Administrator, 23 Upper Long Leys Road, Lincoln LN1 3NJ (01522 526466; email: leekeclerk@gmail.com)

CC number: 527654

Eligibility

People under the age of 25 who live, or whose parents live, in the city of Lincoln. People studying in Lincoln with a home address elsewhere are ineligible.

Preference can be given to students from families on low income, minimum wage, state benefits, with a single parent or living independently.

Types of grants

One-off and recurrent grants, normally in the range of £150 to £500 each term. Grants are given to schoolchildren, further/higher education students and people entering a trade/profession. Support is aimed to help with the cost uniforms, outfits, books, equipment/instruments, fees, educational outings in the UK, educational leisure time activities, study or travel abroad and student exchanges.

Annual grant total

In 2013/14 the foundation had assets of £792,500 and an income of £54,000. Grants to 117 individuals totalled £65,000.

Exclusions

Grants are not given for those in private education.

Applications

Apply in writing to the correspondent. Applications can be submitted by the individual for consideration at any time. Educational costs should be listed either giving the real amount or a fair estimate.

North East Lincolnshire

The Educational Foundation of Philip and Sarah Stanford

£4,000

Correspondent: Eleanor Hine, Clerk, 86 Brigsley Road, Waltham, Grimsby, South Humberside DN37 0LA (01472 827883)

CC number: 529755

Eligibility

People under 25 who live in the ancient parishes of Aylesby, Barnoldby-le-Beck, Bradley, Irby-upon-Humber or Laceby.

Types of grants

Grants of £60 to £100 towards books, clothing or equipment/instruments for college students and undergraduates.

Annual grant total

In 2014 the foundation had an income of £9,500 and a total expenditure of £19,000. We estimate that the total amount of grants awarded to individuals is approximately £4,000.

Exclusions

Grants are not given for subjects and courses available in schools, to help with student fees, travel or living expenses.

Applications

Application forms are available from the correspondent. They can be submitted directly by the individual and should include reasons for the application and plans for the future. The closing date is normally 1 October each year. Applications must be in the applicant's own handwriting.

Other information

Grants are also made to organisations and the foundation provides bibles and food vouchers.

North Lincolnshire

The James Reginald Heslam Settlement

£1,600

Correspondent: Donald Johnson, Executive, 2 Park Square, Laneham Street, Scunthorpe DN15 6JH (01724 281616; email: don.johnson@sbblaw. com)

CC number: 256464

Eligibility

People in need who are resident in, or originally from, Scunthorpe and immediate district.

Types of grants

One-off grants of up to £1,000 towards books, computers, laptops, other electronic equipment and fees for further education.

Annual grant total

In 2013/14 the charity had an income of £2,400 and an expenditure of £1,700. We estimate that the annual total amount of grants awarded to individuals was around £1,600.

Applications

Applications should be made in writing to the correspondent by post or email. Our research suggests that applications should include a CV and details of the applicant's financial situation.

Withington Education Trust

£2,200

Correspondent: Benjamin Lawrence, Trustee, Frederick Gough School, Grange Lane South, Bottesford, Scunthorpe DN16 3NG (01724 860151; email: admin@frederickgoughschool.co.uk)

CC number: 507975

Eligibility

People under the age of 21 who live in the area of the North Lincolnshire council area (comprising Scunthorpe, Glanford and Boothferry).

Types of grants

Grants can be given for a wide range of educational needs, including academic or training courses, fees, maintenance expenses, and non-formal educational pursuits, for example, music, artistic activities, dance, sports and international opportunities. Grants usually range from £50 to £300.

Annual grant total

In 2013/14 the trust had an income of £4,800 and an expenditure of £2,500. We have estimated the annual total amount of grants awarded to be around £2,200.

Exclusions

Grants towards fees for private schooling are not normally given. Our research suggests that general educational necessities, such as books or equipment, are not usually covered.

The parishes of East Halton, North Killingholme, South Killingholme and that part of the district of Boothferry which lies north of the River Ouse are excluded from the area of benefit.

Applications

Apply in writing to the correspondent. Applications can be made at any time and preferably should be supported by the applicant's school or college. Awards are considered each term.

Other information

The trust was set up in 1979 in memory of Peter Withington, headteacher of Frederick Gough Comprehensive School.

South Holland

The Moulton Harrox Educational Foundation

£7,000

Correspondent: Richard Lewis, Administrator, Maples and Son Solicitors, 23 New Road, Spalding, Lincolnshire PE11 1DH (01775 722261; email: john.grimwood@oldershawgroup. com)

CC number: 527635

Eligibility

People up to 25 who live in the South Holland district council area.

Types of grants

One-off or recurrent grants for school pupils and college students, including mature students, to help with books, equipment, fees, clothing, educational outings and study or travel abroad. Preference is given to schoolchildren with serious family difficulties so the child has to educated away from home, and to people with special educational needs. Individuals must re-apply in order to receive the grant in the following year.

Annual grant total

In 2013/14 the foundation had an income of £35,000 and a total expenditure of £17,500. Grants were made to individuals for educational purposes totalling £7,000.

Applications

Application forms are available from the correspondent. Applications should be submitted before 31 August for consideration in September.

The Moulton Poor's Lands Charity

£200

Correspondent: Richard Lewis, Clerk, c/o Maples and Son Solicitors, 23 New Road, Spalding, Lincolnshire PE11 1DH (01775 722261)

CC number: 216630

Eligibility

People in need who live in the civil parish of Moulton.

Types of grants

Our research tells us that the charity mainly makes relief-in-need grants and that only occasionally educational grants are available.

Annual grant total

In 2014 the charity had assets of £928,500 and an income of £34,500. During the year £7,100 was awarded in grants, the majority of which, we believe, was to individuals for welfare purposes. We estimate that educational grants to individuals amounted to no more than £200

Applications

Applications may be made in writing to the correspondent, usually through a trustee. Appeals are normally considered in April and December.

Other information

The charity also manages almshouses, the rent from which makes up a small part of its income.

Spalding Relief-in-Need Charity

£12,700

Correspondent: Richard Knipe, Clerk and Solicitor, Dembleby House, 12 Broad Street, Spalding, Lincolnshire PE11 1ES (01775 768774; email: patrick. skells@chattertons.com)

CC number: 229268

Eligibility

People in need who live in the area covered by the district of South Holland. Preference is given to residents of the urban district of Spalding and the parishes of Cowbit, Deeping St Nicholas, Pinchbeck and Weston.

Types of grants

One-off grants, usually in the range of £100 to £400. Normally payments are made directly to suppliers.

Annual grant total

In 2014 the charity had assets of £1.3 million and an income of £50,000. Grants totalled £30,500, of which £500 was awarded to an organisation (Age UK Spalding). Grants to individuals amounted to £30,000, of which we estimate around £12,700 was given for educational purposes.

Exclusions

Grants are not intended to be made where support can be obtained from statutory sources.

Applications

Application forms can be requested from the charity. They can be submitted directly by the individual or assisted by a social worker/Citizens Advice/other welfare agency, if applicable. Applications are considered fortnightly.

Other information

This charity is connected with the Spalding Almshouse Charity (Charity Commission no. 220077) and share the same body of administration, the Spalding Town Husbands.

West Lindsey

Tyler Educational Foundation

£7,200

Correspondent: Mrs E. Bradley, Correspondent, 22 Market Place, Gainsborough, Lincolnshire DN21 2BZ (01427 010761)

CC number: 527691

Eligibility

People under the age of 21 who live in parishes of Morton and Thornock and are in financial need. Preference may be given for causes and activities related to the Church of England.

Types of grants

Grants are available for general educational needs.

Annual grant total

In 2013/14 the foundation had an income of £8,100 and an expenditure of £7,400. We estimate that the amount of grants given to individuals totalled around £7,200.

Applications

Applications may be made in writing to the correspondent.

Norfolk

Anguish's Educational Foundation

£479,500 (2,872 grants)

Correspondent: David Walker, Clerk to the Trustees, 1 Woolgate Court, St Benedicts Street, Norwich NR2 4AP (01603 621023; email: david.walker@ norwichcharitabletrusts.org.uk; website: www.norwichcharitabletrusts.org.uk)

CC number: 311288

Eligibility

Individuals under the age of 25 who are permanent residents of Norwich and the parishes of Costessey, Hellesdon, Catton, Sprowston, Thorpe-next-Norwich and Corpusty in the county of Norfolk. Preference is given to individuals who live in the city of Norwich and have lost either one or both parents.

Types of grants

Grants can be made towards school clothing, school trips; maintenance costs for university students; fees for school and further education; music, dance and sports training (if applicants are likely to reach professional standard); books and equipment/instruments; and support for childcare, dyslexia and scotopic therapy.

Most assistance is still given to school pupils, but further education and university students are increasingly supported. A few grants are made each year for educational travel including school trips and occasional overseas visits. However, the trustees believe that the most urgent need of parents is help with the cost of school clothing and the majority of grants are made for this purpose.

Annual grant total

In 2013/14 the foundation had assets of £19.8 million and an income of £876,500. Charitable expenditure totalled £595,000. Educational grants to 2,872 individuals totalled £479,500, broken down as follows:

School clothing	40%	£189,000
Further education and school fees	25%	£118,000
University student maintenance support	19%	£93,000
School trips	16%	£76,500
Books and equipment	1%	£1,500
Dyslexia and scotopic therapy and child minding		£500
Musical and dance training		£500

Exclusions

Postgraduates are not supported.

Applications

Apply in writing to the correspondent. Informal enquiries are welcomed prior to application.

Diss Parochial Charity

£500

Correspondent: Sylvia Grace, Honorary Clerk, 2 The Causeway, Victoria Road, Diss IP22 4AW (01379 650630)

CC number: 210154

Eligibility

People in need who live in the town and parish of Diss.

Types of grants

One-off grants can be given to schoolchildren towards fees, books and excursions, and to college students and undergraduates towards fees and books. Grants normally range from £30 to £200.

Annual grant total

In 2014 the charity had assets of £795,000 and an income of £30,000. Grants totalled £8,100, of which £400 was given to local schools and the remaining amount was awarded to individuals. Previously the majority of grants have been welfare related, with a couple of awards made for educational purposes. We estimate educational grants to have totalled £500.

Applications

Applications can be made in writing to the correspondent directly by the individual, through the individual's school/college/educational welfare agency or, if applicable, through another third party on behalf of the individual. They are considered upon receipt.

Other information

The charity also maintains four almshouses.

The Harold Moorhouse Charity

£7,500

Correspondent: Christine Harrison, Trustee, 30 Winmer Avenue, Winterton-on-Sea, Great Yarmouth NR29 4BA (01493 393975; email: haroldmoorhousecharity@yahoo.co.uk)

CC number: 287278

Eligibility

Individuals in need who live in Burnham Market in Norfolk only.

Types of grants

One-off grants are made ranging from £50 to £200 for educational equipment and school educational trips.

Annual grant total

Our research suggests that this charity gives around £15,000 to individuals each year, for both educational and welfare purposes.

Applications

Applications can be made in writing to the correspondent. They should be submitted directly by the individual in any month.

The Sir Philip Reckitt Educational Trust Fund
See entry on page 49

The Charity of Joanna Scott and Others

£82,500

Correspondent: Sam Loombe, Administrator, Hansells, 13–14 The Close, Norwich NR1 4DS (01603 224800)

CC number: 311253

Eligibility

People under the age of 25 who are being educated or live within five miles of Norwich City Hall. Preference is given to families in financial need.

Types of grants

Grants are given towards the costs of uniforms/other school clothing, books, equipment/instruments, fees, maintenance/living expenses, childcare, educational outings in the UK, study or travel abroad and student exchanges. Grants range between £15 and £2,000. The charity also offers interest-free loans.

Annual grant total

In 2013/14 the charity had assets of £2.3 million, an income of £77,500 and made grants to individuals totalling £82,500.

Applications

Application forms are available from the charity's website and can be posted or sent via email.

Other information

Grants are also given to organisations and schools.

Breckland

Swaffham Relief in Need Charity

£1,800

Correspondent: Richard Bishop, Town Clerk, The Town Hall, Swaffham, Norfolk PE37 7DQ (01760 722922; email: reliefinneed@ swaffhamtowncouncil.gov.uk; website: swaffhamtowncouncil.gov.uk)

CC number: 1072912

Eligibility

People in need who have lived in Swaffham for at least 12 months.

Types of grants

Grants are given for school uniforms, clothing and other necessities for those returning to work. They are also given to people who are re-entering education and need help with the cost of books, for example.

Annual grant total

In 2013/14 the charity had an income of £5,300 and a total expenditure of £7,800. We estimate that about £1,800 was given in grants to individuals for educational purposes.

Exclusions

Typically, an applicant is eligible for one grant in three years. The charity's website also states: 'The Charity does not exist to copy or replace other forms of assistance for which you may be able to legitimately claim from the State.'

Applications

Application forms are available from the correspondent. The charity may arrange a visit to the applicant as part of the application process and may contact a GP, vicar, priest, or care worker familiar with the applicant's situation. The trustees meet six times a year to consider applications – in January, March, May, July, September and November.

Other information

Information on the charity is available via the Swaffham Town Council website. The charity supports both individuals and organisations for social welfare and educational needs.

King's Lynn and West Norfolk

Richard Bunting's Educational Foundation (The Bunting's Fund)

£7,000

Correspondent: Christopher Padley, Trustee, Hedges, Creake Road, Burnham Thorpe, KING'S LYNN, Norfolk PE318HW (01328730258; email: padleychris@btinternet.com)

CC number: 311175

Eligibility

Children and young people in need who are under the age of 25 and live in the parish of Burnham Thorpe.

Types of grants

The foundation provides grants, scholarships, bursaries and maintenance allowances to individuals at school, university or any other educational establishment. Financial assistance is available towards the cost of clothing, school uniforms, books, equipment/ instruments, tools, educational outings, travel/study abroad, student exchange and other educational necessities or expenses. People entering a trade/ starting work and students of music or other arts are also supported. Our research shows that grants reach up to £400.

Annual grant total

In 2013/14 the foundation had an income of £4,300 and an expenditure of £7,300. We estimate the annual total amount of grants awarded to be around £7,000.

Applications

Apply in writing to the correspondent. Our research suggests that applications can be made either directly by the individual (if over 18) or by a parent/ guardian. Applications are normally considered in February and September, but emergencies can be dealt with on an ongoing basis.

Other information

The foundation can give financial assistance towards the provision of facilities for recreation, social or physical training for students in primary, secondary or further education, where these are not normally provided by the local authorities.

Hall's Exhibition Foundation

£68,500 (84+ grants)

Correspondent: Christopher Holt, Administrator, 4 Bewick Close, Snettisham, King's Lynn, Norfolk PE31 7PJ (01485 541534; email: mail@ chrisholtphotographic.co.uk; website: www.hallsfoundation.co.uk)

CC number: 325128

Eligibility

People between the ages of 11 and 25 (as of 1 September in the year of the course) who have been resident in the village of Snettisham for at least one year and are in need for financial assistance.

Types of grants

Grants are available to the following groups:

- Students over the age of 11 moving on to secondary education
- Young people over the age of 16 going on to further education/ undertaking A-levels or training

courses – up to £200 per each year of the course
- Students over the age of 18 undertaking higher education at universities/colleges – up to £2,000 per each year of the course. This payment will be awarded in two separate grants

The foundation's website states:

> Grants are awarded to assist students in their secondary and further education courses. They are in addition to any local authority or state entitlement. Grants are not linked in any way to any national or local government education authority policy. It is up to the individual student, with input from parent/guardian as appropriate, to decide just how the money is spent be it on books, materials, uniform/dress, travel costs or, in the case of university students, accommodation costs.

Annual grant total

In 2013/14 the foundation had assets of £1.5 million, an income of £69,500. The amount of grants given to individuals totalled £68,500. The grants were distributed in the following categories:

Students undertaking University/HE courses	34	£58,000
Students undertaking 6th form/FE education courses	36	£7,000
Pupils moving from primary to secondary school	14	£3,000
Other grants	Not specified	£500

Exclusions

No additional grants are made for word processors, computers, normal travelling expenses or work experience costs. Grants must be returned if any year of the course is not completed.

Applications

Application forms are available on the foundation's website or can be requested from the correspondent. More application forms are also distributed in the local area. They can be submitted either directly by the individual or through a third party.

Other information

The trustees note in their annual report for 2013/14 that:

> The foundation gives priority to individual applicants, but should money be available, having satisfied the demands of all individual applicants, then grants requests can be considered from those local organisations and bodies which exist for the benefit/education of such young people.

The King's Lynn General Educational Foundation

£1,000

Correspondent: Andrew Cave, Administrator, Wheelers, 27–29 Old Market, Wisbech, Cambridgeshire PE13 1NE (01945 582547; email: andrew. cave@wheelers-accountants.co.uk)

CC number: 311104

Eligibility

People aged under 25 who have lived in the borough of King's Lynn for no less than two years, or those who have attended school in the borough for no less than two years, who are going on to further education.

Types of grants

One-off grants of £75 to £200 for people at school, college or university or any other further education institution towards the cost of books, equipment, fees and living expenses.

Annual grant total

In 2014 the foundation had an income of £2,200 and an expenditure of £1,300. We estimate that educational grants to individuals totalled £1,000.

Applications

Application forms are available from R G Pannell, 21 Baldwin Road, King's Lynn, Norfolk PE30 4AL. They should be submitted by 30 August each year. The application should be supported by the applicant's previous educational establishment.

Sir Edmund de Moundeford Charity

£4,300

Correspondent: Barry Hawkins, The Estate Office, 15 Lynn Road, Downham Market, Norfolk PE38 9NL (01366 387180)

CC number: 1075097

Eligibility

Individuals in need who live in Feltwell.

Types of grants

One-off cash grants and grants in kind are made: to university students who live in Feltwell and who have left Feltwell School to purchase books; and to assist school leavers.

Annual grant total

In 2014 the charity had assets of £6.2 million and an income of £130,000. Grants totalled £19,100, including £5,000 awarded to a local playgroup. Individuals received grants totalling

£14,100 for both social welfare and educational purposes. They were distributed as follows:

Fuel grants (Christmas)	£9,600
Student grants	£2,800
School leavers	£1,600
Almshouse tenants	£200

We have not included the figures for assistance relating to social welfare in the grant total.

Applications

Applications can be made in writing to the correspondent either directly by the individual or through an organisation such as Citizens Advice or a school. Applications are considered at meetings held quarterly.

Other information

The main purpose of this charity is the provision of almshouse accommodation.

West Norfolk and King's Lynn Girls' School Trust

£17,500 (21 grants)

Correspondent: Miriam Aldous, Administrator, The Goodshed, Station Road, Little Dunham, King's Lynn PE32 2DJ (01760 720617; website: wnklgirlsschoolstrust.org.uk)

CC number: 311264

Eligibility

Girls and young women over the age of 11 who are at a secondary school or in their first years after leaving school or in further education, who live in the borough of King's Lynn and West Norfolk. Awards to older candidates will be made in exceptional circumstances.

Types of grants

One-off and recurrent grants. Grants are provided for school uniforms, books, equipment/instruments, and educational outings in the UK and overseas.

Annual grant total

In 2013/14 the trust had assets of £291,000, an income of £26,500 and made grants were made to 21 individuals totalling almost £17,500.

Applications

Application forms are available on the trust's website. They should be submitted together with a supporting letter outlining the proposed venture or study course, and include two independent references, one of which must be a teacher or tutor who can vouch for the suitability of the course.

Other information

This trust also gives grants to secondary schools within the area.

North Norfolk

Saxlingham United Charities

£5,000

Correspondent: Julie Queen, Correspondent, 22 Henry Preston Road, Tasburgh, Norwich NR15 1NU (01508 470759; email: saxlingham.uc@gmail.com)

CC number: 244713

Eligibility

People who live in the parish of Saxlingham. Our research suggests that applicants for educational support must be under the age of 21 have lived in the parish for at least five years.

Types of grants

Grants of £50–£100 are made towards the cost of books, clothing or tools to young people starting work or in further or higher education.

Annual grant total

In 2013/14 the charity had an income of £9,600 and a total expenditure of £10,100. These are the highest figures in the past five years. We estimate that grants for educational purposes totalled around £5,000.

Applications

Applications may be made in writing to the correspondent. They can be submitted directly by the individual and are usually considered in October.

Other information

Grants are made for both welfare and educational purposes.

Norwich

Norwich Town Close Estate Charity

£125,500

Correspondent: David Walker, Clerk to the Trustees, 1 Woolgate Court, St Benedicts Street, Norwich NR2 4AP (01603 621023; email: info@norwichcharitabletrusts.org.uk; website: www.norwichcharitabletrusts.org.uk)

CC number: 235678

Eligibility

People under the age of 25 living in Norwich. Priority is given to freemen and their dependants.

Types of grants

Grants are given to schoolchildren, further and higher education students, including mature students and postgraduates. Support may cover school clothing and school trips, further education and apprenticeship costs, university maintenance/living expenses, travel costs, postgraduate studies or music, dance and sports tuition (provided applicants are likely to reach a professional standard).

Annual grant total

In 2014/15 the charity had assets of £23.3 million and an income of £909,500. Grants were made totalling £842,500, of which £245,500 was for individuals, including £125,500 for educational purposes. A total of 142 individuals benefitted across all categories. All grants were broken down as follows:

Other bodies	£578,500
Education	£125,500
Pensions	£98,500
Relief in need	£18,500
TV licences	£3,000

Exclusions

Day outings are not assisted (only residential trips).

Applications

Applications may be made in writing to the correspondent. Our research suggests that they should be submitted by June/early July each year for consideration in August.

The charity's website notes: 'Detailed conditions apply to many of these grants – contact us and we can tell you if you are eligible.'

Other information

Awards are made for educational as well as welfare needs, including the provision of pensions. Organisations helping local people are also supported, principally in the field of education (£578,500 in 2014/15).

This is one of the three grant-making charities under the Norwich Charitable Trusts (others are Norwich Consolidated Charities and Anguish Educational Foundation).

The annual report for 2014/15 states that 'no eligible applicant has been refused a grant for lack of available funds'.

Sir Peter Seaman's Charity

£6,500

Correspondent: Air Commodore Kevin Pellatt, Correspondent, Great Hospital, Bishopgate, Norwich NR1 4EL (01603 622022; email: kjp@greathospital.org; website: www.greathospital.org.uk/charities/peter-seaman-charity.htm)

CC number: 311101

Eligibility

People under the age of 21 who live in Norwich.

Types of grants

One-off and recurrent grants (generally under £250) can be given towards all kinds of educational purposes, including starting a new job/career or to help with educational trips, such as Duke of Edinburgh Award Scheme, Raleigh International and so on.

Annual grant total

In 2014/15 the charity had an income of £6,600 and an expenditure of £13,200. We estimate that the amount of grants given to individuals totalled approximately £6,500.

Applications

Application forms can be accessed on the charity's webpage. They can be submitted directly by the individual and are considered quarterly, in March, June, September and December.

Other information

Awards may also be made 'to charitable organisations which support the educational and other needs of young persons living in Norwich'.

Town Estate Educational Foundation

£8,500

Correspondent: David Hook, Trustee, 1 Freemasons Cottage, Mill Road, Hempnall, Norwich NR15 2LP (01508 498187)

CC number: 311218

Eligibility

People under the age of 25 who live in Hempnall and have done so for a year.

Types of grants

Grants are made to help with:

- The costs of educational outings for schoolchildren
- Expenses incurred while at college or university such as books, help with fees and study or travel abroad
- The costs of vocational courses
- Other activities, including athletic expenses and the study of the arts

Grants to individuals are usually made on a percentage basis on production of receipts for courses, books and so on, with a maximum ceiling which is reviewed annually. Each application is considered entirely on merit, but if a grant is made to one person on a particular course, then everyone making an application for the same course receives exactly the same amount or percentage.

Annual grant total

In 2014 the foundation had an income of £16,000 and a total expenditure of £17,300. We estimate that educational grants to individuals totalled £8,500, with funding also awarded to the village primary school and other organisations.

Applications

Applications should be made in writing to the correspondent, including evidence of the course being taken and relevant receipts.

South Norfolk

The Sir John Sedley Educational Foundation

£8,500

Correspondent: Elaine Everington, 29 Mill Grove, Whissendine, Oakham, Leicestershire LE15 7EY (01664474593; email: ellemai@btinternet.com)

CC number: 527884

Eligibility

People under the age of 25 in further and higher education living in the parish of Wymondham and peripheral areas.

Types of grants

The foundation provides scholarships, bursaries and financial assistance towards the cost of books, clothing, equipment/instruments and travel costs. Financial help is also available for people starting work/entering a trade.

Annual grant total

In 2014/15 the foundation had an income of £15,000 and an expenditure of £17,000. We estimate the annual total amount of grants awarded to individuals to be around £8,500.

Applications

Apply in writing to the correspondent. Our research suggests that it is preferable if a supplier's quotation for the requested item is included.

Other information

The trustees have a discretionary power to allocate up to one quarter of the income towards the benefit of the local schools. The foundation also supports charitable organisations and maintains a hall for the benefit of the local area.

Suffolk

Ann Beaumont's Educational Foundation

£10,000

Correspondent: Rose Welham, Correspondent, 55 Castle Road, Hadleigh, Ipswich IP7 6JP (email: rosewelham55@aol.com)

CC number: 310397

Eligibility

Students under the age of 25 years who are in need of financial assistance and live in the parish of Hadleigh.

Types of grants

Grants to help with course books, equipment or educational trips for people at school, college, university or those starting work.

Annual grant total

In 2014/15 the charity had assets of £1.4 million and an income of £46,000. We estimate that the amount of grants given to individuals for educational purposes totalled £10,000.

Applications

Apply in writing to the correspondent, providing evidence of the cost of the books or equipment required. Applications are considered four times a year.

Other information

Grants were made to eight organisations during the year.

Calthorpe and Edwards Educational Foundation

£8,000

Correspondent: Mrs R. Boswell, Administrator, Chegwidden, Beauford Road, Ingham, Bury St Edmunds IP31 1NW (01284 728288; email: rgboswell@care4free.net)

CC number: 310464

Eligibility

People between the ages of 18 and 25 who live in the parishes of Ampton, Great Livermere, Little Livermere, Ingham and Timworth, Troston, Ixworth, Culford, Great Barton, West Stow, Wordwell, Fornham St Genevieve and Fornham St Martin.

Types of grants

Small scholarships and bursaries are available to further/higher education students for the purchase of books, equipment, necessities or expenses for study/travel overseas. Grants are paid termly with a total of around £300 per year and can be awarded for up to three years. People starting work/entering a trade can be assisted with the cost of books, instruments, tools, equipment and clothing/outfits.

Annual grant total

In 2013/14 the foundation had an income of £9,500 and an expenditure of £8,500. We estimate the annual total amount of grants awarded to be around £8,000.

Applications

Application forms can be requested from the correspondent and submitted directly by the individual. Grants are normally considered in October.

George Goward and John Evans

£12,500

Correspondent: Laura Williams, 8 Woodcutters Way, Lakenheath, Brandon, Suffolk IP27 9JQ (07796 018816; email: laurawill@btinternet.com)

CC number: 253727

Eligibility

People under the age of 25 who live in the parish of Lakenheath, Suffolk.

Types of grants

Our research suggests that grants are usually in the range of £25 and £300. Support can be given for people leaving school/starting work for equipment and other necessities and to further/higher education students to help with the maintenance/living expenses and books. Schoolchildren can also receive grants towards uniforms, clothing and educational outings.

Annual grant total

In 2014 the charity had an income of £35,500 and a total expenditure of £27,000. At the time of writing (November 2015) the charity's annual report and accounts for the year were not yet available to view on the Charity Commission register. In previous two years on average about £12,500 a year has been given in about 27 grants to further/higher education students and other young people.

Applications

Applications can be made in writing to the correspondent. They can be submitted either directly by the individual or through a third party, such as a family member, social worker, teacher, or an organisation, such as Citizens Advice. Applications should generally be submitted by February and August for consideration in March and September, respectively. Candidates should provide brief details of their

financial situation and include receipts for the items purchased.

Other information

One eighth of the charity's income is allocated to Soham United Charities. Grants are also made to: other organisations; local primary, secondary, nursery and Sunday schools; and to individuals for welfare purposes.

Hope House and Gippeswyk Educational Trust

£6,000

Correspondent: John Clements, Trustee, 4 Church Meadows, Henley, Ipswich IP6 0RP (email: clements4henley@aol.com)

CC number: 1068441

Eligibility

Children and young people in need who are under the age of 21 and live in Ipswich or the surrounding area.

Types of grants

One-off grants towards the costs of school uniforms/clothing, books, educational outings, travel, fees, maintenance/living expenses and other necessities, Support is given to schoolchildren and higher/further education students.

Annual grant total

In 2013/14 the trust had an income of £11,500 and an expenditure of £12,000. The trust supports organisations as well as individuals. We estimate the annual total amount of grants awarded to individuals to be around £6,000.

Applications

Apply in writing to the correspondent. Our research indicates that applications should be submitted through the individual's school/college or welfare agency, if applicable, for consideration throughout the year.

Hundon Educational Foundation

£8,000

Correspondent: Bernard Beer, Beauford Lodge, Mill Road, Hundon, Sudbury CO10 8EG (01440 786942)

CC number: 310379

Eligibility

Children and young people under the age of 25 living in the parish of Hundon.

Types of grants

Financial support is available to pre-schoolchildren, school pupils, further/higher education students, people in

training and those starting work/entering a trade. Grants are given towards the costs of the course fees, educational outings/visits and for general educational purposes, including books, clothing, equipment/instruments. Our research indicates that grants range from £50 to about £500.

Annual grant total

In 2014 the foundation had an income of £7,500 and an expenditure of £8,500. We estimate the annual total amount of grants awarded to be around £8,000.

Exclusions

The foundation is strictly limited to beneficiaries within the specified area.

Applications

Apply in writing to the correspondent. Applications can be submitted by individuals directly or by their parent/guardian. The trustees meet two or three times a year. Our research suggests that the foundation is well advertised in the village. Applications are considered in March, July and November and should be received in the preceding month.

Mid Suffolk

Gislingham United Charity

£13,900

Correspondent: Robert Moyes, Correspondent, 37 Broadfields Road, Gislingham, Eye, Suffolk IP23 8HX (01379 788105; email: r.moyes1926@btinternet.com; website: gislingham.onesuffolk.net/organisations/gislingham-united-charity)

CC number: 208340

Eligibility

People in need who live in Gislingham. A few years ago the trustees extended the eligibility for support from children under the age of 18 to 'any resident of Gislingham who genuinely needs help towards the cost of education'.

Types of grants

Grants are given to school excursions and necessities, college or university fees, vocational education, retraining and other educational needs.

Annual grant total

In 2014 the charity had an income of £17,100 and an expenditure of £20,500. The chair's report for 2014 states that a total of £15,700 was distributed in grants and awards, 'nearly 90% of which was for educational purposes'.

Applications

Requests for information or help should be sent to the following address: Sheila

Eade, Clerk, Woodberry, High Street, Gislingham, Suffolk IP23 8JD (email: gislinghamunitedcharity@gmail.com) Applications must include reasons for the need, the amount requested and the applicant's address. Applications can be submitted directly by the individual or also verbally via a trustee. The trustees meet every two months.

Other information

The charity gives educational grants (Education Branch – the largest division), grants to individuals in need (Non-Ecclesiastical Branch) and supports ecclesiastical causes (Ecclesiastical Branch – the smallest division). Village organisations are also assisted.

The Non-Ecclesiastical Branch is divided into two 'moieties': 'for the relief of residents of Gislingham in need, hardship or distress' and 'for the provision and maintenance of facilities for recreation or other charitable purposes for the benefit of the inhabitants of the Parish of Gislingham'.

The Mendlesham Educational Foundation

£16,500

Correspondent: Mrs S. Furze, Administrator, Beggars Roost, Church Road, Mendlesham, Stowmarket IP14 5SF

CC number: 271762

Eligibility

People under 25 who live in the parish of Mendlesham.

Types of grants

One-off and recurrent grants are given towards pre-school fees for children with serious family difficulties, and books and equipment for students in further/higher education or apprenticeships.

Annual grant total

In 2013 the foundation had an income of £14,300 and an expenditure of £33,500. We estimate that £16,500 was awarded in grants to individuals for education.

The 2013 accounts were the latest available at the time of writing (October 2015).

Exclusions

Grants are not given for school fees or maintenance expenses. They are not normally available towards the cost of school educational outings or for special educational needs.

Applications

Application forms are available from the correspondent. Applicants should provide details of: their education to date; the course to be taken; other grants applied for; the estimated expenditure; their parents' financial position; and other dependent children in the family. Applications should be made by the individual or through a parent/guardian by mid-September.

Other information

Grants are also made to organisations and Mendlesham CP School.

Suffolk Coastal

The Annie Tranmer Charitable Trust

£25,500 (43 grants)

Correspondent: Mrs M. Kirby, Administrator, 51 Bennett Road, Ipswich IP1 5HX (01473 743694; email: mary.kirby@timicomail.co.uk)

CC number: 1044231

Eligibility

Young people who live in Suffolk who are keen to develop their physical, mental and spiritual capacities through their leisure time activities.

Types of grants

One-off and recurrent grants are given according to need. Awards can be made towards, for example, educational outings, fees, equipment/instruments and travel overseas. Grants range from £40 to £1,000.

Annual grant total

In 2013/14 the trust had assets of £3.8 million and an income of £117,500. Grants to 43 individuals totalled £25,500.

Applications

Application forms are available from the correspondent. They should include details of the specific need, finances and alternative funding sources.

Other information

Grants are also made to other local agencies for the benefit of individuals.

The Mills Educational Foundation

£19,000

Correspondent: Deborah Stace, Administrator, 45 Saxmundham Road, Framlingham, Woodbridge, Suffolk IP13 9BZ (01728 724370; email: info@themillscharity.co.uk; website: www.themillscharity.co.uk)

CC number: 310475

Eligibility

Children and young people up to the age of 24 who live in Framlingham and the surrounding district, or attend a school there.

Types of grants

One-off grants ranging from £50 to £550. Schoolchildren and further/higher education students can be supported for uniforms, other school clothing, books, equipment, instruments, educational outings in the UK and study or travel abroad. People starting work can receive grants for uniforms, other clothing, equipment and instruments.

Annual grant total

In 2014/15 the foundation had an income of £6,100 and an expenditure of £19,500. Grants given totalled approximately £19,000.

Applications

Apply in writing to the correspondent.

Other information

Local primary schools are also supported.

Waveney

Kirkley Poor's Land Estate

£5,300

Correspondent: Lucy Walker, Clerk to the Trustees, 4 Station Road, Lowestoft, Suffolk NR32 4QF (01502 514964; email: kirkleypoors@gmail.com; website: kirkleypoorslandestate.co.uk)

CC number: 210177

Eligibility

Students undertaking their first degree who live in the parish of Kirkley and are in need.

Types of grants

One-off grants of about £100 per term to help towards university degree expenses and can be for up to three years.

Annual grant total

In 2013/14 the charity had assets of over £2 million and an income of £88,000. Grants were made totalling £60,500 and were distributed as follows:

Grants to organisations	£35,500
Grocery voucher scheme	£19,500
Grants to individuals (education)	£5,300

Applications

Applications can be made writing to the correspondent.

Other information

The boundaries of the parish are fully defined on the charity's website. The charity can support both individuals for welfare and educational purposes, and organisations.

Lowestoft Church and Town Educational Foundation

£13,000

Correspondent: Matthew Breeze, Norton Peskett Solicitors, 148 London Road North, Lowestoft, Suffolk NR32 1HF

CC number: 310460

Eligibility

Children and young people between the ages of 5 and 25 who or whose parents are resident in the parish of Lowestoft and who have attended school in the area for at least three years.

Types of grants

Small, one-off grants are available to schoolchildren, higher/further education students or people entering a trade/ starting work. Support is given towards the cost of uniforms/clothing, books, equipment/instruments, tools, travel expenses, educational outings, study/ travel abroad in pursuance of education and other general educational needs.

Annual grant total

In 2014 the foundation had an income of £6,000 and a total expenditure of £19,000. We have estimated the annual total amount of grants awarded to individuals to be around £13,000.

Applications

Application forms can be requested from the correspondent and submitted directly by the individual. Our research indicates that the application will need to be verified by the applicant's place of education.

Other information

Up to one third of the foundation's funding is directed to support local schools, where assistance is not already provided by the local authority.

London

General

The Aldgate and Allhallows Foundation

£36,000 (36 grants)

Correspondent: Richard Foley, Clerk, 31 Jewry Street, London EC3N 2EY (020 7488 2518; email: aldgateandallhallows@ sirjohncass.org; website: www. aldgateallhallows.org.uk)

CC number: 312500

Eligibility

Young people under the age of 25 who have lived in the City of London or the London borough of Tower Hamlets for at least three years and are studying full-time in further or higher education (including postgraduates) on a course of at least one year that will result in a recognised qualification. Priority is given to people from disadvantaged backgrounds.

Types of grants

Most of the foundation's support is distributed by way of undergraduate bursaries to students at Queen Mary University, London. Some grants are available to individuals studying at other courses or institutions. Support can be given towards books, equipment, travel expenses, maintenance and tuition fees. A scholarship programme has now been introduced for students at the St Paul's way trust school.

Annual grant total

In 2013/14 the foundation had assets of £7.5 million, an income of £74,500 and a total charitable expenditure of £291,500. Grants to 36 individual students totalled £36,000.

Exclusions

The foundation's website states that grants are not normally given for:

- courses at private colleges
- fees at independent schools
- repeated years of study
- study for a qualification at the same or lower level than those an individual already possesses

- fees for higher education courses, unless they are for second degrees and a student loan is not available
- medical electives
- individuals with time limited leave to remain in the UK

Applications

Initially in writing to the correspondent specifying the applicant's 'name, address, phone number, email address, age, course, how long they have lived in the City of London or Tower Hamlets, how they heard about the Foundation, and what they need a grant for'. Eligible candidates will then be sent an application form which should include full details of their financial circumstances. Applications are considered throughout the year and can be made at any time by an individual directly or through a third party. Applicants may be invited for an interview. The foundation welcomes informal contact via phone or email prior to application.

Other information

Grants were also made to 21 schools and institutions working for the benefit of young people in the local area (£255,500 in 2013/14).

The annual report and accounts for 2013/14 note:

> Individuals supported through the Aldgate and Allhallows Scholarships Programme at Queen Mary, University of London will hence forward benefit from an award of £1,250 per annum (now raised from the original level of £1,000). The Foundation has also inaugurated a scholarships programme for students at the St Paul's Way Trust School.

> The charity continues to support a mix of charitable and voluntary organisations that directly assist young people in its area. It also supports young people in local primary and secondary schools in ways that go beyond statutory educational provision, through activities that include art, music, theatre, sport, recreational reading and writing. The criteria for grant-making are outlined on the Foundation's website.

Sir William Boreman's Foundation

£12,000 (17 grants)

Correspondent: Andrew Mellows, Head of Charities, The Drapers' Company, Drapers' Hall, Throgmorton Avenue, London EC2N 2DQ (020 7588 5001; fax: 020 7628 1988; email: charities@ thedrapers.co.uk; website: www. thedrapers.co.uk/Charities/Grantmaking-trusts/Sir-William-Boremans-Foundation.aspx)

CC number: 312796

Eligibility

Children and young people under the age of 25 with a household income of £30,000 or less who live in the London boroughs of Greenwich and Lewisham or in that part of the London borough of Newham which was formerly in the Metropolitan Borough of Woolwich. Preference is given to the borough of Greenwich, to practising members of the Church of England and to sons and daughters of seamen, watermen and fishermen, particularly those who have served in the armed forces. Boys and young men pursuing a career in seafaring are also favoured. Applicants should be UK nationals or have a 'settled' status under the terms of the Immigration Act 1971.

Types of grants

One-off grants usually of up to £1,000 are given to higher/further education students and people starting work towards living expenses, travel costs, educational necessities, books, equipment/instruments, childcare costs. Schoolchildren are eligible for assistance with the cost of the school uniforms, sports kits, travel costs and educational outings/visits.

Annual grant total

In 2013/14 the foundation had assets of £3.4 million and an income of £93,500. The total charitable expenditure was around £86,500, of which £12,000 was awarded to 17 individuals.

Exclusions

Grants are not made for:
- Students aged over 25 or pre-schoolchildren
- Non-UK citizens and asylum seekers (only those with full refugee status may apply)
- Postgraduate students who have attained a 2.2 or lower
- Overseas study/travel or exchange visits
- Retrospective grants
- Tuition fees
- Loans or debts not related to education
- Setting up business ventures
- Performing arts courses (acting, dance, drama)
- Private school fees

Applications

Application forms can be found on the foundation's website or can be requested from the correspondent. The trustees welcome unsolicited applications which should be submitted at least four weeks before the meetings held in November, February and June each year. Further guidelines are available on the website. Our research suggests that applicants are expected to have applied for a grant from their local authority and to have received a decision on this before applying to the foundation. Some applicants may be asked to attend a brief interview with the governors.

Other information

The foundation also supports organisations. In 2013/14 about £74,500 was distributed to 19 institutions and organisations.

The Castle Baynard Educational Foundation

£3,500

Correspondent: Mauricia Cebulec-Gardner, Trustee, 17 Fleetwood, 2 Northwold Road, London N16 7HG (020 7249 2490; email: CBEF_Clerk@ hotmail.co.uk)

CC number: 312502

Eligibility

People in need under the age of 25 who/ whose parents are resident or employed in the Castle of Baynard Ward of the City of London or in the former county of Middlesex, or who are/have been in full-time education at any educational establishment closely connected with the corporation of London. Preference may be given to the City of London School and The City of London School for Girls or to people with special educational needs.

Types of grants

Grants range from £100 to £500 and are available to schoolchildren, further/

higher education students and people starting work. Financial assistance is given towards the cost of books, equipment/instruments, tools, materials, events and educational outings, clothing/ outfits, also travel expenses and research.

Annual grant total

In 2013/14 the foundation had an income of £7,000 and an expenditure of £6,000. We estimate the annual total amount of grants awarded to be around £3,500.

Exclusions

Support is not normally available for the course fees or general maintenance.

Applications

Apply in writing to the correspondent. Applicants should provide an sae and include the following details: the purpose of the grant; a CV; evidence of financial need; and a reference of support to confirm their current educational status and financial circumstances. Applications are normally considered in March, June, September and December.

Other information

The foundation also supports a Sunday school at St Andrew by the Wardrobe.

The City and Diocese of London Voluntary Schools Fund

£14,100 (250 grants)

Correspondent: Inigo Woolf, Administrator, 36 Causton Street, London SW1P 4AU (02079321165; email: inigo.woolf@london.anglican.org; website: www.london.anglican.org/ schools)

CC number: 312259

Eligibility

Children and young people under the age of 25 who have attended Church of England voluntary-aided schools in the Diocese of London (i.e. north of the river) for at least two years.

Types of grants

Due to limited funds, support is mainly given towards the costs of school journeys/field trips, music tuition and maintenance costs. Occasionally grants can be given for general educational expenses. Schoolchildren, further/higher education students, people in vocational training or individuals entering a trade/ starting work can be supported. Grants can range up to £500 and are usually one-off.

Annual grant total

In 2014/15 the fund had assets of £1.7 million and an income of £203,000.

A total of £14,100 was spent in grants to 250 individuals.

Exclusions

Retrospective applications are not considered.

Applications

Application forms can be found on the fund's website or requested from the correspondent. Applications should include two references and specify what kind of assistance is required. Applications for individuals under 16 should be completed by a parent/ guardian. The deadlines are: 28 February for summer term journeys, 30 June for autumn term journeys and 30 October for spring term journeys.

Other information

The fund also accepts group applications for school journeys.

Francon Trust

£27,500 (7 grants)

Correspondent: Col. Derek Ivy, Administrator, Smithtown, Kirkmahoe, Dumfries DG1 1TE (01387 740455)

CC number: 10033592

Eligibility

Students in tertiary education and vocational training who were born or brought up and live in London. Support is aimed at 'school examination high achievers' entering vocational training or proceeding to first degree courses, particularly in medicine, architecture, accountancy, insurance, banking, law or other professional business or trade fields, including science and engineering.

Types of grants

Our research suggests that grants range from £1,000 to £3,000 and are normally given in the form of interest-free loans which become gifts on completion of the course after six months of employment in a related occupation. Grants may be in the form of a single payment or a series of successive payments, depending upon circumstances.

Annual grant total

In 2013/14 the trust had assets of £1.2 million, an income of £32,500 and awarded grants totalling £27,500. The trust states that 'approximately seven students per annum are supported'.

Applications

Applicants should contact the correspondent by sending a brief letter. Application forms will then be provided.

The trust's annual report for 2013/14 states:

> The objectives are achieved based upon guidelines established during the early years of operation in accordance with the

wishes of the original benefactors. Potential students for first degree courses are selected in accordance with the guidelines, based upon applications and recommendations from head teachers in support of bright students who have little or no financial means. After application potential students are selected for interview by the Trustees to decide those that should receive support.

Other information

The trustees' annual report for 2013/14 states: 'The charity awards grants to give educational, welfare and social support to needy students in London.'

The Hornsey Parochial Charities

£18,000

Correspondent: The Clerk to the Trustees, PO Box 22985, London N10 3XB (020 8352 1601; fax: 020 8352 1601; email: hornseypc@blueyonder.co.uk; website: www.hornseycharities.com)

CC number: 229410

Eligibility

People under 25 who have lived for at least one year in the ancient parish of Hornsey in Haringey and Hackney. There are maps showing the area of benefit on the charity's website.

Types of grants

Grants of between £350 and £1,200 are given for bursaries, maintenance allowances, clothing, instruments and books.

Annual grant total

In 2014 the charity had an income of £60,000 and a total expenditure of £54,000. At the time of writing (November 2015) the charity's full annual report and accounts for the year were not available to view. In previous years, we have estimated educational grants to individuals to have totalled £18,000.

Applications

Application forms are available to download from the website, where dates of trustees' meetings can also be found. Forms should be completed and returned to the correspondent.

Other information

Grants are also made for welfare purposes.

The Philological Foundation

£24,500 (20 grants)

Correspondent: Stephanie Hallin, Flat 8 Block East, Peabody Buildings, Wild Street, London WC2B 4AH (email: thephilological@gmail.com)

CC number: 312692

Eligibility

Individual recipients of grants must be under 26 years of age and be or have been pupils at a secondary school in the City of Westminster or the London borough of Camden.

Types of grants

Grants are offered towards tuition fees, study/travel costs, educational necessities, such as books, equipment/instruments, materials, clothing or other. Schoolchildren, further/higher education students and individuals in vocational training or people starting work/entering trade can be assisted. Awards are normally in the range from £150 to £2,000.

Grants for education are considered at the following levels: GNVQ; A-level; access; foundation; diploma; first degree; and postgraduate taught degrees. Awards are not ordinarily made for postgraduate research degrees. Apprenticeships will also be considered.

Annual grant total

In 2013/14 the foundation had assets of £1 million and an income of £167,500. A total of £24,500 was spent in grants to individuals and schools.

Exclusions

Support will not be given to individuals who could be assisted by a statutory loan.

Applications

Applicants are invited to email the correspondent to request further information and application forms. The following is noted in the latest accounts:

> Request for information and application forms should be made via email to: thephilological@gmail.com. Trustees normally meet during the third week of September, December, February, April and June. Deadlines for applications are two months prior to a meeting, Further information is available on the web site: www.philological.org.uk.

Other information

Grants are also given to state-funded primary and secondary schools in Westminster or Camden for the provision of recreation or leisure activities such as playground equipment and educational visits.

Richard Reeve's Foundation

£67,500 (196 grants)

Correspondent: The Clerk of Richard Reeve's Foundation, 13 Elliott's Place, London N1 8HX (020 7726 4230; email: clerk@richardreevesfoundation.org.uk; website: www.richardreevesfoundation.org.uk)

CC number: 1136337

Eligibility

People under the age of 25 (in exceptional cases this may be extended to 40) who (or whose parents) have lived, studied or worked in London boroughs of Camden, City of London or Islington for the last 12 months or for at least two of the last ten years.

Types of grants

Grants ranging from £100 to £1,000 are given to students identified by the partner institutions.

The foundation's website states:

> This educational charity makes grants for projects that help children and young people to get the most from their education or to prepare for work. Our area of benefit covers the London Boroughs of Camden, City of London and Islington and our upper age limit is usually 25.

Previously support has been provided to those in further education towards maintenance costs, specialist tuition, fieldtrips and support has also been provided towards equipment and tools needed for those entering work.

Annual grant total

In 2013/14 the foundation had assets of £23.5 million, an income of £487,000 and a total charitable expenditure of £278,000. Grants to 196 individuals totalled £67,500. All awards were made to individuals studying at the specified universities and colleges through their support schemes.

Exclusions

The foundation does not normally provide grants for:
- Computers
- Holidays
- Clothing
- Childcare costs
- Fees at private schools or colleges (except in some exceptional cases and where it is agreed that education within the state system would be inappropriate)
- Overseas trips or placements
- Second degrees
- Postgraduate courses (except those that are essential for certain careers)
- International students who are resident in the UK on a student visa

Applications

Students studying at the partner institutions (City and Islington College, City University London or Westminster Kingsway College) should apply through their student services. Otherwise application forms can be downloaded from the foundation's website or requested from the correspondent. Applications are normally considered at

209

the trustees' meetings in March, June, October and December.

The following information is taken from the foundation's website:

Grants to Organisations

The Foundation seeks to fulfil its charitable objects by making grants to a small number of partner organisations to deliver benefits to people in our area of benefit through projects that maximise value for our beneficiaries through education and training. Projects are usually funded for up to three years so as to increase their effectiveness and impact.

The Foundation's focus will be to bring about a step-change in the following areas:

▶ Raising Literacy and Numeracy among early years and primary school students
▶ Aiding progression into work for 16-21 year olds and others attending schools and higher and further education institutions.

Grants to Individuals

The Foundation does not make grants direct to individuals.

Other information

The foundation also supports local organisations, charities and schools. In 2013/14 grants to organisations totalled £210,500.

The foundation's website states:

The Foundation has a long association with Christ's Hospital and has set aside a small fund for making grants to Christ's Hospital pupils who qualify as beneficiaries, i.e. who come from homes in our area of benefit and qualify for a high level of bursary from the School. The Fund is intended for items such as sports clothing which are compulsory but not provided by Christ's Hospital.

Scotscare

£30,500 (42+ grants)

Correspondent: Willie Docherty, Chief Executive, 22 City Road, London EC1Y 2AJ (020 7240 3718; email: info@scotscare.com; website: www.scotscare.com)

CC number: 207326

Eligibility

Scottish people, their children and widows, who are in need and have lived within a 35-mile radius of Charing Cross for at least two years.

Types of grants

Grants are given for a variety of educational and training needs, including course fees, books and living expenses. Assistance is also given with school uniforms and trips.

Annual grant total

In 2013/14 the charity had assets of £45.6 million and an income of more than £2 million. The amount of grants given to individuals totalled £417,000, of which £30,500 was given in 42 awards to students.

Exclusions

The charity cannot fund postgraduate courses.

Applications

There is an online Scotscare application request form on the website. Alternatively, call the Freephone helpline on 0800 652 2989; the Scotscare team is there to give advice from Monday to Thursday 9am–5pm and on Friday 9am–4pm.

Other information

In addition to making grants, Scotscare also offers a range of services for beneficiaries in the areas of advocacy, employment and training, families, health, housing, money management, mental health, socialising and substance misuse.

The Sheriffs' and Recorders' Fund

See entry on page 45

Sir Walter St John's Educational Charity

£5,000 (1 grant)

Correspondent: Susan Perry, Manager, Office 1A, Culvert House, Culvert Road, London SW11 5DH (020 7498 8878; email: manager@swsjcharity.org.uk; website: www.swsjcharity.org.uk)

CC number: 312690

Eligibility

People under the age of 25 (in practice, aged 16 to 24) who have been resident in the boroughs of Lambeth and Wandsworth for at least six months. Preference is given to the Battersea area. Grants can only be given to students who are following a validated, approved or recognised course and can demonstrate good prospect of successfully completing it. Grants to individuals will only be given in exceptional circumstances and where the award would have a critical effect on the applicant's opportunity to study.

Types of grants

Support is available for core expenditure for attendance of the course – registration fees, travel expenses, books, equipment/instruments. The upper limit for grants is £500 to students aged 16–18 and £750 to students aged 19–25. Lone parents who are in receipt of benefits can receive grants of up to £1,500 towards childcare. Grants above £1,500 may be awarded in exceptional circumstances to

students on foundation or access courses in arts, dance and drama who have good prospects of progressing to higher education afterwards. Students with disability are eligible for grants to meet additional education/training expenditure.

Annual grant total

In 2014/15 the charity had assets of £4.3 million, an income of £162,000. One grant of £5,000 was made to an individual pursuing further education.

A block grant totalling £5,000 was given to the South Thames College to be distributed to eight students and an additional grant of £2,000 for the purchase of computers to be loaned by single parents.

Exclusions

Grants are not normally given to schoolchildren under the age of 16 or full-time university students. Maintenance expenses are not supported and the charity will not usually contribute towards the cost of a computer or laptop.

Applications

Individuals are invited to contact the correspondent for an initial discussion. Eligible individuals will be sent an application form which has to be returned together with the supporting information and evidence.

Students at South Thames College should contact the college's student services directly to find out specific criteria for applications.

Other information

Currently the charity is focusing its funding to support local organisations providing education and training opportunities for children and young people in the area of benefit. Only a small amount of money is allocated annually to support individual students. Block grants are also made to local colleges for distribution to their students.

Truro Fund

£8,500

Correspondent: Richard Martin, Clerk to the Trustees, St Botolph's Church, Aldgate High Street, London EC3N 1AB (020 7929 0520; email: lm800aat@hotmail.com)

CC number: 312288

Eligibility

Children and young people under the age of 21 living or attending an educational establishment in Greater London.

Types of grants

One-off bursaries, scholarships and maintenance allowances are available to schoolchildren, further/higher education students, people entering a trade/profession, people starting work/business or apprentices. Support is given towards the cost of outfits/clothing, books, equipment/instruments, materials, tools, travel/study abroad, also for music and arts studies.

Annual grant total

In 2014/15 the fund had an income of £9,000 and an expenditure of £9,000. Normally around £8,500 is available to distribute in grants and around 12–15 small awards are given every six months.

Exclusions

Our research suggests that grants are not intended to cover fees.

Applications

Apply in writing to the correspondent. Applications should include three references (at least one of which should be from the applicant's educational establishment), evidence of the applicant's date of birth (either a photo page from a British passport or a birth certificate), full financial details and any information concerning the applicant's immigration status (if applicable).

The trustees meet twice a year in April and September to consider applications.

Other information

The fund is an amalgamation of three small charities – The Rt Hon. the Dowager Baroness Truro's Fund (The Truro Fund), The East London Industrial School Fund and the Regent's Park Boy's Home Fund.

The British and Foreign School Society Trust Fund

£3,500

Correspondent: Belinda Lawrance, Administrator, Maybrook House, 97 Godstone Road, Caterham, Surrey CR3 6RE (01883 331177; email: enquiries@bfss.org.uk; website: www. bfss.org.uk)

CC number: 312516

Eligibility

Students in Bermondsey, Bethnal Green, Poplar, Southwark and Stepney. In practise, students need to be studying at London South Bank University, which currently administers grants from this fund.

Types of grants

Grants of £150 to £1,300.

Annual grant total

In 2014 a total of £3,500 was given to the student welfare fund at London South Bank University.

Exclusions

Grants are not given for private education.

Applications

Applications should be made directly to the University Welfare Fund at London South Bank University.

Other information

The British and Foreign School Society is a grant-giving organisation and offers funding for educational projects in the UK and around the world. The society also offers a small number of grants for organisations and individuals through its subsidiary trusts. Eligibility criteria for these subsidiary trusts depend on area of residence and/or particular field of educational activity. In March 2014 we were informed by Steven Ross, a trustee of the society, that money was available from these funds. Visit the website for information on the set criteria.

Sir Mark and Lady Turner Charitable Settlement

£3,000

Correspondent: Katie Styles, Trust Officer, c/o Kleinwort Benson Trustees Ltd, 14 St Georges Street, London W1S 1FE (020 3207 7041; email: katie.styles@kleinwortbenson.com)

CC number: 264994

Eligibility

University students in need living in Highgate, North London.

Types of grants

One-off and recurrent grants between £100 and £500 are given for university tuition fees and necessities, including books or equipment/instruments.

Annual grant total

In 2014/15 the charity had an income of £9,000 and an expenditure of £12,700. We estimate that the annual total amount of grants awarded to individuals for educational purposes was about £3,000.

Applications

Applications may be made in writing to the correspondent. Our research suggests that applicants should include either their telephone number or email address and submit the application by the end of April or October for consideration in early June or December, respectively.

Other information

Grants are also made for general and young people's welfare purposes. Both individuals and organisations can be supported.

Barnet

Elizabeth Allen Trust

£8,900 (12 grants)

Correspondent: Helen Rook, Clerk to the Trustees, PO BOX 1180, ST Albans, Herts AL1 9XP (01727 823206; email: elizabethallentrust@fsmail.net)

CC number: 310968

Eligibility

People in need under the age of 25 who live, attend college of further education or are employed in the borough of Barnet. Priority is given to applicants from the pre-1965 urban district of (High) Barnet.

Types of grants

One-off grants, normally of up to £300, are offered to schoolchildren, further/higher education students and people starting work/entering a trade. Financial assistance is given for general educational expenses, including books, fees, maintenance expenses, equipment/instruments, tools, clothing/outfits, uniforms, travel in pursuance of education, also for study of music and arts.

Annual grant total

In 2013/14 the trust had assets of £788,000 and an income of £28,000. A total of £8,900 was awarded in grants. During the year 24 applications were received, of which 12 were successful.

Exclusions

Grants are not given for private school fees, postgraduate studies, gap year activities or where funding can be received from the local authority.

Applications

Application forms can be requested from the correspondent providing an sae. Applications should include details of the parents' finances and the use of the applicant's student loan. The trustees meet four times a year to consider applications. It is advised that applications for the current year should be made by April.

Other information

The trust also supports local schools.

The Mayor of Barnet's Benevolent Fund

£3,000

Correspondent: Ken Argent, Grants Manager, The London Borough of Barnet, Building 4, North London Business Park, Oakleigh Road South, London N11 1NP (020 8359 2020; email: ken.argent@barnet.gov.uk; website: www.barnet.gov.uk/citizen-home/council-tax-and-benefits/grants-and-funding/grants-for-individuals.html)

CC number: 1014273

Eligibility

Schoolchildren who have lived in the London borough of Barnet for at least a year and whose parents are in receipt of on an income-related statutory benefit (such as Income Support or Child Tax Credit).

Types of grants

Small, one-off grants of up to £60 per child can be given towards school uniforms to pupils transferring from primary to secondary school or starting a new secondary school. Up to two awards can be given to each applicant.

Annual grant total

In 2013/14 the fund had an income of £15,700 and a total expenditure of £15,400. Both figures are the highest in the past five years. Most support is given in relief-in-need grants; therefore, we estimate that educational grants totalled around £3,000.

Exclusions

Children attending East Barnet School, Finchley Catholic High School and The Wren Academy, which operate their own schemes of financial assistance to parents in need.

Applications

Applications have to be made in writing to the correspondent via post or email. Applications can be submitted directly by the individual or through a third party, such as a social worker, health visitor or an advice agency. Candidates should provide full details of their name, address, contact number, confirmation and length of residence in the borough, number and ages of the family members, family income, a proof of entitlement to a benefit, a summary of the applicant's circumstances, details of support requested, a quotation for any items required and information on other sources of funding approached. Consideration takes about a month and the outcome is communicated by a letter. Payments are not made to the applicant directly, but to the school or supplier.

Other information

Grants are mainly made for welfare purposes.

The Hyde Foundation

£8,000 (11 grants)

Correspondent: Robin Marson, Administrator, 1 Hillside, Codicote, Hitchin SG4 8XZ (020 8449 3032; email: marson36@homecall.co.uk)

CC number: 302918

Eligibility

People in education up to first degree level in the ancient parishes of Chipping Barnet and Monken Hadley.

Types of grants

One-off grants in the range of £100 to £6,000. Grants are given to college students, undergraduates, vocational students, mature students, people with special educational needs and people starting work. Grants given include those for music lessons, fees, travel abroad, books, equipment and maintenance/living expenses.

Annual grant total

In 2014 the foundation had assets of £719,000 and an income of £40,000. Grants made to 11 individuals totalled £8,000.

Applications

In the first instance write to the correspondent, who will provide an application form. The trustees meet quarterly in January, April, July and October to consider applications and applications should be received at the end of December, March, June and September respectively.

Other information

In 2014 £2,500 was awarded to the charity Sense to provide enhanced facilities within additional buildings.

The Valentine Poole Charity

£2,000

Correspondent: Victor Russell, Clerk, Forum Room, Ewen Hall, Wood Street, Barnet, Hertfordshire EN5 4BW (020 8441 6893; email: vpoole@btconnect.com; website: www.valentinepoole.org.uk)

CC number: 220856

Eligibility

Young people in need under the age of 26 who live in the former urban districts of Barnet and East Barnet (approximately the postal districts of EN4 and EN5).

Types of grants

One-off grants to schoolchildren for uniforms and people starting work for books, equipment and instruments.

Annual grant total

In 2014 the charity had assets of £645,500 and an income of £67,500. Grants totalled £47,500. During the year, £26,500 was paid in pensions to older people and Christmas grants to 25 families totalled £2,400. Grants totalling £10,600 were also made to individuals. We believe that the majority of these were made for relief-in-need purposes and we estimate that around £2,000 was given for the 'advancement of life'. A further £8,000 was paid in grants to organisations.

Applications

Application forms are available from the correspondent for consideration in March, July and November. Applications should be submitted by a school, welfare agency or other relevant third party, not directly by the individual.

Camden

Bromfield's Educational Foundation

£24,000 (72 grants)

Correspondent: Alison Shaw, Administrator, 5 St Andrew Street, London EC4A 3AB (020 7583 7394; email: info@standrewholborn.org.uk; website: www.standrewholborn.org.uk)

CC number: 312795

Eligibility

People in need under 25 who live (or whose parents or guardians live) in the Holborn area of the London borough of Camden for at least two years.

Types of grants

One-off and termly grants for clothing, books, equipment/instruments, music lessons, computers and maintenance/living expenses.

Annual grant total

In 2014 the foundation had assets of £1.9 million and an income of £74,500. The amount of grants given to individuals totalled almost £24,000. In 2014 a total of 21 families received termly grants and, in addition, 51 children were provided with a school uniform grant. Termly grants are mostly given to families caring for a child with disabilities.

Exclusions

No grants are given for school, college or university fees. Applications for postgraduate studies will not be considered.

Applications

Application forms are available from the website. Details of the applicant's income and expenditure and personal information are required, supported by documentary evidence which will be treated in the strictest confidence. Applications can be submitted at any time, and will be considered within 21 days.

Other information

Priority is given to families of children with disabilities. Grants are also given to organisations.

Hampstead Wells and Campden Trust

£2,600 (10 grants)

Correspondent: Sheila Taylor, Director and Clerk, 62 Rosslyn Hill, London NW3 1ND (020 7435 1570; fax: 020 7435 1571; email: grant@hwct.co.uk; website: www.hwct.org.uk)

CC number: 1094611

Eligibility

Residents of the former metropolitan borough of Hampstead (a map of the area of benefit is available on the trust's website) who are in need.

Types of grants

Grants are given to people at any stage of their education, or who are entering a trade or profession, for uniforms and other clothing, books, equipment, instruments, maintenance, living expenses, childcare and educational outings in the UK.

Annual grant total

In 2013/14 the trust had assets of £16.4 million and an income of £554,000. During the year, the trust gave grants and pensions totalling £507,500, of which organisations received £231,000. Grants to ten individuals for educational purposes amounted to £2,600, with the majority of funding to individuals given for social welfare purposes.

Exclusions

The trustees are unable to offer assistance with course or school fees.

Applications

Applications are accepted on behalf of individuals from any local constituted group, departments/units of Camden Council or the health service, a housing association, advice agency or other voluntary agency where the individual is known. The applying organisation must be willing to receive and account for any grant offered. The trust prefers to receive applications via the appropriate form, which is available to download from the

website; however, it also accepts applications in letter form. There is a list of essential information which must be included in any letter application on the website.

St Andrew Holborn Charities

£33,000

Correspondent: Anna Paterson, Grants Officer, 5 St Andrew Street, London EC4A 3AB (020 7583 7394; email: charity@standrewholborn.org.uk; website: www.standrewholborn.org.uk)

CC number: 1095045

Eligibility

People who are under the age of 25 and who have lived in the area of benefit (a defined area of Holborn; see the website or contact the charity for specific details) for at least two years.

Types of grants

One-off grants of up to £500 are given for educational needs including books, travel, general maintenance and course equipment.

Annual grant total

In 2014 the charity had assets of £10.7 million and an income of £382,000. Grants totalled £292,000, of which £167,000 was given to individuals. One-off grants to individuals amounted to £66,500 and were awarded for both educational and social welfare purposes. We estimate that educational grants to individuals totalled £33,000.

Exclusions

Applications are not considered for postgraduate studies or for equipment already purchased. Students cannot apply for grants for more than three academic years.

Applications

Application forms are available to download from the website, where guidelines can also be found. Applicants must provide evidence that they are a bona fide student on a recognised and accredited course. All applicants are means-tested.

The website gives the following additional information:

> Grants for books, travel, general maintenance and course equipment will be paid by cheque and made out in the name of the student. IT equipment is to be bought is to be bought from Currys PC World using SAH's established purchase arrangements. A copy of the receipt for all other purchases will be requested. No further grant will be considered without receipts.

Other information

This charity is the result of an amalgamation of three trusts: The City Foundation, The Isaac Duckett's Charity and The William Williams Charity. Grants are also made to local organisations.

City of London

The Thomas Carpenter Educational and Apprenticing Foundation (Thomas Carpenter's Trust)

£25,500 (13 grants)

Correspondent: Richard Martin, Administrator, St Botolph's Church, Aldgate High Street, London EC3N 1AB (020 7929 0520; email: lm800aat@hotmail.com)

CC number: 312155

Eligibility

People under the age of 25 who/whose parents have lived or worked for three years in Bread Street and adjoining wards in the City of London, or who attend educational establishment in that area.

Types of grants

Grants of around £500–£3,000 towards general course-related costs, including outfits, fees, books, equipment/tools, study of music or other arts, travel/study abroad and so on. People in schools, universities/colleges or those starting work/entering trade can be supported.

Annual grant total

In 2013/14 the foundation had an income of £31,500 and a total expenditure of £30,500. Grants to 13 individuals totalled £25,500.

Exclusions

Grants are not normally given towards electives or field trips which are not part of a full-time study course.

Applications

Application forms can be requested from the correspondent. They should normally be submitted before 31 July by the individual's parent or guardian, details of whose financial circumstances should be included.

Other information

Applications from local groups for recreational, social and physical training or equipment will also be considered.

The City of London Corporation Combined Education Charity

£32,000 (14 grants)

Correspondent: Barbara Hamilton, Head of Adult Education, Community and Children's Services, City of London, PO Box 270 EC2P 2EJ (020 7332 1755; email: adulteducation@cityoflondon.gov. uk; website: www.cityoflondon.gov.uk/ corporation/lgnl_services/advice_and_benefits/grants/student_awards.htm# hersef)

CC number: 312836

Eligibility

Individuals who are attending secondary schools or higher educational institutions in the City of London or other London boroughs. Priority will be given to courses related to civil engineering and construction, but other branches of engineering, building studies, manufacturing, IT and design will also be considered. A list of approved courses is available from the correspondent.

Types of grants

Support may take the form of: a bursary over an academic year, with possible renewal for further years during the period of eligibility (living, travel and/or tuition expenses); specific grants to assist in the completion of short course or educational project work; help with the costs of attendance at courses or conferences in the UK or overseas.

Grants for staff at maintained schools and academies in London to undertake studies either at educational institutions or other establishments that will further their development as teachers will also be provided.

Annual grant total

In 2013/14 the charity held assets of £1 million. This represents the total assets for the combined funds. There was an income of £39,500 and grants of £32,000 were made to 14 individuals.

Applications

Application forms are available from the correspondent and can be submitted either directly by the individual, or via their school, college or educational welfare agency. Applications must show evidence of financial hardship and be accompanied by a covering letter of support from the head of the institution. Applications should normally be submitted before March.

Other information

This charity was previously called the Higher Education Research and Special Expenses Fund (HERSEF), which received no applications in the year 2010/11. In 2011 a new scheme was approved whereby this fund merged with Archibald Dawnay Scholarships, Robert Blair Fellowships for Applied Science and Technology and Alan Partridge Smith Trust to form the City of London Corporation Combined Education Charity (retaining the charity registration number for HERSEF).

The Mitchell City of London Educational Foundation

£67,000 (26 grants)

Correspondent: Lucy Jordan, Administrator, Ash View, High Street, Orston, Nottingham NG13 9NU (08456001558; email: mitchellcityoflondon@gmail.com)

CC number: 312499

Eligibility

People aged 11 to 19 who are either attending school in the City of London or whose parents have lived or worked there for at least five years.

The 'city' is classified as the area of almost all of postcodes EC3 EC4 and a small area of EC1, EC2.

Types of grants

Awards are given as sixth form bursaries for A-level or IB students within independent education, or in grants to children from single parent families who are within independent education and have been at the school of choice for one year. Support is available towards general educational needs. Choral bursaries may also be provided.

Awards of £2,000 are made to students in need.

Annual grant total

In 2013/14 the foundation had assets of £1.9 million and an income of £89,000. Grants to 26 individuals totalled £67,000. The awards consisted of:

Sixth form bursaries	16
Pupils from single parent families	7
Choral bursaries	3

The foundation also notes that 94 applications and enquiries for awards did not meet the terms of reference of the charity and 11 applications were unsuccessful.

Exclusions

The foundation does not support further or higher education at any other establishment. Second and master's degrees or gap year and other projects are not assisted.

Applications

Apply in writing to the correspondent. Applications can be submitted either directly by the individual or through a third party, such as a parent or guardian, school or education welfare agency, if applicable. Grants are normally considered in March and September.

Other information

The Diploma Award of £2,500 was made to a needy student at Barts and The London Hospital. An award of £2,500 was also made to a needy student at the Guildhall School of Music and Drama.

City of Westminster

The Hyde Park Place Estate Charity (Civil Trustees)

£8,300

Correspondent: Shirley Vaughan, Clerk, St George's Hanover Square Church, The Vestry, 2A Mill Street, London W1S 1FX (020 7629 0874; email: hpppec@ stgeorgeshanoversquare.org; website: www.stgeorgeshanoversquare.org)

CC number: 212439

Eligibility

People under 25 who are residents of the City of Westminster and are studying at schools or colleges in Westminster.

Types of grants

Grants, usually of £50 to £500, are made to schoolchildren, college students and vocational students towards clothing, books, living expenses and excursions.

Annual grant total

In 2013/14 the charity had assets of £12.9 million and an income of £498,000. Grants totalled £154,000, of which £16,600 was awarded to around 120 individuals. The charity makes grants for both social welfare and educational purposes. We estimate that the amount of grants given to individuals for educational purposes totalled around £8,300.

Exclusions

Our research indicates that refugees, asylum seekers and overseas students are not eligible.

Applications

All applications should be made through a recognised third party/organisation and include a case history and the name, address and date of birth of the applicant. Applications are considered on an ongoing basis.

Paddington Charitable Estates Educational Fund

£12,500

Correspondent: Sarah Craddock, Correspondent, 15th Floor, City of Westminster, Westminster City Hall, 64 Victoria Street, London SW1E 6QP (020 7641 2770; email: scraddock@ westminster.gov.uk; website: www. westminster.gov.uk/paddington-charities)

CC number: 312347

Eligibility

People under the age of 25 who are living in Paddington and who are in need of financial assistance to enable them to pursue their education, including primary, secondary and further education and vocational training.

Types of grants

Scholarships and bursaries are available towards educational trips and to allow people to enter into a trade or profession or to study music and other arts. Long-term recurrent grants are made for school and course fees for children who are particularly gifted or in need of special tuition, to enable them to attend special schools. One-off grants are also made towards course fees and maintenance, travel, clothing and other expenses.

Our research suggests that in the past the pocket money scheme would allocate a block grant to the admissions and benefits office of the education department of Westminster City Council, which then distributed about 25 to 30 grants to individuals nominated by schools and educational welfare officers, of £2 per week for children aged 11 to 14 and £2.50 for children aged over 14.

Annual grant total

In 2014 the fund had an income of £87,000 and an expenditure of £92,500. Further information was not available. In the past awards to individuals have ranged from £5,300 to £18,000 a year. We estimate that about £12,500 may be given in grants to individuals for educational purposes.

Applications

Applications should be made in writing by a social services or welfare organisation on behalf of an individual. If in doubt, a telephone call to the correspondent would be useful to establish whether a case is eligible.

Other information

Grants are also made to voluntary-aided schools in Paddington for repairs or physical alterations and to organisations in the area of benefit.

The Paddington Charities consist of the Paddington Welfare Charities and the Paddington Charitable Estates Educational Fund. Further details on the charities can also be obtained from Clerk to the Trustees (tel: 020 7641 1859; email: cheadly-barton@westminster.gov. uk).

Saint Marylebone Educational Foundation

£71,500 (8 grants)

Correspondent: Clerk to the Trustees of Saint Marylebone Educational Foundation, c/o The Parish Administrator, St Peter's Church, Eaton Square, London SW1W 9AL (email: stmaryedf@gmail.com; website: www.stmarylebone.org/images/stories/ Publicity/Posters/Educational_ Foundation.pdf)

CC number: 312378

Eligibility

People aged between 8 and 18 who have lived or been educated in the former borough of St Marylebone and the City of Westminster for at least two years. Preference may be given to individuals experiencing unforeseen circumstances affecting their financial situation or for whom boarding school is a preferred option due to a parental illness or specific educational need.

Support is also given to postgraduate students at the Royal Academy of Music and the Royal College of Music.

Types of grants

Generally recurrent grants for school pupils to help with fees or other educational needs. Awards usually range from £500 to £5,500.

Annual grant total

In 2013/14 the foundation had assets of £786,000 and an income of £152,500. A total of £90,000 was spent in charitable activities. Grants to eight pupils totalled £71,500.

Exclusions

Grants for further/higher education are not provided.

Applications

Apply in writing to the correspondent. Applications should be made by the applicant's parent/guardian or by the individual, if aged over 18. Applications can also be submitted through a third party such as a teacher, school or welfare agency, if applicable. They are considered in January and July.

Postgraduate students should apply through one of the specified schools.

Other information

This information is taken from the 2013/14 annual report: 'Grants were awarded to the Royal Academy of Music and the Royal College of Music to assist 12 post graduate students, a total of £17,500 These grants enabled the students to complete their academic years on their chosen courses.'

St Clement Danes Educational Foundation

£15,500 (20 grants)

Correspondent: Deb Starkey, Administrator, St Clement Danes School, Drury Lane, London WC2B 5SU (020 7641 6593; email: dstarkey@stcd.co.uk)

CC number: 312319

Eligibility

After meeting the needs of St Clement Danes Primary School, grants are awarded to (in order of priority):

- Ex-pupils of St Clement Danes Church of England Primary School
- People who are under 25 years of age and have lived within the Diocese of London, with preference for the City of Westminster, for the majority of their education

Types of grants

Grants to assist with the costs of books, materials, travel, uniform and associated costs for study at college or university. Normally grants sit alongside other grants obtained.

Annual grant total

In 2014 the foundation had assets of £3.4 million and an income of £151,500. 20 grants were awarded to students totalling £15,500.

Exclusions

Grants towards fees are not usually given to pupils in primary and secondary education. No grants are given to overseas students.

Applications

Application forms are available from the correspondent. Applications can be submitted directly by the individual, or by a parent/guardian if the individual is under 18, for consideration in February, May, October or November. They need to be submitted six weeks before the committee meeting.

Croydon

The Church Tenements Charities– Educational and Church Branches

£6,000 (Around 20 grants)

Correspondent: June Haynes, Administrator, Croydon London Borough Council, Taberner House, Park Lane, Croydon CR9 3JS (020 8726 6000 EXT 62317; email: june.haynes@croydon.gov.uk)

CC number: 312554

Eligibility

People under the age of 25 who are living or studying in the London borough of Croydon (including people from overseas studying in Croydon) who are experiencing financial hardship.

Preference is given to people requesting funding below £500 who have not received support from the local authorities or where the applicants have made some effort to raise funds themselves.

Types of grants

Small, one-off grants in the range of £50–£500 mainly to people in primary, secondary and post-school education and training. Support is given towards books, stationery, uniforms, travelling to and from the place of education, music tuition and instruments, also educational outings, study/travel abroad or school fees. People entering a trade may also be supported.

Annual grant total

In 2013/14 the charity had an income of £49,500 and a total expenditure of £41,500. Over the previous four years grants to individuals totalled on average around £6,000 distributed between approximately 20 people each year.

Applications

Application forms can be requested from the correspondent. They are normally considered quarterly, in January, April, July and October. It is helpful to provide as much supporting information as possible.

Other information

The charity also gives grants to youth services, ecclesiastical organisations and supports Archbishop Tenison's School.

The Frank Denning Memorial Charity

£5,000

Correspondent: Angela Haynes – Ranger, Croydon Council, Chief Executive's Department, Zone 4G, Bernard Weatherill House, 8 Mint Walk, Croydon CR0 1EA (020 8726 6000 Ext 60125; email: Angela.HaynesRanger@croydon.gov.uk; website: www.croydon.gov.uk/advice/grants/frankdenning)

CC number: 312813

Eligibility

Students between the ages of 19 and 25 (by 30 April in the year of their application) who/whose parents are resident in the London borough of Croydon and who want to carry out an educational project overseas. The applicant's travel plans must commence between 1 May and 30 April of the year of application.

Types of grants

One-off travelling scholarships of up to £1,000 are available to full-time university or college students for undertaking a specific project abroad as a part of their course of study.

Annual grant total

In 2013/14 the charity had an income of £4,000 and an expenditure of £5,500. We estimate the annual total amount of grants awarded to be around £5,000.

Exclusions

Support is not available for holidays and journeys that have been completed or have already started at the time of application.

Applications

Application forms are available on the charity's website. Applicants who are successful in their initial application are invited for an interview to discuss their proposal with the trustees.

Ealing

Acton (Middlesex) Charities – Educational Charity

£4,700

Correspondent: Lorna Dodd, Clerk to the Trustees, c/o St Mary's Parish Office, 1 The Mount, Acton High Street, London W3 9NW (020 8992 8876; email: acton.charities@virgin.net; website: www.actoncharities.co.uk)

CC number: 312312

Eligibility

Students whose home residence is in the former ancient parish of Acton in West London. Candidates must be over the age of 18 (and normally up to the age of 25) and have entered a full-time course in the UK, usually of at least three years, which will lead to a recognised qualification.

If there is a high demand, priority will be given to students who have spent some part of their education in an Acton school.

Students who have entered on a foundation or other course in arts, music, dance or drama, without grant may also be eligible for help.

Types of grants

Grants of £300 per year to assist with books or equipment. Small awards are also available to encourage local talent, including help with mounting exhibitions if the group or artist is involved is in the Acton area.

Annual grant total

In 2014 the charity had an income of £9,700 and an expenditure of £6,600. The charity's website notes that during the year a total of £4,700 was given 'to students in various stages of further education'.

Exclusions

Anyone outside the area of benefit (there is a helpful map on the charity's website). Grants are not given for courses in private schools or institutions.

Applications

Application forms are available from the charity's website or the correspondent. Proof that the student has started an educational course is required.

Note that any correspondence should be made via post or email only. The charity advises that a quick response is not always possible. The trustees meet twice a year.

Further details on support for artists can be obtained from the correspondent.

Other information

This charity, together with Acton (Middlesex) Relief in Need Charity (Charity Commission no. 211446), forms part of the Acton (Middlesex) Charities. The charities provide welfare, educational and arts grants and also support local schools and carnivals. The website states that 'in present times the charities try to help where other local services fail'.

During 2014 a total of £1,900 was paid to local organisations and artists (through Athawes Art Gallery Fund).

Enfield

The Old Enfield Charitable Trust

£93,500

Correspondent: Personal Grants Administrator, The Old Vestry Office, 22 The Town, Enfield, Middlesex EN2 6LT (020 8367 8941; email: enquiries@toect.org.uk; website: www.toect.org.uk)

CC number: 207840

Eligibility
People in need who live in the ancient parish of Enfield.

Types of grants
Grants are made to students and other residents who are undertaking education or training. Help is given towards living costs, equipment, stationery, childcare costs, travel expenses and so on. People starting work/entering a trade are also supported.

Annual grant total
In 2013/14 the charity had an income of £599,000 and a total expenditure of £640,000. At the time of writing (November 2015) the annual report and accounts for the year were not yet available to view on the Charity Commission's online register.

The charity's website states: 'In a typical year The Old Enfield Charitable Trust administers around £250K in discretionary grants to families, individuals and community groups residing and living within the boundary of the Ancient Parish.' In previous years, educational grants have accounted for around £93,500 of grants made.

Exclusions
The charity will not provide support where local authority or central government should be assisting. Grants are not normally given for second degrees or master's degree courses. Unless there are special circumstances, applications from individuals who have not taken up a loan offered by Student Finance England will not be considered.

Applications
Application forms are available to download from the website. Supporting evidence, which is outlined in a list on the website, must be provided, along with details of the individual's family income and expenditure. Applications that have not seen their supporting documents received by the charity will be deferred. Application forms can be returned to Susan Foss, Education Grants Administrator. Applicants are invited to attend an interview with the charity's Education Committee and, following receipt of a completed application form and supporting documents, the charity will inform the applicant of the date of the next meeting in writing.

Other information
Community grants are also made to organisations. The charity also administers Ann Crowe's and Wright's Almshouse Charity which owns 10 Almshouses that are let to needy people already resident in the ancient parish of Enfield.

Greenwich

Greenwich Blue Coat Foundation

£10,500 (18 grants)

Correspondent: Mr M. Baker, Clerk to the Trustees, 136 Charlton Lane, London SE7 8AB (020 8858 7575; email: bluecoat@baker5.co.uk; website: www.bluecoathistory.co.uk/page829.html)

CC number: 312407

Eligibility
Young people up to 25 years of age who have lived or have been educated in the London borough of Greenwich for at least two years previous to their application. Preference is given to individuals with limited means.

Types of grants
One-off and recurrent grants, normally of around £500, are given to help individuals to further their education, develop life skills or enter a chosen career path. Financial assistance can be given for the course fees, equipment/instruments or other course-related expenses.

Annual grant total
In 2013/14 the foundation had assets of £1.7 million and an income of £49,500. A total of £12,500 was awarded in grants including £10,500 to 18 individuals. Two beneficiaries were awarded grants exceeding £1,000 with a total of £2,600.

Exclusions
Maintenance or travel costs are not normally supported.

Applications
Application forms can be downloaded from the foundation's website or requested from the correspondent. Candidates are required to provide a name of a referee. The trustees usually meet four times a year in January, April, July and November.

The trustees may ask applicants to attend an interview to help determine their suitability for an award.

Other information
The trustees remind that the foundation 'only has a relatively small sum of money available annually and does not therefore usually make large individual awards'.

During the year a grant of £1,700 was given to Blackheath Bluecoat Church of England Secondary School for a school geography field trip.

Hackney

The Hackney Parochial Charities

£11,000

Correspondent: Sarah Bennett, Correspondent, c/o Trust Partnership, 6 Trull Farm Buildings, Trull, Tetbury, Gloucestershire GL8 8SQ (020 3397 7805 or 01285 841900; email: sarah.bennett@thetrustpartnership.com or office@thetrustpartnership.com; website: www.hackneyparochialcharities.org.uk)

CC number: 219876

Eligibility
People in need who live in the former metropolitan borough of Hackney (as it was before 1970).

Types of grants
Help is given towards the cost of books, equipment, tools and examination fees for apprentices and young people at college or university who are not in receipt of a full grant. Grants are one-off, although applicants can re-apply annually.

Annual grant total
In 2013/14 the charity had assets of £5.7 million and an income of £250,000. Grants were made totalling £122,000, most of which appears to be given to organisations. We estimate that about £22,000 was given to individuals for both social welfare and educational needs.

Applications
Applications can be made via a form available on the website or requested from the correspondent. Grants for individuals are considered by the trustees by email on a monthly or bi-monthly basis. Requests must be made through a supporting agency, such as a church or a social worker, details of whom need to be added to the form. Individuals must provide evidence of their postal address, such as a copy of a utility bill.

Other information

In 2008 the charity took over the administration of Hackney District Nursing Association; however, no grants were made out of the Hackney District Nursing Association's funds during the year.

The annual report notes that 'the trustees also make regular small grants to the local ministers' discretionary sick and needy funds to enable the local clergy to assist poor local people, who are in urgent need, without having to make a formal application for a grant each time'.

Hammersmith and Fulham

Dr Edwards and Bishop King's Fulham Charity

£1,200

Correspondent: Jonathan Martin, Clerk to the Trustees, Percy Barton House, 33–35 Dawes Road, London SW6 7DT (020 7385 9387; fax: 020 7610 2856; email: clerk@debk.org.uk; website: www.debk.org.uk)

CC number: 1113490

Eligibility

People in need who are undertaking education or training and live in the old Metropolitan Borough of Fulham. This constitutes all of the SW6 postal area and parts of W14 and W6. Educational support is given on a limited basis. The website gives a detailed list of geographical area eligible for support.

Types of grants

One-off grants are made to individuals for short accredited training courses which are likely to lead to employment; also support with childcare and other needs.

Annual grant total

In 2013/14 the charity had assets of almost £9.3 million and an income of £438,000. A total of 197 grants were made to individuals totalling £123,000 (including educational/training grants). The annual report suggests that the vast majority of grants were given for welfare needs. In the past about 1% of support has been given for educational needs; therefore, we estimate that grants to support education and training totalled about £1,200.

Exclusions

According to the website, the charity does not:

▶ Normally help those who are homeowners
▶ Help those not in the area of benefit
▶ Give cash grants (unless they are to be administered by an agency)
▶ Give grants retrospectively or pay arrears on utility bill
▶ Provide funds for funerals
▶ Provide wheelchairs or electric scooters
▶ Provide computer equipment of any sort, unless you are housebound
▶ Provide dishwashers
▶ Provide laminate flooring
▶ Provide grants for equipment where government, or local government, or any other agency is required to provide that equipment by law

The charity prefers not to satisfy repeat requests and is extremely unlikely to help requests for which funding may be available from other places. Our research suggests that postgraduate courses are not funded.

Applications

Application forms are available from the correspondent or on the charity's website. Applications must be submitted in hard copy either directly by the individual or through a third party. It is important to note that individuals applying directly for a grant will normally be visited at home by the Grants Administrator.

The committee which considers relief-in-need applications, including educational grant applications, meets ten times a year, roughly every four or five weeks. The charity suggests that applications should be submitted around two or three weeks before the next meeting.

Applicants are welcome to get in touch with the charity prior to making a formal appeal.

Other information

The charity gives money to both individuals and organisations, with its main responsibility being towards the relief of poverty rather than assisting students.

There are also Summer Schemes whereby funding is given to help with 'organised activities and day trips for young local people from challenging backgrounds, over the July and August school holidays'. Assistance for longer trips – provided the destination venues are reputable, reasonably priced, and within the UK – may also be given under the scheme. In 2013/14 funding totalling £21,000 was awarded to eight local groups either to run community play schemes or to finance trips (within the UK) for underprivileged children.

In 2013/14 the overall support was distributed between organisations (50%), relief-in-need grants (43%) and Summer Schemes (7%).

It is stated on the website that 'educational grant uptake in the year was minimal, despite increased provision by the charity' during 2013/14.

Harringey

The Tottenham Grammar School Foundation

£331,500

Correspondent: Graham Chappell, Clerk to the Foundation, PO Box 34098, London N13 5XU (020 8882 2999; fax: Available on request; email: trustees@tgsf.org.uk; website: www.tgsf.org.uk)

CC number: 312634

Eligibility

Young people under the age of 25 who/whose parents normally live in the borough of Haringey and who have attended a school in the borough.

Types of grants

The foundation has different types of awards and there are different eligibility criteria for each:

▶ The Somerset Award – generally one-off grant of £250 to students on full-time courses at colleges of further education (or equivalent)
▶ The Somerset Undergraduate Award – recurrent payments (£750 payable in annual instalments of £250) to university students following a full-time degree or an equivalent higher education course of at least two years' duration
▶ The Somerset Special Award – a wide range of grants, to postgraduate students, young sports people at a county standard or higher, musicians at a conservatoire standard and individuals with special needs

The foundation makes a limited number of Somerset Scholarships and Sponsorships each year. Generally, these are made in partnership with Mountview Academy of Theatre Arts and the Harrington scheme.

Annual grant total

In 2013/14 the foundation had assets of £22.8 million and an income of £489,500. Grants, awards and other sponsorship and bursaries totalled £807,000 and grants to individuals totalled £331,500.

Exclusions

Awards are not normally offered to support apprenticeships or courses being followed at schools (including school sixth forms).

Applications

Separate application forms for general and undergraduate awards can be downloaded from the foundation's website. Applications can also be made through a fast-track online system on the website. Candidates are invited to apply from 1 May each year (for the academic year commencing the following September). The closing date for applications for each academic year is 31 January.

Applications for special grants must be made in writing to the correspondent providing the date of birth, relevant documentation, letters of support and other information specific for different categories (see the website for details). For children with special needs, there is an application form for use by the parent, guardian or other appropriate person applying for assistance on their behalf (which can be downloaded from the website).

Other information

Grants are also made to charities, voluntary groups and other organisations who work with young people in the borough of Haringey. Local schools are also supported for the costs of school trips, special educational needs.

Hillingdon

Uxbridge United Welfare Trusts

£12,600 (23 grants)

Correspondent: Mrs J. Duffy, Grants Officer, Woodbridge House, New Windsor Street, Uxbridge UB8 2TY (07912 270937; email: grants.officer@ uuwt.org; website: www.uuwt.org)

CC number: 217066

Eligibility

People under the age of 25 who are in need and live in (or has a parent who lives) or have a very strong connection with the Uxbridge area. The area of benefit covers Cowley, Harefield, Hillingdon, Ickenham and Uxbridge.

Types of grants

One-off grants for people in school, further/higher education and individuals undertaking vocational training or apprenticeships. Grants can be given towards specific needs, items or services, including course costs, books, school uniforms, school trips, travel and transport expenses, computer equipment, instruments, sometimes living expenses and so on.

Annual grant total

In 2014 the charity had assets of £10.7 million and an income of £514,000. The amount of grants given to individuals totalled £102,500. Educational grants from a restricted Lord Ossulton Fund amounted to £12,600 were distributed to 23 individuals.

Exclusions

Our research suggests that grants are not normally given for school fees. Funding is not intended to be provided where statutory support is available.

Applications

Application forms can be requested from the correspondent. They can be submitted directly by the individual or through a social worker, Citizens Advice or educational welfare agency, if applicable. Awards are considered each month. A trained staff member will visit applicants for an interview to better assess their application.

Other information

Grants are also awarded for welfare purposes and may be given to support organisations. The charity also runs almshouses.

Hounslow

Need and Taylor's Educational Charity

£6,000

Correspondent: Julie Cadman, St Paul's Church Office, St Paul's Road, Brentford TW8 0PN (020 8568 7442; email: clerk@ brentfordchiswickmc.org.uk; website: www.brentfordchiswickmc.org.uk)

CC number: 312269

Eligibility

Children in need who are under the age of 21 and live in the former borough of Brentford and Chiswick (as constituted immediately before 1 April 1965). The charity uses the child's eligibility for free school meals as an indicator of need.

Types of grants

One-off grants between £80 and £100 are provided to schoolchildren towards the cost of uniforms, other clothing including PE kits, coats and shoes, school bags and educational equipment (calculators, art tools and so on).

Annual grant total

In 2013/14 the charity had an income of £14,000 and an expenditure of £12,700.

We estimate the annual total amount of grants awarded to be around £6,000. A number of local schools are also supported.

Applications

Application forms can be found on the charity's website and have to be accompanied by the 'applicant's letter'. The application needs to be signed by the headteacher and include specific amounts requested for each individual item and prices inclusive of VAT. The trustees meet quarterly.

Other information

Grants are also made to schools, where support is not already provided by the local authorities.

Islington

Worrall and Fuller Exhibition Fund

£6,000

Correspondent: Minee Pande, Clerk to the Governors, 90 Central Street, London EC1V 8AJ (020 7549 8181; email: mpande@slpt.org.uk)

CC number: 312507

Eligibility

Children and young people between the ages of 5 and 25 who are resident in the old borough of Finsbury (now part of Islington). Preference is given to those who live in the parish of St Luke, Old Street, or whose parents have had their business or employment there in previous years.

Types of grants

The fund awards scholarships, bursaries, maintenance allowances and grants to schoolchildren, further/higher education students and people entering a trade/ starting work. Financial assistance is given towards the cost of books, clothing/outfits, uniforms, equipment/ instruments, other necessities, also travel/study abroad in pursuance of education. Arts and music studies can also be supported.

Annual grant total

In 2013/14 the fund had an income of £18,500 and an expenditure of £12,000. It can also support organisations; therefore, we estimate the annual total amount of grants awarded to individuals to be around £6,000.

Applications

Apply in writing to the correspondent. The trustees meet three times a year to discuss new applications and make decisions.

Other information

The fund can also offer grants for the maintenance of local schools.

Kensington and Chelsea

The Campden Charities

£408,500

Correspondent: Christopher Stannard, Clerk, Studios 3&4, 27A Pembridge Villas, London W11 3EP (020 7243 0551 or 020 7313 3797; website: www. campdencharities.org.uk)

CC number: 1104616

Eligibility

Individuals applying for funding must: have been continuously living in Kensington for at least two years (there is a helpful area of benefit map on the website); be a British or European citizen or have indefinite leave to remain; live in rented accommodation and not be a homeowner; be in receipt of benefits, including housing benefits, or in low paid work.

Types of grants

The charity divides its educational support into two main areas:

- To assist people of working age to obtain employment with grants for course fees, travel, childcare and equipment
- To support university students aged 24 and under

For more information on the employment routes the charity may be able to help with, see its website.

Annual grant total

In 2014/15 the charity had assets of £143.4 million and an income of £2.9 million. During the year, the charity made grants to both individuals and organisations for social welfare and educational purposes. Of £1.9 million awarded, £1.5 million was given to individuals and £405,000 to organisations. Grants to individuals for educational purposes totalled £408,500.

Exclusions

Previous research indicates that the charity will not give funding for: direct payment of council tax or rent; debt repayments; fines or court orders; foreign travel or holidays; career changes; personal development courses; postgraduate studies; computers; individuals whose immediate goal is self-employment; goods and services catered for by central government.

Applications

The charity's website advises that eligible individuals living in the area of benefit should call 020 7243 0551 to apply.

Other information

The charity provides debt advice for all of its beneficiaries through its partnership with Nucleus (nucleus.org.uk).

The Pocklington Apprenticeship Trust (Kensington)

£13,000

Correspondent: Ali Omar, Administrator, Floor 1 Room 127, Town Hall, Hornton Street, London W8 7NX (020 7361 4318; email: ali.omar@rbkc. gov.uk; website: www.rbkc.gov.uk/ educationandlearning/ familyinformationservice/ charitabletrusts.aspx)

CC number: 312943

Eligibility

Young people aged 21 years or younger who were either born in Kensington and Chelsea or whose parent/parents have lived there for at least ten years. Applicants must have a financial need, which is described on the trust's webpage as when 'either the parents/carers/young person receive entitlements such as Housing Benefit, Jobseekers' Allowance, income support or other similar equivalents.'

Types of grants

One-off grants, usually of between £200 and £300, are awarded to schoolchildren, students in further/higher education, vocational students, people starting work and for special educational needs. Grants are typically awarded for books, equipment, instruments and commuting expenses. People starting work may also receive support for uniforms and clothing.

Annual grant total

In 2014 the trust had an income of £6,000 and a total expenditure of £13,500. We estimate that the amount of grants given to individuals totalled £13,000.

Exclusions

Help is only given to attend classes outside the borough if the classes are unavailable within it.

Applications

Application forms are available from the correspondent. Applications are considered at Administration Committee meetings, deadlines for which are updated on the Royal Borough of Kensington and Chelsea Council website.

Other information

There is also support for those who meet the age criteria who are in the care or under the supervision of the borough.

Westway Trust

£25,500

Correspondent: Mark Lockhart, Finance Director, 1 Thorpe Close, London W10 5XL (020 8962 5720; email: info@ westway.org; website: www.westway.org)

CC number: 1123127

Eligibility

Support is available to people who live in the borough of Kensington and Chelsea and are in need.

Our research suggests that educational grants have been available to adults out of work undertaking courses leading to employment, training grants to individuals over the age of 16 wishing to undertake training courses and sports bursaries to people who wish to participate in Westway organised sports activities but lack means.

Types of grants

Our research suggests that the trust can provide the following support:

- Educational grants – up to £1,000 towards fees, books, travel costs and childcare
- Sports training grants – up to £500 towards training courses leading to employment in the sports and fitness industry
- Sports bursaries – training bursary (fitness membership, access to gyms and sports programmes), coaching bursary (equipment, travel competition entry costs) or education bursary (NGB training courses to enter employment as a couch/instructor in the sports and fitness industry). The bursaries are of up to £500, the average award being around £80–£120, and are awarded where candidates can show evidence of registered disability or receipt of universal credits

Annual grant total

In 2013/14 the trust had assets of £38.9 million, an income of £7.7 million and made grants totalling £386,000. Of this amount £14,200 was distributed in educational grants to individuals and £11,600 in performance sports bursaries.

Applications

Application forms and further details can be requested from the correspondent. In the past the sports bursary scheme was open for applications on 1 May and 1 October each year with applications being considered within six weeks of the closing date.

Note that application criteria are subject to change and for the latest updates consult the website.

Other information

The trust offers education and training programmes, runs sports facilities, health and fitness services and provides facilities for arts, culture and other events. Grants are also made to local community groups and charities.

In the past applicants successful in their application for sports training grant were expected to do ten hours of voluntary work on the trust's sports projects and recipients of the sports bursary were required to help with promoting activities and events.

Lambeth

Walcot Educational Foundation (Lambeth Endowed Charities)

£50,000

Correspondent: H. W. J. Valentine, 127 Kennington Road, London SE11 6SF (020 7735 1925; fax: 020 7735 7048; email: office@walcotfoundation.org.uk; website: www.walcotfoundation.org.uk)

CC number: 312800

Eligibility

People, normally under 30 years of age, who are on low income and live in the borough of Lambeth. Individuals currently living outside the area but who are still considered to be Lambeth residents will also qualify for assistance.

Types of grants

The foundation offers:
- Student grants – one-off or recurrent awards of up to £2,000 per academic year to help young people over the age of 18 with the costs of first degree or vocational training, that has a strong likelihood of leading to work. Grants can be given for: course fees (not for private institutions), associated travel costs, books, special clothing, equipment, study/field trips and childcare
- Moving into employment grants – one-off grants for vocational training and related activities are available to people who have been out of work for most of the previous five years and have not gained a degree or qualification in the past ten years. The support is intended to help to move back to work and can be given for costs associated with further education or vocational courses, work experience, necessities, such as clothing and equipment/instruments

- Talented young people awards – to children between the ages of 10 and 18 who have exceptional talents in sports, music, drama, dance or other areas can apply for a grant of £500 to help with tuition fees, equipment or summer schools

Annual grant total

In 2013/14 the foundation had assets of £84.2 million, an income of £2.2 million and a charitable expenditure of £1.7 million. Grants awarded to individuals for educational purposes totalled £50,000.

Exclusions

Grants are not given for:
- Postgraduate studies
- Second degrees
- Personal development courses
- Study at private institutions
- Repayment of debts
- Career changes
- Course fees in cases where it is not clear that the applicant will be able to raise the balance of funds to complete the entire course
- The cost of goods/services already purchased or those provided by the central/local government
- Council tax, rent or other taxes
- Household goods, furnishing, clothing, unless directly related to work or education progress
- Travel abroad and holidays
- Gifts or toys
- Funeral costs
- Court orders or fines

If the applicant already has significant work experience with a reasonable level of responsibility, or a vocational qualification (at NVQ-4 or equivalent), the foundation will not fund further study.

Applications

Application forms are available on the foundation's website or from the correspondent. Applications can be made at any time and a referral may be required by a staff member at an educational institution, social care officer or other professional. The trustees meet six times a year and it is aimed to respond to applications from individuals within six weeks.

Other information

The foundation is made up of four charities – The Cynthia Mosley Memorial Fund, Hayle's Charity, Walcot Educational Foundation and The Walcot Non-Educational Charity. The general financial information given above represents the funds of the four charities and the information on grants for educational purposes concerns the Walcot Educational Foundation only.

The foundation also provides additional services to beneficiaries including careers advice, debt and budgeting advice, capacity building and low cost psychotherapy. Various projects, schools and organisations working for individuals can also be supported.

Lewisham

The (Brockley) Town and Poor Estate

£500

Correspondent: Jane Forster, Trustee, Brooklands, Chapel Lane, Brockley, Bury St Edmunds, Suffolk IP29 4AS (01284 830558; email: binnybops@btinternet.com)

CC number: 236989

Eligibility

Schoolchildren who live in Brockley village.

Types of grants

Our research suggests that grants are given for the purchase of uniforms. In previous years an educational book has also been given to all students in the village on reaching the age of 15.

Annual grant total

In 2014 the charity had an income of £1,400 and a total expenditure of £1,200. We estimate that the amount of grants given to individuals for educational purposes totalled around £500.

Applications

Applications may be made in writing to the correspondent. They should be submitted directly by the individual or a family member.

Other information

Awards are also made for social welfare purposes.

The Downham Feoffee Charity

£1,400

Correspondent: Jo Howard, Clerk, 35 Fieldside, Ely, Cambridgeshire CB6 3AT (01353 665774; email: downhamfeoffees@hotmail.co.uk)

CC number: 237233

Eligibility

Residents of the ancient parish of Downham.

Types of grants

Grants for students attending higher education. Support to people in other education or training may also be given.

Annual grant total

In 2014/15 the charity had assets of £4.6 million and an income of £91,000. The charity gave £1,400 in higher education grants.

Applications

Applications may be made in writing to the correspondent.

Other information

Awards are also made to individuals in need, schools and other public organisations, although its main focus is the provision of housing and allotments. The charity owns 20 houses and 200 acres of agricultural land. Grants to organisations totalled about £21,000 in 2014/15.

Lee (Educational) Charity of William Hatcliffe

£9,000 (21 grants)

Correspondent: Anne Wilson, PO Box 7041, Bridgnorth, Shropshire WV16 9EL (07517 527849; email: annewilsontc@ hotmail.co.uk)

CC number: 312801

Eligibility

Young people under the age of 25 living in Lewisham, with some preference for those living in the ancient parish of Lee.

Types of grants

One-off support for educational and training purposes.

Annual grant total

In 2013/14 the charity had assets of £174,000 an income of £29,000 and a total expenditure of £10,500. A total of 21 grants were awarded totalling £9,000.

Applications

Apply in writing to the correspondent.

Merton

Alf and Hilda Leivers Charity Trust

£11,000

Correspondent: Trust Administrator, Rosewood End, Windsor Road, Chobham, Surrey GU24 8NA

CC number: 299267

Eligibility

Young people in need up to the age of 18 who live or attend school/college in the London borough of Merton. The trust particularly aims to assist in the fields of education, arts, drama, music or athletics.

Types of grants

One-off and recurrent grants to help with the cost of books, clothing, equipment/instruments, educational outings and other essentials for those at school.

Annual grant total

In 2013/14 the charity had an income of £17,000 and an expenditure of £11,500. We estimate that around £11,000 was awarded in educational grants to individuals.

Applications

Apply in writing to the correspondent. Our research shows that applications can be submitted by individuals, their headteacher or a social care worker, if applicable. Applications should specify what funding is requested and give full details of the applicant's circumstances. Grants are usually considered between April and June, although urgent cases can be considered at any time.

Other information

Grants are also made to organisations.

Richmond upon Thames

The Barnes Workhouse Fund

£13,500 (32 grants)

Correspondent: Miranda Ibbetson, Director, PO Box 665, Richmond, Surrey TW10 6YL (020 8241 3994; email: mibbetson@barnesworkhousefund.org. uk; website: www.barnesworkhousefund. org.uk)

CC number: 200103

Eligibility

Students and schoolchildren who have been resident in the ancient parish of Barnes (in practice SW13) for at least six months. Applications are actively encouraged from individuals looking to return to education.

Types of grants

One-off grants are available to students in further education, where local or national authority assistance is unavailable, for costs such as fees, maintenance, educational equipment and books, travel costs and childcare. School uniforms and school trips are also funded.

Annual grant total

In 2014 the fund had assets of £10 million and an income of £617,000.

Grants totalled £207,000, the majority of which was awarded to organisations. Individuals received grants amounting to almost £33,000; of this amount £19,300 was given for social welfare needs and the remaining £13,500 for educational purposes.

Exclusions

The website states that trustees are unlikely to support applications to help with the costs of postgraduate study.

Applications

Application forms are available to download from the website and can be submitted directly by the individual. Small grants for individuals are considered immediately, whereas requests of a more complex nature are considered at the next trustees' meeting. These meetings are held in January, March, May, September and November and, for consideration at one of these meetings, applications must be received by the fund by the 6th of the preceding month. **Note:** The parental income of applicants up to the age of 25 will usually be taken into account. All applicants will be interviewed by representatives of the trustees.

Other information

The Barnes Workhouse Fund provides sheltered accommodation for around 40 residents at its almshouse, Walsingham Lodge, in Barnes.

The fund has an informative website and annual report, which each provide in great detail information on the fund's activities and its history.

The Hampton Wick United Charity

£5,000

Correspondent: The Clerk, Hunters Lodge, Home Farm, Redhill Road, Cobham, Surrey KT11 1EF (01932 596748; email: info@hwuc.org.uk; website: hwuc.org.uk)

CC number: 1010147

Eligibility

Individuals who are under the age of 25 and have lived in the area of benefit (the parishes of St John the Baptist in Hampton Wick, St Mark in Teddington, and St Mary with St Alban in Teddington) for at least 12 months.

Types of grants

Grants have been given towards, for example: tutorial fees and accommodation costs at university; school uniforms; fares to and from school and college; academic books; school and field trips.

Annual grant total

We have no current information on the grant-giving of this charity. At the time of writing (October 2015) financial information had not been submitted to the Charity Commission for any of the years listed on the charity's online record.

We know that previously over £20,000 a year was awarded to individuals in educational and welfare grants. Grants are also awarded to organisations. We estimate the amount given to individuals for educational purposes totalled around £5,000.

Applications

In the first instance, contact the Clerk.

Richmond Parish Lands Charity (RPLC)

£126,000

Correspondent: Sharon La Ronde, Grants Director, The Vestry House, 21 Paradise Road, Richmond, Surrey TW9 1SA (020 8948 5701; fax: 020 8332 6792; email: grants@rplc.org.uk; website: www.rplc.org.uk)

CC number: 200069

Eligibility

People above school age who are in need and have lived in the TW9 TW10 or SW14 areas of Richmond, Ham, Sheen and Mortlake for at least six months prior to application and have no other possible sources of help.

The charity notes on its website: 'Many of our applicants face challenges, such as mental health issues, divorce, homelessness, a criminal record, (long-term) unemployment and/or debt. A significant number are single parents.'

The trustees will favour applicants who have been educated in the borough and/or can demonstrate community links. Occasionally applications from people who work in the benefit area but do not reside in it will be considered but applicants will have to show that the course is directly related to the efficacy of their role in the community and of benefit to the residents.

Types of grants

One-off and recurrent support is given towards fees, equipment, childcare cost and/or other living expenses.

The charity's website states:

> We recognise that especially in today's competitive economy, people may need additional qualifications to find employment or improve their income potential. Some will be building on previous educational achievements, others could be rethinking their career path because of changed circumstances or limited opportunities in their field. We

aim to enable entry to Further and Higher Education Programmes to help: increase job prospects; set up/expand one's own business; achieve independence and/or quality of life.

Support is normally only given for courses in the public sector except where they are unavailable in state-maintained institutions. Grants can range from £50 towards course books to larger recurrent grants over several years for course fees. In 2013/14 beneficiaries ranged from 'A levels to doctorates and a large proportion of applicants gained vocational qualifications'.

Annual grant total

The charity is a grant-maker and housing provider. In 2013/14 it had assets of £85.7 million and an income of £1.86 million. Grants were made to over 1,000 individuals totalling £267,000. Grants for educational purposes totalled £273,000, of which £126,000 was given to individuals.

Exclusions

Schoolchildren are not supported (although the trustees will apply their discretion with regard to applications for assistance for help with uniform or school trips for children of families on low income. Gap year activities are not funded but contributions to trips directly relating to a course of study may be considered.

Applications

Application forms are available online and may be returned via email to the Education Director, Nancy Van den Broeck (email: director@rplc.org.uk). Any enquiries should also be directed to the Education Director. Applications are discussed at intervals during the year.

The application should include details of the applicant's current employment, their income and expenditure, the course undertaken, explain what assistance is needed for, and provide a statement in support of the application. Two references (personal and professional) are required and applicants are usually asked to attend an interview. Applications should be based on financial need and parental income is taken into account up to the age of 25.

Other information

Grants are also made to organisations – regular core funding to charities with a proven track record of serving local community needs and also project or strategic funding. In 2013/14 assistance was given to 106 organisations totalling over £1 million.

Sector Training Grants are offered to 'organisations that serve the needs of our local community' with priority given to 'applications from individuals working for a small or medium sized charity in

Richmond, who are paid employees and wish to undertake a course or programme that is relevant to their position AND that will benefit their current employer'.

Child Poverty Grants are made at the beginning of each academic year to schools in Richmond with children from the beneficial area (£34,500 in 2013/14) and project support grants are available for organisations for educational initiatives and programmes.

The charity also provides welfare support to individuals, including winter fuel assistance and financial help at times of crisis.

The Barnes Relief in Need Charity (BRINC) (Charity Commission no. 200318) is also administered by the Richmond Parish Lands Charity. BRINC seeks to help people in need who are resident in SW14 and also supports local organisations. BRINC and the RPLC use the same application forms, which are held by referral agencies.

The charity has an informative website.

The Thomas Wilson Educational Trust

£31,000 (35 grants)

Correspondent: Karen Hopkins, Administrator, 23 Tranmere Road, Twickenham TW2 7JD (020 8893 3928)

CC number: 1003771

Eligibility

People under 25 who live in Teddington and neighbourhood.

Types of grants

Grants of £100 to £4,500 are given to schoolchildren towards clothing, books, educational outings and fees (only in exceptional circumstances) and to students in further or higher education, including overseas students (depending on how long they have been a resident in Teddington), towards books, fees, living expenses and study or travel abroad. Help may also be given to mature students under 25.

Annual grant total

In 2013 the trust had an income of £154,000 and a total expenditure of £90,500. A total of £31,000 was distributed in educational payments to 35 individuals. The trust granted assistance to 15 pupils to attend school trips or facilitate other educational needs. The remaining 20 awards were to students attending university or on higher education courses.

At the time of writing (October 2015) this was the most recent financial information available for the trust.

Applications

Application forms are available from the correspondent. Applications can be submitted directly by the individual or by a parent or guardian. They are considered throughout the year.

Southwark

Charity of Thomas Dickinson

£1,400

Correspondent: David Freeman, Trustee, Flat 99, Andrewes House, Barbican, London EC2Y 8AY (020 7628 6155)

CC number: 802473

Eligibility

Young people aged 25 or under and in financial need who are living in, studying in or have at least one parent working in the ancient parishes of: St Giles without Cripplegate; St Sepulchre, St George the Martyr or St Olave, Southwark; or St Mary Magdalene, Bermondsey.

Types of grants

One-off grants ranging from £100 to £500 are given to:

- Schoolchildren for uniforms and educational outings in the UK and overseas
- Students in further or higher education for books
- Vocational students for equipment and instruments
- Individuals with special educational needs for uniforms/clothing

Annual grant total

In 2014 the charity had an income of £2,800 and a total expenditure of £2,700. We estimate that educational grants to individuals totalled £1,400, with funding also awarded to organisations.

Applications

Application forms are available from the correspondent, submitted either directly by the individual or via their school/college/educational welfare agency. Applications are usually considered in February/March, June/July and October/November.

Newcomen Collett Foundation

£30,000

Correspondent: Catherine Dawkins, Administrator, 66 Newcomen Street, London SE1 1YT (020 7407 2967; fax: 020 7403 3969; email: grantoffice@newcomencollett.org.uk; website: www.newcomencollett.org.uk/index.html)

CC number: 312804

Eligibility

People under the age of 25 who have lived in the London borough of Southwark for at least two years. Priority is given to individuals who have grown up in the borough of Southwark and are continuing their education/training beyond school-leaving age.

Types of grants

Grants are available to students in tertiary education or undertaking apprenticeships and to people pursuing courses in arts, music, dancing and so on. Support can be given towards equipment/instruments, college fees, course-related necessities (such as travel, books or supplies) and vocational training expenses. Awards are one-off or recurrent and usually of about £500.

Support towards school uniforms is given through the Southwark Education Welfare and Attendance Office.

Annual grant total

In 2013/14 the foundation had assets of £3 million and an income of £404,500. A total of £105,000 was spent on charitable activities. Normally around £30,000 can be awarded in grants to individuals annually. During the year 37 grants totalling £3,000 were given by referral through the Southwark Education Welfare and Attendance Office.

Exclusions

Grants are not given for independent school fees, overseas travel, postgraduate degrees or for retrospective expenditure.

Applications

Application forms are available from the foundation's website or can be requested from the correspondent. Applicants can apply directly providing a supporting statement from a tutor or other qualified person. Applications are considered three times a year, in June, September and December. They should be submitted a month in advance of the meeting (for specific dates consult the website).

Other information

Grants are also given to schools and organisations.

St Olave, St Thomas and St John United Charity

£0

Correspondent: Angela O'Shaughnessy, 6–8 Druid Street, off Tooley Street, London SE1 2EU (020 7407 2530; email: st.olavescharity@btconnect.com)

CC number: 211763

Eligibility

People under the age of 25 who live in the ancient parishes of Southwark St Olave and St Thomas, and Bermondsey Horsleydown St John. In practice this means residents of Bermondsey (part SE1 and all SE16).

Types of grants

Grants for schoolchildren for items such as clothing, travel and fees are only given in very exceptional circumstances. Grants to college students and mature students for books.

Annual grant total

In 2013/14 the charity had assets of £14.3 million and an income of £384,500. Grants totalled £260,500, the majority of which (£214,500) was given to individuals for social welfare purposes. No grants were made to individuals for educational purposes during the year; however, grants to schools amounted to £27,000.

Applications

Apply in writing outlining the need. Applications should be made through a school or similar organisation.

St Olave's and St Saviour's Schools Foundation – Foundation Fund

£47,500 (52 grants)

Correspondent: Cathy Matthews, Administration Manager, Europoint Centre, 5–11 Lavington Street, London SE1 0NZ (020 7401 2871; email: cathymatthews@stolavesfoundation.co.uk or grants@stolavesfoundation.co.uk; website: www.stolavesfoundationfund.org.uk)

CC number: 312987

Eligibility

Students who are under the age of 25 (at the time of the course) and are undertaking higher, further or vocational education courses. They must have lived in the London borough of Southwark for at least two years prior to starting their course. Consideration will also be given to young people wanting to pursue courses in drama, music, sports, dancing, etc.

Types of grants

The following information was provided by the foundation:

Individuals may receive a maximum grant of £2,000 per academic year over 3 years; however, the normal level of funding is around £500 to £700 per application. Grants will be for specific items or to meet specific costs. More than 3 grants (regardless of value) will not be considered other than in the most exceptional of cases at the discretion of the Trustees.

Examples of grants that have been awarded in the past include: money towards the cost of a laptop, printer, books, educational materials, travel expenses, expenses associated with vocational training, musical instruments etc.

Grants can be split into termly payments dependent on the award granted. The second payment will be dependent upon the Foundation receiving a copy of the receipt(s) for the agreed purchases made with the first payment as proof of purchase. The same happens with the third payment.

Annual grant total

In 2014/15 grants to 52 individuals from the Foundation Fund amounted to £47,500.

Exclusions

Grants are not awarded for individual salaries, school fees, domestic bills, childcare, food or payment of debts. Grants are also not awarded towards items that have already been purchased. Grants may only be considered for direct educational needs.

Applications

The following information was provided by the foundation:

Applications should include the following:

- an application grant form [which can be downloaded from the website]
- an official reference from your current (or most recent) course tutor and/or key/youth worker
- proof of enrolment for the current academic year (or, if not yet enrolled, official confirmation of acceptance onto a course showing proof of home address)
- a copy of your Government Student loan/grant award/refusal letter (if applicable)
- copies of your last 2 bank statements
- a short personal statement explaining the reasons why you feel you should be granted funding over and above other applicants and a short explanation as to why you need the items you have requested.

When considering applications from Individuals, the Trustees will bear in mind the following:

- age and residency
- how the grant will explicitly benefit the applicant's education
- whether a formal offer of a place at an educational establishment has been made and accepted
- whether the individual has demonstrated financial hardship
- previous grant awards from the Foundation to the individual
- evidence of items purchased with any previous grant, in the form of copy receipts

- evidence of other funding applications and their results, if known, e.g. bursaries, hardship funds etc
- official references received from previous educational establishment and others
- short personal statement demonstrating need for requested items
- whether the individual has made contact with the Foundation Office to discuss the application
- how much funding will make a real difference to the applicant
- whether the application was received before the deadline date for receiving applications

The Trustees meet four times a year and grant applications can be made at any time. The dates and application deadline dates of the meetings are on the website.

Other information

The foundation fund also considers grants for organisations, youth groups and schools based in the London borough of Southwark.

Tower Hamlets

Stepney Relief-in-Need Charity

£800 (2 grants)

Correspondent: Mrs J. Partleton, Clerk to the Trustees, Rectory Cottage, 5 White Horse Lane, Stepney, London E1 3NE (020 7790 3598; email: jeanpartleton194@btinternet.com)

CC number: 250130

Eligibility

People in need who live within the old metropolitan borough of Stepney.

Types of grants

One-off grants, usually of £100 to £500, for uniforms/clothing, books and equipment, and school trips, for example.

Annual grant total

In 2013/14 the charity had both an income and a total expenditure of £30,500. Grants were awarded totalling £17,500, of which, we believe, around £800 was given for purposes relating to education. In total, 31 grants were made to individuals during the year for both social welfare and educational needs.

Applications

An application form is available from the correspondent and may be submitted either directly by the individual or through a relative, social worker or other welfare agency. The trustees usually meet four times a year, but some applications

can be considered between meetings at the chair's discretion.

Waltham Forest

Henry Green Scholarships in Connection with Council Schools

£2,800

Correspondent: Debbie Callender-O'Neill, Correspondent, The Business Support Team – Charity Trust Fund, Room 001, Waltham Forest Town Hall, Forest Road, Walthamstow, London E17 4JF (email: debbie.callender-oneill@ walthamforest.gov.uk; website: www. walthamforest.gov.uk/Pages/Services/wf-ect.aspx)

CC number: 310918

Eligibility

People under the age of 25 who live in Waltham Forest, are attending a full-time course at the universities of Oxford, Cambridge or London and have attended one or more of the following schools for at least two years: Buxton All-through School Secondary Phase; Connaught School for Girls; George Mitchell Secondary Phase All-through School; Leyton Sixth Form College; Leytonstone School; Norlington School for Boys; or The Lammas School.

In making their decision the trustees may give consideration to the results of any examinations passed by the applicants, their school record, the headteacher's report, financial needs and their ability to profit by further education.

Types of grants

Small annual grants for educational necessities, books, equipment/ instruments or living expenses. Our research suggests that on average grants are from £50 to £200.

Annual grant total

In 2013/14 the charity had an income of £3,700 and an expenditure of £3,000. We estimate the annual total amount of grants awarded to be around £2,800.

Applications

Application forms can be requested from the correspondent or found on the charity's website. They can be submitted directly by the individual by the end of May and will need a supporting statement from the headteacher. Applicants successful in their initial application are invited for an interview which is normally held in September.

Sir George Monoux Exhibition Foundation

£2,500

Correspondent: Duncan Pike, Administrator, Walthamstow Town Hall, Forest Road, Walthamstow, London E17 4JF (020 8496 3592; email: jenny. hall@walthamforest.gov.uk)

CC number: 310903

Eligibility

Further and higher education students in need of financial assistance who are under the age of 25, live in the London borough of Waltham Forest and are pupils or former pupils of the following schools: Belmont Park School; Brookfield House School; Buxton All-through School Secondary Phase; Chingford Foundation School; Connaught School For Girls; Frederick Bremer School; George Mitchell Secondary Phase All-through School; Heathcote School and Science College; Holy Family Catholic School and Sixth Form; Joseph Clarke School; Kelmscott School; Leyton Sixth Form College; Leytonstone School; Rush Croft School; Sir George Monoux Sixth Form College; The Lammas School; Waltham Forest College; Walthamstow Academy; Whitefield School and Centre; William Morris School; and Willowfield School.

In making their decision the trustees may take into consideration results of any examinations taken by the applicants, their school record, the headteacher's report, their financial needs and their ability to profit by further education.

Types of grants

One-off awards ranging from £50 to £100 are available for activities not normally covered by the local authority grants. Such activities include student exchanges and other educational visits overseas, as well as educational visits in the UK. The foundation also aims to 'encourage students to develop their project work'.

Annual grant total

In 2013/14 the foundation had an income of £2,000 and an expenditure of £3,000. We estimate that the annual total amount of grants awarded was around £2,500.

Applications

Application forms are available from the foundation's website or can be requested from the correspondent. The application must be accompanied with a supporting statement and signature of a referee from the applicant's school/college/ university and should be submitted before the end of May. Candidates who are successful in their initial application are invited for an interview which is normally held in September.

North East

General

The Hill Bursary
See entry on page 305

John Bloom Law Bursary

£6,000

Correspondent: Hugh McGouran, Administrator, Wallace House, Falcon Court, Preston Farm Industrial Estate, Stockton-on-Tees TS18 3TX (01642 260860; email: info@ teesvalleyfoundation.org; website: www. teesvalleyfoundation.org)

CC number: 1111222

Eligibility
Students from Tees Valley studying law on a full-time undergraduate course at a UK university.

Types of grants
A bursary of up to £6,000 over three years.

Annual grant total
Payments are given each term totalling up to £6,000 over three years.

Applications
Application forms are available from the Tees Valley Community Foundation website, once the application round is open.

Other information
This fund is administered by the Tees Valley Community Foundation.

The following information was taken from the community foundation's website:

> The John Bloom Law Bursary was established in memory of John Bloom who was a local solicitor and a Trustee of the Foundation. He was passionate about his chosen profession and also about the area in which he was born and worked. His widow set up the Bursary in memory of John with the aim of providing financial assistance to students who have chosen to follow a career in Law. The Bursary supports students intending to study for a full time undergraduate degree in Law at a UK University. The successful candidate for the bursary will be expected to obtain good A-level grades and will be from a background of modest means.

S. Y. Killingley Memorial Trust

£6,500

Correspondent: Dermot Killlingley, Chair, 9 Rectory Drive, Newcastle upon Tyne NE3 1XT (07720 118603; email: trust@grevatt.f9.co.uk; website: syktrust.org.uk)

CC number: 1111891

Eligibility
People aged 18 or over taking part-time courses in language, literature, music or any other arts or humanities subject who live and study in the north east of England or are taking a long-distance course based in the north east of England. The aim of the trust is to help people who are likely to benefit the community and could not afford to study without a grant.

Types of grants
Grants for course fees, books, equipment, materials, travel or childcare and similar expenses. Grants have been for as little as £7 up to £1,300 for postgraduate students.

Annual grant total
In 2014/15 the trust had an income of £8,000 and an expenditure of £7,000. We estimate that around £6,500 was awarded in grants.

Exclusions
No grants are given for living costs.

Applications
Application forms can be obtained from the correspondent or from the trust's website. They should be submitted by post along with a letter of support from a referee such as a teacher. The selection panel meets about three times a year, usually in January, April and September. Applicants may be asked to attend an informal interview.

Other information
Successful applicants are assigned a mentor to provide them with informal support and advice during the course.

Tees Valley Community Foundation Bursaries

£24,000 (6 grants)

Correspondent: Hayley Wilson, Giving Services Co-ordinator, Wallace House, Falcon Court, Preston Farm Industrial Estate, Stockton-on-Tees TS18 3TX (01642 260860; email: info@ teesvalleyfoundation.org; website: www. teesvalleyfoundation.org)

CC number: 1111222

Eligibility
Students in local authority areas of Hartlepool, Stockton on Tees, Redcar and Cleveland, Middlesbrough and Teesside Wide – see separate funds for specific criteria as they will vary.

Types of grants
A number of bursaries ranging from £1,000 to £6,000. See details for each bursary fund.

Annual grant total
In 2013/14 the foundation had assets of £12.6 million and an income of £1.35 million. A total of 325 grants were made totalling £391,500. This included about £79,500 in grants to individuals, of which £24,000 was given in six bursaries.

Applications
Application forms and guidelines for separate funds can be found on the Tees Valley Community Foundation website, once the application round begins.

Other information
Tees Valley Community Foundation administers a number of funds providing funding to organisations and individuals. See the website for the funds currently open for applications.

There is also the Teesside Emergency Relief Fund supporting people who face an unexpected crisis.

County Durham

County Durham Community Foundation

£733,000

Correspondent: Barbara Gubbins, Chief Executive, Victoria House, Whitfield Court, St John's Road, Meadowfield Industrial Estate, Durham DH7 8XL (0191 378 6340; email: info@cdcf.org.uk; website: www.cdcf.org.uk)

CC number: 1047625

Eligibility

Young people who live in the County Durham area.

Types of grants

Grants, usually up to £5,000, are given for a wide range of educational purposes including: course and tuition fees; books; educational, sporting and musical equipment; and travel costs. Bursaries are also awarded.

Annual grant total

In 2013/14 we estimate that the amount of grants given to individuals for educational purposes totalled around £733,000.

Applications

See the website for information on open funds, guidelines and application procedures.

Other information

Grants are also made to organisations and to individuals for social welfare needs.

Lord Crewe's Charity

See entry on page 120

County Durham

Johnston Educational Foundation

Correspondent: Aynsley Merritt, Administrator, CAS Finance Team, Room G123–125, Durham County Council, County Hall, Durham DH1 5UE (03000 261862; email: aynsley. merritt@durham.gov.uk)

CC number: 527394

Eligibility

People under the age of 25 who live, or whose parents live, in the city of Durham.

Types of grants

Grants of generally up to £300 to further and higher education students. Support is given towards general educational needs, such as the cost of books, equipment/instruments, necessities, fees, coaching, accommodation and other educational expenses. Financial assistance is available for travel and volunteering work. People involved in the arts have been also supported.

Annual grant total

In 2014/15 the foundation had an income of £3,800 and no expenditure. Note that charitable giving fluctuates from about £500 to over £1,000 every year.

Applications

Application forms can be requested from the correspondent. Our research shows that applications are considered in February, June, October and can be submitted directly by the individual.

The Sedgefield District Relief in Need Charity (The Sedgefield Charities)

£6,300

Correspondent: John Hannon, Clerk to the Trustees, East House, Mordon, Stockton-on-Tees, County Durham TS21 2EY (01740 622512; email: east. house@btinternet.com)

CC number: 230395

Eligibility

College, university, vocational and mature students who live in the parishes of Bishop Middleham, Bradbury, Cornforth, Fishburn, Mordon, Sedgefield and Trimdon, in County Durham.

Types of grants

One-off grants are made to undergraduates and mature students for books and maintenance/living expenses. Support may also be given towards education and training fees.

Annual grant total

In 2014 the charity had an income of £20,500 and a total expenditure of £26,500. We estimate that the amount awarded to individuals for educational purposes totalled around £6,300.

Applications

Application forms are available from the correspondent and should be submitted by 30 September each year.

Other information

The charity gives to individuals and organisations and awards grants for both educational and social welfare purposes.

The Sedgefield Educational Foundation

£2,000

Correspondent: John Hannon, Clerk, East House, Mordon, Stockton-on-Tees TS21 2EY (01740 622512; email: east. house@btinternet.com)

CC number: 527317

Eligibility

People between the ages of 18 and 25 who or whose parents are resident in the parishes of Fishburn, Sedgefield, Bradbury and Morden.

Types of grants

Small grants to people in full-time further/higher education and training. Our research suggests that recurrent grants are available for the duration of the study. Support is given to help with the cost of books, equipment, fees and living expenses. The trustees normally only help with education higher than A-level and support those courses that are not available at schools. Grants can range from £140 to £300 (depending on the applicant's circumstances).

Annual grant total

In 2014 the foundation had an income of £4,700 and an expenditure of £2,300. We estimate the annual total amount of grants awarded to individuals to be around £2,000.

Applications

Application forms are available from the correspondent. They should be submitted by 30 September for consideration in October.

Other information

Students seeking funds for study or travel abroad and students over 25 may be referred to the Sedgefield District Relief-in-Need Charities, to which welfare applications are also referred. Local schools may also be assisted.

Hartlepool

The Preston Simpson and Sterndale Young Musicians Trust

£5,000

Correspondent: Trust Administrator, Hartlepool Borough Council, Civic Centre, Victoria Road, Hartlepool TS24 8AY (01429 284085)

CC number: 512606

Eligibility

Young musicians between the ages of 15 and 25 who were born in the borough of Hartlepool or have a parent who has lived in the area for at least five years. The grant is designed to support those who have already achieved a good standard in their studies and wish to pursue a career in music. Applicants' achievements should be demonstrated by participation in concerts, membership in bands or orchestras, a minimum standard of Grade V in the Associated Board Examination or equivalent qualification from Trinity College London and genuine intentions to use musical abilities in their future career (such as commitment to GCSE Music).

Types of grants

Scholarships to musicians studying music at any school, college or university.

Annual grant total

In 2013/14 the trust had an income of £6,500 and an expenditure of £5,500. We estimate the annual total amount of grants awarded to be around £5,000.

Applications

Application forms and guidelines can be found on the trust's website or requested from the correspondent. Applicants should also provide two written references, one of which must be from music teacher or head of music. The deadlines for applications are usually in late autumn but for a current deadline consult the website. Handwritten applications will not be accepted.

Northumberland

Allendale Exhibition Endowment

£7,500

Correspondent: Joseph Robinson, Trustee, Amberlea, Catton, Hexham, Northumberland NE47 9QS (01434683586)

CC number: 505515

Eligibility

People under the age of 25 who live, or whose parents live, in the parishes of Allendale and West Allend.

Types of grants

Grants ranging between £50 and £150 are given to students in further/higher education and training, people starting work. Schoolchildren and individuals studying the arts or music studies can also be supported. Funding is given towards the cost of books, equipment/instruments, maintenance, educational outings or study/travel abroad and student exchange.

Annual grant total

In 2013/14 the charity had an income of £8,500 and a total expenditure of £8,000. We estimate the annual total amount of grants awarded to be around £7,500.

Applications

Apply in writing to the correspondent. Applications can be submitted directly by the individual and the deadline is normally at the end of October. Usually, application forms are also placed in the library, post office and local shops.

Blyth Valley Trust for Youth

£5,000

Correspondent: Nathan Rogerson, Blyth Valley Arts and Leisure, Concordia Leisure Centre, Forum Way, Cramlington NE23 6YB (01670 542222; email: nrogerson@bval.co.uk)

CC number: 514145

Eligibility

Children and young people under the age of 21 who live or attend school in the borough of Blyth Valley. The trust will provide financial assistance to attend a centre of excellence or similar establishment and further their activities in a chosen field of arts, sciences or sports. Applicants should be of amateur status.

Types of grants

Grants are provided to support activities in the fields of arts, music, sciences or sports/physical recreation. Our research shows that the trust awards one-off grants, usually between £50 and £250. Support may only be given to those who are able to identify specific centres of excellence which they will be attending.

Annual grant total

In 2014/15 the trust had an expenditure of £5,500. We have estimated the annual total amount of grants awarded to be around £5,000.

Applications

Application forms can be requested from the correspondent and can be submitted either directly by the individual or by a school/college. Applicants are requested to include full details of the activity and provide references. Our research indicates that applicants should apply early (preferably before February each year) in time for the trustees' meeting, usually held in April.

Coates Educational Foundation

£10,000

Correspondent: Andrew Morgan, Trustee, 14 Bell Villas, Ponteland, Newcastle upon Tyne NE20 9BE (01661 871012; email: amorgan@nicholsonmorgan.co.uk)

CC number: 505906

Eligibility

People under the age of 25 who live in the parishes of Ponteland, Stannington, Heddon-on-the-Wall, and the former district of Newburn or are current/former pupils of the Richard Coates Church of England Voluntary Aided Middle School.

Types of grants

One-off grants and bursaries to help with the cost of books, equipment/materials, clothing, educational outings, maintenance and fees. Support can be given to schoolchildren and students at college/university. People starting work/entering a trade can also be helped with the cost of books, equipment/instruments, clothing or travel.

Annual grant total

In 2014 the foundation had an income of £19,000 and an expenditure of £20,500. We have estimated the annual total amount of grants awarded to individuals to be around £10,000.

Applications

Application forms are available from the correspondent. They can be submitted directly by the individual and are normally considered in February and June.

Other information

The foundation also supports local organisations and schools.

Rothbury Educational Trust

£7,000

Correspondent: Susan Rogerson, 1 Gallow Law, Alwinton, Morpeth NE65 7BQ (01669 650390)

CC number: 505713

Eligibility

Higher education students between the ages of 18 and 25 who live or have attended school in the parishes of Cartington, Hepple, Hesleyhurst, Rothbury, Snitter, Thropton and Tosson and the parts of the parishes of Brinkburn, Hollinghill and Netherton that lie within the ancient parish of Rothbury.

Types of grants

Small grants towards general educational expenses, including the cost of books, fees, equipment/instruments, clothing and so on.

Annual grant total

In 2013/14 the trust had an income of £6,500 and an expenditure of £7,500. We estimate the annual total amount of grants awarded to be around £7,000.

Applications

Apply in writing to the correspondent. Our research shows that applications are normally considered in late August/early September and grants are usually advertised in the local newspapers.

Shaftoe Educational Foundation

£18,000 (41 grants)

Correspondent: Peter Fletcher, The Clark, Chesterwood Grange, Chesterwood, Hexham, Northumberland NE47 6HW (01434688872; email: info@ shaftoecharities.org.uk; website: www. shaftoecharities.org.uk)

CC number: 528101

Eligibility

People in further/higher education or vocational training who live, or whose parents live, in the parish of Haydon.

Types of grants

One-off and recurrent grants in the range of about £400 are available to further/higher education students (including mature students) and to people in vocational training or undertaking apprenticeships. Support is available towards the cost of fees, equipment/instruments, tools, books, clothing or other necessities, also study/ travel overseas for educational purposes.

Annual grant total

In 2013/14 the foundation had assets of £5.8 million, an income of £179,000 and a total charitable expenditure of £124,000. Grants to 41 individuals totalled £18,000.

Applications

Application forms can be downloaded from the foundation's website or requested from the correspondent. The trustees meet three times a year, normally in March, July and November.

Other information

The foundation also makes yearly payments to the Almshouse Charity of John Shaftoe and supports schools and organisations in the parish of Haydon or local groups seeking support for educational initiatives.

Tyne and Wear

Cullercoats Education Trust

£2,400

Correspondent: Helen Lawlan, Administrator, 66 Northfield Road, Gosforth, Newcastle upon Tyne NE3 3UN (email: helenlawlan@sky.com)

CC number: 506817

Eligibility

People who live in the ecclesiastical parishes of St Paul, Whitley Bay and St George, Cullercoats.

Types of grants

Grants are made towards religious instruction in accordance with the doctrines of the Church of England and to promote the education, including social and physical training, of beneficiaries.

Annual grant total

In 2013/14 the trust had an income of £5,300 and a total expenditure of £5,000. We estimate that educational grants to individuals totalled £2,400, with funding also awarded to organisations.

Applications

By letter to the correspondent in February or August for consideration in March or September.

Other information

The charity is also known as the Old Church of England School Fund.

Charity of John McKie Elliott Deceased (The John McKie Elliot Trust for the Blind)

£6,700

Correspondent: Robert Walker, Trustee, 6 Manor House Road, Newcastle upon Tyne NE2 2LU (0191 281 4657; email: bobwalker9@aol.com)

CC number: 235075

Eligibility

People who are blind or have a visual impairment and live in Gateshead or Newcastle upon Tyne.

Types of grants

One-off and recurrent grants are given according to need for items, equipment or activities.

Annual grant total

In 2014 the charity had an income of £900 and an unusually high total expenditure of £13,700. Grants are made to individuals for both social welfare and educational purposes. We estimate that educational grants amounted to £6,700.

Applications

Apply in writing to the correspondent.

Sunderland

The Sunderland Orphanage and Educational Foundation

£13,000

Correspondent: Peter Taylor, Partner, McKenzie Bell, 19 John Street, Sunderland SR1 1JG (0191 567 4857; fax: 0191 510 9347; email: petertaylor@ mckenzie-bell.co.uk)

CC number: 527202

Eligibility

Young people under the age of 25 who are resident in or around Sunderland who have a parent who has disabilities or has died, or whose parents are divorced or legally separated.

Types of grants

Student allowances are given to help with the following:

- Maintenance and clothing for schoolchildren
- The costs of education, training, apprenticeship or equipment for those starting work
- The costs of travel to pursue education, the provision of athletic coaching and the study of music and other arts

Annual grant total

In 2013/14 the foundation had an income of £23,500 and a total expenditure of £27,500. Grants are made to individuals for both social welfare and educational purposes. We estimate that educational grants totalled around £13,000.

Applications

Applications should be made in writing to the correspondent. They are considered every other month.

North West

General

Crabtree North West Charitable Trust

£4,400

Correspondent: Ian Currie, Trustee, 3 Ralli Courts, New Bailey Street, Salford M3 5FT (0161 831 1512)

CC number: 1086405

Eligibility
Children and young people up to the age of 18 who are in education in the North West.

Types of grants
One-off grants are given according to need towards general educational purposes and sports causes.

Annual grant total
In 2013/14 the trust had an income of £6,000 and an expenditure of £9,000. We estimate that the amount of grants given to individuals totalled around £4,400. In the past five years the total charitable expenditure fluctuated between £300 and £104,000. Our research suggests that awards to individuals usually total between £5,000 and £10,000 each year.

Applications
Apply in writing to the correspondent.

Other information
Organisations are also supported.

The Fort Foundation

£18,300

Correspondent: Edward Fort, Trustee, Fort Vale Engineering Ltd, Calder Vale Park, Simonstone Lane, Simonstone, Burnley BB12 7ND (01282 440000; email: info@fortvale.com)

CC number: 1028639

Eligibility
According to the trustees' annual report, the foundation operates throughout England and Wales and gives grants to individuals and organisations for general charitable purposes. Our research indicates that young people in Pendle borough and district, especially those undertaking courses in engineering, may be favoured.

Types of grants
Our research suggests that one-off grants of £50–£1,000 are available to schoolchildren, college students, undergraduates and vocational students for uniforms/clothing, study/travel overseas, books and equipment/instruments and excursions.

Annual grant total
In 2014/15 the foundation had assets of £684,000 and an income of £257,500. Grants to individuals were made totalling £27,000, of which £18,300 was given for educational needs, £31,500 for social welfare purposes, £5,300 for health needs and £2,000 for sports.

Exclusions
Our research suggests that awards are not made for fees.

Applications
Applications may be made in writing to the correspondent, directly by the individual. Appeals are considered at any time.

Other information
Grants are also made to organisations and small groups (£183,500 to organisations in 2014). During the year the foundation contributed £29,000 towards funding of a Report on Climate Change.

The Winwick Educational Foundation

£2,700

Correspondent: Ian Sydenham, Administrator, Forshaws Davies Ridgway LLP, 17–21 Palmyra Square South, Warrington, Cheshire WA1 1BW (01925 230000; email: alastair.brown@fdrlaw.co.uk)

CC number: 526499

Eligibility
Further education students who live in the parishes of Emmanuel Wargrave, Lowton St Luke's, Lowton St Mary's, Newton All Saints, Newton St Peter's, St John's Earlestown and Winwick.

Types of grants
Small, one-off and recurrent grants are available to further education students towards general educational needs, including books, equipment/instruments and fees. Grants normally range from £75 to £100.

Annual grant total
In 2013/14 the foundation had an income of 5,500 and an expenditure of £5,400. We estimate the annual total amount of grants awarded to individuals to be around £2,700.

Applications
Apply in writing to the correspondent. Applications should normally be submitted in February and March for consideration in April. They can be made directly by the individual or through a third party, such as the individual's school, college or educational welfare agency, if applicable.

Other information
The foundation supports four specific Church of England primary schools in north Warrington.

Cheshire

Alsager Educational Foundation

£7,000

Correspondent: Catherine Lovatt, 6 Pikemere Road, Alsager, Stoke-on-Trent ST7 2SB (01270 873680; email: colovatt@hotmail.com)

CC number: 525834

Eligibility
Children and young people who live in the parish of Alsager.

Types of grants

One-off and recurrent grants ranging from around £200 to £1,000 are available to schoolchildren and further/higher education students. Support is given towards general educational necessities, including books, equipment/instruments, maintenance, clothing, also travel/study abroad and extra-curricular activities.

Annual grant total

In 2013/14 the foundation had an income of £11,500 and an expenditure of £15,000. We have estimated the annual total amount of grants awarded to individuals to be around £7,000.

Exclusions

Our research indicates that postgraduate students and people who do not have a permanent home address in Alsager cannot be supported. Assistance would not be given for extra tuition expenses.

Applications

Apply in writing to the correspondent. Applications are considered four times per year.

Other information

Both individuals and organisations can be supported. Special benefits are provided to the Alsager Church of England Junior School.

Audlem Educational Foundation

£8,000

Correspondent: Louisa Ingham, East Cheshire Council, People Service, Delamere House, Delamere Street, Crewe CW1 2JZ (01270 686223; email: louisa. ingham@cheshireeast.gov.uk; website: www.audlem.org/services/audlem-education-fund.html)

CC number: 525810

Eligibility

Children and young people under the age of 25 resident in the ancient parish of Audlem, including Buerton and Hankelow and part of Dodcott-cum-Wilkesley and Newhall. Preference is given to individuals who are attending or have attended any maintained school for at least two years.

Types of grants

The foundation awards grants, exhibitions, bursaries, maintenance allowances and other financial support to schoolchildren, further and higher education students or people in training. Grants are made for general educational expenses, educational outings and visits, field courses, equipment/instruments, tools and student exchange.

Annual grant total

In 2013/14 the foundation had an income of £15,000 and an expenditure of £12,000. The foundation also supports local schools; therefore, we have estimated that the annual total amount of grants awarded to individuals was around £8,000. Note that the grants total varies each year.

Applications

Application forms can be found on the foundation's website or requested from the correspondent. The trustees meet three times a year, usually in November, February and July. Applications should be made in advance of these dates. Candidates are also required to provide a confirmation of attendance and receipts for the items purchased or other financial details of the course/trip taken.

Other information

The foundation allocates one third of its income and interest from the investments to support schools in the area of benefit. The remainder is used to award grants to individuals.

Chester Municipal Charities

£46,000

Correspondent: Sharon Green, Administrator, The Bluecoat, Upper Northgate Street, Chester CH1 4EE (01244 403277; email: sharon.green@chestermc.org.uk)

CC number: 1077806

Eligibility

Young people under the age of 25 who are attending or have attended a school in Chester and who are resident in the city.

Types of grants

Grants may come in the form of bursaries/grants paid directly to schools/colleges/universities. Grants are made for education to help with the costs of equipment, educational trips and other expenses. The charity also provides a limited number of bursaries and a programme of funding support in early years education.

Annual grant total

In 2014 the charity had assets of £14.4 million and an income of £364,000. Grants totalled £182,500 and were awarded to individuals for welfare and educational purposes and to organisations. We estimate that educational grants to individuals totalled £46,000.

Applications

An application form is available from the correspondent.

Other information

The charity also manages almshouses.

Cheshire East

The Congleton Town Trust

£5,000

Correspondent: Jo Money, Clerk, c/o Congleton Town Hall, High Street, Congleton, Cheshire CW12 1BN (01260 270908; email: info@congletontowntrust.co.uk; website: www.congletontowntrust.co.uk)

CC number: 1051122

Eligibility

People in need who live in the town of Congleton (this refers only to the area administered by Congleton Town Council).

Types of grants

The principal aim of the trust is to give grants to individuals in need or to organisations which provide relief, services or facilities to those in need. The trustees will, however, consider a grant towards education or training if the applicant is in need. Support can be given in the form of books, tools or in cash towards tuition fees or maintenance.

Annual grant total

In 2014 the trust had an income of £24,500 and a total expenditure of £21,000. Grants are made to individuals and organisations for both social welfare and educational purposes. We estimate that educational grants to individuals totalled £5,000.

Applications

We would advise potential applicants to, in the first instance, contact the correspondent for more information. This can be done using the online form on the website.

Lindow Workhouse Charity

£7,700

Correspondent: John Fallows, Correspondent, 1 Thornfield Hey, Wilmslow, Cheshire SK9 5JY (01625 533950; email: lwt@jfallows.org.uk)

CC number: 226023

Eligibility

Our research suggests that children with special educational needs who live in the ancient parish of Wilmslow can be supported. The charity only serves people in the parish but any cases of real need can be considered, so other educational needs may potentially be assisted.

Types of grants

One-off grants of up to £500.

Annual grant total

In 2013/14 the charity had an income of £10,800 and a total expenditure of £15,600. We estimate that about £7,700 was awarded to individuals for educational purposes.

Applications

Application may be made in writing to the correspondent at any time. They can be submitted directly by the individual or a family member, through a third party (such as a social worker or teacher), or through an organisation (such as Citizens Advice or a school).

Other information

Awards are made for welfare needs as well.

Cheshire West and Chester

The Sir Thomas Moulson Trust

£5,000

Correspondent: Julie Turner, Correspondent, Meadow Barn, Cow Lane, Hargrave, Chester CH3 7RU

CC number: 214342

Eligibility

Students under the age of 25 who live in the villages of Huxley, Hargrave, Tarvin, Kelsall and Ashton, in Cheshire. Preference is given to those resident in the parish of Foulk Stapleford.

Types of grants

One-off grants ranging from £100 to £500 to students in further/higher education towards books, fees/living expenses and study or travel abroad.

Annual grant total

In 2014 the trust had an income of £21,500 and a total expenditure of £10,900. We estimate that around £5,000 was given in grants to individuals for educational purposes.

Applications

Applications may be made in writing to the correspondent. They should be submitted directly by the individual and are usually considered in September.

Other information

Support is also given to the parish church of St Peter, Hargrave and associated buildings/land provided for community use.

The Thornton-le-Moors Education Foundation

£700

Correspondent: Roy Edwards, Trustee, Jesmin, 4 School Lane, Elton, Chester CH2 4LN (01928 725188)

CC number: 525829

Eligibility

People under 25 in full-time education who live in the ancient parish of Thornton-le-Moors which includes the following villages of Dunham Hill, Elton, Hapsford, Ince and Thornton-le-Moors.

Types of grants

The foundation gives grants mostly to students going to university for books and also to local youth groups, mainly the guides, brownies, scouts and cubs.

Annual grant total

In 2014 this charity had an income of £3,400 and a total expenditure of £1,300. We estimate that around £700 was awarded to individuals.

Applications

Apply in writing to the correspondent. The trustees meet twice a year, usually in April and November.

Other information

Grants are also awarded to organisations.

Cumbria

The Burton-in-Kendal Educational Foundation

£3,200

Correspondent: Allison Cummings, Correspondent, 5 Holmefield, Holme, Carnforth, Lancashire LA6 1RY (01524 782331; email: allison.cummings@btinternet.com)

CC number: 526953

Eligibility

People under the age of 25 who are in sixth form education or university/college and living in the parishes of Arnside, Beetham and Burton-in-Kendal, in Cumbria. Applicants must have attended a county or voluntary primary school for no less than two years.

Types of grants

Scholarships, bursaries and maintenance allowances are available as well as financial assistance towards study/travel abroad, books, equipment/instruments, maintenance/living expenses or facilities for social and physical training. Our research suggests that average grants range between £10 and £60 and that

support can also be made to people with special educational needs.

Annual grant total

In 2014/15 the foundation had both an income and an expenditure of £3,500. We estimate the annual total amount of grants awarded to be around £3,200.

Applications

Applications may be made in writing to the correspondent. They are considered twice a year.

Cartmel Old Grammar School Foundation

£5,500

Correspondent: Colin Milner, Administrator, Cartmel Old Grammar School Foundation, Quintaine, Cardrona Road, Grange-over-Sands, Cumbria LA11 7EW (01539535043; email: mrcolinmilner@gmail.com)

CC number: 526467

Eligibility

Children and young people between the ages of 18 and 25 who live in the parishes of Cartmel Fell, Broughton East, Grange-over-Sands, Lower Holker, Staveley, Lower Allithwaite, Upper Allithwaite and that part of the parish of Haverthwaite east of the River Leven.

Types of grants

Small, one-off and recurrent (up to three years) grants of about £90 are awarded to further/higher education students to help with the costs of books, fees/living expenses or study/travel abroad and in the UK. Support is also given for music and arts studies.

Annual grant total

In 2014/15 the foundation had both an income and an expenditure of £11,000. We estimate the annual total amount of grants awarded to individuals to be around £5,500.

Applications

Apply in writing to the correspondent. Applications can be submitted by email (preferably) or via post, providing an sae. Application forms are also distributed in local churches and educational establishments. The trustees meet in November and applications should be submitted by the end of September at the latest.

Other information

The foundation also makes payments to the Brow Edge Foundation and Cartmel General Charities for the benefit of the poor (approximately £1,000 annually) and helps local schools.

Edmond Castle Educational Trust

£1,800

Correspondent: Ellen Clements, Correspondent, c/o Cumbria Community Foundation, Dovenby Hall, Dovenby, Cockermouth CA13 0PN (01900 825760; fax: 01900 826527; email: ellen@cumbriafoundation.org or enquiries@cumbriafoundation.org; website: www.cumbriafoundation.org)

CC number: 1027991

Eligibility

Disadvantaged children and young people under the age of 21, with a preference to those who are or have been looked after/provided accommodation by/under supervision of Cumbria County Council.

Types of grants

Grants reach up to £500 and are awarded to help with the course fees, computers, equipment, special tuition, childcare and any other activity 'which extend opportunities and which make a difference to the lives of young people'. This may include 'activities that help build self-confidence and skills' and those that 'promote civic engagement and leadership'.

Annual grant total

In 2014/15 the trust had an income of £3,200 and an expenditure of £3,800. We estimate that about £1,800 was given in grants to individuals.

Exclusions

Activities which are the statutory duty of the government are not funded.

Applications

Application forms can be found on the trust's website and are separate for people under 18 or in full-time further/higher education and for people over 18 or in vocational training. Where possible, applications should be supported by a third party, such as a social or youth worker, health visitor and so on. Further application guidelines are available on the community foundation's website.

Other information

The trust supports both individuals and organisations. The application process is managed by the Cumbria Community Foundation.

Cumbria Community Foundation

£5,300

Correspondent: The Grants Team, Cumbria Community Foundation, Dovenby Hall, Cockermouth, Cumbria CA13 0PN (01900 825760; fax: 01900 826527; email: enquiries@ cumbriafoundation.org; website: www. cumbriafoundation.org)

CC number: 1075120

Eligibility

People resident in Cumbria. Other restrictions including geographical and age related pertain depending upon the fund being applied to.

Types of grants

One-off and recurrent grants for various amounts for a wide range of needs including travel abroad and in the UK, educational or training activities or preparations to enter a trade or profession, writing and publishing, the arts and sports. Hardship grants are given to older people and the foundation also responds to local disasters, such as floods, to help people affected.

Annual grant total

In 2013/14 the foundation made 19 grants to individuals totalling £10,700. We estimate that the amount of grants given to individuals for educational purposes amounted to around £5,300.

During the year, more than £1.9 million was awarded to organisations in 232 grants.

Applications

The foundation administers numerous funds that give grants to individuals, they have differing eligibility criteria. Applicants should check the website for full details of each scheme and how to apply.

Other information

The community foundation administers funds for both individuals and organisations, some of which may open and close regularly.

The Mary Grave Trust

£53,000

Correspondent: Trust Administrator, Cumbria Community Foundation, Dovenby Hall, Dovenby, Cockermouth CA13 0PN (01900 825760; email: enquiries@cumbriafoundation.org; website: www.cumbriafoundation.org/archives/301)

CC number: 526869

Eligibility

Young people in need aged between 11 and 21 who were born in the former county of Cumberland (excluding those whose parents were resident in Carlisle). Applicants must live, study or have studied (for at least two years, in secondary/further education) within the area of benefit priority being given to Workington, Maryport and Whitehaven areas. Applicants' household income must be less than £490 per week (excluding all benefits).

Students in sixth forms, further education colleges, universities and higher education colleges or in the gaps between these stages can all be considered as well as those at work, in training or involved in youth organisation activities.

Types of grants

Grants of around £1,000 to fund travel overseas in furtherance of education. The full cost of trips up to a set maximum can be provided and additional assistance for clothing and pocket money may also be given. Support is aimed at activities organised by a school/college or other trips, such as field-work expeditions, work-experience visits, specialist study bursaries for art and music schools, gap year activities and Outward Bound-type courses such as Raleigh International.

Annual grant total

In 2013/14 the trust had assets of £1.7 million and an income of £59,500. Charitable expenditure totalled £56,000 and grants to individuals totalled £53,000.

Exclusions

The trust will not fund:

- Individuals born outside the old county of Cumberland
- Individuals born in Carlisle (unless mother resident outside Carlisle at the time of birth
- Trips in the UK of less than three nights' duration
- Family holidays

Applications

Application forms are available from the trust's website or the correspondent. Applications can be submitted by the individual directly or through a school/college. Applicants are required to submit a full copy of their birth certificate and provide information about their financial circumstances. The trustees meet three times a year and applications should normally be received by 2 April, 1 October and 31 December.

Other information

The fund is administered by the Cumbria Community Foundation but is treated as a separate entity.

Hodgson's School Foundation (Wiggonby School Trust)

£25,000

Correspondent: Mrs M. Fleming, Administrator, Flemsyam, Aikton, Wigton, Cumbria CA7 0JA (01697 342829; email: r.fleming123@btinternet.com)

CC number: 526850

Eligibility

People under the age of 25 in further education and training who live in the parishes of Aikton, Beaumont and Burgh-by-Sands or are former pupils of Wiggonby School.

Types of grants

Grants are normally of around £200 and are given to people engaged in further education/training or people starting work/entering a trade. Support can be given to help with fees, living expenses, books, equipment/instruments and so on.

Annual grant total

In 2013/14 the foundation had assets of £152,000 and an income of £31,000. Grants totalled £25,000 and were distributed under the following categories:

Wiggonby School fund	£16,500
Grants to children	£8,000
School prizes	£500

Applications

Applications are normally advertised in the Cumberland News in August. Candidates can request an application from the correspondent. Applications should include the place of further study and details of the qualification aimed for.

Other information

Support is also given to Wiggonby School, where funding is not already provided by the local authority.

Kelsick's Educational Foundation

£73,500

Correspondent: Peter Frost, Clerk, The Kelsick Centre, St Mary's Lane, Ambleside LA22 9DG (01539 431289; fax: 01539 431292; email: john@kelsick.plus.com; website: www.kelsick.org.uk)

CC number: 526956

Eligibility

Apprentices, further and higher education students under the age of 25 who have been resident in the Lake parishes (Ambleside, Grasmere, Langdale and as far south as the river at Troutbeck Bridge) for at least four years.

Types of grants

The foundation offers grants for additional teaching support, extra assistance for pupils with special needs, music, drama lessons, hire of instruments, travel costs for certain educational trips, for undertaking performing arts or sports activities, books for A-levels, books for college and university courses and any other activity which the trustees consider to be of educational benefit. Apprentices can be supported towards the cost of tools, equipment and extra training. First-year higher education students are eligible for the purchase of a computer and all eligible students attending universities or colleges of further education can apply for subsistence grants. Awards will be given to address essential needs and can be one-off or recurrent, ranging from £25 to £3,000.

Annual grant total

In 2014/15 the foundation had assets of £7.2 million, an income of £388,000 and an expenditure of £368,000. The amount of grants given to individuals totalled £73,500.

Exclusions

Tuition fees and residency expenses cannot be supported.

Applications

Application forms can be found on the foundation's website. Grants are considered at quarterly meetings in February, May, August and November. The deadlines for applications are 31 January, 30 April, 31 July and 31 October respectively. Candidates must list detailed costs (with receipts) of the items required. Forms should be submitted directly by the individual or by a parent/guardian, if the applicant is under the age of 18.

Other information

Grants totalling £137,500 were awarded to schools and organisations in the area of benefit in 2014/15.

Carlisle

Carlisle Educational Charity

£10,000

Correspondent: Peter Mason, Assistant Director of Resources, Carlisle City Council, Civic Centre, Rickergate, Carlisle CA3 8QG (01228 817268; email: peterm@carlisle.gov.uk; website: www.carlisle.gov.uk/education_and_learning/carlisle_educational_charity.aspx)

CC number: 509357

Eligibility

Students in further/higher education under the age of 25 who or whose parents live within the Carlisle district. Financial circumstances of the individual's parents and the extent to which they can support the applicant can be taken into account. Generally, preference is given to students with joint family income below £21,000.

Types of grants

Grants ranging from £50 to £500 are available to students in higher/further education and young graduates undertaking higher studies or professional qualification. Support is given for general educational costs or for students travelling in the UK or abroad for educational purposes associated with their course of study.

Annual grant total

In 2013/14 the charity had an income of £11,000 and an expenditure of £10,500. We estimate that grants totalled around £10,000

Applications

Application forms are available on the charity's website or can be requested from the correspondent. Applications should be submitted by September for consideration in the following month.

Copeland

Silecroft School Educational Charity

£2,500

Correspondent: Catherine Jopson, Administrator, Hestham Hall Farm, Millom LA18 5LJ (01229 772525)

CC number: 509580

Eligibility

People under 25 who were born in the parishes of Whicham, Millom, Millom Without and Ulpha.

Types of grants

Recurrent grants are given for a wide range of educational needs for people at university or college, from books, clothing, equipment and other supplementary awards to foreign travel and other educational visits. However, the charity does not give grants for travel to and from the applicant's place of residence.

Annual grant total

In 2014 the charity had an income of £2,400 and a total expenditure of £2,800. We estimate that educational grants to individuals totalled £2,500.

Exclusions

Grants are not given for schoolchildren, people starting work or to students who have not moved away from home to continue their education.

Applications

Application forms are available from the correspondent and can be submitted in September for consideration in November. Applications can be made either directly by the individual, or through their school, college or educational welfare agency.

South Lakeland

The Brow Edge Foundation

£3,000

Correspondent: Robert Hutton, Administrator, 20 Ainslie Street, Ulverston, Cumbria LA12 7JE (01229 585888; email: gordon@421.co.uk)

CC number: 526716

Eligibility

People in need who live in the area of Haverthwaite and Backbarrow, aged between 16 and 25. Preference is given to young people from disadvantaged backgrounds.

Types of grants

Small grants to assist pupils attending schools, institutions or classes for post-16 education.

Annual grant total

In 2014 the foundation had an income of £2,600 and a total expenditure of £3,200. We estimate that the amount of grants given to individuals totalled £3,000.

Applications

Apply in writing to the correspondent. Applications can be submitted directly by the individual. Applicants must state the type of course of study or apprenticeship they are about to undertake.

Robinson's Educational Foundation

£2,500

Correspondent: Ian Jenkinson, Administrator, Milne Moser Solicitors, 100 Highgate, Kendal, Cumbria LA9 4HE (01539 729786; email: solicitors@milnemoser.co.uk)

CC number: 529897

Eligibility

Children and young people under the age of 25 who live in the parish of

Sedbergh, with a preference for people who live in Howgill.

Types of grants

Scholarships, bursaries and maintenance allowances are available to schoolchildren and further/higher education students. One-off grants, in the range of £15 to £1,000 are given towards general educational necessities, including books, fees, equipment, travel costs, study/travel abroad, also music lessons for pupils.

Annual grant total

In 2013/14 the foundation had an income of £13,000 and an expenditure of £5,500. It supports both individuals and organisations; therefore, we estimate the annual total amount of grants awarded to individuals to be about £2,500.

Applications

Apply in writing to the correspondent. Applications can be submitted either directly by individuals or through a social worker/Citizens Advice/welfare agency, if applicable. Grants are normally considered in September.

Other information

The foundation also supports local schools, where assistance is not already provided by the local authority.

Greater Manchester

The Golborne Charities – Charity of William Leadbetter

£1,800

Correspondent: Paul Gleave, 56 Nook Lane, Golborne, Warrington WA3 3JQ (01942 727627; email: p.gleave56@hotmail.com)

CC number: 221088

Eligibility

People in need who live in the parish of Golborne as it was in 1892.

Types of grants

One-off grants usually between £70 and £100, although larger sums may be given. Grants are usually cash payments, but are occasionally in kind, for equipment such as books, school uniforms and instruments, or for excursions.

Annual grant total

In 2014/15 the charity had an income of £6,600 and a total expenditure of £7,300. Grants are made to individuals for both social welfare and educational purposes.

We estimate that educational grants totalled £1,800.

Exclusions

Loans or grants for the payments of rates are not made. Grants are not repeated in less than two years.

Applications

Applications can be made in writing to the correspondent through a third party such as a social worker or a teacher, or via a trustee. Applications are considered at three-monthly intervals. Grant recipients tend to be known by at least one trustee.

The Community Foundation for Greater Manchester (Forever Manchester)

£3,400

Correspondent: The Grants and Awards Officer, 2nd Floor, 8 Hewitt Street, Manchester M15 4GB (0161 214 0940; email: info@forevermanchester.com; website: forevermanchester.com)

CC number: 1017504

Eligibility

People in need who live in Greater Manchester.

Types of grants

Grants are usually one-off.

Annual grant total

In 2013/14 the foundation had assets of £9.6 million and an income of over £3 million. Grants were made totalling £1.3 million, of which £6,900 was given to individuals. A further breakdown was not available; therefore, we estimate that about £3,400 was given for educational needs.

Applications

Visit the foundation's website or contact the foundation for details of grant funds that are currently appropriate for individuals to apply for. The foundation's website states: 'Please contact our awards team on 0161 214 0940 to discuss deadline dates, eligibility and criteria and to receive guidelines and an application pack.'

Other information

The Community Foundation for Greater Manchester manages a portfolio of grants for a variety of purposes which are mostly for organisations, but there also are a select few aimed at individuals. Funds tend to open and close throughout the year as well as new ones being added – check the website for up-to-date information on currently operating schemes.

Manchester Publicity Association Educational Trust

£4,000

Correspondent: Gillian Cosser, Trustee, 7 Heigham Gardens, St Helens, Merseyside WA9 5WB

CC number: 1001134

Eligibility

People over the age of 16 living in Greater Manchester and the surrounding area who either are studying marketing communications, or already work in or aim to enter marketing, advertising and related occupations.

Types of grants

Our research suggests that grants range between £200 and £500 and are given towards the cost of books or fees for education/training, usually to cover the second half of the year.

Annual grant total

In 2013/14 the trust had an income of £80 and an expenditure of £4,200. We estimate that grants totalled about £4,000. Both the income and the total expenditure vary each year.

Applications

Application forms are available from the correspondent. They must be supported by a tutor and are considered on demand.

Mynshull's Educational Foundation

£9,000

Correspondent: Ann Hosker, Administrator, Gaddum Centre, Gaddum House, 6 Great Jackson Street, Manchester M15 4AX (0161 834 6069; email: amh@gaddumcentre.co.uk)

CC number: 532334

Eligibility

Children and young people aged 25 and under who are at school, university or college, on an apprenticeship or attending another educational/training course (except postgraduates). Applicants must be resident or have been born in the city of Manchester and the following adjoining districts: Reddish, Audenshaw, Failsworth, Chadderton, Middleton, Prestwich, Old City of Salford, Stretford, Sale, Cheadle, Heaton Moor, Heaton Mersey and Heaton Chapel.

Types of grants

Grants towards the costs of education, training and apprenticeships, for items such as books, equipment, clothing, uniforms and travel costs.

Annual grant total

In 2013/14 the foundation had an income of £11,500 and a total expenditure of £9,500. We estimate that grants totalled £9,000.

Exclusions

No grants are given for course fees, rent or any other ongoing expenditure.

Applications

Application forms are available from the correspondent which must be completed by a sponsor from the educational establishment.

Rochdale Ancient Parish Educational Trust

£10,000 (23 grants)

Correspondent: Trust Administrator, Wyatt Morris Golland and Co., 200 Drake Street, Rochdale, Lancashire OL16 1PJ (01706 864707; email: info@e-wmg.co.uk; website: www.rochdale.gov.uk/pdf/2009–03–19_Form%20Rochdale_Ancient_Parish_Educational_Trust_v4.pdf)

CC number: 526318

Eligibility

People who live or attend/have attended school in the ancient parish of Rochdale, which includes; Littleborough, Milnrow, Wardle, Whitworth, Todmorden and Saddleworth. Or attend a school in the area of the ancient parish of Rochdale, or have attended a school in the area.

Note: There is no age limit for applicants, but preference will be given to people qualified who are under the age of 25 years.

Types of grants

Grants are one-off and range between £60 and £2,000. Financial assistance is available towards the cost of clothing, uniforms, books, equipment/instruments and tools to enter a trade/profession or undertake educational/vocational courses. In exceptional circumstances the trust may provide scholarships, bursaries, grants and maintenance allowances to attend a further/higher education course or to travel within the UK/abroad in pursuance of education.

Annual grant total

In 2013/14 the trust had assets of £668,000 and an income of £33,500. Grants to 23 individuals totalled £10,000.

Exclusions

Prospective applicants who have received an award in the previous year.

Applications

Application forms can be requested from the correspondent or found on the trust's website together with detailed guidelines. Applicants are required to submit evidence of enrolment on a particular course and specify the required support with approximate costs. The trustees meet three times a year, for application forms to be considered at these meetings, return completed forms by either 20 February, 20 May or 31 August each year.

Bolton

James Eden's Foundation

£27,000

Correspondent: The Trustees, R. P. Smith and Co., 71 Chorley Old Road, Bolton, Lancashire BL1 3AJ (01204 534421; email: info@rpsmithbolton.co.uk; website: www.rpsmithbolton.co.uk)

CC number: 526265

Eligibility

Young people resident in the metropolitan borough of Bolton who are in need of financial assistance, particularly for individuals in further education. Preference is given to people who have lost either or both parents, or whose parents are separated or divorced.

Types of grants

Cash grants of between £400 and £1,500 are given to assist college students and undergraduates with fees, books, equipment/instruments, maintenance/living expenses, educational outings in the UK and study or travel overseas. Parental income is taken into account in awarding grants.

Annual grant total

In 2013/14 the foundation had an income of £18,500 and an expenditure of £27,500. We estimate that grants awarded totalled £27,000.

Applications

Application forms are available from the correspondent, to be returned by the individual before September for consideration in October. If an individual has applied previously the trustees are particularly interested to know about his or her progress.

Other information

Grants are also given to organisations.

Provincial/Walsh Trust for Bolton

£3,000

Correspondent: Joan Bohan, Administrator, 237 Ainsworth Lane, Bolton BL2 2QQ (email: Joan.bohan@ntlworld.com; website: www.pwtb.org.uk)

CC number: 222819

Eligibility

Young people, usually under the age of 25, who live or work within the Bolton metropolitan borough.

Types of grants

Grants are mainly one-off and generally range between £500 and £1,500, although higher awards may be awarded. Applicants will be expected to have raised some money through other sources.

Grants are designed to assist people to achieve their personal goals or small projects (particularly helping others) rather than to provide relief in need. Character development activities, for example, Operation Raleigh or Health Projects Abroad can be supported. Previously grants have been awarded for specialist equipment, tuition costs, sports activities, volunteering expenses, educational travel.

Annual grant total

In 2013/14 the trust had assets of £990,000 and an income of £37,500. A total of £29,000 was spent in grants, of which £3,000 was awarded to individuals.

Exclusions

Grants are not awarded for building projects, commercial ventures or for personal loans. Our research also suggests that students or recent ex-students of Bolton School are not normally assisted.

Applications

Application forms are available on the trust's website or can be requested from the correspondent. Supporting information may be provided but the candidates are requested to limit this to three A4 sheets. The trustees usually meet in April and October, but urgent requests can also be considered.

Other information

This charity is a merge of The Provincial Insurance Trust for Bolton and David Walsh Trust.

Rochdale

Middleton Educational Trust (The Emerson Educational Trust for Middleton)

£1,500

Correspondent: Trust Administrator, c/o 94 Whalley Road, Clayton-le-Moors, Accrington BB5 5DY (07833249318; email: middletonemersontrust@hotmail.com; website: www.rochdale.gov.uk/the_council/more_about_the_council/charitable_trusts.aspx)

CC number: 510495

Eligibility

People who live or attend/have attended school in the area of the former borough of Middleton.

Types of grants

Support is given to schoolchildren, further/higher education students and people starting work. Grants are towards the cost of books, equipment/instruments, uniforms/clothing, educational outings in the UK, study/travel abroad and student exchanges, also apprenticeships, fees and maintenance expenses. Our research indicates that grants are one-off and range between £250 and £500.

The following information was taken from Rochdale borough council's website: 'We can provide assistance for any purpose that promotes the education, training and development of the applicant. Or, helps ease financial barriers to achieve the required education, training or development.'

Annual grant total

In 2013/14 the trust had an income of £8,500 and a total charitable expenditure of £2,000. We have estimated that the annual total amount of grants awarded was around £1,500.

Applications

Application forms can be downloaded from the Rochdale borough council's website or requested from the correspondent. Applications can be submitted by individuals directly or through their educational institution or welfare agency, if applicable. Contact details of a course tutor or other academic professional are requested to support the application. Our research suggests that the trustees meet twice a year, usually in April and September.

The Middleton United Foundation Trust

£1,500

Correspondent: Elaine Foulkes, Administrator, Horse Shoes, Crowberry Lane, Middleton, Tamworth B78 2AJ (0121 308 3107; email: elainehorseshoes44@talktalk.net)

CC number: 528699

Eligibility

Young people under the age of 25 who are in need and live, or whose parents live, in the parish of Middleton or the immediate vicinity.

Types of grants

One-off and recurrent grants usually of up to £300 each. Schoolchildren, further and higher education students and postgraduates can be supported for books, equipment/instruments, educational outings in the UK and study or travel abroad. In addition, schoolchildren can be helped with uniforms/other school clothing and students in further and higher education can be supported with maintenance and living expenses. People starting work can be helped with books and equipment/instruments. Grants can also be made towards the costs of developing a hobby.

Annual grant total

In 2014/15 the trust had an income of £5,900 and an expenditure of £1,700. We estimate that the trust gave out grants totalling around £1,500.

Applications

Applications should be made in writing to the correspondent, giving as many details as possible, for example, the purpose and size of grant requested, the cost of books/equipment, the age of the applicant and a description of the course.

Other information

Grants are occasionally made to organisations.

Salford

The Salford Foundation Trust

£5,000

Correspondent: Peter Colins, Administrator, Foundation House, 3 Jo Street, Salford M5 4BD (01617878170; email: mail@salfordfoundationtrust.org.uk; website: www.salfordfoundationtrust.org.uk)

CC number: 1105303

Eligibility

Young people between the ages of 5 and 25 who are resident in Salford. Preference is given to applicants who have lived in Salford for a minimum of three years.

Types of grants

Grants of up to £500 to fund opportunities that will enable a young person to learn, develop or gain new skills, take part in a character building experience and so on.

The trust also offers special Tony Wilson Awards which 'are made to children and young people who can demonstrate a special talent or ambition in the fields of art or creative skills'.

Annual grant total

In 2013/14 the trust had an income of £4,000 and a total charitable expenditure of £5,500. We estimate the annual total amount of grants awarded to be around £5,000. Previously the grants have been made in four categories of performing arts, sports/recreation, skills/talent development and academic/vocational opportunities.

Exclusions

Funding will not be considered for the following:

▶ Driving lessons
▶ Childcare costs
▶ Higher education course fees and living expenses
▶ Membership fees
▶ Remedial intervention (speech/language/occupational therapies)
▶ Retrospective funding
▶ Standard school/college and sports trips or residential excursions
▶ Activities with political or religious focus
▶ Needs that should be financed by statutory services

Group applications, organised group activities and so forth are not supported.

Applications

Application forms are available from the trust's website or can be requested from the correspondent and can be submitted directly by the individual or a third party (but not someone who will directly benefit from the grant). Applications are decided in four rounds per year: 2 February–13 March, 20 April–29 May, 13 July–28 August, 5 October–13 November. Note that applications can only be submitted by post and have to include two references.

Other information

Among the trust's patrons have been musician Peter Hook, actress Maxine Peake and Sarah Storey MBE.

Stockport

The Barrack Hill Educational Charity (Barrack Hill Trust)

£3,500

Correspondent: John Asquith, Trustee, 24 Links Road, Romiley, Stockport, Cheshire SK6 4HU (0161 430 3583; email: cllr.mikewilson@stockport.gov.uk)

CC number: 525836

Eligibility

Children and young people under the age of 21 who live or whose parents live in Bredbury and Romiley.

Types of grants

One-off grants to assist with general educational expenses. Schoolchildren can be supported towards the cost of uniforms, other school clothing, books and equipment/instruments. Students in full/part-time education can be assisted towards books, study or travel abroad and equipment. People in vocational training may also be helped with the costs of tools, uniforms, equipment and similar needs.

Annual grant total

In 2014 the charity had an income of £9,400 and an expenditure of £7,300. We estimate the annual total amount of grants awarded to individuals to be around £3,500.

Applications

Application forms can be requested from the correspondent. They are usually made available from the local libraries towards the end of the school year as well. Awards are normally considered in September and October.

Other information

The charity also makes grants to organisations and schools in the local area.

The Ephraim Hallam Charity

£3,500

Correspondent: Stephen Tattersall, Correspondent, 3 Highfield Road, Poynton, Stockport, Cheshire SK12 1DU (01625 874445; email: smt@lacywatson. co.uk)

CC number: 525975

Eligibility

People under the age of 25 resident in Stockport.

Types of grants

Grants to support people at any institution of further or higher education, including the study of music and arts, travel costs, vocational training and people starting work.

Annual grant total

In 2014 the charity had an income of £14,600 and a total expenditure of £7,200. We estimate that the amount of grants given to individuals totalled about £3,500, with funding also awarded to local organisations for young people.

Applications

Applications may be made in writing to the correspondent.

Sir Ralph Pendlebury's Charity for Orphans

£1,700

Correspondent: Stephen Tattersall, Correspondent, Lacy Watson and Co., Carlyle House, 107–109 Wellington Road South, Stockport SK1 3TL

CC number: 213927

Eligibility

Orphans who have lived, or whose parents have lived, in the borough of Stockport for at least two years and who are in need.

Types of grants

Our research suggests that grants can be given to schoolchildren towards the cost of clothing, holidays, maintenance and books. Awards are usually of £5 or £6 a week plus clothing allowance twice a year. The main priority for the charity is relief in need.

Annual grant total

In 2014 the charity had an income of £9,800 and a total expenditure of £3,600. We estimate that around £1,700 was awarded in grants for educational purposes.

Applications

Applications can be made in writing to the correspondent. They should be made by a parent/guardian.

Other information

Grants are also made for social welfare purposes.

Wigan

The Leigh Educational Endowment

£19,500

Correspondent: Corporate Director, The Leigh Educational Endowment, Fairhouse Farm, Pocket Nook Lane, Lowton, Warrington WA3 1AL (01942 244991; email: walter.glen@hotmail.com)

CC number: 526469

Eligibility

Children and young people under the age of 25 who live in the former borough of Leigh and are attending any institution of education, approved by the trustees. In practice, further/higher education students who have achieved high A-level results are normally supported.

Types of grants

Grants of between £250 and £500 are available to assist with the course fees, living expenses, books, equipment and other necessities.

Annual grant total

In 2013/14 the charity had an income of £17,500 and an expenditure of £20,500. We estimate the annual total amount of grants awarded to be around £19,500. Our research suggests that usually around 20 individuals are supported annually.

Applications

Normally, applications should be submitted through the individual's college as a part of a list of suitable applicants for the trustees to choose from. Applications should be made in September after A-level results are released. Grants are considered in October.

The Lowton United Charity

£2,000

Correspondent: John Naughton, Secretary, 51 Kenilworth Road, Lowton, Warrington WA3 2AZ (01942 741583)

CC number: 226469

Eligibility

People in need who live in the parishes of St Luke's and St Mary's in Lowton.

Types of grants

Help can be given towards the cost of books, clothing and other essentials for schoolchildren. Support is also available for those at college or university.

Annual grant total

In 2014/15 the charity had an income of £7,300 and a total expenditure of £6,300.

Our research suggests that grants for individuals total about £4,000 each year. About a half is given at Christmas for relief-in-need purposes and the rest are given throughout the year. We estimate that the amount of grants given to individuals for educational purposes totalled about £2,000.

Exclusions

Grants are not given to postgraduates.

Applications

Applications are usually accepted through the rectors of the parishes or other trustees.

Other information

Some assistance may also be given to organisations.

Spencer's Educational Foundation Trust

£1,500

Correspondent: John Beaman, Trustee, School Lane, Church Leigh, Leigh, Stoke-on-Trent ST10 4SR (01889 502401; email: john.beaman@hotmail.co.uk)

CC number: 528442

Eligibility

People under the age of 25 who live in the village of Leigh.

Types of grants

Grants of around £150 are given to people in secondary, further or higher education towards educational necessities, maintenance costs, fees or travel in pursuance of education. Individuals starting work/entering a trade can be assisted with the cost of books, clothing and equipment/instruments.

Annual grant total

In 2014 the trust had an income of £2,400 and a total expenditure of £1,600. We estimate that the amount of grants given to individuals totalled around £1,500.

Exclusions

Applications from people outside the area of benefit will not be considered.

Applications

Application forms can be requested from the correspondent. They are normally considered in September and should be received by August. Our research suggests that grants are paid in arrears after a reference from the educational body is received.

Other information

Some support may be given to local schools where help is not already provided by the local authorities.

Lancashire

Baines's Charity

£4,600

Correspondent: Duncan Waddilove, Correspondent, 2 The Chase, Normoss Road, Blackpool, Lancashire FY3 0BF (01253 893459; email: duncanwaddilove@hotmail.com)

CC number: 224135

Eligibility

Young people in further education or training and those entering a trade who are in need and live in the area of Blackpool and Fylde and Wyre.

Types of grants

One-off grants ranging from £100 to £250. Requests are considered on their merits.

Annual grant total

In 2014 the charity had an income of £20,500 and a total expenditure of £18,900. We estimate that the amount paid in grants to individuals for educational purposes was about £4,600.

Applications

Application forms are available from the correspondent. They can be submitted either directly by the individual or through a social worker, Citizens Advice or other welfare agency. Applications are considered upon receipt.

Other information

Grants can be made to individuals and organisations for both welfare and educational purposes, including support to schools. The charity works in conjunction with John Sykes Dewhurst Bequest (Charity Commission no. 224133).

The Harris Charity

£2,000

Correspondent: David Ingram, Secretary, c/o Moore and Smalley, Richard House, 9 Winckley Square, Preston PR1 3HP (01772 821021; email: harrischarity@mooreandsmalley.co.uk; website: theharrischarity.co.uk)

CC number: 526206

Eligibility

People in need under 25 who live in Lancashire, with a preference for the Preston district, who are in further or higher education.

Types of grants

One-off grants, usually of £250 to £1,000, for equipment/instruments, tools and books, for example.

Annual grant total

In 2013/14 the charity had assets of £3.7 million and an income of £123,500. Grants totalled £87,000 and were mainly made to organisations. The amount of grants given to individuals totalled £4,000 but we were unable to determine how it was distributed.

Exclusions

No grants are available to cover the cost of course fees or living expenses.

Applications

The trustees advertise for applications in the local press twice a year in March and September. Applications must be made using the form, which is available to download from the website, where guidance can also be found. The completed form should be returned to the charity and accompanied by supporting references from a responsible referee such as a school, college, social services, vicar, priest or minister. Applications must be submitted by 31 March or 30 September, with successful applicants notified in July and January respectively.

Other information

The original charity known as the Harris Orphanage Charity dates back to 1883. A new charitable scheme was established in 1985 following the sale of the Harris Orphanage premises in Garstang Road, Preston. The charity also supports charitable organisations that benefit individuals, recreation and leisure and the training and education of individuals.

Superintendent Gerald Richardson Memorial Youth Trust

£4,500

Correspondent: David Williamson, Trustee, Northdene, Stoney Lane, Hambleton, Poulton-le-Fylde FY6 9AF (01253 590510; email: david@ davidwilliamsonaccountants.co.uk)

CC number: 504413

Eligibility

Children and young people under the age of 25 who live or work within 15 miles of Blackpool Town Hall. There is a preference for people with physical or mental disabilities.

Types of grants

Our research suggests that the trust can provide one-off and recurrent grants, typically in the range of £50 to £250. Awards are aimed to encourage children and young people to attend courses and activities of an educational, cultural, sporting, adventuresome or character-building nature. Assistance towards the cost of equipment, instruments, special educational needs, projects, study or travel overseas can also be provided.

Annual grant total

In 2014/15 the trust had an income of £9,000 and an expenditure of £9,500. The trust also supports organisations; therefore, we estimate the annual total amount of grants awarded to be around £4,500.

Applications

Applications should be made in writing to the correspondent, giving details of the individual's age and the cost of the course. Applications should be submitted at least two months before the amount being requested is required. They are considered bimonthly from September and can be submitted either directly by the individual, or via a third party such as a school/college, welfare agency or carer.

Other information

The trust provides funds to youth organisations and schools. Generally, requests for help with major capital projects or where aid from the trust would be insignificant are rejected.

Blackburn with Darwen

It's Your Wish – The John Bury Trust

£14,000

Correspondent: Pamela Rodgers, Trustee, 2 Eckersley Close, Blackburn, Lancashire BB2 4FA (07985 894499; email: info@thejohnburytrust.co.uk; website: www.johnburytrust.co.uk)

CC number: 1108181

Eligibility

Young people between the ages of 10 and 25 who reside within the boundaries of Blackburn with Darwen borough council.

Types of grants

Grants are given to 'promote the mental, spiritual, moral and physical development and improvement' of the individuals. Support can be for a wide range of causes, including purchase of equipment, other necessities, short-term projects, study/ travel overseas, expeditions, personal development opportunities, gaining new skills, travel costs, extra-curricular activities and so on.

Annual grant total

In 2013/14 the trust had an income of £17,000 and an expenditure of £15,000. We estimate the annual total amount of grants awarded to individuals to be around £14,000.

Applications

Application forms can be downloaded from the trust's website together with full terms and conditions. Applicants who are successful in the initial consideration are invited for an interview.

Other information

All grants are expected to be spent within a 12-month period of receiving the award.

The W. M. and B. W. Lloyd Trust

£22,500

Correspondent: John Jacklin, Trustee, Gorse Barn, Rock Lane, Tockholes, Darwen, Lancashire BB3 0LX (01254 771367; email: johnjacklin@homecall.co. uk)

CC number: 503384

Eligibility

People in need who live or have been educated in the old borough of Darwen, Lancashire. Preference is given to single parents.

Types of grants

One-off and recurrent grants are given according to need. Awards are usually of £50–£7,500 (individual grants tend to be at the lower end of the scale). Grants are made to schoolchildren, college students, undergraduates, vocational students and mature students, including those for uniforms/clothing, books, study/travel abroad, equipment/instruments, excursions and awards for excellence. Support is given for sports activities, including equipment and training costs.

Annual grant total

In 2014/15 the charity had an income of £90,500 and a total expenditure of £99,500. At the time of writing (September 2015) full accounts were not yet received by the Charity Commission. In the past about 90% of the overall expenditure was spent in grants to organisations and individuals. We estimate that the amount of grants given to individuals for educational purposes totalled around £22,500.

Applications

Applications may be made in writing to the correspondent. They should be supported by a relevant third party, such as a social worker, doctor, minister or someone who knows the applicant and can endorse their application for help. Applications are considered quarterly, in March, June, September and December. There is also an Emergency Committee capable of making awards at short notice. Applicants are advised to enquire about the other funds (detailed in this entry) administered by the trustees and available to people living in Darwen.

Other information

Grants are made to both individuals and organisations (grants are usually restricted to hospices and hospitals) for educational and social welfare purposes.

The trustees also administer the following funds:

- **The Peter Pan Fund** – for the benefit of people with mental disabilities
- **The Darwen War Memorial and Sick Poor Fund** – originally to help war widows and dependants after the First World War and the sick poor of Darwen
- **The Darwen Disabled Fund** – originally designed to assist with the social welfare of people with physical disabilities in Darwen
- **The Ernest Aspin Donation** – to support sporting activities and in particular training and educating young people in sports
- **The T P Davies Fund** – for the benefit of the residents of Darwen
- **Darwen Probation Volunteers Fund** – supports people in Darwen who have come under the probation and after care service, and their families

The Peel Foundation Scholarship Fund

£7,200

Correspondent: Catharine Oldroyd, Correspondent, Flat 5, The Cove, 275 Inner Promenade, Lytham St Annes FY81AY (01253 794720)

CC number: 526101

Eligibility

Students under the age of 25 resident in or in the neighbourhood of Blackburn who are entering higher education course to obtain a degree. The trustees choose successful applicants based on academic excellence, career ambitions and financial need.

Types of grants

Grants are for general student expenses. The fund may also support people entering a professional trade.

Annual grant total

In 2014/15 the fund had an income of £2,900 and an expenditure of £7,500. We estimate that the annual total amount of grants awarded was around £7,200.

Applications

Application forms can be requested from the correspondent. Candidates must be nominated by the headteacher or principal of their school or college. Our

research shows that applicants may be called for an interview. Candidates must begin their course in the term following the award of scholarships (usually in September), unless excused by the trustees for sufficient cause. Applications are normally considered in July and August and should be submitted in advance.

Other information

The beneficial area more specifically is defined as: the whole borough of Blackburn, except the civil parish of North Turton; the borough of Hyndburn, those parts of the former urban districts of Rishton and Oswaldtwistle which are close to the boundary with Blackburn; the Ribble Valley borough, the civil parishes of Balderstone, Billington, Clayton-le-Dale, Dinckley, Mellor, Osbaldeston, Ramsgreave, Salesbury and Wilpshire.

Blackpool

Blackpool Children's Clothing Fund

£4,500

Correspondent: Alan Rydeheard, Trustee, 96 West Park Drive, Blackpool FY3 9HU (01253 736812)

CC number: 215133

Eligibility

Schoolchildren aged 4 to 16 who live and attend an educational establishment in the borough of Blackpool.

Types of grants

Clothing, footwear and equipment for disadvantaged children in Blackpool. The fund gives vouchers which can be redeemed in participating local retailers and school shop suppliers.

Annual grant total

In 2013/14 the fund had an income of £2,100 and an expenditure of £4,700. We have estimated that the annual total amount of grants awarded was about £4,500.

Applications

Apply in writing to the correspondent. If applicable, applications should be made by a third party, such as education or social work service, on behalf of the applicant. Individuals in need identified by the local education authority are also considered. Applications are administered by the members of student support team.

The Swallowdale Children's Trust

£0

Correspondent: Alexa Alderson, Secretary, PO Box 1301, Blackpool FY1 9HD (07919 154952; email: secswallowdale@hotmail.co.uk; website: www.swallowdaletrust.co.uk)

CC number: 526205

Eligibility

People who live in the Blackpool area who are under the age of 25.

Types of grants

Our research indicates that grants can be given in the form of one-off payments to schoolchildren, college students, undergraduates, vocational students and people starting work towards, for example, clothing and nursery or training fees.

Annual grant total

In 2013/14 the trust had assets of £1 million and an income of £39,500. Grants made during the year amounted to £43,500. Of this total, £9,000 was given to Lancashire Outward Bound, £1,700 to Life Education and £1,000 to Windmill Group. 71 grants to individuals for the relief of hardship totalled £8,600, and no grants were made to individuals for educational purposes.

The annual report for the year also states: 'In association with the Blackpool Gazette the Trust held a '£25,000 Give Away' to promote the aims of the Trust. This had a very positive response and helped a large number of individuals and organisations.'

Applications

Applications must be supported by an independent or professional third party such as a social worker or teacher. An application form is available to download from the website. It should be completed and signed by the relevant parties before being returned to the correspondent. The trustees meet on a bi-monthly basis.

Burnley

Edward Stocks Massey Bequest Fund

£7,000

Correspondent: Chris Gay, Burnley Borough Council, Town Hall, Manchester Road, Burnley, Lancashire BB11 9SA (01282 425011; email: cgay@burnley.gov.uk)

CC number: 526516

Eligibility

People who live in the borough of Burnley and higher education students who have been previously educated in the borough.

Types of grants

The primary purpose of the fund is to assist local individuals and voluntary organisations in the fields of education, science, music and arts. Two Higher Education Student Support Scholarships are considered each year to support students in higher education who have previously been educated in the borough of Burnley.

Annual grant total

In 2014/15 the fund had assets of £1 million and an income of £39,000. Total charitable expenditure was around £50,000, of which grants to individuals and student scholarships totalled £7,000.

Exclusions

Our research suggests that support is not given to people already in receipt of funding from the local authority. It is required that other sources of funding are explored before applying to the fund.

Applications

Application forms can be requested from the correspondent. Applications should be submitted by the end of May for consideration within the following two months. Students seeking scholarships should be nominated by their previous educational establishment and demonstrate great academic achievements, contribution to school/college and/or financial need.

Other information

Support is mostly given to organisations and groups.

The fund also gives grants to the Burnley Mechanics institute trust.

Chorley

The Shaw Charities

£1,000

Correspondent: Ms E. Woodrow, 99 Rawlinson Lane, Heath Charnock, Chorley, Lancashire PR7 4DE (01257 480515; email: woodrows@tinyworld.co.uk)

CC number: 214318

Eligibility

People in need who live in Rivington, Anglezarke, Heath Charnock and Anderton.

Types of grants

Grants to students on first degree courses for books.

Annual grant total

In 2014/15 the charity had an income of £4,400 and a total expenditure of £2,600. We estimate that around £1,000 was distributed in grants to individuals for education.

Applications

Applications can be made on a form available from the correspondent. They should be submitted for consideration in March and November.

Other information

Educational funding from The Shaw Charities is given through the subsidiary charity The Shaw Educational Endowments. The charity also makes grants for social welfare purposes.

Preston

John Parkinson (Goosnargh and Whittingham United Charity)

£2,000

Correspondent: John Bretherton, Clerk to the Trustees, Lower Stanalea Farm, Stanalea Lane, Goosnargh, Preston PR3 2EQ (01995 640224)

CC number: 526060

Eligibility

People under the age of 25 who live in the parishes of Goosnargh, Whittingham and part of Barton.

Types of grants

One-off grants of up to £150 are available to people starting work, entering a trade or preparing for a profession/occupation. Support can be given for tools, books, outfits, payment of fees towards training and courses, also travel expenses or maintenance costs to those who have to travel outside Lancashire to attend an interview or training. Our research suggests that students in further or higher education may be given help towards the cost of books.

Annual grant total

In 2014 the charity had an income of £5,000 and expenditure of £2,400. We estimate that the amount of grants given to individuals totalled around £2,000.

Applications

Apply in writing to the correspondent. Applications are normally considered in May and November.

West Lancashire

Peter Lathom's Charity

£11,000

Correspondent: Christine Aitken, Clerk, 13 Mallard Close, Aughton, Ormskirk L39 5QJ (0151 520 2717)

CC number: 228828

Eligibility

People under 25 resident in West Lancashire.

Types of grants

Cash grants according to need for education and training.

Annual grant total

In 2014 the charity had assets of £1.5 million and an income of £50,000. The charity supports individuals and organisations through three funds: Lathom Educational Foundation; the Welfare Fund; and the Estate or Mixed Account.

During the year, three juniors and five seniors were supported with grants from Lathom Educational Foundation, totalling £2,700 and £3,000 respectively. In addition, individuals received grants totalling £10,500 from the Estate or Mixed Account. We estimate that grants to individuals from this fund for educational purposes totalled around £5,300.

Applications

Applications can be made using a form available from the correspondent. Our research suggests that they should be submitted by 30 September. Awards in all cases are based on financial need as applications always exceed distributable income. Grants are awarded in November/December of each year.

Merseyside

The Girls' Welfare Fund

£4,500

Correspondent: Mrs S. O'Leary, Trustee, West Hey, Dawstone Road, Heswall, Wirral CH60 4RP (email: gwf_charity@hotmail.co.uk)

CC number: 220347

Eligibility

Girls and young women, usually those aged between 15 and 25, who were born in Merseyside. Applications from outside this area will not be acknowledged. Preference will be given to those who are pursuing vocational or further education courses rather than other academic courses.

Types of grants

One-off and recurrent grants, usually of £100 to £1,000, are given for leisure and creative activities, sports, welfare and the relief of poverty. Grants may be given to schoolchildren and students for uniforms/clothing, college students and undergraduates for uniforms/clothing, study/travel overseas and books, vocational students for uniforms/clothing, books and equipment/instruments and to people starting work for clothing and equipment/instruments. The trustees are particularly interested in helping individual girls and young women of poor or deferred education to establish themselves and gain independence.

Annual grant total

In 2014 the fund had an income of £8,700 and a total expenditure of £4,700. We estimate that the amount of grants given to individuals for educational purposes totalled around £4,500.

Exclusions

Grants are not made to charities that request funds to pass on and give to individuals.

Applications

Apply in writing to the correspondent or by email. Applications can be submitted directly by the individual or through a social worker, Citizens Advice, other welfare agency or college/educational establishment. Applications are considered quarterly in March, June, September and December, and should include full information about the college, course and particular circumstances.

Other information

At the time of writing (November 2015) the fund's Charity Commission record described its activities as: 'to assist young women, of non-vocational education, in buying equipment or materials to help gain a qualification and achieve independence'.

The Holt Education Trust

£20,000 (76 grants)

Correspondent: Anne Edwards, Administrator, P. H. Holt Foundation, 151 Dale Street, Liverpool L2 2AH (0151 237 2663; email: administrator@ phholtfoundation.org.uk; website: www. phholtfoundation.org.uk/holt-education-trust)

CC number: 1113708-02

Eligibility

With the exception of a small number of individual students previously supported by the trust, unsolicited applications are no longer accepted.

Further information can be found on the trust's website.

Types of grants

Grants range from £400–£500 for travel bursaries and £1,000 for a small number of selected scholarships. These funds are managed by the institutions concerned and funding enquiries are through recognised channels at the University of Liverpool and Liverpool John Moores University.

Annual grant total

In 2013/14 grants from The Holt Education Trust were awarded to 76 students and totalled £20,000.

Exclusions

The trust's website reminds that the trustees will 'not normally give grants for courses which can be considered as "in-service training" which employers could fund.'

Applications

Grants through The Holt Education Trust are normally available in specific establishments; however, the website notes the following: 'With the exception of students previously supported by the Trust, we are no longer open to grant applications.'

Other information

The Holt Education Trust was established in 1915, in memory of Alfred and Philip Holt, founders of the Liverpool shipping firm, Ocean Steamship Company Ltd. Both brothers took an active interest in the promotion of education during their lifetime, particularly in connection with the Liverpool Institute and Blackburne House Schools. The original trust deed continued the Holts' mission, namely of encouraging higher education among the inhabitants of the city of Liverpool and its neighbourhood by providing scholarships and grants of money to institutions.

The Holt Education Trust, now a subsidiary of its sister charity the P. H. Holt Foundation, is managed by a board of trustees still committed to pursuing the Holt family concern for education. Since 2014, Holt Education Trust has been providing bursaries to Merseyside students studying sciences and vocational training at specific institutions which have a strong association with the trust.

The Sheila Kay Fund

£40,000

Correspondent: Gill Gargan, c/o PSS, 18 Seel Street, Liverpool L1 4BE (email: gill.gargen@skffund.org.uk; website: www.sheilakayfund.org/site)

CC number: 1021378

Eligibility

People in need living in Merseyside (Liverpool, Knowsley, Sefton, St Helens, Wirral) who have a background of work (paid or voluntary) in social/community/voluntary sector and are pursuing education but lack means.

Priority is given to those who have left school with few, if any, qualifications, also people from minority communities who have experienced difficulties in entering education, unemployed people or individuals on low income.

Types of grants

One-off and recurrent grants are made ranging between £50 and £300 for people engaged in social, youth and community work (paid or voluntary) who cannot afford the relevant education or training. Support has been previously awarded for the course fees, childcare, travel expenses and books or materials.

The fund helps people at a wide variety of educational stages, including higher education in social, community and youth work, access courses, GNVQ's, GSE's, counselling qualifications, introductory courses to maths, english and IT, and community courses such as credit union, playwork and capacity building. Priority will be given to funding short/part-time courses or conferences.

Annual grant total

In 2013/14 the fund had assets of £13,500 and an income of £41,500. Charitable expenditure totalled £40,000. Educational grant awards totalled almost £18,000 and a further £22,500 was spent to enable adults to access learning opportunities.

Exclusions

Grants are not given to anyone qualified to a degree standard and beyond.

Applications

Application forms are available on the fund's website and can be submitted by email or post at any time. References are required.

Other information

The fund also offers guidance, information or support materials to individuals and community/voluntary groups and can refer applicants to other funds to obtain further grant support.

Community Foundation for Lancashire and Merseyside

£10,000

Correspondent: Sue Langfeld, Administrator, Community Foundation for Merseyside, Third Floor, Stanley Building, 43 Hanover Street, Liverpool, Merseyside L1 3DN (0151 232 2444; email: info@cfmerseyside.org.uk; website: www.cfmerseyside.org.uk)

CC number: 1068887

Eligibility

People in need who live in Merseyside.

Types of grants

The foundation currently administers three funds which provide grants to individuals for education:

- John Goore Fund – grants of up to £350 to people in higher education and training, particularly adults who need to retrain and improve their skills after a period of unemployment or redundancy
- Joseph Harley Bequest Fund – support is given to young people under the age of 25 who live in Formby for educational projects and activities which are not normally assisted by the public bodies and local authorities
- Sefton Education and Learning Fund – grants of up to £250 are offered to young people under the age of 25 who are resident in Sefton towards the cost of educational materials and courses

Annual grant total

In 2013/14 the foundation had assets of £7.9 million, an income of £2.1 million and a charitable expenditure of £1.8 million. A total of £48,000 was awarded in grants for both educational and welfare purposes to 43 individuals. We estimate that around £10,000 was awarded to individuals in education.

Applications

Application forms can be found on the foundation's website. For further information on application procedure and required supporting documents for each of the funds, consult the website or contact the correspondent.

Other information

The foundation administers a number of funds for various purposes. Most of the funding is given to organisations (£1.3 million to 341 voluntary and community groups in 2013/14); however, individuals in need can also be supported. The funds tend to open and close regularly; therefore, potential applicants should contact the foundation directly for the most recent updates.

John James Rowe's Foundation for Girls

£14,500

Correspondent: Mrs G. Gargan, Administrator, 18–28 Seel Street, Liverpool L1 4BE (0151 702 5555)

CC number: 526166

Eligibility

Girls between the ages of 10 and 22 who live in Merseyside and whose parents are separated/divorced, or whose home conditions are especially difficult, or who have lost one or both of their parents.

Types of grants

Assistance is given for girls at secondary school, further/higher education students and those entering a profession/trade or undertaking apprenticeships. One-off grants are made for equipment/ instruments, clothing, tools, books, also boarding expenses and the cost of holidays. The maximum award is of about £200.

Annual grant total

In 2013/14 the foundation had an income of £13,000 and an expenditure of £15,000. We estimate that the amount of grants given to individuals totalled around £14,500.

Applications

Application forms can be requested from the correspondent or downloaded from The Sheila Kay Foundation's website. Applications can be made at any time directly by the individual.

Liverpool

The Liverpool Council of Education (Incorporated)

£8,000

Correspondent: Roger Morris, Trustee, P. H. Holt Foundation, 151 Dale Street, Liverpool L2 2AH (0151 237 2663)

CC number: 526714

Eligibility

Pupils, students and teachers in Liverpool.

Types of grants

Grants, usually of around £50 to £350, are given according to need.

Annual grant total

In 2013/14 the charity had an income of £16,000 and an expenditure of £16,000. We estimate that grants to individuals totalled around £8,000.

Applications

Apply in writing to the correspondent. Our research suggests that the charity shares its details with the schools in Liverpool at the beginning of each school year.

Other information

The charity acts as a trustee to various charitable funds providing educational support to schools, pupils and teachers in Liverpool.

The Bishop David Sheppard Anniversary Trust

£6,000

Correspondent: Margaret Sadler, Administrator, 5 Hazel Grove, Great Crosby, Liverpool, Merseyside L23 9SH (0151 345 3972; email: margaret.sadler@ hotmail.co.uk)

CC number: 517368

Eligibility

People between the ages of 21 and 49 who live in the Anglican Diocese of Liverpool (which includes Southport, Kirkby, Ormskirk, Skelmersdale, Wigan, St Helens, Warrington and Widnes) and who are doing second-chance learning at a college or training centre.

Types of grants

Grants are provided for books and equipment needed to complete courses or training programmes.

Annual grant total

In 2014 the charity had an income of £7,000 and an expenditure of £6,500. We estimate that grants made totalled approximately £6,000.

Exclusions

No grants are given to students who have had no break from their education (or schoolchildren), to people with good vocational qualifications or on degree courses, or to organisations.

Applications

Application forms are available from the administrator to be submitted directly by the individual at any time.

St Helens

The Rainford Trust

£1,000 (1 grant)

Correspondent: William Simm, Executive Officer, c/o Pilkington Group Ltd, Prescot Road, St Helens, Merseyside WA10 3TT (01744 20574; email: rainfordtrust@btconnect.com)

CC number: 266157

Eligibility

People in need who are normally resident in the borough of St Helens.

Types of grants

One-off and recurrent grants ranging from £100 to £750 are paid directly to the college or other third party organisation. Grants can be awarded to schoolchildren for equipment/instruments, fees, maintenance/living expenses and educational outings in the UK. Further and higher education students and mature students can receive grants for books, equipment/instruments, fees, childcare and educational outings in the UK.

Annual grant total

In 2013/14 the trust had assets of £8.7 million and an income of £229,500. During the year only one grant, of £1,000, was made to an individual for educational purposes.

Applications

Apply in writing to the correspondent. Applications can be made directly by the individual, or through his or her school, college or educational welfare agency. Requests are considered throughout the year. The trust sends out a questionnaire, if appropriate, after the application has been made.

Other information

Grants are mostly made to organisations (£21,700 for educational purposes in 2013/14).

Wirral

Lower Bebington School Lands Foundation

£2,800

Correspondent: S. Green, Trustee, Poulton Hall, Bebington, Wirral, Cheshire CH63 9LN (0151 334 3000)

CC number: 525849

Eligibility

Higher/further education students residing in the area of the parish of St Andrew, Lower Bebington, as it was in 1924.

Types of grants

Small grants of up to £300 are available towards general educational costs, including books, equipment/instruments, necessities, fees and living expenses. Some assistance may also be available towards facilities not normally provided by the local authorities for public school pupils.

Annual grant total

In 2014/15 the foundation had an income of £3,100 and an expenditure of £3,000. We have estimated the annual total amount of grants awarded to be around £2,800.

Applications

Application forms can be obtained from the correspondent. Our research suggests that applications should be submitted by August each year but may be considered at other times if funds are available.

Other information

The trustees inform that 'owing to poor drafting when state education was introduced [the beneficial area] cannot be adjusted to suit current boundary' and further suggest that applicants should 'see the Poulton Lancelyn Lands Foundation (1998) which covers omitted areas'.

South East

General

The Chownes Foundation

£7,800

Correspondent: Sylvia Spencer, Secretary, The Courtyard, Shoreham Road, Upper Beeding, Steyning, West Sussex BN44 3TN (01903 816699; email: sylvia@russellnew.com)

CC number: 327451

Eligibility

Individuals living in Sussex, particularly mid-Sussex.

Types of grants

One-off and recurrent grants.

Annual grant total

In 2013/14 the foundation had an income of £20,000 and a total expenditure of £110,500. Due to its low income, the foundation was not required to submit its accounts to the Charity Commission and so we were unable to determine a total for grants made during the year.

In the most recent year for which accounts were available to view (2012/13), the foundation awarded £17,000 to assist former employees of Sound Diffusion plc. A further £15,700 was given to individuals for other charitable purposes. We estimate that around half of this was given for social welfare purposes. Based on this, we estimate that grants for educational purposes totalled around £7,800.

Applications

Our research suggests that the trustees prefer a one page document and will request further information if they require it.

Other information

The majority of the foundation's funds are committed to long-term support for poor and vulnerable beneficiaries, so only very few applications are successful.

The Ewelme Exhibition Foundation (Ewelme Exhibition Endowment)

£107,000 (10 grants)

Correspondent: James Oliver, Clerk and Trust Manager, 126 High Street, Oxford OX1 4DG (01865 244661; fax: 01865 721263; email: clerk@ewelme-education-awards.info; website: www.ewelme-education-awards.info)

CC number: 309240

Eligibility

Young people (both in state and independent education) aged between 11 and 21 who live in Berkshire, Buckinghamshire, Conock in Wiltshire, Oxfordshire and Ramridge in Hampshire and demonstrate exceptional talent or need.

Types of grants

Grant awards for educational purposes:

- Scholarships or maintenance allowances at school, university or place of learning approved by the governors
- Financial assistance to beneficiaries on leaving school, university or other place of learning to prepare for, or to assist their entry into a trade, profession or calling
- Travel bursaries.
- Providing facilities of any kind not normally provided by the LEAs for recreation and social and physical training
- Financial assistance for the study of music or other arts

In the state sector the foundation provides funds for additional tuition, educational visits, sports, music and arts, also books and equipment for skills training. The trustees note that a large proportion of the endowment income is currently used to support young people in independent education and mostly at secondary education level. Beneficiaries are young people aged under 21 who, in the opinion of the governors, are in need of financial assistance and who have residential qualification in Ewelme and

Marsh Gibbon, the other Estate areas and the counties of Oxon, Bucks and former Berks.

Annual grant total

In 2014 the foundation had assets of £238,000 and an income of £132,500. The amount of grants given to individuals totalled £107,000.

Applications

Application forms can be requested from the correspondent via email. Applications are advertised in the regional press in late September/October and the closing date for submissions is the end of November. Candidates are invited to an interview in February. The foundation requires applicants to provide details of parental income and a testimonial from the school's headteacher.

Other information

Grants are also made to local schools (£8,500 in 2014).

The trustees' annual report for 2014 states:

> Ten children benefited from individual grants during the year and grants were awarded to the three Church of England primary schools within the endowed estate areas to fund facilities and projects for which State funding was unavailable in order to benefit the pupils from financially disadvantaged families.

Kentish's Educational Foundation

£19,500 (24 grants)

Correspondent: Margery Roberts, Clerk to the Trustees, 7 Nunnery Stables, St Albans, Hertfordshire AL1 2AS (01727 856626)

CC number: 313098

Eligibility

Young people in need between the ages of 11 and 35, particularly (but not exclusively) those who are permanently resident in Hertfordshire or Bedfordshire. Preference can be given to people with the family name Kentish or people related to the founder Thomas Kentish (died 1712).

Types of grants

Grants towards costs arising from education at any secondary school, university, further education college or other educational establishment approved for the purpose by the trustees or for the purpose of enabling beneficiaries to study music or other arts or to undertake travel in furtherance of their education. Grants towards the cost of outfits, clothing, tools, instruments or books to help them on leaving secondary school, university or other educational establishment to prepare for, or to enter, a profession, trade or calling. The latest accounts state: 'The policy of the trustees is to award grants to young people who are in secondary schools, further education colleges and Universities, up to first degree level or equivalent, with grants for postgraduate study awarded only in very exceptional circumstances.'

Annual grant total

In 2013/14 the foundation had assets of £1 million and an income of £26,000. The amount of grants given to individuals totalled £19,500.

Grants for higher education/further education	£18,000
Grants for secondary education	£1,000
Grants for travel	£500

Exclusions

Support is normally available up to first degree level.

Applications

Application forms can be requested from the correspondent and can be submitted by individuals directly or through their parents/guardians. Applicants should also provide a copy of their school/tutor report and copies of birth or marriage certificates (for applicants claiming kinship). Grants are normally considered in October/November; therefore, applications should be received by the end of August.

The Mijoda Charitable Trust

£12,000

Correspondent: Jacquie Hardman, Trustee, Oak House, 38 Botley Road, Chesham HP5 1XG (01494 783402; email: jacquie_hardman@hotmail.com)

CC number: 1002565

Eligibility

People who live in Buckinghamshire or Hertfordshire who are undertaking further, higher or postgraduate education in music, the arts or medicine. Beneficiaries are usually under 40 years of age.

Types of grants

One-off and recurrent grants of up to £250 towards fees and study or travel overseas.

Annual grant total

In 2013/14 the trust had an income of £19,000 and an expenditure of £12,500. We estimate that grants totalled around £12,000.

Applications

Apply in writing to the correspondent. A reply will only be sent if an sae is enclosed.

Sarum St Michael Educational Charity
See entry on page 282

The Kathryn Turner Trust (Whitton's Wishes)

£62,500

Correspondent: Kathryn Turner, Founder and Trustee, Unit 3, Suffolk Way, Abingdon, Oxfordshire OX14 5JX (01235 527310; email: kathrynturnertrust@hotmail.co.uk)

CC number: 1111250

Eligibility

Children and young people, individuals with disabilities or special needs in the area of old county of Middlesex. Members of the Royal Navy, Army and Royal Air Force, and their dependants, are also supported.

Types of grants

Grants towards various educational needs, including equipment and necessities.

Annual grant total

In 2013 the trust had an income of £200,500 an expenditure of £200,000 and £62,500 was awarded in grants. At the time of writing (October 2015) this was the most recent financial information available.

Applications

Apply in writing to the correspondent. The trustees meet every three months.

Other information

Organisations and individuals are supported for both educational and welfare purposes.

Bedfordshire

Ashton Schools Foundation

£10,500

Correspondent: Yvonne Beaumont, Administrator, Grove House, 76 High Street North, Dunstable, Bedfordshire LU6 1NF (01582 660008; email: dunstablecharity@yahoo.com)

CC number: 307526

Eligibility

Children and young people under the age of 25 living within the Dunstable area (defined as a radius of six miles from the parish church of the ecclesiastical parish of St Peter).

Types of grants

One-off and recurrent grants, scholarships, bursaries towards general educational needs, including books, equipment/instruments, clothing, maintenance, other necessities, also study/travel overseas, educational outings, study of music or other arts. Schoolchildren, further/higher education students or people starting work/ entering a trade can be supported.

Annual grant total

In 2013/14 the foundation had an income of £21,500 and a total expenditure of £21,500. We estimate the annual total amount of grants awarded to individuals to be around £10,500.

Applications

Apply in writing to the correspondent.

Other information

The foundation also provides annual grants to Manshead, Ashton Middle and Ashton Lower schools in Dunstable.

Chew's Foundation at Dunstable

£6,000 (20–25 grants)

Correspondent: Yvonne Beaumont, Administrator, Grove House, 76 High Street North, Dunstable, Bedfordshire LU6 1NF (01582 660008; email: dunstablecharity@yahoo.com)

CC number: 307500

Eligibility

Children and young people, normally under the age of 25, living within the boroughs of Dunstable and Luton and parish of Edlesbrough who/whose parents are 'in sympathy' with the Church of England and other Christian churches. Our research suggests that a certificate of baptism is required.

Types of grants

The foundation provides scholarships to individuals in education and can assist people undertaking apprenticeships. Support is given towards general educational costs, including books, school uniforms, educational outings, equipment/instruments and so forth.

Annual grant total

In 2013/14 the foundation had an income of £18,000 and an expenditure of £12,500. Previously around 20–25 grants a year have been awarded to individuals. We estimate the annual total amount of grants awarded to individuals to be around £6,000.

Applications

Apply in writing to the correspondent. According to our research, applications should normally be submitted by the end of May to receive a grant around July. Late applications may be considered in December. Details of parental income and the number of dependent children of school age in the family will be taken into account.

Other information

The foundation also maintains the Chew's House and the Old Library (now the Little Theatre).

Flitwick Combined Charities

£5,400

Correspondent: David Empson, Trustee, 28 Orchard Way, Flitwick, Bedford MK45 1LF (01525 718145; email: deflitwick8145@aol.com; website: www. flitwickcombinedcharities.org.uk)

CC number: 233258

Eligibility

Students who have completed their first year at university and are about to start the second, and whose home is the parish of Flitwick.

Types of grants

Grants are of around £100–£250. As a general rule, educational grants are awarded to students at the start of their second year of study in higher education. In exceptional circumstances, one-off grants may be given for other reasons, such as providing sports equipment to a youth group.

Annual grant total

In 2013/14 the charity had an income of £11,100 and a total expenditure of £10,000. We estimate that grants for education purposes totalled about £5,400.

Applications

Application forms are available from the charity's website or the correspondent. The charity's website states: 'Anything not covered by these forms should be sent to us as a short paragraph outlining the reasons for the request and how any money will be spent, **using the contact us form** [emphasis added], following which we will then be in touch for extra information.'

The trustees' meetings are held three times a year and the dates are publicised on the website. Applications need to be submitted a month in advance of the meeting.

Other information

There are three charities The Deacons Dole, The Poors Moor and The Town Lands Charity) collectively known as Flitwick Combined Charities. The objectives of the trustees are to provide both educational and relief-in-need help.

The Harpur Trust

£95,000

Correspondent: Peter Milburn, Grants Manager, Princeton Court, The Pilgrim Centre, Brickhill Drive, Bedford MK41 7PZ (01234 369500; fax: 01234 369505; email: info@harpurtrust.org.uk; website: www.harpurtrust.org.uk)

CC number: 1066861

Eligibility

Adults who are returning to study after a minimum of five years away from formal education and are resident in the borough of Bedford. Schoolchildren who are in receipt of free school meals are eligible for school uniform when transitioning from state upper school to middle school.

Undergraduate bursary applicants should meet the criteria set by their university or college.

Preference is given to people in need, hardship or distress.

Types of grants

Grants are made to help with the cost of further education and training leading to career development. Support can be given for fees, travel costs and necessities. The trust also gives grants towards school uniforms and provides bursaries at the schools it runs as well as undergraduate bursaries for school leavers at the partner schools. Contact the school directly to discuss these awards.

Annual grant total

In 2013/14 the trust had assets of £130 million and an income of £55.3 million. The amount of grants given to individuals totalled £95,000.

The awards can be broken down as follows:

University bursary programme	£57,500
College bursary programme	£20,000
School uniform grants	£12,500
Grants to two individuals	£4,500

Exclusions

The trust will not give grants for PGCE courses and certificates of education or for recreational courses, including academic courses taken for recreational purposes only.

Applications

Adults returning to education may use the form available on the trust's website. It should be submitted by the end of May for courses beginning in September/October. Successful candidates are invited for an interview. Applicants must determine their entitlement to statutory funding before making an application.

Applicants for the university/college bursaries should apply via their schools.

The school uniform grants scheme is advertised to all eligible families in the borough by Bedford schools.

The trustees consider grants five times a year. Applicants are 'encouraged to contact the trust informally for initial guidance on their applications and much advice is given verbally'.

Other information

Most grants are given to registered charities, voluntary organisations and other groups but a small number of grants can be offered to individuals pursuing or continuing vocational education and training, particularly adults returning to education.

Bedford

Alderman Newton's Educational Foundation (Bedford branch)

£5,500

Correspondent: Lynn McKeenna, Correspondent, Bedford Borough Council, Committee Services, Borough Hall, Cauldwell Street, Bedford MK42 9AP (01234 228193; email: lynn.mckeena@bedford.gov.uk; website: www.bedford.gov.uk/aldermannewton)

CC number: 307471

Eligibility

People aged 13 to 25 who have lived in the borough of Bedford (including rural area) for at least three years. Support is available to schoolchildren, higher/further education students and people entering a trade/profession.

Types of grants

The foundation reimburses the expenses for educational necessities such as books, equipment/instruments, stationery, outfits, special clothing and so forth. The upper limit of money available is £500 but in exceptional circumstances can be increased up to £750. Grants are only given when receipts for the items specified in the application are produced.

Annual grant total

In 2013/14 the foundation had an income of £4,500 and an expenditure of £6,000. We have estimated the annual total amount of grants awarded to be around £5,500.

Exclusions

Grants exceeding £750 or travel expenses to and from school would not normally be supported.

Applications

Application forms are available from the foundation's website and can be submitted at any time. A letter from the applicant's educational establishment is required to confirm their attendance and need for the items requested. Details of the applicant's or their parents' income should also be included.

Central Bedfordshire

Potton Consolidated Charity

£38,000

Correspondent: Dean Howard, Clerk, 69 Stotfold Road, Arlesey, Bedfordshire SG15 6XR (01462735220; email: clerk@ potton-consolidated-charity.co.uk; website: www.potton-consolidated-charity.co.uk)

CC number: 201073

Eligibility

People between the ages of 16 and 25 who live in the parish of Potton.

Types of grants

Students aged between 16 and 18 can apply for assistance with the costs of transport to school and college. Students who are aged between 18 and 25 and are in full-time education can apply for higher education grants.

Annual grant total

In 2014/15 the charity had assets of £4.3 million and an income of £152,000. Grants totalled £191,500, of which £153,500 was given to organisations for a range of purposes. Grants to individuals amounted to more than £38,000, the vast majority of which was given for educational purposes.

Applications

Applications can be submitted using the online form or, alternatively, using the appropriate form, which is available to download from the website or from Potton Post Office and the library. Guidelines can be found on the website.

The Sandy Charities

£3,500

Correspondent: Mr P. Mount, Clerk, Woodfines Solicitors, 6 Bedford Road, Sandy, Bedfordshire SG19 1EN (01767 680251; email: pmount@woodfines.co.uk)

CC number: 237145

Eligibility

People who live in Sandy and Beeston and are in need.

Types of grants

One-off grants only, ranging from £100 to £1,000. Schoolchildren can receive grants towards school uniforms and other school clothing and educational outings; and college students, undergraduates and vocational students towards books and equipment/instruments.

Annual grant total

In 2013/14 the charity had an income of £7,700 and a total expenditure of £15,300. Grants are made to individuals and organisations for both educational and social welfare purposes. We estimate that educational grants to individuals totalled £3,500.

Applications

Apply in writing to the correspondent who will supply a personal details form for completion. Applications can be considered in any month, depending on the urgency for the grant; they should be submitted either directly by the individual or via the individual's school, college or educational welfare agency.

Berkshire

The Earley Charity

£1,500

Correspondent: Jane Wittig, Clerk to the Trustees, Liberty of Earley House, Strand Way, Earley, Reading RG6 4EA (0118 975 5663; fax: 0118 975 2263; email: enquiries@earleycharity.org.uk; website: www.earleycharity.org.uk)

CC number: 244823

Eligibility

People in post-school education who live in Earley, the northern part of Shinfield, Winnersh, central, east and south Reading, and the immediate neighbourhood, including Sonning and lower Caversham. Applicants must have lived in the area for at least six months.

In order to check whether you live within the area of benefit, see the map available on the website. If in doubt, get in touch with the correspondent to confirm.

Types of grants

Grants to individuals are generally one-off and do not normally exceed £400 with the majority being relatively small. Support is available to further and higher education students, mature students, people starting work or vocational training and apprenticeships. Assistance is given towards general educational necessities, such as books, tools, equipment, materials or clothing.

Annual grant total

In 2014 the charity had assets of £13.1 million and an income of £1.2 million. Grants totalled £325,000, of which £7,200 was given in 29 awards to individuals. The amount given for educational purposes was not known – the correspondent has informed us that the trustees 'do not record separately the amount awarded for this type of grant'. We estimate that educational grants to individuals totalled around £1,500.

Exclusions

Grants are not generally given:

- To schoolchildren
- Towards student exchange
- For study or travel abroad
- To foreign students studying in Britain
- Where parents contribute to fees
- For postgraduate education
- Towards general living costs
- Outside the area of benefit
- To people who have been awarded three grants in the past or benefitted from the charity within the last two years

Applications

Application forms can be requested from the correspondent. They can be submitted either directly by the individual or through a social worker, Citizens Advice or other welfare agency. Applications for grants under £500 and applications for grants over £500 are considered at separate meetings around five times each year. The dates of these meetings, along with application submission deadlines, are published on the website.

Other information

Support is given to individuals and organisations for welfare purposes.

Wellington Crowthorne Charitable Trust

£10,000

Correspondent: Paul Thompson, Trustee, Wellington College, Crowthorne, Berkshire RG45 7PU (email: pft@wellingtoncollege.org.uk)

CC number: 277491

Eligibility

People who live in the parishes of Crowthorne, Finchampstead, Sandhurst and Wokingham Without. Preference is given to applicants under the age of 25.

Types of grants

Grants are given to 'promote spiritual, moral, mental and physical capacities of individuals'. Previously grants have been awarded for a wide range of overseas gap year projects, Outward Bound expeditions, school trips and international sports events.

Annual grant total

In 2013 the trust had an income of £12,700 and an expenditure of £15,900. We estimate that the amount of grants given to individuals totalled around £10,000.

At the time of writing (November 2015) the annual report and accounts for 2014 were not yet received by the Charity Commission.

Applications

Applications may be made in writing to the correspondent. The trustees' meetings are normally held three times a year, although in urgent cases applications can be considered between the meetings.

Other information

Our research suggests that the trust also supports local youth organisations awarding about £5,000 a year.

The trust is maintained and mainly supported by Wellington College.

Reading

John Sykes Foundation

Correspondent: Vickie Randall, Chief Executive, 23/24 Market Place, Reading RG1 2DE (0118 903 5909; email: mail@johnsykesfoundation.org; website: johnsykesfoundation.org)

CC number: 1156623

Eligibility

Individuals who live in and around Reading who are in need of help and support. A map showing the area of benefit can be found on the website.

Types of grants

Grants are given to individuals for a wide range of needs, including for the following purposes stated on the foundation's website:

- Education – The Foundation wants to give people the opportunity to improve their lives through education and training. The opportunity to develop, grow and learn new skills will enable people to fulfil future hopes, dreams and aspirations
- Arts & culture – Through heritage, culture and arts so much can be learnt and kept for future generations. The charity wants to support individuals that have a talent or special project that they want to create. A project can be a work of art, a musical talent, or may be a restoration project
- Science – The foundation will support the advancement of science and technology. If an individual has a new idea to develop and needs a helping hand the John Sykes Foundation will consider an application for support
- Sport – Amateur sport brings great opportunities for a healthy lifestyle, sporting career and achieving a personal goal. The foundation offers support and encouragement to individuals who live in and around the Reading area that have aspirations or dreams to reach milestones in the world of sport

The foundation has four grant programmes and states on its website: 'Each grant is not currently time specific. The individual grants are structured with a grant total therefore it's important to apply to the correct grant programme.' The four grant programmes are: Minster – grants of £500 or less; Abbey – grants of £2,500 or less; Forbury – grants of £5,000 or less; and Maiwand – grants of £10,000 or less. It is important that applicants apply to the application appropriate for the amount needed.

Annual grant total

John Sykes Foundation was registered in April 2014 and, at the time of writing (November 2015), had not yet submitted any accounts to the Charity Commission. We were, therefore, unable to gather any financial information for the foundation.

Applications

Application forms can be downloaded from the website and should be completed and returned to the foundation's office by post or email. When your application is submitted, you will be sent a notification to confirm it has been received. Your application will be assessed by the trustees and you will be informed whether it has been taken forward to the next stage. Applicants who are unsuccessful at this point will also be notified. If your initial application is successful, you will either be invited to the foundation's office or be visited in your home to discuss your application, financial details, your reason for applying and what you hope to achieve. Following this meeting, you will be informed verbally of the foundation's decision and will receive confirmation in writing.

Note: As the foundation is a newly registered grant-maker and is in the early stages of its development, we would advise potential applicants to consider the information on the website thoroughly before beginning an application.

Other information

The foundation's informative website presents the following information:

The foundation established by John Sykes in 2014 aims to help, support, and transform the lives of people living in and around the Reading area. John not only has a passion for business but his hometown of Reading too. It's from where over the last 15 years he has built his successful companies. He now wants to give something back for the people of Reading and his foundation is set to do just that.

Reading Dispensary Trust

£600 (2 grants)

Correspondent: Walter Gilbert, Clerk, 16 Wokingham Road, Reading RG6 1JQ (0118 926 5698; email: admin.rdt@btconnect.com; website: www.readingdispensarytrust.org.uk)

CC number: 203943

Eligibility

People in need who are in poor health, convalescent or who have a physical or mental disability and live in Reading and the surrounding area (roughly within a seven-mile radius of the centre of Reading).

Types of grants

One-off grants towards course fees, books, computer equipment and software.

Annual grant total

In 2014 the charity had assets of £1.3 million and an income of £49,000. Grants totalled £29,000, of which £1,500 was awarded to five organisations. During the year, 94 grants were made to individuals, the vast majority of which were for what we determine to be social welfare purposes. Of this total, two grants were also made towards the purchase of computer equipment and software. We estimate that grants with purposes related to education totalled around £600.

Exclusions

The charity cannot fund services or goods which are available from statutory sources.

Applications

Application forms can be downloaded from the website, along with guidelines. Applications are usually made through doctors, nurses, social workers or voluntary organisations. Grant applications are considered on the 2nd Tuesday of each month. Further information can be obtained by contacting the Clerk (the office is open on Tuesday and Thursday mornings only, although answerphone messages can be left outside these times).

Windsor and Maidenhead

The Spoore Merry and Rixman Foundation

£156,500 (129 grants)

Correspondent: Helen MacDiarmid, Clerk to the Trustees, PO Box 4229, Slough SL1 0QZ (020 3286 8300; email: clerk@smrfmaidenhead.org; website: www.smrfmaidenhead.org.uk)

CC number: 309040

Eligibility

People under the age of 25 who are in need and live in the former (pre-1974) borough of Maidenhead or the ancient parish of Bray, including Holyport and Woodlands Park.

Types of grants

Grants can be given for general educational needs, including school uniforms, equipment/instruments, tools, books, musical instruments and sporting equipment, school visits, facilities for recreational or social training not normally provided by the local authorities, tuition in music or other arts, travel expenses in the UK and overseas, supplement for college/ university fees, support to people entering a trade, residential courses and special needs and aids, such as laptops for dyslexic children.

Our research suggests that grants are for amounts of up to £5,000 each, although in special cases, such as death of parents, this figure can be exceeded. Families receiving income support can be given up to £3,000 for a student in higher education. Grants of £1,000 (if living at home) or £1,500 (if living independently) per year are offered to people undertaking an apprenticeship.

The foundation encourages young people to return to or to remain in education when they may have dropped out and not achieved GCSE passes.

Annual grant total

In 2014 the foundation had assets of £11.2 million and an income of £533,500. A total of £156,500 was awarded in grants to 129 individuals.

Applications

Application forms can be found on the foundation's website. They can be submitted by post or online by the individual or through an educational institution. Applications for school uniforms should be submitted by a parent or guardian with a supporting statement from a social worker/teacher/ Citizens Advice/health professional. Parents are also required to provide a statement of their income. Applications should not be sent via recorded or registered post – the charity operates with a PO Box address and there is no one to sign a receipt.

Other information

Awards to 51 institutions totalled £171,500 in 2014.

The foundation's website states that 'the trustees are considering setting up bursaries for students from low income families which could cover the entire cost of a university course'.

Every child leaving a local authority-maintained primary school in Maidenhead and Bray receives a dictionary from the trust.

Wokingham

The Polehampton Charity

£2,700

Correspondent: Miss E. Treadwell, Assistant Clerk to the Charity, 114 Victoria Road, Wargrave, Berkshire RG10 8AE (0118 934 0852; email: polehampton.applications@gmail.com; website: www.thepolehamptoncharity.co. uk)

CC number: 1072631

Eligibility

People in need who are under the age of 25 and live in the former ecclesiastical parishes of St Mary the Virgin, Twyford and St James the Great, Ruscombe.

Types of grants

The charity's website notes: 'Educational Grants cover assistance with the purchase of books and tools which are essential for the completion of courses of training at university, college, or other recognised educational establishments, including apprenticeships.'

Our research suggests that awards are generally in the range of £100–£250.

Annual grant total

In 2014 the charity had assets of £2.9 million and an income of £96,000. Grants were made totalling about £41,500. Awards to individuals totalled £7,200. The trustees' annual report notes that £2,700 was given in 10 grants to individuals for educational purposes and £4,500 in three awards – for other needs.

Applications

Applications should be made in writing to the correspondent, including full details of the applicant and their need and giving full costings. They can be submitted directly by the individual or a family member, through a third party (such as a social worker or teacher), or through an organisation (such as Citizens Advice or a school). Applications can be made at any time and are considered at trustee meetings (there are three meetings a year – in February, May and October).

Other information

The charity supports both individuals and organisations for social welfare and educational purposes. Awards to organisations during 2014 totalled £34,000 (£27,000 in grants to schools for equipment and resources and £7,200 in grants to organisations and groups).

The Wokingham United Charities Trust

£2,500

Correspondent: P. Robinson, Clerk, 66 Upper Broadmoor Road, Crowthorne, Berkshire RG45 7DF (01344 351207; email: peter.westende@btinternet.com; website: www.westende.org.uk)

CC number: 1107171

Eligibility

Schoolchildren in need who live in the civil parishes of Wokingham, Wokingham Without, St Nicholas, Hurst, Ruscombe and that part of Finchampstead known as Finchampstead North.

Types of grants

One-off grants, usually between £25 and £150. Grants have been given towards school uniforms and educational visits.

Annual grant total

The annual report and accounts for 2013/14 did not include a figure for grants made from the Relief-in-Need Fund. In previous years, grants have totalled around £5,000 and we have estimated those for educational purposes to have amounted to £2,500.

Applications

Application forms are available from the correspondent or can be downloaded from the website. Applications are considered each month (except August) and can be submitted directly by the individual, or through a social worker, school liaison officer or similar third party.

Buckingham-shire

Amersham United Charities (Amersham and Coleshill Almshouse Charity)

Correspondent: Mrs C. Atkinson, Clerk to the Trustees, 25 Milton Lawns, Amersham, Buckinghamshire HP6 6BJ (01494 723416)

CC number: 205033

Eligibility

People under the age of 21 who live in the parishes of Amersham and Coleshill, Buckinghamshire.

Types of grants

One-off grants for those at school, college or university, or about to start work, to help with the cost of fees (students only), books, equipment, clothing and travel.

Annual grant total

In 2014 the charity had assets of £243,000 and an income of £56,000. The latest accounts state: 'The Trustees have made gifts to various parties in line with the objectives of the Young Persons and Poor Fund during the year.'

The correspondent has previously informed us that, although no grants have been made in recent years, the charity is open to applications from individuals for relief in need and education.

Applications

Applications may be made in writing to the correspondent.

Other information

The main work of the charity is the administration and management of 13 almshouses. Grants can be made through the Young Persons and the Poor Fund. Welfare support can also be given.

Arnold's Educational Foundation

See entry on page 164

Norman Hawes Memorial Trust

£1,000

Correspondent: Madeleine Carrington, Milton Keynes Council, Education Department, 502 Avebury Boulevard, Milton Keynes MK9 3HS (01908 253614; email: madeleine.carrington@milton-keynes.gov.uk)

CC number: 310620

Eligibility

Young people between the ages of 15 and 18 who are in full-time education in Milton Keynes and North Buckinghamshire.

Types of grants

Financial assistance to students travelling abroad for educational purposes. Grants range between £50 and £200.

Annual grant total

In 2013/14 the trust had an income of £3,500 and an expenditure of £1,000. We have estimated that the annual total amount of grants awarded was around £1,000.

Applications

Application forms are available from the correspondent. They can be submitted either by individuals or through their school/college/educational welfare agency, if applicable. Considerations take place in November and February/March, and applications should be made in September/October and January/February respectively.

The Stoke Mandeville and Other Parishes Charity

£16,100

Correspondent: Caroline Dobson, Administrator, 17 Elham Way, Aylesbury HP21 9XN (01296 431859; email: smandopc@gmail.com; website: smandopc.org)

CC number: 296174

Eligibility

People in need who live in the parishes of Great and Little Hampden, Great Missenden and Stoke Mandeville. Applicants should have been resident in the area of benefit for at least two years.

Types of grants

At the time of writing (November 2015), the charity listed the following types of grants on its website:

- Educational grants – annual grants available to all residents of Stoke Mandeville, Great Missenden and Great and Little Hampton parishes in

order to allow them to continue their studies at college or university
- School trips – assistance with the costs of school trips and equipment for residents of Stoke Mandeville who are facing hardship

Annual grant total

In 2014 the charity had assets of £1.9 million and an income of £90,500. Educational grants to individuals totalled £16,100.

Applications

Application forms for educational grants are available to download from the website.

Other information

The charity gives grants to individuals for welfare causes and can also support organisations. The vast majority of funding is given to residents of Stoke Mandeville.

Aleysbury Vale

William Harding's Charity

£143,500 (185 grants)

Correspondent: John Leggett, Clerk to the Trustees, 14 Bourbon Street, Aylesbury, Buckinghamshire HP20 2RS (01296 318501; fax: 01296 318531; email: doudjag@pandcllp.co.uk)

CC number: 310619

Eligibility

People under the age of 25 who live in the town of Aylesbury.

Types of grants

One-off grants are made to schoolchildren towards uniforms, clothing, fees, study/travel overseas, books, educational outings, equipment/instruments, maintenance/living expenses or for special educational needs. Further/higher education students and people in vocational training can also be supported. Facilities for recreation, social or physical training may be provided to people in primary, secondary or further education.

Annual grant total

In 2012 the charity had assets of £23.6 million and an income of £834,000. During the year 185 pupils were supported totalling £143,500. At the time of writing (July 2015) the latest financial information available was from 2012 accounts.

Applications

Apply in writing to the correspondent.

Other information

The charity also owns almshouses, provides relief in need and supports local educational institutions, youth groups and organisations.

Thomas Hickman's Charity

£16,000

Correspondent: John Leggett, Clerk, Parrott and Coales, 14–16 Bourbon Street, Aylesbury, Buckinghamshire HP20 2RS (01296 318500; email: doudjag@pandcllp.co.uk)

CC number: 202973

Eligibility

People who live in Aylesbury town and are in need, hardship or distress.

Types of grants

According to our research, grants can be given for school uniforms.

Annual grant total

In 2014 the charity had an income of £641,000 and a total expenditure of £678,500. A total of 144 grants were made to individuals, amounting to £63,500, although a breakdown of distribution by purpose was not included in the annual report. We estimate that around £16,000 was awarded to individuals for educational purposes.

Applications

Application forms can be requested from the correspondent. They should be submitted either directly by the individual or through a third party, such as a family member, social worker, school or Citizens Advice. The trustees meet on a regular basis and applications are considered as they arise.

Other information

The charity provides almshouses to the elderly, supports the welfare needs of individuals and makes grants to organisations.

Milton Keynes

The Ancell Trust

£3,000

Correspondent: Karen Phillips, Secretary, 78 London Road, Stony Stratford, Milton Keynes MK11 1JH (01908 563350; email: karen.phillips30@hotmail.co.uk)

CC number: 233824

Eligibility

People in need in the town of Stony Stratford.

Types of grants

Our research suggests that grants are given to students for books and are occasionally made to individuals for

welfare purposes and to organisations or groups. Grants may also be given for travelling expenses and other training needs, including apprenticeships.

Annual grant total

In 2014/15 the trust had an income of nearly £8,000 and a total expenditure of £12,100, which is the highest in the past five years. We estimate that about £3,000 was given to individuals for educational purposes.

Applications

Applications may be made in writing to the correspondent at any time.

Other information

The trust owns the sports ground in Stony Stratford, which provides cricket, football, bowls, croquet and tennis facilities. Grants are also made to organisations or groups.

Wolverton Science and Art Institution Fund

£1,900

Correspondent: Karen Phillips, 78 London Road, Stony Stratford, Milton Keynes MK11 1JH (01908 563350; email: karen.phillips30@hotmail.co.uk)

CC number: 310652

Eligibility

People who live, study or work in the parishes of Wolverton or Stantonbury.

Types of grants

The fund awards scholarships, bursaries and grants to schoolchildren, people starting work, further and higher education students, mature students and postgraduates. Particular preference is given to the arts, science and related subjects. Our research suggests that grants can range between £100 and £500 and are given towards the cost of school uniforms, other clothing, books, equipment/instruments, fees and educational outings in the UK.

Annual grant total

In 2014/15 the fund had an income of £5,800 and an expenditure of £3,800. We have estimated that the annual total amount of grants awarded to individuals was about £1,900.

Exclusions

Our research indicates that grants are not available to cover the salary expenses of a project.

Applications

Application forms are available from the correspondent and can be submitted either directly by the individual or through a school/college/educational welfare agency, if applicable. According

to our research, applications are normally considered in February, April, August and October and should be received in the preceding month.

Other information

The fund allocates up to one third of the income to provide benefits to educational organisations not normally provided by the local authorities.

South Buckinghamshire

Stoke Poges United Charity

£8,800

Correspondent: Anthony Levings, Clerk, The Cedars, Stratford Drive, Wooburn Green, High Wycombe HP10 0QH (email: anthony@levings123.wanadoo.co.uk; website: www.stokepogesparish council.gov.uk/village-charities)

CC number: 205289

Eligibility

People who are in need and live in the parish of Stoke Poges and the surrounding area.

Types of grants

Grants, typically ranging between £30 and £1,500, are given for tools, clothing, books and other school equipment. During the year, educational grants were given to assist with the costs of: the second year of support for a MSc student; nursery care; and school uniforms.

Annual grant total

In 2014 the charity had an income of £58,000 and a total expenditure of £13,100. During the year, grants totalled £12,800, of which £8,800 was for educational purposes.

Exclusions

The charity cannot give regular or frequent grants.

Applications

An application form is available to download from the Stoke Poges Parish Council website. It should be completed and returned to: Mike Dier, 34 Hazell Way, Stoke Poges SL2 4DD. There is also the option of applying for a grant online via the website. The guidance notes, which are available to download along with the application form, state: 'If you need any assistance with completion, please contact our Chairman, Trevor Egleton 01753 646090 or Mike Dier 01753 642886'.

Other information

See the Stoke Poges Parish Council website for more information.

Wycombe

The Stokenchurch Education Charity

£38,000

Correspondent: Martin Sheehy, Administrator, Fish Partnership LLP, The Mill House, Boundary Road, Loudwater, High Wycombe HP10 9QN (01628 527956; email: martins@fishpartnership.co.uk)

CC number: 297846

Eligibility

People under the age of 25 who live in the parish of Stokenchurch.

Types of grants

Grants normally range from £5 to £500 and are available for educational expenses and training, including awards for clothing, tools, books, equipment/instruments and study of music and other arts. Schoolchildren, further/higher education students and people entering a trade/starting work or undertaking apprenticeships can be supported.

Annual grant total

In 2013/14 the charity had assets of £2 million and an income of £148,000. Expenditure totalled £45,500 and grants to individuals for educational purposes totalled £38,000.

Exclusions

Grants are not normally made for private tuition and where statutory grants are available. Applications from outside the parish cannot be considered.

Applications

Application forms can be requested from the correspondent. Ordinarily the trustees place an advertisement in the local press and two public places in Stokenchurch in August to invite applications. They should be returned by 30 November each year. Grants are paid in or around April. Applications from outside the parish cannot be considered and are not responded to.

East Sussex

Catherine Martin Trust

£12,000

Correspondent: Trust Administrator, Catherine Martin Trust, The Parish Office, Hove Vicarage, Wilbury Road, Hove, East Sussex BN3 3PB (email: audrey.good14@hotmail.co.uk)

CC number: 258346

Eligibility

Children and young people under the age of 21 who are in full-time education, British born and have lived in the old borough of Hove and Portslade for at least one year. Support is intended to help individuals whose parents cannot work due to ill health or are deceased. It is necessary to demonstrate that applicants' next of kin or other people acting as guardians do not have sufficient means to support the child.

Types of grants

Recurrent grants are available to schoolchildren and further/higher education students for educational expenses, including books, equipment/instruments, clothing, fees, travel and maintenance costs.

Annual grant total

In 2014/15 the trust had an income of £14,000 and an expenditure of £13,000. We estimate that the annual total amount of grants awarded to individuals was around £12,000.

Applications

Apply in writing to the correspondent. Applications can be made by the individual directly or through a third party, such as a relative, solicitor, school/college or educational welfare agency, social/health worker, if applicable. Applications are usually considered in March, June, August, September and December.

The Mrs A. Lacy Tate Trust

£9,700

Correspondent: The Trustees, Heringtons Solicitors, 39 Gildredge Road, Eastbourne, East Sussex BN21 4RY (01323 411020)

CC number: 803596

Eligibility

Schoolchildren who are in need and live in East Sussex.

Types of grants

One-off and recurrent grants are given according to need.

Annual grant total

In 2013/14 the trust had assets of £688,500 and an income of £56,000. Grants were made to 76 individuals totalling £19,500. We estimate that the amount of grants given to individuals for educational purposes totalled around £9,700.

Applications

Applications can be made in writing to the correspondent.

Other information

Grants are also made to individuals in need for relief-in-need purposes and to organisations.

City of Brighton and Hove

The Brighton Educational Trust

£2,800

Correspondent: Mary Grealish, Brighton and Hove City Council, Central Accounting, Room 201, Kings House, Grand Avenue, Hove, East Sussex BN3 2SR (01273 291259; email: accountancy@brighton-hove.gov.uk)

CC number: 306963

Eligibility

People under the age of 25 who have lived in Brighton and Hove for at least two years.

Types of grants

Small, one-off grants, usually between £10 and £250. The trust provides scholarships, maintenance allowances, assists with living expenses and gives support towards the cost of books, clothing, equipment/instruments, tools, educational outings and visits or travel costs in the UK and abroad in pursuance of education. Facilities for recreation, social and physical training for primary, secondary and further education students are provided, where these are not normally paid for by the local authorities. Financial assistance is also available to people starting work/entering a trade and students of music and arts.

Annual grant total

In 2014/15 the trust had an income of £4,800 and an expenditure of £3,200. We estimate the annual total amount of grants awarded to be about £2,800.

Exclusions

No grants are available for postgraduate students.

Applications

Application forms can be requested from the correspondent. The trustees meet twice a year, in April and October. Applications should normally be received by the end of March and September respectively. Our research indicates that applicants should also provide a letter of support from the place of study.

The Brighton Fund

£12,300

Correspondent: The Secretary, Brighton and Hove City Council, Democratic Services, Room 121, Kings House, Hove, East Sussex BN3 2LS (01273 291067 or 01273 291077; email: brightonfund@ brighton-hove.gov.uk; website: www. brighton-hove.gov.uk)

CC number: 1011724

Eligibility

People in need who live in Brighton and Hove administrative boundary. The fund primarily exists for the relief of need, hardship or distress. Applications from individuals applying on their own behalf are not accepted.

Types of grants

Small, one-off cash grants are given for special educational needs of children. Our research suggests that expenditure like nursery childcare costs, excursions and school uniforms can also be funded.

Annual grant total

In 2013/14 the fund had assets of almost £1.3 million and a loss of £47,000. Grants were paid totalling £53,500 – a total of £19,500 to residents over the age of 60, around £24,500 to residents under the age of 60, and £9,300 to residents outside the Brighton area but within the Brighton and Hove city area. Awards are made to individuals for both educational and social welfare purposes. We estimate grants made for educational purposes to be around £12,300.

Exclusions

Only in exceptional circumstances support can be made to someone who is resident outside the Brighton area, or who is only temporarily resident within there.

Applications

Application forms are available from the correspondent or the fund's website and must be submitted either through a third party, such as a social worker, minister or teacher. Applications are considered upon receipt. It usually takes around two to three weeks to receive a decision (unless additional information from the applicant is required).

Other information

The fund also supports older people towards welfare needs. The annual report specifies that 'the trustees after meeting the administration costs of the charity apply the remaining income 70% to residents over 60 and 30% to residents under 60'.

The Oliver and Johannah Brown Apprenticeship Fund

£10,000

Correspondent: Mary Grealish, Administrator, Brighton and Hove City Council, Central Accounting, Room 201 Kings House, Grand Avenue, Hove, East Sussex BN3 2LS (01273 291259; email: accountancy@brighton-hove.gov.uk)

CC number: 306335

Eligibility

People under the age of 25 who have lived in Brighton and Hove for at least five years and are in training for a profession, trade, occupation, service or are undertaking an apprenticeship.

Types of grants

One-off grants of about £10 to £600 are given to help with the cost of fees, outfits/uniforms, travel costs, maintenance expenses, equipment/ instruments, books or other educational needs.

Annual grant total

In 2013/14 the fund had an income of £12,500 and an expenditure of £10,500. We estimate the annual total amount of grants awarded to individuals to be around £10,000.

Exclusions

According to our research, overseas students studying in Britain cannot be supported.

Applications

Apply in writing to the correspondent. Applications can be submitted by the individual directly and are normally considered in September and April. A letter of support from the place of study/ apprenticeship should also be provided.

Miss Laura Soames Charity for Education of Girls (Soames Girls Educational Trust)

£3,700

Correspondent: Mary Grealish, Correspondent, Brighton and Hove City Council, Central Accounting, Room 201, Kings House, Grand Avenue, Hove, East Sussex BN3 2LS (01273 291259; email: accountancy@brighton-hove.gov.uk)

CC number: 306962

Eligibility

Girls and young women under the age of 25 who live in Brighton and Hove.

Types of grants

One-off grants in the range of £250–£500 are available towards general educational costs, including maintenance expenses, course fees, travel, books, equipment/ instruments, materials and clothing. School pupils and university/college students can be assisted.

Annual grant total

In 2013/14 the charity had an income of £7,000 and an expenditure of £3,900. We estimate the annual total amount of grants awarded to individuals to be about £3,700.

Applications

Applications may be made in writing to the correspondent. Our research suggests that applications are considered twice a year, usually in April and September.

Hastings

The Isabel Blackman Foundation

£42,000

Correspondent: Foundation Administrator, Stonehenge, 13 Laton Road, Hastings, East Sussex TN34 2ES (01424 431756; email: ibfoundation@ uwclub.net)

CC number: 313577

Eligibility

People in education who live in Hastings and St Leonards district and require financial assistance.

Types of grants

Scholarships are available to schoolchildren for educational outings and further/higher education students (including mature students and postgraduates) for books, equipment/ instruments, fees, maintenance/living expenses or childcare costs.

Annual grant total

In 2013/14 the foundation had assets of £5.3 million, an income of £290,000 and a total charitable expenditure of £214,500. A total of £42,000 was awarded in educational grants.

Applications

Apply in writing to the correspondent. Applications can be made directly by individuals.

Other information

The foundation also gives grants for education, health, culture, religion, environment, youth or welfare causes. It mainly supports organisations.

The Magdalen and Lasher Educational Foundation

£45,500

Correspondent: Gill Adamson, Administrator, 132 High Street, Hastings, East Sussex TN34 3ET (01424 452646; email: mlc@oldhastingshouse.co.uk; website: www.magdalenandlasher.co.uk)

CC number: 306969

Eligibility

People under 25 who live in the borough of Hastings or who have attended schools in the borough for more than two years.

Types of grants

Scholarships, bursaries or maintenance allowances at higher education institutions for any profession, trade or calling; scholarships and maintenance allowances for education abroad; financial assistance to study music or other arts.

Annual grant total

In 2013/14 the foundation had assets of £4.3 million and an income of £260,000. Bursaries totalling £29,000 and grants to individuals totalling £16,500 were made.

Applications

Application forms are available from the correspondent. The trustees meet every three months.

Other information

The foundation also supports state schools in Hastings.

Essex

Chelmsford Educational Foundation (CEF)

£8,500

Correspondent: Richard Emsden, Administrator, 19 Rushleydale, Chelmsford CM1 6JX (07941 958652; email: remsden@gmail.com)

CC number: 310815

Eligibility

People who live or have been educated in the borough and former rural district of Chelmsford.

Types of grants

Grants are given to people in education and training towards general needs, such as books, fees, tools, equipment, instruments, also travel/study abroad,

study of music, and for any other activities that will help the applicant to achieve employment or qualifications. Awards usually are of up to £500.

Annual grant total

In 2014 the foundation had an income of £18,500 and an expenditure of £17,500. We estimate that the amount of grants given to individuals totalled around £8,500.

Exclusions

Grants are not normally given for school fees.

Applications

Apply in writing to the correspondent. Our research suggests that candidates are interviewed.

Other information

Grants are also available to organisations and schools.

George Courtauld Educational Trust

£2,000

Correspondent: Bryony Wilmshurst, Administrator, c/o Cunningtons, Great Square, Braintree, Essex CM7 1UD (01376 326868)

CC number: 310835

Eligibility

People under the age of 21 who live in, or have parents who live in, the parishes of Braintree, Bocking, Black Notley, Great Notley, Rayne and Cressing. Also eligible are those under the age of 21 who have at any time attended a school in the parishes.

Types of grants

One-off grants of up to £250 are given to schoolchildren and further and higher education students for uniforms/other school clothing, books and equipment/instruments. Grants given include those in the areas of music and other arts and individuals preparing to enter a profession or trade after leaving school or higher education.

Annual grant total

In 2014 the trust had an income of £1,700 and a total expenditure of £2,100. We estimate that grants totalled £2,000.

Applications

Application forms are available from the correspondent. Applications can be submitted at any time, directly by the individual, including an independent letter of support and a written quotation.

Earls Colne and Halstead Educational Charity

£13,000 (50 grants)

Correspondent: Martyn Woodward, Clerk to the Trustees, St Andrew's House, 2 Mallows Field, Halstead, Essex CO9 2LN (01787 479960; email: earlscolnehalstead.edcharity@yahoo.co.uk; website: www.echec.org.uk)

CC number: 310859

Eligibility

Children and young people between the ages of 5 and 25 who have lived for at least one year or attended school in the charity's catchment area in North Essex.

The following parishes are eligible: Alphamstone, Ashen, Belchamp Otten, Belchamp St Paul, Belchamp Walter, Birdbrook, Borley, Bulmer, Bures Hamlet, Castle Hedingham, Coggeshall, Colne Engaine, Earls Colne, Foxearth, Gestingthorpe, Gosfield, Great Henny, Great Maplestead, Great Yeldham, Greenstead Green and Halstead Rural, Helions Bumpstead, Lamarsh, Liston, Little Henny, Little Maplestead, Little Yeldham, Middleton, Ovington, Pebmarsh, Pentlow, Ridgewell, Sible Hedingham, Stambourne, Steeple Bumpstead, Stisted, Sturmer, Tilbury Juxta Clare, Toppesfield, Twinstead, White Colne and Wickham St Paul, the town of Halstead (all in the District of Braintree); and Chappel, Mount Bures and Wakes Colne (all in the district of Colchester).

Types of grants

The charity offers Book Grants for books, equipment/instruments, tools, outfits usually to further/higher education students; and Projects Grants for various educational projects and educational outings to schoolchildren. Priority is given to people studying for a recognised higher education qualification or who are already performing to a high level in the arts or sports.

Annual grant total

In 2013/14 the charity had assets of £1.2 million and an income of £51,500. A total of £13,000 was distributed in grants to 50 individuals.

Exclusions

Tuition fees are not normally supported.

Applications

Application forms can be found online or requested from the correspondent. Applications for Book Grants may be made at any time. Book Grants may cover the costs of further education, including: books, specialist clothing, tools or equipment but usually excluding costs of tuition. All Project Grant applications are considered at meetings of the board of trustees. The trustees normally meet to consider grant applications during February, July and November. The cut-off date for Project Grant applications to be considered at meetings of the trustees is three weeks prior to the date of the meeting. After this, all applications will be closed. See the charity's website for details.

Other information

The charity also gives grants to local schools for educational travel or other purposes and supports voluntary bodies working for the benefit of young people in the charity's beneficial area. A total of £47,500 was awarded to organisations in 2013/14.

Essex Community Foundation

£17,000

Correspondent: Essex Community Foundation, 121 New London Road, Chelmsford CM2 0QT (01245 355947; email: general@essexcf.org.uk; website: www.essexcommunityfoundation.org.uk)

CC number: 1052061

Eligibility

Individuals who can demonstrate a strong current link to Essex either through residence or study. Individual applicants must be able to demonstrate how learning or training would enable them to take the next step in their personal/professional development or career path. In addition you should also clearly state your financial position and need.

Types of grants

Through the Essex Education Fund the foundation provides support for individuals of any age and at any stage in their professional development, further or higher education. Typically the Essex Education Fund has around £18,000 to distribute each year. Grants are likely to be around £1,500; if your request is in excess of this contact the grants team to discuss your needs.

Current funds available for individuals:

Essex Education Fund

To support educational opportunities for people who could not otherwise realise their full potential and whose permanent place of residence falls within the administrative county of Essex. (College and university fees will not be considered).

Annabel and Gerald Malton Charitable Fund

Young people who could not otherwise realise their full potential in musical (or other performing arts) or sporting activities and whose permanent place of residence falls within administrative Essex, Southend or Thurrock.

Belinda Starling Memorial Fund

Young people with an identified talent pursuing a career in the arts and whose literary, drama or music ambitions and talents cannot take root without help and encouragement and whose permanent place of residence fall within administrative Essex, Southend or Thurrock.

Essex and Southend Sports Charitable Fund

To support sporting activities for individuals in Essex, Southend and Thurrock who could not otherwise realise their full potential.

Little Braxted Community and Educational Fund

To support educational opportunities for those under the age of 25 who live within the parish of Little Braxted or Wickham Bishops.

Annual grant total

In 2014 the foundation had assets of nearly £29.2 million, an income of £4.1 million and a charitable expenditure of £2.3 million. Grants awarded from the Essex Education Fund totalled £17,200.

Applications

Application forms are available from the website. They are accepted throughout the year, there are no deadlines. Decisions are made by the Essex Education Fund quarterly – normally in March, June, September and December each year; decisions will be given shortly thereafter. The application guidelines note: 'Include a reference from someone who knows you and can support your request e.g. Teacher/Coach. Your referee cannot be a family member, relative or close friend. Include their telephone number and ask permission for us to contact them if necessary which must be during office hours (9am to 5.30pm). For teachers ensure we can reach them during school holidays.' Contact the grants team, on 01245 356018 before you begin an application.

Other information

Grants in the main are awarded to organisations (299 organisations received grants in 2014).

The following is taken from the 2014 accounts: 'A total of 496 grant payments were made to 299 voluntary organisations and 31 individuals during the period under review. The net amount of grants awarded during the year ended 30 June 2014 totalled over £2 million and the grants distributed totalled £1.8 million.'

Great Bursthead Exhibition Foundation (Billericay Educational Trust)

£14,000

Correspondent: Jennifer Moore, Clerk to the Trustees, The Billericay School, School Road, Billericay, Essex CM12 9LH (01277 655191; email: info@ billericayeducationaltrust.co.uk; website: www.billericayeducationaltrust.co.uk)

CC number: 310836

Eligibility

Young people under the age of 25 who live within a six-mile radius of Billericay (including Noak Bridge, Ramsden Bellhouse, Ramsden Heath and Stock) and are in need.

Types of grants

One-off or recurring grants may be given for up to three years to further/higher education students and people in vocational training or those starting work. Help is given towards general educational necessities, including clothing, tools, instruments and equipment, books, also tuition fees, travel for educational purposes in the UK or abroad, study of music or other arts, recreational activities or physical training.

Annual grant total

In 2013/14 the foundation had an income of £18,500 and an expenditure of £14,500. We estimate that around £14,000 was given in grants to individuals.

Applications

Application forms can be downloaded from the foundation's website and should be submitted by June for consideration in July. Applicants are invited to an informal meeting.

Other information

Previously grants have also been given to schools to help with specific educational projects.

Ann Johnson's Educational Foundation

£19,000 (20 grants)

Correspondent: Jonathan Douglas-Hughes, Clerk, 58 New London Road, Chelmsford, Essex CM2 0PA (01245 493939; fax: 01245 493940; email: douglas-hughesj@gepp.co.uk)

CC number: 310799

Eligibility

People living or educated in Chelmsford and the surrounding parishes, who are under 25.

Types of grants

Help with the cost of books, clothing and other essentials for schoolchildren, including school fees. Grants are also available for those at college or university and towards the cost of books, equipment and instruments, clothing and travel for people starting work.

Annual grant total

In 2013/14 the foundation had assets of £20,500 and an income of £29,500. Grants were awarded to 20 individuals totalling £19,000.

Applications

Application forms are available from: Ravenscroft, Stock Road, Galleywood, Chelmsford, Essex CM2 8PW (01245 260757). The governors meet quarterly to consider applications.

Other information

The foundation also gives funding to local schools.

Braintree

Sir Robert Hitcham's Exhibition Foundation

£6,000

Correspondent: Nicholas Johnson, Trustee, 75 Queen Street, Coggeshall, Colchester CO6 1UE (01376 562915; email: nicjo@btinternet.com)

CC number: 1095014

Eligibility

People under the age of 25 who live in Coggeshall and have left school and are moving on to higher education or training.

Types of grants

Small grants are given towards books, equipment/instruments, clothing/uniforms/outfits, tools and living costs to students and people starting work/entering a trade.

Annual grant total

In 2013/14 the foundation had an income of £6,000 and a total expenditure of £6,500. We have estimated the annual total amount of grants awarded to individuals to be around £6,000.

Applications

Application forms can be requested from the correspondent. Our research suggests that applications are normally considered in early September and should be submitted by the end of August.

Brentwood

The Canon Holmes Memorial Trust

£15,000

Correspondent: John Brown, Trustee, 556 Galleywood Road, Chelmsford CM2 8BX (01245 358185; email: canonjbrown@mac.com)

CC number: 801964

Eligibility

Children between the ages of 7 and 13 who live or have recently lived in the Roman Catholic Diocese of Brentwood and cannot continue their education because their parents/guardians are experiencing financial difficulties as a result of employment problems, marital breakdown, illness or death.

Types of grants

Short-term scholarships and bursaries to continue school education in the moment of crisis. Grants can be given for private school fees.

Annual grant total

In 2014 the trust had an income of £12,000 and a total expenditure of £15,500. We estimate the annual total amount of grants awarded to individuals to be around £15,000.

Applications

Apply in writing to the correspondent. Applications should be made by a parent or guardian and grants will be made directly to the school.

City of Chelmsford

The Butler Educational Foundation

£6,000

Correspondent: Nicholas Welch, Administrator, Duffield Stunt, 71 Duke Street, Chelmsford, Essex CM1 1JU (01245 262351)

CC number: 310731

Eligibility

Children and young people living in the parishes of Boreham and Little Baddow who have attended a public elementary school in the area for at least two years.

Types of grants

Grants are available for general educational expenses, including clothing/uniforms, books, tools, equipment/instruments, maintenance costs, educational visits, fees, equipment for special projects and so on. Financial assistance is available to secondary school pupils, further/higher education students, people entering a trade/starting work or individuals undertaking apprenticeships.

Annual grant total

In 2013/14 the foundation had both an income and an expenditure of £8,500. We estimate the annual total amount of grants awarded to individuals to be around £6,000.

Exclusions

Primary school pupils are not supported.

Applications

Apply in writing the correspondent. The trustees meet three times a year, usually in January, April and October. Our research suggests that normally one of the trustees will visit the applicant.

Other information

The foundation may also assist school libraries in the provision of books and fittings.

Epping Forest

Joseph King's Charity

£35,000 (55 grants)

Correspondent: Catherine Kenny, Secretary, 36 Coopers Hill, Ongar, Essex CM5 9EF (01277 366167)

CC number: 810177

Eligibility

People under 25 years of age who live in the civil parish of Chipping Ongar.

Types of grants

Help with the cost of books, clothing and other essentials for schoolchildren. Help may also be available for students at college or university. Preference is given to the advancement of the Christian religion.

Annual grant total

In 2014 the charity had assets of £1.8 million and an income of £70,500. Educational grants to 55 students totalled £35,000. A further £200 was given towards Sunday special and school club expenses carried out under the auspices of St Martin's Church in Chipping Ongar.

Applications

Apply in writing to the correspondent.

Other information

The trustees' annual report for 2014 states:

> The Charity's aims are to promote the education of persons resident in the Parish of Ongar under the age of 25 years in awarding grants whilst attending schools, colleges, universities other institutions of further education or other educationally beneficial activities. Also to make grants to schools within the Parish of Ongar for benefits of a kind not normally provided by the local authority.

Hampshire

Aldworth's Educational Trust (Aldworth Trust Foundation)

Correspondent: Debbie Reavell, Clerk to the Trustees, 25 Cromwell Road, Basingstoke RG21 5NR (01256 473390; email: reavell@btinternet.com)

CC number: 307259

Eligibility

Children and young people who are either resident or were educated/are attending school in the borough of Basingstoke and Deane.

Types of grants

Grants can be awarded for travel, books, equipment and clothing. As the charity has informed us, most of their grants go to 'school children whose parents cannot afford the costs of residential visits which primary schools make'.

Annual grant total

In 2014/15 the trust had an unusually high income of £26,000 (in the past few years the income has totalled around £2,500 on average) and an expenditure of £1,900. No grants were awarded to individuals during the year, although grants totalling £1,900 were awarded to four schools.

Applications

Apply in writing to the correspondent.

The Ashford Hill Educational Trust

£7,000

Correspondent: Graham Swait, Administrator, Oakview, Yeomans Lane, Newtown, Newbury RG20 9BL (01635 276098)

CC number: 1040559

Eligibility

People who live in the parish of Ashford Hill with Headley or the surrounding area.

Types of grants

Grants are generally given to promote social and physical education. They are given towards the cost of formal education, enhancement of employment prospects, group activities, music, adult education and sporting and recreational activities.

Annual grant total

In 2013 the trust had an income of £7,000 and a total expenditure of £7,200 we estimate that grants awarded totalled around £7,000.

These were the latest accounts available at the time of writing (October 2015).

Applications

Application forms are available from the correspondent. Applications are considered in January, March, July and October.

Bramshott Educational Trust

£2,500

Correspondent: Richard Weighell, Trustee, 107 Haslemere Road, Liphook GU30 7BU (01428 724289; email: info@ bramshotteducationaltrust.org.uk or clerk.bramshott.trust@hotmail.co.uk; website: www.bramshotteducationaltrust. org.uk)

CC number: 277421

Eligibility

Children and young people under the age of 25 who live, or have a parent/ guardian who lives, in the ancient parish of Bramshott, which includes Liphook, Bramshott, Passfield, Conford and the parts of Hammer Vale located in Hampshire.

Types of grants

Grants of up to £250 are awarded for general educational needs which in the past have included equipment/ instruments, tools, school uniforms/ clothing, books, educational trips/visits, specialist courses and tuition, attendance at educational events, also extra-curricular activities, such as music or ballet lessons.

Annual grant total

In 2013/14 the trust had an income of £7,800 and an expenditure of £5,100. The trustees have a discretion to allocate funds to support local schools; therefore, we estimate the annual total amount of grants awarded to individuals to be around £2,500.

Exclusions

The trust's eligibility guidelines remind that 'in order to support as many applicants as possible, the trustees do not fund the whole amount required and do not award grants for expenditure which would reasonably be provided by the local authority'.

The trustees will not consider late, incomplete or retrospective applications.

Applications

Application forms can be found on the trust's website or requested from the correspondent. The deadlines for submission are 15 March for consideration in April and 15 September for consideration in October.

Other information

Up to one third of the yearly income can be allocated to help local schools.

Dibden Allotments Fund

£700 (2 grants)

Correspondent: Valerie Stewart, Clerk to the Trustees, 7 Drummond Court, Prospect Place, Hythe, Southampton SO45 6HD (023 8084 1305; email: dibdenallotments@btconnect.com; website: daf-hythe.org.uk)

CC number: 255778

Eligibility

People in need who live in the parishes of Hythe, Dibden, Marshwood and Fawley in Hampshire. Individuals should have lived in the Waterside area for at least 12 months.

Types of grants

One-off and recurrent grants are given according to need. In previous years, grants have been awarded for school uniforms, other school clothing, books, equipment, fees and living expenses for students in further and higher education, educational outings for schoolchildren and childcare for mature students.

Annual grant total

In 2013/14 the fund had assets of £9.5 million and an income of £391,500. During the year, two grants were made to individuals for educational purposes, totalling £700.

Applications

Application forms are available on the fund's website, where the fund's criteria, guidelines and application process are also posted. It is helpful to supply a supporting statement from a professional such as a health or social worker, midwife or teacher.

Other information

Grants are also made to individuals for social welfare purposes and to charitable and voluntary organisations.

Basingstoke and Dean

The Cliddesden and Farleigh Wallop Educational Trust

£9,500

Correspondent: Alison Mosson, Administrator, 11 Southlea, Cliddesden, Basingstoke RG25 2JN

CC number: 307150

Eligibility

People under 25 who are in need of financial assistance and live within the original boundaries of the parishes of Cliddesden and Farleigh Wallop only.

Types of grants

One-off and recurrent grants. Education is considered in its broadest sense, from help with school projects and trips to college/university courses to music lessons.

Annual grant total

In 2014 the trust had an income of £15,500 and a total expenditure of £19,000. We estimate that educational grants to individuals totalled £9,500, with funding also awarded to organisations.

Applications

Apply in writing to the correspondent. Applications should be submitted through a school or directly by the individual or their guardian to reach the secretary by the end of April, August or December, accompanied by fully documented receipts.

The Robert Higham Apprenticing Charity

£6,000

Correspondent: Roy Forth, Administrator, PO Box 7721, Kingsclere RG20 5WQ (07796 423108; email: kclerecharities@aol.co.uk)

CC number: 307083

Eligibility

People aged between 16 and 25 attending sixth forms, colleges and universities who live in the parishes of Kingsclere, Ashford Hill and Headley.

Types of grants

Grants towards books, specialist equipment and clothing or travelling expenses for those preparing for or engaged in any profession, trade, occupation, service or towards books, study or travel abroad for those studying for A-levels. Grants can be one-off or recurrent and are given according to need.

Annual grant total

In 2014 the charity had an annual income of nearly £7,000 and a total charitable expenditure of £6,000 we estimate that grants made totalled around £6,000.

Applications

Application forms are available from the correspondent. Applications must include a letter outlining the applicant's further education plans. Applications are not accepted from parents.

Fareham

The William Price Charitable Trust

£15,500 (46 grants)

Correspondent: Christopher Thomas, Administrator, 24 Cuckoo Lane, Fareham, Hampshire PO14 3PF (01329 663685; email: mazchris@tiscali.co.uk; website: www.pricestrust.org.uk)

CC number: 307319

Eligibility

Children and young people under the age of 25 who live in the parishes of St Peter and St Paul, Holy Trinity with St Columba and St John the Evangelist (the same area as the original Fareham town parish but not the whole area of the Fareham borough).

Types of grants

The trustees' annual report for 2014/15 states:

> The trustees place their emphasis on assisting and supporting both individuals and educational establishments in the study of those subjects and the pursuit of those activities which in the opinion of the trustees do not command adequate priority in education. The types of projects that are given priority are those that enrich the quality of life and widen horizons, encourage participation and appreciation of the arts, develop good citizenship and encourage help in the community and local environment.

Support can equally be given towards fees, travel costs, outfits/clothing, books or other necessities. In accordance with the provisions of the trust the trustees also seek to promote education in the doctrines of the Church of England. Major grants for educational benefits are normally in the range of £1,000 plus, while the minor hardship grants for urgent needs are of about £100.

Annual grant total

In 2014/15 the trust had assets of £7.2 million, an income of £197,500 and a total charitable expenditure of £137,500. The amount of grants given to individuals totalled £15,500. A total of £12,000 was awarded in hardship grants to 43 people and £3,500 was also awarded to three students in bursaries and grants for college/university fees.

Applications

Where possible applications should be made through a school/college; however, individual applications will be considered, particularly from people in further/higher education. Application forms can be downloaded from the trust's website or requested from the correspondent. Bursaries and college/university grants are considered twice a year, normally in March and September, and applications should be received by the first day of these months. Applications for smaller hardship grants can be made at any time and will be paid through a school/college.

Other information

Grants are also made to churches and schools/colleges (£111,000 in 2014/15) and there is an annual grant to the Fareham Welfare Trust (£11,000).

The Earl of Southampton Trust

£500

Correspondent: Sue Boden, Clerk, 24 The Square, Titchfield PO14 4RU (01329 513294; email: earlstrust@yahoo.co.uk; website: eost.org.uk)

CC number: 238549

Eligibility

People in need who live in the ancient parish of Titchfield (now subdivided into the parishes of Titchfield, Sarisbury, Locks Heath, Warsash, Stubbington and Lee-on-the-Solent).

Types of grants

One-off grants, usually ranging from £25 and £1,000, are given to schoolchildren, college students, mature students and to people with special educational need towards tuition fees, uniforms and books.

Annual grant total

In 2013/14 the trust had assets of £1.65 million and an income of £99,500. Grants amounted to £15,300 and were given for a wide range of purposes. We estimate educational grants (for uniforms and child holiday care) to have totalled around £500, and social welfare grants around £12,300. A further £2,500 was awarded to organisations.

Exclusions

Grants are not given for study or travel abroad, student exchange, tertiary and postgraduate education. The trust will not supply items or services which should be provided for by the state.

Applications

Application forms can be downloaded from the trust's website and must be submitted through a recognised agency (social services, a health visitor, etc.). Applications must include details of medical/financial status and are usually means-tested. They are normally considered on the last Tuesday of every month, although in the event of extreme urgency requests can be fast tracked between meetings.

Other information

The trust runs almshouses and a day centre for old people.

Gosport

Thorngate Relief-in-Need and General Charity

£3,200

Correspondent: Kay Brent, 16 Peakfield, Waterlooville PO7 6YP (023 9226 4400; email: kay.brent@btinternet.com)

CC number: 210946

Eligibility

People in need who live in Gosport.

Types of grants

One off grants usually of between £100 and £500.

Annual grant total

In 2013/14 the charity had an income of £11,200 and a total expenditure of £12,900. Grants are made to individuals and organisations for a wide range of purposes. We estimate that educational grants to individuals totalled £3,200.

Exclusions

No grants are made towards legal expenses.

Applications

Application forms are available from the correspondent. Applications can be made either directly by the individual or through a social worker, Citizens Advice, Probation Service or other welfare agency.

Portsmouth

The Bentley Young Person's Trust

£1,000

Correspondent: John Turner, Trustee, 23 Blackmore Avenue, College Park, Bideford, Devon EX39 3TG (01237 479366; email: john@fundaid.net)

CC number: 1069727

Eligibility

People under the age of 26 who live in Portsmouth and surrounding areas or who have a connection with the area.

Types of grants

Grants to help develop the 'physical, mental and spiritual capacities' of young people.

Annual grant total

In 2014/15 the trust had an income of £3,200 and a total expenditure of around £2,200. We estimate that the annual total amount of grants awarded to individuals was about £1,000.

Exclusions

Direct educational fees are not provided.

Applications

Apply in writing to the correspondent.

Other information

Grants are also made to organisations.

Test Valley

Miss Gale's Educational Foundation (The Gale Trust)

£17,000

Correspondent: John Butcher, Trustee, 58 Wolversdene Road, Andover, Hampshire SP10 2BA (01264 355445; email: gales.trust@yahoo.co.uk)

CC number: 307145

Eligibility

Children and young people in need who are under the age of 25, live in or near Andover and are attending/have attended any school in the area. Preference is given to girls and applicants from families with serious difficulties.

Types of grants

The foundation provides small, one-off grants to schoolchildren, higher/further education students and people starting work/entering a profession. Financial assistance is available towards general educational expenses, including the cost of uniforms/clothing, books, equipment/

instruments, tools, educational outings and study/travel abroad.

Annual grant total

In 2014 the foundation had both an income and an expenditure of £17,500. We have estimated that the annual total amount of grants awarded was just under £17,000.

Exclusions

Our research suggests that grants are not normally given towards the cost of school or college fees or living expenses.

Applications

Apply in writing to the correspondent. Applications can be made by individuals directly or through their educational establishment or welfare agency, if applicable. According to our research, it is required to specify the individual's date of birth, give reasons why the family are not able to provide themselves and explain what the grants is required for.

Hertfordshire

Bosbury Educational Foundation

£6,000

Correspondent: Jane Bulson, Willow End, Southfield Lane, Bosbury, Ledbury HR8 1PZ (email: jane_bulson@hotmail.com)

CC number: 527140

Eligibility

Young people leaving school who live in the parish of Bosbury and have done so for at least three years.

Types of grants

Grants of up to £250 towards books are given to young people on leaving school and going on to further education. Students undertaking university courses of three years or longer are invited to apply for a further grant in their final year. Grants may also be given towards school uniform for children in need.

Annual grant total

In 2014 the foundation had an income of £22,000 and an expenditure of £6,300. We estimate that grants totalled about £6,000.

Applications

Apply in writing to the correspondent. Full details of the course should be included. Applications can be submitted directly by the individual and are considered at any time.

Other information

Note: The parish of Bosbury consists of around 500 people. In previous years the foundation has stated that it is being inundated by applications from outside the parish which cannot be considered due to the deeds of the charity, and these applications will not be acknowledged.

Fawbert and Barnard School's Foundation

£5,000

Correspondent: Pamela Rider, Trustee, 22 South Brook, Sawbridgeworth, Hertfordshire CM21 9NS (01279 724670)

CC number: 310965

Eligibility

People between the ages of 16 and 25 who live within a three-mile radius of Great St Mary's Church in Sawbridgeworth or who attend/have attended school in that area for at least three years.

Types of grants

One-off grants and bursaries to assist further/higher education students. Awards are made to help with the cost of books or materials associated with the course. Grants are usually in the range of £100 to £200.

Annual grant total

In 2014 the foundation had an income of £10,000 and an expenditure of £10,500. We estimate the annual total amount of grants awarded to individuals to be around £5,000.

Applications

Application forms can be requested from the correspondent. Applications should normally be submitted by 30 September. They are considered in October.

Other information

As the grant is awarded once only, students who do not apply during their first year can apply at any time during their period of study.

Support can also be given to organisations.

The Harpenden Trust

£11,300 (92 grants)

Correspondent: Dennis Andrews, Secretary, The Harpenden Trust Centre, 90 Southdown Road, Harpenden AL5 1PS (01582 460457; email: admin@theharpendentrust.org.uk; website: www.theharpendentrust.org.uk)

CC number: 1118870

Eligibility

Children in need who live in the AL5 postal district of Harpenden.

Types of grants

One-off grants are given to assist pupils with the cost of essential school trips.

Annual grant total

In 2013/14 the trust had assets of £4 million and had an income £229,000. The amount of grants given to individuals totalled £63,000, of which £11,300 was given in 92 grants to young people for what we consider to be educational purposes. They were distributed as follows:

General grants	559	£33,000
Utilities grants	78	£16,800
Youth grants	92	£11,300
Christmas parcels	140	£1,700

Grants to individuals for social welfare purposes amounted to £51,500 and a further £41,500 was awarded to organisations.

Applications

Applications should be made in writing to the correspondent, either directly by the individual or, if applicable, through a third party such as a social worker or Citizens Advice. The trust can be contacted by telephone or email, by completing the online contact form, or by dropping into the Trust Centre (between 10am and noon, Monday to Friday).

Other information

The Harpenden Trust was founded in 1948 by Dr Charles Hill. Amongst its activities in the Harpenden community – and with the help of more than 300 volunteers – the trust hosts coffee mornings for older people (Tuesdays at the Trust Centre, 90 Southdown Road and Thursdays at High Street Methodist Church Hall, Lower High Street; both 10am-11am), organises outings for older people and children, and operates a home visiting service to assist families financially and otherwise. Each year, the trust produces and sells its own calendar, of which it donates 50 units each to around 12 local charities to sell for their own funds.

Hertfordshire County Nursing Trust (Hertfordshire Nursing Trust)

£11,000

Correspondent: Nicholas Tufton, Trustee, 11 Highway Street, Barkway, Royston, Hertfordshire SG8 8EA (01763 848888; email: nicholas@ntufton.co.uk; website: www.hertsnursing.co.uk)

CC number: 207213

Eligibility

Nurses who have worked within the community of Hertfordshire for at least 18 months. As defined by the Queen's Nursing Institute, the 'community' means 'working outside a hospital setting'

Types of grants

Financial assistance is available to both individual nurses and groups for various activities, projects and full/part-time courses which contribute to applicant's professional development. It is reminded that any available funding from NHS sources must be exhausted prior to application. Recently grants have been awarded for the following activities/projects/courses: counselling, palliative care, cancer care, mental health, childcare, learning disabilities, asthma tissue viability, systemic psychotherapy, pain management, gerontology nurse prescribing and general nursing degree.

Annual grant total

In 2014/15 the trust had assets of £863,500 an income of £62,500 and a total charitable expenditure of £50,000. Educational grants to individuals totalled £11,000.

Exclusions

Grants are not made retrospectively and cannot be provided for subsistence expenses for conferences or academic courses, such as travel, hotel, food costs and so on.

Applications

Application forms can be found on the trust's website. A completed application form should be accompanied with full details and costs of the course or conference attended. The trustees require the application to be signed by the applicant's manager to confirm his/her support and agreement with the project.

Applications should demonstrate the benefit of the funding to the applicants and their care abilities. In the case of applications for equipment, the application should demonstrate how it benefits the patients/families/carers.

The trust's website also notes that:

> Applications should be for one activity or project ... consideration will not be given to several different courses or conferences in one year. In the case of academic courses, funding must be sought for each academic year and in certain instances for each academic module.

Other information

The trust owns Rosemary House, which comprises ten flats. The flats are let at a rent well below the market levels to nurses who are working or have worked in the community of Hertfordshire. Other welfare support is available to working and retired nurses.

Grants are also made to the Queen's Nursing Institute.

The Hertfordshire Educational Foundation

£10,000

Correspondent: Darren Tyler, Administrator, c/o Finance Accountancy Group, 3rd Floor, North West Block, County Hall, Hertford, Herts SG13 8DN (01992 555157; email: darren.tyler@hertfordshire.gov.uk)

CC number: 311025

Eligibility

Pupils and students up to 21 years who have a home address in Hertfordshire.

Types of grants

The foundation administers three types of grant scheme:

1   Travel scholarships to individuals aged 17 to 21 to undertake approved courses of study, expeditions, voluntary work and other projects in overseas countries. The usual duration is for a minimum of one month and individuals should be able to demonstrate how their project will benefit the local community they are visiting. Scholarships range between £100 and £500

2   Support to primary school pupils taking part in educational visits arranged by their school whose parents, due to exceptional circumstances other than financial, are unable to pay for all or part of the board and lodging element of the visit

3   The Sir George Burns Fund grants to enable young people who have disabilities or are underprivileged aged 16 to 21 to participate in expeditions, educational visits and so on, or to purchase special items of equipment needed for them to become involved in recreational and educational activities. Grants are usually in the range of £50 to £500 and previous awards have covered the costs of laptops and computer software, travel expenses, courses and conferences

Annual grant total

In 2014 the foundation had an income of £20,500 and an expenditure of £26,500. Educational grants to individuals total around £10,000 each year.

Applications

Application forms are available from the correspondent. Applications should be submitted at least a month before the individual travels. The deadlines for travel scholarships and Sir George Burns Fund applications are normally in February, May and October. Guidelines and application forms are available from the foundation's website.

Other information

The foundation has also provided grants to organisations.

Broxbourne

Robert Dewhurst's School Foundation

£5,000

Correspondent: Jill Hempleman, 215 Northbrooks, Harlow, Essex CM19 4DH (01279 425251; email: jillhempleman@yahoo.co.uk)

CC number: 310972

Eligibility

Children and young people under the age of 25 who live within the ancient parish of Cheshunt. Preference is given to people who have attended Dewhurst St Mary's Church of England Primary School for at least two years.

Types of grants

One-off grants to secondary schoolchildren, further/higher education students and people starting work to help with general educational costs, including books, equipment/instruments, tools, materials, clothing, travel, fees and educational outings in the UK.

Annual grant total

In 2014/15 the foundation had an income of £13,500 and an expenditure of £11,500. We estimate that the total amount of grants awarded to individuals was about £5,000.

Applications

Apply in writing to the correspondent. Applications can be submitted directly by the individual or through a school/welfare agency, if applicable.

Other information

The foundation also provides support to Dewhurst St Mary's Church of England Primary School.

The Wormley Parochial Charity

£1,700

Correspondent: Carol Proctor, Trustee, 5 Lammasmead, Broxbourne, Hertfordshire EN10 6PF

CC number: 218463

Eligibility

Students who are over the age of 18 and live in the parish of Wormley as it was defined before 31 March 1935.

Types of grants

Grants are made to schoolchildren or college students, people undertaking training or apprentices, towards essential clothing, equipment, instruments or books.

Annual grant total

In 2014 the charity had an income of £13,000 and a total expenditure of £6,800. Grants are made to individuals and organisations for a range of purposes. We estimate that educational grants to individuals totalled around £1,700.

Exclusions

The charity does not give loans.

Applications

Applications can be made in writing to the charity, either directly by the individual, or through a social worker, Citizens Advice, welfare agency or a third party such as a friend who is aware of the situation. Applications are considered in April and October.

Dacorum

The Dacorum Community Trust

£15,000

Correspondent: The Grants and Finance Officer, The Hub Dacorum, Paradise, Hemel Hempstead HP2 4TF (01442 231396; email: admin@dctrust.org.uk; website: www.dctrust.org.uk)

CC number: 272759

Eligibility

People in need who live in the borough of Dacorum.

Types of grants

Generally one-off grants of up to £500 to schoolchildren for uniforms/clothing, equipment/instruments and excursions, to college students, undergraduates and people starting work for clothing and equipment/instruments and to vocational students, mature students and those with special educational needs for uniforms/clothing, equipment/instruments and childcare.

Annual grant total

In 2013/14 the trust had assets of £111,500 and received an income of £104,000. There were 721 grants made totalling £60,500. Direct grants totalled £35,000 and gifts in kind were costed at £26,000. We have estimated the educational grants total to be around £15,000.

Exclusions

Grants are not normally given for the costs of further or mainstream education and only in exceptional circumstances for gap year travel.

Applications

Application forms are available from the correspondent or can be downloaded from the website. Applications can be submitted by the individual, through a recognised referral agency (such as social services or Citizens Advice) or through an MP, GP or school. Applications are considered in March, June, September and December. The trust asks for details of family finances. A preliminary telephone call is always welcome.

Other information

The trust also gives to organisations.

East Hertfordshire

Newton Exhibition Foundation

£12,500

Correspondent: Anne Haworth, 117 Ladywood Road, Hertford SG14 2TA (01992 550121; email: clerk@ newtonexhibitionfoundation.co.uk)

CC number: 311021

Eligibility

Young people under the age of 25 who are attending/have attended school in the town of Hertford. Preference is given to members of the Church of England. Our research also suggests that grants may be awarded to otherwise eligible applicants who, because of special learning difficulties or disabilities, are attending/have attended schools outside the town.

Types of grants

According to our research, grants between £20 and £400 can be awarded to schoolchildren and further/higher education students (including postgraduates). Financial support is available for general educational purposes, such as uniforms/clothing, books, equipment/instruments, fees, educational outings in the UK and study or travel overseas.

Annual grant total

In 2013/14 the foundation had an income of around £14,000 and a total expenditure of £13,000. We have estimated the annual total amount of grants awarded to be about £12,500.

Applications

Apply in writing to the correspondent. Our research indicates that the application should include the name(s) of schools attended, full details and costs of the support required, also information about any other grants obtained or applied for. Applications can be

submitted either directly by individuals or through their school, welfare agency/ social worker, if applicable.

The Ware Charities

£8,000

Correspondent: Susan Newman, Correspondent, 3 Scotts Road, Ware, Hertfordshire SG12 9JG (01920 461629; email: suedogs@hotmail.com)

CC number: 225443

Eligibility

Schoolchildren, college students and people starting work who live in the area of Ware Town Council, the parish of Wareside and the parish of Thundridge.

Types of grants

Grants are given to schoolchildren, college students, people with special educational needs, people starting work and overseas students, including those for uniforms/clothing, fees, study/travel abroad, books, equipment/instruments and excursions. Grants are also made to undergraduates and vocational students for uniforms/clothing. Awards are not paid to individuals directly, rather through a third party.

Annual grant total

In 2014/15 the charity had an income of £66,000 and a total expenditure of £41,000. Full accounts were not available to view at the time of writing (September 2015). In the past grants to individuals have totalled about 40% of the overall expenditure on average. We estimate that about £16,500 was paid in grants to individuals and of that sum about £8,000 – for educational purposes. Note that grant-making varies annually. On average about 37 awards are made each year to individuals.

Applications

Applications may be made in writing to the correspondent at any time. They should be submitted directly by the individual or a family member. Applications must include brief details of the applicant's income and savings and be supported and signed by a headteacher, GP, nurse, member of clergy or social worker.

Other information

Grants are also made to local organisations and individuals for general welfare needs.

Hertsmere

The Platt Subsidiary Foundation

£3,800

Correspondent: Alan Taylor, Secretary, 57A Loom Lane, Radlett, Hertfordshire WD7 8NX (01923 855197)

CC number: 272591

Eligibility

People under the age of 25 who live in the parishes of Christ Church – Radlett, St John the Baptist – Aldenham or St Martin's – Shenley, and are in need.

Types of grants

Grants in the range of £200–£800 can be given to people planning expeditions away from home, for example, gap year schemes, volunteering opportunities, adventure trips and so on. Community projects are particularly favoured. Applicants are expected to raise a proportion of money themselves.

Annual grant total

In 2014 the foundation had an income of £8,400 and an expenditure of £7,800. We have estimated that the annual total amount of grants awarded to individuals was around £3,800.

Applications

Application forms can be requested from the correspondent. Deadline for applications is normally by the end of March. Applicants are required to attend an interview in April.

Other information

Grants may also be made to organisations.

North Hertfordshire

Hitchin Education Foundation

£17,000

Correspondent: Brian Frederick, Administrator, 33 Birch Close, Broom, Biggleswade SG18 9NR (01767 313892; email: bfred@rmplc.co.uk)

CC number: 311024

Eligibility

People who live in the former urban district of Hitchin and surrounding villages, aged under 25.

Types of grants

One-off grants are given towards the costs of uniforms, books, scholarships and any other educational facilities.

Grants are means-tested, so the applicant's income and size of family are taken into account.

Annual grant total

In 2013/14 the foundation had assets of £1.3 million and an income of £98,000. £17,000 was distributed in grants to individuals consisting of £3,500 in grants of less than £400 and £13,500 in grants of over £400.

Exclusions

Grants are not available for books, fees, travel, living expenses or mature students.

Applications

Application forms are available from the correspondent, either directly by the individual, or through the individual's school, college, educational welfare agency or any third party. They are considered monthly.

Other information

Grants were also made available to four educational establishments.

The Leete Charity

£4,000

Correspondent: Susan Thornton-Bjork, Royston Town Council, Town Hall, Melbourn Street, Royston, Hertfordshire SG8 7DA (01763 245484; email: enquires@roystontowncouncil.gov.uk; website: www.roystontowncouncil.gov.uk)

CC number: 311084

Eligibility

People under the age of 25 going into further education who are either resident in Royston or attending school there.

Types of grants

Small grants to help with the costs of books, travel expenses, equipment/instruments and other educational necessities.

Annual grant total

In 2014/15 the charity had an income of £2,000 and an expenditure of £4,500. We estimate the annual total amount of grants awarded to be around £4,000.

Exclusions

According to our research, grants are not normally available to people starting work or mature students.

Applications

Application forms are available from the Royston town council offices at the town hall or can be downloaded from the council's website. It is requested to submit all the relevant information about the applicant's financial situation and their general background to speed up the consideration. Estimated costs of the items the funding is requested for would also be helpful.

The Letchworth Civic Trust

£41,500

Correspondent: Sally Jenkins, Secretary, Broadway Chambers, Letchworth Garden City, Hertfordshire SG6 3AD (07785 104357; email: letchworthct@gmail.com; website: letchworthct.org.uk)

CC number: 273336

Eligibility

Schoolchildren and students attending college or university who are in need and have lived in Letchworth Garden City for two years or more.

Types of grants

University students who have lived in Letchworth for at least two years will usually receive a grant of £300 towards the costs of books and learning materials. They may apply for a top-up grant of £100 upon reaching their third year of study.

Schoolchildren whose families have great difficulty supporting a school activity, in particular a residential field visit or camp, which the headteacher believes would benefit the pupil, can receive a grant of up to £60 towards the costs.

Bursaries are occasionally available to exceptionally talented musicians, athletes, swimmers, etc.

Annual grant total

In 2013/14 the trust had assets of £725,000 and an income of £71,000. Grants totalled £51,500, the majority of which was distributed to individuals for purposes relating to their education. Grants to individuals were distributed as follows:

Type of grant	No. of grants	Average grant	Total
Grants to university students for educational learning materials	189	£197	£37,500
Grants to individuals for educational or medical support	6	£508	£3,100*
Grants for students with disadvantaged home backgrounds	49	£55	£2,700

*We estimate that grants for medical support amounted to £1,500, and have not included this figure in the total for educational grants.

An additional £8,500 was paid in grants to ten organisations.

Applications

Application forms can be downloaded from the trust's website and should be returned to the trust by post.

Applications are considered in January, March, June, September, October and December and can be submitted by the individual or a third party such as a headteacher, social worker, probation officer or police officer.

Other information

The trust mainly makes grants to schoolchildren and students for purposes relating to their education, although people who have disabilities may also apply for assistance to help with mobility problems. In a typical year about 200 grants are given to individuals, mainly for young people. Around 20 organisations also receive support each year.

St Albans

The 948 Sports Foundation

£10,500

Correspondent: Alexander Bell, Trustee, Old Albanian Sports Club, Woollam Playing Fields, 160 Harpenden Road, St Albans AL3 6BB (01727 864476; website: www.the948sportsfoundation.org)

CC number: 1088273

Eligibility

Young people who attend schools, colleges and universities in St Albans and the surrounding areas.

Types of grants

Grants of up to £1,000 are given according to need to allow individuals to participate in sports and recreational activities.

Annual grant total

In 2013/14 the foundation had an income of £23,500 and a total expenditure of £21,000. We estimate that £10,500 was awarded in grants to individuals.

Exclusions

Retrospective grants are not made and funding is not normally given for holidays or general grants.

Applications

Application forms can be downloaded from the foundation's website or requested from the correspondent. They should be submitted by post at least ten days before the trustees' meeting. Candidates are required to provide copies of accreditation from sport associations and demonstrate evidence of efforts to secure funding from other sources. Awards are only made upon production of an invoice/purchase order/a copy of a receipt.

Other information

Grants are also made to St Albans school and organisations towards projects, equipment and facilities.

The James Marshall Foundation

£142,000

Correspondent: Lynne Machin, Trustees' Office, Unit 6, 17 Leyton Road, Harpenden, Hertfordshire AL5 2HY (01582 760735; email: jmfoundation@ btconnect.com; website: www. wheathampstead.net/jmf)

CC number: 312127

Eligibility

People under the age of 25 who live in Harpenden and Wheathampstead and are in financial need. Priority is given to individuals over the age of 16.

Types of grants

Grants are awarded to pay for, or contribute to: the cost of fees, books, equipment and clothing for vocational training courses such as apprenticeships, GNVQ and BTEC; the cost of books, equipment, accommodation and other course-related expenditure for degrees; in some cases postgraduate degree course fees, books, equipment and accommodation; work-related and self-development opportunities; school trips, school uniform and extra-curricular tuition such as music and sports.

Grants generally range from £50 to £2,000, but can be of up to £4,000.

Annual grant total

In 2013/14 the foundation had assets of £5.4 million and an income of £187,500. Expenditure totalled £155,500. Grants were made totalling £142,000 (£82,500 in Harpenden and £60,000 in Wheathampstead).

The grants were made in the following categories:

Primary/secondary/further education	61
Degree courses	36
Computer	15
Other	7
Medical student	5
Master's and postgraduate education	4
Personal development	2

Applications

Application forms and further guidance can be requested from the correspondent. Applications can be submitted directly by the individual at any time and are considered every six to eight weeks. Applicants should provide details of their parental or other income and state the purpose for the requested grant.

Welwyn Hatfield
Wellfield Trust

£750

Correspondent: Jenny Bayford, Trust Manager, Birchwood Leisure Centre, Longmead, Hatfield, Hertfordshire AL10 0AN (01707 251018 (Monday to Friday, 9.30am to 3pm); email: wellfieldtrust@aol.com; website: www. wellfieldtrust.co.uk)

CC number: 296205

Eligibility

People in need who are on a low income, who live in the parish of Hatfield and are undertaking vocational courses, such as computer or hairdressing training. Schoolchildren in the parish may also be supported.

Types of grants

One-off grants of £100 to £500 to schoolchildren, college students, mature students, people with special educational needs and people starting work. Grants are made to help with, for example, course equipment, school uniforms and school trips.

Annual grant total

In 2013/14 grants to individuals amounted to £14,900, with a further £5,200 given in grants to organisations.

The majority of grants are given for social welfare purposes. We estimate that grants for educational purposes totalled around £750.

Exclusions

Our research indicates that grants are not made for council tax arrears, rent or funeral costs. Applications are not normally considered from individuals who have received a grant from the trust within the last two years.

Applications

There is an application form available to download from the website, which must be completed by the individual or a member of the household in need and a sponsor. The sponsor should be somebody who is familiar with the applicant's personal circumstances such as a social worker or a teacher. Applicants who cannot think of an appropriate sponsor should contact the trust for advice.

The trust's committee meets on the second Tuesday of every month to consider applications which, to be considered at the next meeting, must be submitted by the first Monday of every month.

Other information

The trust also gives to organisations, has a room at a local leisure centre which can be hired free of charge to charitable organisations, and offers a scooter loan scheme. It has a helpful and informative website.

Isle of Wight
The Broadlands Fund (Broadlands Home Trust)

£3,300

Correspondent: Mrs M. Groves, Correspondent, 2 Winchester Close, Newport, Isle of Wight PO30 1DR (01983 525630; email: broadlandstrust@ btinternet.com)

CC number: 201433

Eligibility

Girls and young single women (under the age of 22) in need who are resident on the Isle of Wight.

Types of grants

One-off grants of £100 to schoolchildren, vocational students, people with special needs and people starting work, including those for uniforms/clothing, books, fees, equipment/instruments, travel expenses and educational trips.

Annual grant total

In 2013/14 the fund had an income of £11,300 and a total expenditure of £6,800, which is the lowest in the past five years. Grants are given for both educational and social welfare purposes and we estimate the total amount awarded in educational grants to be around £3,300.

Exclusions

Grants are not made to married women or graduates.

Applications

Application forms are available from the correspondent and should be submitted either directly by the individual or a family member. They should include the applicant's name, date of birth, address, financial details (the family's income and expenditure), details of course undertaken, reference and confirmation of attendance, and specify the support needed. Requests are considered quarterly in January, April, July and October. If you are applying by post, enclose an sae.

Other information

Support to single women or widows who are over the age of 40 is also provided through pensions.

Kent

Cliffe and Cliffe Woods Community Trust (formerly known as Cliffe-at-Hoo Parochial Charity)

£1,000

Correspondent: Paul Kingman, Clerk, 52 Reed Street, Cliffe, Rochester ME3 7UL (01634 220422; email: paul.kingman@btopenworld.com)

CC number: 220855

Eligibility

People in need who live in the ancient parish of Cliffe-at-Hoo.

Types of grants

One-off grants according to need for any educational purpose.

Annual grant total

In 2013/14 the trust had an income of £9,900 and a total expenditure of £4,200. Grants are made to individuals and organisations for both educational and social welfare purposes. We estimate that educational grants to individuals totalled £1,000.

Applications

Apply in writing to the correspondent. Applications can be submitted directly by the individual or a family member, or through a third party such as a social worker or teacher.

Dunk's and Springett's Educational Foundation

£10,000

Correspondent: Andrew Davis, Clerk to the Trustees, Fothersby, Rye Road, Hawkhurst, Kent TN18 5DB (01580 388973; email: dunksclerk@outlook.com; website: www.dunkscharities.com)

CC number: 307664

Eligibility

Children and young people under the age of 25 who live in the ancient parish of Hawkhurst and are in need.

Types of grants

The website notes that grants are made to support local young people 'in various ways, especially those of school-leaving age contemplating apprenticeships or further training'.

Annual grant total

In 2014 the foundation had an income of £9,100 and a total expenditure of £14,800. We estimate that about £10,000 was distributed in grants to individuals.

Applications

Applications should be made in writing to the correspondent at any time.

Other information

The Clerk to the Trustees is responsible for both Dunk's charities. Should you need to contact the correspondent, it is helpful to specify that the query is for the educational foundation not the almshouses charity. The foundation's record on the Charity Commission's website indicates that organisations may also be assisted.

Educational Foundation of James Morris

£2,600

Correspondent: Maria Wells, Trustee, 4 Bybrook Field, Sandgate, Folkestone CT20 3BQ (01303 248092; email: robjhudson@ntlworld.com)

CC number: 307559

Eligibility

Young people who live within the boundaries of Sandgate on a permanent basis.

Types of grants

Our research suggests that one-off and recurrent grants can range from £75 to £275 and are awarded to help further and higher education students with fees, books, equipment/instruments and maintenance/living expenses. Support is also offered towards the cost of school uniforms, books and equipment/instruments for schoolchildren and towards books and fees for people starting work. Mature students can receive help towards books, fees and maintenance/living expenses and vocational students can receive help towards fees.

Annual grant total

In 2013/14 the foundation had an income of £2,800 and an expenditure of £2,800. We estimate that the annual total amount of grants awarded was around £2,600.

Applications

Applications may be made in writing to the correspondent, either directly by the individual or through their school/college or educational welfare agency, if applicable. Our research shows that applications should include particulars of the university or college that the applicant is attending or planning to attend, together with details of the course of study and ultimate ambitions. Applications should be submitted by 15 September for consideration in October.

The Gibbon and Buckland Charity

£5,000

Correspondent: David Harmsworth, Trustee, Hemsted Oaks, Cranbrook Road, Benenden, Cranbrook TN17 4ES (01580 240683; email: daharmsworth@hotmail.com; website: benendenparishcouncil.org/grants-for-young-persons)

CC number: 307682

Eligibility

People between the ages of 16 and 25 who have lived in Benenden for at least three years.

Types of grants

Grants are given to students entering further/higher education, also people starting work and apprentices. Awards are of around £150–£300 and can be given for general educational needs or gap year and similar projects.

Annual grant total

In 2014 the charity had both an income of £24,000 and a total expenditure of around £11,000. We estimate that £5,000 was awarded to individuals.

Applications

Application forms can be requested from the correspondent, downloaded from the Benenden parish council's website and are also placed in the village shop. The trustees meet twice a year with additional meetings being called as the need arises. Applications should be made by 30 September.

Other information

The charity also supports a Benenden Primary School and provides bibles to year six pupils in the school.

The Gibbons Family Trust
See entry on page 286

The Hayes (Kent) Trust

£6,900 (5 grants)

Correspondent: Andrew Naish, Trustee, 2 Warren Wood Close, Bromley BR2 7DU (020 8462 1915; email: hayes.kent.trust@gmail.com)

CC number: 221098

Eligibility

People who live in the parish of Hayes and can demonstrate that they are in need.

Types of grants

One-off grants, generally in the region of £75 to £1,500, are given according to need.

Annual grant total

In 2014/15 the trust had assets of over £1 million and an income of £49,000. Grants were awarded totalling £35,500, of which £16,500 was given to 28 individuals, allocated as follows:

Relief in need	22	£8,900
Advancement of education	5	£6,900
Relief in sickness	1	£400

The trust also awarded £19,500 to 12 organisations: £10,600 for educational purposes (five organisations); £8,000 for relief in sickness (five organisations); and £700 for relief-in-need purposes (two organisations).

Applications

Applications can be made in writing to the correspondent. They should include the full name of the applicant, postal address in Hayes (Kent), telephone number, email, date of birth, and details of why support is required. Applications may include any supporting information and can be made at any time either directly by the individual or through a third party, such as the individual's college, school or educational welfare agency.

Other information

The trust is an amalgamation of the following charities: The Poors Land Cottage Charity; The Poors Land Eleemosynary Charity; The Hayes (Kent) Educational Foundation.

The Hugh and Montague Leney Travelling Awards Trust

£10,000

Correspondent: Lyn Edwards, Awards Group, Education and Libraries, Bishops Terrace, Bishops Way, Maidstone, Kent ME14 1AF (01622 605111; email: leneytrust@hotmail.co.uk)

CC number: 307950

Eligibility

Children and young people over the age of 16 who are attending/have attended within the previous 12 months any county, voluntary or independent school in the county of Kent. The trustees will give preference to individuals in their final year of school showing qualities of leadership. The project should be of a humanitarian nature, in less developed regions of the world, lasting at least four weeks and benefitting the local community.

Types of grants

The trust provides awards of up to £2,500 to travel to all parts of the world in pursuance of education and to gain skills and knowledge for future career.

Annual grant total

In 2013/14 the trust had an income of £8,000 and an expenditure of £10,500. We estimate the annual total amount of grants awarded to be around £10,000.

Applications

Apply in writing to the correspondent. The closing date for applications is 31 January each year. Our research indicates that applications should be submitted by the headteacher or come through an educational welfare agency, if applicable.

Other information

Grants are not intended to cover all costs and other efforts of fundraising, sponsorships, parents' contributions and individual initiative will be taken into account.

Anne Peirson Charitable Trust

£2,000

Correspondent: Ina Tomkinson, Trustee, Tyrol House, Cannongate Road, Hythe, Kent CT21 5PX (01303 260779; fax: 01303 238660)

CC number: 800093

Eligibility

People in need who live in the parish of Hythe and are at any level of their education. Our research suggests that in practice children are mainly assisted.

Types of grants

One-off grants ranging between £50 and £600 given mainly to early years children and schoolchildren for books, educational outings, fees and equipment. Extra-curricular activities are also supported.

Annual grant total

In 2014 the trust had an income of £14,100 and a total expenditure of £8,300. We estimate the amount given to individuals for educational purposes was around £2,000.

Exclusions

Grants are not made where statutory support is available.

Applications

Applications may be made in writing to the correspondent via either Citizens Advice, a social worker, health visitor, school headteacher or other third party. Grants are considered at quarterly meetings of the trustees, but emergency applications can be considered in the interim.

Other information

Grants are awarded to individuals and organisations for both educational and social welfare purposes.

Ashford

Headley-Pitt Charitable Trust

£6,300

Correspondent: Thelma Pitt, Old Mill Cottage, Ulley Road, Kennington, Ashford, Kent TN24 9HX (01233 626189; email: thelma.pitt@headley.co.uk)

CC number: 252023

Eligibility

Individuals in need who live in Kent, with a preference for those residing in Ashford.

Types of grants

One-off grants, usually in the range of £100 and £300. Recent grants have been given to schoolchildren, college students, undergraduates, vocational students, mature students, people with special educational needs, people starting work and overseas students, for various educational purposes.

Annual grant total

In 2014/15 the trust had assets of £2.5 million and an income of £82,500. A total of 62 grants were made to individuals, for both social welfare and educational purposes, totalling £12,600. We estimate that educational grants to individuals amounted to £6,300.

An additional £27,500 was awarded in 94 grants to organisations.

Applications

Applications should be made in writing to the correspondent, either directly by the individual or through a third party.

Hothfield Educational Foundation

£9,000

Correspondent: Pater Patten, Trustee, The Paddocks, Hothfield, Ashford TN26 1EN (01233 620880; email: marianne.highwood@btinternet.com)

CC number: 307670

Eligibility

People under the age of 25 who live in, or have attended school at, the parish of Hothfield. People resident immediately outside the area of benefit or those over

25 may be supported at the trustees' discretion if there are surplus funds.

Types of grants

One-off and recurrent grants are given according to need, in the range of £10–£3,000. Funding is given to help with the cost of books, school clothing, uniforms, educational trips and other essentials for schoolchildren. Further and higher education students can be supported towards books, fees, living expenses and study or travel abroad. People starting work may receive grants towards books, equipment, instruments and clothing.

Annual grant total

In 2014 the foundation had an income of £8,500 and an expenditure of £18,000. We estimate the annual total amount of grants awarded to individuals to be around £9,000.

Applications

Apply in writing to the correspondent. Applications are considered on an ongoing basis.

Other information

Grants are also made to local organisations.

City of Canterbury

The Canterbury United Municipal Charities

£3,500

Correspondent: Aaron Spencer, Furley Page Solicitors, 39 St Margaret's Street, Canterbury, Kent CT1 2TX (01227 863140; email: aas@furleypage.co.uk)

CC number: 210992

Eligibility

People who are in need and have lived within the boundaries of what was the old city of Canterbury for at least two years.

Types of grants

Small, one-off and recurrent grants are made to further and higher education students for books and equipment/ instruments.

Annual grant total

In 2014 the charity had an income of £9,200 and a total expenditure of £7,300. Grants are made for social welfare and educational purposes. We estimate that educational grants to individuals totalled around £3,500.

Applications

Applications can be made in writing to the correspondent through the individual's school/college/educational welfare agency or directly by the individual. They are considered on an ongoing basis and should include a brief

statement of circumstances and proof of residence in the area.

Streynsham's Charity

£3,600

Correspondent: The Clerk to the Trustees, PO Box 970, Canterbury, Kent CT1 9DJ (0845 094 4769)

CC number: 214436

Eligibility

Young people who live or attend school in the ancient parish of St Dunstan's, Canterbury, and are under the age of 21.

Types of grants

One-off grants of up to a maximum of about £300. Help with the cost of books, clothing, educational outings, maintenance and other essentials can be given to schoolchildren. Grants are also available for those at college or university (including mature students), for books, fees, travel and living expenses. People starting work can receive help towards books, equipment/ instruments, clothing and travel.

Annual grant total

In 2014 the charity had an income of £74,000 and a total expenditure of £74,000. A total of £33,500 was awarded to individuals and organisations. Grants to individuals amounted to £24,000, of which £3,600 was given in educational grants and the remainder for social welfare purposes.

Applications

Apply in writing to the correspondent. Applications can be made directly by the individual, through the individual's school/college/educational welfare agency or through other third party on behalf of the individual. They are usually considered in March and October but can be made at any time and should include an sae and telephone number if applicable.

Dartford

Wilmington Parochial Charity

£800

Correspondent: Regina Skinner, Correspondent, 101 Birchwood Road, Dartford DA2 7HQ (01322 662342)

CC number: 1011708

Eligibility

People in need who live in the parish of Wilmington and are receiving a statutory means-tested benefit, such as Income Support, Housing Benefit or help towards their council tax.

Types of grants

One-off grants are available according to need. Our research suggests that grants may be awarded to:

- Schoolchildren for books and educational outings but not clothing, uniforms or fees
- Students in further/higher education for books, fees, living expenses and study and travel abroad, but not to foreign students or for student exchange
- Mature students for books and travel but not fees or childcare

Annual grant total

In 2013/14 the charity had an income of £13,300 and a total expenditure of £8,800. The charity's record on the Charity Commission's website states that about 15%–17% of the expenditure is given for educational purposes. We estimate that about £800 can be given in educational grants to individuals.

Exclusions

Educational support is offered where funding is not provided by the local authorities.

Applications

Applications should be submitted by the individual or through a social worker, Citizens Advice or other welfare agency. The trustees meet in February and November. Urgent applications can be considered between the meetings in exceptional circumstances.

Other information

Grants are also given to local schools at Christmas and to individuals for welfare purposes.

Maidstone

The Mike Collingwood Memorial Fund

£4,200

Correspondent: Peter Green, Trustee, Acorn House, 12 The Platt, Sutton Valence, Maidstone, Kent ME17 3BQ (01622 843230; email: peter@ acornshouse.plus.com; website: www. wealdofkentrotary.org.uk/MCMF.html)

CC number: 288806

Eligibility

Young people who live within a 20-mile radius of 'The Who'd a Thought It' pub in Grafty Green, Kent, where the Rotary Club of the Weald of Kent holds its weekly meetings.

Types of grants

Support can be given to undertake projects, trips and challenges in the UK and abroad, practice towards excellence in a chosen sport or vocation, and similar activities. The fund aims to give learning opportunities which may not be essential for a course, but are a good learning experience and will contribute to the applicant's future career.

Grants and loans are available. Due to limited amount available support is only supplementary and the applicants are expected to raise the balance by other means, ideally, with an entrepreneurial spirit and personal effort.

Annual grant total

In 2013/14 the fund had an income of £7,600 and an expenditure of £4,400. We estimate the annual total amount of grants awarded to individuals to be around £4,200.

Exclusions

The fund is not able to help with recurring costs such as university fees.

Applications

Application forms can be found on the Rotary Club of The Weald of Kent website or requested from the correspondent. Awards are normally made in February and October and applications should reach the trustees a month in advance.

Applications can be submitted by email at: mcmf@wealdofkentrotary.org.uk, or by post to: Derek Lamb, 68 Oak Lane, Headcorn TN27 9TB.

Medway

Arthur Ingram Trust

£97,500 (58 grants)

Correspondent: Margaret Taylor, Administrator, Medway Council, Gun Wharf, Dock Road, Chatham, Kent ME4 4TR (01634 732876; email: margaret.taylor@medway.gov.uk)

CC number: 212868

Eligibility

Young people in need between the ages of 14 and 21 who are in full-time education and live in the Medway council area.

Types of grants

According to our research, grants can be made to:

- Students aged between 14 and 16 whose parents are on a low income and who need assistance with school uniform, books and towards school trips which are identified as being linked to exam-related studies (the maximum grant is £300)
- Students continuing at school or in further education establishments/ training and have attendance of at least 90% unless there are exceptional reasons for absence, such as long-term illness (the maximum grant is £400)

- Students whose courses have been recognised as requiring specialist equipment can be granted advanced payments in kind to the school/ college (the maximum grant is £150)
- Independent students where parental assistance is not possible or appropriate and the student is independent through no fault of their own
- Sixth form students who have been nominated by the school (applications for these bursaries cannot be requested directly from the trust)

Annual grant total

In 2013/14 the trust had assets of £2.1 million, an income of £87,000 and a total charitable expenditure of £108,500. The amount of grants given to individuals totalled £97,500 and was distributed in the following categories:

Bursary grants	35	£91,500
Continuing education	12	£4,400
Uniforms	11	£1,500

Applications

Application forms can be requested from the correspondent. Applications can be made by the individual or through a third party, such as a teacher, school/ college or educational welfare agency, if applicable. General grants can be submitted at any time and are considered on an ongoing basis. Continuing education applications should normally be submitted between July and March and bursaries can be applied for from April to June. Each application is means-tested and evidence of income is required.

Other information

Other grants were given to field trips and school equipment totalling £108,000.

Richard Watts and The City of Rochester Almshouse Charities

£9,100 (13 grants)

Correspondent: Jane Rose, Clerk and Chief Officer, Administrative Offices, Watts Almshouses, Maidstone Road, Rochester, Kent ME1 1SE (01634 842194; fax: 01634 409348; email: admin@richardwatts.org.uk; website: www.richardwatts.org.uk)

CC number: 212828

Eligibility

People in need who live in the city of Rochester and urban Strood.

Types of grants

One-off grants towards specific items required for the course or training, such as books, equipment, special educational

needs, music instruments, educational outings, tours, outfits, school uniforms or similar support. Schoolchildren, university students and people in further education or training can be assisted.

Annual grant total

In 2014 the charity had assets of £20.8 million and an income of £1.2 million. During the year, grants were made to both individuals and organisations, and for educational as well as social welfare purposes. A total of 13 educational grants were made to individuals, amounting to £9,100.

Applications

Application forms can be requested from the correspondent and can be submitted at any time directly by individuals. Evidence of the applicant's financial situation is required and a letter of support – from social services, a doctor, school or other care organisation – is needed in most cases. Applications are considered on a regular basis and candidates will be interviewed before the final decision is reached.

Other information

This charity was founded in 1579 and, aside from making grants, also runs almshouses. There are four main sites: Maidstone Road; Reeves House in Watts Avenue; St Catherine's at the top of Star Hill; and Haywards House on Corporation Street.

Sevenoaks

Kate Drummond Trust

£500

Correspondent: David Batchelor, Trustee, The Beeches, Packhorse Road, Sevenoaks, Kent TN13 2QP (01732 451584)

CC number: 246830

Eligibility

Young people, especially girls, living in Sevenoaks urban district and neighbourhood.

Types of grants

One-off grants are given towards education, recreation or training, including vocational training or people entering a trade.

Annual grant total

In 2013/14 the trust had an income of £7,000 and a total expenditure of £1,100, which is the lowest in the past five years. We estimate that the amount of grants given to individuals for educational purposes totalled around £500.

Applications

Applications may be made in writing to the correspondent. Include an sae if a reply is required.

Other information

The trust owns and operates a residential house offering either a rent-free or subsidised accommodation. Grant making is available when there is surplus money. It can also give grants to organisations and for social welfare purposes.

Shepway

Southland's Educational Charity

£4,300

Correspondent: Mrs U. Wooding, Correspondent, c/o Town Hall, High Street, New Romney, Kent TN28 8BT (01797 362348; email: sacclerk@gmail.com)

CC number: 307783

Eligibility

Children under the age of 25 who are continuing into further education, live in the parish of New Romney and are in need.

Types of grants

Grants are given towards the cost of books, equipment, instruments, fees, maintenance/living expenses, educational outings in the UK and study or travel overseas. Grants are generally in the range of £100 to £500.

Annual grant total

In 2013/14 the charity had an income of £3,700 and an expenditure of £4,500. We estimate that about £4,300 was given in grants to individuals.

Applications

Application forms are available from the correspondent.

Swale

The William Barrow's Charity

£42,500 (39+ grants)

Correspondent: Stuart Mair, Clerk, George Webb Finn, 43 Park Road, Sittingbourne, Kent ME10 1DY (01795 470556; email: stuart@georgewebbfinn.com)

CC number: 307574

Eligibility

Further and higher education students in need who are under the age of 25 and who/whose parents live in the parish of Borden.

Types of grants

Grants are available for general educational necessities, such as books, equipment/instruments, tools and also travel/study overseas or living expenses for students studying away from home. According to our research, schoolchildren can be supported towards the cost of school uniforms/other clothing, educational outings and other necessities. Grants are usually in the range of £350 to £500 and can be given as one-off awards or as two-yearly allowances.

Annual grant total

In 2014 the charity had assets of £6.7 million and an income of £242,500. The amount of grants given to individuals totalled £72,500, of which grants for educational purposes amounted to £42,500. They were distributed as follows:

Grants to pensioners	£30,500
Grants to students	£29,500
Educational grants	£13,000

An additional £52,000 was paid in grants to schools

Applications

Apply in writing to the correspondent. The trustees meet at least four times a year, normally in January, April, July and October.

Other information

The charity also provides funds for alterations/repairs or general school expenses to Borden C.E. Primary School and Borden Grammar School premises.

The Eleemosynary fund gives funding to the elderly, people with disabilities and students away in college/university to help with living costs and the Educational fund supports institutions/schools and individuals in education.

Oxfordshire

Bartholomew Educational Foundation

£2,000

Correspondent: Robin Mitchell, Clerk to the Trustees, 20 High Street, Eynsham, Witney, Oxfordshire OX29 4HB (01865 880665; website: www.eynsham.org/edcharity.html)

CC number: 309278

Eligibility

People under the age of 25 who live in the parish of Eynsham.

Types of grants

Grants are available towards educational travel abroad; study of music and other arts; the cost of tools, equipment/instruments, books and clothing to apprentices and trainees; to schoolchildren and university/college students for general educational needs. Awards are usually in the range of £50 to £200.

Annual grant total

In 2014 the foundation had an income of £4,000 and an expenditure of £2,900. The foundation states that about £2,000 is available for distribution in grants annually.

Applications

Apply in writing to the correspondent. Applications for people under 18 should be made by a parent or guardian.

The following is taken from the foundation's website:

> Write to the Clerk with full details of the person the grant is requested for (name, address, age, what you need the grant for, what cost is involved, etc.). If you are an **Apprentice** or **Trainee** send a list of tools, books, instruments, etc. with their prices and a note of when you expect to start your training. The Trustees meet four times a year, usually in February, May, August or September and November. They will consider your application and will be in touch with you as soon as possible afterwards. Please send in your application the month before the next meeting if you can.

Other information

Local educational bodies can also be supported, after the individual needs have been met.

Charlbury Exhibition Foundation

£11,000

Correspondent: Kathryn Jones, Trustee, Took House, Sheep Street, Charlbury, Chipping Norton, Oxfordshire OX7 3RR (01608810793)

CC number: 309236

Eligibility

People under the age of 25 who live in the ancient township of Charlbury and are going into further or higher education, including vocational courses and apprenticeships.

Types of grants

Recurrent grants for up to three years. Our research shows that grants are of about £100 a year per individual but depend on the foundation's income. Support is given towards general educational costs, necessities and maintenance expenses.

Annual grant total

In 2013/14 the foundation had an income of £13,000 and an expenditure of £11,000. We have estimated that the annual total amount of grants awarded was around £11,000. The amount given in grants varies each year.

Applications

Apply in writing to the correspondent. Applications should be submitted by October and include the individual's age, school, details of course, university/college and so on. People attending short training courses sponsored by Charlbury Youth Organisations can also apply.

Other information

The foundation owns a property and a field in Charlbury, Oxfordshire and uses the rental income from these assets to award grants.

Culham St Gabriel's Trust (The Culham Institute)

£19,500 (12 grants)

Correspondent: Mark Chater, Director, Culham St Gabriel's, 60–62 Banbury Road, Oxford OX2 6PN (01865 612035; email: enquiries@cstg.org.uk; website: www.cstg.org.uk)

CC number: 309671

Eligibility

People who are or intend to become teachers in religious education or are otherwise involved in work, development, research and studies of the Church of England.

Types of grants

Grants are aimed to help further/higher education students and to promote life-long learning of teachers. Financial support is available towards books, equipment, necessities and the costs of classes, lectures, various development opportunities.

Annual grant total

In 2013/14 the trust had assets of £15.3 million and an income of £871,500. The trust's expenditure totalled £980,500. Grants totalled £19,500 and were awarded to 12 individuals.

Exclusions

Grants are not given for work outside the UK, for general running costs, deficit reduction or religious instruction (as distinct from education).

Applications

Application forms can be obtained from the trust's website and should be submitted by January, May and September (specified dates may be subject to change; see the trust's website for further information).

Other information

Grants are also made to organisations and there were 15 awards made totalling £195,900 in 2013/14. The Keswick Hall Trust also received £200,000 during the year.

The Exuberant Trust

£3,200 (About 10 grants)

Correspondent: Megan Boyes, Trust Administrator, 11 St Margaret's Road, Oxford, Oxfordshire OX2 6RU (01865 751056; email: admin@exuberant-trust.org.uk; website: www.exuberant-trust.org.uk)

CC number: 1095911

Eligibility

People up to the age of 30 who are from Oxfordshire and are developing their interest in the arts (music, drama, dance, arts and crafts, jewellery, multimedia and so on). Preference is given to people applying for the first time.

Types of grants

One-off grants of up to a maximum of £500 for a specific project or activity. These awards can be made for tools, training, music lessons, general costs, instruments and so on.

Previous grant recipients include: musicians, designers, jewellers, theatre directors, dancers, performing artists, composers, conductors, DJs, film makers, singers, art promoters, concert organisers, instrumentalists, bands and chamber groups.

Annual grant total

In 2014 the trust had an income of £2,500 and an expenditure of £3,400. We estimate that the amount of grants given to individuals totalled around £3,200. On average around ten individuals are supported annually.

Applications

Full application guidelines are available from the trust's website or can be requested from the correspondent. Applicants are advised to give convincing reasons for applying and are required to provide appropriate references and a budget proposal. The trustees meet four times a year to consider applications and it may take up to three months for grant applications to be processed. If applying by post, remember to enclose an sae.

Other information

The trust's website states that the charity 'raises funds by organising concerts throughout the year and from donations received from its supporters' and notes that 'successful applicants are encouraged to take part in concerts and other activities in support of the trust'.

The Faringdon United Charities

£3,200

Correspondent: Vivienne Checkley, Bunting and Co., Faringdon Business Centre, Brunel House, Volunteer Way, Faringdon, Oxon SN7 7YR (01367 243789; email: vivienne.checkley@buntingaccountants.co.uk)

CC number: 237040

Eligibility

People who are in need and live in the parishes of Great Faringdon, Littleworth or Little Coxwell, all in Oxfordshire.

Types of grants

One-off grants to: schoolchildren for study/travel abroad, equipment/instruments and excursions; mature students for books; people with special educational needs for equipment/instruments; and people starting work for equipment/instruments.

Annual grant total

In 2013/14 the charity had an income of £11,200 and a total expenditure of £13,000. Grants are made to individuals and organisations for both educational and social welfare purposes. We estimate that educational grants to individuals totalled £3,200.

Applications

Applications can be made in writing to the correspondent throughout the year. They can be submitted through Citizens Advice, a social worker or other professional party, directly by the individual or by a non-professional third party on their behalf, for example a neighbour, parent or child.

Henley Educational Trust

£16,500 (87 grants)

Correspondent: Claire Brown, Clerk, Syringa Cottage, Horsepond Road, Gallowstree Common, Reading, Oxon RG4 9BP (0118 972 4575; email: henleyeducationalcharity@hotmail.co.uk; website: www.henleyeducationalcharity.com)

CC number: 309237

Eligibility

People under the age of 25 who live in the parishes of Henley North, Henley South, Bix, Remenham or Rotherfield Greys; or currently attend, or have attended for a minimum of two years, the following qualifying schools or colleges: Nettlebed Primary, Trinity Primary, Valley Road Primary, Sacred Heart RC Primary, Badgemore Primary, Crazies Hill Primary, Henley College or Gillotts School.

Types of grants

Grants can be given to schoolchildren for uniforms, educational outings, music lessons and instruments, educational extra-curricular activities; to people entering a trade/starting work for fees, clothing, equipment/instruments, maintenance expenses or travel costs; young people under 25 can be assisted with the study/travel overseas costs, voluntary work, gap year activities. Pre-school fees for up to three extra sessions may also be provided.

Annual grant total

In 2013/14 the trust had assets of £3.3 million and an income of £142,500 and a total charitable expenditure of £96,500. There were 87 grants made to individuals totalling £16,500.

Exclusions

Funding for pre-school fees is only provided where the extra sessions can be supported by an educational or healthcare professional and are essential to the child's development. The trust will not help merely to allow the parent/guardian to engage in employment.

Applications

Application forms can be obtained from the trust's website. The trustees meet six times a year, in January, March, May, June, September and November. For specific dates see the website. Note that email applications are not accepted. Candidates are required to provide evidence of their financial circumstances and a letter of support from an educational or healthcare professional.

Other information

Grants were also made to schools (£15,000 in 2013/14). Wider educational support to organisations totalled £64,000 during the year.

Cherwell

The Banbury Charities

£44,000

Correspondent: Nigel Yeadon, Clerk, 36 West Bar, Banbury OX16 9RU (01295 251234)

CC number: 201418

Eligibility

People under the age of 25 who live in the former borough of Banbury.

Types of grants

Grants are given to assist people who are preparing for or entering a profession or trade and students who are in higher and further education. Grants are also given to assist young people under the age of 25 who are studying the arts, literature or science.

Annual grant total

In 2014 the charities had assets of £5.6 million and an income of £418,500. A total of 310 grants were made to individuals for both education and social welfare purposes which, with an average of £285 per grant, amounted to £88,500. We estimate that the amount of grants given to individuals for educational purposes totalled around £44,000.

Grants totalling £204,000 were also made to organisations serving the area of benefit.

Applications

Apply in writing to the correspondent. Applicants are encouraged to obtain a letter of support from their social worker, carer or other person in authority to give credence to their application.

Other information

The Banbury Charities is a group of eight registered charities. These are as follows: Bridge Estate Charity; Countess of Arran's Charity; Banbury Arts and Educational Charity; Banbury Almshouses Charity; Banbury Sick Poor Fund; Banbury Welfare Trust; Banbury Poor Trust; and Banbury Recreation Charity.

City of Oxford

The City of Oxford Charity

£15,300 (34 grants)

Correspondent: David Wright, Clerk, 11 Davenant Road, Oxford OX2 8BT (01865 247161; email: enquiries@oxfordcitycharities.fsnet.co.uk; website: www.oxfordcitycharities.org)

CC number: 239151

Eligibility

Children and young people under the age of 25 who have lived in the city of Oxford for at least three years.

Types of grants

One-off grants are given to schoolchildren and college or university students. Assistance can be given with school uniforms, books, materials and also special educational needs.

Annual grant total

In 2014 the charity had assets of £5.5 million and an income of £360,500. Grants made during the year amounted to £92,000, the majority of which was given for the relief of need and sickness.

Grants for educational purposes totalled £15,300. Some of these grants were awarded to schools to help with the costs of school trips for children whose parents are on low incomes or welfare benefits.

Applications

Application forms can be downloaded from the charity's website or requested from the correspondent. Grants are considered quarterly in March, June, September and December. Applications from pupils must be accompanied by a letter of support from an educational social worker/health visitor/welfare worker/similar professional.

Other information

The charity is an amalgamation of a number of charities working for the benefit of the people of Oxford city. It also accepts applications from schools to help with 35% of the full costs of educational trips for children from low income families, supports the social welfare of individuals and maintains almshouses in the local area.

The Charity of Thomas Dawson

£3,000 (2 grants)

Correspondent: Mrs K. Lacey, Clerk and Receiver, 56 Poplar Close, Garsington, Oxford OX44 9BP (01865 368259)

CC number: 203258

Eligibility

Children and young people in need who have lived in the city of Oxford (postcodes OX1 to OX4) for three years, with a preference for those resident in the parish of St Clements.

Types of grants

Help is given with the cost of books, clothing, fees and other essentials for schoolchildren and for people at college or university. Grants are also made for people preparing for entering or engaging in a profession, trade, occupation or service. Awards generally range from £40 to £1,500.

Annual grant total

In 2013/14 the charity had assets of £10.7 million, the majority of which is permanent endowment and unavailable for grant-giving, and an income of £427,000. One quarter of the income is allocated to the Designated Fund for Educational Purposes. During the year a total of £27,000 was given through the fund, the majority of which went to organisations (£24,000) and £3,000 was given to two individuals.

Exclusions

Grants are not normally given for medical sponsorships or electives, or towards accommodation, travel or living expenses.

Applications

Applications may be made in writing to the correspondent, with evidence regarding course fees. **Note:** Applicants can only apply for one degree course.

Other information

Grants may also be made to schools and young people, family and volunteer organisations. One half of the income is applied for the upkeep and repair of the parish church of St Clement and one quarter to The Parochial Charities of St Clements, Oxford.

South Oxfordshire

The Stevens Hart and Municipal Educational Charity (Henley Municipal Charities)

£2,300

Correspondent: Jean Pickett, Henley Municipal Charities, Rear, 24 Hart Street, Henley-on-Thames, Oxon RG9 2AU (01491 412360; email: henleymcharities@aol.com)

CC number: 292857

Eligibility

Children and young people in need of financial assistance who live in the parishes of Bix and Rotherfield Greys or the town of Henley-on-Thames.

Types of grants

Our research shows that grants are awarded up to a maximum of £300 and can be given towards the cost of books, clothing and other educational necessities. Support is mainly for schoolchildren but students at college or university may also be assisted.

Annual grant total

In 2013/14 the charity had an income of £5,400 and an expenditure of £4,600. It provides assistance to local schools; therefore, we estimate the annual total amount of grants awarded to individuals total to be around £2,300.

Applications

Apply in writing to the correspondent.

Other information

The charity also supports local schools in maintenance and special benefits not normally provided by the local authorities.

The Thame Welfare Trust

£6,700

Correspondent: John Gadd, 2 Cromwell Avenue, Thame, Oxfordshire OX9 3TD (01844 212564; email: johngadd4@gmail.com)

CC number: 241914

Eligibility

People in need who live in Thame and the immediately adjoining villages.

Types of grants

One-off grants of up to £1,000 are given to help towards a wide variety of needs to schoolchildren, college students, undergraduates, vocational students, mature students, people with special educational needs and people starting work.

Annual grant total

In 2013/14 the charity had an income of £15,700 and a total expenditure of £28,500. Grants are made to individuals and organisations for a range of purposes. We estimate that educational grants to individuals totalled £6,700.

Applications

Apply in writing to the correspondent. Applications are usually made through social workers, probation officers, teachers, or a similar third party, but can also be submitted directly by the applicant.

Wallingford Relief in Need Charity

£1,000

Correspondent: Jamie Baskeyfield, Correspondent, Wallingford Town Council, 9 St Martin's Street, Wallingford, Oxfordshire OX10 0AL (01491 835373; email: queries@wallingfordtc.co.uk)

CC number: 292000

Eligibility

People in need who live in Wallingford and the neighbourhood (including the former parish of Clapcot).

Types of grants

Help is given towards the cost of bills, clothing and other essentials. The charity gives one-off grants only.

Annual grant total

In 2014/15 the charity had an income of £8,500 and a total expenditure of £4,100. We estimate that grants for educational purposes totalled about £1,000. Our research indicates that overall grants generally total around £6,500 a year.

Applications

Application forms are available from the correspondent. They should be submitted either directly by the individual or through a local organisation. The trustees meet about every three months, although emergency cases can be considered in between the meetings. Urgent cases may require a visit by a trustee.

Other information

The majority of grants are given for welfare needs.

The Wheatley Charities

£2,800

Correspondent: R. Minty, Trustee, 24 Old London Road, Wheatley, Oxford OX33 1YW (01865 874676)

CC number: 203535

Eligibility

People who are under the age of 25 and live in the parish of Wheatley.

Types of grants

Grants are given to help young people prepare for any trade or occupation or to promote their education.

Annual grant total

In 2014 the charity had an income of £4,100 and a total expenditure of £5,800. Grants are made to individuals and organisations for social welfare and educational purposes. We estimate that educational grants to individuals totalled £2,800.

Applications

Apply in writing to the correspondent.

Vale of White Horse

The Hope Ffennell Trust

£7,000

Correspondent: Louis Letourneau, Trustee, Church End, Wytham Abbey, Wytham, Oxon OX2 8QE (01865 203475)

CC number: 309212

Eligibility

People under the age of 25 years who live in the parishes of Wytham and North Hinksey.

Types of grants

Help towards outings and educational visits, books and the study of music.

Annual grant total

In 2013 the trust had an income of £8,000 and a total expenditure of £7,500 we estimate that grants totalled £7,000.

At the time of writing (November 2015) the information provided was the latest available.

Applications

Apply in writing to the correspondent.

The Steventon Allotments and Relief-in-Need Charity

£7,300 (26 grants)

Correspondent: The Clerk, 19 Lime Grove, Southmoor, Abingdon, Oxfordshire OX13 5DN (01865 821055; email: info@sarinc.org.uk)

CC number: 203331

Eligibility

People who are in full-time education in Steventon who are eligible for a student loan. Applications are considered from anyone living in the parish or with a significant connection to the parish.

Types of grants

One-off grants of up to £500 are given according to need for costs associated with higher education.

Annual grant total

In 2014 the charity had an income of £97,500 and a total expenditure of £148,000. Individuals received 15 grants totalling £7,300 for educational purposes.

Applications

Apply in writing to the correspondent. The charity advertises regularly in the local parish magazine. Applications should include full details of the individual's income and expenditure, and will be treated in strictest confidence.

West Oxfordshire

The Bampton Exhibition Foundation

£3,000

Correspondent: Gerald Mills, Trustee, 21 Southlands, Aston, Bampton OX18 2DA (01993 850670; email: geraldmills1937@gmail.com)

CC number: 309238

Eligibility

People under 25 who live in Bampton, Aston, Cote, Weald or Lew and are in need.

Types of grants

Grants are given to schoolchildren, people with special educational needs, students in further/higher education, vocational students and postgraduates

for projects/courses which would be otherwise beyond the means of applicants. Support that can be given includes books, equipment/instruments, fees, maintenance/living expenses, educational outings in the UK, study or travel abroad and so on.

Annual grant total

In 2013/14 the foundation had an income of £22,800 and a total expenditure of £10,000. We estimate that the total amount of grants awarded to individuals was approximately £3,000.

Applications

Apply in writing to the correspondent at any time, including details regarding the proposed project/course, any expenses involved and relevant references. Applications can be submitted either directly by the individual, through the individual's school, college or educational agency, or through another third party such as a teacher or parent.

Other information

The foundation also awards grants to organisations and spends some of its income on the maintenance of a partly listed building.

The Burford Relief-in-Need Charity

£5,100

Correspondent: Anne Burgess Youngson, Whitehill Farm, Burford, Oxfordshire OX18 4DT (01993 822894)

CC number: 1036378

Eligibility

People who are in need and live within seven miles of the Tolsey, Burford.

Types of grants

Grants are given to assist recipients to earn a living.

Annual grant total

In 2014 the charity had an income of £13,200 and a total expenditure of £10,500. We estimate that educational grants to individuals totalled £5,100, with funding also awarded to individuals for social welfare purposes.

Applications

Apply in writing to the correspondent either directly by the individual or, where applicable, through a social worker, Citizens Advice or other third party. Applications should include the individual's full name, address, age, and the number of years they have lived in Burford or their connection with Burford.

Surrey

The Archbishop Abbot's Exhibition Foundation

£4,000

Correspondent: Richard Middlehurst, Administrator, 17 Ashdale, Bookham, Leatherhead, Surrey KT23 4QP (01483 302345; email: richard.middlehurst@ dmhstallard.com)

CC number: 311890

Eligibility

People aged between 11 and 28 who live or attend school in the boroughs of Guildford or Waverley in Surrey. Preference is given to male applicants.

Types of grants

Scholarships, bursaries or maintenance allowances at schools or universities; the provision of clothing and equipment to assist entry into a trade or profession; scholarships for travelling abroad.

Grants range from £250 to £800 and are one-off.

Annual grant total

In 2014 the foundation had an income of £6,300 and a total expenditure of £4,500. We estimate that grants totalled £4,000.

Applications

Application forms are available from the correspondent.

Chessington Charities

£2,000

Correspondent: Mrs L. Roberts, Correspondent, St Mary's Centre, Church Lane, Chessington, Surrey KT9 2DR (07540 144016; email: stmaryschessington@hotmail.co.uk)

CC number: 209241

Eligibility

People in need who live in the parish of St Mary the Virgin, Chessington. Applicants must have lived in the parish for at least one year.

Types of grants

Grants are made for education and training needs. Previously grants have included those for school uniforms, shoes and school trips. Awards are generally in the range of £30–£250 and usually one-off.

Annual grant total

In 2014 the charity had both an income and a total expenditure of £8,500. We estimate grants for individuals for educational purposes to have totalled around £2,000.

Exclusions

Grants are not given to pay debts. The area of benefit is only the parish of St Mary the Virgin and excludes the rest of the Chessington postal area.

Applications

Application forms are available from the correspondent and can be submitted either directly by the individual or through a social worker, Citizens Advice or other agency. Christmas gifts are distributed in November and other applications are considered throughout the year. A home visit will be made by a trustee to ascertain details of the applicant's income and expenditure and to evaluate the need.

Other information

Grants are also given to local organisations which help people who are older or who have disabilities. Individual welfare grants are also available.

Chobham Poor Allotment Charity

£600

Correspondent: Elizabeth Thody, 46 Chertsey Road, Windlesham GU20 6EP

CC number: 200154

Eligibility

People in need who live in the ancient parish of Chobham, which includes the civil parishes of Chobham and West End.

Types of grants

Grants, usually ranging between £100 and £500, are typically made towards the cost of school uniforms and educational outings, trips and visits.

Annual grant total

In 2013/14 the charity had assets of £429,000 and an income of £47,500. Grants to four individuals amounted to £1,200, of which, we estimate, £600 was given for educational purposes.

Applications

Our research indicates that applications can be made in writing to the correspondent.

Other information

The main activities of the charity are the provision and maintenance of allotments, almshouses and relief in need. The charity is also involved in provision/maintenance of recreational and educational facilities. The trustees can support both individuals and organisations; nevertheless, only a small

amount each year is awarded in educational grants.

Epsom Parochial Charities (Epsom Almshouse Charity)

£200

Correspondent: John Steward, Trustee, 26 Woodcote Hurst, Epsom, Surrey KT18 7DT (email: vanstonewalker@ntlworld.com)

CC number: 200571

Eligibility

People in need who are under the age of 25 and live in the ancient parish of Epsom.

Types of grants

One-off and recurrent grants are given according to need are given to schoolchildren, college students, undergraduates, vocational students, mature students, people starting work and people with special educational needs, including awards towards clothing/uniforms, fees, books, equipment/instruments maintenance/living expenses and excursions.

Annual grant total

In 2014 the charity had assets of £1.7 million (most of which is endowment funds) and an income of £89,500. Grants to individuals for educational purposes totalled £200.

Applications

Application forms are available from the correspondent and can be submitted directly by the individual.

Other information

Grants are also made for social welfare purposes. The charity also provides residential accommodation through its three almshouses.

Mole Valley

Leatherhead United Charities

£30,000

Correspondent: David Matanle, Clerk to the Trustees, Homefield, Forty Foot Road, Leatherhead, Surrey KT22 8RP (01372 370073; email: luchar@btinternet.com)

CC number: 200183

Eligibility

People in need who live in the area of the former Leatherhead urban district council (Ashtead, Bookhams, Fetcham and Leatherhead). Preference is given to

residents of the parish of Leatherhead as constituted on 27 September 1912.

Types of grants

Our research indicates that grants are normally one-off and can range from £100 to £750. Support is available for general educational expenses. This charity does not deal with educational needs only, grants are made for the relief of need generally.

Annual grant total

In 2014 the charity had assets of £4 million and an income of £306,500. During the year, 30 grants were made, 27 of which were to individuals and the remainder to organisations. Pension, grants and other charges are listed in the annual report and accounts as having totalled £120,000. We estimate that assistance for social welfare purposes totalled around £30,000.

Applications

Application forms can be requested from the correspondent. Our research suggests that they can be submitted by the individual directly or by a family member. Awards are considered throughout the year.

Other information

The charity also provides residents of Mole Valley District Council with sheltered housing and associated services.

Reigate and Banstead

The Pilgrim Band Trust

£7,500

Correspondent: Gregory Andrews, Trustee, Clevelands, 13 Furzefield Road, Reigate RH2 7HG (01737 244134; email: pilgrim.band@virgin.net)

CC number: 1140954

Eligibility

Children and young people between the ages of 8 and 18 living in Reigate and surrounding areas who want to learn to play an instrument. Young musicians are also supported. Preference may be given to individuals or families with limited means or children with disabilities.

Types of grants

The trust gives an opportunity to children and young people to learn music by loaning the instruments and providing one-to-one or group tuition sessions for acoustic and electric guitars, piano, singing, drums and steel pans. Grants can also be provided for tuition fees to young musicians.

Annual grant total

In 2013/14 the trust had assets of over £4 million, an income of £138,500 and a total charitable expenditure of £117,000. Around £7,500 was given in scholarships and tuition.

Applications

Apply in writing to the correspondent.

Other information

The trust also supports local schools, with priority to state schools, and local music festivals. Most of the charitable expenditure is spent for the activities of the band.

Mary Stephens Foundation

£4,000

Correspondent: John Stephenson, Trustee, Doghurst Cottage, Doghurst Lane, Chipstead, Surrey CR5 3PL (01737 556548; email: john.stephenson24@ gmail.com)

CC number: 311999

Eligibility

People under the age of 25 who live, or whose parents live, in the ancient parish of Chipstead and Hooley, or who have attended Chipstead County First School.

Types of grants

One-off and recurrent grants of up to a maximum of £1,200 a year. Help to people in further education is in the form of books, uniforms and travel expenses. Limited help is given towards fees on a scholarship basis. Grants are given to those qualifying to obtain further education in the broadest possible way, such as for music lessons and field courses.

Annual grant total

In 2013/14 the foundation had an income of £7,000 and an expenditure of £4,500. We estimate that grants totalled about £4,000.

Exclusions

The foundation does not issue grants to pre-schoolchildren or provide loans.

Applications

Applications are considered at quarterly meetings and should be made directly by the individual, or by the individual's head of school or church leader.

Runnymede

The Chertsey Combined Charity

£1,700

Correspondent: Mr M. O'Sullivan, Secretary, PO Box 89, Weybridge, Surrey KT13 8HY (email: info@charity.me.uk)

CC number: 200186

Eligibility

People in need who live in the electoral divisions of the former urban district of Chertsey.

Types of grants

Grants are often given to help towards the cost of books, clothing and other essentials for those at school. Grants may also be given to people at college or university.

Annual grant total

In 2014/15 the charity had an income of £67,500 and a total expenditure of £75,000. The amount of grants given to individuals totalled £3,500. We estimate that about £1,700 was awarded for educational purposes.

Applications

Application forms are available from the correspondent.

Other information

Grants to organisations totalled £51,500 in 2014/15.

The Egham Education Trust

£2,800

Correspondent: Max Walker, Correspondent, 33 Runnemede Road, Egham TW20 9BE (01784 472742; email: eghamunicharity@aol.com; website: www.eghamunitedcharity.org)

CC number: 311941

Eligibility

People in need who are between the ages of 16 and 25 and have lived in the electoral wards of Egham, which is now Egham, Englefield Green, Virginia Water and Hythe, for at least five years.

Types of grants

One-off and recurrent grants in the range of £100–£500 are made towards further and vocational education. Awards may be made to students in secondary school, training college, university or other institution of further (including technical and professional) education. Students undertaking second degree courses may also be assisted.

The trust may:

- Award a grant valid at any secondary school, training college, university or other institution of further (including technical and professional) education. If appropriate they may repeat the grant annually throughout the student's full course of study. Students undertaking second degree courses may also be assisted
- Make grants for initial expenses when a student first leaves home to take up a course
- Contribute towards the costs of outgoings and equipment for Outward Bound, Duke of Edinburgh's Award and similar character and experience-building schemes
- Help with those studies that involve exceptionally costly items, such as musical instruments and specialist project work
- Assist with vocational and professional training course costs and equipment
- Contribute to exceptional travel costs

Annual grant total

In 2014 the trust had an income of £8,900 and a total expenditure of £3,000. We estimate that about £2,800 was awarded in grants to individuals.

Applications

Application forms are available from the trust's website or the correspondent (separate forms for different types of applicants/requests). Applications should include details of other grants and loans secured or applied for. The trustees meet regularly at six weekly intervals to consider applications.

The trust's website states: 'The application is usually followed by a meeting between the applicant and two Trustees, who subsequently present the case to a full meeting of the Trustees.'

Other information

It is further noted on the trust's website:

For undergraduates, the student's entitlement to assistance with fees and student loans from the Student Loan Company will be the principal guide for the Trustees in assessing each application. Likewise, for 16–19 year olds at Sixth Form and FE Colleges, the student's eligibility for help via EMA, free school meals or the Student Bursary fund will be taken into account.

For those seeking help with vocational or post-graduate courses, the Trustees will make an appraisal of the applicant's financial position and the total costs to be incurred.

For Duke of Edinburgh applicants there is a standard scale of payments regardless of parental income.

Waverley

The Witley Charitable Trust

£1,100

Correspondent: Daphne O'Hanlon, Trustee, Triados, Waggoners Way, Grayshott, Hindhead, Surrey GU26 6DX (01428 604679)

CC number: 200338

Eligibility

Children and young people (normally under the age of 20) who are in need and live in the parishes of Witley, Milford and a small part of Brook.

Types of grants

One-off, modest grants ranging from £25 to £300 can be given for educational needs. In the past the trust has supported a pupil to attend a local pre-school.

Annual grant total

In 2014 the trust had an income of £3,700 and an expenditure of £2,400. We estimate that grants for educational purposes totalled around £1,100.

Exclusions

The trust does not give loans or support for items which should be provided by statutory services.

Applications

Applications can be made in writing to the correspondent. Applications should be submitted through nurses, doctors, social workers, clergy, Citizens Advice and so on but not directly by the individual. Awards are usually considered in early February and September, although emergency applications can be considered throughout the year.

Other information

Grants are also given for welfare purposes.

West Sussex

The Bassil Shippam and Alsford Trust

£3,300

Correspondent: Trust Administrator, The Corn Exchange, Baffin's Lane, Chichester, West Sussex PO19 1GE (01243 786111; email: shippam@ thomaseggar.com)

CC number: 256996

Eligibility

Students in need living in West Sussex.

Types of grants

One-off grants ranging from £100 to £1,000 for gap year activities and other educational or personal development projects.

Annual grant total

In 2013/14 the trust had assets of £4.3 million, an income of £159,000 and a total charitable expenditure of £148,000. Grants to individuals for educational purposes totalled £3,300.

Exclusions

According to our research, funding cannot be provided towards academic courses.

Applications

Apply in writing to the correspondent. Applications can be submitted at any time directly by individuals and should include a summary of their proposal. The trustees meet three times a year.

Other information

The trust also supports organisations.

Arun

William Older's School Charity

£8,000

Correspondent: The Honorary Secretary, Parish Office, Church House, Arundel Road, Angmering, Littlehampton BN16 4JS

CC number: 306424

Eligibility

Children and young people aged 25 or under who live in the ecclesiastical parish of Angmering. Our research suggests that the applicant's parents must reside in the parish.

Types of grants

One-off and recurrent grants of up to £500. Grants are given to schoolchildren towards the cost of equipment/ instruments and fees, and to students in further or higher education towards books, equipment/instruments, childcare and educational outings in the UK. Gap year opportunities, volunteering, musical or sports activities or field trips can all be supported.

Annual grant total

In 2014 the charity had an income of £15,200 and an expenditure of £16,600. We estimate that the amount of grants given to individuals totalled about £8,000.

Applications

Applications should be made in writing to the correspondent, giving details about the applicant's income and expenditure, the course being studied and their residence in Angmering. Applications are usually considered in January, May and September.

Other information

Grants can also be made to organisations.

South West

General

The Adams Youth Trust

£65,000

Correspondent: Margaret Pyle, Administrator, Greendale Court, Clyst St Mary, Exeter, Devon EX5 1AW (01395 233433)

CC number: 1067277

Eligibility

Young people principally in the West Country (Cornwall, Devon, Somerset and Wiltshire).

Types of grants

Grants to provide opportunities for education, advancement of personal skills and training.

Annual grant total

In 2013/14 the trust had an income of £4,500 and an expenditure of £105,000. We have estimated that grants and scholarships totalled around £65,000.

Applications

Apply in writing to the correspondent at any time.

Other information

The trust also makes grants to organisations.

Viscount Amory's Charitable Trust

£7,500 (16 grants)

Correspondent: Secretary to the Trustees, The Island, Lowman Green, Tiverton, Devon EX16 4LA (01884 254899; email: office@vact.org.uk; website: www.vact.org.uk)

CC number: 204958

Eligibility

People in need in the south west of England, with a preference for small charities in Devon (due to limited funds).

Types of grants

One-off and recurrent grants are given according to need.

Annual grant total

In 2013/14 the trust had assets of almost £12.5 million and an income of £433,000. The trust awarded £7,500 to individuals, of which £4,000 was awarded for educational purposes. A further £324,500 was given to organisations.

Applications

Apply in writing to the correspondent. Requests are considered every month.

Devon and Cornwall Aid for Girls Trust

£10,000

Correspondent: Frederick Webb, Administrator, 33 Downham Gardens, Tamerton Foliot, Plymouth, Devon PL5 4QF (01752 776612; email: fjwebb@ talktalk.net)

CC number: 202493

Eligibility

Young women between the ages of 16 and 23 who live in the counties of Devon and Cornwall. Preference is given to girls who have lost one or both of their parents.

Types of grants

One-off and recurrent grants ranging from £100 to £350 are offered to further and higher education students or people in vocational training to help with the cost of books, clothing, fees, instruments/tools, IT equipment, travel or living expenses.

Annual grant total

In 2013/14 the trust had an income of £12,500 and a total expenditure of £10,500. We estimate the annual total amount of grants awarded to individuals to be around £10,000.

Exclusions

Grants are not normally awarded for postgraduate and mature students, second qualifications or part-time studies.

Applications

Apply in writing to the correspondent. Applications can be submitted directly by the individual at any time.

Dyke Exhibition Foundation

£2,500

Correspondent: Christopher Stanley-Smith, Correspondent, Grove View, Hodshill, Southstoke, Bath BA2 7ED (email: christopher.stanley-smith@ brewin.co.uk)

CC number: 306610

Eligibility

Further and higher education students (between the ages of 16 and 25) who are resident in Somerset, Devon or Cornwall. Applicants must either have been born in the area, have been resident there for at least three years, or have been attending school in the area of benefit for at least two years prior to application.

Preference is given to individuals who are in most need and those who are, or are about to become, undergraduates of Oxford University or other university.

Types of grants

Grants are given towards fees, accommodation, books and equipment, travel costs or 'any other expense incurred by the student'. Awards usually range between £100 and £300 a year for up to three years.

Annual grant total

In 2013/14 the foundation had an income of £6,400 and an expenditure of £2,700. We have estimated that the annual total amount of grants awarded was around £2,500.

Applications

Application forms can be obtained by sending an sae to the correspondent. Completed application forms must be submitted by the end of February for consideration in April.

The Elmgrant Trust

£1,500 (11 grants)

Correspondent: Amanda Horning, Secretary, Elmhirst Centre, Dartington Hall, Totnes, Devon TQ9 6EL (01803 863160; email: info@elmgrant.org.uk; website: www.elmgrant.org.uk)

CC number: 313398

Eligibility

People living in the South West England (counties of Cornwall, Devon, Dorset, Gloucestershire, Somerset and Wiltshire).

Types of grants

The trust offers one-off grants in the region of £150 to help schoolchildren with the cost of books, equipment/instruments, fees, educational outings/visits. Further/higher education students are also assisted with the cost of books, equipment/instruments, fees, maintenance/living expenses, educational outings in the UK and childcare. People who are furthering their training to improve work prospects are also assisted.

Annual grant total

In 2013/14 the trust had assets of £2.1 million, an income of £66,000 and a total charitable expenditure of £46,000. Grants to 11 individuals totalled £1,500.

Exclusions

The trustees will not provide support towards the following:

▶ Postgraduate study or related expenses
▶ Second and subsequent degrees
▶ Overseas student grants
▶ Expeditions, travel and study projects overseas
▶ Training in counselling courses

Grants will not be given to organisations or individuals who have already received a grant from the trust within the previous two years. Research is rarely funded and support cannot be given retrospectively.

Applications

Applications can be made in writing to the correspondent. Note that online applications are not accepted.

Applications should provide the following details:

▶ Full contact details (name, address, email address, phone number, etc.)
▶ For students – evidence of your attendance or course place
▶ Full list of items required, including costs
▶ Evidence of your financial status and why you need funding – receipt of benefits, low income, etc. (all information is confidential)

▶ Letters of support from a professional person who knows you, for example a tutor, GP, employer or social worker
▶ If a medical condition is part of the application – evidence from the medical professional

The trust's website states: 'We aim to respond to every application we receive with a decision of being short-listed or not within six weeks. The Trustees decision is final and we do not usually enter into further correspondence.'

Our research suggests that the trustees meet three times a year on the last Saturday of February, June and October. It is crucial to submit the application at least one month prior to the meeting.

Other information

The trust also supports organisations, groups and educational establishments throughout the UK with strong preference for those in the South West. Various projects, particularly related to education, arts and social sciences are eligible. Large-scale national organisations would not be assisted. In 2013/14 a total of £33,000 was given in 81 grants to organisations.

Sarum St Michael Educational Charity

£134,000

Correspondent: Clerk to the Governors, First Floor, 27A Castle Street, Salisbury SP1 1TT (01722 422296 (Monday to Thursday mornings); email: clerk@sarumstmichael.org; website: www.sarumstmichael.org)

CC number: 309456

Eligibility

People over the age of 16 who live or study in the Diocese of Salisbury or adjoining dioceses, including Bath and Wells, Exeter, Oxford and Winchester (for exact geographical area see the map on the website). The charity can support:

▶ Individuals in need of financial assistance towards their higher/further education or training
▶ People who are/are about to become teachers or otherwise work with religious education
▶ Research and development of religious education

Types of grants

Grants are available for first degrees (including mature students), diplomas, access courses, Open University courses, vocational courses, postgraduate degrees, gap year activities and projects. Support can be given towards general educational expenses, including fees, necessities, books, equipment, travel, dissertation expenses and so on. Clergy can also

apply for grants to attend conferences and travel.

Annual grant total

In 2013/14 the charity had assets of £5.4 million, an income of £202,000 and a total charitable expenditure of £214,000. The amount of grants given to individuals totalled £134,000.

Exclusions

The charity will not:

▶ Make retrospective grants
▶ Contribute towards maintenance (unless an integral part of a residential course)
▶ Pay money for buildings, fixtures or fittings

Grants for people attending educational establishments are continued only if the applicant remains at that establishment.

Applications

Application forms can be obtained from the charity's website. Grants are considered four to five times a year, normally in January, March, June, August and October. Exact dates of the meetings are available online. Applications can be submitted directly by individuals, preferably by email.

Other information

A total of 80 applications were received during 2014. A total of 24 personal applicants were successful. 40 new awards were made in total, together with 35 grants due from previous years.

City of Bristol

R. W. Barnes Educational Fund

£8,000 (4 grants)

Correspondent: Mr D. Kent, Administrator, Quartet Community Foundation, Royal Oak House, Royal Oak Avenue, Bristol BS1 4GB (0117 989 7700; fax: 0117 989 7701; email: info@quartetcf.org.uk; website: www.quartetcf.org.uk)

CC number: 1080418

Eligibility

Undergraduate students on courses related to mathematics, physics, engineering (aeronautical, electrical, electronics or mechanical), astronomy or oceanography, at Bath or Cambridge universities, Imperial College, other Russell group universities or other universities in the top 40 university rankings, as compiled by 'The Complete University Guide'. Applicants must be UK nationals by birth, demonstrate that their family income is below £40,000 a year and live within either of the following post code areas: all of BS, BA, and TA, DT9, DT10, SP3/7/8, SN10/12/13/14/15, GL9.

Priority is given to students with no family history of higher education, those attending Imperial College, Bath or Cambridge Universities, individuals studying mathematics or physics and people living within BA8, BA9 BA11 post code areas.

Types of grants

Recurrent grants of up to £2,500 a year (for a maximum of four years) are available towards university fees and living costs. Awards are subject to satisfactory academic result.

Annual grant total

The amount of grants awarded from this particular fund was not specified in the Quartet Community Foundation's annual accounts; however, previously awards have totalled around £8,000.

Exclusions

Grants are not awarded to applicants studying civil or chemical engineering.

Applications

Application forms can be downloaded from the Quartet Community Foundation's website and should be returned by August, either by post or email. Applicants will be informed about the outcome in September.

Other information

This fund is managed by Quartet Community Foundation.

The Christ Church Exhibition Fund

£9,000

Correspondent: Ian Millsted, Administrator, 1 All Saints Court, Bristol BS1 1JN (0117 929 2709; email: ccl.charity@btconnect.com)

CC number: 325124

Eligibility

Grants are given to:

- Boys and girls over the age of 11 who live in the city of Bristol and are attending fee-paying schools. Assistance is not, however, given on first entry to fee-paying education. Grants for schoolchildren are calculated in relation to the family's income and actual fees
- Students in higher education up to the age of 25 who have received at least two years' secondary education in Bristol or who have long residential connections with the city

Types of grants

Grants, generally of between £200 and £1,000 a year, are given for fee-paying secondary education, where parents are unable to maintain payments because of changed family or financial circumstances. Grants are awarded to help with the cost of school uniforms, other school clothing, books and educational outings. Occasional help is given to talented pupils at state schools who need help to pay for music lessons. Grants of between £100 and £300 a year are awarded to students unable to obtain discretionary awards or for higher education courses not qualifying for grants. Grants are awarded only for courses in the UK and can be given to help with the cost of books or towards fees and living expenses.

Annual grant total

In 2014 the fund had an income of £13,500 and a total expenditure of £13,000. Based on financial information that is available from previous years, we estimate grants to individuals to have totalled around £9,000.

Exclusions

Grants are not given for trips abroad, for courses outside the UK or for postgraduate study.

Applications

Application forms are available from the correspondent from Easter onwards. Applications should be submitted directly by the individual (student) or by a parent (schoolchildren). Meetings are held in June/July for junior grants, and in September for seniors. Applications should include length of residence in Bristol, how long in present school (schoolchildren) and whether a definite place offer has been received (student).

Other information

Choristers of Christ Church with St Ewen, Bristol, are also eligible for support.

Edmonds and Coles Scholarships (Edmonds and Coles Charity)

£7,500

Correspondent: Jo McNab, Administrator, The Society of Merchant Venturers, Merchants' Hall, The Promenade, Clifton Down, Bristol BS8 3NH (0117 973 8058; email: treasurer@merchantventurers.com; website: merchantventurers.com/charitable-activities/edmonds-and-coles-scholarships)

CC number: 311751

Eligibility

People in need who are under the age of 25 and live in the area of benefit, which includes: Aust, Avonmouth, Bishopston, Brentry, Charlton Mead, Coombe Dingle, Cotham, Durdham Down, Hallen, Henbury, Henleaze, Horfield, Kindsweston, Kingsdown, Lawrence Weston, New Passage, Northwick, Pilning, Redland, Redwick, Sea Mills, Severn Beach, Shirehampton, Southmead, Stoke Bishop, Tyndalls Park, Westbury-on-Trym, Westbury Park and Woolcott Park.

Types of grants

Small grants, usually in the range of £100–£1,000, are available towards general educational expenses, including the cost of books, equipment/instruments or travel. Support can be given to people at school, college/university, or those undertaking vocational training. Awards are not normally made to enable a child to enter private education. Help may, however, be given in respect of pupils already in private education when there has been a change in financial circumstances through, for example, death of a parent, divorce or unemployment, and there are good reasons for avoiding disruption of a child's education.

Annual grant total

In 2013/14 the charity had an income of £11,000 and an expenditure of £8,000. We estimate the annual total amount of grants awarded to individuals to be around £7,500.

Exclusions

At primary and secondary school level, grants are not normally given to enable children to enter private education when parents cannot afford the cost. Help may be given in respect of children already in private education when there is a change in financial circumstances (for example, due to a death of a parent, marriage break-up, unemployment and so on) and there are good reasons for avoiding disruption of the child's education.

Applications

Application forms are available from the charity's website or the correspondent. They can be submitted by the individual or a third party, if the applicant is under 16. Grants are usually considered in February, July and September.

Other information

Our research shows that this charity consults and co-operates with Bristol Municipal Charities in some cases.

Anthony Edmonds Charity

£5,000

Correspondent: Mrs F. Greenfield, Correspondent, 43 Meadowland Road, Bristol BS10 7PW (0117 909 8308; email: fran.greenfield@blueyonder.co.uk; website: www.edmondscharity.org.uk)

CC number: 286709

Eligibility

Young people up to the age of 25 who live in any of the ancient parishes of Henbury, Westbury and Horfield.

Types of grants

Grants are to help with activities of a broadly educational nature including apprentices, courses and less formal projects that can be academic, artistic, technical, social or sporting.

Annual grant total

In 2014 the charity had an income of £17,500 and a total expenditure of £6,000. We estimate that grants totalled around £5,000.

Applications

You can download an application form online or contact the Clerk for a hard copy. Requests can be submitted directly by the individual. The trustees meet to consider applications in March and September.

The Gane Charitable Trust

See entry on page 151

The Redcliffe Parish Charity

£4,000

Correspondent: Paul Tracey, Trustee, 18 Kingston Road, Nailsea, Bristol, North Somerset BS48 4RD (email: redcliffeparishclerk@mail.com)

CC number: 203916

Eligibility

Schoolchildren in need who live in the city of Bristol, with preference for those who live in the ecclesiastical parish of St Mary Redcliffe with Temple – Bristol, and St John the Baptist – Bedminster.

Types of grants

One-off grants, usually of £25–£50. The trustees generally limit grants to families or individuals who can usually manage, but who are overwhelmed by circumstances and are in particular financial stress rather than continuing need. Our research suggests that grants can be for children's school trips and school uniforms.

Annual grant total

In 2013/14 the charity had an income of £8,500 and a total expenditure of £8,400. We estimate that educational grants totalled around £4,000.

Exclusions

Support is not given in the form of loans, for adult education, school/college fees or repetitive payments.

Applications

Awards are made through a third party, for example, social services, housing associations, doctor, health visitor, Citizens Advice or other appropriate body. Applications need to be made in writing on behalf of an individual for consideration each month. Ages of family members should be supplied in addition to financial circumstances and the reason for the request.

Other information

Grants to schoolchildren occur as part of the charity's wider welfare work.

Cornwall

Blanchminster Trust

£255,000 (330 grants)

Correspondent: Jane Bunning, Clerk to the Trustees, Blanchminster Building, 38 Lansdown Road, Bude, Cornwall EX23 8EE (01288 352851; email: office@ blanchminster.plus.com; website: www. blanchminster.org.uk)

CC number: 202118

Eligibility

People who live (or have at least one parent who lives) in the parishes of Bude, Stratton and Poughill (the former urban district of Bude-Stratton). Current or immediate past pupils of Budehaven Community School living outside the area are also considered.

Types of grants

One-off grants are made to schoolchildren, people starting work, further and higher education students, mature students and postgraduates towards uniforms or other school clothing, books, equipment/instruments, fees, maintenance/living expenses, childcare, educational outings in the UK, study or travel overseas and student exchanges.

Annual grant total

In 2014 the trust had assets of almost £11 million and an income of £511,500. During the year, 330 educational grants were made totalling £255,000.

Exclusions

Grants are not given to foreign students studying in Britain.

Applications

In general, applications should be made in writing to the correspondent and should outline exactly what assistance is needed and why. The trust does not have a standard application form, although it will send a 'Financial enquiry' form to individuals seeking assistance. Applications must include details of the applicant's weekly income and expenditure, as well as information on any efforts that have been made to seek help elsewhere.

The trust's website provides this additional information:

Standard Student Grants.

The Blanchminster Trust may support former pupils of Budehaven School who go on to Higher Education. This support usually takes the form of a Standard Student Grant. Applications for a Standard Student Grant must be made between October 1st and December 1st each year.

If you are applying for a Standard Student Grant for the first time, please contact the Clerk in October after you have started your course (01288–352851 or office@blanchminster.plus.com).

If you are applying for a second or subsequent grant, you must complete the form on this site and either email (cut and paste into Word or OpenOffice, delete dots, fill in and email to office@blanchminster.plus.com) or print and send to the Clerk.

Other information

Grants are also made to individuals for social welfare purposes and for community projects.

Carrick

Trevilson Educational Foundation

£2,500

Correspondent: Marjorie Vale, Trustee, Fiddlers Reach, 34 Station Road, St Newlyn East, Newquay, Cornwall TR8 5NE (01872 510318; email: maggie. vale@gmail.com)

CC number: 306555

Eligibility

People under the age of 25 who live in the parish of St Newlyn East and are in need.

Types of grants

Grants are available to schoolchildren, further/higher education students and people starting work or undertaking apprenticeships. Help is given towards books, equipment/necessities, educational outings and other essentials. Awards usually range from £50 to £500.

Annual grant total

In 2014 the foundation had an income of £17,400 and an expenditure of £2,700. We estimate that the amount of grants given to individuals totalled around £2,500. Note that both the income and expenditure vary annually. Over the past five years the charitable expenditure fluctuated between £2,700 and £27,000.

Applications

Applications may be made in writing to the correspondent.

Other information

Some support may be given to local schools and organisations helping people under the age of 25.

Devon

Adventure Trust for Girls

£6,000

Correspondent: Beryl Cuff, Administrator, 28 Lovelace Crescent, Exmouth, Devon EX8 3PR (01395 223606; email: ecuff@btinternet.com)

CC number: 800999

Eligibility

Girls and young women between the ages of 10 and 20 who live or attend school within eight miles of Exmouth Town Hall, south of the M5 and east of the Exe.

Types of grants

One-off grants, usually ranging from £50 to £400, can be provided to girls who wish to travel either on their own or with friends/group/organisation. A wide range of trips can be supported, including summer schools, camps, school exchange programmes and any other adventure that would develop the individual's personality, self-confidence, physical abilities, leadership and team working skills.

Assistance can also be given to girls from low income households to participate in school trips and educational outings.

Annual grant total

In 2013/14 the trust had an income of £6,900 and an expenditure of £6,500. We estimate the annual total amount of grants awarded to be around £6,000.

Exclusions

Areas to the west of the river Exe are excluded. Our research suggests that grants would not be given towards organised school ski trips.

Applications

Application forms can be requested from the correspondent. Our research indicates that applications should be submitted two months in advance of the trustees' meetings, which are normally held every second month.

Individuals who require assistance with the cost of school trips should apply through their school.

Albert Casanova Ballard Deceased (A. C. Ballard Deceased Trust)

£26,000 (120 grants)

Correspondent: Margaret Mary, Trustee, Pengelly, 6 Victory Street, Keyham, Plymouth PL2 2BY (01752 569258; email: ballardplymouth@outlook.com)

CC number: 201759

Eligibility

Boys aged between 11 and 16 who are entering or attending secondary education and live in the city of Plymouth, within seven miles from the Ballard Institute.

Types of grants

One-off grants are offered towards general educational expenses, including school uniforms, other clothing, books and equipment/instruments.

Annual grant total

In 2013/14 the trust had assets of over £1.1 million, an income of £51,500 and a total charitable expenditure of £52,000. Grants to 120 individuals totalled £26,000.

Applications

Application forms can be requested from the correspondent providing an sae up until April. Applications are only considered once a year, in June – the deadline for applications is normally the end of May.

Other information

Grants can also be given to organisations, clubs and schools operating in the area of benefit.

Bideford Bridge Trust

£191,500

Correspondent: P. Sims, Steward, 24 Bridgeland Street, Bideford, Devon EX39 2QB (01237 473122)

CC number: 204536

Eligibility

People in need who live in Bideford and the immediate neighbourhood.

Types of grants

One-off grants, usually ranging from £150 to £500, are given in the following forms:

- Book grants and bursaries for students resident within the parish of Bideford who are attending post-A-level courses
- Hardship grants for other students not resident within the parish, but within the charity's area of benefit
- Discretionary grants to support individuals resident within the parish of Bideford who are attending vocational or apprenticeship training schemes

Grants are also given to assist unemployed people and people who were recently unemployed with business start-up schemes, usually over a period of two years. Alternatively, a loan may be given.

Annual grant total

In 2014 the charity had assets of £15.2 million and an income of £766,000. During the year, educational grants for books, bursaries and vocational and apprenticeship training schemes totalled £83,000. An additional £108,500 was paid to assist individuals who are unemployed with business start-up schemes.

Exclusions

Applications from individuals in Barnstaple, Torrington and the areas beyond this are not accepted. Grants are not given to postgraduates or for computers for personal use.

Applications

Application forms are available from the correspondent, to be submitted at any time during the year by the individual, although a sponsor is usually required. Applications are considered monthly.

The Devon Educational Trust

£32,000

Correspondent: The Clerk to the Trustees, PO Box 86, Teignmouth TQ14 8ZT (email: devonedtrust@talktalk.net; website: devoneducationaltrust.co.uk)

CC number: 1157674

Eligibility

Pupils and students under the age of 25 who live, or whose parents' normal place of residence is, in Devon. Preference is given to applicants from low-income families. Applicants or their parents must be living in Devon on a permanent basis for at least 12 months.

Types of grants

One-off grants of between £100 and £500 to:

◗ Schoolchildren for uniforms/clothing and equipment/instruments

◗ College students and undergraduates for special clothing, study/travel costs, books, equipment/instruments and maintenance/living expenses

◗ Vocational students and people starting work for uniforms/clothing, books, equipment/instruments and maintenance/living expenses

During 2014, grants were also awarded to young people with specific learning difficulties to assist with the costs of one-to-one specialist tuition.

Annual grant total

In 2014 the trust had assets of £1.1 million and an income of £37,000. The trust has stated that charitable grants to individuals totalled £32,000.

Exclusions

Assistance is not normally given to those embarking on a second or higher degree course. However, in some cases the trustees may make a small grant to assist with living costs or the purchase of books, equipment and so on. No assistance is available for the payment of university fees and only in exceptional cases will the trustees consider paying school or boarding fees.

Applications

Application forms are available from the correspondent or can be downloaded from the website. They should include details of two references. The trustees meet three times a year, usually in March, July and November, and applications should be submitted four weeks before the date of the next meeting.

The Gibbons Family Trust

£10,500 (21 grants)

Correspondent: Roger Dawe, Trustee, 14 Fore Street, Budleigh Salterton, Devon EX9 6NG (01395 445259; email enquiries@gibbonstrusts.org; website: www.gibbonstrusts.org)

CC number: 290884

Eligibility

People up to 25 in Devon and the Isle of Thanet area of Kent with a preference for those from East Devon.

Types of grants

Grants towards the maintenance and educational advancement, training and recreation of children and young people.

Annual grant total

In 2014/15 the trust had assets of £2.2 million and an income of £83,000. Grants to 21 individuals totalled £10,500.

Exclusions

No grants are given for private school fees, gap year projects or other types of overseas trips.

Applications

Application forms are available to download from the website with a short covering letter and a supporting statement from a third party such as a school, club, doctor or social worker. Applications must be posted and are not accepted by email.

Other information

Grants were also made to organisations (£66,000 in 2014/15).

The Heathcoat Trust

£167,500

Correspondent: Mrs C. Twose, Secretary, The Factory, Tiverton, Devon EX16 5LL (email: heathcoattrust@ heathcoat.co.uk)

CC number: 203367

Eligibility

Mainly students in secondary and further education who live and study in Tiverton and the mid-Devon area. Occasionally students can be supported for study outside the area if the courses are not available locally. Applicants need to have a personal connection with either the John Heathcoat or the Lowman Companies.

Types of grants

One-off and recurrent grants towards fees.

Annual grant total

In 2013/14 the trust had assets of £19.8 million and an income of £563,000. Grants totalled £732,000 and included £160,000 awarded to organisations. Grants to individuals amounted to £572,000, the majority of which was given for social welfare purposes. Educational grants to individuals totalled £167,500.

Applications

Apply in writing to the correspondent. For A-level applicants who attend East Devon College, application forms are available and should be submitted between April and June each year.

The George Ley Educational Trust

£3,000

Correspondent: James Williams, Trustee, Brendon, Western Gardens, Combe Martin, Ilfracombe, Devon EX34 0EY

CC number: 306788

Eligibility

People who live in Combe Martin.

Types of grants

Grants of up to £200 can be made for books and equipment to higher/further education students or schoolchildren.

Annual grant total

In 2014 the trust had an income of £5,000 and a total expenditure of £3,300. We estimate that the total amount of grants awarded to individuals was approximately £3,000.

Exclusions

Grants are not given for main expenses, such as fees or living costs.

Applications

Applications can be made in writing to the correspondent. The committee meets to consider applications in May and September. Re-applications for future grants can be made by people who have already been supported by this trust.

Dulce Haigh Marshall Trust

£3,800

Correspondent: The Secretary, Heathercombe, Inner Ting Tong, Budleigh Salterton, Devon EX9 7AP (01395 442893; email: info@ dulcehaighmarshalltrust.com; website: www.dulcehaighmarshalltrust.com)

CC number: 286273

Eligibility

Cellists and other string players who are in need of financial assistance, live in Devon, and are under the age of 25.

Types of grants

Grants ranging between £200 and £500 towards tuition fees or the purchase of instruments.

Annual grant total

In 2013/14 the trust had an income of £600 and a total expenditure of £4,000. We have estimated that the annual total amount of grants awarded was around £3,800.

Exclusions

Grants are not given to people who or whose parents have sufficient income to meet their needs. People who do not demonstrate sufficient commitment to learning their instrument will not be supported.

Applications

Application forms are available from the trust's website or can be requested from the correspondent. They should be returned before 1 May. Grants are usually distributed in August each year. Applications can be made directly by the individual and should include a teacher's report. Students may be asked to attend an audition.

City of Exeter

The Exeter Advancement in Life Charity

£7,500

Correspondent: Steven Sitch, Chichester Mews, Exeter Municipal Charities, 6 Southernhay West, Exeter, Devon EX1 1JG (01392 421162; fax: 01392 201551; email: info@ exetermunicipalcharity.org.uk)

CC number: 1002151

Eligibility

Children and young people under the age of 25 who are in need and live in the city of Exeter or within 15 miles of the city centre. Preference may be given to schoolchildren with serious family difficulties so that the child has to be educated away from home.

Types of grants

One-off and recurrent grants of up to £500 a year. Support can be given to schoolchildren towards clothing and uniforms, books, equipment/instruments, fees or educational outings in the UK. Further/higher education students (including mature and postgraduate) can be assisted with the cost of books, equipment/instruments, course fees and related necessities, also study or travel overseas. People in vocational training/starting work can receive help with equipment/instruments, travel costs, outfits and materials. Grants towards study/travel overseas are subject to a minimum study period of six months (unless it is an obligatory part of an approved course).

Annual grant total

In 2014 the charity had an income of £8,000 and an expenditure of £8,000. We estimate the annual total amount of grants awarded to be around £7,500.

Applications

Application forms are available from the correspondent. They can be submitted directly by the individual or through a third party, such as a parent/guardian or educational welfare agency, if applicable. Candidates should provide an academic reference and outline their financial circumstances. Prospective grant recipients are usually interviewed in February, May, August and November.

Note: This charity is comprised of two educational charities: John Dinam School Endowment and Lady Ann Clifford Trust. These two charities have the same criteria, described above, with the exception that John Dinam School Endowment can make grants outside Exeter – up to 15 miles from the city centre. Applicants can only receive a grant from one of these charities. Those living outside the city should apply to John Dinam School Endowment.

Other information

This charity is part of Exeter Municipal Charities. Support for welfare needs is available through The Exeter Relief in Need Charity.

City of Plymouth

The Maudlyn Lands Charity

£2,000

Correspondent: Anthony Golding, Clerk to the Trustees, Blue Haze, Down Road, Tavistock, Devon PL19 9AG (01822 612983)

CC number: 202577

Eligibility

People in need who live in Plympton St Mary and Sparkwell.

Types of grants

One-off grants to help with general educational costs.

Annual grant total

In 2013/14 the charity had an income of £7,500 and a total expenditure of around £8,200. We estimate that about £2,000 was awarded to individuals for educational purposes.

Applications

Applications may be made in writing to the correspondent. They are considered in November.

Other information

This charity also gives grants to individuals for welfare purposes, and to organisations.

The Olford Bequest

£3,300

Correspondent: John Coates, Correspondent, 24 Dolphin House, Sutton Wharf, Plymouth PL4 0BL

(01752 225724; email: johnbcoates@ btinternet.com)

CC number: 306936

Eligibility

Young people from Plymouth schools going to university.

Types of grants

Allowances are available to five students 'who have gained exhibitions or scholarships to universities'. Two of these grants must be awarded to students at Devonport High School for Boys. The charity provides £250 a year for three years to be spent on anything the student wants and not course-related matters.

Some support may also be given to present or past pupils of any school in Plymouth in need of financial assistance.

Annual grant total

In 2014/15 the charity had an income of £4,100 and an expenditure of £3,500. We estimate that grants totalled about £3,300.

Exclusions

Young people from Plymouth schools who are going to university.

Applications

Applications may be made in writing to the correspondent.

Orphan's Aid Educational Foundation (Plymouth)

£2,500

Correspondent: Vanessa Steer, Clerk and Treasurer, 184 Mannamead Road, Plymouth PL3 5RE (01752 703280; email: v_steer@yahoo.co.uk; website: www.plymouth.gov.uk/ modgov?modgovlink=http%3A%2F% 2Fwww.plymouth.gov.uk% 2FmgInternet% 2FmgOutsideBodyDetails.aspx%3FID% 3D385)

CC number: 306770

Eligibility

Children who live in the city and county borough of Plymouth, are of school age and from a one-parent family.

Types of grants

One-off grants of up to £250 for the purchase of school uniforms and shoes.

Annual grant total

In 2014 this charity had an income of £2,500 and a total expenditure of £2,600. We estimate that grants awarded totalled £2,500.

Exclusions

No grants are given for school fees or maintenance, for people starting work or for mature students.

Applications

Application forms are available from the correspondent by email or post, including information about income, expenditure and dependants. Applicants are usually interviewed.

East Devon

Sidmouth Consolidated Charities

£1,700

Correspondent: Ruth Rose, Correspondent, 22 Alexandria Road, Sidmouth, Devon EX10 9HB (01395 513079; email: ruth.rose@eclipse.co.uk)

CC number: 207081

Eligibility

People in need who live in Sidmouth, Sidford, Sidbury or Salcombe Regis.

Types of grants

Our research suggests that one-off grants are available for educational needs, such as computers and books for university students.

Annual grant total

In 2014 the charity had assets of £1.25 million, almost all of which was permanent endowment and unavailable for distribution. The charity's income was £36,500 and a total of £30,000 was spent in awarding grants, which consisted of 'housing needs based' (£23,000) and 'other local needs' (£6,800). No other details were given; therefore, we estimate that the amount of grants given to individuals for educational purposes totalled around £1,700.

Applications

Applications may be made in writing to the correspondent, either directly by the individual or through a social worker, Citizens Advice or welfare agency. Applications are considered at monthly meetings.

Other information

The charity supports both organisations and individuals for social welfare and educational needs.

The charity's record on the Charity Commission's website notes that 'the objects of the John Arthur & William Slade branch are the relief of poverty, need or other hardship for beneficiaries over the age of 60 years who are resident in the area'.

Mid Devon

The Richards Educational Charity

£39,500 (108 grants)

Correspondent: Geoffrey Knowles, Secretary, Silvertrees, 26 Hederman Close, Silverton, Exeter EX5 4HW (01392 860109; email: jmthomas1951@yahoo.co.uk)

CC number: 306787

Eligibility

Young people under 25 who live in the parish of Silverton.

Types of grants

Recurrent grants in the range of £5 to £750 are given to schoolchildren and college students for study/travel abroad, books, equipment/instruments, maintenance/living expenses and excursions. They are also given to undergraduates, vocational students, mature students, and people starting work for fees, study/travel abroad, books, equipment/instruments, maintenance/living expenses and excursions.

Annual grant total

In 2014 the charity had assets of £1.27 million and an income of £228,500 (including proceeds from sales of investments). Educational grants to individuals totalled £39,500 and were distributed as follows:

University students	21	£20,800
Schoolchildren	73	£7,200
Career training	9	£5,800
Further education	3	£2,500
Pre-school	2	£600

A further £2,700 was awarded in four grants to groups.

Applications

Application forms are available at the village post office, school or health centre. They should be submitted directly by the individual or a parent. They are considered regularly.

Other information

Information about the charity is made known throughout the parish, particularly through the places of education for children in Silverton.

Silverton Parochial Charity

£8,100

Correspondent: Michelle Valance, Secretary to the Trustees, 9 Davis Close, Silverton, Devon EX5 4DL (01392 860408; email: secretary@silvertonparochialtrust.co.uk)

CC number: 201255

Eligibility

People in need who live in the parish of Silverton only.

Types of grants

One-off grants, with no minimum or maximum limit, to 'parishioners who are in a condition of need, hardship or distress'.

Annual grant total

In 2014 the charity had an income of £38,000 and paid grants in aid to individuals and community projects totalling £32,500. We estimate that the amount of grants given to individuals for educational purposes totalled around £8,100. It would appear that main support is given for general relief in need.

Exclusions

The charity only supports needs that are not provided for by the state schemes such as social services or state benefit programmes. Grants are not normally made towards state or local authority taxes.

Applications

Application forms are available to download from the website and should be returned to the correspondent or the trustees. The forms can also be obtained from the correspondent or Silverton Post Office. The trustees will need details of the applicant's financial situation (including their income and outgoings) as well as any additional information that may assist the application. The trustees meet eight times a year.

Other information

Grants are also made to people in need who live in the parish and to organisations providing assistance for them. The charity has an informative website.

North Devon

The Vivian Moon Foundation

£16,000

Correspondent: The Secretariat, The Vivian Moon Foundation, c/o Simpkins Edwards, 21 Boutport Street, Barnstaple, Devon EX31 1RP (email: info@vivianmoonfoundation.co.uk; website: www.vivianmoonfoundation.co.uk)

CC number: 298942

Eligibility

People over the age of 18 who have links with North Devon and have an offer of a place on a course of further educational, professional or vocational training which will lead to employment or improve individuals' skills and their career opportunities. Preference is given to people who intend to return to North Devon to work and, ideally, have an employment secured there at the end of their training.

Types of grants

One-off and recurrent grants ranging between £150 and £300 are available to people in further education and training, including college students, vocational students, mature students, people starting work, unemployed people seeking to get into employment or working people who wish to develop their skills. Both full-time and part-time, also sandwich and correspondence courses can be supported. Most applicants are funded partially and on a course or annual basis.

Annual grant total

In 2014 the foundation had an income of £15,500 and a total expenditure of £17, 500 we estimate that the amount of grants given to individuals totalled around £16,000.

Exclusions

First degree applicants are unlikely to be supported, unless in extraordinary circumstances.

Applications

The foundation prefers to receive applications online through its website in order to speed up the process. Applicants who are unable to apply in such way can book computer time at a Pathfinder centre in Barnstaple (01271 345851) or Bideford (01237 405250), or request an application from the correspondent. Applications should provide an email address of one referee. Grants are considered in January, May and September.

Other information

North Devon comprises the area administered by either Torridge or North Devon district council.

South Hams

Parish Lands (South Brent Feoffees)

£10,800

Correspondent: J. Blackler, Correspondent, Luscombe Maye, 6 Fore Street, South Brent TQ10 9BQ (01364 646180; email: southbrent@ luscombemaye.com)

CC number: 255283

Eligibility

Individuals who live or have lived in the parish of South Brent.

Types of grants

One-off and recurrent grants are awarded, generally in the range of £50 to £300. They can be given for general educational needs. Our research suggests that support is mainly given to further education students.

Annual grant total

In 2014 the charity had assets of around £67,500 and an income of £55,000. A total of £32,500 was given in grants. We estimate that educational support to individuals totalled around £10,800.

Applications

Application forms can be requested from the correspondent. They can be submitted at any time either directly by the individual or through a third party, such as a family member, social worker, teacher, or an organisation, for example, Citizens Advice or school.

Other information

Grants are also given to organisations and for welfare purposes. The trustees' annual report from 2014 further specifies that one third of the income of the charity is to be applied for upkeep of the parish church, one third for the benefit of deserving people in need living in the parish and one third to form the endowment of the Parish Lands Educational Foundation (to support the education and advancement in life of the parish children).

Torridge

Great Torrington Town and Lands Charity

£15,000

Correspondent: Ian Newman, Steward, 25 South Street, Great Torrington, Devon EX38 8AA (01805 623517; email: greattorringtoncharities@btconnect.com)

CC number: 202801

Eligibility

People in need who live in Great Torrington.

Types of grants

Our research suggests that grants are usually made to students towards a year out (voluntary work). Requests are also considered for school uniform costs for schoolchildren and for other costs for mature students. Grants to individuals are generally up to £200, although may reach up to £400 in extreme cases.

Annual grant total

In 2013/14 the charity had assets of around £6.2 million and an income of £258,500. The total amount spent on charitable activities for this charity totalled about £453,500, which included

£44,500 in the maintenance of the almshouses. Grants were made totalling £374,000; however, unlike in the past, further breakdown was not given. In previous years educational support has reached around 4% of the overall grant total. We estimate grants to individuals for educational purposes to be around £15,000.

Exclusions

Needs that should be addressed by statutory sources are not funded. The charity cannot make recurrent grants.

Applications

Applications should be made in writing to the correspondent, providing all the relevant personal information.

Other information

The charity is concerned with the provision of almshouse accommodation and affordable rented housing. Grants are provided for organisations with various purposes, local churches, pensioners and other people in need.

Dorset

Cole Anderson Charitable Foundation

£3,300

Correspondent: Martin Davies, Rawlins Davy, Rowlands House, Hinton Road, Bournemouth BH1 2EG (01202 558844; email: martin.davies@rawlinsdavy.com)

CC number: 1107619

Eligibility

Individuals studying medicine, architecture or music who live in Bournemouth and Poole.

Types of grants

Bursaries and grants are given.

Annual grant total

In 2013/14 the foundation had an income of £10,000 and a total expenditure of £6,700. Grants are made to individuals for both social welfare and educational purposes. We estimate that educational grants to individuals totalled £3,300.

Applications

Apply in writing to the correspondent.

Ashley Churchill and Thorner Educational Trust

£6,000

Correspondent: Kay Dawson, Administrator, Clerk's Office, Whetstone's, West Walks, Dorchester, Dorset DT1 1AW (01305 262662; email: info@actet.org.uk; website: www.actet. org.uk)

CC number: 306229

Eligibility

Children and young people under the age of 25 who live within five miles of the county hall in Dorchester or in the civil parish of Crossways. Applicants' household income should be below £30,800 a year.

Types of grants

One-off grants, normally of up to £500, are available to schoolchildren and further/higher education students to help with the cost of fees, books, equipment/ instruments, materials, travel expenses, study/travel abroad and other necessities.

Annual grant total

In 2013/14 the trust had an income of £6,500 and a total expenditure of £6,500. We estimate the annual total amount of grants awarded to individuals to be around £6,000.

Applications

Apply in writing to the correspondent. Applications should outline how the grant will benefit the applicant, include details of parental income and confirmation of course attendance. They can be submitted by the individual directly, through a school/college/ university or through a welfare agency, if applicable. Our research shows that information about applications is also publicised in local schools. The trustees normally meet in September, January and May.

Beaminster Relief in Need Charity

£2,700

Correspondent: John Groves, Correspondent, 24 Church Street, Beaminster, Dorset DT8 3BA (01308 862192; email: jan@hand-n-head. freeserve.co.uk)

CC number: 200685

Eligibility

Individuals in need who live in the parish of Beaminster, Dorset. Preference is given to children.

Types of grants

Grants are generally in the range of £50–£1,000 and are made to schoolchildren and college students for study/travel abroad, books and equipment/instruments, also training needs, sports and recreation. About 50 grants are made each year.

Annual grant total

In 2014 the charity had an income of £13,800 and a total expenditure of £10,900. These are the highest figures in the past five years. We estimate that the total amount of grants awarded to individuals for educational purposes was around £2,700.

Applications

Applications can be submitted in writing to the correspondent by the individual or through a recognised referral agency, such as social worker, doctor or Citizens Advice. The trustees meet throughout the year.

Other information

Grants are also made to organisations and for social welfare purposes.

The Bridge Educational Trust (1996)

£47,000 (41 grants)

Correspondent: Trust Administrator, c/o Piddle Valley School, Piddletrenthide, Dorchester, Dorset DT2 7QL (email: bridgeeducationaltrust@outlook.com; website: www.bridgeeducationaltrust.org. uk)

CC number: 1068720

Eligibility

People in need who were born in or are resident in the county of Dorset, primarily from the parishes of Alton Pancras, Piddlehinton, Piddletrenthide and Plush. Normally the candidates should be approaching the end of their school education or be recent school leavers.

Special consideration is given to:

▶ People who are suffering from hardship or are in difficult family circumstances
▶ Cases where the education, course or activity would not be possible without assistance
▶ Younger children with special educational needs
▶ Older people who are making a late start after interrupted education

Types of grants

One-off and recurrent grants (for a maximum of three years) are offered to people in education at school, college or other educational establishment. Grants are not normally paid to individuals directly. Average grants range from £500 to around £2,000 and are awarded towards fees, study/travel abroad, books, equipment/instruments, excursions and visits, childcare and other expenses.

The following information is taken from the trust's website:

> Payment of a grant is usually made direct to the establishment, organisation or supplier of the course or activity. Where a grant has been awarded for books, equipment or tickets and these can be obtained through the internet at more competitive prices, then by prior arrangement successful applicants may purchase these items on line and will be reimbursed on submission of receipts. Retrospective awards will not be made i.e. if an applicant decides to pay for a course or equipment before an award has been made then the cost will not be refunded.

Annual grant total

In 2013/14 the trust had assets of £1.9 million, an income of £129,000 and made grants totalling £47,000 to 41 individuals for educational purposes.

Exclusions

The trust does not:

▶ Make loans
▶ Provide grants for fees which can be covered by student loans
▶ Give retrospective grants
▶ Support postgraduate degrees
▶ Assist people living in temporary student accommodation while studying at an educational establishment in Dorset, unless their permanent home is also in Dorset

Applications

Applications should preferably be submitted about three to four weeks before one of the regular meetings of the trustees which are normally held in February, May and September.

For a course of study over twelve months, a fresh application is required for the second and subsequent years. Three years is normally the maximum period for a grant to any one person.

An application form is available on request to be completed by the applicant in person (or by a parent in the case of a child under the age of 18). This may be completed and returned either electronically or in paper form.

Completed applications can be sent by post to:

Piddle Valley First School, Piddletrenthide, Dorset DT2 7QL

or by email to:
admin@bridgeeducationaltrust.org.uk

Other information

The trustees' annual report for 2013/14 states:

> The Trust provides grants and bursaries to assist with the education of students of

any sex, race, colour or creed drawn primarily from the parishes of Piddletrenthide (with Plush), Piddlehinton and Alton St Pancras and secondarily from those born or having their main residence in the rural County of Dorset. The Trustees favour applications from residents of the Piddle Valley and, secondarily, from residents of the rural shire County of Dorset.

Clingan's Trust

£44,000

Correspondent: David Richardson, Clerk, Avon House, 4 Bridge Street, Christchurch, Dorset BH23 1DX (01202 484242; email: richardsonfamily@ waitrose.com; website: www. clinganstrust.co.uk)

CC number: 307085

Eligibility

Applicants must be under 25 with the family home and in education at some time in the trust's area of benefit, which broadly covers Christchurch, Highcliffe, parts of Bournemouth to the east of the town centre and other outlying areas to the north and east of Christchurch.

Types of grants

One-off grants of between £100 and £1,000 for any educational need for people under 25. Preference is given to schoolchildren with serious family difficulties where the child has to be educated away from home and people with special educational needs.

Annual grant total

In 2013 the trust had assets of £31,500 an income of £63,000 and a total charitable expenditure of £45,500. The amount of grants given to individuals totalled £44,000. At the time of writing (August 2015) the information provided was the latest available.

Exclusions

The trust is normally unable to consider applicants who have applied for a grant within six weeks of the next meeting.

Applications

Application forms are available from the correspondent or to download from the website. Applications can be made directly by the individual unless under the age of 14. They are subject to deadlines, which are listed on the website, and are considered at meetings, usually held quarterly.

Other information

Funding is also occasionally awarded to organisations (£1,500 in 2013).

Corfe Castle Charities

£33,500 (17 grants)

Correspondent: Jenny Wilson, Clerk to the Trustees, The Spinney, Springbrook Close, Corfe Castle, Wareham, Dorset BH20 5HS (01929 480873; email: jennybear.wilson@virgin.net)

CC number: 1055846

Eligibility

People in need who live in the parish of Corfe Castle.

Types of grants

One-off grants or interest-free loans to students in further or higher education. In recent years grants have been given for books, fees, maintenance/living expenses, educational outings in the UK and study or travel overseas. Schoolchildren have also received one-off grants for uniforms or other school clothing.

Annual grant total

In 2013/14 the charity had assets of £3.25 million and an income of £234,000. A total of 17 grants were made to individuals for educational purposes, amounting to £33,500.

Applications

Application forms are available from the correspondent and can be submitted directly by the individual. The trustees meet monthly, but emergency requests are dealt with as they arise.

Other information

Grants are also made to individuals for social welfare purposes and to organisations.

Dorchester Relief in Need Charity

£1,000

Correspondent: Robert Potter, Trustee, 8 Mithras Close, Dorchester, Dorset DT1 2RF (01305 262041; email: robjoy1@talktalk.net)

CC number: 286570

Eligibility

People in need who live in the ecclesiastical parish of Dorchester.

Types of grants

One-off grants to those in need. In the past grants have been given for school uniforms and excursions, and to people starting work for books and equipment.

Annual grant total

In 2014/15 the charity had an income of £3,200 and a total expenditure of £2,200. We estimate that the amount of grants given to individuals for educational purposes totalled around £1,000.

Applications

Application forms are available from the correspondent and can be submitted through a school/teacher, social worker, health visitor, Citizens Advice or social services.

Other information

This charity also gives grants for relief-in-need purposes.

Gordon Charitable Trust

£7,500

Correspondent: Gerry Aiken, Trustee, 45 Dunkeld Road, Bournemouth BH3 7EW (01202 768337; email: gerry_aitken@hotmail.com)

CC number: 200668

Eligibility

Young people between the ages of 15 and 25 living in the county of Dorset who are in further/higher education or undertaking apprenticeships. Preference is given to individuals who have lived, or whose parents have lived, in the borough council areas of Bournemouth, Poole and Christchurch.

Types of grants

The trust provides scholarships, bursaries and other financial help 'to a very limited extent'. Grants are one-off or recurrent for three or four years (depending on the course) of up to £1,000 per year per individual. Support is towards the cost of books, clothing, equipment/instruments, maintenance/ living expenses. People starting work and music/arts students are also supported.

Annual grant total

In 2014 the trust had an income of £6,000 and an expenditure of £8,000. We estimate the annual total amount of grants awarded to be around £7,500.

Applications

Apply in writing to the correspondent.

Other information

Our research indicates that the trust is reliant upon donations from other sources; therefore, its income is limited and variable.

North Dorset

The William Williams Charity

£95,500

Correspondent: Ian Winsor, Steward, Stafford House, 10 Prince of Wales Road, Dorchester, Dorset DT1 1PW (01305 264573; email: enquires@williamwilliams.org.uk; website: www.williamwilliams.org.uk)

CC number: 202188

Eligibility

People who live in the ancient parishes of Blandford Forum, Shaftesbury or Sturminster Newton.

Types of grants

One-off grants to students, mature students or apprentices embarking on higher education or recognised training schemes.

Annual grant total

In 2014 the charity had assets of £8.2 million and an income of £422,500. Grants totalled £153,000, of which £18,500 was given to organisations. Grants to individuals amounted to £134,500, with £95,500 of this awarded for educational purposes.

Exclusions

The charity's website states:

> Due to the increased number of applications from the three towns and the finite nature of the funds available to the Charity, the Trustees found it necessary, from 2008, to require parental income to be taken into account. Therefore those students whose parental/household annual income exceeds £35,000 net per annum will not generally be considered eligible in the future.

Applications

Application forms are available to download from the website (form 'A' should be completed by the student and form 'B' by the student's parent or guardian). They should be submitted along with a covering letter describing more about the applicant, their education and background, preferably to a trustee from the town in which the student lives (there is a list of trustees' names and contact details on the website), or to the charity's office. There is an annual cut-off date for applications in September, which is stated on the application forms; however, in cases of need, trustees may consider applications outside this timeframe. Following the receipt of both forms before the deadline, a trustee from the town in which the student lives will arrange a meeting to discuss the application.

Purbeck

The Cecil Charity

£16,000

Correspondent: Lord Rockley, Trustee, Lytchett Heath House, Lytchett Heath, Poole BH16 6AE (email: charity@lytchettheath.co.uk)

CC number: 306248

Eligibility

Young people under the age of 25 who live within a ten-mile radius of the parish church at Lytchett Matravers.

Types of grants

Grants, scholarships and bursaries at any secondary school, university, college or other place of education. The provision of clothing, books and equipment and studying abroad.

Annual grant total

In 2013/14 the charity had an income of £23,500 and an expenditure of £17,500. We estimate that grants totalled £16,000.

Applications

An application form is available from the correspondent and can be submitted directly by the individual. Applications are considered in August, November and March.

Weymouth and Portland

The Sir Samuel Mico Trust

£28,000

Correspondent: Howard Jones, Administrator, Edwards and Keeping Unity Chambers, 34 High East Street, Dorchester, Dorset DT1 1HA (01305 251333; email: howardjones@edwardsandkeeping.co.uk; website: www.weymouthtowncharities.org.uk)

CC number: 202629

Eligibility

Young people between the ages of 16 and 24 who reside in the borough of Weymouth and Portland and have been born in the borough, or have resided there for at least ten years. The trust particularly welcomes applications for those on apprenticeships and those wishing to take up professional careers.

Types of grants

One-off and recurrent grants are made to students in further or higher education or those undertaking apprenticeships. Grants are given towards educational course fees, living costs for those on educational courses, equipment, books and assisted places on the Tall Ships Youth Trust ships.

Annual grant total

In 2014 the trust had assets of £826,000 and an income of £42,000. It made grants to individuals totalling £28,000.

Applications

Application forms are available to download from the website or from the correspondent. Applicants must be able to show that they are in difficult financial circumstances and have a desire to extend their education.

Gloucester-shire

Barnwood House Trust

£56,000 (66 grants)

Correspondent: Gail Rodway, Grants Manager, Ullenwood Manor Farm, Ullenwood, Cheltenham, Gloucestershire GL53 9QT (01452 611292; fax: 01452 634011; email: gail.rodway@barnwoodtrust.org; website: www.barnwoodtrust.org)

CC number: 218401

Eligibility

People in need over the age of 18 who live in Gloucestershire, have long-term mental health challenges or a physical disability that affects their quality of life, are on a low income and have little or no savings. Applicants are expected to seek statutory support first.

Types of grants

Opportunities Fund

One-off awards are offered to provide individuals with the opportunity to attempt 'something new that will enable them to move on to employment, volunteering or give them the ability to help others'. It may also be used to fund training or equipment that will enhance their ability to pursue a current hobby. Grants range from £200 to £2,000 (the average award of £850 in 2014) and can be given for training courses, purchase of equipment for sports or other hobbies, towards books, exam fees, educational necessities, specialist work clothing and so on.

Annual grant total

In 2014 the trust had assets of £81.1 million and an income of £3.28 million. Grants were made totalling £557,000, which consisted of £237,000 given to organisations and £340,500 provided to 821 individuals. The website informs that 66 people were assisted through the Opportunities Fund.

About £56,000 was given for educational purposes.

Exclusions

Grants are not usually made to:

- People living outside Gloucestershire
- Those under the age of 18
- People with problems relating to drugs and alcohol – unless they also have physical disabilities or a diagnosed mental illness
- Fund anything normally considered by the Individual Wellbeing Fund such as daily living equipment, computers or holidays
- Fund university fees or associated costs for which statutory grants or student loans are available
- Help retrospectively, or when an item has been ordered prior to the grant application

Applications

Application forms can be downloaded from the trust's website or requested from the correspondent. All applications should be made through, or endorsed by, a social or healthcare professional (an occupational therapist, social worker, health visitor, district nurse or community psychiatric nurse). Applications are considered at quarterly meetings, normally in March, June, September and December.

Other information

Small grants (up to £1,000) are made to local organisations with similar aims (£62,000 in 2014). The trust is also engaged in providing housing accommodation. The Small Sparks grants are offered to 'small groups of people throughout Gloucestershire to get together to do something they enjoy and make a difference to where they live' (66 grants totalling over £16,000 were awarded in 2014).

The Wellbeing Fund of the trust offers support to enable individuals to live independently.

John Edmonds' Charity

£5,000

Correspondent: Richard Mullings, Administrator, 7 Dollar Street, Cirencester, Gloucestershire GL7 2AS (01285 650000; email: rrm@sml-law.co.uk)

CC number: 311495

Eligibility

People under the age of 25 who were born in Cirencester. Our research indicates that people who currently live or were educated in Cirencester are also eligible for support.

Types of grants

Help is given to people entering a trade/starting work. Assistance is towards the cost of education, training or apprenticeships, including fees, equipment/tools, clothing/outfits, travel costs or maintenance expenses. Grants can be made to schoolchildren and students as well. Awards can range from £100 to £500 and are one-off.

Annual grant total

In 2014 the charity had an income of £7,000 and an expenditure of £5,400 We estimate that around £5,400 was awarded in grants to individuals. Our research suggests that about ten awards are made each year.

Applications

Application forms can be requested from the correspondent.

Lumb's Educational Foundation

£12,500

Correspondent: Neville Capper, Trustee, 54 Collum End Rise, Leckhampton, Cheltenham GL53 0PB (01242 515673; email: lumbsfoundation@virginmedia.com)

CC number: 311683

Eligibility

People between the ages of 16 and 25 who live in the borough of Cheltenham and the surrounding parishes. Students from Gloucestershire, especially studying arts and music, can also be considered.

Types of grants

One-off grants in the range of £50–£1,000 towards general education and training. Support can be given for the course fees, books, clothing, equipment/instruments and educational visits in the UK or study/travel abroad. People starting work can be helped with the cost of uniforms/outfits, books and equipment/instruments. Gap year and similar official travel projects are supported.

Annual grant total

In 2014 the foundation had an income of £12,000 and an expenditure of £13,000. We estimate the annual total amount of grants awarded to individuals to be around £12,500.

Exclusions

People who are permanently resident outside the area of benefit are ineligible. Grants are not made towards trips that are not of educational nature. Living expenses or school fees are not supported.

Applications

Application forms can be requested from the correspondent. Once completed they should be returned with a supporting letter, including details of income, expenditure, parents' financial situation and the purpose of the grant. The trustees usually meet in February, April, July, September and November. Candidates are interviewed. Each application is assessed according to need and funds available at the time.

Cheltenham

Higgs and Cooper's Educational Charity

£18,000

Correspondent: Martin Fry, Administrator, 7 Branch Hill Rise, Charlton Kings, Cheltenham GL53 9HN (01242 239903; email: martyn.fry@dsl.pipex.com)

CC number: 311570

Eligibility

People under the age of 25 who were born or live in the former Charlton Kings civil parish. Preference is given to people from single parent families.

Types of grants

Grants are awarded to people in secondary education, further/higher education students and people starting work/entering a trade. Support is mainly given towards educational outings, study/travel overseas, but also for general educational expenditure, including books, equipment/instruments, fees and so on. Grants can also be given for postgraduate degrees and training.

Annual grant total

In 2013/14 the charity had an income of £16,500 and an expenditure of £19,000. We estimate that the annual total amount of grants awarded to individuals was around £18,000. Normally around 30 individuals are awarded each year.

Exclusions

Trips beyond Europe are not likely to be supported.

Applications

Application forms can be requested from the correspondent. They can be submitted directly by the individual and are considered six times a year. Our research suggests that the charity publicises its grants locally in order to increase awareness, as at times there has been a lack of applications.

Other information

The charity also supports local schools, youth clubs and other voluntary organisations broadly connected with the education or recreational pursuits of young people in the area of benefit.

Cotswold

Weston-sub-Edge Educational Charity

£14,000

Correspondent: Rachel Hurley, Administrator, Longclose Cottage, Weston-sub-Edge, Chipping Campden, Gloucestershire GL55 6QX (01386 841808; email: cjhurley@wseg.wanadoo. co.uk; website: www.westonsubedge. com/?page_id=143)

CC number: 297226

Eligibility

People under the age of 25 who or whose parents live in Weston-sub-Edge, or who have at any time attended (or whose parents have attended) Weston-sub-Edge Church of England Primary School.

Types of grants

Grants range from £10 to £500. People at any stage of education who fit the criteria listed above (including people starting work) can be supported for books, equipment/instruments, fees, educational outings in the UK and study or travel abroad. Further and higher education may also be supported for maintenance/living expenses. In cases of special financial need grants can be for uniforms or other clothing for schoolchildren.

Awards have been given for nursery fees, music, dance, drama and sports lessons, after school clubs and trips, residential trips, brownies/cubs, extra tuition, through to grants to university students.

Annual grant total

In 2013/14 the charity had an income of £11,500 and an expenditure of £14,500. We estimate the annual total amount of grants awarded to individuals to be around £14,000.

Applications

Application forms can be requested from the correspondent and should include details of the course, its duration and purpose. Applications should be submitted directly by the individual if over 16, or otherwise by the parent/ guardian. The trustees meet every other month, usually the 4th Monday, in January, March, May, July, September and November. Applications must be received ten days before the meeting to allow time for production and circulation of agenda. A separate form is required for each applicant within a family. Applications should be submitted during or just before the term in which the course or activity takes place. Applications should include all activities for the whole term on one form. Only one application per student per term is allowed. The trustees are unlikely to consider applications which are submitted the term after the event takes place. Receipts for the payment of fees should accompany the application form or be submitted as soon as they are available.

South Gloucestershire

Almondsbury Charity

£3,100

Correspondent: Peter Orford, Secretary, Shepperdine Road, Oldbury Naite, Oldbury-on-Severn, Bristol BS35 1RJ (01454 415346; email: peter.orford@ gmail.com; website: www. almondsburycharity.org.uk)

CC number: 202263

Eligibility

Young people who are in further or higher education and have lived in Almondsbury, Bradley Stoke North, Easter Compton, Patchway or parts of Pilning for at least one year.

Types of grants

One-off grants are made, usually for buying books.

Annual grant total

In 2013/14 the charity had assets of £2.3 million and an income of £69,500. Grants totalled £56,000 and were mainly made to organisations. Grants to 18 individuals from the Education and Relief Fund amounted to £6,200 but we were unable to determine how they were distributed

Exclusions

No grants are made for school or course fees.

Applications

Applications can be made using the appropriate form. Forms are available to download from the charity's website and should be completed and returned to the correspondent along with any other relevant information. The charity does not make cash awards; all grants are paid by cheque against invoices/accounts. Where necessary, applications should be supported by an appropriate person.

The Chipping Sodbury Town Lands

£14,800

Correspondent: Nicola Gideon, Clerk, Town Hall, 57–59 Broad Street, Chipping Sodbury, Bristol BS37 6AD (01454 852223; email: nicola.gideon@ chippingsodburytownhall.co.uk; website: www.chippingsodburytownhall.co.uk)

CC number: 236364

Eligibility

People in need who are aged up to 25 years and live in the parish of Sodbury.

Types of grants

One-off and recurrent grants to aid the promotion of education, including further education courses.

Annual grant total

In 2014 the charity had assets of £9 million and an income of £360,500. Grants totalled £92,000, of which £24,500 was given in grants to individuals for both educational and social welfare purposes. Educational grants totalled £14,800.

Applications

Apply in writing to the correspondent. Grant aid is advertised locally in schools, clubs, associations, churches and other religious orders, in the local press, and the Town Hall.

Stroud

The Stroud and Rodborough Educational Charity

£18,000

Correspondent: Shani Baker, Clerk to the Trustees, 14 Green Close, Uley, Dursley, Gloucestershire GL11 5TH (01453 860379; email: info@ stroudrodboroughed.org; website: www. stroudrodboroughec.org)

CC number: 309614

Eligibility

Children and young people in need who are under the age of 25 and resident in the parishes comprising the Stroud rural district (Bisley-with-Lypiatt, Chalford, Cranham, Horsley, Kings Stanley, Leonard Stanley, Minchinhampton, Miserden, Oakridge, Painswick, Pitchcombe, Randwick, Rodborough, Stonehouse, Thrupp, Whiteshill, Woodchester and Nailsworth urban district).

Types of grants

Grants can be given towards general educational needs, including study/travel overseas, educational activities, equipment/instruments, clothing, books, music and drama lessons, course-related necessities and so on. Primary school pupils have also been assisted to undertake educational and residential school trips. Grants range from £10 to £500.

Annual grant total

In 2013/14 the charity had assets of around £50,000 and an income of £128,500. A total of £45,500 was spent in charitable activities. We estimate that around £18,000 was given to individuals in educational grants. Almost £1,000 was awarded in prizes.

Exclusions

Support is not given in the cases where funding should be provided by the local authority.

Applications

Application forms are available on the charity's website or from the correspondent. The trustees meet four times a year, normally at the end of January, April, July and October. Applications should provide a reference from a teacher and be submitted in advance of the meetings.

Other information

The priority of the charity is to assist Marling School, Stroud High School and Archway School, where support is not already provided by the local authority. The charity also gives grants to local charitable organisations working for the benefit of young people and administers a number of prize funds tenable at local schools.

Somerset

Arthur Allen Educational Trust

£5,500

Correspondent: Allison Dowding, Trustee, Meadow's Edge, High Street, Stoney Stratton, Shepton Mallet, Somerset BA4 6DY (01749 831077; email: adowding.epc@virgin.net)

CC number: 310256

Eligibility

Further and higher education students between the ages of 16 and 25 who were born or live in the parish of Evercreech.

Types of grants

One-off and recurrent grants in the range of £50–£2,000 are available to students attending college, university or sixth form college, also vocational students or people starting work. Support is given towards travel expenses, books, equipment/instruments, study/travel abroad, clothing, maintenance/living expenses and fees.

Annual grant total

In 2013 the trust had an income of £5,900 and an expenditure of £5,800. We estimate that the annual total amount of grants awarded to individuals was around £5,500. At the time of writing (October 2015) the information provided was the latest available.

Applications

Application forms can be either downloaded from the Evercreech village and district website, requested from the correspondent, or collected from the Evercreech Pharmacy. The closing date for applications is 1 October each year and the awards are made in late October/early November. Two references are required.

Prowde's Educational Foundation (Prowde's Charity)

£20,000

Correspondent: Richard Lytle, Administrator, 39 Stanley Street, Southsea PO5 2DS (023 9279 9142; email: mbyrne@vwv.co.uk)

CC number: 310255

Eligibility

Boys and young men aged between 9 and 25 who live in Somerset or the North or East Ridings of Yorkshire. Preference is given to those who are descendants of the named persons in the will of the founder, for those whose parents reside in the foundation's beneficial area and for those whose names were entered in the candidates' book before the date of the scheme. Boys with serious family difficulties causing them to be educated away from home and individuals with special educational needs are also favoured.

Types of grants

One-off grants of around £450 are given to schoolchildren and further/higher education students, including mature students and postgraduates. Support is given towards fees, uniforms and other clothing, books, equipment/instruments and study/travel abroad or in the UK.

Annual grant total

In 2013/14 the foundation had an income of £20,500 and an expenditure of £20,000. We estimate the annual total amount of grants awarded to individuals to be around £20,000.

Applications

Application forms can be requested from the correspondent and can be submitted by individuals directly or through a third party, such as a parent/guardian or a social worker, if applicable. Applications

should include a birth certificate and evidence of enrolment on the course. Grants are normally considered in July and applications should be made by May/June.

Bath and North East Somerset

Richard Jones Charity (Richard Jones Foundation)

£2,500

Correspondent: Peter Godfrey, Correspondent, 'Two Shillings', 24D Tyning Road, Saltford, Bristol BS31 3HL (01225 341085; email: peter.h.godfrey@ googlemail.com)

CC number: 310057

Eligibility

People under the age of 30 who live in the parishes of Chew Magna, Lawrence Stanton Prior, Newton St Loe, Stanton Drew, Stowey-Sutton (all in the area of Bath and North East Somerset).

Types of grants

Small educational grants are available to schoolchildren, college/university students, people starting work or entering a trade, also mature and postgraduate students. One-off and recurrent grants, usually from £30 to £400, are given for course books, equipment, instruments and tools. Occasionally pupils may be helped with the cost of school clothing and further/ higher education students supported towards educational travel.

Annual grant total

In 2013/14 the charity had an income of £11,900 and an expenditure of £3,200. We estimate the annual total amount of grants awarded to individuals to be around £2,500.

Exclusions

Individuals attending private schools are not supported.

Applications

Application forms are available from the correspondent and can be submitted directly by the individual. Grants are normally considered in April and October and applications should be submitted in March and September, respectively. Specific dates of the trustees' meetings and the application deadlines are normally advertised in parish magazines and on parish noticeboards. Candidates may be invited for an interview.

Other information

Small awards are also made to elderly people in need at Christmas time. Schools, clubs and other organisations supporting young people in the area of benefit may also receive grants towards equipment.

Previously the correspondent has stated:

> The majority of our beneficiaries are students at universities and colleges of further education. We would like to attract more applications from school leavers starting to learn a trade for grants towards tools and equipment.... We do on occasions assist school pupils with the cost of extra music lessons and, if they can exhibit exceptional talent, towards the cost of musical instruments. We have also given grants to children for educational visits, camps etc. organised by their schools but it seems that most of the state schools in the area are able to fund needy pupils from their own resources for such activities. We do not, generally speaking, assist pupils at private schools. Very occasionally grants may be made towards the cost of school uniform. Grants have also been given in the past few years to participants in Operation Raleigh expeditions, Outward Bound courses and other ventures of a similar nature.

Ralph and Irma Sperring Charity

£28,000

Correspondent: E. Hallam, Company Secretary, Thatcher and Hallam Solicitors, Island House, Midsomer Norton, Bath BA3 2HJ (01761 414646; email: sperringcharity@gmail.com)

CC number: 1048101

Eligibility

People in need who live within a five-mile radius of the Church of St John the Baptist in Midsomer Norton, Bath.

Types of grants

One-off and recurrent grants are given according to need.

Annual grant total

In 2013/14 the charity had assets of £6.2 million and an income of £218,000. Awards to local causes amounted to £111,500. The charity makes grants to both individuals and organisations although there is no stipulation as to how the income is divided. We have estimated the amount awarded to individuals for educational purposes to be approximately £28,000.

Applications

Apply in writing to the correspondent. Applications are considered quarterly.

North Somerset

Marchioness of Northampton (Wraxall Parochial Charities)

£400

Correspondent: Mrs A. Sissons, Clerk and Treasurer, 2 Short Way, Failand, Bristol BS8 3UF (01275 392691)

CC number: 230410

Eligibility

Residents of the parish of Wraxall and Failand, Bristol who are at any level of their education, in any subject, and are in need.

Types of grants

One-off grants in the range of £50–£100.

Annual grant total

In 2014 the charity had assets of £12,600, an income of £38,000 and a total expenditure of £37,500. There were discretionary payments totalling £900 and Christmas distribution totalling £14,500. It would appear that educational support given depends on the demand and will form part of the discretionary payments. We take it that about £400 may have been contributions for educational purposes. The accounts state:

> Discretionary Payments were granted to the Wraxall Entertainments Committee towards the cost of an outing for local residents, to Wraxall School to allow 2 children to attend after school activities and the provision of a washing machine for a disabled resident. John Lewis Vouchers for Grocery and Clothing were issued to 66 households at Christmas to families with children of school age or under, the over 65's, widows, widowers and to two disabled residents.

Applications

Applications may be made in writing to the correspondent, directly by the individual. They are considered in February, June, September and November.

Other information

Grants are made to individuals and organisations for educational and welfare purposes.

During the year a total of £2,900 was spent on the hire of a mini bus once a week for older residents and those with disabilities to get to shops, health centre, library and chemist in Nailsea.

Nailsea Community Trust Ltd

£2,100

Correspondent: Ann Tonkin, 1st Nailsea Scouts Training and Activity Centre, Clevedon Road, Nailsea, North Somerset BS48 1EH (email: info@nailseacommunitytrust.co.uk; website: www.nailseacommunitytrust.co.uk)

CC number: 900031

Eligibility

Young people under the age of 25 who live in Nailsea, Backwell, Chelvey, Tickenham or Wraxall.

Types of grants

One-off grants usually up to £500. Grants are made to assist with education in the areas of the arts, science, religion, commerce and health care.

Annual grant total

In 2013/14 the trust had an income of £7,200 and a total expenditure of £8,800. Grants are made to individuals and organisations for social welfare and educational purposes. We estimate that educational grants to individuals totalled £2,100.

Exclusions

Applications from outside the area of benefit will not be considered.

Applications

The trust's website states that eligible individuals, or somebody who knows of an individual who may be eligible, should contact the trust by email or in writing. Applicants may be asked for a short interview with a couple of the trustees so a fuller understanding of their situation can be established. All applications are dealt with in confidence.

South Somerset

The Ilchester Relief-in-Need and Educational Charity (IRINEC)

£11,000

Correspondent: Kaye Elston, Clerk, 15 Chilton Grove, Yeovil, Somerset BA21 4AN (01935 421208; website: www.ilchesterparishcouncil.gov.uk/IlchesterPC/irinec-24745.aspx)

CC number: 235578

Eligibility

Students in financial need who live in the parish of Ilchester.

Types of grants

One-off grants to university students for fees and maintenance/living expenses, also travel, books and field trips. College students can be supported towards the cost of travel.

Annual grant total

In 2014 the charity had assets of £502,500 (mainly as a permanent endowment) and an income of £32,500. Educational grants totalled £11,000.

Exclusions

Grants are not available where support should be received from statutory sources.

Applications

Application forms can be requested from the correspondent and should be submitted directly by the individual. Additional information can be obtained from the correspondent. The trustees consider grants at their monthly meetings (held on the fourth Tuesday of each month). Evidence of financial need will be required.

The website states: 'Phone the clerk to talk through your needs to find out if you qualify to be considered for help by the Trustees.'

Other information

Grants are also given for relief-in-need purposes. Organisations may be supported.

The Ilminster Educational Foundation

£16,700

Correspondent: Edward Wells, Administrator, 20 Station Road, Ilminster, Somerset TA19 9BD (01460 53029; email: e.wells125@btinternet. com)

CC number: 310265

Eligibility

People under the age of 25 who live or have attended an educational institution for at least two years in the parish of Ilminster.

Types of grants

Grants of around £200–£400 are available to schoolchildren for educational outings in the UK/overseas and to students at Ilminster-based universities or colleges for general educational expenses.

Annual grant total

In 2013/14 the foundation had assets of £106,700 and an income of £50,500. A total of £16,700 was awarded in grants to students.

Exclusions

According to our research, grants are not made for A-level courses.

Applications

Apply in writing to the correspondent. Our research suggests that applications are normally considered in October and November. They should be submitted in advance to those dates.

Other information

The foundation also makes grants to five local schools, special grants to individuals and an annual grant for the general benefit of the parish of Ilminster.

John Nowes Exhibition Foundation

£500

Correspondent: Joanne Smith, Battens Solicitors, Mansion House, 54–58 Princes Street, Yeovil, Somerset BA20 1EP (01935 846092; email: joanne. smith@battens.co.uk)

CC number: 309984

Eligibility

Children and young people between the ages of 16 and 25 living in the Yeovil parishes (including Yeovil Without) who have a household income of less than £30,000 per annum.

Types of grants

Grants ranging from £150 to £500. The foundation provides scholarships, bursaries, maintenance allowances and grants to support schoolchildren, further and higher education students and people starting work or entering a trade/ profession. Financial assistance is also available to travel/study abroad in pursuance of education, to study music or other arts. The foundation can support people in primary, secondary and further education in provision of facilities for recreation, social and physical training, including coaching in athletics, sports and games, where help is not provided by the local authorities.

Annual grant total

In 2013/14 the foundation had an income of £6,700 and an expenditure of £500. We estimate that the annual total amount of grants awarded was about £500.

Applications

Application forms can be requested from the correspondent and should usually be submitted by 31 August each year.

Taunton Deane

Taunton Heritage Trust

£14,500 (87 grants)

Correspondent: Karen White, Clerk to the Trustees, Huish Homes, Magdalene Street, Taunton, Somerset TA1 1SG (01823 335348 (Mon–Fri, 9am–12pm); email: tauntonheritagetrust@btconnect. com; website: www.tauntonheritagetrust. org.uk)

CC number: 202120

Eligibility

People living in the borough of Taunton Deane that are of school age (generally up to the age of 16). Our research suggests that requests from colleges of further education on behalf of individuals may also be considered depending on circumstances and need.

Types of grants

Grants to schoolchildren are made according to need, towards school uniforms, educational visits and, in exceptional circumstances, computers.

Annual grant total

In 2014 the trust had assets of £5.7 million and an income of £628,500. A total of 332 grants were made, amounting to £95,500, both to individuals for educational and social welfare purposes and to organisations. Grants to individuals for educational purposes totalled £14,500.

Exclusions

Grants are not given: to replace statutory support (supplementary grants may be available); for school trips, school bags or stationery; for retrospective applications; or for further/higher education course fees or books/materials.

Applications

Applications can be downloaded from the trust's website. They must be completed and typed (not handwritten) by a recognised referral agency such as social services or Citizens Advice, for example. Applicants must not complete the forms themselves. Four copies of the completed form must be returned to the trust. The trust asks that, if possible, all information is included on one side of A4 (an accompanying letter should only be sent if absolutely necessary). The referral agency must check and provide details of the type and amount of benefits and/or other income that the applicant is receiving. The applicant's individual/family circumstances must also be described and the need for the grant fully explained. Specific items must be itemised and costed (more information on details to include is listed on the website).

The referral agency officer responsible for submitting the application, and for monitoring the use of any grant, must ensure that they have signed the form. Applications submitted by schools must be signed by the headteacher. If the applicant has moved home in the last 12 months, their previous address should be included. It is also essential (in order to arrange delivery of white goods) to include the applicant's correct telephone number.

Note that the trust cannot accept applications via email.

Other information

The primary role of the charity is to provide sheltered accommodation for people over the age of 60.

Wiltshire

Chippenham Borough Lands Charity

£10,000

Correspondent: The Grants Officer, Jubilee Building, 32 Market Place, Chippenham, Wiltshire SN15 3HP (01249 658180; fax: 01249 446048; email: admin@cblc.org.uk; website: www.cblc.org.uk)

CC number: 270062

Eligibility

People in need who are living within the Parish of Chippenham at the date of application, and have been for a minimum of two years immediately prior to applying.

Types of grants

Usually one-off grants according to need, for things such as help towards travel costs, the provision of equipment to undertake a course or help towards actual course fees, depending on the nature of the course and the individual's personal circumstances.

Annual grant total

In 2014/15 the charity had assets of £13.2 million and an income of £452,500. Grants were given to 47 individuals totalling about £37,000. Grants are made to both individuals and organisations for educational, social welfare and other charitable purposes. Grants paid to individuals for educational purposes totalled around £10,000.

Exclusions

The charity is unable to help towards:

▷ Funding of individual sports people
▷ Direct funding of the local authorities
▷ Religious organisations (except projects with a benefit for the entire community)
▷ First degrees
▷ The provision of carpets or council tax arrears

The charity will not consider an application if a grant has been received within the past two years (or one year for mobility aids) unless the circumstances are exceptional.

Applications

Application forms should be requested from the correspondent. In the first instance get in touch with the charity via phone or email to discuss your requirements. Once received the application will be looked at in detail by the Education/Arts Officer, David Powell. It is possible that the charity will visit, or ask applicants to call in at this stage. Applications are considered every month and can be submitted directly by the individual or through a third party, such as a teacher. The trustees meet monthly.

Other information

The charity was first established in 1554 when Queen Mary granted a Royal Charter to Chippenham. She gave Crown Land to the borough and the income was to be used to pay for two members of parliament and for the upkeep of the bridge over the River Avon. A full history of the charity can be found on its informative and helpful website.

Organisations are also supported. Each of the 14 state schools within the parish is allocated a specific amount annually to enable them to provide activities and/or equipment that they would otherwise be unable to fund and for which they receive no government funding. There is also an annual award, known as the Social Fund, to each school to help with the provision of school uniform and trips for those families on low incomes. In addition, the trustees make annual awards to Wiltshire College Chippenham to enable the presentation of prizes to two students.

Note that after the changes to the parish boundary both the Cepen Park North and Cepen Park South estates are included.

The Community Foundation for Wiltshire and Swindon

£145,000

Correspondent: The Grants Team, Ground Floor, Sandcliff House, 21 Northgate Street, Devizes, Wiltshire SN10 1JT (01380 729284; email: info@wscf.org.uk; website: www.wscf.org.uk)

CC number: 1123126

Eligibility

Individuals in the county of Wiltshire and the borough of Swindon and its immediate neighbourhood. Scholarships are given to university students and support is offered to people in other tertiary education and training.

Types of grants

Currently educational support is given through the One Degree More fund, which offers:

▷ Vocational grants of up to £1,000 to support course costs to people aged between 16 and 25 who live within the boundaries of Swindon or Wiltshire councils and who or whose parents/carers/guardians are in receipt of means-tested benefits
▷ Personal Support Fund grants of up to £1,000 to individuals under the age of 25 who have been in the care of the local authority or who have a disability, and live or attend education in Swindon or Wiltshire and who are, or whose parents/carers are, in receipt of means-tested benefits. The foundation is particularly 'keen to fund 'tools of the trade' or vocational training'
▷ Scholarship grants of up to £5,000 per year (for the duration of a course) to people between the ages of 17 and 24 who have lived in Swindon or Wiltshire for at least two years and are undertaking an undergraduate university degree. Applicants or their parents/carers must be in receipt of means-tested benefits. The website notes that the foundation 'aims to offer scholarships to talented individuals to help them overcome difficult financial circumstances and achieve their potential'

Annual grant total

In 2013/14 the foundation held assets of £17.35 million and had an income of £2.26 million. During the year a total of £800,000 was awarded in grants to 157 different groups (£560,000) and 391 individuals (£240,000, including £71,000 distributed through Surviving Winter Fund). One Degree More programme made awards totalling about £145,000.

Exclusions

The following are not funded:

▷ Postgraduate, master's or PhD courses
▷ Second degrees or gap years
▷ Retrospective expenditure
▷ The promotion of party political or religious causes
▷ Equipment or expenses which should be provided by someone else
▷ Sponsorship costs
▷ School fees
▷ Activities or equipment that is not education related

Applications

Initial applications should be made online using an Expression of Interest form, following the links (specific for each of the three funds). A member of staff will get back to the applicant with a full application form. Application deadlines are specific to each fund and subject to change candidates are advised to consult the website for the most up-to-date details before applying. When applying scholarship grants you will normally need to present a copy of your University Personal Statement. Student awards are paid termly, after a progress report is received.

The Grants Officer responsible for One Degree More programme is Jonathan Whitehead-Whiting (email: jonathan.ww@wiltshirecf.org.uk).

As with any community foundation, funds are likely to open and close – for the most up-to-date information on grant schemes currently operating consult the website.

Other information
The Community Foundation is an amalgamation of two smaller trusts – the Thamesdown Community Trust and the Wiltshire Community Trust.

Organisations and various groups are supported. The foundation also has a separate Surviving Winter fund to help vulnerable people with fuel costs.

The Ewelme Exhibition Foundation (Ewelme Exhibition Endowment)
See entry on page 247

Colonel William Llewellyn Palmer Educational Charity

£2,300 (2 grants)

Correspondent: Chief Accountant on behalf of CFO, Wiltshire Council, Accountancy, County Hall, Trowbridge, Wiltshire BA14 8JN (01225 718584; email: financialplanning@wiltshire.gov.uk)

CC number: 1015681

Eligibility
Children and young people under the age of 25 who live or attend/have attended schools maintained by the local authority in Bradford-on-Avon.

Types of grants
One-off grants are available towards general educational expenses, such as purchase of equipment/instruments, books, uniforms/clothing, also for recreational projects, holiday schemes, music lessons.

Annual grant total
In 2013/14 the charity had assets of £1.7 million and an income of £55,500. A total of £15,000 was awarded in educational grants to individuals and organisations, of which two grants were made to individuals, totalling £2,300. Additional two grants were made to

schools, totalling £2,300, and a further £10,400 was awarded in 11 grants to other groups.

Applications
Our research suggests that applications should not be made directly to the correspondent. Individual applications have to be made on behalf of the candidate by their school as a part of a block application of all pupils who wish to apply. Such block applications should be submitted to the correspondent normally by October for consideration at a meeting in November. Grants are then distributed via the school.

Swindon
The W. G. Little Scholarship and Band Concert Fund

£13,000

Correspondent: Darren Stevens, Administrator, Swindon Borough Council, Civic Offices, Euclid Street, Swindon SN1 2JH (01793 445500; email: customerservices@swindon.gov.uk)

CC number: 309497

Eligibility
Secondary school pupils who have lived within the boundary of Swindon borough council for at least 12 months. Priority is given to pupils who are transferring form primary to secondary school. Only applicants who have previously received a grant from the fund are currently eligible to apply.

Types of grants
Grants are given towards school clothing and are usually of about £50.

Annual grant total
In 2013/14 the fund had an income of £23,500 and an expenditure of £13,500. We estimate that around £13,000 was awarded in grants. Normally several hundreds of grants are distributed each year.

Applications
The Swindon borough council's website notes that new applicants are currently not accepted. Please refer to the website for current information.

Other information
The fund is administered by the Swindon borough council. The council's website states that:

> The use of the fund is being greater aligned to the original aims of the trust, and only those who have previously received an award in 2012/13 will be eligible to re-apply for 2014/15. It is anticipated that 2015/16 will be the final

year of this award process. Awards are not available for new applicants.

The information provided on the Charity Commission record states that the primary aims of the fund are 'under review with the aim of adding in other funds and updating activities'.

Organisations can also be supported, provided their service users are aged 11 to 25 and live within the borough boundary.

Wiltshire
The Rose Charity

£2,000

Correspondent: Charles Goodbody, Trustee, 94 East Street, Warminster, Wiltshire BA12 9BG (01985 214444; email: cgoodbody@mulaw.co.uk)

CC number: 900590

Eligibility
Schoolchildren in need who live in Warminster and the surrounding villages.

Types of grants
One-off grants, ranging from £50 to £500, towards general educational costs, such as books, necessities, uniforms and other clothing, educational outings and so forth. According to our research, music lessons can also be supported.

Annual grant total
In 2013/14 the charity had an income of £4,000 and an expenditure of £2,500. We estimate the annual total amount of grants awarded to be around £2,000 but the amount awarded varies each year.

Applications
Apply in writing to the correspondent. Our research suggests that applications are considered throughout the year and should be supported by the social services/welfare agency or school/college.

Salisbury City Educational and Apprenticing Charity

£880 (5 grants)

Correspondent: Mrs S. Coen, Clerk to the Trustees, Trinity Hospital, Trinity Street, Salisbury, Wiltshire SP1 2BD (01722 325640; fax: 01722 325640; email: clerk@almshouses.demon.co.uk; website: www.salisburyalmshouses.co.uk)

CC number: 309523

Eligibility
Young people under the age of 25 who live in the district of Salisbury. Our research suggests that preference is given

to those resident in the city of Salisbury and/or in secondary education.

Types of grants

One-off educational and apprenticing grants are made ranging from £100 to £200. Awards are available to schoolchildren for educational outings in the UK and study or travel abroad, and to further and higher education students (including apprentices but not mature students or postgraduates) for books, equipment/instruments, fees, educational outings in the UK and study or travel abroad.

Interest-free loans are also made towards the cost of tools and equipment needed to start a trade.

The charity interprets the term education in the widest sense and offers help towards the cost of expeditions, gap year opportunities, educational projects designed to develop character, such as Project Trust, scout jamborees and adventure training, projects abroad and training to obtain qualifications.

Annual grant total

In 2014 the charity had an income of £2,800 and a total expenditure of almost £2,000. The charity's record on the Charity Commission's website states that 'the trustees considered seven applications and approved five grants totalling £880'.

Exclusions

Grants are not made for school uniforms, daily subsistence and living expenses or student exchanges. There is no support available for second degree courses. Regular payments towards fees or expenses are only made in exceptional circumstances.

Applications

Application forms and full guidelines are available on the charity's website. Candidates are advised to contact the clerk as early as possible to discuss an application. Requests are considered monthly and can be submitted through the individual's school, college or educational welfare agency.

Other information

The charity shares the trustees with Salisbury City Almshouse and Welfare Charities (Charity Commission no. 202110), which maintains almshouses and may also provide welfare grants in case of emergency hardship.

Yorkshire

General

Prowde's Educational Foundation (Prowde's Charity)
See entry on page 295

Yorkshire Training Fund for Women

£2,300

Correspondent: Ann Taylor, Trustee, 1 High Ash Close, Notton, Wakefield, West Yorkshire WF4 2PF (01226722155; website: ytfund.wordpress.com)

CC number: 529586

Eligibility

British women over the age of 16 and over who live in, or have connections to, Yorkshire.

Types of grants

One-off grants in the range of £100–£300 are available to women undertaking training courses leading to qualifications for employment that will enable them to become self-sufficient financially. Grants are given towards general necessities, such as books, equipment and instruments.

Annual grant total

In 2014 the fund had an income of £2,500 and an expenditure of £2,500. We estimate that the annual total amount of grants awarded to individuals was around £2,300.

Exclusions

Grants are not given to cover fees and to people on access courses.

Applications

Application forms can be accessed from the fund's website or requested from the correspondent. They should be completed by the individual. Applicants should provide details of two referees and detailed information of their financial position. Completed forms should be returned by 1 May or by 1 December, providing an sae. The application form states that requests should be returned to: The Hon. Secretary, YTF, Mrs Fran Slater, 5 Bede Court, College Grove Road, Wakefield, West Yorkshire WF1 3RW.

Other information

Support may also be given to the Yorkshire Ladies' Council of Education and organisations, especially those working for the benefit of older people.

The fund has previously stated that 'there is a great deal of competition for the grants'.

East Riding of Yorkshire

Christopher Eden Educational Foundation

£7,000

Correspondent: Judy Dickinson, Trustee, 85 East Street, Leven, Beverley HU17 5NG (01964 542593; email: judydickinson@mac.com)

CC number: 529794

Eligibility

Young people under the age of 25 who live in the town of Beverley and the surrounding area or have attended school there. People with special educational needs are given preference.

Types of grants

One-off and recurrent grants in the range of £50–£400 are available to further/higher education students and people undertaking apprenticeships. Financial support is given towards any kind of educational needs, including fees, necessities, books, equipment/instruments, clothing, travel expenses, sports or art studies and so forth.

Annual grant total

In 2014/15 the foundation had an income of £11,500 and a total expenditure of £7,000. We estimate the annual total amount of grants awarded to individuals to be around £7,000.

Applications

Apply in writing to the correspondent. Our research suggests that applications for assistance with university or college costs are considered in October and applications for any other purposes in January, April, July and October. A parent/guardian should complete the application for those under the age of 16. Applications should include full details of the course, information on the applicant's education, income of the parents/applicant and reasons why the help is needed. Incomplete or incorrect applications will not be considered and are not returned.

Other information

According to our research, the foundation has endowed a berth on a sail training schooner and selects a deserving young person for the berth each year.

Alderman Ferries Charity (Hull United Charities)

£4,500

Correspondent: The Chair, Hull United Charities, The Office, Northumberland Court, Northumberland Avenue, Hull HU2 0LR (01482 323965; email: office@hulluc.karoo.co.uk; website: www.hullunitedcharities.org.uk/alderman-ferries.html)

CC number: 529821

Eligibility

People under the age of 25 who are entering secondary, further/higher education or apprenticeships and who have attended school or lived within Kingston upon Hull city boundary for at least two years prior to applying.

Types of grants

Grants ranging from around £300 to £500 are given for fees, books, equipment/instruments, clothing, travel costs and maintenance expenses.

Annual grant total

In 2014/15 the charity had an income of £14,000 and a total expenditure of £10,000. We estimate the annual total amount of grants awarded to individuals to be around £4,500.

Applications

Application forms and detailed guidelines are available on the charity's website or can be requested from the correspondent. The trustees consider grants every December and applications should be submitted by the middle of November.

Dr A. E. Hart Trust

£20,000

Correspondent: Secretary to the Trustees, Williamsons Solicitors, 45 Lowgate, Hull HU1 1EN (01482 323697; fax: 01482 328132; email: admin@williamsons-solicitors.co.uk; website: www.williamsons-solicitors.co.uk/dr-a-e-hart-trust)

CC number: 529780

Eligibility

Young people aged 18 and above for educational training within the boundary of the city and county of Kingston upon Hull.

Types of grants

The trust was established for 'the promotion and encouragement of education by way of bursaries and studentships or scholarships for needy students of either sex residing within the boundary of the city and county of Kingston Upon Hull'.

Assistance is offered to those people who are studying for their 1st degree (or equivalent qualification), PGCE, LPC or BPTC.

Annual grant total

In 2013/14 the trust had an income of £24,500 and an expenditure of £26,500. Previously grants to individuals have totalled around £20,000.

Exclusions

Applications cannot be considered for residents living outside the city boundary or students who are resident in Hull only because they are attending an education institution there. Applicants residing in the surrounding areas of Willerby, Hessle, Anlaby, Hedon, etc. will not be funded.

Applications

Application forms can be obtained by contacting the trust. The grants available from this trust are relatively modest, and are unlikely to have any significant bearing on an applicant's decision to embark on any given course.

The Hedon Haven Trust

£1,700

Correspondent: Ian North, Trustee, 44 Souttergate, Hedon, Hull HU12 8JS (01482 897105; email: iannorth@iannorth.karoo.co.uk)

CC number: 500259

Eligibility

People at any stage or level of their education, undertaking study of any subject, who live in Hedon near Hull. Our research suggests that preference may be given to children with special educational needs.

Types of grants

One-off grants ranging from £50 to £500 are given to schoolchildren for educational outings in the UK and abroad, and students in further/higher education towards study or travel abroad and maintenance/living expenses.

Annual grant total

In 2014 the trust had an income of £3,800 and an expenditure of £3,600. We estimate that the amount of grants given to individuals totalled about £1,700.

Exclusions

Support is not given where statutory funds should be used.

Applications

Applications may be made in writing to the correspondent at any time, enclosing an sae. Requests can be submitted directly by the individual or through a school/college or educational welfare agency.

Other information

Grants are also made to organisations.

The Hesslewood Children's Trust (Hull Seamen's and General Orphanage)

£11,200

Correspondent: Rex Booth, Secretary to the Trustees, 1 Canada Drive, Cherry Burton, Beverley, North Humberside HU17 7RQ (01946 550474; email: detaylor@duttonmoore.co.uk)

CC number: 529804

Eligibility

People under the age of 25 who are in need and are native to, or have family connections with, the former county of Humberside or the district of Gainsborough and Caistor in Lincolnshire. The trust also gives to former Hesslewood Scholars. 'Applicants

must be in need, but must show their resolve to part fund themselves.'

Types of grants

One-off grants, typically of up to £1,000, are given towards: books, school uniforms, educational outings and maintenance for schoolchildren; books for students in higher and further education; and equipment, instruments and clothing for people starting work.

Annual grant total

In 2013/14 the trust had assets of £2.8 million and an income of £88,000. Grants totalled £72,500, of which £34,000 was given to organisations. Grants to or on behalf of specific individuals amounted to £38,000, with those for educational purposes totalling £11,200.

Exclusions

Students who have come to the area to study are not eligible. Loans are not made.

Applications

An application form is available from the correspondent. Applications can be made either directly by the individual or through the individual's school/college/welfare agency or another third party on their behalf. Applicants must give their own or their parents' financial details, state what help is required, and why parents cannot provide the money. If possible, a contact telephone number should be quoted. Applications must be accompanied by a letter from the tutor or an educational welfare officer (or from medical and social services for a disability grant). The deadlines are 16 February, 16 June and 16 September.

Kingston upon Hull Education Foundation

£4,800

Correspondent: Brice McDermid, Administrator, Corporate Finance, City Treasury, Hull City Council, Guildhall Road, Hull HU1 2AB (01482 615010; email: corpfinanceplanning@hullcc.gov.uk)

CC number: 514427

Eligibility

People over 13 who live, or whose parents live, in the city of Kingston upon Hull and either attend, or have attended, a school in the city.

Types of grants

Awards of £80 to £250 are available as scholarships, bursaries or grants tenable at any school, university or other educational establishment approved by the trustees; and towards the cost of outfits, clothing, tools, instruments or books to assist the beneficiaries in pursuance of their education or to prepare them for entering a profession, trade, occupation or service on leaving school, university or other educational establishment.

Annual grant total

In 2013/14 the foundation had an income of £4,800 and an expenditure of £5,000. We have estimated that the total amount of grants awarded in the year was about £4,800.

Applications

Apply in writing to the correspondent. Applications are usually considered in November (closing date mid-October) and February (closing date mid-January). A letter of support from the applicant's class or course tutor, plus evidence of their progress and attendance on the course is needed before a grant is made.

The Sir Philip Reckitt Educational Trust Fund
See entry on page 49

Henry Samman's Hull Chamber of Commerce Endowment Fund

£14,000

Correspondent: Ian Kelly, Administrator, Hull and Humber, Chamber of Commerce, Industry and Shipping, 34–38 Beverley Road, Hull HU3 1YE (01482 324976; fax: 01482 213962; email: i.kelly@hull-humber-chamber.co.uk; website: www.hull-humber-chamber.co.uk/the-chamber/henry-samman-fund.aspx)

CC number: 228837

Eligibility

British citizens who are over the age of 18 and can demonstrate some academic skills in either business methods or a foreign language. Preference is given to young people from Hull and East Riding. Candidates should be studying or planning to study at degree level, although consideration will be given to those slightly under this age limit.

Types of grants

Bursaries to enable individuals to spend a period of 3 to 12 months abroad in connection to their studies of business methods and/or foreign languages. The award is generally of around £100 a month. Longer periods of travel may be funded at the trustees' discretion.

Annual grant total

In 2014 the fund had an income of £7,500 and an expenditure of £14,500.

We estimate that the annual total amount of grants awarded was around £14,000.

Applications

Apply in writing to the correspondent. Applications should include a covering letter, a CV and outline how the award would benefit the applicant's education and training. Candidates may be required to attend an interview. The trustees meet once a year to consider applications, normally in summer.

Other information

The fund was set up in 1917 originally to encourage the study of Russian in a commercial context but has since been extended.

Ann Watson's Trust

£90,500

Correspondent: Karen Palmer, Administrator, Flat 4 The College, 14 College Street, Sutton-on-Hull, Hull HU7 4UP (01482 709626; email: awatson@awatson.karoo.co.uk)

CC number: 226675

Eligibility

People under the age of 25 who live in East Riding, Yorkshire or who attend school in that area.

Types of grants

One-off and recurrent grants are given according to educational need.

Annual grant total

In 2013/14 the trust had assets of £19 million and an income of £421,500. Charitable expenditure totalled £220,500 and educational grants to individuals totalled £90,500.

Applications

Apply in writing to the correspondent. The trustees meet quarterly.

Other information

Grants are also given to local organisations, churches and to individuals for welfare purposes; provision of accommodation and relief in need of poor women who are members of the Church of England, with preference given to widows or unmarried daughters of clergymen of the Church of England.

East Riding of Yorkshire

The Leonard Chamberlain Trust

£14,900

Correspondent: Alison Nicholson, Secretary, 4 Bishops Croft, Beverley, North Humberside, East Yorkshire HU17 8JY (01482 865726; email: alinicholson4@googlemail.com)

CC number: 1091018

Eligibility

People under the age of 25 who live in East Riding of Yorkshire, particularly Hull and Selby, and are in need.

Types of grants

Grants of £50 to £1,000 are given for items such as books.

Annual grant total

In 2014 the charity had assets of £6.2 million and an income of £190,500. Grants totalled £52,000, of which £14,900 was awarded for educational purposes. Relief-in-need grants to individuals amounted to an additional £9,900.

Applications

Our research indicates that application forms can be obtained from the correspondent. They should be returned in August for consideration in September.

Other information

The trust's main purpose is the provision of housing for residents in the area of benefit who are in financial need and it also makes a small number of grants for religious purposes.

Heron Educational Foundation (Heron Trust)

£12,500

Correspondent: Brenda Frear, Trustee, 2 The Bungalows, Humbleton Road, Lelley HU12 8SP (01964 670788; email: mrscrawforth@btinternet.com)

CC number: 529841

Eligibility

People under the age of 25 living in the parish of Humbleton and Flinton and Fitling villages.

Types of grants

Grants are available to pupils entering primary/secondary school and further/higher education students. People entering a trade/profession may also be assisted. Support can be given towards general educational needs, mainly for clothing and books, other necessities.

Annual grant total

In 2014/15 the foundation had an income of £12,500 and a total expenditure of £13,500. We estimate that the amount of grants given to individuals totalled around £12,500.

Applications

Apply in writing to the correspondent.

The Hook and Goole Charity

£13,500

Correspondent: Diane Taylor, Administrator, The Courtyard, Boothferry Road, Goole DN14 6AW (07539269813; email: hookandgoole@ gmail.com)

CC number: 513948

Eligibility

Students and apprentices aged between 16 and 25 who have lived or attended school in the former borough of Goole or the parish of Hook for at least two years.

Types of grants

Grants of between £150 and £400 are given for educational bursaries. Grants are given for books, tools/equipment, living expenses, educational outings and study or travel overseas.

Annual grant total

In 2014 the charity had an income of £12,500 and an expenditure of £13,500. It made grants totalling approximately £13,500.

Applications

Application forms are available from the correspondent. Applications should be submitted directly by the individual by the beginning of September.

The Nafferton Feoffees Charities Trust

£8,900

Correspondent: Margaret Buckton, Secretary, South Cattleholmes, Wansford, Driffield, North Humberside, East Yorkshire YO25 8NW (01377 254293; email: secretary@feoffeetrust.co. uk; website: www.feoffeetrust.co.uk)

CC number: 232796

Eligibility

People in need who live in the parish of All Saints Nafferton with St Mary's Wansford.

Types of grants

Bursaries are available to local students going to a college or university for things, such as educational overseas trips, course materials, laptops, books and so on. Grants are also made to primary and secondary school students for study trips, projects and so on.

Annual grant total

In 2014 the trust had assets of £1.8 million and an income of £47,000. Grants were made totalling £18,500. This included £8,200 in scholarship expenses, £1,200 in grants to individuals and further support to groups and organisations. We take it that about £8,900 was given in educational support.

Exclusions

The trust stated that the parish only consists of 3,000 people and every household receives a copy of a leaflet outlining the trust's work. People from outside this area are not eligible to apply (sometimes help may be given to people from outside the area of benefit but who have very close ties with the parish). Awards are not made to replace or augment statutory support.

Applications

Applications can be made in writing to the correspondent at any time, directly by the individual.

Other information

Grants are also made to local organisations and to individuals for welfare purposes.

The trust is 'made up of three charities known as the Poors Trust, the Town Trust, and the John Baron Trust covering the ecclesiastical parish of Nafferton, Wansford and Pockthorpe and was started in 1890'.

The Rawcliffe Educational Charity

£10,500

Correspondent: Julie Parrott, Administrator, 26 Station Road, Rawcliffe, Goole, North Humberside DN14 8QR (01405 839637)

CC number: 509656

Eligibility

People under the age of 25 who/whose parents live in the parish of Rawcliffe and who have attended one of the local schools.

Types of grants

One-off and recurrent grants of up to £600. Individuals finishing school can be given grants to help upon entering further/higher full-time education. Assistance is given towards the cost of books, equipment/instruments, outfits

and clothing, fees, maintenance/living costs and travel expenses. Apprentices and people starting work are also eligible to apply for help with books, equipment, clothing and travel. The study of music and other arts is also supported.

Annual grant total

In 2013/14 the charity had an income of £9,000 and a total expenditure of £11,500. We have estimated the annual total amount of grants awarded to individuals to be around £10,500.

Exclusions

School fees or study/travel overseas is not normally covered.

Applications

Apply in writing to the correspondent. Applications should include the type and duration of the course to be studied. Candidates must confirm that they are not in receipt of any salary. The awards are normally considered in September.

Other information

Children leaving primary schools and going into secondary education are gifted books.

The Wray Educational Trust (Wray Trust)

£8,500

Correspondent: Judy Dickinson, Trustee, 85 East Street, Leven, Beverley, North Humberside HU17 5NG (01964 542593; email: judydickinson@mac.com)

CC number: 508468

Eligibility

People under the age of 25 who (or whose parents) have lived in the parish of Leven for at least three years.

Types of grants

One-off grants are given to schoolchildren, students in further or higher education and people starting work. Support is available towards general educational costs, including books, equipment/instruments, fees, educational outings, study or travel abroad and musical or sports activities.

Annual grant total

In 2013/14 the trust had an income of £7,000 and an expenditure of £9,000. We estimate that the annual total amount of grants awarded to individuals was around £8,500.

Applications

Application forms are available from the correspondent, who knows many of the people in the village and is always willing to discuss needs. Applications should be submitted by the beginning of January, April, July and October for consideration during that month.

Other information

Grants are also given to local organisations working for the benefit of young people.

North Yorkshire

Bedale Educational and Bedale 750 Charity (The Rector and Four and Twenty of Bedale)

£200

Correspondent: John Winkle, Correspondent, 25 Burrill Road, Bedale DL8 1ET (01677 424306; email: johnwinkle@awinkle.freeserve.co.uk)

CC number: 529517

Eligibility

People under the age of 25 who/whose parents live in the parishes of Aiskew, Bedale, Burrill, Cowling, Crakehall, Firby, Leeming Bar, Longthorne and Rand Grange in North Yorkshire. Preference is given to people with special educational needs or disabilities.

Types of grants

One-off grants in the range of £200–£600 are given to schoolchildren, college students and people in training. Support can be provided towards books, fees, maintenance/living expenses and excursions.

Annual grant total

In 2013/14 the charity had an income of £600 and an expenditure of £430. Both figures vary each year. Charitable expenditure has fluctuated between £0 and £2,500 in the past five years. We estimate that educational grants to individuals totalled around £200.

Applications

Application forms are available from the correspondent. They can be submitted at any time either directly by the individual or their parent.

Other information

Grants may also be made to organisations.

The Gargrave Poor's Land Charity

£8,700

Correspondent: The Trustees, Kirk Syke, High Street, Gargrave, Skipton, North Yorkshire BD23 3RA

CC number: 225067

Eligibility

People who are in need and are permanently resident in Gargrave, Bank Newton, Coniston Cold, Flasby, Eshton or Winterburn.

Types of grants

One-off and recurrent grants and loans are given to: schoolchildren for uniforms, clothing and outings; and students in further or higher education towards maintenance, fees and textbooks. Help is also available to students taking vocational further education courses and other vocational training.

Annual grant total

In 2013/14 the charity had assets of £427,000 and an income of £32,500. Grants totalled £17,300 and were distributed as follows:

Educational assistance	£8,700
Hardship relief	£5,500
Christmas distribution	£3,100

Applications

Applications can be made on a form, which is available from the correspondent, and can be submitted at any time.

The Hill Bursary

£4,500

Correspondent: Hugh McGouran, Administrator, Tees Valley Community Foundation, Wallace House, Falcon Court, Preston Farm Industrial Estate, Stockton-on-Tees TS18 3TX (01642 260860; email: info@ teesvalleyfoundation.org; website: www. teesvalleyfoundation.org)

CC number: 1111222

Eligibility

People residing in Teesside, including Hartlepool, Middlesbrough, Redcar and Cleveland and Stockton on Tees, who are intending to study business economics or accounts on a full-time course at a UK university. Decisions are made based on the A-level results and personal circumstances.

Types of grants

Bursaries of £4,500 over three years.

Annual grant total

This fund is administered by the Tees Valley Community Foundation. Successful applicants receive £500 a term for the three years of their degree.

Applications

Application forms are available from the Tees Valley Community Foundation website, once the application round is open. They should normally be submitted by 29 June.

Reverend Matthew Hutchinson Trust (Gilling and Richmond)

£3,700

Correspondent: Christine Bellas, Oak Tree View, Hutton Magna, Richmond DL11 7HQ (01833 627997; email: cbellas4516@gmail.com)

CC number: 220870/220779

Eligibility

People who live in the parishes of Gilling and Richmond in North Yorkshire.

Types of grants

Grants are given to schoolchildren for fees, equipment and excursions. Undergraduates, including mature students, can receive help towards books while vocational students can be supported for study/travel overseas.

Annual grant total

This charity has branches in both Gilling and Richmond, which are administered jointly, but have separate funding. In 2014 the combined income of the charities was £23,000 and their combined total expenditure was £15,400. Both charities make grants to individuals and organisations for social welfare and educational purposes. We estimate that educational grants to individuals totalled £3,700.

Applications

Apply in writing to the correspondent. Applications can be submitted directly by the individual or through a trustee, social worker, Citizens Advice or other welfare agency.

Other information

Grants are made to organisations including local schools and hospitals.

John Bloom Law Bursary
See entry on page 227

See entry on page 227

Madeleine Mary Walker Foundation

£18,500

Correspondent: Paul Benfield, Trustee, 1 Levington Wynd, Nunthorpe, Middlesbrough TS7 0QD (email: m100pfb@yahoo.co.uk)

CC number: 1062657

Eligibility

People in need of support towards their education up to first degree or equivalent. Priority is given to those living within a 30-mile radius of Stokesley, North Yorkshire.

Types of grants

Assistance can be given towards various educational needs, including the cost of books, equipment/tools, musical instruments, fees, study/travel abroad, field trips and so forth. Grants usually range from £250 to £750.

Annual grant total

In 2013/14 the foundation had assets of £891,000 and an income of £32,000. A total of £18,500 was awarded in grants.

Applications

Applications should be made in writing to the correspondent, providing an sae and a contact telephone number. The trustees usually meet three/four times per year. Applicants may be interviewed.

Yorebridge Educational Foundation

£12,500

Correspondent: Robert Tunstall, Treasurer, Kiln Hill, Hawes, North Yorkshire DL8 3RA (01969 667428; email: bobtunstall@hotmail.co.uk)

CC number: 518826

Eligibility

Students under 25 years of age undertaking full-time courses of further education. Students or parents must live in Wensleydale, North Yorkshire. Preference is given to those with parents resident in the parishes of Askrigg, Bainbridge, Hawes, High Abbotside or Low Abbotside.

Types of grants

One-off grants, typically of £200 a year, towards books, fees and living expenses.

Annual grant total

In 2013/14 the foundation had an income of £16,800 and a total expenditure of £25,000. We estimate that educational grants to individuals totalled £12,500, with funding also awarded to organisations.

Applications

Applications are considered in September/October each year and should be submitted in writing directly by the individual.

Hambleton

The Beckwith Bequest

£4,100

Correspondent: Joy Richardson, Correspondent, 2 Station Court, Tollerton, York YO61 1RH (07929372352; email: richardsonj7@hotmail.co.uk)

CC number: 532360

Eligibility

People resident or educated in the parishes of Easingwold and Husthwaite who are in need of financial assistance.

Types of grants

The charity provides scholarships, bursaries and maintenance allowances. Grants are available to help with general educational costs, including books, equipment/instruments, clothing, travel and so on. Our research indicates that small grants, usually around £100–£150, are available.

Annual grant total

In 2014/15 the charity had an income of £9,600 and an expenditure of £8,400. We estimate the annual total amount of grants awarded to individuals to be around £4,100.

Applications

Applications can be made in writing to the correspondent.

Other information

The charity can also provide facilities or other benefits for educational establishments, where these are not already covered by the local authority.

Scarborough

The Scarborough Municipal Charity

£2,500

Correspondent: Elaine Greening, Flat 2, 126 Falsgrave Road, Scarborough YO12 5BE (01723 375256; email: scar.municipalcharity@yahoo.co.uk)

CC number: 217793

Eligibility

People who have lived in the borough of Scarborough for at least five years.

Our research suggests that in exceptional circumstances support may be given to someone resident outside the area of benefit or living in the borough temporarily.

Types of grants

Small grants can be given towards general education or training needs and purchase of necessities, including books, fees, uniforms, travel, equipment, maintenance/living expenses and excursions. According to our research, college, undergraduate and mature students and people in vocational training can be supported.

Annual grant total

In 2014 the charity had assets of £2.1 million and an income of £185,000. Grants are given for social welfare and educational purposes and, during the year, amounted to £4,900. We estimate that educational grants totalled around £2,500.

Applications

Application forms are available from the correspondent. Our research suggests that they are considered quarterly and the sub-committee of three trustees interview each applicant.

Other information

The trustees are responsible for both the almshouse and the relief-in-need branches of the charity. The majority of the charity's expenditure is spent in direct charitable activities maintaining the almshouses and providing services to the tenants.

Scarborough United Scholarships Foundation

£10,500

Correspondent: Anne Morley, Secretary, 169 Scalby Road, Scarborough YO12 6TB (01723 375908; email: anne.morley169@btinternet.com)

CC number: 529678

Eligibility

People under the age of 25 who live in the former borough of Scarborough and have attended school in the area for at least three years.

Types of grants

Grants are available to schoolchildren, college/university students (including mature students), vocational students and people starting work/entering a trade. Support is given towards the cost of uniforms/clothing, books, equipment/instruments, study/travel overseas and educational outings/visits.

Our research suggests that grants are usually given to those at Scarborough Sixth Form College, Yorkshire Coast College or a college of further education 'where a student is following a course which is a non-advanced course'. Occasionally, loans can be made or second degree and postgraduate students may receive assistance.

Annual grant total

In 2013/14 the foundation had an income of £9,000 and an expenditure of £11,000. We estimate the annual total amount of grants awarded to be around £10,500.

Exclusions

According to our research support is not given towards educational fees.

Applications

Our research shows that the foundation mostly deals with local colleges to ensure potential applicants are made aware of when and how to apply.

York

The Company of Merchant Taylors of the City of York (Merchant Taylors – York)

£10,000

Correspondent: Nevil Pearce, Clerk, U. H. Y. Calvert Smith, 31 St Saviourgate, York YO1 8NQ (01904 557570; fax: 01904 557571; email: clerk@merchant-taylors-york.org; website: www.merchant-taylors-york.org)

CC number: 229067

Eligibility

Young people in education or training in the fields of arts, music and craftsmanship who live in York and the surrounding area.

Types of grants

Bursaries, prizes and other grants of up to £1,000 are available for a wide range of activities under the headings of arts, music and craftsmanship to develop applicants' skills and enhance their career prospects.

Annual grant total

In 2013/14 the charity had assets of £503,500 and an income of £83,500. Charitable expenditure totalled £10,500 and a total of £10,000 was awarded in grants to individuals.

Applications

Application forms can be downloaded from the charity's website or requested from the correspondent. Applications can be submitted at any time and should be sent by email to The Clerk of the Company of Merchant Taylors in the City of York at clerk@merchant-taylors-york.org.

Other information

The charity also maintains the company's hall and premises, almshouses, documents, runs the guild, pays pensions to tailors in the area of benefit and supports individuals and organisations for welfare causes.

York Children's Trust

Correspondent: Margaret Brien, Administrator, 29 Whinney Lane, Harrogate HG2 9LS (01423 504765)

CC number: 222279

Eligibility

Children and young people under 25 who live within 20 miles of the centre of York.

Types of grants

One-off grants, usually of between £100 and £300, are awarded to:

- Schoolchildren for uniforms/clothing, equipment/instruments and excursions
- College students for study/travel overseas, equipment/instruments, maintenance/living expenses and childcare
- Undergraduates for study/travel overseas, excursions and childcare
- Vocational students for uniforms/clothing, fees, study/travel overseas, excursions and childcare
- Mature students for childcare
- People starting work
- Those with special educational needs for uniforms/clothing

Our research suggests that preference is given to schoolchildren with serious family difficulties so that the child has to be educated away from home and to people with special educational needs who have been referred by a paediatrician or educational psychiatrist.

Annual grant total

In 2014 the trust had an income of £96,000 and a total expenditure of £91,500. At the time of writing (November 2015) the trust's annual report and accounts for the year were not available to view. In the most recent year for which we had a grants figure (2012) grants for educational purposes totalled around £6,700.

Exclusions

Grants are not available for private education or postgraduate studies.

Applications

Application forms are available from the correspondent and can be submitted directly by the individual or by the individual's school, college or educational welfare agency, or a third party such as a health visitor or social worker. Applications are considered quarterly, normally in January, April, July and October, and should be received by the trust one month beforehand.

South Yorkshire

Armthorpe Poors Estate Charity

£1,600

Correspondent: Tracey Ellis, 6 The Lings, Armthorpe, Doncaster, South Yorkshire DN3 3RH (01302 355180; email: apecharity@gmail.com)

CC number: 226123

Eligibility

People who are in need and live in Armthorpe.

Types of grants

One-off and recurrent grants of a minimum of £50 are given to schoolchildren who are in need for educational outings and to undergraduates for books.

Annual grant total

In 2013/14 the charity had an income of £10,800 and a total expenditure of £6,800. Grants are made to individuals and organisations for a wide range of purposes. We estimate that educational grants to individuals totalled £1,600.

Exclusions

Applications from individuals outside Armthorpe will be declined.

Applications

Contact the Clerk by telephone who will advise if a letter of application is needed. Undergraduates are required to complete an application form, available from the correspondent, and return it by 31 August.

Beighton Relief-in-Need Charity

£1,800

Correspondent: Diane Rodgers, Trustee, 41 Collingbourne Avenue, Sothall, Sheffield S20 2QR (email: beigtonrelief@hotmail.co.uk)

CC number: 225416

Eligibility

Students who live in the former parish of Beighton and are in need.

Types of grants

One-off grants according to need.

Annual grant total

In 2014 the charity had an income of £10,700 and a total expenditure of £7,400. Grants are made to individuals and organisations for social welfare and educational purposes. We estimate that educational grants to individuals totalled £1,800.

Applications

Apply in writing to the correspondent. Applications can be submitted directly by the individual or through a social worker, Citizens Advice, other welfare agency or a third party such as a relative, neighbour or trustee.

Bolsterstone Educational Charity

£4,300

Correspondent: Cliff North, 5 Pennine View, Stocksbridge, Sheffield S36 1ER (0114 288 2757; email: cliff.north@ virgin.net)

CC number: 529371

Eligibility

Children and young people under the age of 25 who live in the parishes of St Mary's, Bolsterstone and St Matthias', Stocksbridge.

Types of grants

Grants are given towards books, equipment/instruments and other educational needs, not normally provided by the local authorities.

Annual grant total

In 2014/15 the charity had an income of £9,900 and an expenditure of £8,600. It also supports local schools; therefore, we estimate the annual total amount of grants awarded to individuals to be around £4,300.

Exclusions

No grants are given to mature students or people starting work.

Applications

Apply in writing to the correspondent. Our research suggests that applications can be submitted directly by the individual normally for consideration at the beginning of March, July or November.

Other information

The charity also supports a number of local schools.

Barnsley

The Shaw Lands Trust

£12,000

Correspondent: Jill Leece, Clerk, 35 Church Street, Barnsley, South Yorkshire S70 2AP (01226 213434; email: jill.leece@newmanandbond.co.uk)

CC number: 224590

Eligibility

Children and young people under the age of 25 who live within the Barnsley metropolitan borough or have attended school there for at least two years. Preference is given to individuals from households with a low income.

Types of grants

Grants in the range of £300–£750. Support can be given to schoolchildren, further/higher education students or people starting work/entering a trade for various educational needs, including books, necessities, equipment/ instruments, tools, outfits/clothing, uniforms, travel in the UK or abroad in pursuance of education and study of music or other arts.

Annual grant total

In 2013/14 the trust had assets of £1.4 million, an income of £48,000 and a total charitable expenditure of £42,500. Educational grants totalled £12,000.

Applications

Apply in writing to the correspondent. Applications are considered in September.

Other information

At least two thirds of the charity's income is spent supporting local charitable organisations working for young people (£31,000 in 2013/14) with the remainder being allocated to assist individual students.

Sheffield

Church Burgesses Educational Foundation

£124,000

Correspondent: Godfrey Smallman, The Law Clerk, 3rd Floor Fountain Precinct, Balm Green, Sheffield S1 2JA (0114 267 5594; fax: 0114 267 3176; email: sheffieldchurchburgesses@wrigleys.co.uk; website: www.sheffieldchurchburgesses. org.uk)

CC number: 529357

Eligibility

People under the age of 25 who/whose parents have lived in Sheffield for at least three years. Generally individuals below tertiary education level.

Types of grants

Grants can be given for a wide variety of general educational needs, such as books, clothing, equipment and other essentials for schoolchildren. Support for attending independent schools can only be made where the need is clearly demonstrated (for example, unexpected familial or financial difficulties, or special needs of the child).

Special grants are given for one-off special projects, church-based youth and education work, gap year opportunities, summer schools and festivals and extra-curricular activities in arts, music, sports and so on.

Assistance may occasionally be available for those at tertiary education, although no grants are made where support from local authority is available. Postgraduates can only receive funding if there is a special need for retraining or education in a different subject.

Annual grant total

In 2013 the foundation had assets of £145,000 and an income of £259,000. Educational grants to individuals totalled £101,000 and special grants to individuals amounted to £23,000. At the time of writing (September 2015) the information provided was the latest available.

Exclusions

Individuals based in Sheffield on a temporary basis to attend an educational establishment are not eligible. As a general rule higher education courses are not supported.

Applications

Application forms are available from the foundation's website or can be requested from the correspondent. The trustees usually meet four times a year, in January, April, August (emergency cases) and October, but grants can be made outside these times as well. Applications will need to include confirmation of attendance at an educational institution, a reference from a music teacher (if applicable), information of the educational trip to be undertaken and other relevant supporting documentation.

Other information

The following is taken from the foundation's website:

Funding is given to a wide variety of activities which include one-off or special projects in schools, church-based youth and education work, and to other organisations operating in this field.

Grants may also be made to those with special needs as well as to gifted individuals who incur exceptional expenses in developing their skills in the field of the arts and sport. Modest awards are also made to assist participation in gap year expeditions, medical electives and similar activities.

The Foundation gives financial assistance to many musical activities in schools, at Sheffield Cathedral, and more widely in the community and has good links with arts organisations all of which support enables beneficiaries to extend their work with young people.

It is developing schemes with training organisations with a view to helping young men and women through apprenticeships or internships in trades and crafts.

Hollowford Trust

£4,400

Correspondent: Lucy Nunn, Correspondent, Sheffield Dioccsan Church House, 95–99 Effingham Street, Rotherham, South Yorkshire S65 1BL (01709 309135; fax: 01709 512550; email: lucy.nunn@sheffield.anglican.org; website: www.sheffield.anglican.org/hollowford-trust)

CC number: 523918

Eligibility

Young people between the ages of 10 and 25 resident in, or near, the Diocese of Sheffield.

Types of grants

Awards of up to £300 aim to help 'develop [the applicants'] physical, mental and spiritual capabilities, so that they may grow to full maturity as individuals and members of society and so that their conditions of life may be improved'. This may include overseas and UK-based experience, for example, voluntary work or short trips in the UK, and associated costs, such as fees, travel expenses or equipment.

Annual grant total

In 2014 the trust had an income of £10,200 and an expenditure of £13,700. We estimate that about £4,400 was given in grants to individuals for educational purposes.

Exclusions

According to the guidance notes available on the trust's website, funding is not given for:

- repeat applications from an individual or the same group of young people for the same purpose
- musical instruments
- costs towards formal qualifications/education (inclusive of fees for integral course trips)
- activities where evangelism is the primary purpose
- employment of youth or children workers
- grants needed in retrospect of closing dates
- grants to other charitable trusts

Applications

Application forms are available on the trust's website and should be returned to the correspondent at least two weeks in advance of the trustees' meetings. Most recently deadlines for submitting an application were in the second half of January, April, June and September.

Other information

Grants of up to £400 are also available to groups as start-up grants or for UK trips. Funding may also be given for events, concerts or outreach activities.

Sir Samuel Osborn's Deed of Gift Relief Fund

£2,400

Correspondent: Sue Wragg, Fund Manager, South Yorkshire Community Foundation, Unit 3 – G1 Building, 6 Leeds Road, Attercliffe, Sheffield S9 3TY (0114 242 4294; fax: 0114 242 4605; email: grants@sycf.org.uk; website: sycf.org.uk/apply/individuals/sir-samuel-osborns-deed-gift-relief-fund)

CC number: 1140947

Eligibility

Residents of Sheffield, with some preference for former employees of the Samuel Osborn Company (or one if its subsidiaries) and their dependants.

Types of grants

Grants of up to £1,000 are given for costs associated with undertaking any training or education, for example, books, equipment and living costs.

Annual grant total

In 2013/14 the fund had an investment income of £5,500 and made grants totalling £4,900 for social welfare and educational purposes. We estimate that educational grants to individuals totalled £2,400.

Exclusions

Individuals with large personal reserves of money will not be funded.

Applications

Application forms can be downloaded, along with guidelines, from the South Yorkshire Community Foundation's website. The foundation welcomes informal approaches about applications prior to submitting. Applicants with a connection to the Osborn company should include written evidence. The foundation aims to assess cases within 12 weeks of receiving the completed application form with all enclosures.

Other information

The fund is now administered by the South Yorkshire Community Foundation.

The Sheffield Bluecoat and Mount Pleasant Educational Foundation

£14,000 (29 grants)

Correspondent: Godfrey Smallman, Clerk, Wrigleys Solicitors, Fountain Precinct, Balm Green, Sheffield S1 2JA (0114 267 5588; fax: 0114 276 3176; email: godfrey.smallman@wrigleys.co.uk)

CC number: 529351

Eligibility

People under the age of 25 who have lived within a 20-mile radius of Sheffield Town Hall for at least three years and are in need.

Types of grants

One-off or recurrent grants can be made for general educational purposes, including necessities, clothing and outfits, equipment/instruments, maintenance expenses, fees, gap year opportunities, study/travel overseas and study of music, arts, sports or physical education. Support is given to schoolchildren, further/higher education students or people in training and people starting work/entering a trade. In special cases private schooling costs can be assisted.

Annual grant total

In 2013/14 the foundation had assets of £1.5 million, an income of £64,500 and awarded £36,000 in grants. Grants were made to 29 individuals totalling £14,000.

Applications

Apply in writing to the correspondent. Application should also include all the supporting documents and evidence of financial need. The trustees meet twice a year, usually in April and September.

Other information

The foundation also supports local organisations (£22,000 in in 2013/14).

Sheffield Grammar School Exhibition Foundation

£60,000 (110 grants)

Correspondent: Godfrey Smallman, Clerk, 3rd Floor, Fountain Precinct, Balm Green, Sheffield S1 2JA (0114 267 5594; fax: 0114 267 5630; email: godfrey.smallman@wrigleys.co.uk)

CC number: 529372

Eligibility

People who have lived within the city of Sheffield boundary for at least three years (excluding residency for educational purposes). There is a preference for people who are attending/have attended King Edward VII School for at least two years.

Types of grants

Grants are awarded for general educational purposes, including the course costs, study/travel overseas, training and retraining courses, medical electives, childcare costs, field trips, gap year and character building opportunities, sports or musical training. Support can be given to schoolchildren, further/higher education students and people entering a trade/occupation towards outfits, clothing, tools, books, equipment and instruments.

Annual grant total

In 2013/14 the foundation had assets of £2.8 million, an income of £157,500 and a charitable expenditure of £174,500. The amount of grants given to individuals totalled £60,000.

Applications

The trustees' 2013/14 annual report notes that:

Applications are accepted from a wide range of individuals and organisations. Some of the grant programmes have application forms and financial eligibility documentation which requires completion, other applications are taken by letter with supporting documentation

All applications are reviewed by trustees at their quarterly meetings.

Details of how to apply for grants are available from the Law Clerk and his office, both in hard copy and by email.

Other information

In 2013/14 a total of £19,000 was awarded in grants to organisations.

West Yorkshire

Bowcocks Trust Fund for Keighley

£2,500

Correspondent: Alistair Docherty, 17 Farndale Road, Wilsden, Bradford BD15 0LW (01535 272657; email: wendy. docherty4@btinternet.com)

CC number: 223290

Eligibility

People in need who live in the municipal borough of Keighley as constituted on 31 March 1974.

Types of grants

One-off grants of no more than £350 are given according to need.

Annual grant total

In 2013/14 the charity had an income of £9,400 and a total expenditure of £10,200. Grants are made to individuals and organisations for both educational and social welfare purposes. We estimate that educational grants to individuals totalled £2,500.

Applications

Initial telephone calls are welcomed. Applications should be made in writing to the correspondent by a third party.

Lady Elizabeth Hastings' Educational Foundation

£118,000 (203 grants)

Correspondent: Andrew Fallows, Clerk, Carter Jonas, 82 Micklegate, York YO1 6LF (01904 558212; email: leh. clerk@carterjonas.co.uk; website: www. ladyelizabethhastingscharities.co.uk/ grants/education)

CC number: 224098–1

Eligibility

Individuals in education who are in need and live in the parishes of Bardsey with East Keswick, Burton Salmon, Collingham with Harewood, Ledsham with Fairburn, Shadwell and Thorp Arch.

Grants can also be made to people who have at any time attended one of the Lady Elizabeth Hastings schools in Collingham, Ledston or Thorp Arch, irrespective of whether they are still resident in the area of benefit.

Types of grants

One-off and recurrent grants are given according to need can be given to college and university students, schoolchildren or people in vocational training or apprenticeships. Support can be given towards school uniforms, educational outings, sports equipment and musical instruments, university/college fees and associated necessities, tools, books and so on.

Annual grant total

In 2013/14 the foundation had assets of £15.8 million and an income of almost £542,000. Grants were awarded to 203 individuals for educational purposes totalling £118,000.

Exclusions

Grants to purchase computers are only given in exceptional circumstances; however, college and university grants are generally made without conditions and may be used towards buying computer equipment.

Applications

Application forms can be found on the foundation's website or requested from the correspondent. Applications can be completed by the individual directly or by a parent/guardian and must be submitted by post at any time a month in advance of the trustees' meeting. The meetings are held four times a year, in early March, June, October and December.

Other information

The foundation is managed by and derives its income from Lady Elizabeth Hasting's Estate Charity. The foundation also gives yearly payments to designated local schools, organisations and clergy to be applied for the benefit of people in the area of benefit.

Calderdale

The Community Foundation for Calderdale

Correspondent: Grants Department, The 1855 Building (first floor), Discovery Road, Halifax, West Yorkshire HX1 2NG (01422 438738; fax: 01422 350017; email: grants@cffc.co.uk; website: www.cffc.co. uk)

CC number: 1002722

Eligibility

People in need who live in Calderdale.

Types of grants

See the website for details of grants available to individuals.

Annual grant total

In 2013/14 grants were awarded to 349 individuals. Grants from the Individual Fund amounted to £52,000. We believe that the majority of this was awarded for social welfare purposes. We were not able to determine the exact figure for grants made for educational purposes.

Applications

Applications are made through referring agencies. See the website for details of funds open to individuals.

Other information

The foundation also gives to organisations and to individuals for relief-in-need purposes.

Kirklees

Mirfield Educational Charity

£2,500 (5 grants)

Correspondent: Malcolm Parkinson, Clerk, 7 Kings Street, Mirfield, West Yorkshire WF14 8AW (01924 499251; email: Malcolm.Parkinson@ramsdens.co. uk)

CC number: 529334

Eligibility

People under the age of 25 who or whose parents live in the former urban district of Mirfield.

Types of grants

One-off grants ranging from £300 to £1,000 are awarded towards educational costs and opportunities, including tuition fees, travel/study overseas, expeditions, projects, living expenses or necessities.

Annual grant total

In 2013/14 the charity had assets of £1.5 million, an income of £51,000 and a total charitable expenditure of £82,000. Grants to five individuals totalled £2,500.

Applications

Applications may be made in writing to the correspondent. The trustees meet three times a year, in February, May and October.

Other information

The charity also supports organisations, schools and groups.

Leeds

The Bramley Poor's Allotment Trust

£1,800

Correspondent: Marian Houseman, 9 Horton Rise, Rodley, Leeds LS13 1PH (0113 236 0115)

CC number: 224522

Eligibility

People in need who live in the ancient township of Bramley, especially those who are elderly, poor and sick.

Types of grants

One-off grants between £40 and £120.

Annual grant total

In 2014 the charity had an income and expenditure of £3,600. We estimate that grants given to individuals for educational purposes totalled around £1,800.

Applications

Apply in writing to the correspondent. The trust likes applications to be submitted through a recognised referral agency (social worker, Citizens Advice, doctor, headmaster or minister). They are considered monthly.

The Community Shop Trust (also known as The Leeds Community Trust)

£1,500

Correspondent: Lynn Higo, Administrator, McCarthy's Business Centre, Suite 23, Enterprise House, Leeds LS7 2AH (0113 237 9685; fax: 0113 278 3184; email: info@ leedscommunitytrust.org; website: www. leedscommunitytrust.org)

CC number: 701375

Eligibility

Children and young people who are in need and live in Leeds.

Types of grants

Small, one-off grants towards the costs associated with education, music and sports are available through the 'Keen Kidz' programme. In the past, grants have been made towards a computer, learning aids, playgroup fees, a drum kit, DJ mixing decks and sports clothes.

Annual grant total

In 2014 the trust had an income of £23,500 and a total expenditure of £28,500. Due to its low income, the trust was not required to submit its accounts to the Charity Commission and so we were unable to determine how much was given in grants. Based on previous years, we estimate that individuals received around £1,500 in grants for educational purposes.

Applications

Applications can only be submitted by a social worker or care agency on behalf of the individual.

Other information

The trust runs two shops and distributes the profits to local charities, groups and individuals in need, particularly people who are in vulnerable situations.

Kirke's Charity

£1,700

Correspondent: Bruce Buchan, Trustee, 8 St Helens Croft, Leeds LS16 8JY (01924 465860)

CC number: 246102

Eligibility

People in need who live in the ancient parishes of Adel, Arthington or Cookridge.

Types of grants

One-off grants, usually of around £100.

Annual grant total

In 2013/14 the charity had an income of £9,500 and a total expenditure of £7,000. Grants are made to individuals and organisations for both educational and social welfare purposes. We estimate that educational grants to individuals totalled £1,700.

Applications

Apply in writing to the correspondent. Applications can be submitted directly by the individual or through a social worker, Citizens Advice or other welfare agency.

Wakefield

Lady Bolles Foundation

£7,000

Correspondent: Stephen Skellern, Trustee, 6 Lynwood Drive, Wakefield WF2 7EF (01924 250473; email: neil. holland@wakefield-cathedral.org.uk)

CC number: 529344

Eligibility

People under the age of 21 who live in the county borough of Wakefield and are in full-time education. At the trustees' discretion support may be continued up to the age of 24.

Types of grants

Grants are given towards uniforms, clothing, fees, educational outings, books, travel or maintenance expenses. Apprentices and people starting work are also supported.

Annual grant total

In 2014 the foundation had an income of £6,500 and an expenditure of £7,500. We estimate the annual total amount of grants awarded to individuals to be around £7,000.

Applications

Apply in writing to the correspondent. Grants are normally considered in February and October.

Feiweles Trust

£650

Correspondent: Paul Rogers, Trustee, c/o Yorkshire Sculpture Park, Bretton Hall, Bretton, Wakefield, West Yorkshire WF4 4LG (01924 832519; email: patricia. jorgensen-ghous@ysp.co.uk; website: www.ysp.co.uk)

CC number: 1094383

Eligibility

Young artists at the beginning of their career.

Types of grants

The trust provides an annual bursary to an artist or artists at the beginning of their career to allow them to work within local schools, normally for three months. Successful applicants work with children of all ages, are supported by the teacher and can use the surroundings and educational resources of Yorkshire Sculpture Park for the residency. Each year a different area of art is undertaken and to date the artists have explored film, sculpture, poetry, drama, dance, music, creative writing, painting, textile art, physical theatre, art as environment and creative writing with illustration. The award is of up to £10,000.

Annual grant total

In 2013/14 the trust had an income of £5 and a total expenditure of £700. We estimate that about £650 was spent in grants.

Applications

Apply in writing to the correspondent. Our research suggests that applications can be submitted directly by the individual usually before January for consideration in February/March.

The Daniel Gaskell and John Wray Foundation

£8,500

Correspondent: Martin Milner, Clerk, Meadow View, Haigh Moor Road, Tingley, Wakefield WF3 1EJ (07947 611100)

CC number: 529262

Eligibility

People under 25 in full-time education who are living or who have a parent living in the former urban district council of Horbury.

Types of grants

Grants, typically ranging between £50 and £200, can be given towards books, equipment, field trips, travel, course expenses for those at school, college or university.

Annual grant total

In 2014 the foundation had an income of £20,000 and a total expenditure of £17,300. We estimate that the amount of grants given to individuals totalled £8,500, with funding also awarded to local schools

Applications

Applications should be made after advertisements are placed in the local press. The trustees meet annually in September, so applications should be received by the end of August.

Statutory grants and student support

A complete overview of benefits is beyond the scope of this book. There are a number of organisations which provide comprehensive guides, information and advice to students wishing to study in the UK and overseas. Contact details for these organisations can be found in the 'Contacts and sources of further information' section on page 325.

Statutory provision of both educational and welfare support is extremely complex and continuously changing. The following is intended to act as a signpost to helpful sources of information.

This chapter includes information on:
- Schoolchildren (aged 16 and under)
- Further education
- Student support

Schoolchildren (aged 16 and under)

The following benefits are all administered separately by individual local education authorities (LEAs) which set their own rules of eligibility and set the level of grants. The following information covers the basic general criteria for benefits, but you should contact your LEA directly for further information and advice.

Free school meals

In England and Wales, LEA-maintained schools must provide a free midday meal to pupils if they or their parents are in receipt of certain benefits. More information regarding eligibility for free school meals is available from www.gov.uk/apply-free-school-meals.

School clothing grants

In England and Wales, children who attend maintained schools, further education colleges and sixth form colleges may be able to receive help with the costs of their school clothing, including PE kits. However, this is at the discretion of their LEA and the policies on who can receive help and what items help can be given for vary widely from area to area. Check with your LEA to find out what the policy is in your area.

As it is not a legal requirement for schoolchildren to wear a uniform, some local authorities do not provide financial help to help with the purchase of school clothing. Citizens Advice is campaigning to encourage more parents to challenge local authorities that have policies of not providing financial assistance with school uniforms. More information on this is available from www. citizensadvice.org.uk.

More information on school clothing grants across the UK is available from:
- **England and Wales:** www.gov.uk/help-school-clothing-costs (contains a local authority postcode search)
- **Northern Ireland:** www.nidirect. gov.uk/school-uniform-grant
- **Scotland:** www.citizensadvice.org. uk/scotland/education
- **Wales:** www.gov.wales/topics/ educationandskills/schoolshome

School transport

Generally, children who are between 5 and 16 years old qualify for free school transport if they go to their nearest suitable school and live at least two miles from the school, if they are under eight years old and three miles from the school, if they are over eight years old, or if there is no safe walking route to school. There are different requirements for families on low incomes and some LEAs may provide free transport for other reasons. Check with your local LEA for more information.

People who are over 16 years old and in further education may qualify for help with transport costs; this varies in each LEA.

Local authorities also have to consider any disability or special educational needs when deciding whether transport is necessary for a child. If a child has a statement of special educational needs and disability (aka SEND) and has transport requirements written into their statement, the local authorities must meet them. Discretionary grants may also be available from LEAs to cover travel expenses for parents visiting children at special schools.

Pupils living in London can also qualify for free transport on London buses and trams if they are in full-time education or work-based learning. For more information, a helpline is available on 0343 222 1234, or information can be found online at www.tfl.gov.uk.

Further education

Depending on their circumstances and the subject being studied, individuals who are in further education may qualify to receive help with the costs of their course, day-to-day living expenses and childcare. More information on the types of funding available can be found at www.gov.uk/further-education-courses/overview.

Student support

Following drastic changes in the way universities are funded in England, different rules apply depending on whether you started university pre-2012 when the old funding system was in place, or in 2012 or after when the new system was introduced.

More information on financial support available for students can be found at www.gov.uk/browse/education/student-finance

Advice is also available from your LEA. However, note that the busiest time for LEAs is the period between mid-August (when A-level results come out) and about mid-November (by which time most awards have been given). It is probably best not to contact your LEA for detailed advice at this time, unless absolutely necessary. Students should also check with their university or college for other funds that may be available within the institution.

Supplementary grants

Some students are entitled to extra help, and currently this can be applied for through the following supplementary grants:
- National Scholarship Programme
- Childcare Grant
- Parents' Learning Allowance
- Adult Dependants' Grant
- Disabled Students' Allowance

Refer to the Gov.uk site referenced above for current information on the types of grants available.

Further useful contacts include:
- **Student Finance England:** PO Box 210, Darlington DL1 9HJ (tel: 0300 100 0607; website: www.gov.uk/student-finance)
- **Student Finance Wales:** PO Box 211, Llandudno Junction LL30 9FU (tel: 0300 200 4050; website: www.studentfinancewales.co.uk)
- **Student Finance Northern Ireland:** tel: 0300 100 0077; website: www.studentfinanceni.co.uk
- **Student Awards Agency for Scotland:** Saughton House, Broomhouse Drive, Edinburgh EH11 3UT (tel: 0300 555 0505; website: www.sass.gov.uk)
- **For students from other EU countries:** Student Finance Services Non UK Team, PO Box 89, Darlington DL1 9AZ (tel: 0141 243 3570; website: www.gov.uk/studentfinance)

NHS bursaries

Subject to certain criteria, full-time NHS students can apply for a bursary and a grant from the NHS. Part-time students are eligible for reduced bursaries and grants. Eligible courses that lead to professional registration are:
- Medicine or dentistry
- Chiropody, podiatry, dietetics, occupational therapy, orthoptics, physiotherapy, prosthetics and orthotics, radiography, radiotherapy, audiology and speech and language therapy
- Dental hygiene or dental therapy
- Nursing, midwifery or operating department practice

Please visit www.gov.uk/nhs-bursaries/eligibilityfor further current information.

Social Work Bursaries

Social Work Bursaries can help with living costs and tuition fees.

For students in England: Social Work Bursaries, PO Box 141, Hesketh House, 200–220 Broadway, Fleetwood FY7 9AS (tel: 0300 330 1342; website: www.nhsbsa.nhs.uk)

For students in Wales: Care Council for Wales, South Gate House, Wood Street, Cardiff CF10 1EW (tel: 029 2078 0698; email: studentfunding@ccwales.org.uk; website: www.ccwales.org.uk)

For students in Scotland: Scottish Social Services Council, Compass House, 11 Riverside Drive, Dundee DD1 4NY (tel: 0345 60 30 891; email: enquiries@sssc.uk.com; website: www.sssc.uk.com)

For students in Northern Ireland: Social Service Inspectorate, Department of Health, Social Services and Public Safety, Information Office, C5.20, Castle Buildings, Stormont, Belfast BT4 3SJ (tel: 028 9052 0500; email: webmaster@dhsspsni.gov.uk; website: www.dhsspsni.gov.uk)

Teacher training funding

Funding is available for full-time or part-time students on Initial Teacher Training (ITT), Postgraduate Certificate in Education (PGCE) and School-Centred Initial Teacher Training (SCITT) courses through the main student finance avenue. For more details please visit: www.gov.uk/teacher-training-funding.

Department for Education: (tel: 0800 389 2500; website: www.education.gov.uk/get-into-teaching)

Professional and career development loans

A professional and career development loan (PCDL) can be a useful means of helping to finance vocational courses for periods of up to two years, particularly if the course offers the prospect of obtaining a steady, reasonably well-paid job at the end.

Loans of between £300 and £10,000 are given to assist individuals who are aged 18 and over who have lived in the UK for at least three years before the start of the course, and who plan to work in the UK, EU or European Economic Area when the course ends.

They are commercial bank loans which must be paid back after the course has finished. Interest is not paid by the individual for the period of study but is instead covered by the government while you are learning and for one more month after the course is completed (after that the repayment of the loan and the interest is the responsibility of the student).

Full information, including eligibility criteria and how to apply, is available from the National Careers Service website www.nationalcareersservice.direct.gov.uk.

Types of schools in the UK and their funding

This section contains information about and details of the types of schools that exist in the UK, how they are funded and how funding can be obtained to attend them.

Local authority-maintained schools

These schools are funded by the local education authority and include foundation schools, community schools, voluntary-controlled schools, voluntary-aided schools, nursery schools and some special schools. They all follow the national curriculum and are inspected by Ofsted.

The Gov.uk website supplies some information about the different types of schools, how to find one and apply for a place. See www.gov.uk/types-of-school for more information.

Academies

Academies are independently managed schools which are funded directly by the Education Funding Agency and operate outside the control of the local authority. They are set up by sponsors from business, faith or voluntary groups in partnership with the Department for Education and the local authority. In 2015 more than half of all secondary schools had converted, or were in the process of converting, to academy status. Many factors have caused academies to be a controversial current issue; therefore, there exists a wide range of information available about academies from all perspectives. The Department for Education supplies some details (see www.gov.uk/government/policies/academies-and-free-schools).

Free schools

These schools are non-profit, independent, state-funded schools which are not controlled by the local authority. They are similar to academies but are usually new schools, set up as a response to a demand that is not being met by existing schools.

The New Schools Network provides advice about free schools, including how to set one up. See www.newschoolsnetwork.org or call 020 7537 9208 for more information.

Independent schools

Independent schools are independent in their finances and governance, and are funded by charging parents fees (on average £10,500 a year, or £25,000 for boarders). They set their own curriculum and admission policies and are inspected by Ofsted or other approved inspectorates. According to the Independent Schools Council, around 6.5% of schoolchildren in the UK are educated in independent schools, with the figure rising to 18% of pupils for those over the age of 16.

Most independent schools offer scholarships and bursaries to some applicants, ranging from 10% of fees to full fees paid (very occasionally). They are subject to fierce competition and are usually awarded on the basis of academic merit, as well as individual need.

A number of independent schools also offer music scholarships, varying from 10% of fees to full fees paid (including free musical tuition). Candidates are usually expected to offer two instruments at at least grades 6 to 8. Contact the Director of Music at the school you are interested in for more details.

The Independent Schools Directory

The searchable directory lists all the UK independent schools, has an interactive map and offers further details on each school.

Tel: 020 8906 0911

Website: www.indschools.co.uk

The Independent Schools Council Information Service

The Independent Schools Council Information Service is the main source of information on independent schools. It has a website containing detailed information to help families to select the right school and find possible sources of funding.

Tel: 020 7766 7070

Website: www.isc.co.uk

The Independent Schools Yearbook

The Independent Schools Yearbook contains details of schools with a membership of one or more of the Constituent Associations of the Independent Schools Council. It is published by A&C Black and can be bought online.

Tel: 020 7631 5988

Email: isyb@acblack.com

Website: www.isyb.co.uk

The Independent Association of Prep Schools

The Independent Association of Prep Schools is the professional association for headteachers of the leading 600 independent prep schools in the UK and worldwide.

Tel: 01926 887833

Email: iaps@iaps.org.uk

Website: www.iaps.org.uk

The Council of British International Schools

The Council of British International Schools is a membership organisation of British schools of quality, providing British education in Europe and worldwide.

Tel: 020 3826 7190

Email: members@cobis.org.uk

Website: www.cobis.org.uk

Boarding schools

Boarding Schools Association

The Boarding Schools Association serves and represents boarding schools and promotes boarding education in the UK, including both state and private boarding schools.

Very occasionally the local authority may pay for a child's boarding fees, if they have a particularly difficult home situation. A total of 75 children were supported this way in 2011/12, and the new Assisted Boarding Network, which is backed by the government, is pushing for this number to rise to 1,000 by 2018.

Contact the Director of Education or the Chief Education Officer for the area in which you live (if you live outside the UK approach the area with which you have the closest connection).

Tel: 020 7798 1580

Website: www.boarding.org.uk

Maintained boarding schools

These are state schools that take boarders as well as day pupils; they only charge for the cost of boarding, not for tuition. Boarding costs are generally between £8,000 and £13,000 a year. According to the State Boarding Schools' Association, there are 37 state boarding schools in England. They are a mix of all-ability comprehensive schools, academies and grammar schools. They all follow the national curriculum and take the same examinations as pupils in day state schools.

State Boarding Schools' Association

Tel: 020 7798 1580

Email: info@sbsa.org.uk

Website: www.sbsa.org.uk

Music, dance and stage schools

Choir schools

Choir Schools' Association

The Choir Schools' Association is a group of 44 schools which are attached to cathedrals, churches and college chapels around the country. The majority are fee-paying, with nine out of ten choristers qualifying for financial help with fees through the schools.

Tel: 01359 221333

Email: info@choirschools.org.uk

Website: www.choirschools.org.uk

Music schools

There are various specialist music schools in the UK, with no single umbrella body. Contact the school directly for information about fees and funding.

Music and Dance Scheme

This government scheme is designed to help exceptionally talented young musicians between the ages of 8 and 19 and dancers between the ages of 11 and 19. Means-tested fee support and grants are distributed through specialist centres of education and training and conservatoires. Applications should be made directly to the school or centre you wish to attend. A full list of schools is available on the scheme's website.

Website: www.gov.uk/music-dance-scheme

MMA

MMA is the national association for music teaching professionals. It publishes the *MMA Music Directory* annually, a comprehensive guide to music departments and music scholarships in the UK, which can be purchased on its website.

Tel: 01223 312655

Email: membership@mma-online.org.uk

Website: www.mma-online.org.uk

Foundations for Excellence

The Foundations for Excellence website provides information, guidance and signposting in the areas of health and well-being for young musicians and dancers.

Website: www.foundations-for-excellence.org

Dance schools

Council for Dance and Education Training

Information on dance education and training can be obtained from the Council for Dance and Education Training. It is a quality-assurance body of the dance and musical theatre industries and provides information on its recognised schools and teachers.

Tel: 020 7240 5703

Email: info@cdet.org.uk

Website: www.cdet.org.uk

Dance Schools UK

Dance Schools UK provides a directory of dance schools and teachers across the UK and Ireland.

Website: www.danceschools-uk.co.uk

Stage schools

Drama UK

Drama UK was formed after a merger of the National Council for Drama and the Conference of Drama Schools and provides accreditation for vocational drama courses and support for organisations which offer accredited training. It acts as an advocate for the sector and encourages the industry and training providers to work together. Its website provides information about drama training.

Tel: 020 3393 6141

Email: info@dramauk.co.uk

Website: www.dramauk.co.uk

Free Index

Using the Free Index you can browse a list of stage schools in the UK.

Website: www.freeindex.co.uk/ categories/entertainment_and_ lifestyle performing_arts/ stage_schools

Other possible sources of help with fees

Allowances for Crown Servants

The Foreign and Commonwealth Office gives grants to enable children of diplomats and other government servants working abroad to attend boarding schools in the UK.

Tel: 020 7008 1500

Allowances for Armed Forces Personnel

The Children's Education Advisory Service (CEAS) provides expert and impartial advice about the education of children of the armed forces personnel.

Children whose parents are members of Her Majesty's Forces are eligible for an allowance towards boarding education, whether their parent(s) is (are) serving at home or abroad. This is the Continuity of Education Allowance which is available for children who are eight years old and older. Families are expected to contribute a minimum of 10% towards the fees. Contact CEAS to obtain advice and the relevant application form.

Address: Trenchard Lines, Upavon, Pewsey, Wiltshire SN9 6BE

Tel: 01980 618244 (civilian)

GPTN 94 344 8244 (military)

Extra funding is also available for day-school allowances, special educational needs, guardian's allowances and children's visits to parents serving overseas.

Multinational companies

Some multinational companies and organisations help with school fees if parents have to work overseas. A few firms make grants, run scholarship schemes or provide low-interest loans for employees who are resident in the UK. Consult your employer for further information.

317

Alternative routes to employment: apprenticeships

In this section, you will find information on apprenticeships and how to apply for one.

What is an apprenticeship?

Briefly, an apprenticeship is a job that also provides rigorous skills training in order to equip a school-leaver with enough experience to work in their chosen field, and improve their career prospects. At the end of an apprenticeship, the apprentice is awarded a nationally recognised qualification.

Types of apprenticeship

There are approximately 1,500 job roles available in ten different sectors including: agriculture, horticulture and animal care; business, administration and law; construction, planning and the built environment; education and training; engineering and manufacturing technologies; health, public services and care; information and communications technology; and retail and commercial enterprise.

Training duration

Generally, an apprenticeship takes between one and four years to complete. The length varies depending on the level of existing skills of the apprentice, the qualification being obtained and the industry sector.

Main benefits

The main benefits of becoming an apprentice are:
- You earn a wage during your entire apprenticeship
- There is a guaranteed, nationally recognised qualification awarded to you as you complete each stage of your training
- You gain skills and knowledge which can be used across a range of jobs and industries
- Once the apprenticeship has finished there is an opportunity to carry on working, maybe get promoted or go on to higher education in a college or university
- You can learn at your own pace and get support as and when you need it

Entry requirements

Different apprenticeships have different entry requirements depending on the type of work you will do. However, the most important requirements are the following:
- You must be living in England and not taking part in full-time education
- You must be aged 16 or over
- If you took your GCSEs more than five years ago and did not gain a top grade (A or A*), or you do not have good GCSE grades in maths and English you will need to take a literacy and numeracy test

Are there any costs involved?

The National Apprenticeship Service supports, funds and co-ordinates the delivery of apprenticeships throughout England. It will pay the costs of your training depending on your age, with any remaining costs met by the employer if you are aged 23 or under.

How to apply

To apply for an apprenticeship or a traineeship, visit the apprenticeship vacancies' website: www.findapprenticeship.service.gov.uk/apprenticeshipsearch

Application support

If you would like some help on registering, searching and applying for your chosen apprenticeship, please read the 'How to write a winning apprenticeship application' guide at: https://www.gov.uk/government/publications/how-to-write-a-winning-apprenticeship-application

References and further information

All the information presented on this page was taken from the National Apprenticeship Service. For more information, or to view what previous apprentices have to say about their experiences, please visit www.apprenticeships.org.uk.

Company sponsorships

Company sponsorships particularly apply to people in their last year at school who are intending to study a business-related, engineering, or science-based subject at university.

Sponsorship of degree courses

A number of companies sponsor students who are taking degree courses at universities, usually in business, engineering, technology or other science subjects. Such sponsorships are generally for students who are resident in the UK and are taking a first degree course (or a comparable course).

Sponsorship generally takes the form of cash support (i.e. a bursary or scholarship) while at university, with a salary being paid during pre-university and vacation employment or during periods of industrial training at the company concerned. (If the sponsorship is for a sandwich course the placements will be for longer than the vacation and will form an integral part of the course.) Sponsorships are highly competitive but can be of great value to students who, for any reason, do not receive the full grant. They may also help students avoid having to take out a loan.

Each company has its own sponsorship policy. Some sponsorships are tied to a particular course or institution; others are only given for specific subjects. The value of the sponsorship also varies. Additional help can be available in the form of discretionary educational gifts or degree prizes.

Sponsorships do not necessarily offer a permanent job at the end of the course (unless the student is classed as an employee). Equally, the student does not usually have to take up a job if offered by the company, although there may be at least a moral obligation to consider the offer.

Students should not decide on a course simply because there may be sponsorship available, they should choose the course first and seek sponsorship afterwards if appropriate.

In most sponsorships it is the student, not the company, who has to make arrangements to get on the course. Indeed some companies will only sponsor students who have already been accepted on a course. However, most university departments have well-established links with industry and actively encourage students who are seeking sponsorship.

Students should apply for sponsorships as early as possible in the autumn term of the final academic year before moving to university.

Further information

Individuals are advised to identify major institutions working in the industry they intend to follow and see what schemes are available. An example of such an institution is The Engineering Development Trust (www.etrust.org.uk), which runs a number of schemes for individuals who wish to pursue a career in STEM subjects.

Funding for gap years and overseas voluntary work

Gap years have traditionally been a popular choice with school-leavers looking to travel, volunteer, work or broaden their horizons in some other way before embarking on university life. With increasingly high costs of education many feel the need to be extra careful in choosing a career path. A short pause between leaving school and continuing education may be a smart rather than just adventurous decision. A 'mini-gap', for example, during the summer holidays can equally add valuable experience and skills to a CV and is seen by many universities and potential employers as an advantage in what is a very competitive job market.

There are some opportunities to participate in voluntary work, expeditions and other activities which can be funded or partly funded through charities, bursaries and schemes. For further information on support available in this area see 'Study, work and voluntary work overseas' on page 45. The charities in this section include:

1   Charities that can provide funding towards study or work overseas
2   Grant-makers that can offer support towards volunteering opportunities

Generally, most grant-making charities have quite specific criteria which apply to all eligible applicants; it is important to keep this in mind and not assume that you can apply just because you wish to travel to a particular area or place. Likewise, some grant-makers have a particular preference for a certain type of project, for example conservation or one that involves working for the benefit of the local community. They may also give within a specific catchment area, so it can be useful to look at local grant-makers first. Many of the local charities in this guide will give grants under terms such as 'travel overseas' or 'personal development activities'. This allows them to give broadly to a number of different activities which may fall into these categories, such as gap year projects, voluntary work overseas and so on.

It cannot be over-emphasised that it is your responsibility to check that you are eligible for funding from any charity to which you intend to apply. Please do not apply if you are in doubt of your eligibility; where appropriate, contact the organisation for further clarification.

If you are successful in gaining financial support, remember that it is always a good practice to keep charities informed of the progress of your project and what you have achieved by doing it. This might even be a requirement of accepting the funding. You may also be asked to act as an ambassador to the charity back in the UK by giving talks or presentations on your experiences. This might be something to think about when making your application, particularly if the organisation is keen to involve past participants in promoting its scheme.

It may help your cause if you raise some of the funds yourself; this might give you an edge over other applicants and prove how dedicated and determined you are to succeed. You may also find it useful to break down the total costs of your project and apply to several different grant-makers for smaller amounts of money, as this could increase your chances of securing the right amount of funding.

There are other alternatives to funding gap year projects and voluntary work overseas. Many large volunteer organisations provide funded or partly funded volunteering and exchange schemes that will allow you to take part in voluntary work at a minimum cost. Some can offer bursaries to cover specific costs such as the project fee or flight fare, and others may ask you to fundraise a block amount of money but will pay for all your necessary costs in return.

Below are a few fully or partly funded voluntary schemes available to young people living in the UK.

The European Voluntary Service (EVS)

EVS is a fully funded youth volunteering scheme run by the British Council, the UK's national agency for the Erasmus+ programmes. EVS provides opportunities for young people to volunteer in another European country for two weeks to twelve months.

The scheme is open to all young people aged 17 to 30 who are resident in the UK or one of the other participating programme countries.

EVS placements can be in all member countries of the European Union, the European Economic Area, pre-accession countries and countries neighbouring EU, including Western Balkans, Eastern Partnership countries, Russian Federation or Southern Mediterranean.

Most placements last from six to twelve months and priority is usually given to longer-term placements; however, short-term placements are also available. Placements can be organised in variety of sectors, such as social, cultural, environmental and sports, and are chosen by the volunteers themselves.

All EVS projects are fully funded by European Commission grants, which are applied for by the applicant's sending organisation. The grant covers the costs of travel, food and accommodation, insurance, training and living expenses and provides volunteers with a modest living allowance.

In order to take part in an EVS project, volunteers have to find a suitable host organisation to volunteer with and a sending organisation from their own country to sponsor them.

More information onprogramme countries, sending organisations, host organisations, projects and other information regarding EVS can be found on the European Youth Portal website (www.europa.eu/youth/en).

Note that applicants are advised to plan their projects, preferably six months in advance (as the process can take this long to complete).

In addition to applying for a volunteer placement with EVS directly, it is also possible to organise a placement through certain volunteering organisations that are linked to the EVS programme. The Inter-Cultural Youth Exchange (www.icye.org.uk) and International Voluntary Service (www.ivsgb.org) will help volunteers through application processes and will sometimes carry out administration work on their behalf. If you are interested in volunteering with EVS, it may be worthwhile contacting one of these organisations for help.

Lattitude Global Volunteering

Lattitude Global Volunteering is a UK-based volunteering organisation and registered charity (Charity Commission no. 272761) that organises volunteer placements in developing countries for 17- to 25-year-olds and offers bursaries and funded projects for applicants in need of financial help. Volunteers can take part in a number of different projects such as camps and outdoor education, and environmental, medical and community projects. More information about the opportunities Lattitude Global Volunteering can offer is available from the charity's website (www.lattitude.org.uk).

The Jack Petchey Foundation

The foundation supports young people aged 11 to 25 who live in Essex or London who are raising money in order to be involved in a voluntary project or participate in events that will benefit others in society. Grants are given to cover up to 50% of the cost of the project (but no more than £300 per person). Full details of eligibility criteria and how to apply can be found on the foundation's website (www. jackpetcheyfoundation.org.uk).

Project Trust

Project Trust is an educational charity which specialises in overseas volunteering placements for school-leavers. People between the ages of 17 and 19 are given training and support to undertake voluntary teaching and social care projects abroad lasting about 8 to 12 months. Living allowances are provided by the trust or the overseas host. More details on the opportunities available can be found on the trust's website (projecttrust.org.uk).

Other helpful contacts

www.igapyear.com
iGapyear.com provides advice on how to put together a proposal for a funding application as well as offering other information on gap year and volunteering opportunities.

www.gapyear.com
An online community where backpackers and gap year travellers can meet, chat and share experiences.

www.idealist.org
Idealist.org is an independent, online network of non-profit and voluntary organisations that provide information on voluntary opportunities worldwide.

www.eurodesk.eu/edesk
The website holds information on European policies and opportunities for young people.

www.yearoutgroup.org
Year Out Group is an association of organisations running gap year and volunteering projects. The website provides general information for people planning to take a year out and offers the details of member organisations.

Volunteer organisations
www.vsointernational.org
www.frontier.ac.uk
www.raleighinternational.org

Contacts and sources of further information

Many people in education and training need financial advice and help from time to time. It is usually best to contact the following people or organisations as a starting point:

- The educational institution you are studying at
- Your local education authority
- Your local Citizens Advice or other welfare agencies

These organisations will be in the best position to point you in the right direction for further or more specialist advice if necessary. For resources that offer information and advice in specific areas readers should also see the details listed in the preceding sections:

- Statutory grants and student support (p. 313)
- Types of schools in the UK and their funding (p. 315)
- Alternative routes to employment: apprenticeships (p. 319)
- Company sponsorships (p. 321)
- Funding for gap years and overseas voluntary work (p. 323)

We have put together the following list of organisations that provide information and guidance on a broad range of issues.

General

Citizens Advice

England: 03444 111 444

Wales: 03444 77 20 20

Scotland: 03454 04 05 06

Northern Ireland: contact local bureau

Provides free, independent, confidential and impartial advice to everyone on their rights and responsibilities. Find your local bureau or get advice online at www.citizensadvice.org.uk.

Department for Education

Piccadilly Gate, Store Street, Manchester M1 2WD (tel: 03700 002288; website: www.gov.uk/dfe).

Department of Business, Innovation and Skills (further and higher education)

1 Victoria Street, London SW1H 0ET (tel: 020 7215 5000; email: enquires@bis.gsi.gov.uk; website: www.gov.uk/bis).

Department of Education for Northern Ireland

Rathgael House, Balloo Road, Rathgill, Bangor, County Down BT19 7PR (tel: 028 9127 9279; email: mail@deni.gov.uk; website: www.deni.gov.uk).

Education Scotland

Denholm House, Almondvale Business Park, Almondvale Way, Livingston EH54 6GA (tel: 0131 244 3000; email: enquires@educationscotland.gov.uk; website: www.educationscotland.gov.uk).

Gov.uk

Website: www.gov.uk

General advice and information on government services.

The Money Advice Service

Holborn Centre, 120 Holborn, London EC1N 2TD (tel: 0800 138 7777 (English), 0800 138 0555 (Welsh); Typetalk: 18001 0300 500 5000 [Mon–Fri 8am–8pm, Sat 9am–1pm]; email: enquiries@moneyadviceservice.org.uk; website: www.moneyadviceservice.org.uk/en; an online chat facility is also available).

The Money Advice Service helps people manage their money, through a free and impartial advice service. It also works in partnership with other organisations to help people make the most of their money. It is an independent service set up by the government.

The Prince's Trust

Prince's Trust House, 9 Eldon Street, London EC2M 7SL (tel: 0800 842842; website: www.princes-trust.org.uk)

A youth charity that helps change young lives. The trust can help people aged 13 to 30 who are unemployed or struggling at school to transform their lives.

Welsh Assembly Education and Skills

Cathays Park, Cardiff CF10 3NQ (tel: 03000 603300 – English; 03000 604400 – Welsh; email: Customer Help@Wales.GSI.Gov.uk; website: www.wales.gov.uk).

Children

Child Poverty Action Group (CPAG)

Child Poverty Action Group, 30 Micawber Street (tel: 020 7837 7979; email: info@cpag. org.uk; website: www.cpag.org.uk).

Child Poverty Action Group in Scotland, 94 Duke Street, Glasgow G4 0UW (tel: 0141 552 3303; email: staff@cpagscotland.org.uk).

CPAG publishes a number of guides which include information on state benefits and entitlements for both schoolchildren and students.

National Youth Advocacy Service

Tower House, 1 Tower Road, Birkenhead, Wirral CH41 1FF (tel: 0151 649 8700; helpline: 0800 808 1001 [Mon–Fri 8am–8pm, Sat 10am–4pm]; email: main@nyas.net or help@nyas.net; website: www.nyas. net).

Youth Access

1–2 Taylors Yard, 67 Alderbrook Road, London SW12 8AD (tel: 020 8772 9900; email: admin@ youthaccess.org.uk; website: www. youthaccess.org.uk – an online directory of information, advice and support services for young people).

Further and continuing education

City and Guilds

1 Giltspur Street, London EC1A 9DD (tel: 0844 543 0000; email: centresupport@cityandguilds.com; website: www.cityandguilds.com).

City and Guilds provides support to learners and training providers.

Department for Business, Innovation and Skills

Department of Business, Innovation and Skills (further and higher education): 1 Victoria Street, London SW1H 0ET (tel: 020 7215 5000; email: enquires@bis.gsi.gov.uk; website: www.gov.uk/bis).

Learning and Work Institute

Chetwynd House, 21 De Montfort Street, Leicester LE1 7GE (tel: 0116 204 4200; email: enquiries@ learningandwork.org.uk; website: www.learningandwork.org.uk).

Higher Education

The National Union of Students (NUS)

NUS UK, Macadam House, 275 Gray's Inn Road, London WC1X 8QB (tel: 0845 521 0262; email: online form; website: www.nus. org.uk).

NUS Scotland

Papermill Wynd, McDonald Road, Edinburgh EH7 4QL (tel: 0131 556 6598; email: mail@nus-scotland.org. uk).

NUS-USI

42 Dublin Road, Belfast BT2 7HN (tel: 028 9024 4641 email: info@ nistudents.org).

NUS Wales

2nd Floor, Cambrian Buildings, Mount Stuart Square, Cardiff CF10 5FL (tel: 029 2043 5390 email: office@nus-wales.org.uk).

The Open University (OU)

The Open University, PO Box 197, Milton Keynes MK7 6BJ (tel: 0300 303 5303; email: online form; website: www.open.ac.uk).

Scholarship Search

Website: www.scholarship-search.org. uk

Search scholarships in the UK for pre-university, undergraduate and postgraduate learning.

Student Awards Agency for Scotland

Gyleview House, 3 Redheughs Rigg, Edinburgh EH12 9HH (tel: 0300 555 0505; email: online form; website: www.saas.gov.uk).

Student Cashpoint

Website: www.studentcashpoint.co.uk

A website giving information on student grants, loans, bursaries, scholarships and awards.

University and Colleges Admissions Service (UCAS)

Rosehill, New Barn Lane, Gloucestershire GL5 3LZ (tel: 0371 468 0468; website: www.ucas.com).

UCAS can also be contacted via social media.

Applications for full-time university degree courses must be made through UCAS (part-time degree courses and the Open University are not covered by UCAS – apply directly to the university).

Careers

National Careers Service

Website: www.nationalcareersservice. direct.gov.uk; tel: 0800 100900; an online chat service is also available.

Provides information, advice and guidance to help people make decisions on learning, training and work opportunities. The service offers confidential and impartial advice, supported by qualified careers advisers.

Not Going to Uni

Mountcharm House, Ground Floor 102–104, Queen's Road, Buckhurst Hill IG9 5BS (tel: 020 3691 2800;

email: info@notgoingtouni.co.uk; website: www.notgoingtouni.co.uk).

Opportunities for people leaving school or college that are outside the traditional university route, including apprenticeships, sponsored degrees, diplomas, gap years, distance learning and jobs.

Prospects

Graduate Prospects, Booth Street East, Manchester M13 9EP (tel: 0161 277 5200; website: www.prospects.ac.uk).

Graduate careers website for jobs, postgraduate courses, work experience and careers advice.

Students with disabilities

Disability Rights UK

Ground Floor CAN Mezzanine, 49–51 East Road, London N1 6AH (tel: 0800 328 5050; email: students@disabilityrights.org; website: www.disabilityrightsuk.org).

National pan-disability organisation led by people with disabilities that provides advice to students with disabilities.

Lead Scotland

Princes House, 5 Shandwick Place, Edinburgh EH2 4RG (tel: 0131 228 9441; email: enquires@lead.org.uk; website: www.lead.org.uk).

Set up to widen access to learning for young people and adults with disabilities and carers across Scotland.

Study overseas

The British Council

British Council Customer Service UK, Bridgewater House, 58 Whitworth Street, Manchester M1 6BB (tel: 0161 957 7755; email: general.enquiries@britishcouncil.org; website: www.britishcouncil.org).

Advice and publications on educational trips overseas.

Erasmus

British Council, Erasmus Team, 1 Kingsway, Second Floor, Cardiff CF10 3AQ (tel: 029 2092 4311; email: erasmus@britishcouncil.org; website: www.erasmusplus.org.uk).

Erasmus enables higher education students, teachers and institutions in 31 European countries to study for part of their degree in another country.

Overseas students

Refugee Women's Association

Print House, 18 Ashwin Street, London E8 3DL (tel: 020 7923 2412; email: info@refugeewomen.org.uk; website: www.refugeewomen.org.uk).

Provides advice and guidance on education, training, employment, health and social care for refugee women throughout London.

United Kingdom Council for International Students' Affairs (UKCISA)

9–17 St Alban's Place, London N1 0NX (advice line: 020 7288 4330; website: www.ukcisa.org.uk).

UKCISA provides information for overseas students on entering the UK, as well as general advice.

Other funding or sources of help

Community Foundations

12 Angel Gate, 320–326 City Road, London EC1V 2PT (tel: 020 7713 9326; website: www.ukcommunityfoundations.org).

These local organisations sometimes have a pot of money available for individuals to apply for. Use this website to identify your local community foundation.

Money Saving Expert

Website: www.moneysavingexpert.com

British consumer finance information and discussion website providing information and journalistic articles to help people save money.

Prisoners' Education Trust

The Foundry, 17 Oval Way, London SE11 5RR (tel: 020 3752 5680; website: www.prisonerseducation.org.uk).

Access to a grants programme to enable prisoners in England and Wales to study through distance learning. The trust also provides advice and support, influences policy and advocates best practice.

Index

948: The 948 Sports Foundation 266

Abbot's: The Archbishop Abbot's Exhibition Foundation 276

Aberdeen: Aberdeen Endowments Trust 147

Aberdeenshire: Aberdeenshire Educational Trust 147

ABF: ABF The Soldiers' Charity (also known as The Army Benevolent Fund) 97

Able: Able Kidz 19

ABTA: ABTA LifeLine (The ABTA Benevolent Fund) Bursary 78

Acton: Acton (Middlesex) Charities – Educational Charity 216
The Tom Acton Memorial Trust 60

Actors': The Actors' Children's Trust (TACT) 103

Actuaries: Company of Actuaries Charitable Trust Fund 68

Adams: Ted Adams Trust Limited 80
The Adams Youth Trust 281

Adolph: Gustav Adolph and Ernest Koettgen Memorial Fund 68

Adventure: Adventure Trust for Girls 285

AIA: The AIA Education and Benevolent Trust 68

Air: The Air Pilots Benevolent Fund 124
Air Pilots Trust 67

Airey: The Airey Neave Trust 93

Aitchison: The Christina Aitchison Trust 23

Aldgate: The Aldgate and Allhallows Foundation 207

Aldworth's: Aldworth's Educational Trust (Aldworth Trust Foundation) 260

Alenson: The Alenson and Erskine Educational Foundation 193

Allen: Arthur Allen Educational Trust 295
Elizabeth Allen Trust 211

Allen's: Allen's Charity (Apprenticing Branch) 193

Allendale: Allendale Exhibition Endowment 229

Al-Mizan: Al-Mizan Charitable Trust 3

Almondsbury: Almondsbury Charity 294

Alsager: Alsager Educational Foundation 231

Altrusa: Altrusa Careers Trust 17

Alvechurch: The Alvechurch Grammar School Endowment 188

Amber: The Amber Trust 23

Amersham: Amersham United Charities (Amersham and Coleshill Almshouse Charity) 253

Amiel: The Barry Amiel and Norman Melburn Trust 93

Amory's: Viscount Amory's Charitable Trust 281

Ancell: The Ancell Trust 254

Anderson: Anderson Barrowcliff Bursary 68
Cole Anderson Charitable Foundation 289
The Andrew Anderson Trust 87

Anglo: The Anglo Jewish Association 41

Anglo-Czech: The Anglo-Czech Educational Fund 30

Anglo-Swedish: Anglo-Swedish Literary Foundation 30

Anguish's: Anguish's Educational Foundation 199

Angus: Angus Educational Trust 149

Annie: The Annie Tranmer Charitable Trust 205

Apothecaries: The Worshipful Society of Apothecaries General Charity Limited 80

Arlidge's: Arlidge's Charity 178

Armenian: Armenian General Benevolent Union London Trust 30

Armthorpe: Armthorpe Poors Estate Charity 307

Arnold: Arnold Educational Foundation 167

Arnold's: Arnold's Educational Foundation 164

Arrol: The Arrol Trust 37

Artistic: The Artistic Endeavours Trust 54

Arts: Arts Trust of Scotland 135

Ashford: The Ashford Hill Educational Trust 260

Ashley: Ashley Churchill and Thorner Educational Trust 290

Ashton: Ashton Schools Foundation 248

Athletics: Athletics for the Young 85

Athlone: The Athlone Trust 10

Atwell's: Lawrence Atwell's Charity (Skinners' Company) 4

Audlem: Audlem Educational Foundation 232

Australian: The Australian Music Foundation in London 60

Avenel: The Avenel Trust 135

Awards: Awards for Young Musicians 61

Ayrshire: Ayrshire Educational Trust 135

Babington's: Babington's Charity 159

Bailey: The Ernest Bailey Charity 160

Baines's: Baines's Charity 240

Baker: Josephine Baker Trust 104

Ballard: Albert Casanova Ballard Deceased (A. C. Ballard Deceased Trust) 285

Bampton: The Bampton Exhibition Foundation 276

Banbury: The Banbury Charities 274

Banffshire: Banffshire Educational Trust 146

Bank: The Bank Workers Charity 105

Barnabas: The Barnabas Trust 87

Barnes: R. W. Barnes Educational Fund 282
The Barnes Workhouse Fund 222

Barnet's: The Mayor of Barnet's Benevolent Fund 212

Barnwood: Barnwood House Trust 292

Barrack: The Barrack Hill Educational Charity (Barrack Hill Trust) 239

Barristers': The Barristers' Benevolent Association 111

Barrow's: The William Barrow's Charity 272

Barry: The William Barry Trust 51

Bart: The Lionel Bart Foundation 55

Bartholomew: Bartholomew Educational Foundation 272

Baxter: Alan Baxter Foundation (ABF) 69

Baylies': Baylies' Educational Foundation 171

BBC: BBC Performing Arts Fund 61

Beacon: Beacon Centre for the Blind 24

Beaminster: Beaminster Relief in Need Charity 290

Beaumont's: Ann Beaumont's Educational Foundation 203

Beckett's: Beckett's and Sergeant's Educational Foundation 166

Beckwith: The Beckwith Bequest 306

Bedale: Bedale Educational and Bedale 750 Charity (The Rector and Four and Twenty of Bedale) 305

Beighton: Beighton Relief-in-Need Charity 307

Belfast: Belfast Association for the Blind 133

Benlian: The Benlian Trust 31

Bennett: The Oli Bennett Charitable Trust 9

Benney: Benney Arts Foundation 55

Bentley: The Bentley Young Person's Trust 262

Bestway: The Bestway Foundation 31

Bewdley: The Bewdley Old Grammar School Foundation 190

Bideford: Bideford Bridge Trust 285

Bilton: The Bilton Poor's Land and Other Charities 179

Bingham: The Bingham Trust 161
The Bingham Trust Scheme 169
Bingham United Charities 2006 167

Bird: The Dickie Bird Foundation 85

Birmingham: The Birmingham and Three Counties Trust for Nurses 113
Birmingham Bodenham Trust 183

Bishop: Jim Bishop Memorial Fund 37

Black: Black Family Charitable Trust 5
The Black Watch Association 99

Blackman: The Isabel Blackman Foundation 256

Blackpool: Blackpool Children's Clothing Fund 242

Blanchminster: Blanchminster Trust 284

Blatchington: The Blatchington Court Trust (BCT) 24

Blue: Blue Coat Educational Charity 166

Blyth: Blyth Valley Trust for Youth 229

BMA: BMA Charities Trust Fund 81

BMTA: The BMTA Trust Ltd 26

Bolles: Lady Bolles Foundation 311

Bolsterstone: Bolsterstone Educational Charity 308

Bomford: The Douglas Bomford Trust 70

Book: The Book Trade Charity 109

Boreman's: Sir William Boreman's Foundation 207

Bosbury: Bosbury Educational Foundation 262

Bowcocks: Bowcocks Trust Fund for Keighley 310

Bowdler's: Bowdler's Educational Foundation 175

Brackley: The Brackley United Feoffee Charity 167

Bramley: The Bramley Poor's Allotment Trust 311

Bramshott: Bramshott Educational Trust 260

Brentnall: The Alan Brentnall Charitable Trust 5

Bridge: The Bridge Educational Trust (1996) 290

Bridgnorth: The Bridgnorth Parish Charity 175

Brighton: The Brighton Educational Trust 255
The Brighton Fund 256

British: The British Airline Pilots' Association Benevolent Fund (BALPA) 124
British Council 31
The British Institute for the Study of Iraq (Gertrude Bell Memorial) 31
The British Institute of Archaeology at Ankara (British Institute at Ankara) 93
The British Kidney Patient Association 20
British Society for Antimicrobial Chemotherapy 81
British Veterinary Nursing Association 81

Broadlands: The Broadlands Fund (Broadlands Home Trust) 267

Brockley: The (Brockley) Town and Poor Estate 221

Bromfield's: Bromfield's Educational Foundation 212

Brow: The Brow Edge Foundation 236

Brown: The Oliver and Johannah Brown Apprenticeship Fund 256
The John and Nellie Brown Farnsfield Trust 168

Bunting's: Richard Bunting's Educational Foundation (The Bunting's Fund) 200

Burchett: The Rainer and Doreen Burchett Charitable Foundation (The Burchett Foundation) 62

Burford: The Burford Relief-in-Need Charity 276

Burton: Consolidated Charity of Burton upon Trent 176

Burton-in-Kendal: The Burton-in-Kendal Educational Foundation 233

Busenhart: The Busenhart Morgan-Evans Foundation 104

Butchers': The Worshipful Company of Butchers' Educational Charity 90

Butler: The Butler Educational Foundation 259

Buttle: Buttle UK – School Fees Programme 27

Calder: Dr John Calder Trust 136

Calderdale: The Community Foundation for Calderdale 310

Calthorpe: Calthorpe and Edwards Educational Foundation 203

Cambrian: Cambrian Educational Foundation for Deaf Children in Wales 151

Cameron: The Cameron Fund 114

Campden: The Campden Charities 220

Canadian: The Canadian Centennial Scholarship Fund UK (CCSF) 32

Cannon: M. R. Cannon 1998 Charitable Trust 51

Canterbury: The Canterbury United Municipal Charities 270

Cardiff: Cardiff Further Education Trust Fund 156

Carers: Carers Trust 9

Careswell: The Careswell Foundation 171

Carlisle: Carlisle Educational Charity 235

Carne: The Richard Carne Trust 55

Carnegie: The Carnegie Trust for the Universities of Scotland 136

Carpenter: The Thomas Carpenter Educational and Apprenticing Foundation (Thomas Carpenter's Trust) 213

Carpenters: The Carpenters Company Charitable Trust 91

Cartmel: Cartmel Old Grammar School Foundation 233

Cassel: Sir Ernest Cassel Educational Trust (The Cassel Trust) 32

Castle: The Castle Baynard Educational Foundation 208
Edmond Castle Educational Trust 234

Catenian: Catenian Association Bursary Fund Limited 39

Cattle: The Joseph and Annie Cattle Trust 26

Caunt: The Francis Bernard Caunt Education Trust 159

Cecil: The Cecil Charity 292

Chamberlain: The Leonard Chamberlain Trust 303

Chance: The Chance Trust 187

Charlbury: Charlbury Exhibition Foundation 272

Charles: Charity of Charles Clement Walker (The Walker Trust) 175

Chartered: The Chartered Institute of Journalists Orphan Fund 109
The Chartered Institute of Management Accountants Benevolent Fund 105

The Worshipful Company of Chartered Secretaries and Administrators Charitable Trust 122

The Chartered Society of Physiotherapy Charitable Trust 82

Chelmsford: Chelmsford Educational Foundation (CEF) 257

Chertsey: The Chertsey Combined Charity 278

Chessington: Chessington Charities 276

Chester: Chester Municipal Charities 232

Chew's: Chew's Foundation at Dunstable 248

Children: Children of the Clergy Trust 120

Children's: The Children's Boot Fund 185

Chippenham: Chippenham Borough Lands Charity 298

Chipping: The Chipping Sodbury Town Lands 294

Chizel: The Chizel Educational Trust 5

Chobham: Chobham Poor Allotment Charity 277

Choir: The Choir Schools' Association Bursary Trust Limited 62

Chownes: The Chownes Foundation 247

Christ: The Christ Church Exhibition Fund 283

Christ's: Christ's Hospital Endowment at Potterhanworth 193

Church: Church and Town Allotment Charities and others 164
Church Burgesses Educational Foundation 308
The Church Tenements Charities– Educational and Church Branches 216

Churchill: The Winston Churchill Memorial Trust 45
Churchill University Scholarships Trust for Scotland 33

City: The City and Diocese of London Voluntary Schools Fund 208
City and Guilds Bursaries 51
The City of London Corporation Combined Education Charity 214

Clerkson's: Faith Clerkson's Exhibition Foundation 167

CLIC: CLIC Sargent (formerly Sargent Cancer Care for Children) 20

Cliddesden: The Cliddesden and Farleigh Wallop Educational Trust 261

Cliffe: Cliffe and Cliffe Woods Community Trust (formerly known as Cliffe-at-Hoo Parochial Charity) 268

Clingan's: Clingan's Trust 291

Coachmakers: The Coachmakers and Coach Harness Makers Charitable Trust 1977 70

Coates: Coates Educational Foundation 229

Coats: Coats Foundation Trust 91

Coffey: The Coffey Charitable Trust 5

Cole: Charities of Susanna Cole and Others 38

Colitis: The National Association for Colitis and Crohn's Disease (Crohn's and Colitis UK) 20

Collings: John Collings Educational Trust 10

Collingwood: The Mike Collingwood Memorial Fund 270

Community: The Community Foundation for Wiltshire and Swindon 298
The Community Shop Trust (also known as The Leeds Community Trust) 311

Company: The Company of Merchant Taylors of the City of York (Merchant Taylors – York) 307

Congleton: The Congleton Town Trust 232

Conservative: Conservative and Unionist Agents' Benevolent Association 29

Corfe: Corfe Castle Charities 291

Corporation: The Corporation of Trinity House, London 83

Costume: The Costume Society 55

Council: Council for British Research in the Levant 53

County: County Durham Community Foundation 228

Courtauld: George Courtauld Educational Trust 257

Cowbridge: The Cowbridge with Llanblethian United Charities 157

Cowell: Cowell and Porrill 194

Crabtree: Crabtree North West Charitable Trust 231

Craft: Craft Pottery Charitable Trust 56

Creative: Creative Scotland 137

Crewe's: Lord Crewe's Charity 120

Cross: The Else and Leonard Cross Charitable Trust 62
The Cross Trust 137

Culham: Culham St Gabriel's Trust (The Culham Institute) 273

Cullercoats: Cullercoats Education Trust 230

Cumbria: Cumbria Community Foundation 234

Cutlers: The Worshipful Company of Cutlers General Charitable Fund – Captain F. G. Boot Scholarships 47

Cwmbran: The Cwmbran Trust 157

Dacorum: The Dacorum Community Trust 264

Daily: Daily Prayer Union Charitable Trust Limited 39

Dain: The Dain Fund 114

Dairy: The Dairy Crest and National Farmers' Union Scholarship Fund 108

Dawson: The Dawson and Fowler Foundation 161

Deeping: Deeping St James United Charities 194

Denning: The Frank Denning Memorial Charity 216

Devlin: The Thomas Devlin Fund 133

Devon: Devon and Cornwall Aid for Girls Trust 281
The Devon Educational Trust 285

Dewhurst's: Robert Dewhurst's School Foundation 264

Diamond: Diamond Education Grant (DEG) 17

Dibden: Dibden Allotments Fund 260

Dickinson: Charity of Thomas Dickinson 224

Dickson: Peter Alan Dickson Foundation 33
The Alec Dickson Trust 37

Diss: Diss Parochial Charity 200

Dixie: The Dixie Educational Foundation 163

Dixon's: Henry Dixon's Foundation for Apprenticing – administered by Drapers' Charitable Fund 51

Dorchester: Dorchester Relief in Need Charity 291

Downham: The Downham Feoffee Charity 221

Drake: Francis Drake Fellowship Trust Fund 85

Drexler: The George Drexler Foundation 105

Driver: The Ann Driver Trust 56

Dronfield: Dronfield Relief in Need Charity 160

Drummond: Kate Drummond Trust 271

Duffy: The Marie Duffy Foundation 60

Dumfriesshire: The Dumfriesshire Educational Trust 144

Duncan: The Duncan Trust 87

Dundee: City of Dundee Educational Trust Scheme 137

Dunk's: Dunk's and Springett's Educational Foundation 268

Dunn: The W. E. Dunn Trust 171

Duveen: The Duveen Trust 38

Dyke: Dyke Exhibition Foundation 281

Dyslexia: Dyslexia Institute Limited (Dyslexia Action) 26

E: Miss E. B. Wrightson's Charitable Settlement 62

EAC: The EAC Educational Trust 10

Eagle-Bott: Elizabeth Eagle-Bott Memorial Fund 25

Earley: The Earley Charity 250

Earls: Earls Colne and Halstead Educational Charity 257

East: East Lothian Educational Trust 138

Eden: Christopher Eden Educational Foundation 301

Eden's: James Eden's Foundation 237

Edinburgh: Edinburgh Association of University Women – President's Fund 17

Edmonds: Edmonds and Coles Scholarships (Edmonds and Coles Charity) 283

Anthony Edmonds Charity 284

Edmonds': John Edmonds' Charity 293

Educational: The Educational Charity of John Matthews 153

Educational Foundation of James Morris 268

Edwards: Dr Edwards and Bishop King's Fulham Charity 218

Austin Edwards Charity 180

William Edwards Educational Charity 180

The Roger Edwards Educational Trust (formerly the Monmouthshire Further Education Trust Fund) 156

Egham: The Egham Education Trust 278

Elland: The Elland Society 87

Elliott: Charity of John McKie Elliott Deceased (The John McKie Elliot Trust for the Blind) 230

Elmgrant: The Elmgrant Trust 282

Elwes: The Monica Elwes Shipway Sporting Foundation 86

EMI: EMI Music Sound Foundation 63

Emmott: The Emmott Foundation Limited 13

Engineers: The Worshipful Company of Engineers Charitable Trust Fund 71

English: English Speaking Union of the Commonwealth (English Speaking Union) 33

Epsom: Epsom Parochial Charities (Epsom Almshouse Charity) 277

Equity: Equity Charitable Trust 102

Erasmus: Erasmus Mobility Grants 33

Esdaile: Esdaile Trust Scheme 1968 138

Essex: Essex Community Foundation 258

Evans: Freeman Evans St David's Day Denbigh Charity 154

Ewelme: The Ewelme Exhibition Foundation (Ewelme Exhibition Endowment) 247

Exeter: The Exeter Advancement in Life Charity 287

Exhall: The Exhall Educational Foundation 179

Exuberant: The Exuberant Trust 273

Eyre: Monica Eyre Memorial Foundation 9

Family: Family Action 5

Faringdon: The Faringdon United Charities 273

Farmer: Farmer Educational Foundation 194

Fashion: The Fashion and Textile Children's Trust 111

Fawbert: Fawbert and Barnard School's Foundation 263

Feiweles: Feiweles Trust 311

Fenton: The Fenton Arts Trust 56

Fenton Trust 6

Fermanagh: The Fermanagh Recreational Trust 133

Ferries: Alderman Ferries Charity (Hull United Charities) 301

Fife: Fife Educational Trust 138

Finnart: Finnart House School Trust 42

Finzi: The Gerald Finzi Trust 63

Fishley: The Fishley Educational and Apprenticing Foundation 188

Fishmongers': Fishmongers' Company's Charitable Trust 27

Fitzmaurice: The Caroline Fitzmaurice Trust 138

Flitwick: Flitwick Combined Charities 249

Follett: The Follett Trust 13

Fort: The Fort Foundation 231

Foster: Alfred Foster Settlement 106

Frampton: Frampton Educational Foundation 194

Francon: Francon Trust 208

French: The French Huguenot Church of London Charitable Trust 10

Gainsborough: Gainsborough Educational Charity 195

Gale's: Miss Gale's Educational Foundation (The Gale Trust) 262

Gane: The Gane Charitable Trust 151

Gardeners': Gardeners' Royal Benevolent Society (Perennial) 108

Gardner's: Gardner's Trust for the Blind 25

Gargrave: The Gargrave Poor's Land Charity 305

Garnett: The Zibby Garnett Travelling Fellowship 77

Gaskell: The Daniel Gaskell and John Wray Foundation 312

General: General Charity (Coventry) 186

George: George Goward and John Evans 204

The Ruby and Will George Trust 106

George's: St George's Police Children Trust (formerly St George's Police Trust) 118

Gibbon: The Gibbon and Buckland Charity 268

Gibbons: The Gibbons Family Trust 286

Gibbs: The William Gibbs Trust 11

Gilbert: Reg Gilbert International Youth Friendship Trust (GIFT) 48

Gilchrist: Gilchrist Educational Trust 13

Ginsburg: The Jean Ginsburg Memorial Foundation 63

Girls: The Girls of The Realm Guild (Women's Careers Foundation) 17

Girls': The Girls' Welfare Fund 243

Gislingham: Gislingham United Charity 204

Glamorgan: The Glamorgan Further Education Trust Fund 151

Glasgow: Glasgow Educational and Marshall Trust 139

The Glasgow Highland Society 139

The Glasgow Society of the Sons and Daughters of Ministers of the Church of Scotland 139

Go: Go Make it Happen: A Project In Memory of Sam Harding 52

Golborne: The Golborne Charities – Charity of William Leadbetter 236

Goldie: The Grace Wyndham Goldie (BBC) Trust Fund 110

Goldsmiths: The Goldsmiths Arts Trust Fund 91

Gordon: Gordon Charitable Trust 291

GPM: The GPM Charitable Trust 122

Grand: The Grand Lodge of Antient, Free and Accepted Masons of Scotland 125

Grantham: Grantham Yorke Trust 182

Grave: The Mary Grave Trust 234

Great: Great Burstead Exhibition Foundation (Billericay Educational Trust) 258

Great Torrington Town and Lands Charity 289

Greater: The Community Foundation for Greater Manchester (Forever Manchester) 236

Green: Henry Green Scholarships in Connection with Council Schools 225

Greenwich: Greenwich Blue Coat Foundation 217

Greenwich Hospital 100

Grey's: Lady Dorothy Grey's Foundation 176

Guildry: The Guildry Incorporation of Perth 140

Gur: Gur Trust 42

Gurney: The Gurney Fund for Police Orphans 117

Hackney: The Hackney Parochial Charities 217

Hallam: The Ephraim Hallam Charity 239

Hall's: Hall's Exhibition Foundation 201

Hampstead: Hampstead Wells and Campden Trust 213

Hampton: The Hampton Wick United Charity 222

Hanna: The Hanna and Zdzislaw Broncel Charitable Trust (The Broncel Trust) 54

Harding's: William Harding's Charity 253

Harpenden: The Harpenden Trust 263

Harpur: The Harpur Trust 249

Harris: The Harris Charity 240

Harrison: The Geoffrey Harrison Foundation 78
Audrey Harrison Heron Memorial Fund 168

Hart: Dr A. E. Hart Trust 302

Hastings': Lady Elizabeth Hastings' Educational Foundation 310

Hatton: Hatton Consolidated Fund (Hatton Charities) 179

Hawes: Norman Hawes Memorial Trust 253

Haworth: The Haworth Charitable Trust 57

Hayes: The Hayes (Kent) Trust 268
The Carol Hayes Foundation 6

Hayman: Ruth Hayman Trust 34

Hazell: The Walter Hazell Charitable and Educational Trust Fund 110

Hazel's: Hazel's Footprints Trust 46

Headley-Pitt: Headley-Pitt Charitable Trust 269

Heathcoat: The Heathcoat Trust 286

Hedon: The Hedon Haven Trust 302

Heim: George Heim Memorial Trust 6

Hellenic: The Hellenic Foundation 94

Help: Help for Heroes 97

Henley: Henley Educational Trust 273

Henry: The Nora Henry Trust 34

Herd: The Anne Herd Memorial Trust 149

Hereford: Hereford Municipal Charities 173
The Hereford Society for Aiding the Industrious 173

Herefordshire: The Herefordshire Community Foundation (known as Herefordshire Foundation) 174

Heron: Heron Educational Foundation (Heron Trust) 303

Hertfordshire: Hertfordshire County Nursing Trust (Hertfordshire Nursing Trust) 263
The Hertfordshire Educational Foundation 264

Hervey: The Charity of Hervey and Elizabeth Ekins 164

Heslam: The James Reginald Heslam Settlement 198

Hesslewood: The Hesslewood Children's Trust (Hull Seamen's and General Orphanage) 302

Hewley's: Lady Hewley's Charity 88

Hickman's: Thomas Hickman's Charity 254

Higgs: Higgs and Cooper's Educational Charity 293

Higham: The Robert Higham Apprenticing Charity 261

Higher: The Higher Education Academy 69

Highland: The Highland Children's Trust 148

Highlands: Highlands and Islands Educational Trust Scheme 140

Hill: The Hill Bursary 305

Hilton: Hilton Educational Foundation 160

Hitcham's: Sir Robert Hitcham's Exhibition Foundation 259

Hitchin: Hitchin Education Foundation 265

Hockerill: The Hockerill Educational Foundation 69

Hodgson's: Hodgson's School Foundation (Wiggonby School Trust) 235

Hollowford: Hollowford Trust 309

Holmes: The Canon Holmes Memorial Trust 259

Holt: The Holt Education Trust 244

Holywood: The Holywood Trust 144

Honourable: The Honourable Company of Master Mariners and Howard Leopold Davis Charity 84

Hook: The Hook and Goole Charity 304

Hope: The Hope Ffennell Trust 275
Hope House and Gippeswyk Educational Trust 204

Horne: The Horne Foundation 165

Hornsey: The Hornsey Parochial Charities 209

Hothfield: Hothfield Educational Foundation 269

Howat: James T. Howat Charitable Trust 146

Hughes: The Robert David Hughes Scholarship Foundation 154

Hundon: Hundon Educational Foundation 204

Huntingdon: Huntingdon Freemen's Trust 192

Huntingdon's: John Huntingdon's Charity 193

Huntly: Huntly Educational Trust 1997 147

Hutchinson: Reverend Matthew Hutchinson Trust (Gilling and Richmond) 305

Hyde: The Hyde Foundation 212
The Hyde Park Place Estate Charity (Civil Trustees) 214

Hylton: The Hylton House Fund 21

IAPS: IAPS Charitable Trust 27

IdeasTap: IdeasTap Limited 57

Il: Il Circolo Italian Cultural Association Limited 94

Ilchester: The Ilchester Relief-in-Need and Educational Charity (IRINEC) 296

Ilminster: The Ilminster Educational Foundation 297

Incorporated: The Incorporated Benevolent Association of the Chartered Institute of Patent Attorneys 111

Independent: The Independent Dancers Resettlement Trust (Dancers' Career Development) 104

Ingram: Arthur Ingram Trust 271

Institute: The Institute of Actuaries Research and Education Fund 68
The Institute of Materials, Minerals and Mining (IOM3) 67

Institution: The Benevolent Fund of the Institution of Civil Engineers 71
The Institution of Engineering and Technology (IET) 71
Institution of Fire Engineers 84
The Benevolent Fund of the Institution of Mechanical Engineers (IMechE) – known as Support Network 72

Insurance: The Insurance Charities 106

International: The British and Foreign School Society – International Link Scholarship Scheme 46

ISTRUCTE: The ISTRUCTE (Institution of Structural Engineers) Educational Trust 72

It's: It's Your Wish – The John Bury Trust 241

James: The Michael James Music Trust 104

Jarvis: The Jarvis Educational Foundation 172

Jeffreys: Dame Dorothy Jeffreys Educational Foundation 155

Jewish: The Jewish Widows and Students Aid Trust 42

Jobson's: George Jobson's Trust 195

John: John Bloom Law Bursary 227
John Sykes Foundation 251

Johnson: The Dorothy Johnson Charitable Trust 165
Johnson Matthey Public Limited Company Educational Trust 122

Johnson's: Ann Johnson's Educational Foundation 259

Johnston: Johnston Educational Foundation 228
The Brian Johnston Memorial Trust (The Johnners Trust) 86

Jones: The Charity of Doctor Jones 157
The Geoffrey Jones (Penreithin) Scholarship Fund 152

Richard Jones Charity (Richard Jones Foundation) 295

The Thomas John Jones Memorial Fund for Scholarships and Exhibitions 152

Jones': Elizabeth Jones' Scholarships for Boys and Girls of Aberavon and Margam (Elizabeth Jones' Trust) 152

Jones': Edmund Jones' Charity 153

Journal: The Journal Children's Fund (in conjunction with the Royal Antediluvian Order of Buffaloes) 125

Kathleen: The Kathleen Trust 64

Kay: The Sheila Kay Fund 244

Kelsick's: Kelsick's Educational Foundation 235

Kennedy: Helena Kennedy Foundation 14

Kentish's: Kentish's Educational Foundation 247

Kesteven: The Kesteven Children in Need 195

Killingley: S. Y. Killingley Memorial Trust 227

King: The King Henry VIII Endowed Trust – Warwick 181

King's: Joseph King's Charity 259

The King's Lynn General Educational Foundation 201

King's: The King's Norton United Charities 183

Kingston: Kingston upon Hull Education Foundation 302

Kirk: The Peter Kirk Memorial Fund 47

Kirke's: Kirke's Charity 311

Kirkley: Kirkley Poor's Land Estate 205

Kirton-in-Lindsey: Kirton-in-Lindsey Exhibition Foundation 195

Kitchings: Kitchings Educational Charity 196

Kitchings General Charity 197

Kochan: The Kochan Trust 196

Kroliczewski: The Jeremi Kroliczewski Educational Trust 35

Lancashire: Community Foundation for Lancashire and Merseyside 245

Laney's: Bishop Laney's Charity 191

Lathom's: Peter Lathom's Charity 243

Leaders: The Leaders of Worship and Preachers Trust 88

Leadership: The Leadership Trust Foundation 174

Leatherhead: Leatherhead United Charities 277

Leathersellers': The Leathersellers' Company Charitable Fund 14

Lee: Lee (Educational) Charity of William Hatcliffe 222

Leeds: The Duchess of Leeds Foundation for Boys and Girls 39

Leeke: Leeke Church Schools and Educational Foundation 197

Leete: The Leete Charity 266

Leigh: The Leigh Educational Endowment 240

The Leigh Educational Foundation 181

Leivers: Alf and Hilda Leivers Charity Trust 222

Leney: The Hugh and Montague Leney Travelling Awards Trust 269

Letchworth: The Letchworth Civic Trust 266

Lethendy: The Lethendy Trust 140

Leverhulme: Leverhulme Trade Charities Trust 6

Levy: The Joseph Levy Memorial Fund 21

Ley: The George Ley Educational Trust 286

Lincolnshire: Lincolnshire Community Foundation 196

Lindow: Lindow Workhouse Charity 232

Link: The Link Foundation 47

Little: The W. G. Little Scholarship and Band Concert Fund 299

Liverpool: The Liverpool Council of Education (Incorporated) 245

Llanidloes: Llanidloes Relief-in-Need Charity 153

Llewellyn: Colonel William Llewellyn Palmer Educational Charity 299

Lloyd: Owen Lloyd Educational Foundation 155

The Lloyd Foundation 107

The Doctor Dorothy Jordan Lloyd Memorial Fund 91

The W. M. and B. W. Lloyd Trust 241

Lloyd's: Lloyd's Patriotic Fund 98

Logan: The Logan and Johnstone School Scheme 140

Longford: The Frank Longford Charitable Trust (Longford Trust) 43

Lovell: P. and M. Lovell Charitable Trust 7

Lower: Lower Bebington School Lands Foundation 246

Lowestoft: Lowestoft Church and Town Educational Foundation 206

Lowton: The Lowton United Charity 240

Lumb's: Lumb's Educational Foundation 293

Lyon: The Dr Thomas Lyon Bequest 98

Macfarlane: The Macfarlane Walker Trust 64

Mackichan: The Catherine Mackichan Trust 66

Mackmillan: The Mackmillan Educational Foundation 187

Maddock: Maddock, Leicester and Burslem Educational Charity 177

Magdalen: The Magdalen and Lasher Educational Foundation 257

Manchester: Manchester Publicity Association Educational Trust 237

Mapletoft: Mapletoft Scholarship Foundation 197

Marchioness: Marchioness of Northampton (Wraxall Parochial Charities) 296

Marillier: The Marillier Trust 18

Marine: The Marine Society and Sea Cadets 112

Market: The Market Harborough and The Bowdens Charity 162

Marr: The C. K. Marr Educational Trust Scheme 143

Marshall: The James Marshall Foundation 267

Dulce Haigh Marshall Trust 286

Martin: Catherine Martin Trust 255

Martin's: John Martin's Charity 189

Martindale: The Hilda Martindale Educational Trust 18

Maskell: The Dan Maskell Tennis Trust 86

Mason's: Sir Josiah Mason's Relief in Need and Educational Charity 184

Mathew: Mathew Trust 140

Maudlyn: The Maudlyn Lands Charity 287

Maxell: Maxell Educational Trust 176

Maxton: Maxton Bequest 141

McAlpine: The McAlpine Educational Endowments Ltd 11

McCosh: The Alice McCosh Trust 74

McGlashan: The McGlashan Charitable Trust 141

Measures: The James Frederick and Ethel Anne Measures Charity 172

Mendlesham: The Mendlesham Educational Foundation 205

Meningitis: Meningitis Now (formerly known as Meningitis Trust) 21

Merchant: The Merchant Taylors' Company Charities Fund (Livery and Freemen Fund) 125

Merlin: The Merlin Trust 74

MFPA: The MFPA Trust Fund for the Training Of Handicapped Children in the Arts 22

Mico: The Sir Samuel Mico Trust 292

Middlecott's: Sir Thomas Middlecott's Exhibition Foundation 196

Middleton: Middleton Cheney United Charities 167

Middleton Educational Trust (The Emerson Educational Trust for Middleton) 238

The Middleton United Foundation Trust 238

Mihran: Mihran Essefian Charitable Trust (The Mihran and Azniv Essefian Charitable Trust) 35

Mijoda: The Mijoda Charitable Trust 248

Milford: Milford Haven Port Authority Scholarships 158

Millichip: The Adam Millichip Foundation 22

Millington's: Millington's Charity (Millington's Hospital) 176

Mills: The Mills Educational Foundation 205

Milton: Milton Mount Foundation 39

Miners': Miners' Welfare National Educational Fund (MWNEF) 116

Mining: Mining Institute of Scotland Trust 73

Mirfield: Mirfield Educational Charity 310

Mitchell: The Mitchell City of London Educational Foundation 214

Mitchells: The Mitchells and Butlers Charitable Trusts 184

Monke: Thomas Monke 159

Monmouth: Monmouth Charity 156

Monmouthshire: The Monmouthshire County Council Welsh Church Act Fund 156

The Monmouthshire Farm School Endowment 75

The Monmouthshire Further Education Trust Fund 156

Monoux: Sir George Monoux Exhibition Foundation 226

Moon: The Vivian Moon Foundation 288

Moorhouse: The Harold Moorhouse Charity 200

Moray: Moray and Nairn Educational Trust 141

Morgan: The Morgan Trust Scheme 1982 149

Morgan's: Minnie Morgan's Scholarship 157

Morris: The Henry Morris Memorial Trust 191

Morris-Jones: The Sir John Henry Morris-Jones Trust Fund 153

Mott: The Mott MacDonald Charitable Trust 73

Moulson: The Sir Thomas Moulson Trust 233

Moulton: The Moulton Harrox Educational Foundation 198

The Moulton Poor's Lands Charity 199

Moundeford: Sir Edmund de Moundeford Charity 201

Mountsorrel: Mountsorrel Educational Fund 162

Muirhead: The Muirhead Trust 18

Murray: Gilbert Murray Trust – International Studies Committee 93

Music: The Music Libraries Trust 64

Mylne: The Mylne Trust 40

Mynshull's: Mynshull's Educational Foundation 237

Nafferton: The Nafferton Feoffees Charities Trust 304

Nailsea: Nailsea Community Trust Ltd 296

Narberth: Narberth Educational Charity 158

NASUWT: NASUWT (The Teachers' Union) Benevolent Fund 107

National: The National Police Fund 118

National Trainers' Federation Charitable Trust (N. T. F. Charitable Trust) 123

Need: Need and Taylor's Educational Charity 219

New: New St Andrews Japan Golf Trust 145

Newcomen: Newcomen Collett Foundation 224

Newfield: The Newfield Charitable Trust 182

Newspaper: The Newspaper Press Fund (Journalists' Charity) 110

Newton: Newton Exhibition Foundation 265

Newton's: Alderman Newton's Educational Foundation (Bedford branch) 249

NFL: The NFL Trust 18

NFU: The NFU Mutual Charitable Trust Centenary Award 75

NIACRO NIACRO 44

Nichol-Young: Nichol-Young Foundation 191

Nickerson: The Joseph Nickerson Charitable Foundation 14

Nightingale: The Nightingale Fund 82

Noon: Viquaran Nisa Noon and Firoz Khan Noon Educational Foundation (Noon Educational Foundation) 35

Norfolk: The Norfolk (Le Strange) Fund 126

North: North East Area Miners' Social Welfare Trust Fund 117

North of Scotland Quaker Trust 40

The North Yorkshire Fund Educational Travel Award 48

Northamptonshire: Northamptonshire Community Foundation 165

Northern: The Northern Counties Children's Benevolent Society 11

Norton: Norton Folgate Trust 92

The Norton Foundation 183

Norwich: The Norwich French Church Charity 40

Norwich Town Close Estate Charity 202

Nottingham: Nottingham Gordon Memorial Trust for Boys and Girls 168

The Nottingham Roosevelt Memorial Travelling Scholarship Fund 48

Nowes: John Nowes Exhibition Foundation 297

Nuffield: Nuffield Farming Scholarship Trust 75

Oadby: The Oadby Educational Foundation 164

Ogden: The Ogden Trust 53

Old: The Old Enfield Charitable Trust 217

Oldacre: The John Oldacre Foundation 76

Oldbury: The Oldbury Educational Foundation (The Oldbury Charity) 187

Older's: William Older's School Charity 279

Olford: The Olford Bequest 287

Orphan's: Orphan's Aid Educational Foundation (Plymouth) 287

Osborne: The Osborne Charitable Trust 7

Osborn's: Sir Samuel Osborn's Deed of Gift Relief Fund 309

Ouseley: The Ouseley Trust 64

Overall: Richard Overall Trust 22

Oxford: The City of Oxford Charity 274

Paddington: Paddington Charitable Estates Educational Fund 215

Pain: The Pain Trust (The Pain Adventure Trust) 38

Palmer: The Palmer and Seabright Charity 186

Palmer Educational Charity (The Palmer Trust) 187

Pantyfedwen: The James Pantyfedwen Foundation (Ymddiriedolaeth James Pantyfedwen) 14

Parish: Parish Lands (South Brent Feoffees) 289

Parkinson: John Parkinson (Goosnargh and Whittingham United Charity) 243

Parsons: Daniel Parsons Educational Charity 187

Peel: The Peel Foundation Scholarship Fund 242

Peirson: Anne Peirson Charitable Trust 269

Pendlebury's: Sir Ralph Pendlebury's Charity for Orphans 239

Perkin's: Perkin's Educational Foundation 172

Perry: The Perry Family Charitable Trust 172

The Sidney Perry Foundation 15

Perth: Perth and Kinross Educational Trust 150

Peveril: Peveril Exhibition Endowment 168

Philip: The Philip Bates Trust 57

Philological: The Philological Foundation 209

Pilgrim: The Pilgrim Band Trust 277

Pilkington: Roger and Miriam Pilkington Charitable Trust 49

Platt: The Platt Subsidiary Foundation 265

Plowden: Anna Plowden Trust 78

Pocklington: The Pocklington Apprenticeship Trust (Kensington) 220

Podde: The Podde Trust 40

Polehampton: The Polehampton Charity 252

Police: The Police Dependants' Trust Limited 119

Poole: The Valentine Poole Charity 212

Poppyscotland: Poppyscotland (The Earl Haig Fund Scotland) 98

Potton: Potton Consolidated Charity 250

Powis: Powis Exhibition Fund 88

Presbyterian: The Presbyterian Orphan and Children's Society 134

Preston: The Preston Simpson and Sterndale Young Musicians Trust 228

Price: The William Price Charitable Trust 261

The Lucy Price Relief-in-Need Charity 181

Primrose: John Primrose Trust 145

Prince's: The Prince's Trust 7

Printing: The Printing Charity 110

Prisoners: Prisoners of Conscience Appeal Fund 43

Prisoners': Prisoners' Education Trust 44

Professional: Professional Footballers' Association Educational Fund 123

Professionals: Professionals Aid Council 8

Provincial: The Provincial Grand Charity 126

Provincial/Walsh: Provincial/Walsh Trust for Bolton 238

Prowde's: Prowde's Educational Foundation (Prowde's Charity) 295

Puri: The Puri Foundation 35

Queen: The Queen Elizabeth Scholarship Trust 92

Queen's: The Queen's Nursing Institute 82

Railway: The Railway Benefit Fund 124

Rainford: The Rainford Trust 246

Ramsay: Peggy Ramsay Foundation 57

Rank: Allan and Gerta Rank Educational Trust Fund 42

Rawcliffe: The Rawcliffe Educational Charity 304

Rawlet: The Rawlet Trust 178

Rawlins: The Thomas Rawlins Educational Foundation 162

RCN: The RCN Foundation 114

Reading: Reading Dispensary Trust 251

Reardon: Reardon Smith Nautical Trust 84

Reckitt: The Sir Philip Reckitt Educational Trust Fund 49

Red: The Red House Home Trust 148

Redcliffe: The Redcliffe Parish Charity 284

Reedham: Reedham Children's Trust 28

Reeve's: Richard Reeve's Foundation 209

Reid: Rhona Reid Charitable Trust 82

Renfrewshire: Renfrewshire Educational Trust 141

Reuben: Reuben Foundation 29

RFL: The RFL Benevolent Fund (Try Assist) 123

Richards: The Richards Educational Charity 288

Richardson: Superintendent Gerald Richardson Memorial Youth Trust 241

Richmond: Richmond Parish Lands Charity (RPLC) 223

Risley: Risley Educational Foundation 161

Robinson: The Andrew Robinson Young People's Trust 186

Robinson's: Robinson's Educational Foundation 236

Rochdale: Rochdale Ancient Parish Educational Trust 237

Rose: The Rose Charity 299

Ross: Ross and Cromarty Educational Trust 148

Ross Educational Foundation 174

Rossiter: The Stuart Rossiter Trust Fund 66

Rotary: The Rotary Foundation Scholarships 49

Rothbury: Rothbury Educational Trust 229

Rowe's: John James Rowe's Foundation for Girls 245

Royal: The Royal Air Force Benevolent Fund 100

Royal Artillery Charitable Fund 100

The Royal Bath and West of England Society 76

Royal British Legion Women's Section President's Award Scheme 98

The Royal Caledonian Education Trust 99

The Royal College of Organists 65

Royal Geographical Society (with the Institute of British Geographers) 95

The Royal Horticultural Society (RHS) 76

The Royal Liverpool Seamen's Orphan Institution (RLSOI) 112

The Royal London Society 44

The Royal Masonic Trust for Girls and Boys 126

The Royal Medical Benevolent Fund (RMBF) 115

The Royal Medical Foundation of Epsom College 116

The Royal Merchant Navy Education Foundation 113

Royal National Children's Foundation 28

The Royal Naval Benevolent Trust 101

The Royal Naval Reserve (V) Benevolent Fund 101

The Royal Navy and Royal Marines Children's Fund 101

The Royal Navy Officer's Charity 101

The Royal Pinner School Foundation 106

Royal Society of Chemistry Benevolent Fund 121

Royal Television Society 79

The Royal Ulster Constabulary – Police Service of Northern Ireland Benevolent Fund 134

RSABI: RSABI (Royal Scottish Agricultural Benevolent Institution) 108

Ruabon: Ruabon and District Relief-in-Need Charity 155

Rugeley: The Rugeley Educational Endowment 177

Rushworth: The Rushworth Trust 65

Rutland: The Rutland Trust 169

Sacro: Sacro Trust 45

Sailors': Sailors' Society 84

Sailors': Sailors' Children's Society 113

Saint: Saint George's Trust (FSJ (UK) TA SSJE) 41

Saint Marylebone Educational Foundation 215

Salford: The Salford Foundation Trust 238

Salisbury: Salisbury City Educational and Apprenticing Charity 299

Salter: The George and Thomas Henry Salter Trust 173

Samman's: Henry Samman's Hull Chamber of Commerce Endowment Fund 303

Sandra: Sandra Charitable Trust 83

Sandy: The Sandy Charities 250

Sarum: Sarum St Michael Educational Charity 282

Saunders: The Peter Saunders Trust 152

Saxlingham: Saxlingham United Charities 202

Scarborough: The Scarborough Municipal Charity 306
Scarborough United Scholarships Foundation 306

Scargill's: Scargill's Educational Foundation 159

Scarr-Hall: Scarr-Hall Memorial Trust 8

Schilizzi: Schilizzi Foundation in Memory of Eleutherios and Helena Veniselos (The Schilizzi Foundation) 36

Scientific: The Worshipful Company of Scientific Instrument Makers 53

Scotscare: Scotscare 210

Scott: The Charity of Joanna Scott and Others 200

Scott's: Joseph Scott's Educational Foundation 184

Scottish: Charities Administered by Scottish Borders Council 142
Scottish Building Federation Edinburgh and District Charitable Trust 69
Scottish Chartered Accountants' Benevolent Association 107
Scottish International Education Trust 142

Seaman's: Sir Peter Seaman's Charity 202

Sedgefield: The Sedgefield District Relief in Need Charity (The Sedgefield Charities) 228
The Sedgefield Educational Foundation 228

Sedgley: The Sedgley Educational Trust 187

Sedley: The Sir John Sedley Educational Foundation 203

Shaftoe: Shaftoe Educational Foundation 230

Shardlow's: Victoria Shardlow's Children's Trust 11

Sharma: Dr Meena Sharma Memorial Foundation 19

Shaw: The Shaw Charities 243
The Shaw Lands Trust 308

Sheffield: The Sheffield Bluecoat and Mount Pleasant Educational Foundation 309
Sheffield Grammar School Exhibition Foundation 309
The Sheffield West Riding Charitable Society Trust 88

Shelroy: The Shelroy Trust 50

Sheppard: The Bishop David Sheppard Anniversary Trust 245

Sheriffs': The Sheriffs' and Recorders' Fund 45

Sherriff: The R. C. Sherriff Rosebriars Trust 102

Shippam: The Bassil Shippam and Alsford Trust 279

Shipston-on-Stour: Shipston-on-Stour Educational Charity 180

Shropshire: The Shropshire Youth Foundation 175

Sidmouth: Sidmouth Consolidated Charities 288

Silcock: The Silcock Trust 120

Silecroft: Silecroft School Educational Charity 235

Silverton: Silverton Parochial Charity 288

Sloane: The Sloane Robinson Foundation 36

Smith: The Marc Smith Educational Charity 163

Smith's: Thomas Herbert Smith's Trust Fund 163

Snowdon: Snowdon Trust (Formerly known as The Snowdon Award Scheme) 22

Soames: Miss Laura Soames Charity for Education of Girls (Soames Girls Educational Trust) 256

Social: The Social Workers' Educational Trust 85

Society: The Society for Relief of Widows and Orphans of Medical Men (The Widows and Orphans) 116
Society for the Benefit of Sons and Daughters of the Clergy of the Church of Scotland 121
The Society for the Education of the Deaf 25
The Society for Theatre Research 58
Society of Antiquaries of London 54

Sola: Sola Trust 89

Sons: Sons and Friends of the Clergy 121

Soothern: Soothern and Craner Educational Foundation 186

South: The South Square Trust 58
South Wales Institute of Engineers Educational Trust 74

Southampton: The Earl of Southampton Trust 261

Southland's: Southland's Educational Charity 272

Spalding: Spalding Relief-in-Need Charity 199
The Spalding Trust 89

Speak: John Speak Foundation Foreign Languages Scholarships Trust Fund (John Speak Trust) 66

Spencer's: Spencer's Educational Foundation Trust 240

Sperring: Ralph and Irma Sperring Charity 296

Spiers: The Spiers Trust 143

Split: Split Infinitive Trust 58

Spondon: The Spondon Relief-in-Need Charity 160

Spooner: W. W. Spooner Charitable Trust 50

Spoore: The Spoore Merry and Rixman Foundation 252

Saint: St Andrew Holborn Charities 213
St Clement Danes Educational Foundation 215
Sir Walter St John's Educational Charity 210
The Foundation of St Matthias 89
St Olave, St Thomas and St John United Charity 224
St Olave's and St Saviour's Schools Foundation – Foundation Fund 224

Stafford: The Stafford Educational Endowment Charity 178

Stanford: The Educational Foundation of Philip and Sarah Stanford 198

Stationers': The Stationers' Foundation 79

Stein: The Stanley Stein Deceased Charitable Trust 12

Stephens: Mary Stephens Foundation 278

Stepney: Stepney Relief-in-Need Charity 225

Stevens: The Stevens Hart and Municipal Educational Charity (Henley Municipal Charities) 275

Steventon: The Steventon Allotments and Relief-in-Need Charity 276

Stewardship: The Stewardship Trust Ripon 41

Stickford: The Stickford Relief-in-Need Charity 197

Stirlingshire: Stirlingshire Educational Trust 144

Stocks: Edward Stocks Massey Bequest Fund 242

Stoke: Stoke Golding Boy's Charity 163
The Stoke Mandeville and Other Parishes Charity 253
Stoke Poges United Charity 254

Stokenchurch: The Stokenchurch Education Charity 255

Stokes: The Stokes Croft Educational Foundation 41

Strasser: The Strasser Foundation 177

Stratford-upon-Avon: Municipal Charities of Stratford-upon-Avon – Relief in Need 180

Streynsham's: Streynsham's Charity 270

Stringwise: The Stringwise Trust 65

Stroud: The Stroud and Rodborough Educational Charity 294

Student: Student Disability Assistance Fund (SDAF) 23

Studley: Studley College Trust 77

Sunderland: The Sunderland Orphanage and Educational Foundation 230

Sutherland: The Erik Sutherland Gap Year Trust 50

Sutton: Sutton Coldfield Municipal Charities 184

INDEX

Swaffham: Swaffham Relief in Need Charity 200

Swallowdale: The Swallowdale Children's Trust 242

Swann-Morton: The Swann-Morton Foundation 83

Swansea: The Swansea Foundation 158

Talbot: The Talbot House Trust 59

Talisman: The Talisman Charitable Trust 8

Tate: The Mrs A. Lacy Tate Trust 255

Taunton: Taunton Heritage Trust 297

Tees: Tees Valley Community Foundation Bursaries 227

Thame: The Thame Welfare Trust 275

Thaw: The John Thaw Foundation 59

The: The Norwich Jubilee Esperanto Foundation (NOJEF) 66

Thomas: The Charity of Thomas Dawson 274

Thorngate: Thorngate Relief-in-Need and General Charity 262

Thornton: The Thornton Fund 90

Thornton-le-Moors: The Thornton-le-Moors Education Foundation 233

Thornton-Smith: Thornton-Smith and Plevins Trust 12

Thorold's: Dame Margaret Thorold's Apprenticing Charity 196

TIKO: TIKO Foundation 16

Torch: The Torch Trophy Trust 87

Torchbearer: Torchbearer Trust Fund 90

Tottenham: The Tottenham Grammar School Foundation 218

Town: Town Estate Educational Foundation 203
Town Lands Educational Foundation 192

Trades: The Trades House of Glasgow 146
Trades Union Congress Educational Trust 127

Trans-Antarctic: The Trans-Antarctic Association 48

Trevilson: Trevilson Educational Foundation 284

Truro: Truro Fund 210

Trust: The British and Foreign School Society Trust Fund 211

Turath: Turath Scholarship Fund 94

Turner: Sir Mark and Lady Turner Charitable Settlement 211
The Kathryn Turner Trust (Whitton's Wishes) 248

Turton: The T. A. K. Turton Charitable Trust 12

The Tutbury General Charities 178

Educational Foundation 199

and Barbara Tyre

a Ullmann Travelling ship Fund 60

Uxbridge: Uxbridge United Welfare Trusts 219

Vegetarian: The Vegetarian Charity 29

Viner: George Viner Memorial Fund 79

Virgin: Virgin Atlantic Be The Change Volunteer Trip Scholarship 50

Walcot: Walcot Educational Foundation (Lambeth Endowed Charities) 221

Walker: C. C. Walker Charity 188
Madeleine Mary Walker Foundation 305

Wall: The Wall Trust 59
The Thomas Wall Trust 52

Wallace: The Charles Wallace India Trust 36
John Wallace Trust Scheme 145

Wallingford: Wallingford Relief in Need Charity 275

Walsall: Walsall Wood (Former Allotment) Charity 188

Walwyn's: Walwyn's Educational Foundation 189

Ware: The Ware Charities 265

Warsop: Warsop United Charities 168

Warwick: Warwick Apprenticing Charities 182

Water: The Water Conservation Trust 77

Watson: The Watson Scholarship for Chemistry 179

Watson's: Ann Watson's Trust 303
John Watson's Trust 143

Watts: Richard Watts and The City of Rochester Almshouse Charities 271

Webster: Webster and Davidson Mortification for the Blind 25

Wellfield: Wellfield Trust 267

Wellington: Wellington Crowthorne Charitable Trust 251

Wessex: The Wessex Young Musicians Trust 65

West: West Dunbartonshire Trusts 145
West Lothian Educational Trust 149
West Norfolk and King's Lynn Girls' School Trust 202

Weston-sub-Edge: Weston-sub-Edge Educational Charity 294

Westway: Westway Trust 220

Wheatley: The Wheatley Charities 275

White: Charity of Sir Thomas White, Warwick 182

White's: Sir Thomas White's Northampton Charity 166

Whitehead's: Sydney Dean Whitehead's Charitable Trust 59

William's: Dr Daniel William's Educational Fund 154

Williams: The William Williams Charity 292

Williamson: Williamson Memorial Trust 16

Wilmington: Wilmington Parochial Charity 270

Wilson: The Thomas Wilson Educational Trust 223
The Wilson Foundation 166

Wine: The Wine Guild Charitable Trust 92

Winwick: The Winwick Educational Foundation 231

Withington: Withington Education Trust 198

Witley: The Witley Charitable Trust 279

Witting: S. C. Witting Trust 16

Wokingham: The Wokingham United Charities Trust 252

Wolverton: Wolverton Science and Art Institution Fund 254

Women's: Women's Continuing Ministerial Education Trust 90

Worcester: Worcester Municipal Exhibitions Foundation (Worcester Municipal Charities) 189

Works: The Institution of Works and Highway Management (Bernard Butler) Trust 74

World: World Friendship 37

Wormley: The Wormley Parochial Charity 264

Worrall: Worrall and Fuller Exhibition Fund 219

WR: The WR Foundation 16

Wray: The Wray Educational Trust (Wray Trust) 304

Wrexham: The Wrexham (Parochial) Educational Foundation 155

Wright's: Elizabeth Wright's Charity 192

WRNS: The WRNS Benevolent Trust 102

Wylde: The Anthony and Gwendoline Wylde Memorial Charity 173

Wyles: Toby and Regina Wyles Charitable Trust 9

Yardley: Yardley Educational Foundation 185

Ymddiriedolaeth: Yr Ymddiriedolaeth Ddarlledu Gymreig (The Welsh Broadcasting Trust) 80

Yorebridge: Yorebridge Educational Foundation 306

York: York Children's Trust 307

Yorkshire: Yorkshire Ladies' Council of Education (Incorporated) 19
Yorkshire Training Fund for Women 301

Zobel: The Zobel Charitable Trust 9